The History Of Devonshire

Thomas Moore (writer on Devon.)

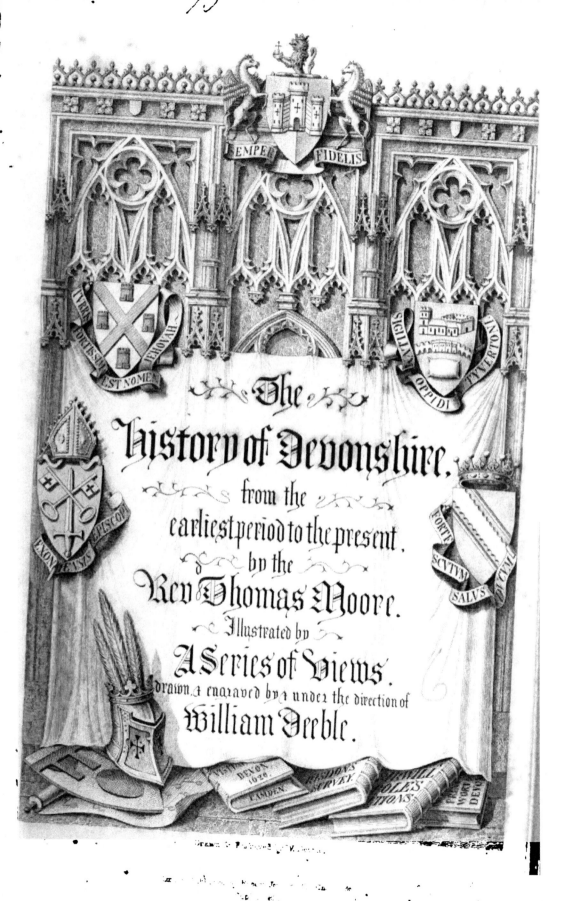

The
History of Devonshire,
from the
earliest period to the present.
by the
Rev. Thomas Moore.
Illustrated by
A Series of Views.
drawn & engraved by & under the direction of
William Deeble.

THE GUILDHALL, EXETER.

TO THE RIGHT WORSHIPFUL THE MAYOR, RECORDER, ALDERMEN AND COMMON COUNCIL OF
THE CITY OF EXETER, THIS PLATE IS MOST RESPECTFULLY INSCRIBED
BY THE PUBLISHERS.

THE MARKET PLACE, ASHBURTON.

THE

HISTORY AND TOPOGRAPHY

OF

DEVONSHIRE.

INTRODUCTION.

OPOGRAPHICAL descriptions, histories, and statistical illustrations of the different counties and principal towns in the Kingdom, constituting, as they do, one of the most valuable branches of English literature, are at present multiplied to an extent which shows them to be as interesting and acceptable to the public, as they are useful and important. In manufactures and the mechanical arts the division of labour renders a degree of excellence in execution, as well as the quantity of production, indefinitely greater than would otherwise be possible; so in this popular and valuable department of literary occupation, what could not be accomplished by one individual, or by a few, is easily effected, in the most masterly style, by numbers employed on the various districts and localities of the country. Men of the first talents and of the highest intellectual attainments as well as industry, have contributed in this way to the general aggregate of information; and

by their separate labours and researches a stock of knowledge is accumulated, in a high degree useful and interesting, not only to the antiquary, the historian, the
geographer and the statesman, but to men of science and
to general readers. It is desirable therefore to render productions of this kind as acceptable as possible to the public
generally; and with this view, in the high state of refine-
ment to which the arts of design and engraving have at
present arrived in this country, a valuable improvement
has of late been introduced, by the successful application
of these arts to the illustration, the embellishment and
the enriching of such works as well as others. Graphic delineations convey ideas at once, and in a manner
much more vivid and complete than verbal descriptions;
and may be used therefore with great advantage, if indeed they are not indispensably necessary, to give just
conceptions of the antiquities, picturesque scenery, ornamental buildings, curiosities, and modern improvements of
the different counties. Works, intended to illustrate in
this manner the Topography and History of several districts, are in the course of publication; no attempt, however, of a similar description has been made, as yet, with
respect to the County of Devon. But as this county, not
only the largest, with the exception of Yorkshire, but also
on several accounts one of the most important, abounds
with grand and beautiful scenery, as well as with antiquities, and with seats of the nobility and gentry, it may justly
be expected to supply abundant materials for the operations of the artist, not less than the topographer and historian. It occurred therefore to the projectors of the present
undertaking, that there was sufficient room for a work
differing in its design from any that have preceded on the
same subject, and in the instance just mentioned at least,
having greatly the advantage of them. If a series of
engravings illustrative of the principal antiquities, towns,
curiosities, the seats of the nobility and gentry, public
buildings, modern improvements, and the fine and romantic scenery of the county, were prepared from original

drawings, in the best style of the arts, to accompany "The History and Topography of the County of Devon," the latter being rendered as complete as possible; a work might be produced, in a great measure novel in its character, and acceptable to the public in general, but to the inhabitants of Devonshire especially. Such is the object of the present publication. In the engravings particular attention will be paid to the antiquities; and with respect to the literary part of the undertaking, by collecting together into one view whatever is of importance, from the most valuable publications already existing on the subject of Devon, or any other books, ancient or modern, from which useful information can be obtained, as well as from personal investigation and original communications,—no pains will be spared to render this work as comprehensive, as interesting and as useful, as the nature of its subject demands.

The following are the topics intended to be treated of in the course of the work. The description of its surface will be followed by a general history of the county, ancient and modern; together with an account of its antiquities, its geological features, natural history, rural œconomy, and the state of trade and commerce; ecclesiastical history, general biography, and brief histories of the nobility and distinguished families connected with the county; and finally, a particular and historical description of the different towns, sea-ports, harbours, curiosities, &c. including every topic of general interest which a parochial survey can supply.—From this statement it will appear that the plan is extensive; and in the execution of it every effort will be made to render the whole as complete as possible.

BOOK I.

GENERAL DESCRIPTION,

—◆—

CHAPTER I.

ETYMOLOGY, EXTENT, DIVISIONS, PICTURESQUE
SCENERY, &c.

BOOK
I.
———
Origin of
the name.

 ONCERNING the origin of Danmonium, the ancient name of Devonshire and Cornwall united, and of the modern appellation of the former of these counties, the following conjectures occur in the most respectable antiquarian works.   According to Camden *, Danmonii is the name given by Solinus to the ancient Britons of these two counties; but Ptolemy calls them Damnonii †, though in some copies Danmonii occurs, more correctly, the transposition of the two letters being easy, and so common a practice in ancient names as to be of little consequence. "This name," he observes, "if not derived from the mines of tin, called by the Britons *moina*, seems to be taken from their dwelling under mountains, the inhabitants generally living in the valleys, which in British are called *Danmunith*, and on this account the County of Devon is still called by the Britons *Duffneint*, or the low valley."   Sammes ‡, however, supposes Danmonium to be of Phœnician origin.   "As the Silures," he says, "derive their name from the Phœnicians, so likewise did the Danmonii, the inhabitants of Cornwall

* *Britannia*, Gough's edit. p. 1.
† Such is the name also in Richard of Cirencester.
‡ British Antiquities illustrated by Aylett Sammes, p. 58.

and Devonshire, in which two counties the Phœnicians were very conversant, by reason of their abounding in tin. Upon this account some have derived this name from *moina*, in the British tongue signifying *mines;* but the question is, whence the *dan* or *dun* proceeds. In the ancient British language, as also in the Phœnician, *dun* or *tun* (for in composition we have both ways) signifies *hill*, and *dan* of the British is *down* of the Phœnicians and English, and signifies *low*. Now whether we derive them from *dan*, from their low habitation in valleys, or, which is righter, from *dun*, or *tun*, and *moina*, signifying *hills of tin*, I find, both ways, they are of Phœnician derivation." Gale* also makes the name to signify a *hill of mines, Dun Mwyn*.

In the Saxon Chronicle † Devonshire is called Defnascyre, Defenascyre, Defnanscire, Defenanscyre, and Defenum ‡, derived, according to Camden, from *Deuffneynt*, and "whence," he observes, "comes the Latin name *Devonia*, and the common contraction *Denshire* §; and not from the Danes, as some unlearned sciolists maintain." "The original name," says another writer, "of

* Gale's Itin. Ant. p. 183.

† An. 851, 878, 894, 977, 997, 1001; see also An. 823, 901, 961, 1017, 1044, 1046, 1048, 1051.

‡ In a note contributed by Mr. Richard Taylor, he observes, that Defenum, from its plural form, should seem to be the appellation not of the district but of the inhabitants.

The nominative plural is given by Lye . . . . Defan, *Devonienses;* and we find in the Saxon Chron. Genitive Plur. Defena, Defna, Dena; Dat.&Abl.Plur. Defenum.

Defena-scire, *Devoniensium provincia*, is therefore formed in the same way as Engla-land, *Anglorum terra*. It is one of those nouns which has its nominative plural in *n;* and Defenas and Denas in Bishop Gibson's index are erroneously given, not being written with an s in the places referred to. He gives the following from several ancient historians: *Deveneschire*, Bede. *Deuensire, Dauenescyre*, Henry of Huntingdon. *Daveneshire*, Hoveden. *Devenchire, Devenschyre*, Knihton.

§ This contraction might be in use in Camden's time, but is unknown at present, except in an agricultural practice called Denshiring, because it was once peculiar to this county, and which consists in paring the surface, and burning the turf for manure. Risdon mentions this contraction as in use in his time, as does also Westcote in his unpublished MS. in the British Museum.

this district, though it was afterwards included with Cornwall under the general appellation of Danmonium, was *Dyvnaint;* and by this term it is frequently mentioned in ancient Welsh MSS. The import of the name is descriptive of the country, and implies *deeps* or *hollows;* and hence the people might call it *Dyvni, Dyvniad, Dyvnoni, Dyvnonywyr, Dyvnonvys,* and *Dyvnwys,* all implying the inhabitants of glens, or deep valleys*."

Boundaries.

Devonshire is bounded on the north by the Bristol channel, which divides it from South Wales and the south-east of Ireland. The Tamar was appointed by Athelstan as the western boundary, and has remained such, with a little variation, from his time to the present. This river rises on the ridge of Shorten Moor, and falls into the sea at Plymouth, separating this county from Cornwall with the exception of a few miles, where the boundary is a small stream, called Marsland Water, which also rising in Shorten Moor, near Wooleigh Borrow, a short distance from the source of the Tamar, and running in an opposite direction, falls into the Bristol Channel. Devonshire, however, extends westward beyond the Tamar for seven miles in length, and two in breadth, at Werrington, including besides that of Werrington, the parish of North Petherton, as it does also the mansion and part of Mount Edgecombe. These

* Beauties of England and Wales, vol. iv. p. 7. Cambrian Register, vol. vii. p. 7. Risdon mentions another derivation of the name: " Others would," " he observes, " that the county should take denomination of the many rivers rising in it; Avon, in the British tongue, being the name of a river, and therefore De-avon, but this is mere conjecture," unsupported by any authority.—Survey of Devon, edit. 1811, p. 2.

In Westcote's MS. also is the following passage: " I would call this county *Avonshire,* De-avonshire, and so by contraction *Denshire.* Avon in the old British language is the name for fleet waters, as wells, rills, brooks, streams and rivers; and this province abounds more with waters and rivers than any other that I have read of. I am induced to believe it may with as good reason take name from them as from mines, valleys, or Danes. *De-Avon* also, or *Devon, the county of rivers,* requires less alteration of letters than any other." He also objects to the derivation of Devon from *Deuffneynt,* &c., because the Welsh have another and more ordinary and more significant word for valleys. This conjecture, however, is inconsistent with the name given to Devonshire in ancient Welsh MSS.—Westcote's MS. Mus. Brit. Bibl. Harl. 2307, p. 5.

places are subject to the civil authority of Devon, but are taxed as belonging to Cornwall, and are under the jurisdiction of the archdeacon of the latter county. On the other hand, Cornwall exceeds its ancient limits near North Tamerton, having a small slip of land on the eastern bank about two miles square, and another, not a square mile in extent, opposite Saltash. Devonshire is bounded on the south by the English or British Channel. The eastern boundary being artificial, the county is separated from Dorsetshire and Somersetshire by a line passing near the following places : Lyme Regis, Uplyme, Axminster, Ford Abbey, Chard, Whitstanton, Otterford, Church Stanton, Red Ball, Holcombe Rogus, Clayhanger, Moorbath, Dulverton, Hawkridge, and the borders of Exmoor to Linmouth on the Bristol Channel. A small portion of land belonging to Dorsetshire is inclosed in Devonshire in the hundred of Axminster, including Sachland and Dalwood. This hundred is also in part divided by a narrow slip of land belonging to the same county.

The most remarkable places on the northern coast Remark-
able points
on the
coast. are Bull Point, Morte Bay, Baggy Point, Barnstaple or Bideford Bay, Portledge, and Hartland Point, eleven miles from which is Lundy Island. This coast, from the eastern extremity of the county to the headland of Hanton, is high and rocky, and within land the hills are steep and the valleys narrow. About Bideford, to some distance, the land gently declines towards the sea, and from Portledge to the western extremity the rocks are bold and prominent. On the English Channel, near the harbour of Plymouth, is Bigbury Bay, whence the land runs out into the sea to a considerable extent, as far as Start Point ; but again retiring forms Start Bay, at the extremity of which is Dartmouth harbour. The coast beyond, shooting out into a promontory called Berry Head, forms the western extremity of Torbay, where there is a good road for shipping, but no port. Further on are Babbicombe Bay, Teignmouth, Exmouth, Sidmouth, and Seaton, where was once a capacious port, which is now reduced to an inconsiderable creek. Great part of the cliffs from Exmouth to Lyme Regis are almost perpendicular, and nearly 400 feet in height. That on the west side of Sidmouth is said to be the highest in England.

Extent, divisions, and population.

Devonshire is about 280 miles in circumference, and by trigonometrical survey contains an area of 1,650,560 statute acres. Its greatest length is about 69 miles, and its greatest breadth 64*. It is now divided into 33 hundreds and 471 parishes. Diocese, Exeter. Jurisdiction, Devonshire and Cornwall. Petty Sessions 20. Acting magistrates 167. It contains one city, (Exeter,) and 37 market towns, and returns 26 members to parliament; namely, two for the county, two for Exeter, and two for each of the following boroughs: Ashburton, Barnstaple, Beeralston, Dartmouth, Honiton, Oakhampton, Plymouth, Plympton, Tavistock, Tiverton, and Totness.

Though this county is the second in the kingdom in extent of territory, it is the fourth in respect to the number of its inhabitants, being exceeded in population by Yorkshire, Middlesex and Lancashire.

The total population, by returns to parliament

In 1801, was 343,001
In 1811 383,308
In 1821 439,040
Of whom the Males in 1821 were 208,229
Females 230,811

Number of families in 1821.

Employed in agriculture 37,037
Employed in trade and manufactures 33,984
Not comprehended in either of these classes . . . 19,692
Total . . . 90,713
Number of inhabited houses in 1821 . . 71,486
Uninhabited 3082
Houses building 756

The average mortality for 10 years is found to be as 1 to 44 of the population.

* Introduction to Risdon's Survey, 1811, p. ii. This Introduction, we understand, was written by John Taylor, Esq. F.R.S., and Treasurer of the Geological Society.

Amount of sums expended for the relief of paupers in each of the following years, ending on 25th March.

Years.	£	Years.	£
1815–16	198,608	1819–20	249,908
1816–17	215,173	1820–21	234,090
1817–18	247,910	1821–22	207,686
1818–19	260,191	1823	201,887 *

To a traveller entering this county, the most remarkable features of its surface appear to be an almost constant succession of hills and valleys;—of hills generally of a similar height, often steep and precipitous, on the eastern side especially, with their tops rounded and sloping, cultivated to their very summits, or skirted with woods and coppices, but sometimes rising into mountainous elevations; with intervening valleys in a state of high cultivation, and finely diversified by inclosures, meadows, orchards, woods, and water. In other parts extensive moors and barren wastes, broken and shattered rocks in solitary grandeur, and the wild disorder of their primitive state, form a striking contrast with scenes of rich fertility and the most luxuriant vegetation; the whole being intersected by large and numerous rivers, or smaller currents, sometimes falling over precipices, dashing over rocky bottoms and through deep ravines, with sides almost perpendicular, fringed with shrubs and trees among projecting rocks, or winding quietly through open plains, and expanding into noble estuaries, with frequent views of the sea from both the shores. From these circumstances Devonshire abounds with the most picturesque and romantic scenery, as well as with open and extensive views, where rocks and hills and vales, woods and rivers, and inclosures, gentlemen's seats, and towns and villages, together with the sea, give so much richness, variety and magnificence to the whole, that this county has sometimes been denominated, with reference also to the mildness of its climate, the Italy of the West. To this it may be added, that every one who has taste to admire, and has been in the habit of observing with at-

The surface.

* See Powell's Statistical Illustrations of the British Empire.

BOOK
I.
_____

tention, the beauties of natural scenery, is well aware how much the aspect of such views depends on the state of the atmosphere, and especially on the combined effect of light and shade occasioned by passing clouds ; and this circumstance is adverted to here, because there is no county, perhaps, the beauty of which is more affected by it than Devonshire, where the clouds continually rising from the sea, and driven by brisk winds over a surface so much diversified, by contrasts and varieties of brilliant lights and deep shade, produce effects on the landscape the most striking, beautiful, and even grand. Even in winter the surface of the county is by no means destitute of attractions.

On the eastern extremity of the county are the Blackdown Hills, so called from their dreariness, being a continuation of the ridge which runs through a great part of the Kingdom. White Down, between Collumpton and Tiverton, Broad Down and East Down, are rude and barren tracts. Passing from Honiton to Exeter through one of the richest vales in the kingdom, with a continual succession of the finest views, on approaching Haldon a noble contrast opens on the traveller, by the gradual rising of the hills into moors and commons bordering upon Dartmoor, on which High Tor, a rock with a divided summit, forms a conspicuous object in the distance. "The vale of the Exe differs widely in appearance from this mountainous district, but in some parts has a billowy, irregular surface, with considerable elevations, particularly between Tiverton and Exeter, and the latter place and Collumpton. The central and northern parts preserve the vale character. The area of this district contains about two hundred square miles *." The south of Devon is a fine, richly wooded, well cultivated country, generally level, with the exception of numerous hills in the South Hams, which are in some instances precipitous and wild. "This latter district is frequently termed the

* Beauties of England, vol. iv. p. 8.

Garden of Devonshire, from its fertility. Its natural
boundaries are Dartmoor, and the heights of Chudleigh
on the north; Plymouth Sound on the west; Torbay on
the east; and on its southern point the English Channel.
Its area, including the rich vale of the Dart, extends
nearly 250 square miles. In many parts, especially towards the north, the scenery is picturesque and romantic.
The surface in the west is extremely diversified, not only
from the number, narrowness, and depth of the valleys,
the sides of which generally rise with a steep ascent from
the banks of the streams that divide them, but from the
wild and rude state of the rocky hills, which are rent and
broken in a singular manner*." Roborough is a down
of some extent, formed by a ridge of hills between the
Plym and the Tamar. Dartmoor, so named from the Dart
to which it gives rise, as it does to most of the rivers in
Devonshire, constitutes the south-west part of the county
on the north of the South Hams. " On approaching this
tract from the south and south-east, the eye is bewildered
by an extensive waste, exhibiting gigantic tors, large
surfaces covered with vast masses of scattered granite
and immense rocks, which seem to have been precipitated from deep declivities into the valleys. These huge
fragments, spread in wild confusion over the ground, have
been compared to the ponderous masses ejected by vol-
canoes, to the enormous ruins of formidable castles, and
to the wrecks of mountains torn piece-meal by the raging
elements. Dartmoor, and the waste called the Forest of
Dartmoor, include between two and three hundred
thousand acres of open and uncultivated land. Of these
Dartmoor alone is supposed to comprise upwards of
80,000†." Swampy declivities unfit for cultivation also
abound in many parts of this district. The hills between
Tiverton and South Molton are dreary, and have no attractions, except by contrast with the finer portions of
the county; and of a similar character is the Down be-

---

* Beauties of England, vol. iv. p. 7, 8.   † Ibid. p. 6, 7.

tween Challacombe and the Bristol Channel. Exmoor in its general features resembles Dartmoor, and is usually described as belonging to Devonshire : but, says Mr. Lysons *, " I am assured on good authority, that although very extensive commons adjoining the forest, and scarcely separated from it by any visible boundaries, are in this county, yet the whole of the forest itself is in Somersetshire." The little vale of the Culme is more level than any other part of the county. The lowest spot is said to be between Chudleigh and Ashburton, near the lignite coal-works of South-Bovey †. Other valleys and combes will be noticed more particularly when the rivers are described; and the different character of the soils of the county will be described when the subject of agriculture comes under consideration. The whole aspect of the country is doubtless greatly changed since the time of Risdon; for he observes, " The greatest part of this county is in its own nature barren, and full of breaks and briars ;" a description forming the most striking contrast with its present state, since it is exceeded by none perhaps in richness, fertility, and picturesque beauty, comprising features of every kind, from the wild mountain, impetuous torrent and trackless bog, to the wooded vale and the beautiful meadow, with the quiet stream winding its course undisturbed to the ocean ‡.

Height of the principal hills. The forest of Dartmoor is considered the highest ground in the county, its mean height being estimated at about 1782 feet above the level of the sea, and its highest point at 2090. Rippon Tor is said to be 1540 ; Salsbury Castle, in the parish of High Bray, 1500 ; Chapman's Barrow, between Challacombe and Parracombe, 1200 ; Butterton Hill, near Ivybridge, 1200 ; Black Down, near Tavistock, 1160 ; Hoardown Gate, three miles from Ilfracombe, 800 ; Great Hangman Hill,

* Magn. Brit.   ‡ Introduction to Risdon's Survey, p. xi.
    † Mr. Polwhele observes, that this is said to be the lowest land in the island ; and the editor of Risdon also remarks, that it is considered to be below the level of the sea. But if this be the fact, where does the water of this district discharge itself?

800 ; Great Haldon and Black Down, 800 ; and Little Hangman Hill, 600. Lesser heights are High Bellever, Essery, Steeperton, Ham, Mist, Row and Crackern Tors on Dartmoor ; Castle Lawrence on Pen Hill, and Belvedere in Powderham grounds.

From the perpetual recurrence of hills in this county, and their steepness, together with the depth and narrowness of the roads between fences, consisting of high mounds surmounted by coppice wood, forming altogether a barrier thirty feet in height, travelling, in a great part of Devonshire is unpleasant, all prospect of the country being shut out, except on the open tops of the hills, and where there are no inclosures, whilst the country abounds every where with the finest distant views, and exhibits in numerous parts of it the most picturesque and beautiful scenery. The following are enumerated by Mr. Lysons * and others, as the most remarkable instances of both. The views from Haldon, overlooking the rich vale of the Exe, with its estuary and finely ornamented banks ; those of Black Down, over the vale of Culme ; from Pinhoe and other heights in that vicinity, overlooking Exeter with the same fine country and the river. From Little Haldon is a commanding view of the Channel, the Exe, and the Teign†. On Holcombe Down are seen, to the west, Teignmouth, with the river and the adjacent hamlets, Shaldon Hill and the Ness, the coast from the Bay of Babicombe to Tor-point, the detached rocks called Oar Stone and Lead Stone, over the hills of Torbay, and beyond that the Dartmouth and Brixham hills ;—on the east, with Dawlish lying rather on the left beneath, a most extensive line of coast with its creeks and bays, and passing the Beacon Point, Sidmouth Bay, Seaton and Lyme Regis, with the island of Portland, computed at a distance of sixty or seventy miles. In the intermediate space the river Exe, with the numerous objects of attraction on its banks. The large tract of

* Magn. Brit.   † Note 13 to " Devon, a Poem," by J. Gompertz, Esq.

Haldon on the north, and at a distance the stupendous hills of Dartmoor and Haytor Rock, frowning with sublime grandeur above the numerous intervening swells. From the heights of Dartmoor on the side towards Plymouth; and the magnificent view from High Tor or Haytor Rock, overlooking the vale of Teign to Teignmouth on the sea. The view from Brent Tor churchyard; from the height above Torquay, and from Mamhead. The singularly picturesque view from Morwell Rock, overlooking the Tamar into Cornwall. The view from the higher grounds in Tawstock Park, overlooking Barnstaple and its bay; and that from Portlemouth church, extending over the estuary of the Aven, with Kingsbridge, Salcombe, Ataborough, South Pool, &c. Nor ought the ride from Honiton to Exeter, which is one of the finest in the kingdom, to be forgotten in the list. The views also about Powderham, Exmouth, and Teignmouth, especially at high water, are rich and beautiful beyond description. Picturesque scenery, however, is chiefly to be found near the sources of the principal rivers. The road from Bampton to Tiverton, by the side of the Exe, abounds with the finest views of this description. The upper part of the East Teign and of the Dart, particularly about Holme Case and bridge, are highly picturesque. There is much fine scenery on the wooded banks of the Tamar, the Tavy, the Taw, and the Plym, especially about Bickley Mill, the Erme, the Creedy, the Mole, and other rivers. The ride from Moreton Hampstead to Lustleigh is through a finely wooded vale. There is much beautiful scenery in Widdon Park and in the neighbourhood. The scenery of the little river Lyn is well known and much admired, as is that at Ivy Bridge and Lydford Bridge, with its waterfall and cascades; and also that of Combe Martin and Ilfracombe. The Valley of Stones near Linton is a rude and romantic specimen of rocky scenery; and though Mr. Lysons thinks it somewhat overrated in comparison with similar views in the north-west of Yorkshire and other parts of the kingdom, the rocks, he admits, which skirt this valley towards the sea, are magnificent. The scenery about the romantic village of Clovelly, Sir J. Hamlyn Williams's park, and of the new drive from the Bideford road, called the Hoby, are among the most singularly beautiful. Torquay is spoken of as a little terrestrial paradise *. The houses, which are all built of a kind of marble found on the spot, are scattered among the hills and valleys, commanding one of the most delightful views of the surrounding country and of Devonshire scenery, together with Torbay. The views from Mount Edgecombe Park, and other commanding situations about Plymouth, are highly and justly celebrated. Babbicombe is also one of the most singularly romantic and delightful places in Devonshire: it is a hamlet built in a rock. And finally, the village of Milton, in the parish of Buckland Monachorum, situated in a deep and narrow ravine, has much attracted the notice of artists.—For a more particular description of each of these views, other opportunities will occur in the course of this work, and plates will be given in illustration of their principal beauties.

The climate of Devon is so highly celebrated for its mildness and salubrious qualities, that it is not unusual for invalids, particularly in cases of consumption, to retire hither for the recovery of their health. Its superiority in this instance to other counties, arises in part from its abounding with hills, but chiefly from its vicinity to the sea. The wind, two-thirds of the year from the west and south-west, crossing an immense extent of ocean, is regularly warmer than in more inland counties; and being seldom languid, serves to purify the air and to correct the extremes both of heat and cold. In summer the intenseness of the former is moderated by strong and refreshing breezes from the sea and the hills, and in winter the frosts in the southern portion of the county are not so severe, nor does the snow lie so long as in

Climate.

* Note 9 to "Devon, a Poem," by J. Gompertz, Esq.

other districts.   Even in December a languid sort of spring is said to be observable ; and shrubs that will not live in the colder parts of the island flourish here.

It is a notion generally prevalent, that more rain falls in the western counties than in any other ; but Mr. Polwhele, who resided here, gives it as his opinion, founded on observation, that this is not the case in Devonshire. Among the hills, of course, more rain falls than in the valleys.   Immense quantities of moisture, rising from the sea, are condensed by the superior cold of these elevations ; and the clouds thus formed, being attracted and intercepted in their course by the hills, discharge themselves in torrents.   Thus on Dartmoor especially, the rains are so frequent and heavy, and the storms so severe, as to form, it is said, the chief obstruction to its cultivation.   No attempt at winter farming, in the forest, can be made by the modes in general use in the county. The roots of the corn sown in autumn, if forward in its growth at the close of the year, are laid bare, and its stems torn from the ground ; and in young plantations many hundred thousand trees have been destroyed by the violence of the tempests. The climate, however, with all its severities, is decidedly healthy : the inhabitants on the borders of this district attain to great ages ; and since there have been residents in it, it has been ascertained that no prevalent disease follows the most inclement seasons *.   The natives indeed of Devonshire in general, and of this neighbourhood especially, have always been mentioned as singularly healthy and robust.   Plymouth, Tiverton, and Ashburton, are proverbially wet ; but in the more open and level parts of the country, the rains in this county, as Mr. Polwhele maintains, are not, on an average, more frequent and copious than in others ; and fogs abound less here than in many other quarters of the island.   Clouds indeed are continually rising from the sea ; but these are not stagnant vapours, or injurious to health : and though there may be much moisture in

* Additions to Risdon's " Survey," p. 407—409.

the atmosphere, it is never allowed to be stationary; for the wind so near the sea being seldom at rest, scatters the clouds, dissipates the vapours, and preserves the purity of the air. Among the mountains, and on the northern and eastern coasts, the air may be too keen and severe for those who are not accustomed to it, but is not in any degree injurious to the natives. From the great variety in the surface of the county, and the different position of the several districts, corresponding variation may be expected in the climate. By the winds from the north on the open moors, every bush and shrub is nipped and withered; and it is a common opinion that in the quality also of the air in the north and south of Devon there is considerable difference: in the former, it is said to be rendered fretting and acrimonious to strangers, by a mixture of particles of salt from the sea, except when purified by the frequent rains; whilst in the south, on the contrary, abounding with gentle hills and refreshed by salutary breezes, the climate is mild, balmy, and salubrious. In this quarter vegetation begins a fortnight or three weeks sooner than in the north, where the snow in winter sometimes lies to a considerable depth.

Tempests of extreme violence have occasionally taken place in Devonshire, and the appalling circumstances of several are familiar to the public, particularly of that which destroyed the Eddystone Lighthouse, on November the 27th, 1703, when Mr. Winstanley, the architect, together with the building itself, was washed into the sea; the hurricane of February the 15th, 1760, when the Ramillies, a second-rate man-of-war, was lost, with 734 men on board, near Plymouth Sound; and the tempest in 1781, which, although it was not perceived even at Salisbury, laid waste this county in a manner the most terrific. But as catastrophes of this kind are probably not more frequent here than in other mountainous districts near the sea, it is unnecessary to enter further into this subject*. It is

Storms.

* Several other storms are described in Mr. Polwhele's Devonshire, vol. i.

remarkable, however, that notwithstanding the violence of many tempests on this coast, thunder-storms are said to be less frequent and less destructive in this county than in any other part of England, except Cornwall. The summits of the numerous hills break the clouds in their passage, which after discharging their contents are dispersed in scattered fragments; and this circumstance may furnish the reason why such storms are less numerous, and occasion less mischief, than in other places.

Parts of the county favourable to health.

The following are mentioned by Mr. Polwhele as some of the situations distinguished by circumstances favourable to health or otherwise. The dry air of Offwell on the borders of Dorset and its vicinity is remarkable for its salubrious qualities; but that of Smeaton is to be avoided as pernicious, on account of the stagnation of sea water by which it is surrounded. Exeter, situated on a descent in the midst of a fine, open, richly cultivated country, with an atmosphere clear, dry and airy, and so mild that the snow in winter seldom lies, is considered as singularly healthy. Exminster, from its marshes, is subject to intermitting fevers. Moreton Hampstead, on the contrary, sheltered as it is by hills, enjoys the dry air of the moor in its vicinity, without its keenness, and is considered as one of the most healthy spots in the county. Agues, in Mr. Polwhele's time, were not unfrequent at Bovey Heathfield. The air of Salcombe, on the southern coast, is so mild and salubrious that medical practitioners have been accustomed to call it the Montpellier of England. Some parts of Dean Prior are unwholesome; but Bideford, near the sea, though on the northern coast, is considered as a healthy spot. To this brief enumeration it may be added, that the places on the southern coast generally, and especially those that are frequented by visitors in the bathing season, as Sidmouth, Exmouth, Dawlish, Teignmouth, and Torquay, are to be preferred, not less as situations highly favourable to health than for their other attractions.

CHAPTER II.

RIVERS AND SPRINGS.

DEVONSHIRE, as is well known, abounds more with rivers, brooks and springs, than any other English county; a circumstance to be attributed, no doubt, to the number and elevation of its hills, which attracting the clouds and vapours as they arise from an immense tract of sea, and intercepting their progress, receive from these never-failing reservoirs sufficient and abundant supplies of moisture; without our having recourse to the absurd notion that the sea forces up its waters through the pores and internal ducts and channels of the earth even to the summits of the hills. This latter notion indeed is too puerile and unphilosophical to merit notice, if it had not been advocated by some persons whose talents and opinions in other respects are certainly deserving of regard. Mr. Polwhele, in his attempt to explain the manner in which the springs and rivers of Devonshire are supplied, adopts this strange hypothesis, and speaks of the sea as acting as a sort of forcing engine to convey its waters, purified and become lighter in their passage through the earth, to a considerable distance inland, and even to the summits of elevated districts. But by what doctrine of natural philosophy this action of the sea can be explained, he has omitted to state. On the principle of the hydrostatic balance, it is well known that the waters of the ocean, wherever they might be able to penetrate, would in no instance rise above the level of the sea, except indeed when they might meet with a perfect vacuum above them; and even in that case their elevation would be trifling, not exceeding thirty-two feet; so that if from the pores of the earth the atmospheric air could be excluded, and a vacuum could take place, even that supposition would not answer the purpose of this groundless hypothesis. There

c 2

BOOK
I.

is no other principle that could be impressed into its service but that of capillary attraction, which in this case would, if possible, be still more ridiculous. Nor is there the slightest occasion to have recourse to any supposition different from the commonly received opinion on this subject. The immense and inconceivable quantities of moisture that arise from the earth, and especially from the sea into the atmosphere by universal and incessant evaporation, and which are condensed and again discharged or deposited upon the earth's surface, in rains, and dews, and mists, are amply sufficient to supply all the springs and streams with which it abounds. The reduction and failure of these streams and springs, moreover, in seasons of great and long continued drought, afford plain indications from whence their supplies are obtained.

The rivers.

The principal rivers of this county are the Axe, the Otter, the Exe, the Teign, the Dart, the Erme, the Yealme, the Plym, the Tamar, the Tavy, and the Torridge,—all of which are more or less navigable. The chief of the smaller ones are the Bovey, the Bray, the Coney, the Coly, the Creedy, the Culm or Columb, the Little Dart, the Dawl, the Kenn, the Lenmon, the Lyd, the Lynn, the Mole, the Oke, the East and West Okements, the Sid, the Tindal, the Tynhay, the Tale, the Walden, the Wray, and the Yeo.

The Axe.

" The Axe," (supposed to be the Alænus of Ptolemy,) says Leland *, " riseth a mile east from Bermistre (Berminster), a market-town in Dorsetshire, at a place called Axnoble, a ground belonging to Sir Giles Strangeways, in a moor on the hanging of a hill, and thence runneth south-west four miles to Ford Abbey, standing in Devonshire on the furthest rise of it ; and hereabout it is a *limes* to Devonshire and Somersetshire." After crossing an angle of Dorsetshire it proceeds to Axminster, a market-town three miles beyond, having received two brooks from the parish of Hawkschurch in Dorsetshire ; a

* Leland's Itin. vol. iv. p. 43.

short distance below Axminster bridge it also receives
the Yarty; and passing between Colyford and Musbury,
and under a bridge of two stone arches called Axbridge,
beyond which it receives the Cole, it falls into the sea
between Axmouth on the east and Seaton on the west.
The whole of its course is little more than fifteen miles.
The principal bridges over this river are those on the
roads to Honiton and Colyton, and Axbridge on the road
from Sidmouth to Lyme.

The smaller river *Yarty* rises on the borders of Dorsetshire, about two miles south-east of Otterford in that
county; and passing by Yarcombe on its western bank,
proceeds between Stockland and Membury to Dalwood,
below which it falls into the Axe near Kilmington.

The *Coly* rises about two miles north of Cotleigh in
Devonshire; and passing that place and Widworthy, washes
the foot of the hill on which Colyton stands; and after
passing by Colyton Park and Colyford, falls into the Axe
half a mile below that place.

The *Sid*, a small stream scarcely deserving the name
of river, rises a short distance north of Sidbury; and
passing that place and through Sidford, falls into the
sea at Sidmouth.

The OTTER rises at the upper end of Honiton vale
near Otterford, in Somersetshire, to which, as well as to
several other places on its banks, it gives name. From
its rise it runs about four miles to a village called Up-
Ottery, and thence to Monkton; and proceeding between
Honiton and Combe Raleigh to Fenton Bridge, by Ottery
St. Mary on the east, between Fen-Ottery and Harpford
to Newton Poppleford, it passes Colyton Raleigh and
Otterton, about two miles below which it empties itself
into the sea at Ottermouth, its course in this county being
about twenty-five miles. This is not a large river, as it
seldom exceeds twenty feet in width and three in depth,
having a gravelly bottom. The principal bridges are at
Up-Ottery, Fenton Bridge, Newton Poppleford, and Otterton.

CHAP.
II.

The Yarty.

The Coly.

The Sid.

The Otter.

The little river *Tale* falls into the Otter about a mile above Ottery St. Mary.

The most beautiful and important river of Devonshire is the EXE, the ancient *Isca*, the source of which is in Somersetshire, on Exmoor, to which it gives name. About three miles north-east of Exbridge, at a place called Excross, according to Leland, it issues from a bore about five inches in diameter, in sufficient quantity to turn a mill, and is soon joined by several streams, as the Barle and Dunsbrook *. A few miles from its source the Exe abounds with picturesque scenery. From Helebridge on the road to Dunster there is a fine romantic view northward of a beautiful narrow vale, inclosed by hills of considerable elevation, the sides of which are covered by luxuriant woods, with rocks occasionally interspersed, raising their bold fronts among the trees several hundred feet above the level of the sea. Both the Exe and the Barle are broad shallow streams, clear, rapid, flowing over rough, rocky beds, and forming in their course a continual succession of waterfalls †. At Exbridge the river enters the county of Devon, and passing the village of Highleigh and Oakford Bridge, it receives the Batham, a small river which, rising near Clayhanger and passing through Bampton, falls into the Exe about a mile below that town. The Exe, entering the parish of Tiverton and running under Cove Bridge, takes its course towards the south, dividing the parish of Stoodley and Washfield from Pitquarter in Tiverton. It then washes the foot of the precipice on which the castle and the church of Tiverton stand, and passing the Exbridge separates the higher town from Westex : here it is joined by the Lowman, or Leman ; and proceeding thence beneath Backwood to

* Archdeacon Hale observes, that some few miles from where the Exe rises, towards the west, is a large standing lake always full, the depth of whose bottom is unknown. It opens a passage under ground, and breaks out again a few miles distant. Hence we may presume it receives its name of *Mole's Chamber.*—Polwhele's Devon, vol. i.

Mr. Polwhele's conjecture that this lake is the crater of an extinct volcano will be noticed in our view of the Geology of the county.

† Collinson's Somersetshire.

Bickleigh Bridge, about a mile below that town, it receives the Little Dart, which takes its rise a short distance from Batterleigh. Passing between Silverton and Thorverton, it crosses by Up-Exe to Dinniford Bridge. Near Netherex chapel it receives a small stream from Thorverton, and further on, about a mile from Bamford Speke, it is joined by the river Columb. Before it passes under Cowley bridge * it also receives the Creedy; and a little below that bridge a branch is divided from it, which is again united to it above Exeter, where the Exe passes under a modern bridge, which separates that city from the parish of St. Thomas. Here it supplies a navigable canal to Topsham, and passing under Countesswear bridge, is joined by the canal, and meets the tide a short distance above that village. At Topsham it receives the Clyst about four miles below Exeter, where it suddenly widens its bed to upwards of a mile, and becomes navigable for ships of several hundred tons. From this place the Exe rolls on a majestic stream between a constant succession of the richest and most varied scenery on both its banks, having the woods and castle of Powderham on the west, and the pleasant village of Lympstone, with gentlemen's seats, on the east. In this part of its course it receives several little tributary streams; one near Exminster, a pleasant trout brook, called the Kenn, at Powderham, and a small river from Lympstone on the opposite bank. Having passed Starcross on the west, the river makes a sudden turn towards the east, finding a barrier to its direct course in a vast sand-bank, that extends nearly two miles from east to west, called the Warren †. Thus turned and contracted in its channel, it winds round between this barrier

---

* "Cowley bridge of twelve arches under the gut and causey." Leland's Itin. vol. iii. p. 38. Cowley bridge was washed away some years since, and another has been erected in its place.

† "There lieth a great vast plain, and barren sandy field, at the west side and very point of Exmouth haven; and in the west part of this haven mouth a little above this sand goeth in a creek, a mile or thereabout into the land. Some call it Kenton Creek."—Leland's Itin. vol. iii. p. 46.

and a flat projecting point which runs out from the town of Exmouth, and rushes over a small bar of sand near the Cheekstone, into the British Channel. The course of the Exe, including all its windings, is estimated at about seventy miles. This river is a pure pellucid stream till it is joined by the Creedy, which imparts to it a reddish colour from the soil through which the latter flows; and from this junction the Exe continues polluted and muddy till it enters the sea.

Of the subsidiary rivers that fall into the Exe, the following is a brief account. (The Batham and the Little Dart have been sufficiently noticed before.)

The Low-man.

The *Lowman,* or *Leman,* called by the Saxons Sunning-brook, or *Slow River,* rises near Chipstaple in Somersetshire, and passing by Up-Lomon, which takes its name from standing highest on the banks of the river, enters the parish of Tiverton near Lowman Mill, divides Tincombe quarter into two nearly equal parts, and proceeding through the village of Craze Lomon, to which it gives name, arrives at Tiverton, and after passing under Little Selver Bridge falls into the Exe.

The Culm.

The *Culm,* or *Columb*,* also makes its first appearance in Somersetshire, in the parish of Otterford; and passing through Church Staunton, Hemiock, by Columbstock, Uffculme, and Collumpton (so named from the river), and through Bradninch, Silverton and Stoke, falls into the Exe about a mile below Stoke bridge. The course of this river is rather rapid, and its bed is of sand, and stony.

The Creedy.

The *Creedy* rises north-west of Crediton, near Morchard Bishops, and descending rapidly, passes near Woodfordsworthy, between Langford and Upton Helions to Crediton, to which it gives name; and where it is joined, says Risdon, by a brook called Forton. Three miles and a half lower down it runs under Newton bridge of four

---

* "The Culme," Risdon says, " descendeth from divers heads under the Black Down hills, by the confines of this county, near Church Stanton."—Survey, p. 81.

S. W. VIEW OF EXETER CATHEDRAL.

CASTLE.

arches; and about two miles and a half further on, having passed under another stone bridge of two arches, enters the Exe a little above Cowley bridge. The Creedy, as before observed, is generally of a reddish colour from the soil, and imparts this colour to the Exe,

The little river *Yeo* rises about two miles from Colebrook, near which village it runs, and, passing near the bartons of Yeoford and Yeoton, falls into the Creedy not far from Crediton.

The *Clyst* has its source in an estate called Clyst William, the proper name being Clyst-well-head, about a mile and a half east of the parish church of Plymtree, and passing Clist St. Lawrence, Broad Clist, St. Mary's Clist, and St. George's Clist, falls into the Exe near Topsham. This river, notwithstanding the shortness of its course, gives name to nearly a dozen places, being the general denomination of the parishes and villages through which it passes. It is a dull, sluggish stream.

The *Kenn* rises near Dunchideock, and running by Kenford and Kenn, falls into the Exe between Kenton and Powderham.

The preceding are the rivers which have their sources in the east, and chiefly on Exmoor or its vicinity. The following are those which rise on Dartmoor, called by Risdon " The mother of many rivers." The first on the southern coast is

The TEIGN*, or East Teign, rising on Dartmoor, a short distance north of Gidley, from two heads, which meet near Holy Street, and proceeding thence to Chagford by Whiddon Park and Moreton Woods, near Dunsford, Christow, Hennock, Chudleigh, Teigngrace and King's Teignton, after passing under Teign bridge, spreads into a wide estuary, and falls into the sea between Shaldon and Teignmouth, its course being about thirty miles. The principal bridges over the Teign are those on the

The Yeo.

The Clyst.

The Kenn.

The East Teign.

* " So called," says Risdon, " by the Britons, for that it is straightly pent with narrow banks."—Survey, p. 132.

The West
Teign, or
Bovey.

Waterfall
at Canon
Teign.

The Becky
and its
waterfalls.

roads from Exeter to Moreton Hampstead, Ashburton, and Totness.

The *West Teign*, or *Bovey* river, rises also on the border of Dartmoor, a short distance from North Bovey, and, passing that place and Bovey Tracey, falls into the East Teign not far from Teigngrace. Halwell brook, the small river Hayne, Radford brook, and the little but romantic river Becky in the parish of Manaton, all have their sources in or near Dartmoor, and fall into the Bovey; as does also the river Wrey, which rises near Moreton Hampstead.

In the course of these rivers, especially near their sources, there is much to attract the attention of the artist, and of all indeed who have a taste for what is romantic and beautiful in natural scenery. The country through which the Teign passes being full of rocks which are often precipitous, this river rushes on sometimes over beds of granite; at others, flows through a finely wooded country, and is often pent up in deep and narrow valleys; whence the sound of its waterfalls, and the roar occasioned by its tumultuous passage over rocky bottoms, may be heard at a considerable distance.—One of the most remarkable of its waterfalls is at Canon Teign, where, though in its usual state there may be nothing singularly striking in its appearance, after much rain a large body of water rushing down a craggy precipice, foaming beneath and struggling among the granite rocks, cannot fail to produce a grand and beautiful effect. The water of this river, like that of all the rivers of Dartmoor, is tinged by the peat or turf of a brown colour, and when swollen with rain is almost black.

The course of the *Becky* previously to its arrival at the Bovey, becomes sometimes invisible among rocks of granite in a state of great rudeness and disorder; and hence may have arisen a notion that it works its way through a subterraneous passage. In summer when the springs are low it is lost entirely among the rocks,

but in winter and after rain it rises into view, and often
exhibits scenes of singular beauty,—the most remarkable
of which is a cascade called Becky Fall, than which
nothing can be more romantic. The following is the
substance of Mr. Polwhele's animated description of this
fine but difficult subject for the pencil of the artist. The
little river winding its way over a rough and stony bottom, at one time foams along as if ready to force a passage through every obstruction, and at another seems to
lose itself silently beneath the rocks, till at length rushing full in view, and reaching a precipice of moor-stone,
it tumbles from the summit in one collected mass, with
a roar almost deafening; while the foam of the waters
dashing from one enormous bed of rock to another
equally abrupt and vast, sprinkling the oak and ash and
holly that overhang the torrent, envelops the whole of
the scene in a sort of magic obscurity. The distance
from the beginning to the termination of the fall is at least
one hundred feet. After this interruption the river pursues its course through a gloomy valley, in exact accord-
ance with the character of this magnificent cataract.

The DART, the Durius of Richard of Cirencester*,
gives name to Dartmoor, in which it takes rise near
Craumere Pool, on an elevated swampy spot, in a direct
line between Oakhampton and Crockern Tor: near its
source is a granite pillar twelve feet in height. Higher
up, the rivers take a contrary direction, flowing towards
the north. This elevated part of Dartmoor is covered with
rushes and coarse grass, and appears to be totally incapable of cultivation. The river receives its name, no
doubt, from its swiftness, its current over descents generally steep being unusually rapid and always brisk.
Winding its course through a fine romantic country, it is
celebrated as one of the most picturesque rivers in the
kingdom. As the eye ranges over Dartmoor there appears to be an interminable succession of barren ridges,

CHAP.
II.

The Becky
Fall.

The Dart.

* Book i. ch. 6. § 18. In old writings, says Mr. Polwhele, it is called
Darant.

D 2

the outline being varied only by slight indentations or
lofty tors.   Longford Tor, near the Dart, is completely
conical, and has a singular and striking effect.   As the
river approaches Two Bridges it rolls through a valley
close to Wistman's Wood, the remains of the ancient
forest; and at Two Bridges it crosses the turnpike road.
Further on, winding over the moor, it has on one side Tor
Royal, the seat of Sir Thomas Tyrwhitt, and on the other
Prince Hall, the estate of the late Judge Buller.   " The
views on this part of the moor," says Mr. Jones, " are
worthy of observation on the evening of a fine day, when
some of the distant hills put on a deep blue, and others
are tinged by the bright rays of the setting sun, which
generally descends in clouds, and affords even to the
solitary wilds of Dartmoor features which may attract
the attention of the artist or the traveller.   There is in
this district a stillness, a want of life and activity, and a
sombre dignity of expression in its black barren pastures,
which can only be observed in similar ranges of uncultivated land : the few cottages scattered about the valleys, surrounded by small gardens separated from the
heath by a stone wall and a heap of turf, are likewise
interesting objects in a scene marked by an absence of
variety *."

A few miles beyond Two Bridges the Dart, approaching the lower part of the vale of Widdecombe, rolls over
a shallow bed among scattered rocks.   In the breaks of
the hills distant and indistinct views are caught of the
southern parts of the county.   At Dartmeet, where there
is a noble view in the bottom of a romantic valley, a bridge
of two arches is thrown over the river near the junction
of two auxiliary streams.   Close by are some flourishing
plantations around a farm-house called Brimpts, on the

* See " A Guide to the Scenery in the Neighbourhood of Ashburton,
Devon," by the Rev. J. P. Jones, to which the writer of this work is indebted for the greater part of this description of the river Dart. This little
publication, as the descriptions are founded on actual observation, is
really interesting and valuable, and an indispensable companion to any
visitor who wishes to explore this part of the county.

side of the hill directly opposite to which is a lofty barren
heath, with a winding road leading down to the bridge.
Near the latter are a cottage, and the remains of an ancient bridge formed of large flat slates,—a specimen of
the original mode of crossing the Dartmoor streams before the introduction of arches *.   On the summit of the
hill opposite Brimpts there is an extensive view, which
takes in the prison and a considerable part of the moor ;
and a little further on is Shapiter Tor, a conical pile of
rocks forming one side of a wide valley, at the extremity
of which is a farm-house, a pleasing object in the midst
of this superabundance of rocks and heathy pastures. As
the river approaches Holne, the vale becomes deeper
and the sides of the hills are lofty and precipitous.   On
a projecting rock above Spitchwick is a magnificent view
of the course of the stream along the rocky valley, amidst a
succession of barren hills, where the water appears white
with foam, and its murmurs are distinctly heard. It then
passes at the foot of Holne Moor and Bench Tor, near
which it enters on the inclosed country and assumes a
new appearance, the banks being thickly clothed with
woods for several miles.   On the left is Spitchwick, the
seat of Lord Ashburton, the plantations of which are extensive and flourishing in the midst of a barren country
and downs covered with furze and rocks. The finest part
of the scenery in this spot is along the banks of the river,
which is very romantic, the broad extent of Dartmoor rising
beyond, and with its blue rugged expanse closing the prospect.   On leaving Spitchwick you immediately enter the
woods of Buckland-in-the-Moor, a retired and delightful
spot.   The view extends along the vale of the Dart, and
embraces a long range of hills and woods.   In the lower
part of the plantations a small stream joins the Dart,
and a road has been formed along the banks of the river.
The beauty and magnificence of the scenery here can

* There are several bridges of this kind on the upper part of the Dartmoor rivers. They consist of rude pillars covered with flat stones, sometimes so large as to render it difficult to conceive how they were placed
there.

hardly be described*. Newbridge, at the foot of a steep descent crowned with a mass of rude rocks, crosses the Dart, and connects Widdecombe with Holne. The walks along the river are enchanting, and the scenery sublime. Holne Chase, with its woods and rocky summits, extends about two miles along the banks of the stream. Beyond the Chase, near Holne Bridge, is Holne Park, the seat of Sir Bourchier Wrey, Bart. Behind the park the hills rise to a considerable height, and on the summit of one of the loftiest is Hembury Castle, an earthwork thrown up, perhaps, by the Danes. Passing Holne Park, the Dart proceeds to Buckfastleigh, where in a beautiful wooded vale about a mile from the village, on the banks of the river, are the remains of the great Cistercian Abbey. At Dartbridge the river crosses the turnpike road, and is joined by another stream of some size. The church of Buckfastleigh is on a hill just above the bridge. Pursuing its course through a fine fertile country and the most beautiful scenery, between Dartington and Little Hempton, the Dart flows in placid beauty beneath the high hill which is distinguished by the castle and church of Totness. About three miles below, it receives a small river called Harbern, which, rising on the borders of Dartmoor a short distance north of Rattery, gives name to Harberton†. In the vicinity of Harberton is the vale of Dean Burn, a most enchanting and romantic spot, where are several picturesque waterfalls. The neighbourhood of Torbryan is full of rocks and tors, among which rises a brook, which soon empties itself into the Dart. Passing by Ashpreington, Cornworthy, and Dittisham to Dartmouth, the river empties itself into the sea about a mile below, where on the rocks of the western

---

* For an excellent description of the whole scenery in this vicinity, see the " Guide " before referred to.

† " Harbertoun water cummith out of a well spring, and so renning about a two miles, passith thorough a stone bridg caullid Rastel-Thens in two miles lower to Bowbridge, and ther goith into salt water that creketh into the land out of the maine streame of Dartmouth haven."—Leland's Itin. vol. iii. p. 31.

bank is an ancient fort or castle. The Dart is navigable
to Totness ; and a short distance below that town receiving the tide, the river rolls a majestic stream between
hills and dales richly wooded and interspersed with cottages and villas, disclosing new beauties at every curve,
and forming altogether a scene well calculated to gratify
a taste for the grand and beautiful. The adjacent country varies perpetually both in form and in its attendant
features. The eminences which inclose the Dart become
at last almost mountainous, while the river, winding between
their rocky bases, passes the striking position called
Kingsweare on the east, and the irregular town of Dartmouth on the west. The whitened fronts of the houses
ranged above each other on the side of a steep hill,
beautifully interspersed with rocks and wood, with the
walls of the castle and its romantic church in the distance, form a grand and beautiful close to the scene *.
The course of the Dart is about forty miles. The principal bridges are those at Holne, Buckfastleigh, Ne-
therton and Totness.

A few miles from Dartmouth on the coast of Start Slapton
Bay, south-west of Slapton, is a fresh-water lake about Lake.

* Beauties of England, vol. iv.

BOOK
I.

two miles in length, which is generally reckoned a curiosity, as it is separated from the sea only by a sand-
bank, and has no apparent outlet. There is nothing,
however, peculiar to it which cannot be accounted for
without difficulty. The lake is supplied by several brooks
in its vicinity, which are prevented from running into the
sea by the height of the beach. The bank that forms
the line of separation is sometimes broken through by
the weight of the water in the lake, or by the violence
of the sea in a tempest; but when this is not the case,
the fresh water oozes through the sand in sufficient
quantity to prevent the lake overflowing.

The Aven.

The AVEN, the next river on the southern coast of
Devon, rises also in Dartmoor, a short distance north of
Brent Beacon, and immediately before it passes Brent
runs under Leedy bridge, then between Diptford and
North Huish, passes Aveton Giffard and Bigbury, discharging itself into the sea at Aven Mouth. The principal bridges on this river are Brent or Leedy bridge
on the road from Totness to Modbury, Geran bridge
on the Dartmouth road, and another at Aveton Giffard.

View at
Brent or
Leedy
bridge.

The Aven flows through a fertile country rich in interesting views. Immediately before it passes under
Brent or Leedy bridge it pours down a ledge of rocks,
not much higher indeed than a common weir; but the
height of the arch of the bridge beautifully covered with
ivy, and the waterfall seen through the arch, together
with the picturesque approach of the stream towards the
bridge, afford an assemblage of romantic objects so finely
harmonized, that it has been preferred even to the Becky
Fall, and considered much superior to the cascades or
the cataract at Lydford bridge *. It is not half a mile
from the great western road.

The Erme.

The ERME also rises on Dartmoor not far from Peter
Cross Tor, and passing Ivy bridge, Ermington, and near

* Polwhele's Devon.

Halbeton, falls into Bigbury Bay at Ringmore[*]. Ivy bridge, well known and much celebrated for its romantic scenery, on the great western road, and another on the road from Modbury to Plymouth, are its principal bridges. The course of this river is only about thirteen miles; but, short as it is, it abounds with admirable views. In the parish of Ermington there is a hill rising behind the church, overlooking the windings of the river; and from this spot there is also a fine view of the picturesque village of Ermington, and of Ivy, Lyd and Secars bridges, with an extensive inland prospect over the different valleys through which the beautifully serpentine course of the river may be seen.

The YEALME rises north of Cornwood, being collected from several springs in a large vale of lean and hungry land at the foot of Dartmoor, and from small streams in the same vicinity. The most conspicuous hill in this quarter rises above its source, and is called by the country people the Shell-top, from its resemblance to a limpet-shell. Passing Cornwood, which it divides into two nearly equal parts, and crossing the Plymouth road at Lee Mill bridge, the river proceeds to the village of Yealmton, to which it gives name, and thence to Newton Ferrers, falling into the sea about two miles below, opposite the Mewstone west of Bigbury Bay. The principal bridges over the Yealme are on the great road to Plymouth and on the Modbury road. The course of this river, over a bed of moor-stone and gravel, is generally rapid. A large body of water is usually collected by it from the rains during the winter, but in dry summers the whole stream through the greater part of its course is barely sufficient for a mill. Three miles from its mouth, however, it is navigable for sloops and small brigs to Kitley-quay, and for barges and boats still higher.

The Yealme.

---

[*] " This river risith by north est, and runnith upon great rokky stones with no small noise. Some say that part of Philippe, king of Castille's navie was driven toward the mouth of this water, wher is no harbour but periculus rokkes."—Leland's Itin. vol. iii. p. 28.

Further upwards, from the approach of the hills towards each other, several romantic views occur in its passage between steep and narrow banks not two hundred yards from each other.

The Silver.   The *Silver*, a small clear stream, rises about half a mile north of the Plymouth road, and running through Brixton over a bed of gravel, and for the most part between banks of clay, falls into the Yealme near Kitley, about two miles from its mouth.

The Plym.   The PLYM rises on Dartmoor about three miles north of Walkhampton, and passing by Meavy church, between Brickleigh and Shaugh, after separating the parish of Plympton St. Mary from that of Eggbuckland, proceeds by Plympton to Saltram. From Plympton it forms a wide estuary, which after becoming narrow again at Oriston, joins the Tamar in Plymouth Sound.

The
Meavy.   The little river *Meavy* rises also on Dartmoor, and after passing Sheepstor falls into the Plym in the parish of Meavy.

The Tavey.   The *Tavey* rises in the northern extremity of Plympton parish, and after running through Newnham Park becomes a considerable stream, and joins the Plym at Newbridge.

The
Tamar.   The TAMAR head is a short distance from two tumuli called Wooleigh Burrows, in the parish of Morwinstow, in a basin about eighteen inches in diameter. The ridge near the Burrows easterly is the boundary of Devon and Cornwall, not far from which spot these counties are separated by the Tamar, which serves that purpose nearly the whole of its course. About a mile from its source this river runs between two elevations, East Youlston and West Youlston, having a narrow channel between both. It soon becomes a considerable stream, and ten miles from its source passes Tamarton, to which it gives name, where leaving a stone bridge it continues south till it enters the parish of St. Stephen, at the corner of which it receives a plentiful stream called the Werrington. In this quarter it has Devonshire on both

sides of it, the village of Werrington being on the west. About a mile and a half lower down it receives the Aterey, which runs under the walls of Launceston, and shortly after, at Polston bridge, becomes a wide and rapid stream. Proceeding nearly south, and receiving brooks from both counties until it has passed Grainston bridge, the river increases in width, and flows under a high stone bridge called Horsebridge, and by Leland Howtebrige, *i. e.* Highbridge. The last bridge in its course is in the parish of Calstock and is called Newbridge *. It becomes a wide estuary near Beer Alston, and receives the Tavy below Beer Ferrers; and having formed a creek in the parishes of Batsfleming and Landulph, and passing Saltash, (an ancient Cornish borough,) it expands into the spacious harbour called the Hamoaze, near the entrance to which is Plymouth Dock, or Devonport. It then falls into Causand Bay, or Plymouth Sound, between Mount Edgecombe and Stonehouse, after a course of about forty miles. Its principal bridges are Bridgerule, Tamarton, Palton, Grainston bridges, Horsebridge and Newbridge in the parish of Calstock. The following are the rivers that fall into the Tamar.

The *Week* rises near Pancrasweek, and, running between Bridgerule and Pyworthy, empties itself into the Tamar nearly opposite North Tamarton. The *Derle*, rising near Pyworthy, and the *Deer* near Holsworthy, join their streams and fall into the Tamar about a mile and a half below their junction. Lower down about half a mile the Tamar receives the *Claw*, which rises near Clawton, and runs near Tetcot. The Week, the Derle, the Deer, and the Claw.

The *Werrington* on the west side of the Tamar, rising in Cornwall, forms the boundary which separates the parishes of Petherwin and Werrington in Devonshire from the former county, and after passing through Werrington Park falls into the Tamar a short distance below. The The Werrington. The Cary.

* "This New Bridge," says Leland, "was of the making of the abbots of Tavestock, and maintained by them; for Tavestock Abbey had fair possessions thereabout."—Itin. vol. iii. p. 57.

Cary rises near Ashwater, and passing by Virginstow falls into the Tamar between Upper Newbridge and Polston bridge.

The Lyd.
Romantic scenery at Lidford bridge.

The *Lyd* rises on Dartmoor, and passing by Lidford forms a cataract that is much admired. The whole of the scenery indeed in this vicinity is in the highest degree romantic and beautifully picturesque. After issuing from the moor this little river seems to have worn itself a very deep channel through the solid rock, dashing between high banks irregular and broken, in some places variegated with herbage, in others rude and bare, with tremendous rocky projections, and in some parts overshadowed by majestic trees. The view down from the bridge on the Tavistock road into the deep gulf below is appalling. The rude projecting sides of this fissure, not more than seven or eight feet asunder, support the bridge. About half way down, the trunks of fallen trees rest suspended, with huge fragments of rocks severed from the parts above; their bare and rugged points, with the spars from every crevice, and the white foam of the river dashing among the rocks at the bottom about sixty feet below, are scarcely discernible through the gloom, nor can more than a faint murmur of the waters be heard so high. Whether this small stream has really scooped itself so deep a passage through the rocks, or whether the fissure has been occasioned by some convulsion of nature, must be left to naturalists to determine *.

The cascade and cataract of the Lyd.

The Lidford cascade, which is near the bridge, is also considered as a great curiosity. It is formed by a small stream running into the Lyd over a romantic rock finely clothed with wood. The streamlet winding its course

---

* This spot, as Mr. Polwhele relates, has served the purpose of suicide. The following is an astonishing instance of deliberation and firmness in the perpetration of such an act. A Captain Williams rode thirty miles from Exeter to this place with no other object in view. After endeavouring to make his horse leap the parapet of the bridge, but in vain, he dismounted, threw himself over, and was dashed to pieces: the horse returned to the inn. And a few days after a poor man of the village, in the paroxysm of a delirious fever, also threw himself over the bridge, and met with a similar fate.

down this eminence in a manner the most graceful for about two hundred feet, meets with a projection of the rock near the bottom, which gives it the appearance of a beautiful fountain. Below, in a deep and narrow valley, with sides almost perpendicular and thickly wooded, the whole scene is enchanting. Fine as the cascade is, however, the cataract of the river Lyd itself, which runs through the valley, is much superior as to picturesque effect. A short distance below the bridge, among alpine scenery of the wildest and most romantic description, is one of the finest waterfalls in the county. After raging among the rocks, the river thunders down about thirty feet in the gloomy recesses, foaming among fragments scattered in all directions and with the rudest grandeur. About two miles east of Lidford bridge the water runs partly under ground at a place called Skidhole. After passing Coryton, Marystow and Lifton, the Lyd falls into the Tamar nearly two miles south of Polston bridge.

The small river *Tinhay* falls into the Lyd near Lifton. The Tinhay.

The *Tavy* rises on Dartmoor, and after passing between St. Mary Tavy and Peter Tavy, and running through a deep valley and by Tavistock, (to which place it gives name,) proceeds thence near Whitechurch and Buckland Monachorum, as well as between Beer Ferrers and Tamerton Foliot, and falls into the Tamar opposite Landulph. The banks of the Tavy, with the beautiful remains of the abbey, the walls of which run a considerable distance by the side of it forming a delightful public walk, are highly interesting and romantic. Large rocks also intercept the progress of the river from the town, by which means many pleasing cataracts and little bays are formed that delight the eye of the observer. The Tavy.

The little river *Stour* rises also on Dartmoor, and passing near Sampford Spiney, Walkhampton and Buckland Monachorum, falls into the Tavy near the latter place. The Stour.

The TORRIDGE rises, at the distance of a few yards only from the source of the Tamar, (the latter running southward and the former towards the north,) from two The Torridge.

springs on a pretty level summit of a very high common
near Wooleigh Burrows mentioned before; and after running about fifty miles in the north-west part of the county
a course the most circuitous, with numerous windings
and abrupt doublings, falls into the Bristol Channel near
Appledore. Not far from its source it passes between
East and West Putford, then between Bulkworthy and
Abbots Bickington, near Newton Petrock, between Sheb-
bear and Bradford, near Black Torrington and Shipwash;
between Meeth and Idderleigh, and between Dawland,
Dalton, and Beaford on the east, and Huish and Little
Torrington on the west, to Great Torrington. Thence,
leaving Frithelstock and Monkleigh on the west, the
river proceeds to Wear Gifford, and near Lancross to
Bideford, where it becomes a wide and rapid stream,
flowing between Appledore and Instow, near which it
unites with the estuary of the Taw, and both together
fall into Barnstaple Bay about two miles below. The
water of this river has generally a dark brown tinge from
the moorland through which it passes. At Bideford it
becomes clear and salt, and the colour of it is a light
green. Its bed consists of a light umber-coloured sand
fit for manure, and of some gravel useful to potters.

The Wal-
dron.

The little river *Waldron* rises near Bradsworthy on
the borders of Cornwall, and, after running near Sut-
combe and Milton Dameral, falls into the Torridge near
Bradford.

The Ock,
or Oak-
ment.

The *Ock*, or *Oakment*, descends from Dartmoor in two
streams called the East and West Oakment, which passing the park unite near the town of Oakhampton; and
proceeding thence between Jacobstow and Exborne, and
near Monk Oakhampton, the river falls into the Torridge
nearly opposite Meeth.

The Taw.

The TAW rises on Dartmoor near Craumere Pool, passes
near Belston, crosses the Oakhampton road between Stic-
kle-path and South Zeal Chapels, and runs near South
Tawton, North Tawton, Bundley, Brushford, Nymet Ro-
land, Egglesford, about a mile and a half west of Chawley

and Chumleigh; leaving High Bickington and Atherington about the same distance to the west, and Warkleigh and Chittlehampton to the east. Proceeding under New Bridge by a course beautifully serpentine, it divides Tawstock and Tawton, and about two miles below it passes Barnstaple under an excellent stone bridge of nineteen arches, when by a broad estuary, having Pilton, Ashford and Heanton Punchardon on the north, and Fremington on the south, it proceeds to Instow, where it joins the estuary of the Torridge after a course of about sixty-eight miles. The chief bridges over the Taw are at Humberleigh, New Bridge, and Barnstaple.

A small stream called the *Little Dart* rises near Rakenford, and passing near Witheridge, East and West Worlington, Cheldon and Chumleigh, falls into the Taw about a mile and a half from the last-mentioned town.

: The river *Bray* rises in the vicinity of Exmoor, a short distance south of Parracombe; runs near Challacombe, between Charles and High Bray, near East Buckland, through Earl Fortescue's grounds at Castlehill, under Filleigh bridge near Sutterleigh, and New Place in King's Nympton, falling into the Taw near Newnham bridge.

The *Mole* rises in Exmoor about two miles north of North Molton, from which place, passing by South Molton and George Nympton, it joins the Bray nearly opposite Sutterleigh. Several nameless streams rising south of Exmoor join the Mole.

The *North Yeo* rises in two streams south-west of Parracombe in the parish of East Down, where are numerous springs of the purest water. One of these streams runs near Arlington and Laxhore, and the other near Bratton Fleming, and having united form the Yeo, which runs by Yeoton, near Goodleigh, and between Pilton and Barnstaple, near which town, after a course of about ten miles, it falls into the estuary of the Taw. There is a bridge over the Yeo between Pilton and Barnstaple. This river turns many mills, particularly those at Rawleigh, where is a great woollen and cotton manufactory in the parish of

CHAP.
II.

The Little Dart.

The Bray.

The Mole.

The North Yeo.

Pilton. It also supplies Barnstaple with water carried in pipes from Rawleigh Mills.

The Lyn.

The river *Lyn* rises on Exmoor, and after a course of about ten miles, having passed near Brendon, falls into the sea at Linmouth, commonly pronounced Lymouth, near Linton, to both of which it gives name. This little river is highly interesting from the romantic scenery through which it passes. It makes its way over numerous huge rocks with great rapidity into the Bristol Channel. A short distance from the sea it forms a fine cascade over a fall of about fourteen feet, which is particularly beautiful when the river is swelled by the rains.

The preceding is a brief sketch of the rivers of Devonshire. Smaller streams and springs, descending from almost every hill in the county, are exceedingly numerous, and of course cannot be specified.

Craumere Pool.

It is observable that several of the Dartmoor rivers take their rise near Craumere Pool in the morass with which it is surrounded to the extent of two miles; as the Teign, the Dart, the Lyd, the Ockment, the Tavy, and the Taw. This pool is in fact a great bog, which in the winter is converted by the rains into a lake. It is of an oblong form, about one hundred and fifty feet in length and eighty in breadth. The water in it gushes from a bed of gravel beneath a stratum of peat bog. It is situated about the centre of Dartmoor, at a considerable elevation among the hills, about twelve miles from Moreton Hampstead, eight from Tavistock, and six from Oakhampton. It is not correctly placed in the maps, and is found with great difficulty.

Changes in the beds, &c. of rivers.

That all rivers from natural causes undergo, in a greater or less degree, perpetual changes in the elevation of their beds and in the direction of their courses, as well as in the depth if not in the rapidity of their streams, is well known. Whilst their banks in some places are constantly being worn away, in others they are receiving considerable additions. Some streams, dashing over rocks, have worn themselves deep channels in the solid stone; and in the lower and more level parts of the country depositions of sand, soil, gravel, and other materials, brought down by currents and inundations, serve to elevate the adjacent lands as well as the beds of rivers; and from this cause, together with accumulations of 'sand and pebbles thrown up by the sea, their mouths especially are liable to great and important alterations. The more mountainous and rocky the countries through which they pass, the more violent are their currents, and the more sudden and extensive the inundations which ensue upon heavy rains and thunder storms, the clouds being attracted and intercepted in their course by the hills. These characteristics belong particularly to the rivers of Devonshire. Rising chiefly on Dartmoor at great elevations, and passing over rocks and declivities, their currents are rapid, and their floods often sudden and tremendous. This, however, appears to have been the case in a much greater degree in former periods than at present. The whole country then abounded with woods, and a great part of Dartmoor is supposed to have been an extensive forest, some vestiges of which are still remaining. Hence larger quantities of moisture were supplied for the currents, and the torrents and inundations were occasionally appalling. Evidences of this are found in numerous places in the vicinity of the rivers. The following is an abstract of some of the principal changes enumerated chiefly by Mr. Polwhele as the effects of these causes. At Tiverton the alterations in the bed and the course of the river Exe are remarkable. In 1771 St. Peter's church and tower were declared to be in danger from the encroachments of this river; and that it was navigable much higher than at present there is no doubt. Anchors have been found at Cowley bridge, far above the present navigation. Formerly mills were at work on the banks of the river a little under the road towards this bridge, from which spot the water has now retired to a considerable distance. In the suburbs of Exeter some of the lands now dry were once overflowed. Half a century ago a man digging for a well in his garden in the parish of St. Thomas, found first a stratum of sand, after this several other strata of different kinds; and under the whole, about fifteen feet deep, a bed of hazel leaves five or six inches thick, on the removal of which nuts swam about on the surface of the water. Hither therefore, it should seem, they must have been drifted and afterwards covered.

Many of the massy stones near the rivers of Dartmoor have been evidently moved to a considerable distance, and some of them worn smooth by the violence of the torrents, which were so much greater before the removal of the woods.

On the banks of the stream that runs below Chudleigh Rock, a short distance above the cataract, is a large rock close to the bed of the rivulet, covered with a number of curious cavities, some of which are two feet in depth and a foot in circumference: there are several smaller ones communicating with each other by means of lips' perforated in the rock. These cavities have been formed by the action of the water rushing with violence over the rock during the winter floods, and whirling round stones, which soon create hollows in the soft limestone rock. Similar basins may be observed on the banks of rapid rivulets in various parts of the county *.

The river Yealme must have changed its course materially, as the two stone bridges of Torr and Puslinch seem to indicate, which instead of being at right angles with the stream are now approaching to a parallel with it. The Lyd, as mentioned before, is a remarkable instance of a river fretting and wearing out its bed to a great depth among the rocks. This circumstance is taken notice of by Risdon as well as Polwhele, and Camden has the following observation respecting it: " The little river Lyd is so confined by the rocks at the bridge, and falls down so high a precipice to such a depth in the ground, which

* From information with which the writer was favoured by the Rev. J. P. Jones, of North Bovey.

it continually hollows for itself, that to the astonishment of travellers the water is not seen, but only the noise heard *." Other instances of alteration in the course and beds of the rivers will be adverted to, when the singular changes that have occurred on the coast are described.

THE SPRINGS.

To ascertain the prevailing qualities of the springs of a country is certainly of some importance,—not as a matter of mere curiosity, but in reference to geology, and in a considerable degree to the health of the inhabitants in their vicinity. They are the sources of rivers; they give indications of the strata among which they take their rise; some of them are medicinal; and at any rate the inquiry whether the water in general use is salubrious or otherwise, is deserving of attention. It is proper therefore to take some notice of the springs of Devonshire; and as Mr. Polwhele, who resided in the county, has taken more pains with this subject than any other writer on its topography, the following is given as a sketch, with additions, of those which he has described.

Beginning with the eastern part of the county, it may be observed, that the country between the Axe and the Otter abounds with excellent water. Two springs are deserving of notice that rise at the two extremities of a stratum of limestone in the parish of Widworthy, a mile distant from each other, the water of which is remarkably pure and warm: over every meadow through which they flow a most luxuriant vegetation is diffused. The one runs into the Coly, and the other into a rivulet on the western side of this parish. At the head of the Beer a pure spring rises out of a flinty rock, and runs in a clear current through the town of Ottery St. Mary; and in the middle of the town is a spring that sparkles with all the brilliancy of the Bristol waters, but without their warmth. Another spring, rising near a house called Paradise, has been used medicinally as a solvent for the stone.

Remarkable springs.

* Brit. vol. i. p. 25.

Between the Otter and the Exe, among a variety of springs the most remarkable are those at Tidwell, of which Risdon gives the following account : " The ponds at Tidwell, maintained by springs, continually whelm and boil up, not unlike that wonderful well in Derbyshire which ebbeth and floweth by just tides. These springs are so warm, that whilst all the waters around are frozen they are free from ice in the coldest weather; when abundance of wild fowl flock hither, to the no little pleasure and profit of the place."

Near St. Leonard's Chapel, Exeter, on the road to Topsham, is Parker's Well, famed for its medicinal qualities. Mineral springs, towhich there was formerly much resort, are found in the parish of St. Sidwell. Just above Hill's Court there is a pleasant water moderately impregnated with iron. The water of Exeter in general is said not to be good; but to that which issues from the northern rock, below the castle, great virtues have been attributed. This spring is never dry. The water with which the Bedford Circus is supplied issues from a spring remarkably fine and the most salubrious in the city. The conduit is supplied by springs in the parish of St. Sidwell.

Between the Exe and the Teign mineral springs are numerous. Gubb's Well is in the parish of St. Thomas. Near Cleve is a chalybeate of considerable strength; and also near the brow of the hill above Pocomb bridge an agreeable strong chalybeate is found; and another in the vale immediately under Longdown on the right hand leading from Exeter. The brackishness of the water at Exminster is remarkable. In that neighbourhood several chalybeate springs occur, as well as in the road near an estate called Wracombe, in this parish. The water of a spring in Ugbrooke Park, near the Swiss bridge, is impregnated with iron. At Haldon House the water sparkles like champagne, and is equal to that of the Circus at Exeter. On Little Haldon there is a remarkable spring called Whitwell, or Witywell, headed with stone work, and formerly much resorted to. On an estate in the parish

of Ideford there is a chalybeate, the water of which resembles those of Bristol. But of all the springs in this
part of the county the waters of Kingsteignton have the
strongest impregnation of iron. The stream called the
Mole, the source of which is in Whiteway estate in the
parish of Kingsteignton, buries itself in Kingswood, a
part of Landridge in Bishopsteignton; and after running a
mile and half under ground, rises again near the town of
Kingsteignton, forming a part of Fairwater spring, which
turns the mills of the latter town. Fairwater stream is
never known to fail, and is the most pleasant as well as
the most wholesome water in Devonshire; it is colder
in summer than at other times, and never freezes. The
water in Mr. James Templar's canal is impregnated with
ochre, and that at the Bovey head has a similar appearance. In one of the coal-pits on the Heathfield there is a
large pool, the water of which is as warm as some of the
Bath springs; but it is remarkable that an adjoining pool,
separated by the space of a foot only, is quite cold. The
tepid spring is green, and has an ochreous incrustation.
There are strong chalybeates at Ilmington. At Ashburton,
and near the banks of the Dart, there are springs saturated with ochre.

Near Brixham in Torbay, at the foot of a large ridge
of hills, is Laywell, a remarkable spring that ebbs and
flows very sensibly. In some fevers the common people
think it medicinal: this notion, however, appears to be
superstitious, and it is worthy of notice only as an intermitting fountain. It is certainly a curiosity, and has
been observed formerly by men of science very minutely.
The water rises in a large basin with an area of about
twenty feet. By a careful observation of a great number
of fluxes and refluxes it was found to ebb and flow, when
it proceeds regularly, about eleven times in an hour; but
occasionally to intermit, and to have no motion whatever
for an hour or more. It is also observed in summer to
rise generally about an inch and one-eighth, sometimes
an inch and three-quarters, and at other times not more

Laywell.

than an inch.　Two accounts were sent about a century ago to the Royal Society, and inserted in the Philosophical Transactions: the first by Dr. William Oliver [*], who made observations upon it twice with considerable care in the year 1693.　His description of it on the whole corresponds with what is now known of the spring; but he makes no attempt to account for its remarkable phænomena.　He observes however, justly, that there is no evidence of its communication with the sea, as it issues from an elevation above the level of high-water mark, at the distance of a mile; nor is the water of the spring at all brackish, but soft and pleasant to the taste, being used by the people in the neighbourhood for culinary purposes. In addition to this it must also be observed, that the frequency and irregularity of its fluxes and refluxes demonstrate that it has no connection whatever with the tides of the ocean.—The other account of this remarkable spring is by Mr. John Atwell, F.R.S. in the year 1732 [†], who states at large the particulars of his own observations, and at the same time suggests an ingenious and satisfactory hypothesis to account for the phænomena of intermitting springs in general, and of this in particular.　As this communication contains matter of curiosity and interest, the substance of it, as follows, may be acceptable to the reader.　Upwards of a mile from the sea, upon the north-east side of a range of hills, there is a constantly running stream which discharges itself near one corner into a basin about eight feet in length and four and a half in breadth, the outlet of which is at the furthest end from the entrance of the stream, and of sufficient height for the purpose of making observations on the rise and fall of the water.　Outside of the basin also are three springs which run constantly, but with streams subject to a like variation of increase and decrease with the main spring; they are evidently branches of the latter.　After much rain, moreover, when springs in general are high, upon

[*] Phil. Trans. vol. xvii. for the year 1693, pp. 908 and 910.
[†] Ibid. vol. xxxvii. page 301.

the flux or increase of this fountain several small additional streams are observed to break forth both in the bottom of the basin and on the outside of it, which disappear again when the ebb or decrease takes place. At the time when Mr. Atwell saw them they were more than sufficient to turn an overshot mill, of which the stream in the basin might be about one-half.

When this gentleman and his companion arrived at the spot, they were informed, by a man at work near, that the spring had flowed and ebbed about twenty times that morning, but had ceased to do so about an hour before they came. Mr. Atwell observed the stream more than an hour by his watch, without perceiving the least variation in the height of the water in the basin. After leaving it for a short time, on their return the man informed them the spring began to flow and ebb about half an hour after they left, and had continued to do so ten or twelve times. In less than a minute they saw the stream coming into the basin, and those on the outside beginning to increase and flow with great violence. The water in the basin rose perpendicularly about an inch and a quarter; nearly two minutes after it began to sink; and in two minutes more it had fallen to its usual height, where it continued stationary for about two minutes longer. From repeated observations it appeared that at that time the rise, descent and pause were made in about five minutes and a little more. By the mark on the stones it was evident the water had risen, before they returned, about three quarters of an inch higher; and it appeared also that some little abatement was perceptible both in the perpendicular height and in the time of rising and sinking, while the period of the pause seemed to lengthen. From a comparison of his own account with Dr. Oliver's just mentioned, Mr. Atwell concluded that the flux and reflux took place about nine or ten times in an hour, except when it ceased to ebb and flow altogether.

Mr. Atwell's hypothesis, which can scarcely fail to be interesting to the intelligent observer, is briefly this. He supposed the phænomena of this spring to be occasioned by two streams, or springs, one of which passes through two caverns, or natural reservoirs, with a syphon, thought not to be uncommon in the bowels of the earth, belonging to each, and meets with the other stream or spring, in a third reservoir without a syphon, from which they issue to the surface of the earth in conjunction. The effect of this arrangement it will be difficult to understand without an engraving, which is here subjoined.

Suppose the reservoir E F to be constantly supplied by the stream H; the water Y will then issue regularly into the open air at the vent K. But suppose this reservoir to receive at Q the water of another spring G, coming through two other caverns A B and C D, each having a syphon M L N and P O Q; the stream at K would then

Drawn by T.M. Baynes.

Engraved by W.Deeble.

ILFRACOMBE.

THE NEW BRIDGE, TOTNES.

flow and ebb with intervals of intermission, when it would
issue regularly in a smaller quantity, being supplied only
by the stream H.

To explain this, it must be observed that the cavern
A B will retain all the water that comes into it by the
spring G until this water rises to the top of the syphon L,
when this syphon beginning to play will empty the cavern
till the water has sunk below its upper mouth M. This
syphon, however, must be large enough to discharge more
water than is supplied by the spring G. After the water W
has sunk below M, the syphon will cease to play till the
cavern is filled again, when it will play as before. The
second cavern C D therefore will be supplied with water
by the syphon M L N, but not constantly, and only
when the syphon plays. The syphon P O Q will draw
off the water X in the cavern C D in a similar manner,
and supply the reservoir E F, though with intermissions,
provided also that this syphon have a larger bore than
M L N; so that the water issuing at K will flow constantly, in consequence of being supplied by the stream
H; but when the syphon P O Q plays, an increased issue
will take place at K; and when this syphon stops, it will
be reduced to its usual quantity. This will take place
regularly so long as the cavern C D is supplied by the
syphon M L N; but that syphon, it has been shown, will
also intermit, and the consequence will be, that when the
cavern C D ceases to be supplied by the syphon M L N,
the flowing and ebbing at K will stop till C D is again
supplied by M L N. And it is obvious that the width of
the lower syphon 'may be in such proportion to the upper,
that the former may empty the cavern C D in a few minutes, whilst the latter may continue for hours, or days,
before it has emptied the cavern A B; and hence it appears that by this very ingenious hypothesis all the phænomena of Laywell may be explained. It is well known
there are many caverns in the bowels of the earth, for
in mining, numbers have been discovered; nor is it at all
absurd to suppose that some of these may communicate

BOOK
I.

with each other or with the open air by means of natural syphons. It is of no signification how crooked and
irregular these water-courses may be, provided they retain all the properties of the syphon; that is, if they be
air-tight, the upper bend be towards the top of the
cavern, and the inner leg shorter than the outer.——
Similar explanations of other kinds of intermitting
springs, and of such as have a regular flux and reflux,
may be seen in Mr. Atwell's paper on the subject in the
Philosophical Transactions *.

The southern parts of Devon in general have the advantage of clear and wholesome water. Near Totness
are several excellent chalybeate springs. About Newton
Ferrers, the whole country abounding with lime rock, the
springs are clear and salubrious. The parish of Brixton
is remarkable for pure inodorous water. Of the singular
wells at Stonehouse, three of the finest ebb and flow, and
hence it is inferred that they communicate with each
other; but, as the water is soft and fit for every purpose
of common use, on what the supposition is founded that
they have communication also with the sea, does not appear. Out of certain pits in the moors about Patrickstow
brackish water issues, at the distance of twelve miles
from the sea. The water that springs up in the granite
district in general, about Dartmoor, is remarkably clear
and good.

The parish of Clannaborough is near the centre of the
county, and remarkably high; yet no part is better supplied with warm springs. In the parish of Swimbridge is
a singular mineral spring, efficacious in illness occasioned
by a reduced state of the system. At Barnstaple, springs
of the purest and best water abound, of which ale is made,
said to be superior to that of Burton. Warm springs
abound also in the neighbourhood between the Mole and
the Exe. In North Molton is a noted spring called

* Artificial intermitting springs or fountains may be formed by inclosing, in the side of a hill, a large chest containing an apparatus constructed upon the principles explained above.

Holywell, held in estimation by the common people as CHAP. medicinal. At Bampton, in a part called Shaltern Street, II. is a spring more strongly impregnated with iron than any other in the county.

The preceding description, it will be seen, affords ample evidence that chalybeate springs abound in Devonshire.

From the powerful and incessant action of the sea on Changes its shores, changes, in many instances of great magni- on the coast. tude and extent, are continually taking place; the sea in some districts gaining, and in others losing ground in an equal proportion. Whilst in various quarters the sea is re- tiring, the whole extent of the coast exposed to the vio- lence of the Atlantic is in a state of constant diminution, and there can be no doubt that the western extremity of the island was formerly of much greater extent than at present. The following are instances of alterations that have taken place on the coasts of Devon*. Many centuries ago there was a harbour at Seaton of considerable extent and depth. Leland, who wrote about the year 1538, takes notice of this circumstance in the following terms†. " Ther hath been a very notable haven at Seton; but now ther lyith between the 2 pointes of the whole haven a mighty rigge and barre of pible stones in the mouth of it, and the ryver of Ax is dryven to the very est point of the haven caullid Whitcliff, and ther at a very smaul gut goith into the sea. The town of Seton is now but a meane thing, inhabited by fisharmen. It hath been far larger when the haven was good." The harbour of Ax- mouth, says Mr. Polwhele, on the east side of the river, probably grew into use as that of Seaton fell into decay; but at length, however, the sea threw up such quantities of sand as rendered both harbours, by its constant accu- mulation, inconvenient and unsafe. In the year 1788, from a spot called Southdown, belonging to Mr. Rolle,

* Selected chiefly, though not entirely, from Mr. Polwhele's " Devon- shire," he having paid much attention to this subject.
† Itin. vol. iii. p. 38—47.

BOOK
I.

about half a mile from Beer, a large portion of the cliff, undermined no doubt by the sea, gave way, and sunk to a depth of about two hundred feet perpendicular. This fall forced up large rocks more than thirty feet above the level of the water, about one hundred yards from the land : and it is remarkable that the stone which was thus driven above the water, is of a very different kind from that which is found among the strata of the cliff. A greater quantity of rain than usual had fallen previously to the cliff giving way. The washing of the sea, together with the action of the frosts, the rain and the winds, has apparently formed the cliffs of Sidmouth, which are believed to have been once regular hills with sides sloping towards the water. In some parts, portions of them have evidently descended not long since ; others, being gradually undermined by the sea, have a threatening aspect, and at no great distance of time considerable falls may be expected. " Less then an hundred" (now nearly five hundred) "yeres since," says Leland *, "shippes usid the haven of Budleigh or Ottermouth, but it is now clene barrid." At Salterton there are considerable defalcations of the shore, and before many years have elapsed some of the houses will probably be tumbled into the sea. In the mouth of the Exe great changes have formerly taken place, and are still going on, for it was once much to the south of Exmouth towards Starcross. At that time the bar of sand was connected with the main land at Exmouth, and on this bar stood a fort. The river however forced itself a passage, and running towards Exmouth entirely altered its course. A cannon ball was found on the Starcross side, with several vestiges of the fortification. At present the Exe appears to be returning to its ancient channel. The vast accumulation of sand at Exmouth produced the great change in its mouth ; and the channel itself, formerly deep, but now full of banks and shallows, has become dangerous to shipping ; whilst on

* Itin. vol. iii. p. 46.

the Starcross side the sands are visibly yielding to the force of the current. About a century ago the Warren consisted of three hundred acres, but it is now reduced to less than two hundred, more than fifty having been washed away in twenty years. The tremendous storm in November, 1824, created a breach through the Warren into the Bite, which continued open for about twelve months; this is now closed up entirely by a fresh accumulation of sand. After a passage has been made in this quarter, which will probably be effected at no very distant period, the river will resume its former channel. The sea was accustomed to flow beyond Powderham Mill over the whole flat commonly called the Sod, which is at present intersected by Lord Courtenay's canal. In digging in this marsh, shells are met with as well as at Exmouth. A boat also, and some timber, were not long since discovered several feet deep, a sufficient proof that the ground has been raised. From ancient records* it appears that an arm of the sea extended to the very walls of Exeter, and the place where vessels lay at anchor for the loading and unloading of all kinds of merchandize is still called the Water-gate. The best lands in the valley beneath the city appear to have been once overflowed, and the ancient boundaries of the stream may even now be traced up and down the river. The haven on the east part of West Teignmouth, called the Poles, is almost choked by a shoal of sand thrown up by the sea. At East Teignmouth much ground has been lost, as is apparent from the situation of the church. The decrease of the cliffs along the whole coast is evident. The site of the houses at Old Teignmouth formerly burnt by the French, is now many feet below high water mark; and the cliffs at Sidmouth have lost many acres within remembrance, as have those also at Exmouth and those further on towards Teignmouth.

The surface of the present marshes of King's Teignton

* Palkian MSS. referred to by Mr. Polwhele.

is nearly on a level with the top of the old Roman arches, which were not long since laid open at the bridge; and as there is not the least inclination in the strata, it is evident these arches have not sunk, but that the adjacent land has been raised eight feet by measurement since the time of the Romans.

The whole of Bovey Heathfield, though now the lowest part of Devon, has been also raised considerably. Firs, poplars, and other trees, have been frequently dug up in this quarter; some lying near the surface, with their branches, leaves and roots, entire; others buried deep, petrified, and resembling agate in colour: they have been found in great numbers where the coal-works now are. Out of the bogs of this district the horns of the Elk, or Mouse Deer, have also been dug; and it has been imagined that the Bovey coal, which in burning emits an unpleasant smell, is pine wood. Strata of mud, sand and clay, alternate in the Heathfield, but no shells are discovered. Large stakes driven into the ground have been frequently found here, to the depth of more than nine feet. All these circumstances plainly demonstrate that Bovey Heathfield and the marshes thence to Teignmouth have been greatly raised above their former level; nor does there seem any reason to doubt that the whole of this district was once the bed of a river, or an arm of the sea. This extensive alteration has been effected probably by the gradual deposition of sand and soil, and by occasional and violent inundations, carrying down stones, earth and trees, from the higher lands in the neighbourhood. Further westward the cliffs have been greatly diminished; and at Torbay especially large tracts of land have been submerged. In confirmation of the common opinion, that a great part at least of this bay was once a wood, there appear to be sufficient indications. At low water whole trees have been dug up and drawn on shore. There is also an account of a meadow of several acres in the parish of Painton, now covered by the sea. In Tor Abbey Sands the roots of trees, as if once flourishing on the spot, have been seen at low water. The late George Cary, Esq. of Tor Abbey, built a strong sea wall along the meadows in front of the abbey, only a few years since, to repel the encroachments of the waves ; and a part of this wall was washed away in the great storm, November 23rd, 1824, by which the whole southern coast suffered much. Leland observes, that fishermen have often taken up with their nets in Torbay "musons of hartes." From these circumstances has arisen the opinion that Torbay was in former times a forest. New Totness Bridge and the adjoining grounds were not long since covered by the tide ; and the tradition is, that the whole street within fifty paces of East-gate was anciently under water. Here is a stone on which Brutus is fabled to have stepped out of his vessel when he first landed at Totness. Little more than a century ago there existed a considerable village in the north-eastern extremity of Slapton Sands, called Under-Cliff Lakes, which has now entirely disappeared ; and not many years since several houses and ten acres of land were carried away by the sea.

At Plymouth along the sides of the hill called the Hoe, or Haw, overlooking the Sound, runs a bed of sea-beach between three and four feet above the level of the present high water mark. It is in a state approaching to petrifaction, and lies in natural strata. If the sea ever rose to this spot, the present site of Plymouth must have been under water. The most probable supposition, however, is, that the elevation of this sea-beach was produced by some violent convulsion, perhaps volcanic, for its strata are not parallel with the present surface of the sea, but form an angle with it of five or six degrees. In the time of Henry VIII. the tide nearly reached the last bridge on the Tamar, in the parish of Calstock, from which spot it is now retired.

On the northern coast large fragments of cliff have been submerged in various places. At Santon hundreds of acres of good land have been overwhelmed by the sand of the sea, or washed away by the waves. Here, says Ris-

BOOK
I.

don, a tree was found under a hill of sand, which the inhabitants had undermined for manure until it fell down and produced the discovery. In other parts the sea has been excluded. The low grounds between Merton and Petrockstow are remarkable for their salt and brackish water, and might in ancient times have been an arm of the sea. No shells, however, are found here; but trees are often discovered lying in different directions among the strata, in some instances fifteen or twenty feet below the surface. Many of them are large, and lie so intermingled as to obstruct the labourer in digging for clay: on some of them nuts and leaves are found. They were probably torn from the neighbouring hills, and carried hither by some violent convulsion, contributing with other materials to raise the valley above the level of the ocean.

The parts of the coast of this county that have gained on the sea bear no proportion to those that are retiring. Both on the southern and northern side great quantities of land are continually disappearing. In the time of Edward I. Cornwall was much larger than at present. The island of St. Nicholas is said to have been at a remote period more than three times its present size. In other parts of the globe the sea is retiring to a considerable extent, but in this quarter the land is in a state of continual diminution.

CHAPTER III.

THE NAVIGATION OF THE RIVERS AND CANALS.—THE RAIL-ROADS.•

CHAP.
III.

Navigation of the rivers.

WITH the exception of Cornwall there is no county in the kingdom that possesses so great an extent of coast as Devonshire, which consequently ranks second only in the participation of the incalculable benefits, direct and

• For the following information respecting the navigation of the rivers and canals, the writer of this work is indebted to Mr. Dymond, Surveyor, Exeter; and for the account of the rail-ways to Mr. Dawson, Surveyor, of the same city.

CHAP. III.

contingent, which vicinity to the sea presents. On her northern coast there is direct and easy communication with the Severn, Wales, and Ireland, together with the north-western portions of England and Scotland; whilst the British Channel, which washes her southern shores, affords to her merchants an opportunity of receiving the various productions of the European continent and of the whole world. There is perhaps no point in the county of Devon which is distant thirty miles from the sea; and hence it is manifest, that, whilst her coasts are thus extensive, it is impossible she should possess many rivers of great magnitude or of much extent of navigation; yet considering the short course to which these rivers are necessarily limited, the body of water they convey, on account of the high and numerous hills among which they flow, is unusually large, and their channels, as they approach the sea, are broad and deep in proportion. As there is no district of the kingdom so much intersected by streams as Devonshire, these numerous rivulets, uniting before they reach the ocean, form in some cases rivers sufficiently navigable to be of vast importance to the country on their banks.

The AXE, the most eastern river of the county, can scarcely with accuracy be termed navigable, as it only admits of boats passing about four miles up the stream at high water. At the mouth of this river a small harbour and pier are being erected at the present time by J. Hallett, Esq., the proprietor of the lands adjoining, which afford good shelter for fishing-boats and other small vessels. *The Axe.*

The next river on this coast, the OTTER, is navigable only at high water for boats as far as the village of Otterton, about two miles and a half from Ottermouth. *The Otter.*

There is of necessity no trade, either import or export, on these streams.

The EXE, in a commercial view, is one of the most important rivers in the county. Vessels of from four to five hundred tons burden can cross the bar at Exmouth at *The Exe.*

high water. The harbour within, which is called The Bite, is commodious, affording good anchorage and shelter for any vessels that can pass the bar, and having sufficient depth for them to float at low water. All the heavy colliers and the larger class of merchant ships lie in The Bite, and discharge their cargoes into lighters for Topsham and Exeter. Vessels of about two hundred tons can proceed to Topsham, where considerable business is carried on in ship-building and in general trade. Vessels of nearly the same tonnage reach Exeter by means of the canal. The river itself is navigable for barges to the village of Weir only, two miles above Topsham and eight from Exmouth. The tide flows within half a mile of the quay at Exeter, to the foot of a weir erected across the river called St. James's Weir. Boats can reach this place at high water. The tonnage both in export and import on the Exe is very considerable, the latter forming by far the largest proportion. This consists principally of coals for the supply of Exeter and the neighbourhood north and west of the city, together with an extensive and populous district contiguous to the river; besides foreign timber of various kinds, and general merchandize. Large quantities of culm and limestone are also constantly brought into the river for the supply of several extensive lime works on its banks, lime forming the principal manure of the neighbourhood. The culm is brought from Wales, and the limestone from the great range of calcareous rock, or marble quarries, situated in Torbay and on the adjacent coast. The lime produced from this stone is of excellent quality, and admirably adapted to the agricultural purposes of the district; not however so suitable for building as the lime made from the blue lias stone found near Lyme and Charmouth in Dorsetshire. The exports on the river Exe consist of paper, butter, cider, native timber (principally oak and elm), manganese, and woollen manufactures.

The Teign.   The TEIGN is navigable for barges about six miles above Teignmouth to a place nearly adjoining the town of Newton Bushell. Vessels of from two to three hun-

dred tons can pass over the bar; but there is not sufficient
water in the harbour for them to float at low water. The
Teign, although a small and short river, has an extensive
export trade, greater as it respects tonnage than any
port in the county, with the exception perhaps of Plymouth. This export consists almost exclusively of clay,
conveyed to Liverpool, and up the Mersey to Runcorn, the
entrance to the Duke of Bridgewater's canal, by which
means it is conveyed to the Staffordshire potteries; and
of granite, brought down from the Hay Tor quarries, which
are very extensive, and now in full work, employing about
three hundred men. From these works immense quantities of granite of the finest quality are constantly exported to London and other large towns. It is in contemplation to cut a canal from the navigable part of the
Teign to the town of Newton Bushell, the distance being
less than a mile; and it is the opinion of those who are
interested in the undertaking, that there is a reasonable
probability of such a work paying good interest on the
capital required for completing it.

The beautiful river DART forms one of the most secure
harbours in the kingdom, and is of sufficient depth to
allow frigates to sail up the stream as far as the town of
Dartmouth, as well as to float in safety at low water.
Sloops and other vessels can pass above the town, and
heavy barges reach the bridge at Totness, nine miles from
the mouth of the river. The navigation terminates just
above the latter town, at a weir across the river, beyond
which barrier of course the tide does not flow. From the
Dart are exported some beautiful marbles, one species
of a black colour being considered particularly valuable;
great quantities of cider, of which in some years seven
or eight thousand hogsheads have been shipped; and latterly ready broken stones for forming roads in the neighbourhood of London. This latter article is obtained on
the banks of the river; and the getting it from the quarries and breaking it affords employment to a great
-number of persons. Formerly there was a considerable

trade from this harbour to the Newfoundland fisheries ;
but of late years this has been greatly diminished, if not
annihilated.

The branch or arm of the sea which extends from Salcombe to the town of Kingsbridge is called a river, although the only stream that flows into it at Kingsbridge is of
the smallest class. It is, however, a navigable creek or inlet
of great importance to that town and the adjacent country.
This creek has several arms, all of which are navigable
for boats or barges. Sloops of from eighty to one hundred tons burden can come up to Kingsbridge Quay at
high water, the distance from hence to the mouth of the
harbour being about six miles. The tide does not flow
above the town. The traffic of Kingsbridge is not very
considerable ; a little is still done in the woollen trade,
and a small quantity of manufactured goods is shipped
for the East India Company. Kingsbridge is also in some
degree celebrated for its blankets. The agriculturists in
this neighbourhood export considerable quantities of corn,
principally wheat ; and Kingsbridge itself carries on a
somewhat extensive export trade in malt, for which article
it has long been noted. The maltsters of this town appear to possess some cheap and superior mode of conducting their business, as they can afford not unfrequently
to import barley from Norfolk and the eastern counties,
and notwithstanding this to export their malt to London,
Liverpool, and other great markets.

The Aven.   The AVEN is more considerable as a river than that
which empties itself at Kingsbridge ; but the tide-way is
less extensive, and it does not possess the same facilities
for navigation. It is navigable for barges to Aveton Gifford only, nor does the tide flow beyond that place, which
is about three miles and a half from the sea. There is no
export or import trade peculiar to this river, nor is it the
medium of any traffic of much importance.

The Erme.   The ERME is navigable for vessels of from ten to fifteen
tons for about three miles from its mouth, to a small quay
two miles below the town of Modbury. The tide makes

its way about half a mile further up the stream. There is a small import trade of coals, limestone, and general merchandize for the supply of Modbury and the neighbourhood, but no export of importance.

The YEALME about three miles before it empties itself into the sea expands into a wide estuary, which may be more properly denominated a creek or an arm of the sea than a river. This inlet, with its branches, insinuating itself into the land in various directions, is of great advantage to the agriculturists on its banks. It is not navigable, however, nor does the tide flow more than three miles. There is no trade upon it of importance carried on.

The PLYM is a small river, and navigable only three miles above Plymouth. The beautiful and extensive sheet of water called the Lara, which sweeps the woods of Saltram the seat of the Earl of Morley, is formed by the estuary of the Plym. Although Plymouth itself is a port of so much importance, possesses such an excellent harbour, and carries on so extensive a trade both foreign and domestic, yet the river Plym partakes of no portion of its consequence, and the upper part of the Lara itself is navigable at high water for small barges only. There are some quarries of slate and flag-stone on this estuary, from which considerable quantities are conveyed for exportation.

The TAMAR, as it respects navigation, is by far the most important in the county, and is worthy of notice as forming the boundary, through nearly the whole of its course, between Devonshire and Cornwall. As the town of Devonport, all the extensive Government dock-yards and works, and the whole of the harbour, are in the county of Devon, the Tamar is usually, and perhaps with propriety, included among the rivers of this county: it is however, notwithstanding, through the greater part of its course wholly in the county of Cornwall. The river separates the counties, but the water itself is in Cornwall, and that county accordingly repairs most of the bridges which cross the Tamar. It is navigable, and the tide

flows more than eighteen miles above Devonport, to the
bridge called New Bridge, which is on the turnpike road
between Callington and Tavistock. To this place barges
ascend at high water. A quay which was formerly adjoining the bridge has been disused for some years ; but
about three miles down the river from this place are
situated Morwelham Quays, which vessels of from one
hundred to one hundred and fifty tons burden can reach
with perfect safety ; and very considerable exportations
take place from thence of copper ore, raised from the
mines in the neighbourhood, and brought hither by the
Tavistock canal and rail-road. From Morwelham, as the
river pursues its course towards the sea it increases in
width and becomes much deeper. Being joined by the
Tavy from Devonshire, and a little below Saltash by the
St. Germain's river from Cornwall, it expands here into a
magnificent harbour called Hamoaze, where any number of first-rate ships of the line can lie in safety at anchor.

On the Tamar no trade is carried on peculiar to itself,
except it be the exportation of copper ore just mentioned.
There are however very large quantities of limestone and
culm conveyed to various lime-kilns along the banks of
the river. Some part also of the sand in the river is
used as manure ; but this branch of traffic is not carried
to any great extent, as the sands are much mixed with
ingredients not adapted for agricultural purposes.

The Tavy.   The estuary of the TAVY, which empties itself into the
Tamar about five miles above Devonport, is of great width ;
but the tide does not flow more than three miles up the
stream, to a place called Liphill. The river is navigable
for barges of about forty or fifty tons burden to Maristow,
the seat of Sir M. M. Lopez, Bart., which is about two
miles and a half from its mouth. The sands of the Tavy
are also used as manure, being of a quality similar to those
the Tamar. At the point called Tavy-Tail, which is the
place where the waters of the Tamar and the Tavy meet,
there are valuable beds of oysters, which are private pro-

perty except during the time of Lent. Through the whole of this season the public have liberty to take whatever quantity they can raise,—a privilege of which all who have it in their power are glad to avail themselves ; but as the oyster beds are situated considerably under low water mark, it is only those who are possessed of a dredging apparatus that can participate in the benefit to be derived from this singular custom.

On the northern coast of Devonshire there are only two rivers which are navigable, the Torridge and the Taw, and these unite about two miles before they empty themselves into the sea.

The TORRIDGE is navigable for small craft to a village called Weir Gifford, which is about eight miles above the mouth of the harbour. Vessels of about sixty or seventy tons burden can, by striking their masts and passing Bideford Bridge, ascend to the basin of the Torridge canal, which is about one mile below Weir Gifford. Bideford, on the Torridge, about five miles from the sea, is a place of very considerable trade, and vessels of about two or three hundred tons burden can lie at the quay of this town ; there is not, however, sufficient depth for them to float at low water. Besides the trade of Bideford, many of the merchants of this place are large ship-owners, and the quay in consequence presents a very animated appearance. Bideford is the principal port in the county for the exportation of corn, large quantities of which are annually sent to various parts of the kingdom.

The tide flows in the river TAW, by which means it is rendered navigable to a place called New Bridge, near Bishop's Taunton, which is three miles above Barnstaple and eleven from the sea. The navigation of the Taw above Barnstaple Bridge is chiefly confined to the conveyance of limestone, coals, and culm. At this town the Taw becomes an important river. Here is an excellent quay, at which vessels of two hundred tons can lie, and considerable business is transacted, much in the same manner and in the same branches as at Bideford. Barnstaple, although a larger town, does not as a port possess so many advantages as Bideford. The navigation of the Taw is longer, narrower, and more intricate than that of the Torridge, and the vessels which can reach Barnstaple Quay are consequently inferior in respect of tonnage to those which find ready access to Bideford.

CANALS.

TheExeter
ShipCanal.

The Exeter Ship Canal, which is the property of the Mayor and Chamber of the City, now extends from Exeter to a place, on the western bank of the river, called Turf. It is nearly six miles in length; the average depth is about eleven feet, and it is capable of carrying vessels of nearly two hundred tons burden. The original canal was one of the most ancient in the kingdom. Previously to the year 1311 boats and barges came up the natural channel of the Exe, direct from Exmouth to the bridge at Exeter; but in that year a dispute arose between Hugh Courtenay, Earl of Devon, and the Mayor of Exeter, relative to a decision of the latter respecting the right of receiving three baskets of fish which were then in the market*. The Earl from that time appears to have done all in his power to injure the interests of the city; and as an effectual means for accomplishing his purpose, he choked up and destroyed the channel of the river below, built

---

* Hoker's account of this transaction is as follows. Isabella de Fortibus, Countess of Aumerle and Devon, an ancestor of the Courtenay family, had built certain weirs upon the river Exe (the property and seniority of which belonged to the city), one on the west side of the river in the parish of Exminster, and the other on the east in the parish of Topsham, leaving a space in the middle of thirty feet for the passage of boats and vessels to the quay at a place called the Water-gate; but Hugh Courtenay, the third of that name, and Earl of Devon, being incensed against the city, from some cause or other which Hoker does not state, as the most effectual way of gratifying his resentment, in the year 1313 completely destroyed the navigation of the river to Exeter, by filling up the opening between the weirs with timber and stones. At the same time he formed a quay at Topsham, where he compelled all vessels entering the port to lade and unlade their merchandize, on the payment of certain dues for his own benefit; from which place the different wares were conveyed to the city by horses, carts and waggons. After him his

two weirs across the river, and formed a quay at Topsham.
In order to restore a water communication between Topsham and Exeter, which the introduction of the woollen
trade now rendered more necessary, an act of parliament
was obtained in the reign of Henry VIII., in the year
1539, to enable the Mayor and Chamber to remove the
obstructions in the river: but this being found impracticable, another act was procured, for cutting a canal from
the city to the river above the town of Topsham. The
expense of this work was defrayed by the Mayor and
Chamber, and by voluntary subscriptions in the parishes
of the city and surrounding country; and so great was
the public anxiety to accomplish the work, that several
parishes contributed large portions of their church plate
for this purpose. The canal was from time to time improved and extended, and in 1675 was so far enlarged
as to be capable of bringing vessels of one hundred tons
burden at all tides up to the city quay. No very important alterations were made in the Exeter canal from
this period until the year 1824, when the Mayor and
Chamber commenced a variety of extensive improvements,
which are not yet wholly completed. They have erected
new gates and locks, and extended the canal nearly two
miles further down the river. They have also begun to
make a very capacious basin or floating dock opposite the

nephew, Edward Courtenay, Earl of Devon, continued and increased this
mischievous annoyance in various ways; and, to render the obstruction
more complete, under pretence of erecting certain mills, threw two other
weirs across the river, the one at St. James's and the other at Lampre-
ford, by which means not only was Exeter deprived of its haven, but the
whole vicinity, in the course of time, overflowed with salt water. Application for redress was made by the citizens in the proper quarter; various writs and commissions of inquiry were granted by the king, and
verdicts against the Earls were obtained. Such, however, was their influence and power, and such the iniquity of these times, that the law was
not suffered to have its due course against them, nor could any justice
be obtained. But at length, after many attempts and at great expense; a
water-course and passage was restored by means of the old canal, begun
in the year 1564, by which boats and vessels of fifteen or sixteen tons
conveyed goods to Exeter, and discharged their cargoes at the old quay
called the Water-gate.—See "The Antique Description and Account of
the City of Exeter by John Vowell, alias Hoker, Gent.," page 8.

quay at Exeter. Having obtained an act of parliament for carrying on these works, they have already expended large sums upon them; and it may be hoped they will eventually reap the reward due to so spirited an undertaking. The principal exports of Exeter are serges and other woollen goods, paper, and manganese. The imports are general merchandize, timber, coals, and limestone.

Mr. Templar's Canal.

There is a small canal which was executed by the father of the present George Templar Esq., of about two miles and a half in length, connecting the navigable part of the river Teign, near the town of Newton Bushell, with a rail-way which extends about seven miles further to a very elevated point called Hay Tor, being in the heart of the Dartmoor granite district. The rail-way, which is remarkable for being made wholly of granite, was laid down at his sole expense by the present Mr. Templar, late of Stover House, without an act of parliament. The canal and rail-way still remain private property, but have passed into the possession of His Grace the Duke of Somerset.

The principal traffic upon them is a coarse clay, shipped from the port of Teignmouth for the Staffordshire potteries; granite, of which some thousand tons are annually exported to London and other places; and within a very short period iron ore *, of which metal considerable quantities have been discovered in working the granite quarries on Dartmoor. No coals are found in Devonshire, and all ores are in consequence sent in a dressed state into Wales to be smelted.

Tamar Navigation.

An act of parliament was obtained in 1796, by a Company styling themselves "The Tamar Manure Navigation Company," for making cuts and canals and otherwise improving the navigation of the river Tamar from Morwelham Quay in the parish of Tavistock in the county of Devon to the immediate vicinity of the town of Launceston in Cornwall. About three miles only of this un-

* This work is at present discontinued.

dertaking was completed at an expense of £11,000 ; the works were carried on principally under the direction of one of the proprietors. The return to the shareholders is at present very small. Besides the canal and rail-road, the Company hold in perpetuity, under Lord Mount Edgecumbe and the Duke of Cornwall, an extensive fishery on the river Tamar, which is not however at present a source of the least profit ; the reserved rents paid to the lords in fee being greater than the amount for which the Company can now let the fisheries to the fishermen on the river.

The Tavistock Canal* was undertaken in the year 1803 under an act of parliament : one of its principal objects was by tunneling through Morwell Down to explore that tract of mineral country with a view to the discovery of tin and copper mines. It commences at the town of Tavistock, being there supplied with water from the river Tavy, and extends to the navigable part of the river Tamar at Morwelham Quay. It is an open narrow canal for about three miles in length to the part of the hill where the tunnel enters it, whence it is driven through solid rock for more than two thousand five hundred yards ; which excavation, together with the open canal, was completed in about fourteen years. The other end of the tunnel, being about two hundred and forty feet above the river Tamar, is connected with it by a rail-way forming an inclined plane, on which goods are raised and lowered by water power.

On the Tavistock side of the tunnel and about five hundred yards from its entrance, is an aqueduct where the canal is carried across a vale by means of an embankment of considerable length. About the middle of this valley an arch of great solidity was constructed, affording a passage under it for the river Lumborn, with a foot-path on each side of the stream, forming an opening of eighty feet in length and thirty feet in height, the summit of

* The writer was favoured with this account of the Tavistock Canal by John Taylor, Esq., who superintended the construction of it.

which receives the embankment, over which the canal is continued at an elevation of fifty feet above the surface of the river beneath.

A collateral cut north of the main line from the aqueduct to Mill Hill Bridge and Quarries is also completed, which is chiefly used for the conveyance of slate, stone, limestone, &c.

In the progress of the works some mines were discovered. The principal one, Wheal Crebor, situate near the north entrance of the tunnel, was discovered in the year 1804 and continued working for several years; large quantities of copper ores were obtained with considerable profit, a part of which was expended on the completion of the tunnel and other works, and the remainder afforded some dividends to the proprietors. From 1812 to 1817 were the years of its greatest prosperity; since which time it has been gradually declining, and at present there is little or nothing doing there. The traffic on the canal still affords a small rate of interest to the proprietors.

This undertaking, the completion of which cost the proprietors about £70,000, was divided into four hundred shares. The canal serves for the transport of copper ores and lead from the mines, and slate from the quarries in the district to the place of shipment; also coals, timber, stone, &c. to the town of Tavistock and the neighbourhood, considerable quantities of which are conveyed by it.

The Bude Canal.

The Bude Canal, as it respects length, is by far the most considerable in the county. Bude Haven is situated in the north-eastern extremity of Cornwall, near the town of Stratton. The harbour is dry at low water, and its bed is formed of a fine bright yellow sand composed almost wholly of shells. This sand, from time immemorial, has been used as a manure for the surrounding country. Before the canal was cut, the harbour presented a very animated appearance at every return of low water during the tilling season, being thronged with waggons, carts, pack-horses, and herds of mules and asses, loading and carrying off the sand into the interior of the country. A canal had been many times projected for the more ready transit of this necessary article, and various lines had been marked out; but it was not until the year 1817 that the surveys for the present line were begun. A Company was then formed in shares of fifty pounds each, and an act of parliament was obtained in 1819. The works were immediately commenced under the direction of James Green, Esq. engineer. The haven was first improved by the erection of a pier, extending from the western side of the harbour, nearly two thirds across its mouth, to some rocks called the Great and Little Chappel Rocks. The canal begins in the low lands just above the town of Bude, and is here capable of admitting vessels of from sixty to seventy tons burden. After running about two miles in a south-easterly direction, it is brought to the foot of the first inclined plane at a place called Marhamchurch. This plane is 826 feet in length and has an elevation of 122 feet. The canal from hence is on a smaller scale, carrying boats of only five tons burden. It proceeds on a level upwards of two miles, in an easterly direction, to another plane, which has an elevation of 225 feet, and is 907 feet in length. About a mile beyond this plane the canal crosses the turnpike-road from Bideford to Launceston at a place called the Red-post, and then diverges into two branches. The first branch, which is called the Bude and Holsworthy Canal, after stretching a little to the north crosses the river Tamar, and thus enters the county of Devon. Here is another inclined plane, much smaller than the two former, the summit of which forms the commencement of the summit level of the canal. A little beyond this part a branch stretches off in a northerly direction, to meet an extensive reservoir, covering, when full, an area of seventy acres, formed on the river Tamar, at a place called Alfordisworthy. This branch, which forms a continuation of the summit level, is about three miles and a half in length, and is used as a feeder to the canal and for the purposes of navigation. The distance from Bude Harbour to the reservoir is thirteen miles and a quarter. The main branch of the Bude and Holsworthy line continues the same summit level, and extends in nearly an easterly direction, crossing the turnpike-road from Holsworthy to Torrington within three quarters of a mile of the former place, and terminates about two miles and a half beyond that town at a place called Blagdon Moor. This point is upwards of sixteen miles from Bude Harbour. The second branch of the canal from Red-post is called the Bude and Launceston Canal, and follows without much variation the course of the Tamar on the Cornish side of the river, until it reaches within three miles of the town of Launceston; it here terminates, at a point called Druxton Bridge, twenty-one miles and a half from Bude Harbour. There are no locks or tunnels in this line, but its descent is accomplished by means of three inclined planes. The whole of these works form an internal water communication, through the counties of Devon and Cornwall, of upwards of thirty-five miles. They were completed in the year 1826, and cost about £128,000. As yet no return has been made to the shareholders for the capital invested.

The Torridge Canal.

The Torridge Canal is on a very small scale, and was cut without the authority of parliament in the year 1823, at the sole expense of the Right Hon. Lord Rolle, through whose lands the line passes. The canal commences about two miles above the town of Bideford, on the navigable part of the river Torridge, and ascending a small inclined plane runs between that river and the new turnpike-road from Bideford to Torrington, about two miles, when it crosses the valley of the Torridge by a lofty stone aqueduct of five arches, which, finely harmonizing with the surrounding grand and romantic scenery, produces a beautiful effect. The canal continues its course near that of the river, skirts the hill on which the town of Torrington stands, and terminates a short distance further up the valley of the Torridge. Considerable traffic is carried on upon this canal, and the noble proprietor has erected several excellent lime-kilns and mills on the line, which are of great benefit to the agriculture of the surrounding district.

W. Dawson, del.

AQUEDUCT OVER THE TORRIDGE, NEAR TORRINGTON.

The Grand Western Canal.

Few schemes of this kind have more frequently occupied public attention, than that of forming a navigable communication between the Bristol Channel and the southern coast of the kingdom. Numerous modes and lines have been projected; the most eminent engineers have devoted their abilities to the work, and immense sums have been expended in surveys and preliminary arrangements: but the grand scheme has never been carried into effect: no such communication has as yet been opened. In 1794 the late Mr. Rennie laid down a line for the whole work, which was intended to extend from the town of Topsham on the river Exe, to the navigable part of the river Tone adjoining the town of Taunton, with branches to the towns of Tiverton and Collumpton. The total length of canal would have been about forty-four miles, and the elevation to be overcome was 326 feet. A Company was formed, an Act obtained, and the work begun;

but of this magnificent undertaking only twelve miles were ever completed, and this unfortunately in the centre of the line, thus affording of course no communication with either of the Channels. The whole of the funds of the Company were exhausted on this comparatively small portion of the work, which in its present state forms what is called The Tiverton or Western Canal. The line commences on the side of a hill just above the town of Tiverton, and, running in an easterly direction, passes the towns of Halberton, and Sampford Peverell; thence, inclining a little to the north-east, it skirts the extensive lime-stone quarries of West Leigh and Cannons Leigh in the parish of Burlescombe, and terminates about a mile to the east of the village of Holcombe Rogus. The traffic on this canal is necessarily very limited, being chiefly confined to the carriage of coals for the adjacent parishes, and lime-stone from West Leigh to some lime works at Tiverton. In the present year (1829) endeavours have been making to convert this line of canal to some more profitable purposes, and several meetings have been held between the shareholders, and the proprietors of the Bridgewater and Taunton Canal, to consider whether their interests may not be mutually promoted by effecting a junction of their works; but nothing has yet been definitely arranged.

Other lines of communication between the English and Bristol Channels have at different periods been projected, especially that from the town of Seaton and Beer, near Axminster, on the southern coast, to the river Tone; many engineers of eminence have repeatedly reported on these lines. In 1822 a survey was made under the direction of James Green, Esq., and an act of parliament obtained for a boat canal communication between the two Channels, but the work was never begun. In 1824 that stupendous work, the English and Bristol Channel Ship Canal was projected, and the whole lines marked out and surveyed under the united care of Mr. Telford and Mr. Green. This line of communication was calculated

Drawn by T.H Williams

Engraved by W. Deeble

PLYMOUTH SOUND, ST NICHOLAS ISLAND & MOUNT EDGCUMBE.

BUCKFASTLEIGH ABBEY,

DEVON.

for the transit of vessels of two hundred tons burden from
one Channel to the other, without shifting their cargoes,
and the estimated expense was one million and three
quarters. An Act was obtained in the following year, but
no progress whatever has been made in the work.

A Company of shareholders was established and an
act of parliament obtained in the year 1801, for cutting
a canal from Exeter to Crediton. The length would have
been about eight miles. Soon after procuring this Act,
the work was commenced just above the city. When about
half a mile only was completed, however, owing to a
variety of unforeseen difficulties and expenses, the proceedings were suspended, and finally abandoned. The
lands which the Company had purchased, and their other
remaining property, were disposed of a few years since,
and the Company may now be regarded as entirely dissolved. The shareholders in this speculation calculated
on receiving a handsome return for the capital intended to
be invested, from the transport of lime, coals, and general
merchandize for the supply of Crediton and the surrounding country.

A new canal and rail-way, communicating from the
Cann slate works to the Catwater, were opened on the
20th November 1829, by the passage of boats and waggons containing large quantities of paving stones and
slate from the quarries. This improvement has caused a
considerable increase to the trade of the port; the Cann
slate being known to be of a superior quality, and being
now generally used in London and other cities of the
empire.

From the preceding descriptions it will be perceived
that the inland navigation of Devonshire is not proportionate to the magnitude of the county and the extent of
its coasts. The rivers, with the exception of a few near
the sea, are generally small; and the rapidity of their
descent among the hills, frequently over rocky bottoms,
renders them altogether unfit for the passage even of

BOOK
I.

boats. This deficiency is by no means adequately supplied by the few canals at present existing in the county.
That inland navigation, however, is of vast importance to
any country, as a general principle, will scarcely be con-
troverted ; and it is maintained by those who have paid
most attention to the subject*, that a canal, when completed, if judiciously projected and skilfully executed,
cannot fail to continue an increasing source of revenue to
its proprietors, of fertility to the land near its banks by
the supplies of manure which it will furnish, and of wealth
and comfort to the inhabitants in its vicinity by the facilities which it will afford to trade and commerce. And
to this may be added, that the expense of keeping canals
in repair is trifling, when compared with the perpetual and
enormous consumption of corn for the maintenance of
horses used in other modes of conveyance. Gentlemen of
landed property in the county may perhaps consider these
remarks worthy of attention, especially when it is remembered that land-carriage is in many parts of Devonshire
rendered extremely difficult and expensive by the numerous and steep hills with which it so much abounds, and
that this county is said to possess peculiar advantages for
the formation of canals.

It is however objected, that such undertakings are frequently hazardous and unprofitable speculations to adventurers : rail-roads consequently in many instances are
taking the lead of them, and it is even expected that some
of the old canals will be dried up and converted into rail-
roads. But how far the failure of canals in various instances may be owing to their being improvidently undertaken; to their being executed on a scale too large
and expensive, or to palpable mismanagement and want
of skill in constructing them ; and how far rail-roads may
be rendered more conducive to the objects in view than
canals, are questions which the writer of this work will

* See some valuable remarks on this subject in the Introduction to the
last edition of Risdon's Survey, p. 29, by the Editor, than whom none can
be better qualified to form an adequate and correct judgement respecting it.

not pretend to determine. If self-moving or steam carriages should be brought to perfection, and rendered effective by general application, as the projectors of them
anticipate, these, in conjunction with rail-ways, there
can be no doubt would prove an acquisition of incalculable benefit. At any rate, the subject of these observations, as intimately connected with the value of land
and the general prosperity of the country, is of real importance, and well deserves the utmost attention of practical œconomists, men of science, and gentlemen of property.

THE RAIL-ROADS.

The Plymouth and Dartmoor Rail-road originated with **The Ply-**
Sir Thomas Tyrwhitt, and to his exertions its accomplish- **mouth and**
Dartmoor
ment is to be principally attributed. The whole was **Rail-road.**
executed at the expense of a Joint Stock Company, incorporated by act of parliament 59 Geo. III., and further
powers were given them by subsequent acts of the 1st and
2nd Geo. IV. The rail-road commences at Prince Town,
near the prison of war on the forest of Dartmoor, and
terminates at Sutton Pool in the borough of Plymouth ;
the whole length, on account of the windings of the road,
extending to twenty-four miles. It is chiefly used for the
conveyance of granite from Dartmoor to Plymouth, where
this material is shipped for the metropolis and various
other parts of the kingdom. Large blocks of this stone
are also used in the construction of the surface of the
Plymouth Breakwater. The rail-road is also applied for
general use, to the importation of lime, sea sand, coals,
building materials, and other commodities ; and to the exportation of peat, slate, and agricultural produce.

About four miles from Plymouth the rail-road passes
through a tunnel six hundred and thirty yards in length,
excavated principally through rock. A great part of this
tunnel is one hundred feet below the surface of the earth.
On account of the hills and vales with which this district abounds, the excavations and embankments on the

BOOK
I.
line of rail-way are very considerable, the latter in many places being forty feet in height, and of great length. After passing through the tunnel and proceeding by the rail-way through the woods, the scenery for the distance of five miles is exceedingly rich and beautiful, and in short may be said to be one of the most interesting specimens of woodland scenery in the county.

The rail-way next traverses Roborough Down, and then the Moor, until it arrives at Prince Town, where it terminates at the market-house, which is situated about 1460 feet above the level of the sea. The road is laid with cast-iron edge rails, calculated to sustain waggons containing six tons each. The works were executed under the direction of Mr. Roger Hopkins, civil engineer and mineral surveyor. The entire cost, including the purchase of land and the expense of obtaining three acts of parliament, amounted to about £66,000.

Rail-road from Teigngrace.
There is another short rail-road (before alluded to, page 66) from Teigngrace, which communicates with the Newton Abbot canal and the Hay Tor granite works. This road is about six miles and a half in extent, and is composed of the native granite. These works are under the direction of a Joint Stock Company, whose office is in Broad Street, London. The columns for the New Post Office, and much of the materials for the New London Bridge, were obtained from the quarries at Hay Tor, conveyed down the rail-road to the Newton canal, and from thence to the Teign, where they were shipped for London.

THE PUBLIC ROADS.

The Great Western Road.
The Great Western Road enters Devonshire between the ninth and tenth mile-stone from Bridport; proceeds to Axminster, twelve miles; and through Kilmington and the hamlet of Wilmington to Honiton, nine miles and a half; from thence it passes through Honiton Clist and Heavitree to Exeter, sixteen miles. From Exeter it proceeds through Alphington to Chudleigh, nine miles;

and thence through Bickington to Ashburton, nine miles
and a half. It then passes through Buckfastleigh, Dean
Prior, and South Brent, to Ivybridge, thirteen miles; and
thence through Plympton to Plymouth, about eleven
miles : its whole course through the county being about
seventy-four miles.

Another road from Exeter to Plymouth branches out
at Alphington, and passes through Kenford and over
Haldon to Newton Abbot, fifteen miles; from thence it
proceeds to Totnes, eight miles; and thence by Ivybridge
to Plymouth, twenty-three miles. There is also a new
line of road, beginning near Chudleigh, through Newton
Abbot, Totnes, Ermington, Yealmton, and over the new
Lara Bridge to Plymouth.

A turnpike-road also branches off from Alphington
through Exminster to Starcross, eight miles; from Starcross to Dawlish, four miles; and from thence to Teignmouth, three miles. And another road from Exeter to
Teignmouth passes over Haldon, through Ashcombe,
fifteen miles.

From Newton Abbot there is a turnpike-road, through
Abbots Kerswell, to Tor Mohun and Torquay, and from
thence through Berry Pomeroy, with branches to Paignton, Brixham, and Kingswere. And from Ashburton
there is a turnpike-road to Totnes, which passes through
Staverton and Dartington, eight miles. The road from
Ashburton to Tavistock, twenty miles, comes into the
turnpike-road from Exeter to Tavistock at Two Bridges,
eight miles from the latter town.

From Totnes there is a turnpike-road through Harberton Ford to Kingsbridge, twelve miles; and another
from Totnes to Dartmouth through Townstall, ten miles.
From Dartmouth a turnpike-road passes through Morleigh
to Modbury, twelve miles. There is now, however, a
nearer road, over the ferry at Overton, by means of a boat
called the Flying Bridge.

The great road from London to Falmouth and the Land's-
End branches off at Exeter, passes through Crockernwell,

eleven miles from Exeter; thence through South Zeal and Sticklepath to Oakhampton, twelve miles; and thence through Bridestow and Lifton. It leaves the county at Polston Bridge, about two miles beyond Lifton and forty from Exeter.

Another road from Exeter to the Land's End passes through Moreton Hampstead, twelve miles, and over Dartmoor to Tavistock, twenty miles; about three miles beyond which it enters Cornwall, passing over New Bridge. This road is not much used, and in winter, on account of the severity of the weather on the Moor, is almost impassable.

The turnpike-road from Tavistock to Plymouth and Devonport is about fourteen miles, and from the latter place there is another turnpike-road to Saltash Ferry. From Tavistock to Ivybridge a turnpike-road passes through Walkhampton and Meavy; and at a short distance from the former of these towns a road branches off to Two Bridges on Dartmoor on the road from Moreton Hampstead to Tavistock.

Another turnpike-road from Tavistock to Launceston passes through Milton Abbot and Bradstone to Graiston Bridge. The principal road from Plymouth to the north of Devon proceeds through Tavistock, fourteen miles; to Oakhampton, fifteen miles; and thence through Hatherleigh to Torrington, eighteen miles. From Torrington a road branches off to Bideford, and another to Barnstaple and Ilfracombe.

There is a turnpike-road from Exeter to Topsham, continued through Lympstone to Exmouth, nine miles; from whence the road proceeds, through Littleham, Withecombe Raleigh and Otterton, to Sidmouth, and thence through Salcombe Regis and Colyford to Lyme Regis, which is just within the limits of Dorsetshire. Another road, and the shortest, from Exeter to Sidmouth passes through Heavitree and Newton Poppleford, about fifteen miles. A road branches out from the great road through Honiton to Exeter, at a place called Fairmile, leading

through Ottery St. Mary to the road just mentioned as
leading from Sidmouth to Lyme. There is also a direct
road from Honiton through Sidbury to Sidmouth.

The great road from Bath and Bristol to Exeter enters
Devonshire near the inn called the Red Ball, passes through
the hamlet of South Appledore and the village of Willand
to Collumpton, and thence through Broad Clist to Exeter.
Another road from Bath enters Devonshire at the distance
of about a mile from Church Staunton; and, passing
through Up-Ottery and Rawridge, proceeds to Honiton,
and thence to Exeter.

From Honiton a road passes through Awliscombe to
Collumpton, eleven miles; and from thence to Tiverton,
about five miles. From Tiverton there is a road through
Halberton and Sampford Peverel to the Bath road near
South Appledore. There is also a turnpike-road from
Tiverton to Bampton, seven miles, passing through a
beautifully wooded vale by the side of the Exe: from
Bampton it continues to Dulverton in Somersetshire,
leaving Devonshire at Exe Bridge, about two miles beyond
the former place: a branch of this road crosses a portion
of Somersetshire, and, entering Devonshire between five
and six miles from Bampton, proceeds to South Molton.

A direct road from Tiverton to South Molton, nineteen
miles, passes through Calverleigh, Loxbear and Racken-
ford. From South Molton the turnpike-road to Barnstaple, twelve miles, passes through Filleigh within sight
of Earl Fortescue's house and grounds, Swimbridge, and
Landkey. From Barnstaple there is a turnpike-road
through Pilton and Marwood to Ilfracombe, ten miles;
from this road another branches out at Pilton to Combe
Martin, from which place there is a road to Linton and
Lymouth. A new line of road also from Barnstaple to
Ilfracombe has been made lately.

The road from Exeter to Barnstaple, forty miles, passes
through Crediton; thence through Chawley to Chumleigh;
and thence through Burrington, High Bickington, Atherington, and Bishops Tawton, to Barnstaple. A new road

also from Exeter to Barnstaple, forty-four miles, has been
recently opened. From Chumleigh a road branches off to
South Molton, eight miles; and from this latter, about
a mile from Chumleigh, another road branches off, leading to Barnstaple through Chittlehampton. Through
Atherington and Chittlehampton there is also a turnpike-
road from Torrington to South Molton, sixteen miles.

The turnpike-road from Barnstaple to Hartland passes
through Eastleigh to Bideford, eight miles; and thence
to Hartland, thirteen miles.

The turnpike-road from Bideford to Torrington, about
six miles, passes through no village; but the road from
Torrington to Oakhampton passes through Little Torrington and Petrockstow to Hatherleigh, eleven miles; and
thence to Oakhampton, seven miles. From Hatherleigh
there is a turnpike-road to Holsworthy, about thirteen
miles; continuing thence to Stratton in Cornwall, leaving
Devonshire about four or five miles beyond Holsworthy.

From Oakhampton there is another turnpike-road to
Exeter, passing through Crediton, eighteen miles. This
road also passes through North Tawton and Bow, or
Nymet Tracey, but is now little used.

There is a turnpike-road from Crediton to Tiverton,
twelve miles. Another from Exeter to Tiverton, fourteen
miles, passes through Stoke Canon to Silverton; and from
this place there are two roads, one through Butterleigh,
and the other through Bickleigh, to Tiverton.

Devonshire abounds in all parts with the best materials for the formation of roads, and for keeping them
in good repair. Formerly, however, travelling in this
county was in many places exceedingly inconvenient, from
the state of neglect in which they remained. At present
this district partakes of the general improvement·in this
respect, and the principal roads are in excellent condition.
Further and great improvements, however, are still admissible, and in some parts are being carried on, though
not to the extent that is desirable. One feature in the
rural œconomy of this county, which must strike every

stranger on entering it as remarkable, is the height of the banks and of the hedges on their summits, wherever there are inclosures. These, it is true, afford important shelter for the cattle in a country abounding so much with hills, and consequently exposed to the power of the winds and rain. They afford, moreover, a continual supply of coppice wood for various useful purposes. Still, however, they keep the roads in bad condition, by intercepting the action of the sun's rays and the wind, which would otherwise render them dry and clean : this is particularly seen where the roads are narrow, which in Devonshire is often the case. Another disadvantage is the frequent and steep ascents up the hills in this county. If therefore the roads could be thrown more open by lowering the height of the fences ; if they could be widened, and, instead of passing over the tops of the hills, be carried along the sides of them, or through the valleys, great and valuable improvements might still be effected. Nor will these considerations be thought of little value by any one who is at all aware of the vast importance of good roads to the agriculture, the trade and commerce, and consequently to the prosperity, of the country.

A description of what relates to the surface of the county being thus concluded, it may be proper to proceed to its General History

BOOK II.

GENERAL HISTORY.

———

CHAPTER I.

ORIGINAL POPULATION, &c.

BOOK
II.
———

S in extensive views of natural scenery objects in the distance, in proportion as they recede, diminishing gradually, become indistinct and at length invisible; so in the perspective of time, any thing like a regular series of events and facts in early periods is either wholly lost in obscurity, or so blended with the shadowy distortions of fable as to render altogether impossible the distinction between reality and fiction. Investigation therefore into the origin and ancient history of the inhabitants of Britain, as in the case of all other nations, seems to be little better than loss of time, and labour that might be employed to much better advantage on other topics of inquiry. We have to traverse ages of ignorance, superstition and credulity, with no guides but tradition and conjecture; and even if, in any case, some appearance of genuine history can be extracted, by the most laborious research, from the rubbish of invention accumulated for ages, but little revenue of instruction will be the result. "The convulsions of a civilized state," says Mr. Hume, " usually compose the most instructive and the most interesting part of history; but the sudden, violent and unprepared revolutions incident to barbarians, are so much guided by caprice, and terminate so often in cruelty, that

they disgust us by the uniformity of their appearance;
and it is rather fortunate for letters that they are buried
in silence and oblivion. The only certain means by which
nations can indulge their curiosity in researches concerning their remote origin, is to consider the language, names
and customs of their ancestors, and to compare them with
those of the neighbouring nations. The fables which are
commonly employed to supply the place of true history,
ought to be entirely disregarded." Documents relative
to the early periods of British history, upon which any
dependence can be placed, are entirely wanting. The
Druids were the depositories of whatever knowledge then
existed, and even they were not allowed by their superstition or their policy to commit to writing any account
of their mysteries, though on other subjects, it is said,
they made use of the Greek letters *. No authentic history
respecting the state of this country can be traced prior to
the invasion of it by the Romans ; and even after that period, the counties of Devon and Cornwall were so remote
from the principal settlements of that people, and had so
little concern with their most important transactions, that
scarcely any information of much value respecting this
district can be obtained from Roman historians.

Of the various conjectures respecting the original in- The fable
habitants of this island, the story of Brutus, a hero of of Brutus.
Trojan extraction, who was generally believed in ancient
times to have conquered and given his name to Britain,
may, with propriety perhaps, receive some notice here,
especially as he is said to have landed with his troops,
commenced his operations, and performed his chief exploits, in Devonshire ; for, absurd as it is, this narrative
has the support of tradition, was once generally received
as true, and was believed even by most of the men of
learning in the sixteenth century, by many in the seven-
teenth, and by some even in the last. On one occasion
it received countenance from Royal authority, as it was on

* The Triads are supposed to be Druidical remains.

BOOK
II.
the ground of the subjection of Scotland as well as England by Brutus, that Edward I., among other considerations, founded his claim to the supremacy of the former
of these kingdoms against the pretensions of Pope Boniface VIII., who affirmed it to belong to the demesnes of
the Roman church, as part of St. Peter's patrimony *. On
these accounts some writers † have considered it to be
fiction, founded upon truth; and both Camden ‡ and
Sammes, as well as others, have thought it of sufficient
importance to merit the trouble of refutation ; though the
former, with his usual candour, disavows his intention of
rejecting it altogether, and still admits that the ancient
Britons might have descended in part at least from a
Trojan race ; and as the adventures attributed to Brutus
are still occasionally alluded to, although with contempt,
a short account of them may possibly be gratifying to
readers who are unacquainted with them. The story is
briefly as follows :—Geoffrey of Monmouth in the reign
of Henry II. published a history of Britain, derived, as
he pretended, from British documents ; in which he relates, that Brutus, of Trojan extraction, son of Silvius,
grandson of Ascanius, and great-grandson of Æneas,
having lost his mother at his birth, and killed his father
by accident in hunting, as had been foretold by magicians,
fled his country, and made his way to Greece. Having
collected together a considerable number of followers, he
rescued from slavery the descendants of Hellenus, the son
of Priam, defeated one Pandarus, an unknown king of
the Grecians, married the daughter of that prince, and,
setting sail with the remainder of his forces in 324 ships,
landed on a deserted island named Leogetia, where he
found a temple of Diana, and was directed by the oracle
to proceed to a western island beyond Gaul, in which
would found another Troy and give rise to a race of kings
by whom the world would be subdued. Sailing thence

* Hume's History of England, book i. chap. xiii.
† Sheringham *De Ang. Gent. Orig.*
‡ *Brit.* Introd. p. iii.

by the Pillars of Hercules, where he escaped the Sirens, CHAP.
and afterwards by the Tyrrhenian seas, which, unfortu- I.
nately for the truth of this story, are in an opposite direction, he came into Aquitaine, routed in a pitched battle
Galfar the king, with twelve princes of Gaul, and founded
the city of Tours, for which fact Geoffrey cites Homer.
After having overrun Gaul, he crossed the sea to the
island of Great Britain, which he found inhabited by
giants, whom he defeated, with their monstrous chief
Goemagot (or Gogmagog), and left his name to Britain
in the year of the world 2855, 334 before the first Olym-
piad, and 1108 before Christ*. The victory over this
champion of the Britons, however, is assigned personally
to Corinæus the companion of Brutus, who succeeded,
after a desperate struggle, by precipitating the giant
over the cliff between Plymouth and the sea, now called
the *Hoe*†, and afterwards received the government of the
western territories as the recompense of his valour. This
founder of the western kingdom is represented to have
had numerous successors who shared his honours: and
" if," says Mr. Polwhele ‡, " when facts are wanting, we
are willing to seize upon fable, we may contemplate for

* " The time of Brutus's landing," says Sammes, (p. 157) " is sup-
posed to have been about the year of the world 2887, and after the uni
versal deluge 1231. The Count Palatine places it in the year 2855, and
Holinshed in 2850, and after the destruction of Troy 66. There is no
Chronology, however, of any importance till the time of Julius Cæsar."
The story of Brutus and his descendants is related at large in Holinshed's Chronicle, and occupies the whole of the five chapters of the
Second Book.
† Others affirm, that the cliff at Dover was the scene of this contest.
‡ Historical Views, chap. i. sect. ii. p. 22. He also observes, " The
annalist informs us, with all the gravity of truth, that about the time of
the prophet Samuel, Guendolen, the daughter of our hero, enjoyed Danmonium as her paternal inheritance. The most remarkable of her successors were Heninus, who married a daughter of king Lear, and his son
Cunedagius, who filled the throne at the time of the building of Rome;
and the two brothers Belinus and Brennus, to the first of whom were
allotted Loegria, Cambria or Danmonium; to the second, all from the
river Humber to Cathness [Caithness] in Scotland. To Belinus and Brennus is ascribed the demolition of Rome: and, what is rather remarkable
with respect to the sacking of that great city, there is only the difference
of twenty years between the British Chronology and the Roman Fasti."

BOOK
II.

more than a thousand years the imaginary princes of Danmonium." The place where Brutus landed with his troops is said to have been Totnes, where at that time was a haven; and the stone is still pointed out on which he first set his foot.

Fabulous as this narrative is on the face of it, and fit only to be thrown among the rubbish of similar stories abounding in ancient chronicles, still, say Sheringham* and others, it ought not to be condemned altogether; it may contain truth mixed with fable: nor was it the invention of Geoffrey, for the most ancient writers on British affairs have delivered similar narratives. Such, moreover, was the opinion concerning their origin, universally prevalent among the Britons at the time of the Saxon invasion. Henry of Huntington, a contemporary with Geoffrey, affirms, that he " found these things in diverse histories." Sigebertus, a Frenchman, about one hundred years before Geoffrey, mentions the chief exploits of Brutus, and asserts that all these events were related in the ancient histories of Britain; and the whole, he concludes, agrees with what is observed by Bede†, that the ancient Britons came from Armorica, which, the story says, was named Brittany from Brutus, and that from thence this island received its name. Nennius, also, who lived about the ninth century, relates the history of Brutus, and affirms that he had taken it from the Roman annals, the chronicles of the Holy Fathers, and the histories of the Scots and Saxons, as well as from the traditions of his ancestors, and from the monuments of the ancient inhabitants of Britain. To all this it may be added, that the Cambro-Britons affirm that they sprung from Brutus the Trojan, who had three sons, of whom Cambrus reigned in the west, whilst Brutus himself gave his name to the whole island.

* *De Ang. Gent. Orig.* p. 9.
† *Hist. Eccles.* lib. i. cap. i. Bede's observation is in the following words: " In primis autem hæc insula Brittones solum a quibus nomen accepit, incolas habuit, qui de tractu Armoricano, ut fertur, Brittaniam advecti, australes sibi partes illius vindicarent."

Notwithstanding all this, however, it is to be observed[*],
that the credit of this story is supported chiefly by the
testimony of Geoffrey of Monmouth, a writer of no authority, and of whom his contemporaries especially speak
in the most contemptuous and indignant language, as a
bold inventor of falsehoods, or the most credulous retailer
of ridiculous fables[†]. It is indeed of little importance,
whether this invention be attributed to Geoffrey of Monmouth, Henry of Huntington, or Sigebertus one hundred
years before. If however this Sigebertus, or any other
individuals, had collected, together with the name of
Brutus, a few transactions of some such person, the probability is, that the composing of his genealogy, the arrangement of the circumstances of his life, the time of his
entrance into Britain, and the succession of his line, depend entirely on the credit of Geoffrey and the truth of
his narrative. To say nothing of the absurdity of his
geography, and of his quoting Homer for the founding of
Tours, it is not in the slightest degree credible, that the
rude Britons should have preserved in writing a history
so circumstantial as that which he pretends to have made
use of; and even if he had in his possession an account
of some such prince as Brutus and his successors, collected from tradition in ages of barbarism and credulity,
this does not render the matter at all more worthy of belief. In the period fixed for the exploits of this successful
adventurer, all history, except that of the Scriptures, is
little better than fable. It is an instance of vanity common to most nations, among whom are the Greeks and
Romans, to derive their origin from some celebrated hero
of celestial extraction, and this miraculous tale of Brutus
is on a par with the rest of these poetical fictions. In
Geoffrey's story, therefore, there is nothing to set in competition with the authentic narratives of credible historians, such as Cæsar, Tacitus, Gildas, and others of more

---

[*] Sammes's *Brit. Ant. Illustr.* p.157–160. Camden's *Brit.* Introd. p.iv.
[†] Particularly William of Newbury.—Sammes, p. 158. See also
Scriverius in his preface to the Antiquities of Ancient Batavia.—She-
ringham, p. 8.

ancient date, who make no mention of such a person as Brutus, though they could scarcely have failed to have had some information of exploits of so much magnitude and extent as those attributed to him, had they been real. Cæsar * on the contrary observes, that all he could learn upon inquiry was, that the interior parts of Britain were inhabited by those who were natives of the island, and the maritime parts by others who had crossed over from Belgium. Of the origin of these natives therefore he had heard nothing. Tacitus, moreover, who had taken pains to inform himself on the subject, remarks†, Whether the first inhabitants of Britain were natives, or imported, is a circumstance involved in the uncertainty inseparable from the history of barbarous nations. No such Roman annals as those mentioned by Nennius are now known. Bede, William of Malmesbury, and other writers before 1160, seem not even to have heard of the name of Brutus. And as to Brittany in France deriving its name from him, after he had reduced it to subjection before his conquest of this island, it is to be observed, that Britain was known by this name long before the former country had received that appellation; and Hume affirms‡, that during the dreadful devastations of the Saxons under Hengist in the time of Vortimer, many Britons, deserting their native country, took shelter in the province of Armorica, where, being charitably received by a people of the same language and manners, they settled in great numbers, and gave the country the name of Brittany.

And with respect to any degree of authority § or confirmation which may seem to be given to this fabulous story by Edward I. in his letter to the Pope for the purpose of vindicating his claim to the supremacy of Scotland, this is at once set aside by the following considerations. That prince, it appears, had applied to the

---

* Cæsar and Tacitus seem to have adopted the notion, that the aborigines of this and other countries sprung out of the earth like mushrooms.

† *Vito Agric.* cap. ii.

‡ History of England, vol. i. chap. i.

§ Sammes's *Brit. Ant.* p. 159. Sheringham *De Ang. Gent. Or.* p. 128.

monks and friars throughout the kingdom to search for
facts in favour of his title in any records to which they
might have access ; and the story of Brutus was by them
brought forward on this occasion in a new dress, from
the manufactories of fraud and imposition in which it had
been previously modelled.   But, to place the nullity of
this authority beyond the possibility of a doubt, it is asserted in this same letter, that (in conformity with the in-
tercessions of Athelstan and St. John of Beverley * with
Heaven, that some indubitable sign might be given for
the conviction both of present and future generations
that the subjection of Scotland belonged of right to the
kings of England) that prince drew his sword, and cleft
a rock near Dunbar an ell in length, the mark of which
then clearly remained ; besides, as further proof, the notice which was taken of the miracle in honour of St. John
in the religious services of Beverley church, about every
week throughout the year †.   Edward, no doubt, was a
monarch of too much understanding to be deluded by
tales like these, and, with a policy not uncommon, in-

---

* Archbishop of York and preceptor of the venerable Bede, who attributes several miracles to him.

† This curious document may be seen in Rymer's *Fœdera*, vol. i. pars ii.
p. 932, the edition of 1816, under the superintendence of the Government Commissioners. The passages referred to in this letter of Edward I.
are here given, as follow, in order that it may be seen that no misrepresen-
tation of its statements has been made :—" Sub temporibus itaque Ely et
Samuelis prophetæ, vir quidam strenuus et insignis, Brutus nomine, de
genere Trojanorum, post excidium urbis Trojæ, cum multis nobilibus
Trojanorum, applicuit in quandam insulam, tunc Albion vocatam, a gi-
gantibus inhabitatam : quibus suâ et suorum devictis potentiâ et accisis,
eam nomine suo Britanniam, sociosque suos Britones appellavit ; et ædi-
ficavit civitatem quam Trinovantum nuncupavit quæ modo Londinia no-
minatur.

" Et posteà regnum suum tribus filiis suis divisit ; scilicet,

" Locrino primogenito illam partem Britanniæ quæ nunc Anglia dicitur :

" Et Albanacto secundo natu illam partem quæ tunc Albania, a nomine
Albanacti, nunc vero Scotia nuncupatur :

" Et Cambro filio minori partem illam, nomine suo tunc Cambria vocatam quæ nunc Wallia vocitatur.

" Reservatâ Locrino seniori regiâ dignitate.

•   •   •   •   •   •   •

" Est dignum memoriâ, quòd Adelstanus, intercedente Sancto Johanne

tended only to combat the claims of Boniface with his
own weapons, legend, miracles and imposture. But enough,
and probably too much, of this once popular tale. It remains only to be added, that writers the most respectable
and the most learned in the antiquities of the country,
now agree in rejecting it altogether; nor would it have
been noticed here but for the reasons already mentioned.
Whether any portion of truth is comprised in this fable,
it is impossible now to ascertain. Totnes, however, will,
no doubt, relinquish the honour of having first received
this redoubted conqueror of the island, whose descent
was from Jupiter himself, Venus being the mother of his
great-grandfather.

Whether this island was first peopled by colonies from
the opposite coast of Europe, or by sea from the east, has
been a subject of dispute among writers of the greatest
antiquarian research; but the probability is obviously in
favour of the former of these opinions. As the white cliffs
of Albion are visible from the continent in their nearest
approach, it is reasonable to suppose that no long period
would elapse before the inhabitants of the opposite coast,
either from motives of curiosity, interest, or a desire of
emigration, would visit and form settlements here. The
similarity also of language, customs and manners, especially among the Druids, is sufficient to afford confirmation to this opinion. However, the inhabitants of the
West of England are said to have been the most ancient.
They are also believed to have been a people differing in
their manners and customs, as well as language, from the

de Beverlaco, quondam archiepiscopo Eborum, Scottos rebellantes ei di-
micavit; qui, gratias devotè agens, Deum exoravit, petens quatenus, in-
terveniente beato Johanne, sibi aliquod signum evidens ostenderet quatenus tam succedentes, quàm præsentes cognoscere possent, Scotos Anglorum regno, jure subjugari; et videns quosdam scopulos, juxta quendam
locum prope Dumbar' in Scotiâ, prominere, extracto gladio de vaginâ,
percussit in silicem: qui lapis, ad ictum gladii, Dei virtute agente, ita
cavatur, ut mensura ulnæ longitudini possit coaptari; et hujus rei hac-
tenus evidens signum apparet, et in Beverlac' ecclesiâ in legendâ Sancti
Johannis, quasi singulis ebdomadis per annum, ad laudem et honorem
Sancti Johannis, pro miraculo recitatur: et de hoc exstat celebris me-
moria, tam in Anglia, quàm in Scotia, usque ad præsentem diem."

rest of the islanders; though it is possible this notion may have arisen from the circumstance of their retaining for a longer period their ancient character and state, in consequence of having had less intercourse than other districts with the more modern and more civilized visitors or invaders of Britain *.

The short notices of this part of the country which occur in Ptolemy's Geography, may be properly introduced here, as they may serve to gratify the curiosity of the reader who is unacquainted with them; and although Ptolemy is not a guide that may be followed with safety, the ancient names of places which he gives may be of some use hereafter. Ptolemy flourished in the reigns of the emperors Trajan, Hadrian and Antoninus Pius, and wrote his Geography about A.D. 144. This work abounds with errors, but there are two especially which affect the whole geography of the island. He has made the extent of England decline from its real situation, and entirely changed the position of Scotland, representing it as extending in length from east to west instead of from south to north.—His longitude is computed from Alexandria in Egypt, the place of his residence.

On St. George's Channel, the Hibernian or Vergivian Sea, between Britain and Ireland, he mentions,

Οὐέξαλα εἴσχυσις—ις—νγ, λ΄. Vexala æstuarium 16.00—53.30; probably the bay at the mouth of the river Brent in Somersetshire.

Ptolemy's Geography.

---

* Of the first colonization of this country the following is the statement which occurs in the Saxon Chronicle. "The Britons were the first inhabitants of this country: they came from Armenia, and first settled in the south of Britain; but afterwards it came to pass, that the Picts came from the south of Scythia, with long ships, but not in great numbers, and they first landed in the north of Ireland. They entreated the Scots to permit them to abide there, but were refused The Scots however offered them advice, and said, ' We know another island, east of this, where you may settle, if you choose; and if you meet with opposition, we will assist you, in order that you may obtain the conquest of it.' The Picts then departed, and came to the northern parts of this island, for the Britons had possession of the south, as mentioned before, and the Picts took their name from the Britons. Afterwards the Scots passed from Ireland into Britain, and conquered some part of it."

Ἡρακλέους ἄκρον—ιδ—νγ. Herculis promontorium, 14.00—53.00. Hartland Point.

Ἀντιονέσταιον ἄκρον τὸ καὶ Βολέριον—ια—νβ, λ′. An tivestæum promontorium, quod etiam dicitur Bolerium, 11.00—52.30; Cape Cornwall, or the Land's End: called Antivestæum perhaps from the British words *An diüez tir*, which signifies the end of the land; and Bolerium from *Bel e rhin*, the head of a promontory *.

Δαμνόνιον τὸ καὶ Ὄκρινον ἄκρον—ιβ—να, λ′. Danmonium, quod etiam dicitur Ocrinum promontorium, 12.00—51.30. The Lizard Point in Cornwall, called Ocrinum, probably, from *Och rhen*, a high promontory. Lizard appears to be also of British derivation, from *Lis ard*, a lofty projection †.

On the southern coast, after the promontory Ocrinum, he mentions,

Κενίωνος ποτ. ἐκβολαὶ—ιδ—να, λ′δ. Cenionis flu. ostia. Mouth of the river Cenion, 14.00—51.45; supposed to be Falmouth Haven, from the British *Genou*, a mouth; of which there is still some vestige in the name of the neighbouring town Tregony ‡.

Ταμάρου ποτ. ἐκβολαὶ—ιε, γο—νβ, ϛ. Tamari flu. ostia, 15.40—52.10. The mouth of the river Tamar, from *Tam a rav*, gentle river §.

Ἰσάκα ποτ. ἐκβολαὶ—ιζ—νβ, γ. Isacæ flu. ostia, 17.00—52.20. Mouth of the river Exe.

Ἀλαίνου ποτ. ἐκβολαὶ—ιζ, γο—νβ, γο. Alæni flu. ostia, 17.40—52.40. Mouth of the river Alænus, supposed to be the Axe; so called from *A laün iü*, the full river ‖.

Next to the Dutoriges (the inhabitants of Dorsetshire), on the most western quarter, Ptolemy places the Danmonii, Μεθ᾽ οὓς δυσμακώτατοι Δουμνόνιοι ἐν οἷς πόλεις, among whom are the following cities:

Οὐολίβα—ιδ, λ′δ—νβ, γ. Voliba, 14.45—52.20.

---

* Baxter, p. 19, 36.
‡ Ibid. p. 77. Camd. *Brit.* p. 16.
‖ Ibid. p. 10.

† Ibid. p. 186.
§ Baxter, p. 222.

Placed by Camden * and Baxter † at Grampound, but by CHAP.
Horsley ‡ at Lostwithiel. L.

Οὔξελα—ιε—νβ, λ'δ. Uxela, 15.00—52.45. Probably near Bridgwater; supposed however, by Camden §
to be Lostwithiel; by Baxter ‖, Saltash; and by Horsley ¶, Exeter.

Ταμαρὴ—ιε—νβ, δ. Tamara, 15.00—52.15. Tamerton, according to Baxter ** and Camden ††, who are
probably right; but Horsley ‡‡ thinks it was Saltash.

Ἴσκα—ιζ, λ'—νβ, λ'δ. Isca, 17.30—52.45. Exonia,
Exeter.

Λεγίων δευτέρα σεβαστὴ—ιζ, λ'—νβ, λ'ιβ. Legio se-
cunda augusta, 17.30—52.35. The *Second Legion*, called
the *August*, is here stationed by Ptolemy at Exeter, but
this seems to be a mistake; for there is the fullest proof
that the head quarters of this legion were, for the greater
part of its time in Britain, at Isca Silurum, or Caerleon,
the city of the legion, in Monmouthshire, and no other
evidence that they were ever at Isca Danmoniorum or
Exeter. If this legion were ever placed here, this could
not have been its chief station §§. At the time when the
Notitia Imperii was written, it was quartered at Rutupæ,
or Richborough in Kent, from whence it was soon after
removed to the Continent.

The following translation of a passage relative to the
geography and ancient inhabitants of the West, from Richard of Cirencester, is also important, and must not be
omitted ‖‖. " In this arm," (the West of England) " was

* p. 17.   † p. 254.   ‡ p. 378.   § p. 18.   ‖ p. 257.
¶ p. 378.   ** p. 221.   †† p. 25.   ‡‡ p. 376.
§§ This legion came into Britain, A.D. 43, in the reign of Claudius,
under the command of Vespasian, who was afterwards emperor, and continued here nearly four hundred years, to the final departure of the Romans.
On this account it was called Britannica. It had a principal share in all
the great actions and great works of the Romans in this island, and particularly in building the several walls of Hadrian, Antoninus Pius, and
Severus. From inscriptions still remaining, it appears that this was the
only legion employed in a body on the wall of Antoninus in Scotland.—
Henry's Hist. of Great Britain, vol. i. Appendix II. and VIII.

‖‖ See the edition dedicated to the Bishop of Cloyne, with the notes,
book i. chap. 6. § 16. Richard, who received his denomination from the

BOOK
II.

Richard
of Ciren-
cester.

the region of the Cimbri *, whose country was divided from that of the Hedui by the river Uxella (the Parret). It is not ascertained whether the Cimbri gave to Wales its modern name, or whether their origin is more remote. Their chief cities were Termolus and Atavia (both uncertain, probably in Devonshire). From hence, according to the ancients, are seen the Pillars of Hercules, and the island Herculea (Lundy Island), not far distant. From the Uxella a chain of mountains, called the Ocrinum, extends to the promontory known by the same name.

"Beyond the *Cimbri* the Cornabii inhabited the extreme angle of the island†, from whom that district perhaps obtained the name *Cornubia* (Cornwall), which it retains to this day. They possessed the cities *Musidum* (near Stratton), and Halangium (Carnbre). But as the Romans never frequented these almost deserted and uncultivated parts of Britain, their cities appear to have been of little consequence, and therefore neglected by historians : the promontories Bolerium and Antivestæum, however, are mentioned by geographers.

"Near the above-mentioned people, on the sea coast towards the south, and bordering on the Belgæ Allobroges, dwelled the Danmonii, the most powerful people of all (validissima gens omnium), which reason appears to have induced Ptolemy to assign to them all the country extending into the sea like an arm ‡. Their cities were Uxella (Bridgwater), Tamara (on the Tamar), Voluba (on the Tavey), Cenia (on the Fal), and Isca (Exeter), the mother of all, situated on the river of the same name. Their chief rivers were the Isca (the Exe), the Durius (the Dart), the Tamarus (the Tamar), and the Cenius (the

place of his birth, flourished from the middle to the latter end of the 14th century. He took much pains to gain information, and was a learned as well as industrious writer. So long as he followed his Roman guides, says Whitaker, he may be safely depended upon, but otherwise not.

* They occupied the south-west part of Somerset, and north of Devon.
† The north and west of Cornwall to the Land's End.
‡ Cornwall, Devon, Dorset, and part of Somerset. Their real territory, however, was Devonshire and the south-east part of Cornwall.

Fal). Their coasts present three promontories, which will CHAP.
be briefly noticed hereafter. This region, it appears, was L
well known to the Phœnician, Grecian, and Gallic merchants, by means of the metals with which it abounded.
On account of the great quantity of tin which it produced
they had much intercourse with this country; remarkable
proofs of which are the three promontories already referred
to, namely, *Hellenis* (probably Berry Head), Ocrinum
(the Lizard Point), and Κριοῦ μέτωπον (Ram's Head),
and the names of cities, which indicate a Grecian and
Phœnician origin.

"Beyond this arm in the ocean are situated the Syg-
diles, which are also denominated Æstromenides and
Cassiterides."

But who were the Cimbri which Richard places in the The Cim-
north of Devonshire, whilst the Danmonii inhabited the bri.
south? They are mentioned by Pliny, Strabo, Mela, Tacitus, and Plutarch; but with respect to their origin antiquarians do not agree. They are spoken of as coming
originally from Scythia, and also as the same with the
Cimmerians. They are said to have occupied, in ancient
times, the peninsula which stretches out into the German
Sea, and is known by the name of the Cimbric Cherso-
nesus, but afterwards to have spread themselves by conquest, in great numbers, to the south and south-east.
Homer mentions the Cemmerii as inhabiting the northern
and north-western regions approaching the pole.

The opinion of so respectable an antiquarian as Camden ought not to be slighted. "After the settlement of the
ark (he observes) on the mountains of Armenia, the families, which were numerous, dispersed to all quarters; nor
did the western part stop till some of them reached Britain; so says Theophilus of Antioch. Europe, we are
told by learned writers, was allotted to Japhet and his
posterity, who passed on, leaving their names to places.
His eldest son Gomer gave birth and name to the Gome-
rians, afterwards called Cimbri and Cumerians in these
extremities of Europe. The name of Cimbri, or Cimri,

prevailed in Germany and Gaul. From these Gomeri I always supposed that our Britons derived both their origin and their name, which is a proof of their origin. The proper and peculiar name of the Britons proves this. They call themselves *Kumero, Cymero, Kumeri,* a British woman *Kumeræes,* and the language *Kumeraeg:* nor do they know any other names. Gaul was the ancient seat of the Gomeri, our neighbours. From the name there seems to be an indication that Britain was peopled from Gaul; but above all from their situation, religion, manners, and language. The name of both was Gomeri, and by contraction Cimbri."

With respect to the origin of the Cimbri, however, Sammes[*] is of a different opinion from Camden, whom he considers as mistaken in believing them to be the descendants of Gomer. They are supposed, he observes, to be relics of the ancient Cimmerii, (by contraction Cimbri,) for which we have the authority of Diodorus Siculus and Plutarch. They were a Scythian nation, the offspring of Magog; for Josephus observes, they were called Magogœi, and afterward Scythœ by the Greeks. They are supposed to have formed a settlement in Cœlosyria, and to have built Magog, which was afterwards called by the Greeks Hieropolis. A fierce and warlike portion of them lived upon the Euxine and the Bosphorus. In subsequent periods they were called Germani, Celtæ, Galatæ, and Galli, having conquered these people and taken their names. From a branch of this nation proceeded our British ancestors. Whether they had entered the north-eastern part of the island before the Phœnicians landed in the west, cannot be ascertained.

Such are the opinions of these learned antiquaries relative to the Cimbri. As to the Danmonii, Mr. Polwhele imagines them to have been the primitive colonists of the country; but Mr. Whitaker and some of the most eminent antiquaries of the present day maintain that the

[*] p. 11—15.

Drawn by T H Clarke

Engraved by Wm Deeble

INTERIOR OF THE LADY CHAPEL

EXETER CATHEDRAL.

London Published by Robert Jenning & Cheapside, 1830

PLYMOUTH, THE BREAKWATER, &c.

London, Published by Robert Jennings & Co. Cheapside Jan.y. 1831.

Danmonii were the Belgic invaders, and that the abori- **CHAP.**
ginal inhabitants of the country were the Cimbri, some **I.**
of whom in consequence of these invasions continued to .
occupy the north-west of Devonshire, whilst the Danmonii, as appears from the preceding extract from Richard
of Cirencester, occupied the coast on the south, opposite
Gaul.

The Belgæ are described by Cæsar in the beginning of The Belgæ.
his Commentaries. They were a numerous and powerful
nation, who inhabited a great part of Gaul, and whom
Cæsar found considerable difficulty in reducing to subjection.—Many arguments concur, says Henry*, in proving
that all the ancient inhabitants of Britain came originally
from Gaul at different periods and with various leaders ;
and among them were the Belgæ. As one wave impells
another, these successive colonies drove each other forward until the whole island was covered with population.
But the time and other circumstances of their arrival are
buried in impenetrable obscurity. Richard of Cirencester
informs us, that the Belgæ entered the country about three
centuries and a half before Christ ; but there is no proof
that they had not made previous expeditions hither. As
to their first introduction into Britain, history is silent ;
but with respect to some of the latest colonies that settled
here not long before the Roman invasion, and who inhabited the southern parts of the country, we learn from
Cæsar† that the sea-coast was peopled with Belgians
drawn hither by the love of plunder and of war. Passing
over from different parts, and settling in the country, they
still retained the names of the different states from which
they had descended. The last of these colonies, which
arrived in Britain but a few years before Cæsar, was conducted by Divitiacus, king of the Hedui, one of the most
powerful nations of Gaul, who, having obtained a footing
on the British coast, continued to reign over the Belgæ
in this island, as well as his ancient subjects on the Con-

---

* Hist. of Brit. vol. i. p. 245.   † De Bell. Gal. lib. v. cap. 10.

tinent. The principal settlements of the Belgæ in Britain were in the present counties of Hampshire, Wiltshire, and Somersetshire; but it seems they had also made inroads into Devonshire, and many of the previous inhabitants were driven before them into Ireland. It appears also from Richard of Cirencester, that prior to the coming of Cæsar the war was carried on against the Belgæ by the natives under Cassibelinus, whose second son Theomantius was at that period duke of Danmonium. There are numerous remains of fortresses in this county which evince that at a remote period it had been the scene of frequent warfare; and it seems probable that many of these were formed by the ancient Britons as a defence against the attacks of the Belgæ and other invaders. We have, however, no historians of these early periods [*].

The Ostidamnii and Cossini.

Camden[†] also mentions it as highly probable that the Ostidamnii and Cossini, two other British tribes, were seated within these limits; and Baxter[‡] speaks of them as the keepers of the flocks and herds of the Danmonii. But however this might be, the Danmonii, according to Whitaker[§], having conquered the Cimbri and Cornabii, and usurped their dominions, this was the name by which the inhabitants of Devonshire and Cornwall were then distinguished.

The Phœnicians.

Much has been said and written on the subject of the commercial intercourse of the Phœnicians with Great Britain for different metals, and particularly with Devonshire and Cornwall for tin and lead, as mentioned by Richard of Cirencester. Of the commencement of this intercourse, and its extent, little of course is known; but of the fact there is no doubt. This people, called Canaanites by the Hebrews, and according to Bochart known also by the names of Syrians, Assyrians, Syro-Phœnicians and Sidonians, were the earliest and most active traders of which, together with the Egyptians, we have any account. In-

* Lyson's *Mag. Brit.* part vi. p. 4.   † *Brit.* p. 1.
‡ *Gloss. Ant. Brit.*
§ Hist. of Manchester, vol. i. book i. chap. iii.

genious and excelling in manufactures, they were skilled
in the working of metals, jewelry, timber, stones, and in
architecture, of which the temple of Jerusalem was a
proof, since they were employed on that edifice as the principal artificers. Inhabiting the coasts of the Levant, with
Tyre and Sidon for their chief towns, and being an enterprizing people, their commerce was most extensive. They
appear to have traded to Assyria, Babylon, Arabia, and
even India. At a very early period they explored the
seas not only in their own neighbourhood, but to a considerable distance. As navigators they were the boldest
and most experienced, as well as the greatest discoverers,
of ancient times, and formed many settlements, both on
the coasts of the Mediterranean, and also beyond the
Pillars of Hercules, or the Straits of Gibraltar, of which
they have left traces in the names which they gave to
different places. Affecting no empire but that of the seas,
they engrossed the whole commerce of the western world,
and extended their trade to all the known parts which
they could reach. Their merchants are mentioned in the
Scriptures as equal to princes ; and hence their country,
small as it was, became the grand storehouse for the necessaries and luxuries of the times.

It was nothing, extraordinary, therefore that they discovered the British Isles, and established a trade with them.
The reality of their traffic, however, with Devonshire and
Cornwall, depends not upon conjecture but upon authentic
history. Their arrival at the Scilly Isles, and their trade
in tin, are attested by Strabo, Diodorus Siculus, and Sa-
linus *. Many words are enumerated which are the same
in the Phœnician and the ancient British, and especially
the names of towns in Cornwall derived from the Phœnician language, which was a dialect of the Hebrew. Hercules was one of the deities of the Phœnicians ; and Hartland Point was called the Promontory of Hercules ; and
Lundy Island, Herculea. Bochart and Sammes derive the

* Sammes, p. 54—58.

κ 2

BOOK
II.
Greek name Βρετανικη from the Phœnician or Hebrew
words ברת אנך, *Barat-anac,* the land of tin.   Cassiterides, from κασσίτερος, tin or lead, is a translation of this
name, first given to the Scilly Isles, but afterwards, it
should seem, transferred to the British Islands in general;
and the Greeks, finding the Phœnician name generally prevailing at a subsequent period, called them Βρετανικαι*.

We learn from Strabo, that the Phœnicians had been
accustomed from a very early period to visit the Cassiterides from Spain, for the sake of traffic, especially in tin†,
but were extremely careful to conceal from all other traders
the course which they took.   Herodotus, who flourished
about 450 years before Christ, and who had travelled for
the purpose of obtaining knowledge, in geography espe-

---

* Such is the opinion of these distinguished antiquaries. Camden,
however, (*Brit.* Introd. p. xix.) apparently on very slight grounds, derives the name of Britain from *Brith* (painted), because the natives painted
their bodies. "But," says Whitaker in his *Manchester,* (B. i. C. i. p. 10.)
" the appellation of Britain has been tortured for ages by the antiquarians, in order to force a confession of its origin and import from it. And
erudition, running wild in the mazes of folly, has eagerly deduced it from
every word of similar sound, almost in every known language of the globe.
But the Celtic is obviously the only one that can lay any competent claim
to it. The first denomination of the island was *Albion,* (Plin. lib. iv. c. 16.
Richard, p. 1.) a name that was evidently conferred upon it before it was
inhabited, and while its *alb-ion,* or *heights,* were only viewed at a distance
from the opposite shore of Gaul. The second was *Breatin, Brydain,* or
Britain, a name not applied to the region, but bestowed on the inhabitants
not previously born on the Continent by the original settlers of the country,
but assumed or received at their first removal into the island; and it is
derived from a Celtic word denoting separation or division."
With respect to the name *Albion,* others think it was so called from
the white appearance of its cliffs.
† Sammes, pp. 1, 2, &c. 36. Of the early navigation of this people, and
their trade in this article especially, we read in the Scriptures, upwards of
one thousand years before the Christian æra. In the Psalms it is observed,
" They go down to the sea in ships, and occupy their business in great
waters." " Tarshish," (the city of Tartessus near the Pillars of Hercules,)
says Ezekiel, " was thy merchant by reason of the multitude of all kinds
of riches; with silver, iron, tin and lead, they trade in thy fairs," that is,
the fairs of Tyre. Jesus the son of Sirach, speaking of the glory of So-
lomon, says, " Thou didst gather gold as tin, and didst multiply gold as
lead." And Homer mentions tin more than once as one of the metals
in the shield of Achilles, and in the greaves for his legs.—See Polwhele's
Historical Views, pp. 120, 121.
Tin was also found both in Spain and Portugal, but was discovered
much more plentifully in Britain.—Whitaker's Manchester, vol. ii. p. 41.

cially, to Tyre, Egypt and Assyria, where it was most likely to be obtained, confesses his ignorance of the western countries, and that he knew nothing of the Cassiterides *, whence tin and amber were derived; nor did he know whether Europe was bounded by land or sea. A curious instance, moreover, is given by Strabo of the care which was taken by the Phœnicians to conceal their navigation to this island. A Phœnician trader, finding himself closely watched by a Roman vessel, ran his ship on shore and destroyed it rather than disclose the secret; and on account of his fidelity he was indemnified for his losses out of the public treasury of his country†. The merchants of Carthage were more successful than the rest. Anxious to share the trade of their brethren of Cadiz, who were the original adventurers from Phœnicia, Hanno and Hamilco undertook separate voyages of discovery. Having passed the Straits of Gibraltar, the former turning to the left explored the coast of Africa; and the latter, sailing towards the north, after passing the coasts of Spain, crossed the ocean, and in the fourth month discovered the object of his voyage. The Æstromenides ‡ were distant two days' sail from the sacred isle of the Hibernians, which was situated near the isle of the Albions.

Little is known respecting the commerce of the Greeks with this island; but we are informed that Pytheas, the most celebrated navigator of the Grecian colonists of Marseilles, had the good fortune, 330 years before Christ, to discover the Cassiterides§. They were at that time ten in number, abounding in tin and lead, and were divided, by a narrow but boisterous strait, from the coast of the Danmonii. The largest was called Silura or Sygdelis, the origin, no doubt, of the modern name Scilly. And thus successive discoveries threw open the trade to different nations ‖.

CHAP.
I.

The Greeks.

* Strabo, iii. 175.   † See Lingard's Hist. of Engl. ch. i. p. 11.
‡ So the tin islands were called by Richard of Cirencester, and in the journal of Hamilco, which was extant as late as the fifth century.
§ Plin. ii. 75.
‖ Upon the increase of the Roman empire the Greeks discontinued their voyages to the Western Ocean.

BOOK
II.

Ancient
mode of
traffic in
tin.

Lucius Crassus, a Roman, at length taught the natives to work their mines to greater advantage; and so abundant was the annual exportation, that the surplus of tin was bought up by factors on the coast of the Mediterranean, and conveyed over-land even to the remote provinces of India *. A less expensive course, however, was afterwards adopted. The British miners cast their tin into square blocks, and, it is said, conveyed it to the Isle of Wight as the general emporium †. From thence it was exported by Gallic traders to the mouth of the Seine, the Loire, or the Garonne, and ascending these rivers was carried across the country by horses till it could be conveyed by water to the cities of Marseilles or Narbonne ‡. In return for this metal, so highly prized by the ancient nations, the Britons received articles of inferior value to their possessors, but of high estimation among uncivilized people; namely, salt, earthenware, and brass. Tin was originally the sole article of commerce; but to this were soon added hides in large quantities from the interior of the country; lead; and, what was the most valuable of all, iron.

The mines of the Scilly Isles appear to have furnished the original supplies of tin, but were by no means sufficient to meet the extensive demands for this article in various and very distant quarters of the globe. Cornwall and Devonshire participated largely in the trade; and the latter county abounds with the vestiges of the ancient tin mines on Dartmoor and the vicinity: and of the great importance of the trade in this article to the county in former periods, there is sufficient evidence in the appointment of four stannary jurisdictions, with an equal number

---

* Plin. xxxiv. 17.

† The name given to this general emporium in a passage of Diodorus Siculus (lib. v. cap. ii.) is *Ictis*; and it is the common opinion that by this is meant the Isle of Wight: but he adds, this island was so near the main land that the passage to it at low water was dry, and the people conveyed their tin to it in carts. Borlase, therefore, supposes it to be one of the Scilly Isles, and Mr. Polwhele the island of St. Nicholas; both suppositions in the highest degree improbable. On the whole, it seems altogether uncertain what island was intended by Diodorus.—See Polwhele's Historical Views, p. 124—138.

‡ Plin. iv. 22. xxxiv. 17. Cæs. v. 12.

of stannary courts and coinage towns ; namely, Plympton, Tavistock, Ashburton, and Chagford. By these were chosen*, from time to time, at the direction of the Lord Warden, certain jurats to meet in a general sessions of parliament on Crockern Torr, with power to make laws for the regulation of the mines and the trade in tin. It appears also that in former periods Devonshire produced greater quantities of tin than Cornwall; for so late as the reign of King John, the coinage of tin was farmed for £100 yearly, whilst that of Cornwall was only one hundred marks. And Mr. Polwhele is of opinion that the stannary parliament was the continuation of a similar court among the ancient Britons; as the place where they met in the open air, on one of the tors of Dartmoor, would never have been selected in any modern period for such a purpose.

The method of mining among the Danmonii was, no doubt, of the simplest description, as the tin ore was probably at that time procured with as little difficulty as stones at present†. The mines were then not deep as they now are, but confined to the surface. Before the time of the Romans the mode of procuring this metal was probably, in technical language, by *shoding* and *streaming*‡. *Shodes* consist of loose stones scattered on the sides of hills, and in other situations, sometimes distant a furlong or more from their lodes, and sometimes found in great numbers together, forming one continued course from one to ten feet deep, which is then called a *stream*, from the process used to separate the earthy matter from the ore, which consists in passing a stream of water over it. *Shoding* is described as a method of finding mines of tin by digging small pits, in order to trace out the lodes of tin by the scattered and loose stones or fragments of ore. In *streaming*, the miners sink a shaft three, five, or seven fathoms in depth to the rock itself, or clay, on both of

* Camden's Additions to Devonshire, p. 32.
† The notion of the ancients concerning the discovery of metals, by the burning down of woods which melted them from the ore, is extremely probable.
‡ Polwhele's Historical Views, chap. i. sect. vi. p. 104.

BOOK
II.

which the tin frequently lies in strata at different depths. The stratum of tin may be from one to ten feet in thickness, or more, and in breadth from one fathom to a very considerable extent. The size of the ore, which is rounded, is from that of a walnut to the finest sand, the latter making the principal part of the stream, which is intermixed with gravel and clay. When the miner has traced the *stream*, he digs an open trench in the lowest part of the spot where it is found, which serves to draw off the water and the waste with it in proportion to the strength of the current*. By proceeding in this manner the ore is procured; and in some such way as this the Danmonians in all probability obtained the metal. It has been before observed, that there are the plainest vestiges of ancient tin mines in Devonshire. There are numerous *stream-works* on Dartmoor and its vicinity, which have lain forsaken for ages. In the parishes of Monaton, Kingsteignton and Teigngrace, are many old tin-works of this kind, which the inhabitants attribute to the British period. The Bovey Heathfield has been worked in the same manner; and indeed all the valleys from this spot to Dartmoor bear traces of the same mode of procuring the ore. These might, it is true, be works of a subsequent period; but the traditions of the country and the simplicity of the mode of operation, render it probable that they belong to the time of the ancient Britons†.

That lead was also familiar to the western Britons, is

---

* Several circumstances concur in proving that the veins of tin ore found beneath the surface of alluvial ground in low situations or valleys, have been carried down by currents to the places where they are now found.

† Many of the stream-works, or repositories, are of very ancient date, as they occur considerably below the present level of the rivers. Human skulls, and the horns of the elk or stag, have been found in the beds of sand which cover them. In St. Bazey Moor, Cornwall, there is a depth of twenty feet of alluvial soil. The first stratum next the surface is composed of gravel, containing a little tin ore: this lies upon a bed of dark combustible peat earth. Immediately under this lies a bed of stream-tin about five feet thick. Great part of this has been wrought at a very remote period, and before iron instruments were in use; for several wooden pickaxes, made of oak, holm and box, were discovered in it a few years since. Stream-works sometimes extend under the sea in Cornwall.—See Rees's Cyclopedia, *art.* Stream-tin.

admitted; and Mr. Whitaker asserts that the Scilly Isles
were worked for this metal by the aborigines, and those
of the Peak by the Belgæ*. And that the Danmonii were
acquainted with iron before the time of the Romans, there
can be no doubt. An observation of Cæsar seems to favour
this supposition. Tin, he remarks, came from the interior,
and iron was found in the maritime parts, but in small
quantities. Gold and silver were also discovered in this
country, as we learn from Strabo† and Tacitus‡. As gold
is in the present day frequently found in small quantities
intermixed with tin, there can be no doubt that such was
the case in former periods.

Concerning the method made use of by the Britons in
preparing these metals for use, nothing is now known. But
with respect to tin especially, from the ready fusibility of
this metal, in the separation of it from its native dross they
would find no difficulty. Among the rocks there are often
veins of earth where the tin is found, and to extract, melt,
purify, and afterwards by means of moulds to shape it into
cubical figures, would require but little ingenuity; and
from their well-known skill in other useful arts, we readily
infer this would be found by the ancient Britons an easy
task. The tin, when fused and beaten into squares, (says
Mr. Whitaker,) was formed by the original Britons in all
probability, and by the Romans certainly, into cups, basins and pitchers, some of which have been transmitted to
the present age. A basin was found some years ago, in
Cornwall, four inches and a half in diameter§.

At present our attention is confined to the early inhabitants of Devonshire, and a fitter opportunity will occur
hereafter of entering more largely into the history of
mining in this county.

That the Druids abounded in Devonshire, and were conversant particularly with Dartmoor and its vicinity, is the

* Whitaker's Manchester, vol. ii. p. 40.   † lib. iv.
‡ Vit. Agric. cap. xii.
§ Whitaker's Manchester, vol. ii. p. 41.

BOOK
II.
___

commonly received opinion ; and the cromlech, the logan
stones, the rock basins, the circles, stone pillars, and what
are supposed to be rock idols, are adduced as unquestion-
able proofs of the fact ; whilst some who have investigated
these subjects can discover no satisfactory indications of
Druidism in the county, and are disposed to doubt the
existence of it there altogether. Both opinions have been
carried, no doubt, to the extreme, and the truth in all probability lies between. What are considered as the Druidical remains will be described hereafter, when the antiquities of the county come under consideration ; but at present
it may be sufficient to observe, in the first place, with respect to the cromlech, that there are different conjectures
among antiquarians respecting the design of these singular
erections ; some considering them as used for the purpose
of preparing the sacrifices, and others as connected with
astronomy, being in both cases Druidical ; whilst others
view them only as sepulchral monuments for some distinguished individual, or memorials of some remarkable event,
and as having no connection with ancient superstitions.
The logan * stones are clearly inartificial. They would
suit the purposes of the Druids extremely well ; but that
they were applied to such uses, seems to be matter merely
of conjecture. Some of the rock basins may be excavations
produced by natural causes, but the form of others is much
too regular, and affords indications of design which leave
no room to doubt of their being artificial ; nor is it easy to
imagine from what their origin could be derived, if not from
Druidical superstition. The notion of Dr. MacCulloch and
others, that rock basins have been formed by the action of
water, air and frost on the softer parts of the stone in all instances, seems to be entirely unfounded ; for, if such were
the case, how comes it to pass that they are found only on
the tops of the tors, and sometimes on the logan stones ?
This, if the writer is not mistaken, is a singular fact, and
tends to strengthen the idea that these tors and logan

* That is, logging or rocking, from the Cornish *log*, to rock.

stones were appropriated by the Druids to their religious CHAP.
rites. If the basins were excavations produced by natural I.
causes, why are they not found on numerous other rocks
and in different situations? This circumstance, in conjunction with their regularity and the peculiar form
common to many of them, seems to leave little room for
scepticism. At least some of the circles in Devonshire,
which are entirely different from the remains of British
cottages on the Moor, must surely be regarded as Druidical; and although many of the stone pillars might be
erected as guides to travellers, or as memorials, the form
of others, and especially their situation in the vicinity of
remains confessedly British, afford sufficient indications
of their connection with the religious ceremonies or judicial proceedings of the Druids. And with respect to
what are considered as rock idols on the Moor, these are
evidently rocks in their natural state without the slightest
traces of art. They might, or might not, be consecrated
to the ancient religious worship of the Britons. In the
earlier periods of Druidism, at least, no idols were allowed, but afterwards, it should seem, they, with other
corruptions, were introduced *.

On the whole, there can be no room for scepticism that
Devonshire affords sufficient proofs of the prevalence of
Druidism in the county in early periods. Besides, the
religion of this district was without doubt similar to that
of the rest of the island. This consisted of the worship
of a plurality of fictitious deities, accompanied by imposing ceremonies, magnificent processions, and mysterious rites, admirably calculated, by deluding the senses,
captivating the imagination and inspiring terror, to prostrate the understanding, and hold the minds of a barbarous people in complete subjection. Of this super-

---

* In Lucan s well-known description of the sacred wood, rude images
are mentioned:

. . . . "Tum plurima nigris
Fontibus unda cadit, simulacraque mœsta deorum
Arte carent, cæsisque extant informia truncis."
Pharsalia, lib. iii. lin. 412.

stition, latterly cruel in the extreme, as well as absurd, the Druids were the priests.   Nor will it be denied that few districts of the country afforded situations more suitable to their purpose than the lofty hills and romantic tors, the solitary wilds and ancient woods and streams, of Devonshire.   Such being the case, a brief sketch of the power, the principles and the customs of these ancient ministers of superstition, may not be unsuitable here, especially as it may serve hereafter to assist in forming just ideas of what are supposed to be the Druidical remains of the county.   Many authors have treated largely on these subjects ; and as their works are not more numerous than expensive, it is presumed that an epitome of Druidism, comprising the leading features of this most powerful and extensive superstition, derived from the best sources of information, will not be deemed a useless digression.

Much information is obtained respecting the Druids from ancient and authentic writers, who had the best means of inquiry ; and although the greater part of their descriptions relate to the Continent, they are not less applicable to Britain, for it is certain that the religious principles and the practice of both were similar.   This we learn from Cæsar, who also affirms, that such of the Gauls as were desirous of becoming thoroughly instructed in the principles of their religion, were accustomed to travel for that purpose into this country *, so that it might seem Druidism in Britain was the parent stock.   This religion in its origin was pure, inculcating the belief of one God, the creator and preserver of all things ; but by degrees, in the course of many ages, it had accumulated a hideous mass of corruption, until in the time of the Romans it had degenerated into the most extravagant and cruel superstition.

The power of the Druids.

Of the power of these priests over the minds of all

---

* De Bell. Gal. lib. vi. cap. 13. He also observes, respecting Druidism, " Disciplina in Britannia reperta atque in Galliam translata esse existimatur."

ranks in the state, the most singular accounts are on
record. According to Cæsar, two orders only in Gaul
were held in any estimation, the Druids [*] and the nobles,
and of these the authority of the former was paramount:
such also was the case in Britain. No religious rite,
whether public or domestic, could be performed without
a Druid. As these venerated fanatics or deceivers were
believed to be acquainted with the counsels of the Deity,
and to hold converse with the gods, neither the prayers
nor the sacrifices of the people were allowed to be offered
but by them. In time of peace and war, by friends and
foes, their mandates were observed and implicitly obeyed.
And often have they stepped in between hostile armies,
eager for battle with swords drawn and spears pointed,
and at once pacified them, as though wild beasts had been
suddenly tamed by enchantment [†]. Their persons were
held sacred ; they were exempt from taxes and military
duties ; and such were the honours by which they were
distinguished, that sons of the nobles were devoted to
the sacred office, and even princes were ambitious of
being admitted into their fraternity [‡]. All, however, were
not of equal rank. They were divided into different orders, the whole being subject to a supreme head, the
Archdruid, the Pontifex Maximus, or High Priest, whose
station in Britain is supposed to have been in the Isle of
Anglesea, where he generally resided in great splendour,
surrounded by numerous attendants of his own order [§].

[*] The common derivation of the name Druid is from the Celtic or
British word *derw*, an oak, on account of their veneration for that tree.
However, as Mr. Higgins says, " the meanings given to the word *Druid*
are very numerous, but not more numerous than nonsensical. The Greeks
derive it from δρῦς, an oak ; but how absurd to derive a word of an ancient language from a modern one!" &c. He gives other derivations,
but seems to prefer that of Mr. Davies from Taliessin, the Welsh bard,
who considers it as a compound word composed of the Welsh, i. e. Gaelic
or Celtic word, *gwydd* a priest, and *dar* superior, a superior priest, or
chief priest.

See a splendid and very learned work on " The Celtic Druids" by
Godfrey Higgins, Esq. chap. iii. sect. vii.

[†] Diodorus Siculus, lib. v. cap. ii. Strabo, lib. iv. p. 197.

[‡] Cæs. *De Bell. Gal.* lib. vi. cap. 13. Cicero *De Div.* lib. i. Pompon.
Mela, lib. iii.   [§] Rowland's *Mon. Ant.* p. 83.

BOOK
II.

This high office was in general hereditary, but occasionally the archdruid succeeded to his situation by the election of his fraternity*; and such were the honours and emoluments attached to the station, that the contest for it sometimes occasioned a civil war†. The number of the Druids is uncertain; but there can be no doubt it was exceedingly large in proportion to the rest of the people. We learn from Cæsar, that both Gaul and Britain were much addicted to superstition; and the necessary consequence was a numerous retinue of priests, probably more numerous than in any of the Roman Catholic countries of the present day; for we are informed on the same un questionable authority, that the people were persuaded, that the greater the number of Druids, the more abun dant would be their harvests, and the greater their prosperity.

In the pursuit of power no order of priests have been more successful than the Druids. All ranks in the state were in fact prostrate at their feet, and kings bowed without hesitation to their dominion. The adjusting of disputes and the administration of justice were entirely in their hands. They were the makers of the laws, and no sentence could be pronounced on criminals but by them. They also were the judges of merit, and assumed to themselves the distribution of rewards *.

The whole of this power was founded of course on the superstition and credulity of the people; but, when once established, the means which they adopted to uphold and give it strength remained, so long as its source continued, perfectly irresistible. The principal of these means was the sentence of excommunication pronounced on individuals and tribes indiscriminately, who did not comply with their decrees. Nothing could carry with it greater terror, and consequently be more effective; for by this sentence not only were the unhappy victims of it rendered incapable of participating in any of the religious ceremo-

• " The Celtic Druids," chap. vii. sect. ii.
† Cæsar, lib. vi. cap. 13.

nies, but in fact outlawed, detested and avoided by their countrymen, and exposed to all sorts of injuries without the means of redress; for even those who from motives of compassion might be disposed to render them the slightest assistance or relief, were themselves exposed to all the calamities of a similar malediction[*]. Another instrument by which their power was supported was divination, which always constituted a principal part of the religion of those times. No battle could commence, nor indeed any affair of importance be undertaken, till the auspices had been consulted by the Druids, and pronounced to be favourable; nor could there be any difficulty in rendering these consultations conducive to their own views of interest or ambition. And to this it may be added, that tradition says, as certain dues were paid them annually by each family, the people were compelled, on the last evening of October, to put out their fires, in order to renew them on the following day at the sacred fire in the temple; and if their dues were not paid, light being refused, the winter must be passed in the most deplorable condition; for should their neighbours venture to supply them, they as well as themselves were immediately placed under the terrific sentence of excommunication.

Of the influence of education in a state, none who aspire at dominion can be ignorant. The Druids, on the principle that knowledge is power, seized this mighty engine, and converted it to their own use exclusively. No person was permitted to take share in public employments who had not been educated in their establishments; and the supposition that institutions, similar to monasteries and colleges, were prevalent among them, is highly probable; for it is difficult to imagine how else the youths committed to their care could be provided for and instructed. Children of the highest classes were sent to their schools, and admitted into their order: those of Gaul, also, were frequently sent into Britain; nor was

* Cæs. *De Bell. Gal.* lib. vi. cap. 13.

BOOK
II.
___

their education completed in less than twenty years. The Druids, like the Pythagoreans and other philosophers of antiquity, adopted the practice of requiring their pupils to commit their doctrines to memory; and their young bards especially learned in this way twenty thousand verses before their course of discipline was finished. Their pupils are said to have been taken to the most secluded situations among the woods and rocks and caves, in order that no interruption might impede their studies, and that no knowledge of the doctrines taught in their institutions might transpire. But, above all, these youths were not permitted to have any intercourse with their parents until the age of fourteen. In all this the most consummate policy is discovered [*].

Their
different
orders.

The Druids were generally divided into three principal orders :—the *Druids*, properly so called; the *Bards;* and the *Eubages* or *Vates*, prophets, denominated by the Gauls and Britons *Faids*. The whole, however, of these classes were frequently called *Druids*. The first of them were the Priests, and were employed in all the offices of religion, except the parts allotted to the others, and, in the absence of the Faids, probably in theirs also. They were by far the most numerous, and were held in the highest honour. The Bards were the heroic, historical, and genealogical poets of Germany, Gaul, and Britain; but are said carefully to have avoided the subject of religion, though some think differently. The Vates composed hymns in honour of the gods, which they sung to their harps at their religious solemnities. They were also the pretended prophets of all the Celtic nations, who believed them to be inspired by the gods, and favoured with divine revelations. These orders have been supposed to bear some resemblance to those of the religious officers among the Hebrews, who had their Priests, Levites (who were the Bards), and Prophets [†].

---

[*] " The Celtic Druids," chap. vii. sect. vi. Cæs. lib. vi. Pompon. Mela, lib. iii. cap. ii. Lucan, lib. i.

[†] Henry's Hist. of Brit. 4to, vol. i. Strabo, lib. iv. p. 197. Diod. Sic. lib. v.

Many of the Druids seem to have lived a kind of collegiate or monastic life; and as the service of each temple
required a considerable number, they must have had their
dwellings near the spot. Others led a more secular and
public life; and, as no sacred rite could be performed without them, they must have resided in courts and great families. Some appear to have retired and lived as hermits;
and whilst many had wives and families, others observed
a life of celibacy.

Among the attendants on the offices of religion, there Druid-
were also Druidesses; and when Suetonius invaded the esses.
Isle of Anglesea, his army were actually terrified by the
frantic behaviour of a large number of these females.
They are said to have been divided into three classes.
The first were under a vow of perpetual virginity, and
lived in sisterhoods; they practised divination, &c. The
second class were married, but devoted their services to
religion. And the third, which was the lowest, performed
the most servile offices, and attended on the Druids.

With respect to the property of the Druids there is no Property
certain information; but it is probable some land was al- of the
lotted to their use, particularly in the isles of Anglesea, Druids.
Man, Harris, &c.* Part of the offerings, which were
often great and always frequent, fell to their share. Cattle
and spoils taken in war were dedicated to their gods.
From their consultations about the success of enterprizes,
from the administration of justice, the practice of medicine, but especially from the instruction of pupils, large
emoluments would naturally arise; and, as before observed, they levied annually dues or taxes on every family; besides that many of them were often sumptuously
entertained by the nobles and princes of the times. From
all these sources their revenues must have been very considerable. The private property, moreover, of those of them
who belonged to noble families, no doubt would be large,
and their influence consequently of great importance.

* Henry's Hist. of Brit., vol. i.

With respect to their principles, the Druids had two
sets of opinions different from each other: the one communicated only to the initiated, who were solemnly
sworn to secresy; and, in order to prevent the promulga-
tion of the doctrines imparted, they were taught only in
the deepest recesses of the woods and in caves, were never
committed to writing, and never communicated to women.
This is to be lamented, as their secret doctrines were in
all probability much purer than those which they taught
in public. A few hints only are gathered from the Greek
and Roman writers, who knew little of them. They appear to have believed in the great doctrine of a Supreme
Being, and taught many things about the nature and per-
fections of the Deity, as well as the immortality of the
soul, which was probably one of their secret opinions.
To this they added the Pythagorean notion of the me-
tempsychosis, or transmigration of souls, which was probably their public doctrine, intended for the amusement
and benefit of the people *; whilst from some writers it
should seem their real sentiment was, that the soul after
death ascends to some upper orb, and enjoys a more
sublime felicity. Their secret doctrines were the most
rational, but were of no benefit to the public in general,
as the Druids appear to have adopted the notion, that
ignorance is the mother of devotion, and that the common
people could be led, not by reason, but by their senses,
their passions, and their imaginations under the influence
of superstition. Such is the reason assigned by Strabo†
in this instance for their conduct. Their public instruc-
tions were delivered from little eminences, many of which
are still remaining, and these declamations are said to
have made great impression on the surrounding multitude. With their mythology moral precepts were intermixed, and their system of ethics was short and simple,
but, with some alloy, excellent. *Worship the gods, Do no
evil,* and *Be valiant in battle,* with the expectation of re-

* Cæsar, lib. vi. cap. 13. Diod. Sic. lib. v.   † lib. i.

wards or punishment hereafter, formed the subjects of
their public addresses.

The similarity between all the ancient systems of idolatry is remarkable, and clearly points to the same origin.
The objects of this worship are divided into two classes:
sensible objects, chiefly the celestial bodies, as the sun,
moon and stars; and distinguished men, as founders of
nations, princes, legislators, successful warriors, and in-
ventors of the useful arts; some of them being also intended to represent the different attributes of the Deity
personified.

The Supreme Being was adored by the Gauls and Britons under the name of *Hesus* (in the Hebrew *Hizzus*),
expressing his omnipotence *: nor was his worship at first
accompanied by barbarous ceremonies; but when a plurality of gods was introduced, Hesus was degraded to a
particular deity, and corresponded to Mars, as the chief
divinity of these warlike nations, who endeavoured to pro-
pitiate him by the most cruel rites †. *Teutates* was another name, attribute, or character of the Supreme Being,
compounded of *Deu Tait*, or God the Father, and worshiped
by the same people as a particular divinity; but when sunk
into idolatry, they reduced him also to the sovereign of
the infernal world, Dis or Pluto, and accordingly worshiped him with rites consistent with the stern and gloomy
character of the god. Others, however, are of opinion
that this deity corresponded to Mercury ‡. Another object of their adoration was *Taranis*, the god of thunder,
from *taran*, thunder, which was considered as the voice of
God §, and in the times of gross idolatry was worshiped
with the most inhuman ceremonies.

* Ps. xxiv. 8.
† Et quibus immitis placatur sanguine diro
   Teutates, horrensque feris altaribus Hesus
   Et Taranis Scythiæ non mitior ara Dianæ.
                       Lucan. *Phars.* lib. i. lin. 445.
‡ Baxter, *Gloss. Brit.* p. 277. Cæs. lib. vi. cap. 18. Dionys. Hali-
carn. lib. i. p. 16.
§ As in the sublime poetry of the Hebrews: Job xl. 9; Ps. xxix. 3, 4, 5.

BOOK
II.

Among the celestial bodies the sun was the most ancient and the most universal object of idolatrous worship, and was adored by the ancient Britons with great solemnity and pomp in various places, under names in their language said to be expressive of its nature and qualities, as Bel, Belinus, Belatucardus, &c. To this illustrious object of worship the famous circles of stones, several of which still remain, seem to have been chiefly dedicated; and in these temples, as they are sometimes called for want of a more appropriate name, the Druids kept their sacred fire, as a symbol of the divinity, and whence, as they were usually situated on eminences or in open situations, they had a full view of the heavenly bodies. The moon also, as next in splendour and utility to the sun, was an object of adoration scarcely inferior in ancient times, and among the Gauls and Britons the worship of both was similar. The circles dedicated to each were of the same construction, and contiguous*. According to Cæsar, the moon was the chief divinity of the Germans, on account of her favourable influence on their nocturnal and predatory expeditions; nor did they enter on any enterprize whilst she was in a state of obscurity.

A large proportion of the ancient gods having been distinguished men, it is more than probable that all the deities of human origin were the same in Gaul and Britain as in Greece and Rome: in fact, the only question is, which of them borrowed from the other; and there appears to be no reason to doubt that the Greek and Roman gods were the copies, not the originals. They were Saturn, Jupiter, Mercury, and other princes of the royal family of the Titans, who reigned with much splendour both in Asia and Europe in the Patriarchal ages. These deities belonged to the Celtæ by birth, and were rulers of the Celtic tribes who peopled Gaul and Britain, and all their names in Celtic were expressive†.

* Martin's Description of the Western Isles.
† Henry's Hist. of Brit. vol. i.

Saturn, whose name in that language signifies *martial* or *warlike*, was one of the greatest of these Titan princes, having dethroned his father, subdued his brother Titan, and extended his empire over the greater part of Europe: he was worshiped chiefly in the west. As a great warrior and a cruel and vindictive deity, human victims were offered to avert his wrath.

Jupiter was the youngest son of Saturn, but a still more renowned and distinguished prince than his father, whom he also dethroned. Having been far more enterprizing and successful than his elder brothers Neptune and Pluto, they acted only as his vicegerents. His true name was *Jow*, which in the Celtic signifies *young*, and he was so called because he was the youngest brother, and had performed great exploits in early life. To this name the Latins afterwards add *pater*, retaining however the original name alone in all the cases but the nominative. Distinguished by his talents, and reigning over an extensive empire, he came at length to be considered by the Greeks and Romans, as well as the Gauls, Britons, and many other nations, the greatest of the gods.

Mercury was the favourite son of Jupiter and Maia, and being the most accomplished prince of all the Titan race, he received from Jupiter, during his own life, the government of Europe. In Celtic his name is a compound of *mercs*, merchandize, and *wr*, a man, because he protected commerce as well as learning, eloquence, and the arts. Thieves also claimed his protection. He was worshiped by the Gauls and Britons *.

Besides these they had many other imaginary deities, whose origin was human, but whom it is not necessary to describe in detail. They had also several goddesses; as Andraste or Astarte (supposed to be Venus or Diana), Onvana, Minerva, Ceres, Proserpine, &c.; and according to Gildas the number of their gods was greater than that

---

* Cæs. lib. vi. cap. xvii. Cæsar says the Gauls worshiped Mercury, Apollo, Mars, Jupiter, and Minerva; and that they had generally the same notions of these gods as other nations, although they chiefly worshiped Mercury, and of him they had many images.

BOOK
II.

of the Egyptian deities; and there was scarcely a river, lake, mountain or wood, which was not supposed to have some divinity or spirit presiding over it *. The serpent also appears to have been held in great veneration by the Druids, and to have received from them some kind of religious homage †.

Their
worship.

The worship of the Druids was expressed in four ways, corresponding to their different wants; songs of praise and thanksgiving, prayers and supplications, offerings and sacrifices, and the various arts of divination. The ancient Britons were fond of poetry, and appear to have made great use of it, accompanied by music at their religious solemnities. Sacred poems, composed by the Faids, now entirely lost, are said to have been sung to the harp at their worship; and it is to be feared this music was also used to drown the cries of their victims. Prayers, as in the case of all nations, constituted a principal part of their religious worship, and particularly accompanied the sacrifice, as with the Jews, the priest laying his hand on the head of the victim. Pliny ‡ has recorded one of these prayers by the officiating Druid, who, when he began the sacrifice, prayed to God " to give a blessing with his own gift to them that were honoured with it." Offerings, originating in the same feeling of interest or gratitude, as in the case of presents by dependants to princes and benefactors, were of various kinds, and consisted chiefly of things which they considered as most excellent and useful to themselves, or most acceptable to the gods. As this mode of worship was much encouraged by the Druids, their sacred places were crowded with pious gifts, ex-

---

* *Hist. Gildæ*, cap. ii.

† See " The Celtic Druids" (before referred to), ch. vii. sect. xl. Of this the famous *Anguinum* affords some indication. This was the serpent's egg, or a congeries of small snakes rolled together, and incrusted with a shell formed by a sort of viscous gum, or the saliva of the mother serpent: it was used as a charm by the Druids, and worn as such by themselves. It is described, with the mode of obtaining it, by Dr. Borlase (p. 141); and Pliny (lib. xxix. cap. xiii.) also describes one of these charms, which he says he had seen, and mentions instances in which it had been used.

‡ *Hist. Nat.* lib. xvi. cap. xliv.

pressions of gratitude, the fulfilment of vows, trophies and warlike spoils piled up in a heap in their consecrated groves, or by the side of a hallowed lake. Instances of the violation of these sacred deposits scarcely ever occurred, and in such case the severest punishments with tortures certainly followed[*]. Of sacrifices, the most common were living creatures, such chiefly as were used for food, as sheep, goats, oxen, and other animals. These were examined with the greatest care, and afterwards slain, with various ceremonies, by priests appointed for the purpose. On some occasions the victims were entirely consumed by fire; but most commonly they were divided into three parts; one for the altar, another for the priest, and a third for the person who brought the sacrifice, to feast with his friends.

The opinion has been entertained[†] that the Druids offered no human or other sacrifices of animals; and it would be highly gratifying to the common feelings of humanity if this opinion could be shown to be well founded; but, unfortunately, the evidence of this fact is too clear and decisive to admit a doubt on the subject. There cannot surely be better testimony than Cæsar's, for no one had more ample means of ascertaining the real state of the case; and though his inclination and his interest might afford him sufficient temptation to exaggerate the faults of the people whom he had attacked and subdued, still it cannot be believed that he would have ventured so gross a calumny, when it would have been so easily refuted. Besides, his representation not only remains uncontradicted, but is confirmed by the most respectable writers near his own time[‡]. His statement,

---

* Cæs. lib. vi. cap. xvii.
† So Dr. Smith thinks, p. 36. See "The Celtic Druids," ch. vii. § xiii.
‡ Strabo, lib. iv.
"Et vos barbaricos ritus, moremque sinistrum
Sacrorum, Druidæ, positis repetistis ab armis.
Solis nosse Deos, et cœli numina vobis,
Aut solis nescire datum; nemora alta remotis
Incolitis lucis."—*Lucan*, lib. i. lin. 451.
See also the passage already quoted, p. 107.

BOOK
II.

which is ample and explicit, is as follows: "On account of their propensity to superstition, those of the Gauls who were suffering under dangerous diseases, or were conversant in battles and other perils, either offered men as victims, or made a vow to immolate themselves; and in conducting these sacrifices they made use of the Druids, for they had adopted the notion, that the anger of the gods could not be otherwise appeased than by substituting the life of one man for the life of another. They had public sacrifices of this kind appointed. Others had images of immense size, the limbs of which, being formed of twigs interwoven, were filled with living men, who, fire being applied, were consumed by the flames surrounding them *. Criminals who had been detected in the commission of theft or any other crime, were the victims which they considered as most acceptable to the gods; but when the supply of these was deficient, they had recourse to the innocent for victims." Cæsar, it is true, is speaking here of the Gauls; but he has elsewhere represented the religious customs of the Britons to be the same †.

Dr. Borlase enumerates additional circumstances of

* The form of this image is not mentioned by Cæsar; but Mr. Higgins thinks it was that of a bull, as they were accustomed to sacrifice bulls, and carried one to war with them, &c. "The Celtic Druids," ch. vii. sect. xiii.

† In Mr. Polwhele's "Historical Views" (p. 29) is the following most singular passage, which he seems to think important, as he has transferred it verbatim into his History of Devonshire (p. 141): "Mr. Bryant is of opinion that this mystical sacrifice" (the slaughter of an only son by a person of distinction by way of atonement) "was a typical representation of the great vicarial sacrifice that was to come. At first there is no doubt that the Druids offered up their human victims with the same sublime views. The Druids maintained, 'quod pro vita hominis nisi vita hominis reddatur, non posse aliter deorum immortalium numen placari.' This mysterious doctrine is not of men, but of God! It evidently points out THE ONE GREAT SACRIFICE FOR THE SINS OF THE WHOLE WORLD. These strange remarks surely need no comment. The most savage rite of one of the most cruel superstitions that ever existed, originated, it seems, in divine revelation, and was typical of what Mr. Polwhele considers the most important arrangement of the Christian economy!! Could an unbeliever have aimed a severer sarcasm, or one that is more unjust, at this best of all systems of religion, in which mercy is so conspicuously and so uniformly blended with justice?

KITLEY.

THE SEAT OF EDMUND POLLEXFEN BASTARD ESQ[r]. M.P. FOR DEVON.

To whom this Plate is respectfully inscribed

London, Published by Jones & Co.ne. Temple of the Muses, Finsbury Square.

LARTINGTON MANOR HOUSE, DEVON.

London Published by Robert Jennings 62 Cheapside Feb 1 1830

cruelty with which these horrid rites were attended.
According to his account, the Druids were extremely
lavish of human blood : not only criminals, captives, and
strangers were slain at their sacrifices, but their own disciples were put to death without mercy, if wilfully tardy
in coming to their assemblies. " The more precious the
victim, the more acceptable to the gods," was one of their
maxims ; hence princes and even their children were sacrificed on special occasions. But in order to reconcile
to their fate those who thus suffered, the Druids held that
after death they were deified, or at least were translated
to a superior state of being, where they enjoyed great
felicity. Death was inflicted by a variety of modes.
Some were shot with arrows; others were crucified in
their temples ; some were impaled in honour of their
gods, and then, with many besides who had suffered in
a different manner, were offered up as a burnt sacrifice.
Others were bled to death ; and their blood, received in
basins, served to sprinkle their altars. Some were struck
across the chest or the back with a sword, that by the
direction in which the body fell, by the convulsion of the
limbs, or by the flowing of the blood, the Druids might
foretell what would come to pass *. Strabo observes that
the monstrous image mentioned by Cæsar for the sacrifice of men, was partly filled with fuel, and also with several kinds of wild beasts, as they might imagine, perhaps,
that by a variety of expiring groans and howlings the
gods would be terrified into a compliance with their so-
licitations. During this horrid ceremony trumpets were
sounded without intermission to drown the cries of the
victims, as it was accounted ominous if the lamentations
of children, parents, or other friends were heard distinctly
whilst the victims were being consumed. In the mean time
prayers were offered up to the gods with uplifted hands,
and with great solemnity and fervour. Pliny even thinks
that, after the entrails had been properly examined, the
Druids ate part of the human victim. Intemperance in

* Diod. Sic. lib. v. cap. ii. Strabo, lib. iv.

drinking generally closed the scene, and the altar was
always consecrated afresh by strewing oak leaves upon
it before another sacrifice could be offered.

It is to be feared there is too much truth in this terrific
narrative, nor can much be said in palliation. It is not a
sufficient excuse that our British ancestors were not more
barbarous than others, and that the most civilized nations
of antiquity were guilty of similar atrocities, as the
Egyptians, Phœnicians, Carthaginians, and even the
Greeks and Romans; nor did the latter nation entirely
abandon the horrible custom of sacrificing human victims
until about a hundred years before Christ. Such scenes
however, it is affirmed, took place but seldom, and on occasions only of great national calamity*. The common
sacrifices of the Druids are supposed to have been inof-
fensive.

The following harmonious and spirited lines from Carrington's " Dartmoor†," correspond with this gloomy
subject.

> .... " Unnumbered shapes
> By nature strangely formed,—fantastic—vast—
> The silent desert throng! 'Tis said that here
> The Druid wandered. Haply have these hills
> With shouts ferocious, and the mingled shriek,
> Resounded, when to Jupiter upflamed
> The human hecatomb. The frantic seer
> Here built his sacred circle; for he loved
> To worship on the mountain's breast sublime,—
> The earth his altar, and the bending heaven
> His canopy magnificent. The rocks
> That crest the grove-crowned hill he scooped to hold
> The lustral waters; and to wondering crowds
> And ignorant, with guileful hand he rocked
> The yielding Logan. Practised to deceive,
> Himself deceived, he sway'd the fear-struck throng
> By crafty stratagems; and (falsely deemed
> The minister of Heaven) with bloodiest rites
> He awed the prostrate isle, and held the mind
> From age to age in superstition's spell."

The whole account serves to show the inestimable
value of the Christian religion.

The ancient Britons, as well as all other nations, be-

---

* Diod. Sic. lib. vi.   † p. 79.

lieving that the gods whom they worshiped possessed the CHAP.
government of the world, and were not unwilling on proper I.
occasions to discover future events to their worshipers,
were greatly addicted to divination, and, according to
Pliny*, excelled in it so much that they might have
given a lesson to the Persians themselves. The methods
they made use of in the practice of this art were in general similar to those adopted by other nations of antiquity; as observations on the flight of birds, the inspection of the entrails of victims, &c. One of a most horrible nature has already been described, that of putting a
human being to death with circumstances of great bar-
barity. Other methods of a harmless description were
numerous, but need not be specified.

As the gathering of the misletoe by the Druids was a Gathering
religious ceremony conducted with the utmost solemnity, of the
a description of it cannot with propriety be omitted here. misletoe.
Much of their attention was devoted to the study and the
practice of medicine; but their proficiency in this important
science was limited to the notions prevalent in times of
the greatest ignorance and superstition, for they connected
with it the rights of magic and divination. Three or four
plants are pointed out to us by the ancients, as the peculiar favourites of the Druids; of which one of the principal was *vervain*, used in casting lots and in foretelling
future events, as well as in anointing persons to prevent
fevers: another was the *samolus*, probably the wild trefoil, still called in Ireland *seamrog*, shamroc; and a third
selago, a kind of savin; but, above all, the misletoe, which
they might be said in fact to deify†. Pliny's account of
the ceremonies used in gathering it is as follows: "The
Druids (for so the Gauls call their magicians or wise men)
esteemed nothing so sacred as the misletoe, and the tree
on which it grows, provided it be an oak. These priests
are careful to choose for their religious rites such groves
as consist only of oaks; nor do they offer any sacrifice,

* *Hist. Nat.* lib. xxx. cap. i.
† Whitaker's Manchester, vol. ii. book i. chap. i.

BOOK
II.

or perform any religious ceremonies, without branches or leaves of this tree, so that they may seem very well to derive their Greek name from hence.   Certain, however, it is, that whatever they find growing upon this tree, besides its own natural productions, whether misletoe or any thing else, they esteem as a gift sent from heaven, and as a sign that the god whom they worship has made choice of that tree.   But as the misletoe is scarce, and but seldom to be met with, on the oak in particular, when it is discovered they gather it with great devotion and many ceremonies.   And in the first place they are especially careful to observe that the moon be exactly six days old (for on that day they begin their months and their new years, as also their several ages, or periods of thirty years), because on that day they think the moon has obtained sufficient influence, though she is not yet half full, or arrived at the end of her first quarter.   They call this plant in their own language ' *all-heal*,' for they consider it as a remedy for all maladies whatever.   And when they are about to gather it, after having made all suitable preparation for their sacrifices and the banquet under the tree, they bring to the place two young bulls, which have not yet been put to the yoke, and whose horns are then bound for the first time.   After this the priest, clothed in a white garment, ascends the tree, and with a golden hook cuts the misletoe, which is received by those below in a white sagum *.   They then sacrifice the victims before mentioned, offering with great devotion many prayers, that the deity would bless this gift to the benefit of those upon whom it might be conferred.   They moreover suppose that it renders every animal fruitful, though barren before, that drinks a decoction of it, and they also believe it *to be a* cure for all sorts of poisons : so frivolous and superstitious are many of the prevalent customs of religion †."   The whole of these ceremonies are concluded with feasting, music, dancing, and other diversions.

* A military cloak or square piece of cloth.
† Plin. *Hist. Nat.* lib. xvi. cap. xliv.

Stated periods for religious worship being indispensable, such seasons were observed by the ancient Britons not less than by other nations; and when their propensity to superstition is considered, there can be little doubt that daily sacrifices were common among them, at the hours perhaps of noon and midnight, the former devoted to the sun, and the latter to the moon or infernal deities[*]. The Britons were not ignorant of the ancient division of time into weeks of seven days, for there is the best evidence that this was known, not only to the Egyptians, Greeks and Romans, but to barbarous nations generally. The Druids named the days of the week after the planets, and Mr. Higgins thinks it probable that they set apart one day in seven for religious purposes[†]. They measured their time by nights, not by days. Their religious ceremonies, as well as their military expeditions, were regulated by the age and aspect of the moon. Their year, as we have seen, was divided into lunar months, and a cycle of thirty years was one of their divisions of time, though it is unknown with what design. The tenth of March was their new-year's day, and the festival of the misletoe was to be celebrated as near it as the age of the moon would allow.

The first of May was also a great annual festival in honour of Bellinus (Apollo), or the sun. On this occasion fires were kindled in all their sacred places, and on the tops of their *cairns*[‡], and numerous sacrifices were offered. In Ireland and Scotland the first of May is still called *Bellein*, the fire of Bell, or Bellinus. Other annual festivals were Midsummer-day and the first of November; the former to implore a blessing on the fields, and the latter to return thanks for the harvest, as well as for the payment of their yearly contributions to the Druids. Nay, it is not improbable that all their gods and goddesses, as well as their sacred groves, lakes, fountains and hills, had their annual celebrations, so that the Druidical calendar

[*] Lucan, lib. iii. ver. 423. From this passage in Lucan, it should seem that the hours of noon and midnight were the times when the gods were supposed to visit their sacred places.

[†] " The Celtic Druids," chap. vii. sect. viii.

[‡] Toland's Hist. of the Druids.

BOOK
II.

Places of
worship.

was as much crowded with holy-days as that of the Roman Catholics of the present day.

In ancient Britain the places of worship were also numerous, but of a kind entirely different from those in use at present. It was an article of the Druidical creed, that it was unlawful to erect covered temples to the gods, or to worship them within walls and under roofs *. For this reason, as well as for the convenience of astronomical observations, the places consecrated to their superstitious rites were in the open air, and usually on eminences, where a full view of the heavenly bodies, to whose honour many of their ceremonies were devoted, might be obtained. To avoid interruption and for the purpose of concealment, they not only retired to the deepest recesses of the woods and mountains for the purpose of giving instruction to their disciples, but they also selected these secluded spots in which to perform many of their religious ceremonies. Groves were planted for the purpose in the most suitable situations, and with the trees which they preferred, chiefly the oak; in their veneration for which, as well as in other instances, they bore considerable resemblance to the priests of many other nations, and even to the Hebrew patriarchs. These sacred groves were watered by fountains or rivers, and encompassed by mounds or ditches to prevent intrusion. In the centre of them was a circular area, inclosed with a single or double row of large stones, set perpendicularly in the earth. This constituted what has been called their temple, within which stood the altar for the sacrifices †. In some of the more magnificent erections

* Tacit. *De Mor. Ger.* cap. ix.

† The following quotation from Lucan is so highly poetical, whilst it serves at the same time to illustrate our subject, that it is hoped no apology is necessary for its introduction here.

  "Lucus erat longo nunquam violatus ab ævo,
    Obscurum cingens connexis aëra ramis,
    Et gelidas altè summotis solibus umbras.
    Hunc non ruricolæ Panes, nemorumque potentes
    Silvani Nymphæque tenent, sed barbara ritu
    Sacra deum, structæ sacris feralibus aræ
    Omnis et humanis lustrata cruoribus arbos.
    Si qua fidem meruit Superos mirata vetustas,
    Illis et volucres metuunt insistere ramis,

of this kind, as in the instance of Stonehenge, they laid
huge stones on the tops of the pillars, and thus formed a
kind of circle in the air. Near these sacred erections were
placed the carnedds, or holy mounts; their cromlechs,
which some antiquaries consider as stone tables for the purpose of preparing their sacrifices; and also other things
which were used in the celebration of their religious rites.

As the Druids did not allow their opinions on subjects
of philosophy, any more than those of religion, to be committed to writing, but used every precaution for their concealment, their proficiency in knowledge cannot now be
ascertained. There is no doubt, however, that for the times
in which they lived, their learning, though it may have
been overrated, was considerable. They have been classed

> Et lustris recubare feræ: nec ventus in illas
> Incubuit sylvas, excussaque nubibus atris
> Fulgura, non ullis frondem præbentibus auris,
> Arboribus suus horror inest. Tum plurima nigris
> Fontibus unda cadit, simulacraque mœsta deorum
> Arte carent, cæsisque extant informia truncis.
> Ipse situs, putrique facit jam robore pallor
> Attonitos: non vulgatis sacrata figuris
> Numina sic metuunt: tantum terroribus addit,
> Quos timeant non nosse deos. Jam fama ferebat
> Sæpe cavas motu terræ mugire cavernas,
> Et procumbentes iterum consurgere taxos,
> Et non ardentis fulgere incendia sylvæ,
> Roboraque amplexos circumfluxisse dracones.
> Non illum cultu populi propriore frequentant,
> Sed cessere deis: medio cum Phœbus in axe est,
> Aut cœlum nox atra tenet, pavet ipse sacerdos
> Accessus, dominumque timet deprendere luci."
>
> *Phars.* lib. iii. lin. 399. Cumberland's edit. 1760.

The above passage is thus translated by ROWE:

> " Not far away for ages past had stood
> An old unviolated, sacred wood;
> Whose gloomy boughs, thick interwoven, made
> A chilly, cheerless, everlasting shade:
> There, not the rustic Gods nor Satyrs sport,
> Nor Fawns and Sylvans with the Nymphs resort;
> But barbarous priests some dreadful power adore,
> And lustrate every tree with human gore.
> If mysteries in times of old received,
> And pious ancestors be yet believed,
> There nor the feathered songster builds her nest,
> Nor lonely dens conceal the savage beast;

with the Sophi or Philosophers among the Greéks, the
Magi among the Persians, the Gymnasophists and Brach-
mans among the Indians, and the Chaldeans among the
Assyrians. Physiology, or natural philosophy, as we are
informed *, was their favourite study. On these subjects
many disputations took place in their schools. Systems
and hypotheses were delivered to their pupils in verse, but
were not allowed to be recorded. Two of their tenets have
been preserved by Strabo; one, that the universe will
never be entirely destroyed, but will undergo a succession
of changes and revolutions; sometimes by the predominance of water, and sometimes of fire: and another, that
with respect to the origin of the universe they maintained
the existence of two principles, God intelligent and om-

> There no tempestuous winds presume to fly;
> Even lightnings glance aloof, and shoot obliquely by.
> No wanton breezes toss the dancing leaves,
> But shivering horror in the branches heaves.
> Black springs with pitchy streams divide the ground,
> And bubbling tumble with a sullen sound.
> Wood images of forms misshapen stand,
> Rude and unknowing of the artist's hand;
> With hoary filth depraved, each ghastly head
> Strikes the astonished gazer's soul with dread.
> No gods, who long in common shapes appeared,
> Were e'er with such religious awe revered:
> But zealous crowds in ignorance adore,
> And still the less they know, they fear the more.
> Oft (as fame tells) the earth in sounds of woe
> Is heard to groan from hollow depths below;
> The baleful yew, though dead, has oft been seen
> To rise from earth, and spring with sudden green,
> With sparkling flames the trees unburning shine,
> And round their boles prodigious serpents twine.
> The pious worshipers approach not near,
> But shun their gods, and kneel with distant fear:
> The priest himself, when or the day, or night,
> Rolling have reached the full meridian height,
> Refrains the gloomy paths with wary feet,
> Dreading the demon of the grove to meet;
> Who, terrible to sight, at that fixed hour,
> Still treads the round about his dreary bower."

* Cic. *De Div.* lib. i. Diod. Sic. lib. v. cap. 31. Strabo, lib. iv. Mela,
lib. iii. cap 12. Ammian. Marcell. lib. xv. cap. 9. "Multa præterea de
sideribus atque eorum motu, de mundi ac terrarum magnitudine, de rerum
naturâ, de deorum immortalium vi ac potestate disputant; et juventuti
tradunt."—Cæs. *De Bell. Gal.* lib. vi. cap. 14.

nipotent, and matter. Their knowledge of astronomy has been supposed to have been considerable, but has probably been much exaggerated. It might be in reference to this science that the circle was the favourite figure of the Druids, as appears from the form of what are called their temples, and even of their houses. What are considered as their remains in Anglesea are remarkable. A place there, called *Cerrig-Brudyn*, that is, the astronomer's stones, or circles, is supposed to have been an observatory of the Druids; and Caer Edris, or Idris, their place of residence. The sun and moon were not only the objects of their worship but of their study, as well as the stars, which they distinguished from the planets. They are supposed also to have been acquainted with the constellations, and with the signs of the zodiac. But to whatever knowledge they had of astronomy they added the absurdities of astrology.

They appear to have been acquainted with arithmetic, and though strangers to the Arabic characters, might probably make use of the Greek. To a knowledge of geometry they added an acquaintance with the geography of their own country especially, and probably of others. Their progress in the science and practice of mechanics is evinced by some of their remains. Rude as the original structures might be, how they could be completed without the aid of mechanical power, it is difficult to conceive; as, for instance, placing the huge stones on the pillars of their cromlechs, or on those of their larger circles. They were the medical practitioners of the times; but their knowledge of the science of medicine appears to have been exceedingly limited, and was connected with magic. In their practice of surgery a few healing plants only were in use, of which the misletoe or " all-heal" was a sort of panacea.

Rhetoric, however, is a subject which they diligently studied and taught to their pupils *. One of their gods

* Mela, lib. iii. cap. 2.

was the patron of eloquence, called Ogmius, whom they conceived of as an old man, because eloquence is never so powerful and persuasive as in the aged.   Teaching in their schools, discoursing to the people on religion and morality, pleading in courts of judicature, arguing in the great councils of the nation, and haranguing at the head of armies, afforded them numerous opportunities for the exercise of this art; and the effect of their public speaking, it appears, was on some occasions wonderful.

It has been disputed whether they could read or write; but what Cæsar has observed relative to their use of the Greek letters, settles this question, and shows that they could.

Their judicial proceedings.
In their judicial capacity we have seen that they held the highest rank in the state, for they not only made but administered the laws.   Strabo informs us *, that the highest opinion was entertained of their justice; and that this was the reason why the management of judicial proceedings, whether public or private, was committed to them.   Their discipline was exceedingly strict; their moral principles on the whole excellent, and their general conduct correct; for otherwise it would not have been possible for them to maintain, even with the aid of superstition, so powerful in ages of barbarism and ignorance, the paramount ascendancy which they constantly possessed over the minds of all ranks.

No accurate information is to be obtained relative to their methods of proceeding in the discharge of their judicial functions, or the periods when they assembled for this purpose.   Two law terms, however, are mentioned as observed in ancient times by the Welsh; a custom which they probably received from their British ancestors; the one from the ninth of May to the ninth of August; and the other from the ninth of November to the ninth o. February.   Their laws, which are said to have been on the whole good, were composed in verse, but never written.

* *Geog.* lib iv.

CHAP.
I.

Particular members of the order of Druids were appointed to execute the office of judges. Their courts appear to have been held in the open air, as well as their religious assemblies, and generally on eminences, to which all might have access, and hear and observe the proceedings. These places of judicature, which were sometimes called *Gorseddau*, are supposed to have been near their temples, or perhaps the same places might serve the purposes both of religion and of judicature, as the Druids were the sole agents in both*. In every state one of these places was appointed, and perhaps also in the district of each clan or tribe. The archdruid, whose chief residence in Gaul was at Dreux in the Pais Chartrain, and in Britain in Anglesea, was the supreme judge in the last resort, from whose decision there was no appeal. At the former of these places was held annually a grand assembly for the administration of justice, and the adjustment of disputes in a consecrated place; and as Cæsar observes immediately after his account of this meeting, that the practice of the Druids in Britain was similar, it is highly probable that a like custom prevailed also in this country†: there is however no positive evidence of this fact. According to Dion Chrysostom, the Druids in their judicial functions on some occasions appeared in great magnificence, sitting on thrones of gold, and were sumptuously entertained by sovereigns.

Such then was the religion of the Danmonii, and such the principles, the progress in knowledge, the power and customs of its ministers. As the influence of Druidism was retained in Britain and the adjacent islands longer than any where else, the retreats of Danmonium would not be among the first where this singular hierarchy would yield to the precarious force of foreign assailants. At the

Decline of Druidism.

* Cæsar observes that their annual assembly for the purposes of judicature in Gaul was held *in loco consecrato.*—*De Bell. Gal.* lib. vi. cap. xiii.

† See Rowland's Account of the *Bryn-Gwyn* or *Brein-Gwyn*, i. e. the supreme, or royal tribunal in Anglesea.—*Mona Antiqua*, pp. 89, 90. See also "The Celtic Druids," chap. vii. sect. i. & ii.

N 2

BOOK
II.

period of the first Roman invasion, fifty-five years before the commencement of the Christian æra, the superstition of the Druids, and their absolute dominion over the minds of their countrymen were at the zenith; but as the Roman legions advanced, this tremendous power, after a formidable resistance, gave way, and gradually declined. The common practice of the Romans in treating with forbearance the religious prejudices and customs of the nations which they subdued, was as wise as it was liberal; but in this instance, contrary to their usual policy, they displayed the most inveterate animosity against the religion and the persons of the Druids, arising in part, perhaps, from abhorrence of the cruel rites of this superstition, but chiefly, no doubt, from motives less honourable to their humanity. The Druids were every where the assertors of their country's freedom and independence, or rather of their own; and their influence in inspiring courage into their armies was irresistible. Hence the Romans, finding it impossible to subdue the Britons without extinguishing the power of the Druids, compelled the people wherever their arms were successful to build temples to their own gods, passed several laws against human sacrifices, deprived the Druids of all authority in civil affairs, and showed them no mercy when they were found trespassing. By these means their power was annihilated in Gaul by Claudius in the year 45; and by the same emperor about that time they were also persecuted in the south-eastern parts of Britain, whence many of them fled to Anglesea, their favourite resort. Here, however, they were not suffered to remain long undisturbed. Suetonius Paulinus, governor of Britain under Nero, finding this to be the seat of disaffection, determined to subdue it; and, tarnishing his victories with cruelty, not only cut down their groves, destroyed their temples, and overturned their altars, but burnt many of the Druids in the fires which they had prepared for the Romans [*]. Those who did not

* Tacit. *Ann.* lib. xiv. cap. 3.

submit fled into Scotland, Ireland, and the smaller British isles, where they retained their influence. Their principles, however, remained in the country much longer, and were the sources of great mischief, obstructing the operation even of the Christian religion after it had made considerable progress. The consequence of this determined resistance was many edicts of the emperors, and afterwards canons of councils in the sixth, seventh and eighth centuries, against their worship. Even in the eleventh century Canute made a law strictly forbidding all his subjects to worship the gods of the Gentiles, as the sun, moon, fire, rivers, fountains, hills, woods, or trees of any kind. And as the Britons were not expelled completely from Devonshire until the time of Athelstan, it is reasonable to suppose that some modifications of their ancient superstition remained with them; nor could a retreat be easily found more suitable for their purpose than the wilds of Dartmoor and those of Cornwall*.

Some apology may be necessary for the length of this digression; but there is a terrific and mysterious grandeur in the principles, the customs, and the power of the Druids, which renders the subject interesting in itself; and the preceding detail may serve to illustrate their remains in Devonshire hereafter to be described.

CHAP. I.

At the time of the Roman invasion, Great Britain was divided into many petty states, governed by kings, or supreme rulers under some other name. In each of these states were several subordinate chieftains, who had considerable influence in public affairs. Cæsar† mentions no less than four kings, at the same time, in the county of Kent. The power of these petty sovereigns, however, was sufficiently limited; their chief prerogative being the command of the forces in time of war: they were in fact, as we have seen, little better than agents of

Government and laws of Danmonium.

* "The Celtic Druids," ch. vii. sect. 3.—Henry's Hist. of Brit. vol. i. —See also Toland's History of the Druids.
† De Bell. Gal. lib. v. cap. 22.

the Druids, both in civil affairs and in their military operations. Such was the first step in the progress of civilization, the original form of government being the patriarchal. The constitutions of the small kingdoms of
Britain might resemble each other, but were by no means
precisely similar. The privileges of different sovereigns
varied, and their interests were not the same. Having
no common principle of union, and no supreme head,
under whose management the discordant powers of the
whole might have been concentrated, their divisions and
quarrels among themselves, according to Tacitus, contributed not a little to the success of the Roman arms.

There is no evidence that the government of Danmonium differed in any respect from that of the other parts
of the island. This district was probably divided into
cantreds, or rather *cantrefs*, which signifies a division of
a hundred towns or villages, and is a compound of the
two British words *cant* a hundred, and *trev* or *tref* a
village or town. Wales it seems, according to its lesser
divisions, was distributed originally into *bôds*, supposed
to have been the mansions of the chiefs on their first
settlement, several of which formed a *trev*, or township,
and a hundred of these trevs constituted a cantrev, which
was again divided into two or more *combôts* or lordships,
possessing distinct jurisdictions* and separate courts.
Similar to these, in all probability, were the civil divisions
of Danmonium†; but to attempt to determine the number of cantrevs in this district, or to assign their limits
and the various townships which they comprised, would
be idle, as we have here no guide but conjecture. There
seems to be no reason to doubt, however, that these
ancient divisions furnished the models of those which
prevail in our own time, the trevs corresponding to the
present townships, the cantrevs to the hundreds, and the
kingdoms or dukedoms to the counties, although their
boundaries and extent might be altogether different.

* Rowland's *Mona Antiqua*, essay i. sect. x.
† Risdon's Survey, last edit. p. 14. Polwhele's Historical Views, p. 16.

Little is known of the laws by which these jurisdictions were governed, except what has been already stated in the account of the Druids. Their punishments, like those of all nations but little advanced in civilization, were severe in the extreme. It has been also supposed, that between the judicial decisions of the Druids and the present common law of England, there was considerable resemblance; and even the rudiments of trial by jury have been thought to be traced in some of their institutions [*].

As the learning and degrees of knowledge among the ancient Britons is a subject which historians have neglected, materials are wanting for an account of this kind that would be at all satisfactory; and, indeed, it is highly probable there was little worthy of being recorded. But however small might be their progress in this respect, sufficient is known to show that they were not in the savage and barbarous state represented by some historians. Whatever knowledge the Druids possessed, they endeavoured, it is true, to conceal from the people in general; but still, from the number of their pupils, their own acquisitions in science must have been considerably diffused, and the multitude themselves, who are spoken of as an inquisitive race, could scarcely fail to become in some degree partakers of the benefit. Equally fruitless would it be to attempt to trace the progress of their language, or to mark its different stages of improvement, and the additions it received especially from the Phœnicians and the Greeks. It may be sufficient to observe, that at the time when the Romans first invaded Britain, the language of the country was a dialect of the Celtic, which was at that time spoken by the Gauls and several other nations. And of the ancient British, what was called the Cornu-British or Cornish, is another dialect, which was in use also in Devonshire, and continued to be spoken in this county, at least in conjunction with the Saxon, until the tenth century, when the Britons were driven by Athelstan beyond the Tamar.

Learning and language of the Danmonii.

In architecture the progress of the Danmonii appears

* Higgins's "Celtic Druids," ch. vii. sect. ix.

BOOK
II.

to have been insignificant, as they were in all probability destitute of the necessary tools for such purposes. A few ancient bridges near the sources of the rivers on the Moor, and the British cottages in the same district, are of the rudest description. The latter are always circular, very small, and found in little clusters near each other. The remains of them are the foundations only, consisting of unhewn stones, without cement, rising a foot or two above the surface of the ground, having had the sides completed perhaps of wood, or more probably of turf, with thatched roofs of reeds or straw. The stones of the other circles also, exhibit no traces of art or labour in their form.

ANCIENT BRIDGE ON DARTMOOR, SUPPOSED TO BE BRITISH.

As the ancient inhabitants of this county seem to have differed little in the other arts of life, and in manners and customs from their neighbours, it is unnecessary to enter further into the subject. From their intercourse with the Phœnicians, and afterwards with the Greeks, however, some writers have thought the progress of civilization in these respects was earlier among them than in some other parts of the island.

CHAPTER II.

HISTORICAL EVENTS.

THE British period supplies no remarkable occurrences for the pen of the historian upon which implicit reliance can be placed. We arrive, however, at length, at the æra of authentic history, and have to deal with writers of credit and distinction. But the period during which the Romans occupied this island, being remarkable in general for internal tranquillity, as the power of this victorious people was too well established to admit of insurrections, this also is barren of events. However, that Devonshire was soon in the occupation of these irresistible invaders, and that Exeter was a Roman station of considerable importance, there is abundant evidence.

It has been said the Romans were instigated to their attack upon Britain by the beauty and magnificence of its pearls, and the prospect of obtaining the valuable metals with which it was supposed to abound. The reason which Cæsar himself gives, was that some of the British tribes had afforded aid to his opponents in Gaul; but the true cause was, without doubt, that boundless ambition by which he was actuated in all his proceedings. In his first attempt, having landed on the coast of Kent on the sixth of August, in the year 55 before the Christian æra, according to his own account he made no advances into the country. In his second, the following year in the month of May or June, with five legions, two thousand horse, and about eight hundred ships, he crossed the Thames and took the capital of Cassibelanus, but did not penetrate further than St. Albans; and on account of the unsettled and precarious state of affairs on the continent, he was shortly compelled to return, leaving his conquests in Britain rather nominal than real. With the west of England Cæsar therefore had no intercourse whatever. And on account of the subsequent civil wars in the very heart of the Roman empire, and the pacific policy of

CHAP. II.

The Romans.

Augustus and his successor, Britain was suffered to enjoy undisturbed tranquillity for nearly a century.

No further attempt was made upon the island till A.D. 43 by Plautius the Roman general under Claudius, who was soon after followed by the emperor himself, and made important and extensive conquests in the south. After various and most destructive conflicts between the Roman legions under different commanders, and the Britons, who contended with the utmost intrepidity and desperation for their freedom and independence, it was reserved for Vespasian with Julius Agricola finally to establish the dominion of the Romans in the island.

It has been said that the Danmonii joined the Belgæ, and fought with the most determined valour in their resistance to the progress of the Roman legions; nor is there any improbability in this. Geoffrey of Monmouth also relates that Exeter was besieged by Vespasian, and relieved by Arviragus, between whom and the Roman general a battle ensued, in which neither party could claim the victory; but Geoffrey is a writer of so little credit, that no dependence can be placed on this fact. On the whole, it seems most probable that the several tribes of the Danmonii, when the neighbouring districts were subdued, finding opposition useless, submitted quietly to the Roman power, and never afterward joined in any revolt against the usurpers. The Romans therefore were under no necessity of building forts or keeping strong garrisons in this part of the country; and this may be the reason why no monuments of their power now remain, and why so little notice is taken of it by the Roman writers. And hence, perhaps, these ancient Britons might be permitted to live unmolested for some time at least under their own princes, and governed by their own laws, a privilege which we know was granted by the Romans to some other states.

At first, for 150 years, the Roman territories in Britain formed but one province: by the emperor Severus they were divided into two; and, at length, when the whole country was conquered, they were again divided into five. Danmonium, under the Roman sway, is generally spoken of as forming a part of *Britannia Prima* * ; but, says Henry †, in the most perfect state of the Roman government, it was comprehended in that province of Britain which was called *Flavia Cæsariensis*.

That Devonshire, notwithstanding the little notice taken of it by their historians, was not undervalued or neglected by the Romans, is abundantly evident from the remains of the roads which they formed or improved, and the multiplicity of Roman coins which have been found in the county. And that Exeter was a Roman station of considerable importance, there can be no doubt. It is the last station in the west mentioned in the Itinerary of Antoninus ‡, who travelled through Britain A.D. 140, by the name of Isca Dumnuniorum. The principal Roman roads meet in it as a centre, and numerous Roman coins and some penates have been found in it. Dr. Stukeley, in his account of his visit to this city at the beginning of the last century, mentions the following remains of Roman antiquity. " Dr. Holland," he observes, " supposes the castle to have been a Roman work originally, and it is not unlikely that it was their prætorium or garrison. In Corry-lane, over-against St. Paul's church, is a little old house called King Athelstan's, said to have been his palace, built of large square stones, and circular arches over the doors : it seems to have been originally a Roman building, though other later works have been added to the doors and windows. One arch of South Gate seems to be Roman §. No doubt the walls of the city are upon the Roman foundations for the most part, and a great number of antiquities have been found here. In digging behind

* It is thus spoken of by Richard of Cirencester.
† Hist. of Brit. vol. i. p. 230.
‡ Iter 15. Moridum, (supposed to be Seaton,) he also mentions as another Roman station in this county.
§ Mr. Polwhele mentions some old Roman arches, laid open some time ago at the bridge at King's Teignton. See page 54 of this volume, (or 4to edit. p. 38).

thé Guildhall in Pancras-lane, they found a great Roman
pavement, of little white square stones, eight feet deep.
A pot of Roman coins of two pecks was dug up two years
ago near St. Martin's church.   I saw some of them in
Dr. Musgrave's possession, of Gordian, Balbinus, Philip-
pus, Julia Mæsa, Geta, Gallïenus, and the like. Mr. Land-
ham, surgeon of this city, has many of them*."   The
subsequent account of Roman antiquities discovered at
Exeter, was also read before the Antiquarian Society by
the president Dr. Milles, in 1779†.   "Roman penates
were discovered last July in digging a cellar under the
house of Mr. Upham, situated in High-street at the corner
of Broad Gate.   They were found within a very small
space, and not more than three or four feet below the
present pavement of the street. They consisted of five
figures, executed in a taste far superior to the generality
of statues found in Britain, and therefore the workmanship
of a foreign artist, and of an early period.   The first is a
female, the drapery having been executed with great elegance, perhaps Ceres or Fortune, but uncertain.   The
next, two statues of Mercury; one of them four inches
and a half long, and the other four and a quarter.   The
fourth was a figure of Mars, or a Roman soldier, two
inches and a half high; and the last only two inches and
a quarter, from its delicacy and the dress of the hair, supposed to be Apollo.   These penates were found surrounded
by a considerable number of oyster-shells, known from
their size and form to come from Budleigh.   In the same
mass were also various fragments of urns of different forms,
sizes, colours, and kinds of earth; some of a dark brown,
and others of a bright red; the latter, in particular, very
highly glazed, and much adorned with fancy borders and
human figures executed in very elegant taste.   These
were much injured, not by the workmen who found them,
but at some former period.   With them was found also
a large Roman tile, lying on the natural earth, which was

* *Itinerarium Curiosum*, published in 1724, p. 150.
† Archæologia, vol. vi. p. 1.

certainly not its original position. No medal or coin was
found with them ; but on the opposite side of the street,
when the foundations of a house were dug up, two years
ago, some small remains of a tessellated pavement were
discovered, with a few Roman medals, one of them a Trajan, a large brass *."

Mr. Oliver† also observes, that lately coins have been
found of Agrippa, Tiberius, Vespasian, Trajan, Aurelius,
and Constantine. From all this it is evident that Exeter
was a place of much importance in the latter periods of
the Roman government especially.

At length, about A.D. 448, from the formidable attacks
of the northern barbarians on the empire, the Romans
were compelled to withdraw the legions by which Britain
had been kept in subjection, and which were now become
necessary to its protection, having been the masters of the
island nearly four centuries. Before their departure they
assisted the natives to erect anew the wall of Severus,
exhorting them to arm in defence of their independence.
Being freed from foreign domination, the Britons appear
to have returned to their original form of government by
their own princes. The Scots at that time inhabited Ireland; but the Picts, who had possession of the northern
parts of Britain, taking advantage of the departure of the
Romans, passed the rampart within which they had been
hitherto confined, advanced southward, and made dreadful havoc in the country. The resistance of the Britons
against an enemy so ferocious and determined, was too
feeble to be effective. Their martial spirit, not more

* In a note to Jenkins's History of Exeter (page 6) it is stated that
numerous Roman coins were discovered, particularly in the late alterations in the castle. They are chiefly of the later emperors: a gold one
of Nero, two brass ones of Julius Cæsar, and two base silver ones of Ca-
rausius, are the best preserved. Some years since, in digging for the
foundation of a house at the upper end of Musgrave's Alley, a colossal
head of the empress Julia Donna, and an ancient lamp with a crescent
embossed upon it, were found. Roman coins also, and bones of animals,
have been discovered in digging the ground on St. David's-hill. And in a
note (page 7,) it is stated, that Sir Lawrence Palk, Bart. discovered urns
with Roman coins, in one of the barrows on the northern part of Haldon.

† See the History of Exeter, by the Rev. George Oliver, part. i. ch. 1.

necessary than just in self-defence, by long and tranquil subjection to a foreign power, was entirely subdued; and the evil being greatly augmented by internal divisions, occasioned by contentions among themselves for the supreme power, their condition soon became truly deplorable. After repeated application to the Romans for assistance, but in vain, the unhappy Britons sunk into a state of despondency and became helpless. In this state of things, Vortigern, prince of the Danmonians, and descended probably from the ancient line of kings, his name in British signifying a chieftain, was chosen, notwithstanding his numerous vices, to the sovereignty of Britain, or had obtained it by his valour and enterprising spirit. At his instigation the Saxons were invited to their assistance in resisting these barbarians from the north of the island. No step could have been more fatal than this. The old Saxons, the Angles, and the Jutes, the three most powerful nations of Germany, came over, and Vortigern assigned them a situation in the east of the island. At first their services were of the greatest importance in driving the enemy back to their own territories; but at length preferring Britain to their native country, in breach of the fairest professions, they resolved to gain possession of it for themselves. After fresh reinforcements they joined the Picts and Scots in their sanguinary depredations, and eventually became the masters of those whom they had been employed to assist. After spreading devastation and ruin from one end of the island to the other, in less than a century they wrested the whole from the original and rightful possessors, with the exception of Wales, Cornwall, and part of Devonshire.

The
Saxons.
How long Exeter remained a British city is uncertain; and although the Danmonians appear to have defended their territories with great bravery and perseverance, the earliest military transaction recorded by our historians, relating to this county, is a battle, in the year 614, at Bampton (Beamdune *), in which Cynegilsus, king of the

* Sax. Chron. an. 614.

West Saxons, vanquished the Britons with great slaughter, the latter having lost, says the Saxon Chronicle, 2046 men.

According to Matthew of Westminster, Exeter being held by Brien, nephew of Cadwallo, the British king, was besieged by Penda, king of Mercia, in 633; and Cadwallo, who had some time before been driven from his kingdom by the Saxons, returned; and having collected an army, at the head of a thousand men appeared before the city, defeated the enemy with great slaughter, and took Penda himself prisoner, whom he retained until he had sworn allegiance to his conqueror *. After this nothing of importance occurs relative to Devonshire until the invasion of the Danes.

During the Saxon Heptarchy this county was comprehended in the kingdom of Wessex, and continued to be so until the incorporation of the whole into one monarchy by Egbert.

After the union of the Heptarchy under Egbert, the prospect of prosperity and quiet was soon overclouded by the appearance of a new horde of barbarians from the north towards the close of the eighth century; namely, the Norwegian and Danish pirates, who made a conspicuous figure in the history of Europe for more than two centuries, and who were destined eventually to become the scourge of this country in particular. Their first inroads into this island were about the year 787, but on what part of the coast precisely, seems to be uncertain. From the Saxon Chronicle and Henry of Huntington, it appears " that in the reign of Bertric, king of Wessex, the Danes landed in England from three ships, for the sake of plundering the country. Being observed by the king's chief officer of that district, he, not knowing who they were or whence they came, rode securely amongst them, and endeavoured to drive them to the king's town † or camp, but was imme-

The Danes.

* Lysons's *Mag. Brit.* vol. vi. part i.
† cyninзеꝗ tune, *Chron. Sax.* an. 787. " ad regium castrum," Henry of Hunt. lib. iv. It seems scarcely worth a dispute where these savages (if

diately slain. These were the first ships of the Danes that made an attack upon the English." Aud hence Hume and Henry justly infer that their first attempt on this country was on the coast of Wessex.

Having made an alliance with the Britons in Cornwall, the Danes came with a fleet to that county in the year 806, and made inroads into Devonshire. They were met, however, by Egbert in person, and after a severe contest were totally defeated. But whilst England was throughout in a state of anxiety and alarm from these lawless rovers, that valiant and able monarch died, and with him the English lost their best defence.

The great Alfred had scarcely come to the throne before he was compelled to take the field against the Danes. In the year 876 these ravagers had seized upon Wareham in Dorsetshire, the very centre of Alfred's dominions; but this prince soon reduced them to such extremities, that they were glad to enter into treaty with him, gave him their best hostages, and took the oath to depart the kingdom, which was held the most sacred among northern nations, a pledge which they had never given to any nation before. Disregarding, however, all moral obligations, they suddenly fell upon Alfred's army; and having routed it, marched westward, and took possession of Exeter. In the year 877 we find them in this city again, when their fleet, sailing westward to their assistance, was wrecked in a storm, and 120 ships destroyed. An army by land at

this expression is admissible) first landed; but Mr. Lysons says, "Some modern writers have supposed erroneously that the first landing of the Danes was at Teignmouth, having been led into the mistake by the similarity of the name. On consulting the ancient historians, it will be very evident that it was at Tynemouth in Northumberland, where they first landed in 787. Their first ravages were in the North of England." —*Mag. Brit.* vol. vi. part i. If Mr. Lysons alludes to the Saxon Chronicle, the words "king's town" are evidently not a proper name. Ingram's translation of the passage is as follows: "A.D. 787. This year king Bertric took Edburga the daughter of Offa to wife. And in his days came first 3 ships of the North-men from the land of robbers. The reve then rode thereto, and would drive them to the king's town; for he knew not what they were; and there was he slain. These were the first ships of the Danish men that sought the land of the English nation."—Ingram's Saxon Chronicle.

Drawn by R. Browne Esqr Arch.t

Engraved by W. Deeble

N.W. VIEW OF EXETER CATHEDRAL.

London. Printed by Robert Jennings & Co. Poultry Mar. 1, 1830

Drawn by H Worsley

Engraved by T Brigham

SUTTON POOL & CUSTOM HOUSE, PLYMOUTH.

London Published by Fisher Son & Co. Newgate St Chapman Ward & Co.

the same time, when pursued by Alfred, took refuge in the castle, where however they were soon compelled to submit, to give fresh hostages, and take a new oath, of which in this instance they were more observant *.

After the Danes had left this district, and, according to their stipulations with Alfred, retired into Mercia, they again received numerous reinforcements of their country-men, in consequence of which they ventured once more to return into Wessex, and having seized Chippenham, which was then a royal city of some importance, they overran the whole country A.D. 878†, spreading, as usual, de-vastation and misery wherever they went. The West Saxons, animated by the brave example of their king, were the last that submitted to the dominion of these un-principled and ferocious barbarians; but in consequence of the victory just mentioned, they were at length com-pletely dispirited, thinking it useless to contend with an enemy whom no treaties could bind, and whom nothing could restrain but superior force. Some fled into foreign countries and into Wales, others concealed themselves in the woods and forests, whilst many were compelled to submit to the conquerors. The great Alfred stood alone. Being entirely deserted, except by a small band of faith-ful adherents: these he was at length compelled by ne-cessity to disband, and retired to conceal himself in the disguise of a peasant‡.

Somersetshire being one of the counties most favourable to his interests, afforded him an asylum. Here, having collected by degrees a small but faithful company of ad-herents, from the place of his retreat near the junction of the Thane and Parret, which he named Athelingay, the Isle of the Nobles, now called Athelney, he made frequent excursions upon the enemy, and subsisted on the spoils;

* *Chron. Sax.* ann. 876, 877. Asserius, p. 8.
† *Chron. Sax.* an. 878.
‡ The story of his treatment in the cottage of a neatherd appears to be true: it is related by several historians, and particularly by Asser, who might have had it from the king himself. Asser. p. 9. Matth. West. p. 170. *Chron. Sax.* an. 878.

BOOK
II.

and the success which attended these adventures did not fail to inspire new hopes. In the mean time, in the winter of 878, the Danes, with Hubba for their general, having ravaged the southern shores of Wales, crossed the channel to the northern coast of Devonshire, and from twenty-three vessels landed their troops in the vicinity of Apple dore.

The battle of Kenwith Castle.

Alarmed at this new debarcation, Oddune earl of Devonshire, and several thanes, fled for security to the castle of Kenwith. This place had at that time no fortification but a loose wall of stones, erected after the manner of the Britons; but its position on the summit of a lofty rock rendered it impregnable. Hubba did not venture to hazard an assault, but, intercepting all communication with the country, waited quietly in expectation that want of provisions and even of water would soon compel the garrison to surrender. Oddune, thus driven to the necessity of some desperate expedient, made an unexpected sally before sun-rise, fell upon the enemy's camp, slew the Danish chief himself, with twelve hundred of his men, and drove the remainder to the fleet. Among the trophies of this victory was the *Reafen*, the famous standard of the Raven, woven in one noon-tide, with many incantations, by the three sisters of Hubba. In this mysterious banner the superstition of the Danes led them to place implicit confidence. If it appeared, as they advanced to battle, to flap its wings, this was considered as a sure omen of victory; if it hung without motion in the air, they anticipated nothing but defeat*. Hubba was buried on the shore, near his ships, and, according to the custom of northern nations, covered with a heap of stones; whence the spot received the name of Hubbastone. All vestiges of the tomb have been long swept away by the waves, but traces of the name remain; the spot is now called Wibblestone.

Alfred had lain secure in his retreat about twelve months,

* Lingard's Hist. of Engl. vol. ii. chap. iv. Asser. p. 30. *Chron. Sax.* an. 878.

when news arrived of this prosperous event, and he lost
no time in taking advantage of the favourable turn of his
affairs.   Leaving his retreat*, he summoned the chiefs
of his subjects with their followers, by private messengers,
to meet him at Brixton on the borders of Selwood Forest
in Somersetshire; where on the appointed day, near the
midsummer of the year 878, considerable numbers assembled from the counties of Somerset, Wilts and Hants,
elevated with joy and inspired with fresh courage by
the sight of their beloved king, whom they had supposed to be dead.   He conducted them without delay to
the camp of the Danes, whom he attacked unexpectedly
in the most unguarded quarter.   The enemy, surprised at
the appearance of an English army with Alfred at their
head, made but a feeble resistance, and were soon completely routed with great slaughter.   Alfred pursued the
remainder of their forces to a fortified camp, to which they
had fled for safety, where being speedily reduced to extremities, they were glad to give him hostages, and took
their usual oaths to quit his territories.   Guthrum, their
king, offering to become a Christian, was soon afterwards
baptized, with Alfred for his sponsor.   As East-Anglia and
Northumberland had been desolated by the Danes, Alfred
appointed these districts for the residence of Guthrum
and his followers; and the greater part of them settled
peaceably in their new quarters†.

We learn however from the Saxon Chronicle, that
Guthrum and his successor Guthred being dead, the Danes
of Northumberland and East-Anglia rose against the authority of Alfred, and an immense host of them sailing
southward in about one hundred ships, landed on the coast
of Devonshire and besieged Exeter, whilst a fleet of forty

* *Chron. Sax.* an. 878. The story of Alfred's visit to the enemy's camp
in the disguise of a harper, has a romantic and legendary appearance.
The silence moreover of Asser on this subject, renders it very suspicious.
Had the story been true, he could scarcely have failed to be acquainted
with it; and had he known it, there is the greatest improbability that he
would have omitted the relation of so extraordinary an occurrence.

† William of Malmsbury. *Chron. Sax.*

BOOK
II.

Siege of
Exeter.

sail landed another swarm on the northern coast of the
county.   Alfred was at that time preparing to attack the
Danes at Bamfleet, where another party of them had encamped; but receiving information of this event, and
leaving troops in London sufficient for its defence, he
marched with great expedition into the West, and came
upon the enemy so unexpectedly, that they raised the
siege of Exeter with precipitation, whilst Alfred pursued
them to their ships with great slaughter *.   And on the
same authority we learn that in the year 897 six of their
ships arriving at the Isle of Wight, proceeded to the shores
of Devonshire, where they did much mischief, as well as
in many other places on the southern coast; but being
afterwards pursued by the king's ships, they were at
length dispersed and destroyed.

His son and successor, Edward, surnamed the Elder,
in the year 918 held a wittenagemote at Exeter.

Alfred, in the vigour of his age, after a life of real glory,
died on the 6th of October in the year 900, or 901.

Until the reign of Athelstan the Cornish Britons had
occupied the country from the Land's-End to the river
Exe, and possessed one half of Exeter itself; but soon
after his accession to the throne, probably about the year
926, that prince subdued and intimidated both them and
the Britons in Wales.   The chiefs of the latter waited upon
him at Hereford, where they stipulated to confine their
countrymen within the right bank of the Wye, and to pay

Athelstan
compels
the Britons
to retire
beyond the
Tamar.

him a yearly tribute.   It appears to have been about the
same time that he vanquished Howell, king of Cornwall,
near Exeter, and compelled the Britons to retire beyond
the Tamar, fortifying the city with a strong wall of stone,
flanked by lofty towers, and encompassed with a fosse.
As he frequently honoured Exeter with his presence, it
was also probably about this time that he held a wittenagemote here, as his father Edward had done before him,
when he made the celebrated laws at this place, which

* Chron. Sax. ann. 894 & 897.

may be seen in Brompton's Chronicle, p. 850, and in
Twisden, an. 952*.

CHAP.
II.

Battle of
Brunan-
burgh or
Axmin-
ster.

In the year 938 was fought the battle of Brunanburgh,
or Brundune, the most celebrated that had then occurred
in England, and distinguished among old historians by the
name of the "great battle." It is described by the Saxon
Chronicle in the lofty strains in which the ancient poets
were accustomed to recite the achievements of their kings
and chieftains. Concerning the locality of this conflict
historians are not agreed, though in general they suppose
it to have taken place in Northumberland. The scene of
action has also been laid in the vicinity of Axminster;
and though there is at least great difficulty in settling the
question, there are strong reasons for supposing this to be
true. The circumstances of the conflict are the following.
After Athelstan's victories in Scotland his enemies renewed their confederacy, and acting with greater precaution than they had hitherto done, employed a long time
in making preparations for a formidable invasion of England. The multitude of the confederates consisted of
five nations, Norwegians, Danes, Irish, Scots and Britons;
and at length, every thing being in readiness, the allies
collected their forces, and proceeded on their expedition.
In the inflated and exaggerated style of a contemporary,
in the English army waved a hundred banners, and around
each banner were arranged a thousand warriors†. The
battle continued through the whole day; but the conflict,
though long doubtful, at length terminated in favour of
the English. Constantine king of the Scots with difficulty
saved himself by flight, and Anlaff the Irish chief, who
continued the battle longer, was at last compelled also
to fly. Five kings, says the Saxon Chronicle, twelve
chieftains, and many thousands of their followers, were
left dead on the field.

Lingard especially, whose learning and diligence of

* Lingard's Hist. of Eng. vol. i. chap. iv. Lysons's *Mag. Brit.* vol. vi.
part i. Hist. of Exeter by the Rev. G. Oliver, chap. ii.
† Lingard's Hist. of Eng.

research give great weight to his opinions on such subjects, relates this battle as having taken place in Northumberland, and asserts that Athelstan in his way to the
scene of action, visiting the church of Beverley in Yorkshire, offered his dagger on the altar, making a vow to
redeem it if he returned victorious; and on his return
after the victory, performed his vow by redeeming the
dagger from the church with an ample grant of the most
valuable privileges.   On the other hand, the following
reasons for supposing that this is the battle which took
place at Axminster are deserving of attention.   The true
situation of Brunanburgh, where it was fought, is not
known with certainty, nor do historians agree as to its
locality.   In a " *Role* " from an old Chronicle in French
of the chiefs who came over with William I. to England,
preserved in Leland's *Collectanea**, it is stated that a
very large fleet of foreigners arrived at Seaton in Devonshire about this time, whom Athelstan engaged with great
bravery and conquered.   Five kings were slain, and were
buried in the cemetery of Axminster.   On the part of the
English king were also slain eight earls of the highest
distinction, who were buried in the same place.   This battle,
it is added, began at Brundune near Colyton, and continued to Axminster, which was then called Bronebury.
The cartulary of Newenham Abbey at Axminster also relates that the battle began at Colyton, and continued to
Axminster, and that Athelstan founded a collegiate minster of priests there, to pray for the souls of the earls and
others slain in the battle.   The former name of the town,
it seems, was Branbury, corresponding with that of Brunanburgh in the ancient historians.   It is also evident
that its modern name arose from the minster founded by
Athelstan on the Axe, in consequence of this battle; and
tradition also says, that the names of both Kingsfield and
Warlake in the vicinity have their origin in this event.
That the two accounts refer to the same battle can scarcely
be doubted, when their exact correspondence in the main

* Vol. i. p. 203.   Polwhele's Devonshire.   Lysons's *Mag. Brit.*

circumstances is considered; and if this be not the conflict that took place near Axminster, what other occurrence of this kind is there in the history of those times
that can be attributed to this situation? The circumstances of Athelstan, it is true, both before and after the
battle, seem to point to the north as the scene of action:
but on the contrary it may be observed, that the army of
the confederates came by sea to the place where the
battle was fought; and if they issued from the north with
the king of the Scots at their head, the short distance
into Northumberland would scarcely have rendered this
necessary. The fugitive Northmen moreover, according
to the Saxon Chronicle, immediately after their defeat
took refuge in Ireland, and went to Dublin in disgrace,
which they would be able to do much more conveniently
from Devonshire than from Northumberland. On the
whole, perhaps, we may safely conclude that this celebrated battle was the one that took place near Axminster.

This splendid victory entirely crushed the enemies of
Athelstan, and confirmed his own ascendancy. Till the
reign of Alfred, his predecessors had been styled kings of
Wessex. Athelstan finally established the kingdom of
England. He did not, however, continue long to enjoy
his successes, but died in the year 940, regretted by his
subjects, and admired by surrounding nations.

After the death of Athelstan, owing in part to the vigour
and warlike spirit of his successors, and in a great measure
also to the employment furnished to the Danes by their
establishment in France, this country enjoyed a long period of freedom from the depredations of this piratical
people. But in the reign of Ethelred, distinguished as
it was by imbecility, cowardice and cruelty, fresh swarms
of these barbarians poured into England from the continent, and, assisted by their countrymen already established
here, spread desolation and carnage through the country:
Devonshire especially suffered severely from their destructive incursions.

BOOK
II.

Ravages of
the Danes
on the
north and
west of De-
vonshire.

In the year 997 a Danish fleet sailed round the Land's-End into the mouth of the Severn, ravaging the coasts of Cornwall, Wales and Devonshire, burning the towns, and plundering and destroying the inhabitants wherever they went.   On their return they sailed up the Tamar, laying waste the country on both its banks, and proceeding to Lidford, set fire to that place, destroying whatever came in their way.   On this occasion they also plundered and burnt the abbey and church of Tavistock, and carried back to their ships an immense booty*.

About this period the appalling ravages of the Danes, who swarmed like locusts through the country, were at their height.   Marking their progress every where with fire, carnage and desolation, in the year 1001 they again arrived in Devonshire; and after burning Teignton, and the villages in that neighbourhood, they landed at Exmouth, with Sweyn the king of Denmark at their head.   Proceeding towards Exeter, the citizens, having made the best preparation the time would allow, opposed a brave resistance to his attempt upon the city, and the tyrant did not succeed.   The united forces of Devon, Somerset and Dorset, hastily collected under Cola the English general, and Edsy the sheriff, came to their relief; and a desperate battle was fought at Pinhoe, near the city.   Though the English encountered the barbarians with determined resolution, they were eventually overpowered, and the Danes remained masters of the field of battle.   But despairing of success against the city, the next day, having set fire to Pinhoe, Broad Cliat, and other villages in the neighbourhood, they returned laden with spoils to their ships, and proceeded to the Isle of Wight†.

Battle of
Pinhoe.

In the year 1002 Ethelred, instigated by a spirit of rashness and revenge common to weak princes, carried into execution a measure which has left a stain upon his memory never to be effaced.   Scarcely were the rejoicings

* Chron. Sax. an. 997. Mat. Westm.
† Chron. Sax. and Simeon of Durham.

occasioned by his nuptials with Emma, sister of Richard II.
duke of Normandy, concluded, than he gave orders for
the massacre of the Danes throughout the kingdom. On
the festival of St. Brice, the 13th of November, the un-
suspecting victims, together with their wives and families,
were seized and butchered with such circumstances of ag-
gravated cruelty as have seldom occurred. The Danes, it
is true, who were already settled in the country, in conjunction with the swarms of invaders from the Continent,
had conducted themselves in a manner sufficiently atrocious to provoke severe retaliation; and Ethelred was induced to believe that the design they were meditating was
to wrest the government from his hands, and to effect the
destruction of himself and his family. Nor does it appear
that the whole of the Danes were exterminated on this occasion; and the massacre was in all probability chiefly confined to the northern adventurers, whom the king had retained in his service to fight his battles, but whose fidelity
nothing could secure. These considerations, however, afford but little extenuation of the cruelty and cowardice of
this transaction. The most illustrious of the sufferers on
this occasion was the sister of Sweyn, Gunhelda, who had
embraced Christianity, and had married Paley, an earl who
had been naturalized. After her husband and children had
been slaughtered in her presence, she is said, in the agonies
of death, to have foretold the severe revenge which her
brother would assuredly inflict. Never had prophecy a
more complete and terrible accomplishment. The next year
Sweyn, with his fleet of barbarians, appeared off the western coast, and prepared to effect his bloodthirsty purpose.
Like a vulture eager for his prey, he lost no time in his
approach to Exeter. The citizens, however, having put
themselves in a posture of defence, the city might have
been saved but for the treachery or neglect of Hugh the
governor, a Norman earl, who was indebted for his situation to the influence of Emma, Ethelred's queen. Having
made every effort that was possible in its defence, the citizens were at length compelled to surrender, and dreadful

CHAP.
II.

Exeter de-
stroyed by
Sweyn.

were the consequences. Sweyn, instigated to fury by
the recollection of the failure of his former attempt, in addition to revenge for the fate of his countrymen, spared
nothing. Slaughtering the inhabitants without discrimi-
nation, demolishing the fortifications, pillaging whatever
might suit his purpose, and destroying what remained, he
left the city a heap of ruins. Having sated his revenge
in this instance, he departed with his spoils, to carry on
the work of destruction in Wiltshire.

No event of importance afterwards occurs in our historians relative to Devonshire till the reign of William I.
From the time of Athelstan, Exeter being furnished with
fortifications of considerable strength, had gradually increased in population and prosperity; and though nearly
destroyed by Sweyn, it received from Canute, who endeavoured in some measure to repair the injuries of his father,
various proofs of the royal favour, and had again risen from
its ashes, so that in the beginning of William's usurpation
it assumed courage to offer some resistance to his authority.
During the king's absence in Normandy discontents and
insurrections every where prevailed; and though in part
quelled after his return, they still lingered in the northern and western extremities of the kingdom. The inhabitants of Devonshire and Cornwall, but especially of
Exeter, were animated by the most inveterate hatred against
the invaders. A small squadron of Norman mercenaries
had been driven by a tempest into the harbour, and were
treated by the populace with insult and cruelty *. Sensible of their danger, the citizens had repaired and made
additions to their fortifications, and sent emissaries to excite a similar spirit in other towns. They were strength-
ened by the accession of the neighbouring inhabitants both
of Devonshire and Cornwall; and when William sent to
require their oaths of fealty and the admission of a garrison into the city, they returned a peremptory refusal,
but at the same time expressed a willingness to pay him

* Lingard's Hist. of Engl.

the dues, and to perform the services which had been ex-
acted by their native sovereigns. It was not to be expected that the usurper would submit to conditions dic-
tated by those whom he considered as his subjects.
Advancing with his army to inflict severe chastisement on
the insurgents in the year 1067, he was met at some distance from the city by the wiser and more considerate of
the magistrates, who saw the futility of resistance, was
offered the submission of the inhabitants, and received
hostages for their fidelity. An unexpected mutiny of the
populace however broke this agreement; and when William approached the walls, to his astonishment he found
the gates barred against him, and a crowd of inhabitants
on the walls bidding him defiance. With a view to in-
timidate them, he deprived one of the hostages of his
eyes, but without effect. The siege lasted eighteen days,
and the royal forces suffered severe losses in different assaults. The citizens however, finding resistance unavail-
ing, at length submitted, but on conditions that could
scarcely have been expected, for William was not destitute of generosity, when his temper was not hardened by
policy or passion. They took the oath of allegiance, and
admitted a Norman garrison; but their lives, property,
and immunities were secured, and the conqueror took the
necessary measures to prevent the plundering of the city*.
Githa, the mother of Harold, previously to the siege
had taken refuge in the city, and had, no doubt, instigated the citizens to resistance; but perceiving their disposition to submit, she retired secretly with a number of
others and fled to Flanders. The conqueror repaired the
city, and is said to have rebuilt the castle, which had
been destroyed by Sweyn, and which is therefore considered as a specimen of Norman architecture†.

Godwin, Edmund, and Magnus, the three sons of Harold, after the battle of Hastings had sought a retreat in
Ireland, and meeting with a favourable reception there,

CHAP.
II.

Exeter be-
sieged by
William I.

The defeat
of Harold's
sons.

* Lingard's Hist. of Engl.   † Oliver's Exeter.

P 2

had projected an invasion of England.   They hoped that
the exiles, returning with sufficient forces from the countries into which they had fled, would at once commence
hostilities, and rouse the indignation of the English
against their haughty conquerors.   With these expectations they landed in Devonshire about the year 1069,
but found Brian, son of the Count of Brittany at the head
of some foreign troops ready to oppose them; and being
defeated in several actions, they were obliged to retreat
to their ships with great loss, and returned to Ireland *.

About this time the disaffected Saxons, having taken
up arms in Devonshire, attempted to gain possession of
Exeter; but the citizens, warned by what had so recently
taken place when besieged by William, refused to admit
them.   The king sent some forces to their relief, by whom
the assailants were defeated with great slaughter†.

Upon the accession of William Rufus, the favourers of
Robert duke of Normandy took up arms, and Exeter
was laid waste by Robert Fitz-Baldwin‡.

The contests for the succession on the death of Henry I.
produced civil commotions throughout the country.   About
that time every petty chief was ambitious to rise into
consequence by erecting his fortress, assembling a body
of military retainers, and setting the law at defiance.
To repress these local tyrants or engage them in the interest of the king was a task of no little difficulty, and
Stephen, on his accession, had sufficient employment for
all his activity and skill.   On the revolution occasioned
by that event, however, Exeter set an example of un-
shaken fidelity to the lawful sovereign.   Baldwin de Ri-
pariis, Redvers, or Rivers, the second earl of Devon, was
the first to rear the standard of the empress Matilda, the
only daughter of Henry I., and to bid defiance to the
usurper§.   As baron of Oakhampton he was governor of
Exeter castle, where he retired with his family and pre-

* Stow.   Hume, vol. i. ch. iv.
† Lysons, vol. vi. part. i.   *Oderic. Vital.*   ‡ *Ibid.*
§ Oliver's Exeter, part. i. chap. v.

pared for a vigorous defence of the place. In the year 1136 Stephen invested the city, but met with a resistance from the skill and determined spirit of the besieged, which cost him much. The circumstances of the attack and defence as related by an eye witness, exhibiting a specimen of the method of warfare at that time, may not be unacceptable. When the king invested the castle, the besieged mounted the walls, and treated him with scorn and defiance. Sometimes they sallied out from the secret passages, when least expected, and put many to the sword ; at others they sent showers of arrows, darts, and other missiles on the assailants. On the other hand, the king and his barons laboured with the utmost ardour to distress the garrison. A strong and well armed body of foot assailed the barbican, and after a fierce and bloody struggle carried it. Next he beat down with his engines the bridge of communication between the castle and the town. After which he erected lofty towers of wood to protect his men in their discharges from the walls. He gave the besieged no rest day or night. Sometimes his men, approaching the walls on a machine supported by four wheels, engaged hand to hand. Sometimes he drew up all the slingers of the army, and threw into the castle an intolerable shower of stones. At other times he employed the most skilful engineers to undermine the foundations of the walls. He made use of machines of different kinds, some of which were very lofty, for inspecting their operations within the castle ; and others very low, for battering and beating down the walls. The besieged, making a bold and masterly defence, baffled all his attempts with the most astonishing dexterity, but in vain. After having maintained the defence three months they were at length compelled to surrender by want of water. The siege cost Stephen no less than 15,000 marks†. The clemency, however, with which he treated the besieged after the surrender did him honour.

CHAP. II.

Exeter besieged and taken by Stephen.

* Oliver's Exeter, par. i. ch. v.
† See Polwhele's Devonshire ; and *Gesta Stephani.*

In the mean time some knights who held Plympton castle for the earl entered into treaty with the king for the surrender of their fortress ; and a party of two hundred men being sent to take possession of it, destroyed the castle, and laid waste the earl's extensive manors *. Baldwin himself escaped to the Isle of Wight, which was his own lordship ; where the king followed, and sent him into exile.   In the reign of Henry II. however he returned, and regained his honours, and the whole of his domains, which in Devonshire were very extensive.

After this, few events relative to Devonshire occur in history till about the middle of the fifteenth century. The French indeed made several attacks upon the maritime towns, which will be noticed in their proper places.

In the reign of Richard I. Dartmouth is said to have been burnt, but the chronicles of this reign are silent on the subject.

Exeter, the faithful city, was repeatedly honoured with the presence of majesty in former periods.   Henry III. occasionally held his court in the castle.   During the unfortunate disputes between him and his barons this city supported the royal cause, and obtained a charter, dated March the 4th, in the twenty-first year of the king, confirming his former grants ; and it is not improbable that he frequently repeated his visits.   And in the year 1286 Exeter was also visited by Edward I. with his queen. Here he passed his Christmas, and held a parliament, in which was passed an Act to remedy the abuses of coroners.   He was also one of the principal benefactors of this city†.

In the reign of Edward III., the French repeated their attacks on the coasts of Devon.   In the year 1338 they landed at Plymouth with a design to set fire to the town, and would no doubt have succeeded but for the vigorous exertions of Hugh Courtenay earl of Devon, and other gentlemen, who hastened to its defence with all the men

* *Gest. Steph.* Lysons.   † Oliver's Exeter.

they could collect, killed five hundred of the French, and put the rest to flight[*].

In the year 1350, according to Stow[†], some French pirates, after an unsuccessful attempt upon the Isle of Wight, sailing towards the coast of Devonshire, set fire to Teignmouth, and proceeded to Plymouth, but found it at that time so well defended that they desisted from their designs upon it, but laid waste the neighbourhood, and carried off a knight prisoner.

After the celebrated battle of Poictiers, Edward the Black Prince landed in 1357 with his illustrious prisoners, John king of France and the Dauphin, and proceeded thence to Exeter, where they were honourably entertained, at the expense of the mayor and citizens, during their stay of three days.

A gallant exploit is mentioned by Walsingham of the men of Portsmouth and Dartmouth in the year 1383, when they took five French ships; the whole of the crews except five persons having been killed in the action[‡].

In the reign of Henry IV. the French under the command of Monsieur de Castel landed in considerable numbers at Plymouth, plundered the town, and burnt six hundred houses; after which, according to Stow, they landed at Blackpool, two miles from Dartmouth; where they were immediately attacked, and repulsed by the country people. On this occasion the women united with the men in the assault, behaved with great courage, and rendered important service. The commander himself of the invading forces was slain; three barons and twenty knights were taken prisoners, and conducted to the king by the countrymen, who returned with their purses filled with gold. The king however, it is added, reserved the prisoners for a more valuable ransom[§].

* Stow.
† Annals, p. 237. It is remarkable that the French historians should magnify the burning of this place, which is scarcely known in English history, into an important event. Teignmouth is spoken of as a great port, and the vessels are metamorphosed into frigates and men of war.— Lysons's *Mag. Brit.* vol. vi. part ii.
‡ Lysons's *Mag. Brit.*   § Walsingham. Stow's Annals, p. 329.

During the destructive contests between the Houses of York and Lancaster, Devonshire being remote from the general scenes of action, we have no account of a battle in the county. This district however had a share in the anarchy and confusion that prevailed through the country, and some blood was shed. Several riots and murders are mentioned as having taken place, occasioned by Thomas Courtenay earl of Devon, and Lord William Bonville baron of Shute, the former a partizan of the House of Lancaster, and the latter of that of York. Holinshed* describes a rencontre between the two barons and their retainers in the year 1455. The parties met at Clist Heath, near Exeter; and after a sharp conflict, in which several were killed and wounded on both sides, Lord Bonville was victorious. Approaching Exeter after the fight, the gates of the city were opened to receive him and his party, which so much increased the animosity long subsisting between the Courtenay family and the citizens, that the earl was determined on revenge. His purpose however was defeated by death, for in the contest between Henry VI. and Edward IV. he was shortly after beheaded at York.

Fight at
Clist
Heath.

Exeter besieged by
Sir Hugh
Courtenay.
In the 10th year of Edward IV. 1469, the citizens being divided in their attachment to the two claimants of the crown, Exeter was in considerable danger and alarm. At that time, the Duchess of Clarence being there, Lord Dinham, Lord Fitzwarren, and the Baron Carew, partizans of Henry, entered the city accompanied by a thousand men in arms. And Sir Hugh Courtenay, on the part of Edward, collecting as many forces among his friends as the time would allow, laid siege to the city, broke down the bridges, and, stopping all communication with the country, sent a message to the mayor, requiring him to open the gates or deliver up the leaders of the hostile forces within. The latter, on the contrary, demanded that the keys should be delivered up to them, and that nothing should be done but by their orders.

* Vol. iii. p. 644.

In this dilemma, the magistrates, after due deliberation, resolved not to comply with either party; but, exerting
their best endeavours to pacify both, resolved to maintain
their own authority in the city. as a trust committed into
their hands by the reigning monarch. . Barricadoing the
gates, fortifying the walls, and appointing the soldiers to
their proper stations, they made every necessary preparation for defence. Provisions beginning to fail, no means of
affording relief, which the exigencies of the case required,
were neglected by the magistrates, and the people. submitted with patience to the inevitable deprivations. The
clergy of the city however interfered, and by their mediation
pacific measures were adopted; and about twelve days
after this disturbance began the siege was raised.*
Shortly after. this a battle ensued, in which the Lancastrians were worsted. The Duke of Clarence and the
Earl. of Warwick fled to Exeter on the 3rd of April,
1470, and remained at the bishop's palace a few days,
whilst ships were prepared at Dartmouth for their retreat
to France. The king followed with an army of forty
thousand men, and entered the city on the 14th of the
same month, attended by the principal noblemen in his
service. Being too late in the pursuit, after resting three
days he returned to London. Not long afterwards,
however, the Duke of Clarence and the Earl of Warwick, returning to England with the Earls of Pembroke
and Oxford, and a small body of troops, landed at Exmouth, Dartmouth and Plymouth. The scenes that ensued resemble more the fictions of romance than events
of real history. In no longer space than eleven days
after his landing, Warwick was left, by the flight of Edward, sole master of the kingdom†.

In the year 1472, on the day on which the great battle
of Barnet was fought, in which Warwick was slain and
the Yorkists were. completely victorious, Margaret the
queen landed at Weymouth, with her son Edward, a
youth of great promise, about eighteen years of age, sup-

The cause of Marga-ret and her son Ed-ward es-poused in Devon-shire.

* Hoker's Exeter, p. 26. † Hume's Hist. of Engl.

VOL. I. Q

BOOK
II.

ported by a small body of forces.   Hearing of the fatal
catastrophe of Barnet, and foreseeing at once the appalling results of this calamity, her courage, by which she
had hitherto been supported under so many disasters, at
length forsook her.   At first she took refuge in the abbey
of Beaulieu (Bewley) ; but being waited upon by the
Duke of Somerset and Thomas Courtenay earl of Devon,
with other persons of distinction, who encouraged her to
hope for success in future, she resumed her former firmness, and determined to employ all her resources in re-
covering her fallen fortunes.   Each of her noble adherents
raised what men he could in Dorsetshire, Somersetshire
and Wiltshire, and proceeding to Devonshire, they mus-
tered their forces, and set up the standard of Henry at
Exeter.   Hence they sent for Sir John Arundell, Sir
Hugh Courtenay, and many other gentlemen in whom
they could place confidence, and by their means raised
the whole powers of Devonshire and Cornwall in their
favour.   Having thus collected a large army, they
proceeded, increasing their forces as they advanced, to
Bath, where they met the queen and her son.   They
were soon however intercepted in their further progress
by the expeditious Edward, at Tewkesbury, where a decisive battle ensued on the banks of the Severn, in which
the Lancastrians were totally defeated on the 4th of
May.   The Earl of Devon, and many other persons of
distinction, with upwards of three thousand of their
followers, were slain, and the army entirely dispersed.
Queen Margaret and her son, being taken prisoners,
were treated with great indignity; and the day after the
battle the unfortunate prince was murdered in the most
barbarous and dastardly manner, almost in the presence
of the king himself, by the Dukes of Clarence and Gloucester, Lord Hastings, and Sir Thomas Gray*.

    On the usurpation of Richard III., in consequence of
the dissatisfaction that prevailed throughout the country,
many of the principal persons in Devonshire and Corn-

* Holinshed, vol. iii. p. 686.

wall joined in the confederacy formed by the most distinguished nobility in favour of the Earl of Richmond. Among these were the heads of the Courtenay family, whose influence at that period both in Devonshire and Cornwall was of the greatest importance. Peter Courtenay, third son of Sir Philip Courtenay of Powderham, then bishop of Exeter, took an active part against the usurper, and encouraged the Marquis of Dorset to proclaim Henry earl of Richmond in the city on the 18th of October 1483.

After the death of the Duke of Buckingham, Richard came to Exeter, where he had before sent Lord Scroop, with a special commission to try the confederates; in consequence of which a Court was held for that purpose at Torrington, where the Marquis of Dorset, Peter Courtenay bishop of Exeter, Sir Edward Courtenay his brother, and about five hundred others, who had found means to escape, were outlawed; and Sir Thomas St. Leger, who had married the sister of Richard himself, and Thomas Rayme, Esq. were found guilty of high treason, and beheaded at Exeter*. The bishop was fortunate in making his escape out of the kingdom, for in the sequel he proved highly instrumental in fixing the crown on the head of Henry VII., and for this important service he was honoured with the mitre of Winchester†.

On his visit to the city, Richard met with a reception which could not fail to be highly gratifying to his ambition. At the east gate he was received by the mayor, aldermen, and common council, in due form, and was congratulated by the recorder in a set speech ‡, for which he

---

* Jenkins's Exeter.

† Oliver's Exeter, part i. chap. xi.

‡ "an elegant oration,"—Jenkins. The following anecdote is told by Risdon and by Westcote (MS. p. 60): When Richard visited the castle, he inquired its name; and being told it was Rugemont, he was much alarmed, and said to some of his attendants, that in consequence of an ancient prophecy, his days would not be many after he had seen Rugemont, mistaking this name for Richmond. The prophecy was fulfilled in less than a year by Richmond in Bosworth Field. This anecdote, if true, and there is no reason to doubt it, serves to illustrate the observation, that bad men are prone to superstition.

was rewarded by the city with a scarlet gown. The mayor delivered to the king the maces and keys of the city gates, and presented him with a purse of two hundred gold nobles. Having returned the maces and the keys, he was conducted to the bishop's palace, where he was elegantly entertained during the time of his stay, at the expense of the city. Having visited the principal places, and expressed himself highly pleased with what he saw, he returned to London delighted with his reception at Exeter*.

In the year 1497, in consequence of a subsidy granted by parliament to Henry VII., for the prosecution of the war against the Scots, violent insurrections took place in Cornwall, where the impost was particularly felt as an oppressive grievance. The insurgents were instigated and headed chiefly by two individuals, Thomas Flammock, a lawyer, and Michael Joseph, a smith, men of rash and enterprising spirit. Having assembled in considerable numbers, they marched towards Exeter, where they created great alarm; but the citizens, apprised of their intention, put themselves in arms, barricadoed the bridge, and opposed their entrance into the city. The rebels despairing of success in this quarter, and impatient of delay, proceeded to Taunton, where they were joined by Lord Audley, who assumed the command, marched with them to London, the insurgents conducting themselves peaceably on the road, and encamped at Blackheath. The king had

* That Richard has had even panegyrists as well as defenders, who have endeavoured to show not only that he was at least as good as the generality of princes about that period, but even better than some of them, and especially than his successor Henry VII., is well known. Those who wish to see what has been said in his favour will consult "The Praise of King Richard III." by Sir William Cornwallis, London, 1617; "The History of the Life and Reign of Richard III." by George Buck, Esq. London, 1646 ; and Horace Walpole's "Historic Doubts." It is comparatively of little consequence that the magic of Shakspeare's genius has fixed indelibly in the public mind exaggerated notions of the deformity of his person; the deformity of his mind, it is to be feared, whatever doubts may be raised as to some of the enormities with which he is charged, is but little diminished by his advocates.

The flattering reception which Richard received at Exeter on this occasion appears to have been the effect of intimidation. After the late confederacy against him, so sudden a change of sentiment can scarcely be supposed to be real.

suffered them to proceed thus far, in order that he might
have them the more easily and completely in his power.
Being there attacked by the royal forces, they were
speedily subdued, having 300 slain, and 1500 taken prisoners. Lord Audley was beheaded with circumstances of
peculiar indignity; Flammock and Joseph were hanged,
and, according to the barbarous custom of the times, their
quarters were exposed in different places.

Scarcely had this disturbance subsided, when the rebellion in support of Peter Warbeck spread great alarm
throughout the country. Some years before the pretensions of this mysterious personage * had created a considerable sensation in England, and conspiracies, which had
occasioned considerable anxiety to Henry, had been formed
in his favour. Affirming himself to be Richard duke of
York, the second son of Edward IV., whom Richard III.
was supposed to have murdered in the Tower, his cause
was espoused by the King of France, by the Duchess of
Burgundy, and by many of the English nobility, who were
disgusted with Henry's government. On the present occasion, having previously landed in Ireland, by the advice
of his associates there, and at the request of the insurgents in Cornwall, he determined to take advantage of the

CHAP.
II.

Peter
Warbeck.

* The arguments adduced by Horace Walpole in his " Historic
Doubts," have been thought by some to be conclusive. His own opinion
on the result of them is thus expressed : " For the younger brother, the
balance seems to incline greatly on the side of Perkin Warbeck, as the
true duke of York; and if one was saved, one knows not how or why to
believe that Richard destroyed only the elder." He adds, " We must
leave the whole story dark, though not so dark as we found it."

A reply to these " Doubts" was soon afterwards published, in 1768,
by F. W. G. of the Middle Temple; at the close of which the author observes, " I hope I have plainly and satisfactorily proved my arguments
will balance the scales, chiefly from the authorities alleged by Mr. Walpole." Both should be read to form a just opinion on the subject.

Mr. Buck's account of Warbeck is the following : " Richard duke of
York, son of Edward IV., was sent beyond sea by his friends, in order to
save him from destruction here. He had a liberal education under the
care of a worthy gentleman in Warbeck, a town in Flanders; but was
kept very private, in the time of his uncle, his friends not daring to ac-
quaint him with it. After Richard's death, knowing Henry of Richmond
to be a cruel enemy to the House of York, they committed the prince, for
greater safety, to Charles of Burgundy, and his duchess Margaret, aunt
to the prince." Hist. of Richard III., by George Buck, Esq. p. 87.

discontents in that county, and directing his course to Whitsand Bay, he proceeded to Bodmin the centre of the insurrection. Encouraged by the favourable reception he met with here, he assumed the title of Richard IV. King of England. The men of Cornwall had not learnt wisdom from the disastrous termination of their late attempt. Three thousand of them offered their services to the adventurer, and before they reached Exeter that number was doubled. Having resolved to besiege the city, he formed his army into two divisions, and whilst one scaled the walls, he commanded the other to set fire to the opposite gate. The former attempt was repulsed with considerable loss, and the latter was counteracted by the ready contrivance and intrepidity of the besieged, who themselves also set fire to the gate, and supplying it constantly with fuel, prevented the entrance of the assailants, whilst they were sinking a deep entrenchment and forming bulwarks within. In the several assaults the enemy lost about 200 men. The king having heard of the siege, dispatched a small body of light horse, under the command of Lord Daubeney, to the relief of the city; but in the mean time Edward Courtenay earl of Devon, Lord William his son, Sir Edmund Carew, Sir Thomas Trenchard, Sir Thomas Fulford, Sir John Halwell, Sir John Crocker, and others, accompanied by the inhabitants of the vicinity, arrived in time to decide the contest. In the last assault the earl was hurt in the arm with an arrow, and many of his companions were wounded, though but few were slain. Warbeck, finding his attempt upon the city hopeless, immediately retired, and proceeded towards Taunton*. The remainder of his story is well known; but, to render the account complete, it may be told in few words. Mustering his forces at Taunton, on the 20th of September, he seized the castle, and seemed determined to make a stand; but being closely pursued by the Earl of Devonshire, hearing of the formidable preparations which the king had made to crush him, and

* Holinshed, vol. iii..p. 781.

finding himself deserted by his men, he secretly withdrew CHAP. from his army, and with sixty horsemen fled to the New II. Forest in Hampshire, where he took refuge in the monastery of Beaulieu, or Bewley, near Southampton. Being induced, by the king's promise that his life should be spared, to forsake that sanctuary, he was conducted to the Tower. Having escaped thence, he took refuge in the monastery of Shyne, and was again pardoned at the intercession of the prior, but was placed in the stocks at Westminster and Cheapside, where he was compelled to read aloud to the people his confession of imposture, and was then conducted back to the Tower; whence forming a design to escape a second time, by murdering the lieutenant, he was shortly after executed at Tyburn.

The king had followed the Duke of Buckingham with Henry a considerable army to oppose Warbeck, but on his ap- VII. visits proach to Taunton, finding the adventurer fled and his Exeter. troops dispersed, proceeded to Exeter, where many of the rebels, who had been taken prisoners, were sent. Having thanked the citizens for their loyalty and determined courage in defending the city, he gave orders for the speedy trial of the prisoners, most of whom were found guilty : the ringleaders were executed on Southernhay, and the rest were pardoned. On this occasion, by granting a fresh charter to the city, he also settled some disputes relative to the election of the mayor and other officers.

Henry having determined to depress all the chiefs who favoured the line of York, Lord William Courtenay, son of the Earl of Devonshire, was taken and kept a prisoner during the remainder of this reign*.

From this time Devonshire appears to have remained in Disturb- a state of general tranquillity till the third year of Edward ances oc- VI., 1549, when commotions, occasioned by the change of by the religion, spread with rapidity through the county, and for change of some time threatened serious consequences. As Hooker religion. was living at Exeter at the time, and relates the whole of these proceedings from his personal knowledge, the sub-

* Polwhele's Devonshire.

stance of his account, with some additions, is the best that can be given *. These disturbances began at Sampford Courtenay, about fourteen miles west of Exeter, on Whit-Monday, 1549, the day after the Act for reforming the church service had been put in force. When the priest of this place was preparing to repeat the liturgy as the day before, William Underhill a tailor, and Segar a labourer, with others, interfered to prevent him; and the whole of the parishioners eventually uniting, compelled him to conduct the services of the church in the Roman Catholic form as before. The news of this transaction spread with great rapidity throughout the county : the common people received it with the greatest demonstrations of joy, and were unanimous in their determination to have the same course adopted in every parish. They assembled in clusters in various quarters, and the whole county was in a state of disorder. In this state of things, the magistrates in the neighbourhood of Sampford, after holding a consultation on the best method of proceeding, resolved to seek a conference with the leaders of the disaffected. This took place in an adjoining field, and continued for some time; but no measures whatever were the result. As the magistrates and their attendants were more numerous than the rioters, the disturbances might easily have been suppressed ; and the circumstance of no steps being taken for this purpose, led to the suspicion that the magistrates were favourable to the wishes of the people, and gave them the greatest encouragement to proceed.

Government being apprised of this rebellion, sent into Devonshire, with all expedition, Sir Peter and Sir Gawen Carew, for the purpose of quieting the people, in conjunction with the magistrates, by gentle methods, if possible, but by others, if necessary ; and Lord Russell, afterwards Earl of Bedford, was also dispatched with a similar commission.

The two former of these gentlemen on their arrival at Exeter, after holding a consultation with the sheriff, Sir

* Hoker's Exeter, p. 33.

hat
ord
iit-
the
t of
lav
rer.

THE CHURCH & REMAINS OF THE EPISCOPAL PALACE, HASTINGS, SUSSEX.

Peter Courtenay, and the magistrates of the county, proceeded immediately to Crediton, where the insurgents were
assembled, with a design, which they then thought feasible, The rioters
of reducing them to order by reason and persuasion. This attacked at
expectation, however, was soon found to be erroneous. Crediton.
The rioters, aware of their intention, had provided themselves with whatever weapons their circumstances supplied, entrenched the roads, formed a rampart at the end
of the town, and furnishing some adjoining barns with
men and ammunition, pierced loop-holes in the sides for
their shot. On their approach, the gentlemen, finding their
entrance into the town thus obstructed and all conference
refused, notwithstanding the smallness of their number,
formed the rash determination of making their way over
the barrier by force, but were speedily compelled to relinquish the attempt, with the loss of some of their number
and the injury of others. In this dilemma, a servant of
Sir Hugh Pollard suddenly set fire to the barns; in consequence of which the whole of the rioters quitted the
town, dispersing about the neighbouring country, and the
gentlemen, finding all further proceedings at that time
useless, returned to Exeter.

The news of this event serving only to alarm and ex- St. Mary
asperate the people still more, they assembled in many Clist for-
parts of the county in larger numbers, making preparations tified.
for defence as if an enemy were approaching, particularly
at St. Mary Clist, a village belonging to Lord Russell,
who was then lord lieutenant of the county. This they fortified in the best manner circumstances would allow, entrenched the roads, laid trees across the bridge, and planted
upon it some cannon, which they had procured from Topsham. As "trifles light as air" serve, in cases like this, to increase the flame when once enkindled, the expostulations of
Mr. Walter Raleigh (the father of the great and celebrated
man of that name) with an old woman on her way to the
church, being grossly misrepresented by her to the congregation, and falsely construed into threats of immediate
punishment for adhering to the Catholic mode of worship,

insignificant as it may seem, appears to have acted at this time as a powerful cause of adding to the violence of the ferment. Mr. Raleigh being afterwards met by the insurgents, his life was in great danger; and though he was then protected by the bravery of some sailors who happened to be with him, on a subsequent occasion he was seized by the people, and till the commotions were terminated was kept a prisoner at St. Sidwells, where his life was often threatened.

At St. Mary Clist another attempt was made by pacific proposals to reduce the rioters to order; and on the promise of safety to their persons, some gentlemen entering the village, a conference ensued. All the concession, however, that could be obtained from the people was the assurance that they would remain quiet, on the condition that no alteration should take place in the form of religious worship from the state in which it was left by Henry VIII., until the King came of age. As this of course gave no satisfaction, when the people understood that their terms were rejected, their turbulence, together with their numbers, increased, and they immediately made every addition in their power to their means of defence and annoyance; several gentlemen were made prisoners, and others, being favourable to the views of the insurgents, suffered themselves to be taken, with the design of lending them assistance.

Lord Russell being at that time at Sir Hugh Paulet's in Somersetshire, Sir Peter Carew, who had arrived there with an account of the state of affairs, was sent by him to lay the whole before the Council. After reproving him for increasing the irritation of the people at Crediton, and receiving his complete exculpation of his conduct, they resolved upon a further experiment of conciliatory measures by a pacific proclamation, including an offer of pardon to all who should return quietly to their allegiance. This step, however, served no purpose but to give the insurgents additional encouragement to prosecute their designs with increased vigour. Arranging their forces in some sort of order, they appointed as leaders of the different bodies, men selected from the lowest class, and of the worst character. The insurrection, however, began now to assume a more formidable aspect; for in a short time it obtained the support of some of the discontented gentry both of Devonshire and Cornwall, among whom were Sir Thomas Pomeroy, Mr. John Berry, and Mr. Coffin of Devonshire; and in Cornwall Mr. Humfrey Arundell, Mr. Winslade, and several others, who undertook the command of the rebel forces.

Their number being now very considerable, they resolved to lay siege to Exeter; but as a preparatory step they sent a message to the mayor, requiring him to join their party, and admit them into the city. After a consultation with his brother magistrates, though some of them were strongly attached to the Roman Catholic form of worship, yet being determined notwithstanding to maintain their allegiance and submission to the laws, a positive refusal to comply with the requisition was returned. After a second message to the same purport, and a still more peremptory refusal, both parties prepared for the contest. The rebels being convinced, and with apparent reason, that the majority of the citizens were of the same religious persuasion with themselves, and that they had many friends within the walls, on the 2nd of July invested the city to the number of about two thousand, and immediately took possession of the suburbs.

At this time there were many other insurrections in various parts of the kingdom, as in Oxfordshire, Yorkshire, Norfolk, and Suffolk, though no where were these disturbances so formidable as in Devonshire. They arose from different causes; but the rebels in this county had entertained the hope that the disaffected in other quarters would unite with them in their attempt to restore the religion to which they had been accustomed. In this expectation they were disappointed. Their numbers notwithstanding kept continually increasing, till in the end, it is said, they amounted to about ten thousand [*]: and

* Holinshed, vol. iii. p. 1002. Fox's Acts and Mon. Hayward s Life and Reign of Edward VI., p. 55.

so confident at this period were they of success in their
attempt upon the city, that many of them brought their
wives and horses with panniers to carry off the spoils.
According to Fox and others *, the number of Roman
Catholic priests in this lawless multitude was very considerable, who not only instigated the people to their desperate enterprise, but even headed their forces. And, that
nothing might be wanting to procure success, the insurgents carried with them into the field the host under a
canopy in a cart, together with images, crucifixes, tapers,
holy water, and whatever else of this kind their superstition led them to believe might be calculated to render
a Superior Power propitious to their undertaking †.

All the circumstances of the siege are described at great
length by Hooker ‡, but a minute detail of them on the
present occasion would be tedious. Their first step was
cutting off all communication with the city, by making
trenches and placing trees across the roads, breaking down
the bridges, and appointing guards in proper stations to
prevent the approach of any individual §. Planting small
cannon in various quarters, setting fire to the gates, un-
dermining the walls, and making use of numerous stra-
tagems, they left nothing untried to accomplish their purpose. All their efforts, however, were baffled by the vigilance, activity, and superior skill of the besieged. Ram-
parts were raised within the city, and fires kept constantly
burning between them and the gates: the place of their
mine being discovered, a counter-mine was sunk, and the
water let in, which rendered this attempt abortive. Several sallies were also tried with some success.

The greatest peril, however, to the city was internal.
The besieged were assailed within by two of the most
dangerous enemies to its safety, namely, Discord and
Famine. Of the two parties in the city, the majority were

* Acts and Mon. Strype's Mem. of Cranm. vol. i. ch. x. Holinshed,
vol. iii. p. 1002.

† Fox. Hayward, p. 55.

‡ This name in the title-page of his History of Exeter is spelled Hoker,
in the body of the work Hooker. The latter is the present method of
spelling the name.

§ Hayward, p. 55.

in favour of the old religion. Individuals of this party exerted every effort to prevail upon the magistrates to open the
gates to the besiegers: but failing in this, they entered into
conspiracies, held secret communications with the enemy
without, tampered with the soldiers to deliver up the castle; and with such arms as they were able to procure, endeavoured, by raising disturbances, to become masters of
the city. The firm and judicious conduct of the magistrates, however, and of the more respectable part of the
citizens, who formed associations and paraded the streets
day and night, continually on the watch to prevent disor-
derly conduct, rendered every effort of the disaffected un-
availing. Famine was not so easy to contend with. As
all entrance into the city had been closed for some time,
their means of subsistence were nearly exhausted. Having no flour, they made bread of bran; and even horse-
flesh at length became acceptable food[*]. In this extremity, the humane, prudent and active exertions of the
higher classes, as well as the patient endurance and resolution of the people in general, were deserving of the
highest praise.

In the mean time Lord Russell, finding himself too
weak to encounter the rebels in the field, had been compelled to keep at a distance; for Government, instead of
troops, had sent him nothing but proclamations. By the
first of these, which has been mentioned before, a free
pardon was offered to those of the insurgents who should
return to their duty: by the second, the lands, goods,
and chattels of the rebels were offered to any who could
obtain possession of them: by a third, at a subsequent
period, martial law was ordered to be put in force; and
by a fourth, the commissioners were commanded to put
down all illegal inclosures. By means of Lord Russell
the insurgents had also attempted to negotiate with the
Government, or rather to prescribe terms of accommodation. They first sent through his hands eight articles, a

* Hayward. p. 55. Holinshed, vol. iii. p. 1002.

compliance with which they insisted upon as indispensable to their submission; and these were afterwards increased to fifteen*.   A long and elaborate answer to the latter was composed by Cranmer, and sent to the rebels, at the conclusion of the commotions.   Both may be seen in Strype's Memorials.   A reply to the eight articles by the Council, in which each is discussed at length, is preserved

* These articles, as affording a curious specimen of the dictatorial spirit of the insurgents, so strongly contrasted in their object with the spirit of the present times, though the principle, founded on the prejudices of education, is the same in both cases, will not be out of place if inserted here.

" I. We will have all the general councils and holy decrees of our forefathers observed, kept and performed: and whosoever shall gainsay them, we hold them as heretics.

" II. We will have the law of our sovereign lord King Henry VIII. concerning the Six Articles, to be used again, as in his time they were [1].

" III. We will have the mass in Latin, as was before, and celebrated by the priest, without any man or woman communicating with him.

" IV. We will have the sacrament hang over the high altar, and there to be worshiped, as it was wont to be; and they which will not consent, we will have them die like heretics against the holy Catholic faith.

" V. We will have the sacrament of the altar but at Easter delivered to the people; and then but in one kind.

" VI. We will that our curates shall administer the sacrament of baptism at all times, as well in the week day, as on the holy days.

" VII. We will have holy bread and holy water every Sunday, palmes and ashes at the time accustomed, images to be set up again in every church, and all other ancient and old ceremonies used heretofore by our mother, holy church.

" VIII. We will not receive the new service, because it is but like a Christmas game; but we will have our old service of Latin, mass, evening song, and procession in Latin, as it was before.   And so we the Cornish men, whereof certain of us understand no English, utterly refuse this new English.

" IX. We will have every preacher in his sermon, and every priest at mass, pray especially by name for the souls in purgatory, as our fathers did.

" X. We will have the Bible, and all books of Scripture in English, to be called in again.   For we are informed, that otherwise the clergy shall not of long time confound the heretics.

" XI. We will have Dr. Moreman and Dr. Crispin, which hold our opinions, to be safely sent unto us; and to them we require the King's

[1] The inhuman Act of the Six Articles, passed in the reign of Henry VIII., inflicted death by burning, with forfeiture of goods and lands, upon all who should speak against transubstantiation; and made it felony and forfeiture of lands to defend the communion in both kinds, marriage of priests or others who had made vows of chastity, or to say any thing against the necessity of private masses and auricular confession.

by Fox and Holinshed*. In addition to these, a supplication was sent by the insurgents to the King, which was also answered by the Council†. To the whole of the articles, though much pains were taken to convince the people of their error, a peremptory refusal was given. At first other grounds of complaint were insisted upon by the disaffected, as for instance the inclosure of lands‡; but the priests, who, as we are informed by the historians, were throughout active instigators of the commotions, contrived to give to the whole of their demands a religious turn, and in the composition of the articles their interference is sufficiently manifest.

The tardiness of Government in sending the necessary supplies of men and money for the suppression of the rebellion, might arise in part from the demand upon its resources occasioned by the many other insurrections in the kingdom, and partly also from the wish of the Council to effect their purpose by mild and conciliatory measures, if possible. Lord Russell, however, continued some time at Honiton, and finding the few men with him be-

Majesty to give some certain livings, to preach among us our Catholic faith.

" XII. We think it very meet, because the Lord Cardinal Pole is of the King's blood, that he shall not only have his pardon, but also be sent for to Rome, and promoted to the King's Council.

" XIII. We will that no gentleman shall have any more servants than one to wait upon him, except he may dispense one hundred mark land. And for every hundred mark we think it reasonable that he should have a man.

" XIV. We will that the half part of the abbey lands and chantry lands in every man's possession, however he came by them, be given again to two places, where two of the chief abbeys were within every county, where such half part shall be taken out, and there to be established a place for devout persons, which shall pray for the King and the common wealth. And to the same we will have all the alms of the church box given for these seven years.

" XV. For the particular griefs of our country, we will have them so ordered, as Humphry Arundel and Henry Bray, the King's Mayor of Bodmin, shall inform the King's Majesty, if they may have safe conduct in the King's great seal to pass and repass with an herald of arms."— Strype's Memorials of Archbishop Cranmer, Oxford 1812. Append. XL.

* vol. iii. p. 1003. Hayward, p. 55.   † Fox, and Strype.

‡ Strype's Mem. of Cranm. vol. i. ch. x. Hayward, p. 55. Holinshed, vol. iii. p. 1002.

ginning to desert, he had commenced his retreat into Dorsetshire, but was by Sir Peter Carew persuaded to return.   In this state of perplexity three merchants of Exeter, Mr. Thomas Prestwood, Mr. John Bodley, and Mr. John Periam, gentlemen of large property, obtained for him on their own credit a liberal supply of money ; and shortly after receiving a further supply from Government, he procured sufficient additions to his forces to enable him to advance against the enemy.   Being informed that a party of them were on their march to attack him, and had proceeded to Fenniton Bridge six miles on the road ; on his arrival there, he found some of them in occupation of the bridge, and the rest stationed in the adjoining meadow prepared to give him battle*. The bridge was taken with some difficulty, and in this attempt Sir Gawen Carew was wounded in the arm with an arrow. The rebels in the meadow were attacked at the same time, and after a stout resistance completely overthrown and put to flight.   But whilst the soldiers were employed in collecting the spoils, a fresh party of Cornish men, about 250, under the command of Mr. Robert Smith of St. Germains, came up ; and though they fought with great obstinacy and vigour, were at length also routed and dispersed.   In both battles about three hundred of the enemy were slain.

Fight at Fenniton Bridge.

A report having arisen that the whole country was in arms, Lord Russell returned with his little army to Honiton ; but finding this to be a false alarm, he found means of sending a letter to Exeter, assuring the besieged that he would shortly be with them for their deliverance. The arrival of this information was in the highest degree seasonable ; for the city was at that time in a state the most precarious and uncertain.   Speedily afterwards Lord Grey of Wilton and Sir William Herbert arrived at Honiton, with a body of German horse and about three hundred Italian arquebusiers under Baptista Spinola†. With these forces

* Hayward, p. 55.   † *Ibid.*

in addition to his own, amounting in the whole, however, to little more than a thousand *, Lord Russell resolved, without delay, to attempt the relief of Exeter, which was then reduced to great extremities; and accordingly, after sending another letter of encouragement to the citizens, he set out from Honiton on the 3rd of August; but leaving the direct road, he proceeded over the downs to Woodbury, and encamped near a windmill. The rebels at St. Mary Clist, having heard of his arrival, marched out to the attack. The contest was severe, but in the end they were entirely defeated, and most of them slain. A thanksgiving was ordered for the victory, and a minister of the name of Coverdale preached on the occasion †.

In the mean time the rest of the insurgents, having heard of this defeat, resorted in great numbers from all quarters to St. Mary Clist, to the amount of about six thousand men, and prepared to defend themselves. About nine o'clock the next morning, being Sunday, Lord Russell arrived at this place, and finding all the entrances blocked up, divided his forces into three parts for the attack, and after some conflict the barriers were taken. But when the army had passed on the road, Sir Thomas Pomeroy, the rebel commander, having concealed himself behind some bushes, in company with a trumpeter and drummer, sounded an alarm, and the stratagem succeeded. The Royal forces, supposing this to be an ambush and alarmed at the danger of being surrounded, retreated with precipitation, leaving the baggage in the road. The insurgents lost no time in following; and took the waggons laden with ammunition and money, as well as the cannon, which they planted in different places, and employed in their defence.

The stratagem, however, was speedily discovered, and the Royal forces returned: but finding it impossible to enter the streets with any probability of success, as every

* Hayward.
† Government had given a commission to three preachers to attend' Lord Russell for the purpose of convincing the people of their errors. Cranmer afterwards composed sermons to be read to them with the same view.

BOOK
II.

house was fortified and full of armed men, the town was set on fire. The rebels assembled in an open space, and after a fierce encounter were finally repulsed with great slaughter; their loss on this occasion being about a thousand men. Sir William Francis, who led on the Royal forces to the attack, was killed in the approach to the town.

Battle of
Clist
Heath.

Proceeding toward Clist Heath, after clearing the bridge which they found fortified, observing a multitude of the rebels assembled on Woodbury Hill, and expecting a fresh encounter, Lord Russell commanded the prisoners, which were numerous, to be killed, and the order (inhuman, indeed, but said to have been rendered necessary by the circumstances of the case) was immediately put in execution. Mustering all the forces they were able to collect, the rebels in the vicinity of Exeter assembled with all expedition at Clist Heath, where they formed entrenchments, and placed their cannon in the night, which at day-break they discharged with great effect on the Royal army encamped on the neighbouring hill. Lord Russell resolving to terminate the affair at once, the arrangement which he made of his forces rendered the escape of the rebels impossible. Though they fought with a degree of valour and desperation, which Lord Grey observed he had never seen equalled, in the end they were so completely overthrown, that few, if any, remained. This defeat decided the whole contest; for the party that surrounded the city, being driven to despair by these repeated failures of their confederates, immediately raised the siege, and dispersed in the night, to the no small joy of the citizens, who were then reduced to the last state of distress. After the battle the army marched to Topsham, carrying with them on a horse-litter the body of Sir William Francis, which was afterwards interred in Exeter cathedral with military honours.

Exeter re-
lieved.

The next day, being the 6th of August, early in the morning Lord Russell marched to Exeter, and as the city was destitute of provisions, encamped in St. John's fields *

* At present Barnfield and the adjoining fields.

adjoining Southernhay. Liberal supplies were shortly procured from the surrounding country, by the army, for the
famished citizens ; many of them, however, died through
excessive eating, after long abstinence from food.   The
siege had lasted upwards of a month; and the magistrates,
as an expression of their gratitude for its happy termination, appointed the 6th of August to be observed annually
as a day of thanksgiving ; a custom which is continued
to the present day, the mayor, chamber, and incorporated
trades going in procession to the cathedral, where a sermon is preached by the mayor's chaplain.

The flames of rebellion, however, were not yet totally
extinguished.   Great numbers of the Devonshire and
Cornish insurgents were still assembled at Sampford
Courtenay, and, reckless of consequences, having fortified
the place, were determined to try the issue of another
battle. Lord Russell, who the day after his arrival at
Exeter had been reinforced by one thousand Welshmen
under the command of Sir William Herbert, ordered the
whole of his army, which now amounted to eight or ten
thousand, with Sir William at their head, to disperse
them. The latter, however, defended the town with desperate resolution, and killed some of the assailants, among
whom was a young Welshman, named Ap Owen, much
respected : but in the end the greater part of the rebels, who
were resolved neither to fly nor be taken prisoners, were
put to the sword.   The rest, taking refuge in Somersetshire, were pursued thither by Sir Peter Carew and Sir
Hugh Paulet, with a considerable part of the army; and
most of them being slain or taken prisoners, the rebellion
was finally suppressed.   The number of the slain in these
several battles was estimated at about four thousand.

The atrocities committed by the army after the rebels
had been entirely defeated, admits of no vindication, and
can scarcely be palliated. Finding a disposition in the
people to continue the disturbances whenever opportunity
allowed, Lord Russell ordered the soldiers to scour the
country ; and parties of them sent out for that purpose,

exceeding, no doubt, the design of their commander, set fire to the houses, destroyed the property of the unresisting inhabitants, and spared neither friend nor foe, reducing the country for many miles to a state of desolation, from which it did not recover for many years *.

After this, Lord Russell proceeding into Cornwall for the purpose of inflicting summary retribution on the guilty, caused the leaders of the rebellion in that county who fell into his hands to be executed by martial law †; and returning to Exeter opened a commission for passing sentence on the numerous prisoners in custody. The leaders of inferior rank were executed in the city; but the principals, Arundel, Winslade, Berry, Coffin, and Holmes, were sent to London, and, after trial, were executed there. The common people received a general pardon, and were dismissed to their respective homes. One execution in Exeter, however, is mentioned as remarkable, namely, that of the vicar of St. Thomas's, of the name of Welsh, who had been appointed to the living by Lord Russell, the patron. This man had some qualities which had rendered him popular, and by his influence over the rebels had prevented the city on one occasion from being set on fire.

* Hoker, and Jenkins.

† Hayward relates the following anecdotes, which, if true, serve to show that justice, at that time at least, could be sported with. The provost marshal, Anthony Kingston, after the suppression of the rebellion invited himself to dine with the mayor of Bodmin, who had been active in promoting the disturbances; and in the morning directed the mayor to prepare a gallows immediately, as in the afternoon an execution must take place. The mayor completed the order in time. And after a sumptuous dinner, Kingston requested him to ascertain whether the preparation for the execution was complete: being informed that it was, he told the mayor that he himself must prepare to be executed on the gallows which he had erected. Expostulations were in vain, and the mayor was accordingly executed that afternoon.—The other anecdote is that of a trick played by a miller on his own servant. This man at the same time expecting a visit from Kingston, for a similar purpose, went out of the way and concealed himself, telling his servant to personate him, and if any one called to say that he was the miller. The man faithfully obeyed the order; and Kingston coming to the mill, ordered him for execution: and though the man, discovering the trick which had been played him, fully explained the whole, it was of no avail: he was executed.—History of the Life and Reign of Edw. VI. p. 60.

These circumstances interested many of the peaceable inhabitants in his favour. But he had been an active insti-
gator and principal leader of the rebellion throughout. He
had, moreover, caused an unoffending individual, who
happened to be a zealous Protestant, to be put to death ;
and it seems was accessory also to the death of a Mr. Hel-
lions, one of the gentlemen who had gone to Sampford
with a view to pacify the rebels. His conduct on the
whole left no room for mercy, and he was executed, with
circumstances of unnecessary insult, on the tower of the
church in which he had officiated ; where his body remained suspended till the restoration of popery in the
reign of Mary *.

The brave defence of Exeter by the citizens received
every where the most merited applause, and the Lord
Protector sent a letter, in the name of the King, thank-
ing them for their courage and fidelity, and assuring them
of his protection. The next year, with the advice of the
Privy Council, the King renewed their charter, confirmed
their privileges, and granted the corporation for ever the
valuable manor of Exe Island, or Exeland, of which they
had been deprived unjustly from the time of William I.
To this account it remains to be added, that Sir Thomas
Pomeroy, though the principal of the rebels, found the
means of making his peace, although at a great sacrifice.
The Pomeroys had been a flourishing family for a long
period in the county of Devon ; but Sir Thomas, on the
total defeat of the rebels, compounded for his life by
yielding up his lands and castle at Berry to the Lord Protector Edward Seymour Duke of Somerset ; and Berry
Castle has continued since that time in the possession of
the Somerset family †.—Such was the termination of this
unhappy rebellion.

We are told by Stow ‡, that in the reign of Mary, A.D.
1554, information was brought to the Court that Sir Peter

* Jenkins, and Hoker.   † Polwhele's Devonshire
‡ Annals, p. 618.

and Sir Gawen Carew, and Sir Thomas Derry, with various others, were in arms in Devonshire, to resist the coming of Philip of Spain into the country, and that they had taken possession of Exeter and its castle. But he gives no information as to the result, nor whether any punishment was inflicted on the leaders of this insurrection. The several histories of Devonshire take no notice of this occurrence; and we find that the two former of these gentlemen were living in the reign of Elizabeth; for Sir Gawen Carew received a small pension from the city, as an expression of gratitude for his great services; and Sir Peter Carew in 1754 was elected by the citizens one of their representatives in parliament, in the room of Thomas Williams, Esq. deceased *.

In the long and prosperous reign of Elizabeth, no event of importance occurs peculiar to Devonshire. Exeter contributed, with other commercial towns, her proportion of three ships manned and armed to the fleet collected for the purpose of resisting the Spanish invasion, and voted a loyal address to the Queen, who in returning thanks to the citizens for their loyalty, authorized them to bear the motto *Semper fidelis* on the city arms†. The principal fleet was stationed at Plymouth, and the gentlemen of Devonshire exerted themselves with great zeal in fitting out all the ships they could procure. By their intrepidity and skill they contributed greatly to the success of the various attacks on the Spanish armada. The Devonshire worthies whose names are most distinguished on this great occasion were, Sir Francis Drake, Sir Martin Forbisher, Sir John Hawkins, Sir Humphrey Gilbert, Sir Walter Raleigh, Sir Robert Cary, and Edward Fulford, Esq. at that time sheriff of the county.

No period of English history is more interesting or momentous than those of the civil wars in the time of Charles I.

---

* Jenkins.   † *Ibid.* p. 128.

and the Revolution; nor was the share which Devonshire had in these events of inferior importance. In the former of these periods, we find that the whole of this county was at the beginning of the contest in possession of the Committee of the Parliament*. In the year 1642, Exeter was placed, though in opposition it is said to the general wishes of the citizens, by the Earl of Bedford, who had been appointed lord lieutenant of the county by the Parliament, in a state of military preparation adverse to the King. With twenty-five pieces of ordnance, a strong garrison, and a numerous body of soldiers quartered in the city ready for service, it was in an excellent state of defence[†]. The Earl of Stamford, the Parliamentary general, was appointed governor. Plymouth was also active in its measures in support of the Parliament. This important station, during the absence of its governor Sir Jacob Astley, whom the King had appointed major-general of foot, was seized by the inhabitants and strongly fortified. The Earl of Ruthven was soon afterwards made governor. The north of Devonshire in particular was also remarkable for the spirit of disaffection.

We are told by Vicars[‡], that about this time Sir Edmund Fortescue the sheriff, and a zealous royalist, whose head-quarters, with a small number of men, were at Plympton, happening to be at Modbury with some other gentlemen of distinction in the county, and about two thousand men in arms, was unexpectedly attacked on a sudden by a party of five hundred horse from the garrison of Plymouth; and the Royalists being seized with a sudden panic, under the impression that the forces of the enemy were more numerous, took flight, and Sir Edmund Fortescue and the other gentlemen were taken prisoners and sent to London.

After the defeat of the Parliamentary army on Braddock

CHAP.
II.

The civil
war in the
time of
Charles I.

* Clarendon (Oxford edit.), vol. ii. book vi. p. 191.
† Vicars, part ii. p. 172.
‡ *Ibid.* p. 226.

Down near Liskeard, on the 19th of January, by means
of which the Royalists became again entire masters of
Cornwall, and having taken Saltash, they quartered themselves at Tavistock*. And Sir John Berkeley, the gallant
general of the Royalists, who with a body of horse was
active in scouring the country in all quarters, took many
prisoners ; and prevented Sir George Chudleigh, an active
officer for the Parliament at that time and acting as commander-in-chief for the Earl of Stamford in Devonshire,
from collecting the body of forces in the county which he
was zealously attempting.　In one of these expeditions
Sidney Godolphin, a young gentleman of great promise
on the side of the Royalists, was killed at Chagford.
In the month of February, Sir Nicholas Slanning, being
entrenched at Modbury with two thousand men, after a
battle which lasted from two o'clock in the afternoon to
four the next morning was defeated by the Devonshire
Clubmen†, who took five pieces of ordnance and a considerable number of prisoners : and the same day Sir Ralph
Hopton, who was at that time stationed before Plymouth,
was driven from his quarters by the Earl of Stamford ‡.
About this time a treaty of peace between the two counties of Devonshire and Cornwall being proposed, a cessa-
tion of hostilities, ratified by a solemn oath, commenced,
and the Royalists retired into Cornwall§.

　This state however of comoarative tranquillity in times

* Clarendon, vol. ii. book vi. p. 198—200.

† About this time a new body of men rose into notice, under the appellation of Clubmen, who excited considerable attention during the whole
of the ensuing campaign. The first object of their hostility was the Royal
party ; they were also declared enemies to popery. They appear to have
originated chiefly from two causes, namely, the unparalleled rapine and
barbarities to which they were exposed, from the dissoluteness of the
King's forces, and the levy which was attempted to be made among them to
serve in his army. At first they were probably armed with such weapons
as offer themselves to rustics ; but they retained the same appellation
afterwards when they assumed an air of greater discipline, and were
openly led by the gentlemen of their respective counties. They were
numerous in Devonshire.—Godwin's Commonwealth, vol. i. chap. xvii.

‡ Vicars, part ii. p. 271.

§ Clarendon, vol. ii. book vi. p. 203.

like these, did not promise to be of long continuance, and was in fact shortly after interrupted. The Parliament, having collected large supplies of money by the imposition of a new tax which was levied in Devonshire equally on friends and foes, were enabled to increase their forces; and Sir James Chudleigh, the son of Sir George, the Earl of Stamford being ill at Exeter, went as their major-general, the night before the treaty expired, with a considerable party of horse and foot, into Cornwall*. Attempting to surprise Launceston, the head-quarters of the Royalists, he was repulsed: but on his return he is said to have met with Sir Ralph Hopton's army, and to have given it a total defeat. Vicars gives a full description of this affair, as a brilliant action worthy to be commemorated by a pyramid, for which he proposes an inscription. He states that only one hundred and eight of the Parliamentary soldiers were engaged; and the spot near Bridestowe, where the victory was achieved, he calls Reber Down†. Clarendon, however, calls it Bradock Down; and speaks of the action as a night skirmish, which, though the only check upon the success of the Cornish Royalists, inspired them with great terror, and threw them into greater disorder than on any other occasion‡.

About the middle of May the Earl of Stamford, with an army of fourteen hundred cavalry and five thousand four hundred foot, having thirteen pieces of brass cannon, one mortar, and an abundant supply of ammunition and provisions, marched into Cornwall, and encamped on the top of a hill near Stratton, the only part of Cornwall that was distinguished by disaffection to the King. The Royalists stationed at Launceston did not amount to half the number, and were nearly destitute of provisions as well as ammunition.

Earl of Stamford marches into Cornwall, and is defeated at Stratton.

The Earl, thinking himself secure, dispatched Sir George Chudleigh, with a party of twelve hundred horse, to attack Bodmin by surprise, where the sheriff and the

* Clarendon, vol. ii. book vii. p. 400.
† Vicars, part ii. p. 315.   ‡ vol. ii. book vii. p. 407.

principal gentlemen of the county were assembled. This measure, though well designed, in the result proved to be unfortunate; for the Royalists at Launceston, perceiving this to be a favourable opportunity, proceeded to attack the camp at Stratton, their stock of provisions allowing only a biscuit a day to each man, and their forces consisting of no more than two thousand four hundred infantry, with two pieces of cannon, and a body of five hundred cavalry, under the command of Sir John Digby. The battle commenced on the morning of the 16th, and continued with various success till five o'clock in the afternoon; when the Royalists, finding their ammunition nearly exhausted, resolved to march up the hill where the enemy was stationed, without firing till they arrived at the top. The conflict there was desperate, but terminated in the defeat of the Parliamentarians. Sir James Chudleigh, with thirty officers and seventeen hundred men, were taken prisoners; and the whole of the artillery and baggage, with seventy barrels of powder and a large quantity of provisions, fell into the hands of the victors *. Sir James Chudleigh on this occasion was accused of treachery, and, according to Clarendon, unjustly; but whether incensed at the charge that was brought against him, or induced by the liberal treatment he received from his captors, after remaining a prisoner ten days, he joined the Royal party. Vicars however states, that a letter from Sir James to his father was afterwards intercepted in Devonshire, in which he declares it to have been his intention from the first to go over to the Royalists whenever a suitable opportunity should offer, and the object of which was to persuade his father to follow his example†.

After his defeat the Earl of Stamford fled to Exeter, and Sir George Chudleigh, having been successful at

* Clarendon, vol. ii. book vii. p. 401—403. Dugdale's Short View of the late Troubles of England, p. 183. In consequence of this victory, Sir Ralph Hopton, the commander of the Cornish Royalists, was soon after raised to the dignity of Lord Hopton of Stratton.

† Vicars, part ii. p. 340.

Bodmin, soon followed. The Cornish army under the command of Sir Ralph Hopton, having returned solemn thanks for the victory on the field of battle, and stopping a day and night to refresh themselves on the spoils, marched into Devonshire, intending to attack either Exeter or Plymouth: but receiving information that the King had dispatched Prince Maurice and the Marquis of Hertford with a considerable body of cavalry to join them, and that Sir William Waller was about to be sent by the Parliament into the West, with a fresh army recruited by the fugitives from the battle of Stratton, they determined to advance eastward, their numbers being daily increased by fresh accessions of volunteers in Devonshire. Having established some small garrisons near Exeter as a check upon that city, they proceeded to Tiverton, whence they dispersed a regiment of foot under the command of Colonel Ware of Halberton; and advancing thence, joined Prince Maurice and the Marquis of Hertford at Chard *.

It is remarkable that, though no part of the kingdom was so well affected towards the King as Cornwall, the Royalists had no forces in Devonshire, except a small party at Columb-John, the seat of Sir John Acland, three miles from Exeter, which, however vigilant and enterprising, were of little avail in keeping the Parliamentarians in check. The Earl of Warwick, moreover, was sent with a fleet to reconnoitre the coasts of Devonshire, and to take advantage of any favourable opportunity that might occur. For these reasons the Marquis of Hertford sent Sir John Berkeley back into Devonshire, with Colonel Howard's regiment of horse, who being joined by a considerable number of the gentlemen of the county, and others favourable to the cause of the King, fixed his quarters within a mile of Exeter, where the Earl of Stamford then was with a force at least equal, and stationed his guards even at the gates of the city †.

Such was the posture of affairs on the arrival of the

CHAP.
II.

Exeter besieged by Prince Maurice.

* Clarendon, vol. ii. book vii. pp. 401—412.
† *Ibid.* vol. ii. p. 421.

s 2

King's forces under the command of Prince Maurice, who, after the refusal of his summons to surrender, invested the city, and commenced a close siege. The Parliament, having received information of its danger, sent orders to the Earl of Warwick to attempt its relief; and in order to divert the forces of the enemy from the city, the admiral made a feint of landing at various places on the coast, which compelled Colonel Berkeley with his cavalry to attend his progress with the view of resisting his attempts. The fleet at length entered the Exe; but soon found the attempt to relieve the city entirely frustrated by the vigilance and dexterity of Berkeley, who being supplied with cannon by the Prince, and taking possession of some points of land which commanded the river, kept the enemy employed, till, the tide retiring, they were obliged to depart, after discharging their shot from the fleet for three hours, leaving three of their ships for want of sufficient depth of water, one of which was burnt, and the other two taken possession of by the Royalists in sight of the rest. During these transactions, the garrison of Plymouth being greatly increased in numbers, and having an uninterrupted line of communication with Barnstaple and Bideford, in the north, which was the principal seat of disaffection, the commander of the forces in these quarters resolved to unite, and compel the Royalists to raise the siege of Exeter: nor would there have been any difficulty in this, had corresponding exertions been made by the besieged themselves in support of this design. But Colonel Berkeley being apprised of their purpose, sent Sir John Digby with a regiment of cavalry into the north, with a view to interrupt their operations. His quarters were at Torrington, where, by fresh supplies from Cornwall, his forces amounted to about three hundred horse and seven hundred foot. The Parliamentarians at Bideford and Barnstaple, with a superior force of about twelve hundred foot and three hundred horse, under the command of Colonel Bennet, proceeded to the attack; but on their approach, being seized with a sudden panic and thrown into disorder,

Colonel Digby, taking advantage of this circumstance, obtained an easy victory, but pursued the enemy with great slaughter, and took about two hundred prisoners. The fort of Appledore, which commanded the rivers to Barnstaple and Bideford, being surrendered a few days after, these towns also submitted, with the promise of pardon. The earl of Stamford had protracted the siege of Exeter, with the hope of obtaining relief; but after these successes of the Royalists, as no reinforcements arrived, and his ammunition began to fail, he at length consented to surrender; and the articles were signed on the 5th of September, after a blockade of eight months and nineteen days. Sir John Berkeley was appointed governor by the Prince when he left the city *.

Exeter surrendered.

Sir John Digby, having increased his forces to three hundred foot and eight hundred horse, was sent about the close of the siege to Plymouth, with an order to blockade this garrison; and a short time before he arrived, Sir Alexander Carew, a member of the Parliament, who commanded the fort and island of St. Nicholas in Plymouth harbour, had offered to deliver up his charge to the Royal party, on the promise of pardon; and Sir John Berkeley, who was then lying before Exeter, gave him all the assurance of this in his power: but being unwilling to entrust his safety to any thing short of a written document under the great seal, and as this occasioned delay, a servant in whom he had confided took this opportunity of betraying his design, and he was immediately seized in the fort by the townsmen, sent prisoner to London, and afterwards beheaded on Tower Hill†.

Sir John Digby sent to blockade Plymouth.

The surrender of Exeter having set the army of the Royalists at liberty, as it was the opinion of many that if Prince Maurice had marched immediately to Plymouth this garrison would at that time have been given up, it was a great error that he did not‡. But being unac-

---

* Clarendon, vol. ii. book vii. p. 503. Dugdale's Short View, p. 187. Oliver's Exeter, ch. xiii.

† Clarendon, p. 593. Vicars, part iii. p. 29.   ‡ Clarendon.

Siege of
Dartmouth
by Prince
Maurice.

quainted with the real state of affairs there, he allowed
himself to be persuaded to direct his course to Dartmouth, which was considered as an easy conquest. In
this, however, his expectation was disappointed; for it was
not till after a month's siege, in which he lost many of
his men by sickness, that this garrison surrendered, which
event took place on the 4th of October. On this occasion Sir James Chudleigh, who had joined the Royalists
at Stratton, received a wound from a musket-shot, of
which he soon after died. The Prince, after the surrender, placed a garrison in the town, under the command of
Colonel Seymour, a gentleman of Devonshire, and immediately marched to Plymouth*.

In the mean time Colonel Digby had for several weeks
carried on the blockade of this garrison, having his quarters at Plymstock, and batteries at Oreston and Batten,
and a guard at Hoo, consisting of about three hundred
foot and a troop of horse. By these means all supplies
of provisions from the surrounding country were cut off,
and an attack was planned by the blockading army upon
Mount Stamford, a fort so called after the Parliamentary
general, the Earl of that name. But the garrison of Plymouth having received by sea, on the 31st of September,
an addition to their forces of five hundred men under the
command of Colonel Wardlaw, accompanied by Colonel
Gould, by an unexpected attack defeated the guard at Hoo,
adjoining Mount Stamford, on the 9th of October, took
fifty-four prisoners, including a captain and an ensign,
with three barrels of powder, and put the rest to flight†.

Siege of
Plymouth
by Prince
Maurice.

About this time Prince Maurice arrived, with his army
considerably reduced by the siege of Dartmouth, but still
consisting of five regiments of cavalry and nine regiments
of foot. His head-quarters were at Widey House, and
his troops were stationed at Plympton, Plymstock, Causand, Egg Buckland, Tamarton, &c.‡ He lost no time

* Vicars. Dugdale's Short View, p. 187.
† Narrative of the Siege published in 1644, and attested by Colonel
Gould and the principal officers engaged in the defence of the place.
‡ Vicars. Clarendon, vol. ii. book vii. p. 596.

in making arrangements for an attack on Mount Stamford, the possession of which was indispensable to the success of his attempt upon Plymouth. After the preparatory operations on the part of the assailants, and the equally skilful and determined measures of defence by the assailed, as well as various skirmishes, the assault commenced on Sunday the 5th of November. A battery of upwards of two hundred cannon was kept continually at play by the Royalists, with a force which it was impossible to withstand, and a breach in the works was effected. This however was repaired in the night : but the next day, after the battery had resumed its operations with similar success, about one o'clock a general assault of both horse and foot decided the affair. The captain of the fort having but seven men out of thirty-six remaining to manage the guns, having no provisions, his ammunition being nearly exhausted, and all hope of relief being cut off by the enemy who surrounded him, after the most courageous defence was compelled to surrender. The terms however were honourable. The soldiers were allowed to march out with their arms and colours flying, and the captain with any piece of ordnance which he should choose. The assailants lost four or five officers in the assault and a considerable number of men, whilst the assailed lost among the officers only one lieutenant and a few men with some prisoners which were exchanged the next day *.

On the same day an attempt was made upon the fort at Lipson, but without success.

The loss of Mount Stamford, however, did not in the result prove so serious an injury to the town as was expected; for its defence employed the best troops of the garrison, and exposed them to continual danger ; whereas they were enabled now to concentrate their forces for the defence of the town itself, where they were in greater safety. But unhappily divisions dispirited the inhabitants

* Narrative. Vicars, part iii. p. 75.

BOOK
II.

themselves. A considerable party of Royalists within wished for the surrender of the garrison; and those who had remained neuter, being now terrified with the state of affairs, seemed disposed in this instance in favour of their views. For these reasons, immediately on the surrender of Mount Stamford, Colonel Wardlaw, the commander-in-chief, took possession of the fort and island of St. Nicholas, as well as the castle and magazine, at that time under charge of the mayor, placed them in the hands of Parliamentary officers on whose fidelity and courage he could rely, and furnished them with a liberal supply of provisions and ammunition, of which they had before been destitute. This measure had the best effect; for it gave confidence to the inhabitants, and served to unite them in the defence of the town, as they now saw there was both a determination and ability in their commanders for this purpose. At the same time the leaders of the disaffected were seized and confined, a proceeding which gave additional strength to the unanimity of the people. Taking advantage of this disposition, Colonel Wardlaw proposed to all the inhabitants to engage in a solemn vow and protestation to defend the towns of Plymouth and Stonehouse, and the fort and island of St. Nicholas, to the last extremity; and this protestation was very generally adopted, and sent up to Parliament and registered *.

* A copy of this protestation, which is given at the end of the Narrative of the Siege, and is also preserved by Vicars, (part. iii. p. 77.) is as follows: " I, A. B. in the presence of Almighty God do vow and protest, that I will to the utmost of my power faithfully maintain and defend the towns of Plymouth, Stonehouse, the fort and island, with all the outworks and fortifications to the same belonging, against all forces now raised against the said towns, fort and island, or any part thereof, or that shall be raised by any power or authority whatever, without the consent and authority of both Houses of Parliament; neither will I by any way or means whatsoever contrive or consent to the giving up of the towns and fortifications aforesaid, or any parcel of them, into the hands of any person or persons whatsoever, without the consent of both Houses of Parliament, or of such as are authorized hereunto by them: neither will I raise or consent to the raising of any force or tumult; nor will I by any way or means give or yield to the giving of any advice, counsel, or intelligence to the prejudice of the said towns and fortifications, either in whole or in part; but will withal faithfully discover to the mayor of Ply-

Drawn by J. Gandy, Arch.   Engraved by W. Deeble.

INTERIOR OF THE CHOIR

EXETER CATHEDRAL.

London. Published by Robert Jennings. 63 Cheapside. May 1. 1830.

PLYMOUTH FROM BIRY HILL.

London, Published by Fisher, Son & Co. Newgate Street 1831.

On the 11th of November a party of cavalry and musketeers being sent to Thornhill for the purpose of guarding the wood and hay, disregarding their orders, pursued some cavalry of the Royalists, and killed a captain and a few of the common men; but, having ventured too far in the pursuit, drew upon them the main body of the enemy's horse, and, in their efforts to make good their retreat, Major Leyton, after receiving five wounds, was taken prisoner. And on the 28th of the same month the besiegers planted their battery against Lipson Fort, and cannonaded it for three hours, but without success.

On the 3rd of December a formidable attempt was made by the Royalists on Lara Point, which was eventually defeated with great gallantry by the besieged. Three hours before daybreak four hundred musketeers surprised the guard on that spot, and took three pieces of ordnance; but the alarm being given, one hundred and fifty horse and three hundred musketeers from the town were ready shortly after to fall upon the enemy, when Prince Maurice, with the best part of his army, namely, five regiments of cavalry and four of foot, advanced under protection of their cannon, and the besieged were immediately put to the rout. In their retreat, part of the enemy's horse were mixed with the fugitives, and coming within pistol-shot of the walls, were either killed or taken prisoners. At length a stand being made by the fugitives on the hill above Lipson Fort, and a fresh supply of troops coming to their assistance, they were enabled to maintain their ground for four hours. A summons from the Royalists to the fort to surrender was answered by the cannon; and being again reinforced by a considerable number of troops

mouth, and to the commander-in-chief there, whatsoever design I shall know or hear of hurtful thereunto. Neither have I accepted any pardon or protection, nor will accept any protection from the enemy. And this vow and protestation I make, without any equivocation and mental reservation whatsoever; believing that I cannot be absolved from this my vow and protestation, and wishing no blessing from God on myself or my posterity, if I do not truly and sincerely perform the same. So help me God!"

from the town, the besieged renewed their attack with great spirit on the Royalists, who soon began to retreat, and were driven across the sands at low-water, with the loss of a great part of their number, both horse and foot. The gallantry of the besieged on this occasion was conspicuous, for the number of the assailants exceeded theirs in the proportion of ten to one. The failure of this attempt appears at that time to have saved the town; for had the Royalists maintained the ground which they had gained, the besieged would probably have been obliged to quit their outworks, and the walls of the town, which were then being built and in an unfinished state, were not sufficiently secure to enable them to defend it long *.

The Royalists, being thus repulsed, suffered the besieged, according to their general custom, to remain quiet for fifteen or twenty days; nor did any rencontre take place, except in a trifling attack upon a small outwork, in which they were repulsed, and in numerous light skirmishes, chiefly for cattle which had strayed without the works; or for the sake of bravado, and in ambuscades formed by the guards of the town.

The last attempt of the besiegers.

At length, however, they commenced their preparations for an attack upon Magdalen Fort, in the parish of St. Andrew; and the besieged in the mean time giving additional strength to their works, and finding the batteries of the enemy to be within musket-shot, placed their cannon in a position to counteract them with the greatest effect. And on the 18th of December the Royalists commenced their last attempt by opening a battery on the fort. The besieged, however, having the advantage of higher ground, employed their cannon on the works of the enemy with so much effect, that in two days their batteries were silenced. During the night of the 20th, which being dark and rainy, together with the remissness of the guard, prevented the discovery of their proceedings, the besiegers had raised some works near the fort which might have cut

* Narrative of the Siege. MS. List of the Mayors of Plymouth, with notes.

off its communication with the town; and the next morning the guard, consisting of about sixty men, sallied out with a view of destroying these works, but found them protected by two or three hundred men, and were obliged to desist till assistance arrived. About nine o'clock, a supply of horse and foot being in readiness, they advanced to the attack; and, though twice repulsed, on the accession of some fresh troops eventually took possession of the works with considerable slaughter.

The next day the besiegers were perceived to be preparing to remove their cannon, and on the 25th of December, the day on which the Prince had promised his army an entrance into Plymouth, they withdrew their forces for the present, after the garrison had sustained the siege upwards of three months, from the 15th of September. The town had a day of fasting and humiliation on the loss of Mount Stamford, a thanksgiving on the preservation of Lara Point, and another after the raising of the siege.

When the Royalists had departed, their forces were quartered at Plympton, Modbury, and Tavistock: but in their retreat they cleared the country of provisions, driving off the whole of the cattle, and even burning the corn and hay in the vicinity. Prince Maurice, moreover, caused a proclamation to be published, threatening the usual penalties both to the persons and estates of all who should be concerned in conveying provisions into Plymouth; so that the town was in fact still exposed to the dangers and sufferings of a blockade*.

* The following singular coincidence is related both by Vicars and in the Narrative of the Siege: it is also mentioned in the MS. List of the Mayors of Plymouth. During the latter part of the siege, when the fresh provisions were exhausted and the poor were consequently in great distress, an immense quantity of pilchards came into the harbour within the barbican, which the people took up with great ease in baskets, obtaining by this means not only an ample supply for the time, but also sufficient to be salted for future use. Such an occurrence had never taken place before. The Narrative also commemorates the great humanity and courage of the women during the greatest dangers, who at the risk of their lives brought supplies to the men employed in the garrison.

The principal officers in the army of the Prince on this occasion were the Earls of Marlborough and Newport, Lord Mohun, Lieutenant-general Wagstaff, Major-general Basset, Sir Thomas Hele, Sir Edmund Fortescue, Sir John Grenville, Sir Richard Cave, Sir James Coburne, Sir John Digby, Sir Peter Courtenay, and Sir William Courtenay *.

Visit of the Queen to Exeter.

About the middle of April 1644 the Queen, who had been residing with the King for some time at Oxford, as that city was in danger of a siege by the Parliamentary army under the command of the Earl of Essex, removed to the West, a district in which greater security was expected. Having arrived at Exeter, she was welcomed there with acclamation, and Bedford House was fitted up for her reception. During her stay, on the 16th of June, she gave birth to the Princess Henrietta, who was christened by Dr. Burnett in the cathedral on the 3rd of the ensuing month. In the mean time Essex was making rapid advances towards Devonshire. On the 15th of June Prince Maurice, being informed of his approach, raised the siege of Lyme Regis in Dorsetshire, which had resisted all attempts to reduce it since the 20th of April. On the 26th of June Essex arrived at Chard in Somersetshire, and during his stay there the Queen sent a messenger to him desiring a safe-conduct to Bath for the recovery of her health; and afterwards a second messenger, requesting similar protection for her removal to Bristol; to which Essex returned an answer to the following effect: " That if Her Majesty pleased, he would not only give her a safe-conduct, but attend her himself to London, where she might have the best advice and means for the restoration of her health; but as to either of the other places, he could not obey Her Majesty's desires without direction from Parliament." The irony and gratuitous insult of this answer is to the last degree disgraceful, and is the more extraordinary as utterly opposed to the usual urbanity and

* For all the circumstances of the siege here enumerated, see Narrative of the Siege *passim*, and Vicars's Parl. Chron. part iii. p. 111.

generosity of disposition for which Essex is said to have been remarkable. The Queen in her situation at that time was surely entitled to humane and liberal treatment even from an enemy; and from one whose best feelings were not for the moment annihilated by the fatal influence of civil commotions or fanaticism, would certainly have obtained it. On the 5th of July the Earl arrived at Tiverton, and as he was then too near for the Queen's safety, about the 10th of this month she left Exeter, and proceeded under the protection of Prince Maurice into Cornwall, whence she embarked on the 14th at Falmouth in a Flemish ship, accompanied by a number of other vessels sent by the Prince of Orange. Warwick, the Parliamentary admiral, had ordered several ships to wait at Torbay to intercept her passage; but the wind being favourable, though one of his frigates approached so near as to discharge several shots at Her Majesty's ships, she escaped, and landed the next day at Le Conquest, a small town in Little Britanny *.

No military operations of any note took place this year in Devonshire till the arrival of Essex, except before Plymouth. But about the time that the Queen commenced her journey into the West, in the middle of April, Sir Richard Grenville advanced with his forces, consisting of horse and foot, within two miles of that garrison; when Colonel Martin, at that time governor of the town, marched out with the greater part of the troops under his command, and after a sharp contest took two companies prisoners, two barrels of powder, and forty of the cavalry. About two days after, Sir Richard's cavalry again advanced towards the town, and were again repulsed by troops from the garrison, and pursued to Plympton Bridge, near which the army was stationed †. And in the beginning of July he was defeated a third time not far from Plymouth. The

SirRichard Grenville's defeats before Plymouth.

* Rushworth's Historical Collections, part iii. vol. ii. p. 672—684. Historical Discourses, by Sir Edward Walker, pp. 11 and 41 & 42. Oliver's Exeter, ch. xiii. Clarendon, vol. ii. part ii. p. 765.
† Vicars, part iii. pp. 215, 216.

garrison offering to take the field with Lord Roberts the
Parliamentary general, who was ordered into Cornwall, a
party of them proceeded about seven miles from the town,
beat up the quarters of the Royalists, and took part of their
cavalry prisoners; being afterwards pursued by Sir Richard
Grenville, his troops were repulsed in great disorder and
with considerable loss: Major Wisheart and Colonel Arundel were killed, Colonel Digby wounded, and Sir Richard
Grenville himself escaped with difficulty *.

Proceed-
ings of the
Earl of Es-
sex in De-
vonshire.

About the same time, while the Earl of Essex was at
Tiverton, Prince Maurice having drawn off the greater
part of the garrison from Barnstaple to attend the Queen,
the townsmen rose and took possession of it; and when
the Prince sent Colonel Digby with some forces to that
town, they were repulsed with loss.   The townsmen had
applied to Essex for assistance, and the Earl dispatched
Lord Roberts with a strong party of horse, who placed
the garrison there in a state of security †.

Essex made no attempt upon Exeter, but protracted
his stay at Tiverton to the 18th of July, and about this
time a skirmish took place between the Earl's horse and
Lord Paulet at Cheriton, where the latter suffered considerable loss ‡.   In the mean time Prince Maurice, after
attending the Queen, had drawn his forces together and
fixed his quarters at Oakhampton, his army being increased by additions from the besiegers at Plymouth to
five thousand foot and two thousand cavalry. With these
troops, about the 18th of July, he returned to Crediton,
being resolved either to give battle to Essex, or prevent
his advancing. The King, however, was at the same time
in pursuit of the Earl with a considerable army; and Prince
Maurice hearing that His Majesty had advanced to Il-
chester, marched the whole of his forces to Heavitree
near Exeter, intending to wait there for orders from the
King. On the same day Essex removed his quarters, with

* Vicars, part iii. pp. 265, 266.
† Ibid. Rushworth, part iii. vol. ii. p. 684.
‡ Rushworth, part iii. vol. ii. p. 690. Whitelocke, p. 92.

an intention either to surprise the Prince at Crediton, or to raise the siege of Plymouth *.

But upon news of the King's approach, and the junction of Lord Hopton's forces with the Royal army, the Earl of Essex called a council of war, in which it was determined to march immediately to the relief of Plymouth, and thence into Cornwall, where the vicinity of the sea would afford greater facility of obtaining supplies, or of escape. This measure, however, was in direct opposition to the wish of the Earl of Essex, whose first design was to return and give battle to the King; a design in which the superiority of his own judgement was afterwards discovered: but he was prevailed upon to alter his intention, chiefly by Lord Roberts of Lanhydroc, a man of great powers but of an intractable disposition, who had persuaded the Earl that by his influence in Cornwall more favourable pros pects of success were presented in that county †. Some time before this, Prince Maurice had appeared before Plymouth, but after a short stay had raised the siege, and left the charge of the blockade to Sir Richard Grenville. On the approach of the Earl of Essex with his army, that general abandoned the blockade, and at the same time withdrew the garrison from Mount Stamford, which had been occupied by the Royalists since its capture in the preceding November. And on the 23rd of July the Earl of Essex sent a party to attack Sir Richard Grenville's house at Tavistock, at that time garrisoned, which was soon taken with two hundred prisoners, some cannon, a considerable quantity of muskets, plate, and money to the amount of £3000 ‡.

On the 26th §, Essex entered Cornwall, after a stout resistance from Sir Richard Grenville at Newbridge; and

CHAP.
II.

Charles I.
arrives at
Exeter:

* Walker, p. 42.
† Clarendon, vol. ii. part ii. p. 765.
‡ Vicars. Rushworth, part iii. vol. ii. p. 690.
§ Walker says the 20th; but this must be a mistake, as it is inconsistent not only with the other account, but with his own observation, that Essex was making his way into Cornwall at the moment the King was at Exeter, which was on the 26th. p. 47.

on the same day the King, after stopping a night at Honiton, arrived at Exeter, where he was received with every
demonstration of attachment.   About a mile from the city
he was met by Prince Maurice, the Earl of Bristol, Lord
Paulet, Sir John Berkeley, governor of the city, and most
of the principal gentlemen and commissioners of the two
counties of Somerset and Devon. At the city gates he was
welcomed by the mayor and aldermen and a vast con-
course of people with great joy and acclamation. He went
immediately to Bedford House, where he first saw his in-
fant daughter Henrietta.   In the afternoon of the same
day a council was held, in which it was resolved to follow
the Earl of Essex into Cornwall, and the next morning
the King proceeded to Crediton*. Here he reviewed, on
the 27th, the army of Prince Maurice, consisting of four
thousand well armed infantry, and made a general muster
of his forces.   On the 29th he proceeded to Bow, a small
village, where he quartered that night, having no provisions but what had been left by Prince Maurice, who

enters
Cornwall.

was a day's march in advance of him.   On the 30th he
proceeded to Oakhampton, and the next day quartered at
Lifton, near the Tamar; and on the 1st of August entered
Cornwall by Polston Bridge†.

In the mean time the Earl of Essex, in a state of uncertainty as to the King's intentions, had proceeded to
Bodmin, and thence to Lostwithiel, where, after a skirmish
with the forces of Sir Richard Grenville, he took possession of Fowey, the harbour of which was convenient
for the purpose of obtaining a supply of provisions by sea.
The King was quartered at Liskeard, and several skirmishes
took place, in which some of the officers of Essex were
taken prisoners.

The tide
of events
turns
against
Essex.

The tide had now turned against the Earl, and his
situation became precarious. In the beginning of his expedition into the West he had been successful in all his proceedings; by his engaging and popular behaviour he had

* Walker, p. 47.   Rushworth, part iii. vol. ii. p. 690.   Clarendon.
† Walker, pp. 48 & 49.

ingratiated himself with the people, and the eastern part of CHAP. Devonshire had furnished considerable additions to his II. forces*. But the army of Waller, who had for some time attended the marches of the King, was now defeated and dispersed, and His Majesty was consequently at liberty to join his forces with those of Prince Maurice and others in the West, without danger of an attack upon his rear. The flattering prospects of success and accession to his forces which Lord Roberts had engaged to substantiate by his influence in Cornwall, had entirely disappeared, as the Earl now found no county was more favourable to the King. Between the Parliament and the Earl a misunderstanding had also for some time taken place. He had undertaken this journey into the West in opposition to the express orders of the Parliament; and though they did not venture to resent this, they had before, as well as since, treated him with considerable indignity. Notwithstanding this mutual jealousy, he now wrote to the Parliament for assistance; stating that the King, having arrived in Cornwall, had taken measures for preventing his obtaining the necessary supplies of provisions; and as in this country, from the nature of its inclosures, a general engagement could not be attempted with any rational prospect of success, he requested that an army might be immediately sent into the West to fall upon the King's rear. The request was reasonable, but was followed by no beneficial result. Colonel Middleton was indeed afterwards sent by the Parliament with two thousand cavalry, but was too late, as the contest was decided before his arrival.

At this time Lord Wilmot, a popular general in the King's army, was sent a prisoner to Exeter on the charge of high treason, but as nothing serious could be alleged against him, it was not the King's intention to proceed to extremities; and on the same day Lord Percy, another general officer, was removed and Lord Hopton appointed

* Whitelocke.

BOOK
II.

The King
tries the
fidelity of
Essex.

to the command in his place, which was a promotion generally approved *.

Thinking this to be a favourable opportunity for attempting the fidelity of Essex, the King with his own
hand wrote him a letter on the 6th of August, with a view
to induce him to bring over his forces to the Royal party,
assuring him of his anxious desire of peace, and making
the most advantageous offers " on the word of a king,"
which was a favourite expression of Charles, usually annexed to his promises. And, as this had no effect, on the
8th the officers of the army, with Prince Maurice at their
head, addressed another letter to the Earl, pledging themselves for the fulfilment of the overtures of the King. The
answer of the Earl, which did honour to his firmness and
consistency, was to this effect; That it was not in his
commission to be concerned in a treaty, nor could he betray the trust committed to him by the Parliament. He
immediately sent to the Parliament the letters which he
had received, and on the 18th of that month a day of prayer
was appointed by the two Houses for the safety of his
army. Shortly after he wrote another letter to the Parliament, giving an account of an attempt to blow up his
magazine, which had very nearly taken effect, and de-
claring that the army which could hold out longest against
the want of provisions must prove victorious †.

The Earl
of Essex
escapes to
Plymouth.

In short, after various skirmishes and movements of
both armies in sight of each other, without either of them
venturing to commence an attack for eight or ten days,
the King contrived to make such a disposition of the
forces under the command of Prince Maurice, Sir Richard
Grenville, and himself, that the Earl of Essex was inclosed
in the vicinity of Fowey, and all means of obtaining the
necessary supplies were cut off not only by land but by
sea; so that, finding that in a few days he should be destitute
of provisions, he gave orders to Sir William Balfour, the

* Clarendon, vol. ii. part ii. p. 766. Rushworth, p. 693.
† Rushworth, part iii. vol. ii. pp. 692, 693. Walker, p. 49.

commander of his cavalry, to break through the King's army, and make his escape in the best manner possible: and though the King by means of deserters had intelligence of this design, and had arranged his forces in two columns near the route by which they must pass, the whole of the cavalry in the night, which fortunately for them was rendered more obscure by mist and rain, escaped through them in silence without the firing of a musket. In the morning they were discovered at a distance, and pursued with some loss, but passed through Devonshire with little molestation, and arrived safe in London. The next day, the 1st of September, the Earl of Essex made his escape with his principal officers from Fowey by sea to Plymouth, leaving General Skippon with the infantry to make the best terms he could. The officers and men were allowed to march, unarmed, attended by a guard, to Poole in Dorsetshire, and the stores surrendered were found to consist of thirty-eight pieces of cannon, one hundred barrels of powder, and about six thousand stand of arms*. The Earl of Essex remained two days at Plymouth, and having appointed Lord Roberts governor of that garrison, proceeded to London, where he was received by the Parliament with no diminution of respect.

Colonel Middleton, with the Parliamentary forces sent for the relief of Essex, arrived in Devonshire about the time of the capitulation, and on the 3rd of September was within eight miles of Torrington. Sir William Balfour, with the fugitive horse, was quartered at Egg Buckland in his route from Cornwall, and on the 4th of September had a skirmish with Sir John Berkeley at Tiverton, which was then in his possession; and on the following day, finding themselves in danger, the cavalry of Colonel Middleton and Sir William Balfour made their escape over Exmoor to Taunton†.

Colonel Middleton arrives in Devonshire.

On the 4th of September the King, having given orders for the cannon and ammunition to be sent after him,

The King returns.

* Clarendon, vol. ii. part ii. p. 767. Rushworth. Walker, pp. 79, 80.
† Walker, p. 80.

BOOK
II.

marched his forces to Liskeard, and the next day crossed the Tamar and quartered at Tavistock, where he stayed several days to collect his forces, to refresh the infantry, and to wait for the arrival of the arms and ammunition taken in Cornwall. During his stay there, at the request of the gentlemen in the vicinity who were his friends, the King, with little expectation of success, reluctantly consented to proceed to Plymouth with the design of obtaining possession of that garrison.

The King
before Ply-
mouth.

Accordingly on the 9th of September His Majesty left Tavistock, and quartered that night within four miles of Plymouth, and the next day advanced near the town. The forces of the King were quartered near Magdalen Fort, those of Prince Maurice at Lipson Works, and the King himself occupied Widey House. On the 11th His Majesty summoned the town to surrender, offering a general pardon, and freedom from a garrison, except in the Fort and Island of St. Nicholas. To this the following answer was returned the next day.

" May it please Your Majesty

" The town of Plymouth is kept for the service of the King and Parliament ; to which purpose we intend to defend it to the utmost of our power against all violence and hostility which shall be urged upon us, the soldiers and inhabitants of this town having several times by solemn oaths obliged themselves thereunto ; and doubt not of enjoying still that Divine protection which thus long hath blest their arms.

" JAMES KERR,
" JOHN CAWSE, Mayor."

At a council of war it was determined, for want of sufficient forces, not to attempt an assault or a close siege; and the blockade was again committed to Sir Richard Grenville, whose forces, however, did not at that time exceed five hundred foot and three hundred horse; though this number was afterwards increased, and Plymouth suffered much distress from the blockade. On the 14th the

King drew off his army from Plymouth, and returned to Tavistock, having lost thirteen men [*].

In the mean time General Goring, a distinguished officer of the King, with a party of cavalry had summoned Barnstaple, which was then in distress for want of ammunition and provisions. But before an answer could be returned, Sir Francis Doddington had taken possession of Ilfracombe, with twenty pieces of cannon, twenty barrels of powder, and about two hundred stand of arms. This greatly facilitated the success of the attack on Barnstaple, which surrendered on the 17th of September on the conditions proposed by the garrison, who left on their departure fifty pieces of cannon and a considerable quantity of small arms [†].

On the 16th the King marched his forces to Oakhampton, and the next day himself, with his own troop and the principal officers of his Court, proceeded to Exeter, leaving the army to return by easy marches through Crediton, Bradninch and Collumpton to Tiverton, where they were quartered on the 21st. His Majesty remained at Exeter nearly a week, in order to provide clothing and other necessaries for the army, which was considerably reduced in numbers, and had become discontented for want of their pay. The money requisite for these purposes was raised by a levy on the several towns of Devonshire. Whilst here, the King also appointed some troops in proper stations to protect the city from incursions by the Parliamentarians from the garrisons of Lyme and Taunton. Having arranged these affairs, and leaving at Exeter the greater part of the artillery taken in Cornwall, on the 23rd of September he proceeded to Honiton, and overtaking his army on the road from that place, quartered the same night at Chard [‡]. The Princess Henrietta remained at Exeter.

In the month of October Sir Richard Cholmondeley, who had been left at Axminster with a party of horse

CHAP. II.

Goring takes possession of Barnstaple.

The King at Exeter on his return.

[*] Walker, pp. 84 & 85.　　　　[†] Ibid.
[‡] Walker, p. 87. Clarendon, vol. ii. part ii. p. 765 &c.

BOOK
II.

Fresh as-
sault on
Plymouth
by Gren-
ville.

Mount
Stamford
retaken by
the gar-
rison.

Prince
Charles at
Barn-
staple.

waiting for orders to assist in blockading Lyme, was attacked by some forces of the Parliamentarians, when he
himself was killed in the skirmish *.

In the beginning of the year 1645 the blockade of
Plymouth still continued; and on the 10th of January Sir
Richard Grenville alarmed that garrison by an unexpected
assault at eleven o'clock at night, in four several quarters
at once, with about six thousand troops; and from the
suddenness of the attack, though the victory was severely
contested, he gained possession of the four principal outworks. From these, however, he was speedily dislodged
by the brave and vigorous exertions of the garrison, and
was repulsed with great loss, having many slain and more
wounded. By this defeat his forces were greatly dispirited.
And about the same time Sydenham House, which was
garrisoned by the Royalists, was taken by Colonel Hol-
born, with about one hundred prisoners, among whom were
several officers and persons of distinction †.

A short time after this, fresh advantages were gained by
the garrison of Plymouth. On the 18th of February
Mount Stamford was retaken from the Royalists, with
three hundred stand of arms, and Sir Richard Grenville
was again defeated. This victory was reckoned of so much
importance that a day of thanksgiving was appointed on
the occasion ‡.

Lord Roberts was governor of Plymouth at this time,
and in the month of May the garrison petitioned the Parliament for his continuance in that office. But this being
refused, it was ordered that the government of the town
should be lodged in the hands of five of the principal inhabitants, and Colonel Kerr was appointed the military
governor §. Sir Richard Grenville was superseded in the
command of the forces in this vicinity, and the blockade
was committed to Sir John Berkeley in the month of June.

In the same month, the plague being at Bristol, Prince
Charles, who had been appointed general-in-chief of the

* Walker, p. 87.   † Vicars, iv. 96.   ‡ Ibid. p. 112.
§ Whitelocke, p. 140.

Royal forces in the West, removed to Barnstaple; and
tidings of the fatal battle of Naseby arrived whilst he remained in that town. Lord Goring was defeated by Sir
Thomas Fairfax in Somersetshire, and arrived also at
Barnstaple in the month of July. The above disasters,
as might be expected, spread the greatest consternation
among the Royalists in Devonshire and Cornwall. In
August and September the Prince was at Exeter, and in
the latter month the blockade of Plymouth was again en-
trusted to Sir John Digby*.

About this time the Club-men, who were numerous in
the West, and capable of rendering important service to
whatever party they might support, having shown during
the successes of the King a disposition to unite their efforts in his favour, after the victories of Sir Thomas Fairfax, declared themselves on the side of the Parliament†;
and from this period nothing but a continual series of
disasters attended the cause of Royalty. Nor will this
appear to be extraordinary, when the conduct of the King's
principal generals and his forces is considered. Goring was
an officer of great courage and military talents, but un-
principled, and actuated by an unbounded propensity to
licentiousness and debauchery. When not engaged in
battle, himself and his officers spent their time in the most
scandalous disorders; and his followers, imbibing the spirit
of their leader, lived at free quarters, and plundered without restraint both friends and foes. Nor were the rapacity,
oppression and extravagance of Sir Richard Grenville less
notorious, and the commissioners of Devonshire laid before the Prince repeated complaints of his conduct. These
were grievances, however, which the Prince wanted either
ability or inclination to redress. Nothing could form a
stronger contrast to all this than the character of the Parliamentary army. Consisting chiefly of Independents and
fanatics, they were fired by religious enthusiasm and the

The Club-men join SirThomas Fairfax.

Shameful conduct of the King's officers and of his armies.

* Clarendon. † Whitelocke. Vicars, iv. p. 196.

BOOK
II.
love of freedom; when not employed in military duty, their time was spent in devotional exercises, and they went into the field of battle chanting psalms. To the disorders and licentiousness of the Royal forces were added dissensions, jealousies and fears among all the officers. Another obstacle to the success of the Royalists served also not a little to increase the difficulties and dangers of their situation. The contributions raised in Devonshire, to the amount of £2000 weekly, were by no means adequate to the expenses of the blockade of Plymouth, the support of the several garrisons in the county, and other military demands. Circumstances so disheartening, together with the late important victories of the Parliamentarians in other quarters, left little room for the Royalists in the West to expect a more favourable result of their future exertions *.

SirThomas Fairfax enters Devonshire.

In the midst of these disasters Sir Thomas Fairfax entered Devonshire; and though the Royalists had then most of the garrisons in the county in their possession, as Tiverton, Exeter, Dartmouth, Barnstaple, and Torrington, he found no difficulty in speedily reducing the whole of Devonshire as well as Cornwall to subjection.

Skirmish with Goring.

On the 11th of October Fairfax was at Chard, and on the 13th, part of his army advanced to Axminster. Intelligence having arrived that Goring with fifteen hundred horse had formed the design of forcing his way through these troops, or breaking up their quarters that night, with the intention, if possible, of joining the King, Commissary-general Ireton gave orders to the troops to be in readiness for his reception. This design, however, was not carried into execution; for Goring, together with Lord Wentworth, Lord Miller, and the best part of their cavalry, having left their quarters near Exeter, and passing through Honiton about twelve o'clock at night, arrived on Blackdown, fell in with a detached part of Ireton's troops,

* Clarendon.

and after taking prisoners about forty foot and twenty dragoons, favoured by the darkness of the night, made their escape [*].

On the 14th Sir Thomas Fairfax and the main army marched from Chard, through Axminster, to Honiton, and lay on their arms that night in a field, waiting for Goring; but no attempt being made, the next day they proceeded to Collumpton, where Lord Miller was with three hundred dragoons and other forces, who on the approach of Fairfax took flight: they were pursued, and some prisoners were taken.

Having gained information from the prisoners that their party were gone to Tiverton, Sir Thomas gave orders to General Massey with some cavalry, and Colonel Welden with a brigade of foot, to besiege that garrison; and these troops soon possessed themselves of the town, but not of the church and castle, which were strongly fortified. After stationing some troops at Bradninch, Silverton, and Columb-John, with a view to obstruct the supplies to Exeter, and to prevent the Royal troops advancing eastward, General Fairfax on the 17th proceeded with his army to Tiverton. After the refusal of the governor, Sir Gilbert Talbot, to surrender, four batteries were opened on the 19th; and whilst a council of war was sitting, in which it was determined to storm the garrison that afternoon, a ball struck the chain of the drawbridge, which immediately fell; and, without waiting for orders, the troops rushed forwards and speedily made themselves masters first of the churchyard, and soon afterwards both of the church and the castle. Sir Gilbert Talbot, after a brave defence, was taken prisoner, with about twenty other officers and two hundred soldiers. Among the former was Major Sadler. This officer having formerly belonged to the Parlia mentary army, received sentence of death for his treachery; but finding means to make his escape, he fled to Exeter, and being there detected, it is said, in some traitorous

CHAP.
II.

SirThomas
Fairfax at
Honiton.

Tiverton
besieged
and taken.

[*] Sprigge's England's Recovery, part iii. chap. iii. p. 134. Rushworth's Historical Collections, part iv. vol. i. p. 94.

correspondence, he was shot on Southernhay. There was now no garrison in the interest of the King between Exeter and London to interrupt the progress of the Parliamentary forces *.

Troops sta-
tioned near
Exeter.

Tiverton being thus reduced, on the 20th of October, Sir Thomas Fairfax with his army removed to Silverton and the parts adjacent, where at a council of war, though his first intention was to besiege Exeter, it was now re-solved to relinquish that design for the present, to station troops in the vicinity of the city, to cut off all intercourse with the surrounding country, and annoy the eastern parts of the county. On the 22nd they marched to Newton St. Cyres, where intelligence arrived that Goring had re-moved the night before from Exeter to Oakhampton; and the next day they proceeded to Crediton, and were in-formed that he had retreated to Tavistock. On Sunday the 26th, General Fairfax returned to Silverton, the next day proceeded to Topsham, and stationed garrisons at Bishop's Clyst, Stoke Canon, and Poltimore †.

Sir Thomas
Fairfax
quarters at
Ottery St.
Mary.

As the winter was advancing and the troops of Fairfax wanted rest and refreshment, he proceeded to Ottery St. Mary, and fixed his head-quarters there for several weeks. About the time of his arrival there he received intelligence that Lord Goring's cavalry, to the amount of nearly five thousand, were arrived in the South Hams, being quartered at Totnes, Newton Bushel, and so near as Chudleigh, and that Lord Grenville had returned from Cornwall with a fresh supply of foot to Oakhampton. But the King's generals had for some time been weary of the war, and a trumpeter now arrived from Prince Charles, requesting a safe passage for Lord Hopton and Lord Culpepper to the King on a pacific message; and another messenger ar-rived from Lord Goring, with a proposal for both armies to unite and compel the King and Parliament to agree to terms of pacification. Both applications were unsuccess-

* Sprigge, p. 136–144. Rushworth, part iv. vol. i. p. 94. Vicars, iv. p. 300.
† Sprigge, pp. 147, 148. Rushworth, p. 94.

ful.   Fairfax was at Ottery from the 15th of November
to the 2nd of December; and whilst there, great sickness
prevailed in his army, carrying off eight or nine daily for
several weeks. Some of these were officers, among whom
was Colonel Pickering[*].

During this time, the attempts to obtain peace proving
abortive, Lord Goring took shipping at Dartmouth for
France, with a design, it is said, of procuring fresh
troops for the spring, leaving the command of his cavalry to Lord Wentworth. And the King's generals, encouraged by the mortality in the army of Sir Thomas Fairfax, exerted their best efforts to raise a fresh supply of
forces both in Devonshire and Cornwall under the command of Prince Charles. Proclamations were issued for
this purpose; and by drafts from the quarters near Plymouth, and some infantry from Dartmouth and Barnstaple,
together with the recruits raised by Sir Richard Grenville
in Cornwall, they had collected together a formidable body
of troops, amounting to about nine or ten thousand, which
were quartered at Tavistock and Oakhampton, with two
thousand under the command of Sir Richard Grenville.
With these forces it was their design to compel Sir Thomas
Fairfax to desist from the blockade of Exeter[†].

On the 6th of December, on account of the sickness in
his army, the general removed his forces to Tiverton, which
was supposed to be a more healthy situation. And the
next day, having intelligence of the enemy's design, after
a council of war, some troops were sent under the command of Sir Hardress Waller to take possession of Crediton, and the blockade of the eastern side of Exeter was
committed to him. An attempt was made on the 14th
by a small party on Powderham, where the King had a
garrison, but without success. A temporary garrison was
formed by the besiegers in the church, and victualled from
Nutwell House, which was also a garrison of the Parliament, but was soon evacuated. And during the month of

Margin notes: Goring goes to France. Fresh recruits added to the Royal forces under Prince Charles.
Fairfax removes to Tiverton.
Several garrisons taken from the King.

* Sprigge, p. 151. Rushworth, p. 95.   † Sprigge.

December Sir Thomas Fairfax took three strong garrisons belonging to the King, Fulford House, Canon Teign, and one called Callington House, which is said to have been west of Exeter. The command of the two former were given to Colonel O'Key, who had a skirmish with some of the King's troops near Chumleigh, and took Lord Chichester's house at Eggesford. Sir Thomas Fairfax had a rendezvous of his army at Cadbury Fort on the 26th of December, and on the 29th Ashburton was taken, and garrisoned for the Parliament *.

A bribe offered to Colonel Kerr to betray Plymouth.

We are informed by Vicars, that in the month of January 1646, Colonel Kerr, who was then governor of Plymouth, was offered by Sir John Digby £10,000 to deliver up that garrison, which had so long resisted all attempts to reduce it, to the King's troops. This offer was immediately rejected; the governor was presented with £500 by the Parliament, and assured of further preferment. And on the 1st or 2nd of this month the garrison of Plymouth took what Vicars calls Canterbury (probably Kinterbury) Fort, near the town, and afterwards the church and churchyard of St. Budeaux, with one hundred and forty prisoners, among whom were Major Stukeley and other officers†.

The head-quarters of the Parliamentary army continued at Tiverton till the 8th of January, on which day Sir Thomas Fairfax proceeded on the march westward to Moreton; but Sir Hardress Waller, with two regiments, intending to mislead the enemy respecting the route of the main army, advanced to Bow, where in a skirmish he took some prisoners; whilst at the same time a detachment of horse and foot under the command of Lieutenant-general Cromwell proceeded that night to Crediton, and on the 9th to Bovey Tracey, where he fell in with a part of Lord Wentworth's brigade, and dispersed them. On this occasion were taken by the Parliamentarians four colonels, three lieutenant-colonels, five majors, eleven

Success of Cromwell at Bovey Tracey.

* Sprigge, p. 157–160.
† Parl. Chron. iv. pp. 339, 340. Sprigge, p. 163.

captains and other officers; four hundred horse; three hundred stand of arms, and one hundred prisoners of the common soldiers, besides one hundred and fifty head of cattle and other provisions intended for the relief of Exeter. Cromwell pursued the fugitives to Ilsington, where they had occupied the church, which they quitted on his approach[*].

On the 10th Fairfax proceeded with his army to Ashburton, and the next day to Totnes, which was quitted by the King's forces on his approach. Whilst halting there, and preparing for the siege of Dartmouth, he sent strong detachments of troops in pursuit of the King's forces towards Tavistock; and on the approach of this party towards Plymouth, thinking it to be the van of the whole army, they hastily quitted their works in the vicinity of Plymouth, and finally abandoned the blockade of that garrison. About this time also the garrison of Oakhampton was reduced. Prince Charles and many of the King's troops fled into Cornwall[†].

About the same time Sir Francis Drake's house, which was strongly fortified by the King's troops, was also taken[‡].

Whilst staying at Totnes, Sir Thomas Fairfax having called together by proclamation the friends of the Parliament in the county, about three thousand attended, out of whom he formed a regiment, which was placed under the command of Colonel Fowell. On the 12th of January he sent two regiments with orders to besiege the garrison of Dartmouth, on the 18th followed them himself with his army, and the summons to surrender being refused, commenced storming the town about eleven o'clock the same night. The Parliamentary Vice-admiral Batten, who happened to be lying with a squadron in the vicinity, assisted materially at the siege. The contest was vigorous and severe, but short; and the town and castle, Townstall church,

CHAP. II.

Blockade of Plymouth finally abandoned.

Dartmouth besieged and taken.

---

[*] Vicars, iv. p. 341. Rushworth, part iv. vol. i. p. 96. Sprigge, p. 164.
[†] Vicars, pp. 341, 348. Rushworth, part iv. vol. i. p. 96. Clarendon.
[‡] Vicars, iv. p. 348.

BOOK
II.

Mount Boone, and Kingswear Fort were surrendered the next day. About one thousand prisoners were also taken, with one hundred and twenty cannon mounted, and two ships of war. On this occasion the general behaved with his accustomed moderation and humanity. The Cornish prisoners were set at liberty, and two shillings allowed to each to carry them home. Commissioners were also appointed to restore the property taken belonging to those who had adhered to the Parliament in the town. The general received the warm thanks of the Parliament for this victory. After the conclusion of this affair, a French ship, not knowing that the garrison was taken, entered the harbour with dispatches from the Queen, Lord Goring, and others; and though the captain, when he discovered the real state of the case, threw the packet overboard, according to his orders, it was afterwards recovered, and the letters were sent up to the Parliament, by which means some important discoveries were made [*].

Lord Hopton appointed commander-in-chief of the King's forces.

On the 15th of January Lord Hopton, one of the most respectable of the King's generals, was appointed commander-in-chief of the Royal forces; Lord Wentworth ordered to command the foot; and Prince Charles about this time began to exercise his authority with some wholesome severity, by committing Grenville to prison, first at Launceston and then at St. Michael's Mount, for refusing an appointment to command the foot. But measures of prudence and vigour were now too late: the King's cause was becoming every day more desperate [†].

Powderham surrendered.

On the 19th the army of Fairfax began to move forward, but returned to Totnes on the 21st, marched to Newton Bushel on the 24th, and the next day to Chudleigh; and on the same day Powderham Castle surrendered to Colonel Hammond, who had been sent with a detachment to take possession of it; and soon after the Royalists are said to have abandoned a garrison at Sir

[*] Sprigge, p. 165–177. Vicars, iv. p. 348–352. Rushworth, part iv. vol. i. p. 96–99.

[†] Clarendon, vol. ii. pp. 559, 560.

Peter Byrne's [*]. On the 27th of January Exeter was summoned, but refused to surrender; nor was the siege attempted at that time, as the army was called off by Lord Hopton's forces in the north. Detachments, however, were stationed at several places west of Exeter, and Colonel Shapcote began to blockade Exmouth; so that by these, together with the garrisons already mentioned, the approaches to the city were obstructed on all sides. The command of the blockading forces was given to Sir Hardress Waller, who fixed his head-quarters at Alphington in the beginning of February.

Lord Hopton had proceeded to Cornwall for the purpose of increasing his forces, and of collecting provisions for the relief of Exeter, which was now reduced to distress. He returned on the 6th of February, and fixed his quarters at Torrington, where he had not continued above four days before Sir Thomas Fairfax approached with his army. On the 10th this general was at Crediton, where he continued, waiting for fresh supplies, till the 14th. Thence he proceeded to Chumleigh within eight miles of Torrington, with an army of six thousand foot, three thousand horse, and five hundred dragoons. On the 16th he had a general rendezvous of his forces at Ashreigny within six miles of Torrington, and on his march took Mr. Rolle's house at Stephenstone, which was then occupied by a party of the King's dragoons. Such was the negligence of the officers and soldiers in the vicinity, that Lord Hopton was ignorant of his approach; but as soon as the news arrived, he lost no time in making the best preparation for a defence of the place, which so short a notice would allow, by drawing together as large a number of horse as possible within, and stationing the rest on a common on the east side of the town. Sir Thomas Fairfax arrived the same evening, and about eight o'clock the attack began. After a severe contest for about an hour, Lord Hopton's cavalry were driven into the town, the barricadoes were passed, and such was the consternation of the troops

CHAP.
II.

Approaches to Exeter blockaded.

Torrington taken by Fairfax.

* Whitelocke.

within, who were at the same time in part disaffected, that the whole, both horse and foot, immediately fled, leaving their general with a few other officers to provide for their own safety. Lord Hopton and Lord Cassel were both wounded on this occasion, and fled into Cornwall. The next day a terrible occurrence took place : a number of prisoners were confined in the church, where was the magazine with about eighty barrels of powder. These, whether by accident or design is unknown*, were set on fire; blew up the church and a great part of the houses in the town; killed about two hundred prisoners, and some of the assailants in the churchyard. Six hundred prisoners, three thousand stand of arms, and the whole of the baggage and money fell into the hands of the victors. A thanksgiving was appointed in London for this victory, which may be justly considered, indeed, as the *coup de grace* to the cause of the King in the West†.

On the 17th of February Sir Thomas Fairfax sent a party to take possession of Holsworthy, then in possession of the King's forces; and on the 19th he placed a garrison at Tavistock House, and returned to Stephenstone, Torrington being in a state of desolation through the late explosion at the church.

Fairfax enters Cornwall and subdues it.

Lord Hopton remained two or three days at Stratton, where he was joined by about a thousand or twelve hundred foot, part of his scattered forces. The army of Sir Thomas Fairfax followed on the 23rd. On his approach Prince Charles fled to Scilly, and afterwards into France. Lord Hopton also retired as Fairfax advanced: on the 11th of March the small number of forces which he had been able to collect were disbanded and dispersed, and the whole of Cornwall speedily reduced without bloodshed to subjection to the Parliament‡.

---

* Vicars gives credit to a report that Lord Hopton gave £20 to one of his party to set fire to the powder: but Vicars was a fanatic and a violent partizan, and therefore easily misled.

† Clarendon, vol. ii. p. 561. Vicars, iv. p. 365–367. Rushworth, part iv. vol. i. p. 100. Sprigge, p. 185.

‡ Rushworth, p. 104–110. Clarendon, vol. ii. p. 564–566. Vicars, iv. p. 400. Sprigge, p. 202.

On the 15th of March the fort of Exmouth surrendered, with thirteen pieces of iron ordnance, seventy-two
muskets, and twelve barrels of powder. Powderham had
surrendered to Colonel Hammond in the month of January,
but it should seem was afterwards again occupied by the
Royalists, if the statement of Vicars be correct, that it
was retaken about the middle of this month by Sir Hardress Waller *.

On his return from Cornwall Sir Thomas Fairfax visited
Plymouth on the 25th of March, and met his army at Oakhampton on their route from that county on the 28th. The
next day they marched to Crediton, which they quitted on
the 30th, and proceeded, himself to Columb-John, and the
army to Silverton.   On the 31st the general summoned
Exeter; and at a council of war, called by Sir John
Berkeley the governor, as the city was in want of provisions, and as an attempt to defend it would serve no purpose
but to occasion the loss of many lives and every way increase the distress, it was agreed to negotiate upon honourable terms. Commissioners were appointed for that purpose; on the part of Sir Thomas Fairfax,—Lieutenant-
General Hammond, Colonel Sir Hardress Waller, Colonel
Edward Harley, Colonel Lambert, Commissary General
Stane, and Major Watson; and in behalf of the city,—Sir
Henry Berkeley, Sir George Cary, Colonel Ashburnham,
Colonel Godolphin, Captain Fitzgerald, Mr. John Weare,
Mr. Robert Walker, and Mr. Thomas Knight. Previously
to the commencement of the negotiations three forts were
delivered up to Sir Thomas Fairfax,—St. Downes, in St.
David's parish, on the north side of the city; Mount
Radford; and a very strong house in the parish of St.
Thomas.   The place appointed for the meeting of the
commissioners was Poltimore, the seat of Sir John Bamp-
fylde.   The discussion of the terms of surrender commenced on Friday the 3rd of April, and continued with

Exeter sur-
rendered
to Fairfax
after his re-
turn from
Cornwall.

* Vicars, iv. p. 404. Vicars, on account of his public situation, had the
best means of information : his statements are generally founded on the
reports of events sent up to the House of Commons as they occurred.

unremitting assiduity till the following Wednesday. The
next day, April the 9th, the articles were signed; and on
Monday the 13th, at twelve o'clock, the Parliamentary
forces entered the city. The articles, twenty-four in
number, were in substance as follows:—That the city,
garrison, castle, &c., with all the ordnance, arms, ammunition, provisions, and furniture of war, shall be delivered
up on Monday the 13th of April; that no plundering by
the Parliamentary army shall be allowed; that the Princess
Henrietta, with her governess * and her household, shall
have liberty to pass with her plate, money and goods,
within twenty days, to any place in England or Wales,
and to remain there till the King's pleasure shall be known,
suitable carriages being provided for the purpose; that
neither the cathedral nor any other church shall be defaced; that the governor, officers, common soldiers, and
clergymen shall march out of the city with their horses,
arms, baggage, private property, and with their colours flying, under convoy either to Oxford, or to Helston in Cornwall, and that their quarters on the march shall be free;
that all officers, *clergymen*, and common soldiers, who may
so choose, shall have liberty to depart, with their arms,
to a foreign country, for which purpose a passage shall
be provided for them at the expense of the Parliament;
that no reproaches shall be allowed on their departure
from the city, no search shall take place, nor any of their
property be taken from them; that a general indemnity
shall be granted, with the exception of those that are excepted by Parliament, and with the exception also of the
payment of two years purchase by the besieged for their
estates; that all of them shall have liberty to apply to the
Parliament for indemnity and composition for their estates; which if not granted, they shall have four months
allowed for treating with the Parliament, or for going beyond sea; that no alterations shall be made in the charter,
privileges, or government of the city; that the inhabitants

* Lady Dalkeith.

of the city shall provide nothing more than lodgings for the soldiers; that no oath shall be imposed upon the garrison, except one not to fight against the Parliament; and, finally, that hostages shall be delivered on both sides for the fulfilment of these articles, four to be chosen by Sir Thomas Fairfax, and two by Sir John Berkeley [*].

On the 10th of April Fairfax proceeded to Barnstaple, which was still held for the King, as a garrison of considerable importance, by Sir Allen Apsley the governor. But as it was not in a state to be long defended, it surrendered on the 12th, on terms similar to those of Exeter. On the 15th the general returned to Exeter, and stayed four days for the purpose of arranging the affairs of the city, and on his departure he appointed Colonel Hammond to be the governor. On the 18th, having incorporated the men raised by Colonel Shapcote, Colonel Weare, and Colonel Frye into one regiment, and left it to garrison the city, he began his march to Oxford [†].

Thus had this distinguished general finally subdued to the Parliament the whole of the West, leaving the unfortunate King no prospect of restoring his desperate fortunes; and it must be confessed that his moderation, prudence, and humanity, contributed not a little to his success. Whilst he remained in Exeter, no cause for dissatisfaction appears; but no sooner had he arrived at Salisbury on the 23rd, than he received complaints of the shameful breach of many of the articles by the troops left to garrison the city. In fact, few of them were afterwards observed. Horses, arms, or any articles of use or value which the soldiers chose to appropriate, were seized by them without the slightest regard to the treaty. A considerable sum was demanded of the citizens, it appears, in lieu of plunder, and free quarters for the troops; and the city receiver, who had become obnoxious to their displeasure by his attachment to the King, was removed.

CHAP. II.

Barnstaple surrendered.

Disgraceful behaviour of the Republican troops at Exeter.

[*] Sprigge, p. 231–236. Vicars, iv. p. 411. Rushworth, part iv. vol. i. p. 261–264.
[†] Sprigge, p. 243. Rushworth, p. 266. Vicars, iv. p. 412.

x 2

The churches were plundered, and applied to the most indecent purposes. The chapter-house they converted into a stable for their horses, and the bishop's palace, the deanery, and canons' houses into barracks for the soldiers. Thirteen of the parish churches were exposed to sale by the public crier. The cathedral was divided into two parts, by erecting a wall between the choir and the nave; the one for the religious services of the Presbyterians, and the other for those of the Independents. The barbarians also demolished the beautiful stained glass in the windows of the cathedral, defaced the sculptured ornaments, and especially the sepulchral monuments. They removed the ancient statue of Edward the Confessor's Queen, mistaking it for that of the Virgin Mary. They destroyed the organ, carrying the pipes about the streets in derision; ordered the bishop's throne, a singular monument of Gothic art, to be taken down; and fired their muskets at the altar-piece, the marks of which are said to be still visible. In short, they seem to have been subject to little restraint from any principle of decency, taste, honour, or humanity *.

Mount
Edge-
combe
surren-
dered.

Mount Edgecombe surrendered to Colonel Hammond on the 21st of April. This was the last garrison in Devonshire which held out for the King, except Charles-Fort at Salcombe Regis, which was defended by the gallant governor, Sir Edmund Fortescue, till the beginning of June, when it surrendered upon honourable terms to the governor of Plymouth†.

On the 19th of December, 1653, Oliver Cromwell was proclaimed Protector, at Exeter, with great military pomp.

Insurrec-
tion in the
time of
Cromwell.

At no distant period a conspiracy was entered into by the Royalists throughout England, and the 14th of February, 1655, was appointed as the day of general rising; but by the vigilance of Cromwell, and his secretary Thurloe, the design was completely frustrated. It was in the West only that this conspiracy broke out into action.

* Mercurius Rusticus, A.D. 1685. Rushworth, part iv. vol. i. p. 266.
Oliver's Exeter, chap. xiii. Jenkins, p. 164.
† Lysons. Whitelocke. Vicars, iv. p. 436.

John Penruddock, Edward Penruddock, Hugh Grove,
Robert Duke, gentlemen of Wiltshire, Francis Jones, of
Surry, and several other gentlemen, with about one hundred and fifty horse, entered Salisbury at the time of the assizes, proclaimed Charles II., seized the Judges, and having
taken away their commissions set them at liberty. Being
disappointed in their hope of considerable accession to
their forces, after wandering from place to place with no
more than two hundred horse, they were discouraged and
fled into Devonshire. At South-Molton they again proclaimed the King, but were encountered by Major Cook
and defeated. Many prisoners were taken; among whom
were John Penruddock and Grove. Thurloe gives a
list, with the names of one hundred and eighteen who
were confined at Exeter, where, as they were in great
distress, the citizens did themselves honour by affording
them every assistance and relief in their power. The prisoners pleaded a promise of pardon made to them by Cook
before their surrender; but the Major positively denied
having given them any such pledge. It was also urged
by their captors that they had before participated in the
benefits of the Act of Oblivion, and had been allowed to
compound for their estates; nor was it of any avail for them
to reply that this favour was received from the Parliament,
and that it was not against them, but against the usurpation of the Protector, that in the present instance they had
taken arms. A special commission was appointed in the
spring of 1655 to try them; and the attorney-general,
Prideaux, was sent down to Exeter to conduct the prosecution. Most of them were found guilty*. Penrud- Execu-
dock and Grove were beheaded in the castle, several were tions.
hanged at Heavitree, and the rest were transported to Bar-
badoes. This insurrection, slight as it appeared, occasioned considerable alarm to Cromwell, but in its results

* In Thurloe's Collection of State Papers it is said, that of the thirty
who were tried on the 18th of April, 1655, twenty-six were found guilty
of high treason and condemned, three were acquitted, and against one
of the name of Rivers no indictment was found by the Grand Jury.

proved highly serviceable to his cause, as it evinced the reality of the conspiracy, and supplied a pretext for measures of rigour against the Royalists, which tended greatly to strengthen his authority *.

Richard Cromwell was proclaimed at Exeter with the usual solemnities three days after the death of his father, which happened September 3rd, 1658 †.   After the resignation of the high and arduous office of Protector, which he soon found to be necessary, the officers of the army having assumed the reins of government, and restored to their places ninety-two members of the Long Parliament ‡ expelled by Cromwell, the utmost discontent and consternation prevailed among all parties in the country. In many counties resolutions were formed to rise in arms, and a day was fixed for this purpose.   And though the vigilance of the Parliament and their agents prevented any plans concerted by combinations of this kind being carried into effect, commotions in several parts took place. In Exeter particularly, in 1659, numbers of the common people put themselves in arms, and declared for a free Parliament.   This happened at the general quarter sessions, when the magistrates and many of the principal gentlemen of the county were assembled in the castle; on which occasion the following remonstrance was drawn up by them, and presented to the Parliament by the recorder, Thomas Bampfylde, Esq.

Remonstrance of the gentry of Devon presented to the Parment.

"To the Right Honourable William Lenthall, Esq.
      Speaker of the Parliament.

" We, the gentry of the county of Devon, finding ourselves without a regular government, (after your last interruption,) designed a public meeting to consult remedies, and which we could not so conveniently effect till this week of our general quarter sessions at Exon, where

* A Collection of State Papers by John Thurloe, Esq. Secretary, first to the Council of State, and afterwards to the two Protectors, Oliver and Richard Cromwell, vol. iii. 306. Ludlow's Memoirs, 4to, 1771, p. 218. Parliamentary History, vol. iii. p. 1477.
   † Oliver's Exeter, chap. xiii.
   ‡ Parliamentary History, vol. iii. p. 1547.

we found divers of the inhabitants groaning under high
oppressions and a general defect of trade, to the utter
ruin of many, and fear of the like to others, which is as
visible to the whole county, that occasioned such disorders as were no small trouble and disturbance to us, which,
by God's blessing upon our endeavours, were soon suppressed, and quieted without blood; and though we find,
since our first purposes, an alteration in the state of affairs
by your establishment at the helm of government, yet
conceive that we are but in part redressed of our grievances,
and that the chief expedient will be the recalling all those
members who were excluded in 1648, and sat before the
first force upon the Parliament, and also by filling up
vacant places, and all to be admitted without any oath,
or engagement previous to their entrance, for which things
if you please to take a speedy course, we shall defend you
against all opposers and future interruption with our lives
and fortunes; for the accomplishment whereof we shall use
all lawful means, which we humbly conceive may best con-
duce to the peace and safety of the nation*."

Other remonstrances of a similar tendency were transmitted to the Parliament from various counties; but by
the dispersion of the troops about the country, insurrections were suppressed.

The next year, 1660, Charles II. was proclaimed in
London on the 8th of May, and on the Friday following
in Exeter, with unusual magnificence and rejoicings. In
the year 1670, a new citadel having been built at Plymouth, the King, accompanied by the Duke of Monmouth,
came by sea on the 17th of July to view it, and was lodged
in the Old Fort, the houses in the citadel not being finished.
He returned by sea as far as Dartmouth, and thence
proceeded to Exeter, where he was received with great
demonstrations of joy, and presented with £500. He
stayed at the deanery one night. On this occasion he
promised to present to her native city the portrait of his
sister Henrietta, late Duchess of Orleans, who had died

*Charles II.
proclaim-
ed, and
visits Exe-
ter and
Plymouth.*

* Jenkins, page 170. Polwhele.

suddenly on the 29th of the preceding month, supposed
by poison. The next year he performed his promise, and
the picture may still be seen in the Guildhall. In the
month of August 1676, Charles II. accompanied by the
Duke of York, again visited Plymouth, dined at Mount
Edgecombe, stayed two nights, and returned by sea. On
this occasion the King touched for the evil in St. Andrew's
church. Towards the close of his reign he demanded the
charter of Exeter, but presented the city with a more ample
charter the following year, 1684. About the same time
Plymouth was treated in a similar way, as well as most
other boroughs, and the reception of the new charter was
celebrated in that town with the greatest rejoicings and
demonstrations of loyalty *.

James II.
succeeds to
the throne.

The only circumstance that can give pleasure to the
friends of just government in contemplating the reign of
James II. is its brevity. From its commencement the
most gloomy apprehensions were justly entertained by the
best part of the nation, of his designs, and the general discontents occasioned even by his earliest measures afforded
a favourable opportunity for attempts to stifle the rising
tyranny in its infancy. His solemn pledge to maintain the
Protestant religion and the rights of the people, first to
the Privy Council, and afterwards in his opening speech
to the Parliament, obtained no confidence; for the measures which he immediately adopted, showed a determination too plainly to effect by degrees the restoration of
Popery, to overthrow the liberties of the people, and to
govern, if possible, without a Parliament, and in defiance
of the laws†. Hence arose in the first year of James's

* Oliver's Exeter, chap. xv. MS. List of the Mayors of Plymouth, with
notes. Jenkins, pp. 171, 176, 180. In this reign, at the summer assizes
of 1682, three poor aged women, Temperance Lloyd, Mary Trembles,
and Susannah Edwards, natives of Bideford, were tried for witchcraft,
were convicted, and actually executed at Heavitree on the 25th of
August. The deluded women seemed even to imagine themselves possessed of this art, for they confessed that many parts of the evidence
against them were true. Such was the deplorable ignorance and superstition of the times! Happily these were the last who suffered in England for this imaginary crime.
† The Secret History of the Reign of Charles II. and James II. p. 117.

government two attempts to check these abuses; the one in Scotland by the Duke of Argyle, and the other in concert with him, and intended to be simultaneous in the West, by the Duke of Monmouth, a favourite son of Charles II. by Lucy Walter, to whom some believed the King had been privately married *: both attempts, however, especially the latter, were too feeble, both in preparation and the manner in which they were conducted, to afford the slightest hope of success, notwithstanding the favourable circumstances in which they were undertaken.

The Duke of Monmouth began the preparations for his expedition in Holland about the time that Argyle sailed for Scotland, but having narrowly escaped an arrest by Skelton, the English envoy, did not reach the English coast till after the failure of Argyle's attempt, nor does he appear to have been made acquainted with that failure before his arrival. He landed at Lyme without opposition on Thursday the 11th of June 1685, with three small ships, his company consisting, according to Dr. Burnet, of no more than about eighty of his faithful friends †, with five hundred stand of arms, and little money, the Duke having been obliged to pawn his jewels for a small sum in Holland. Immediately on his landing having offered up devout thanksgivings for his preservation at sea, the three or four following days were spent in enlisting men, for the common people flocked to him in crowds, though the gentry stood aloof. On the following Sunday morning, three hundred of his men took Bridport by storm, with many prisoners; but being attacked by a small party of the King's troops, they were compelled to retreat with the loss of three or four men on each side, eight of the Royal party being taken.

The Duke immediately published a manifesto, in which, after charging James with the poisoning of his brother, Charles II., and numerous encroachments on the liberties

CHAP. II.

The Duke of Monmouth lands in the West.

---

* Granger's Biographical History of England, vol. iii. pp. 194, 195.
† In Welwood's Memoirs and the Life of James II. they are estimated at about 150; and in the Appendix to Dalrymple's Memoirs, at about 200.

and religion of the people, he gave the most solemn assurances that he came for the sole purpose of redressing the grievances of which they had so much reason to complain, and of maintaining the just rights of the nation, which he enumerated. This manifesto was ordered by Parliament to be burnt by the common hangman, a bill of attainder was passed against the Duke, and a reward of £5000 offered for his capture whether dead or alive. The Duke's gentleness and affability however, together with the nature of his undertaking, won the hearts of the people, and the whole country was open to him for nearly a fortnight.

The Duke of Monmouth at Axminster.

On the Monday after his landing he marched to Axminster, and by this time his forces amounted to about two thousand foot and three hundred horse; and had he possessed a sufficient supply of arms, this number might have been greatly increased. After a march of two miles he discovered the Duke of Albemarle, who had been sent into the country by the King to raise the militia, and who had designed to quarter that night at Axminster, and the next day to lay siege to Lyme. The Duke of Monmouth wishing if possible to attach him to his interest, addressed a letter to him for that purpose, signed JAMES REX. But the Duke of Albemarle replied that "he never had been a rebel, and never would be one." The militia however which he commanded, like that of the rest of the kingdom, partaking of the sentiments of the people, were disaffected, and could not be depended upon. The Duke therefore did not think the risk of a battle to be safe, and retreated. Had the Duke of Monmouth pursued the fugitives as was to have been expected, he might have obtained from them the necessary supply of arms, and have marched without obstruction to Exeter, which was then but ill prepared for defence. But as his troops were undisciplined, he had not sufficient confidence in them on this account to venture on a battle as yet; he wished moreover to make his way up the country, and therefore proceeded to Taunton. In that town he met

with the most flattering reception *, and the hearty congra-
tulations and good wishes for his success which he every
where experienced on his march, showed the extreme un-
popularity of the existing Government.   Besides, as the
militia could no where be confided in by the King, it was
a considerable time before James could muster an army
of sufficient force to encounter Monmouth, and he was
under the necessity of sending to Holland for three regiments to assist him.   But the Duke lost the opportunity
by delay and want of vigour, in addition to the deficiency
of his means.   The forces collected by the King, under
the command of the Earl of Feversham, did not exceed
two thousand foot and five hundred horse, whilst the
troops of Monmouth amounted to six thousand, very deficient however both in discipline and arms.   From the
superiority of the King's little army in both these respects,
in the battle that ensued at Sedgemoor, near Bridgewater,
the Duke's forces, though they fought with great courage,
were speedily overthrown and dispersed; and he himself
was taken, disguised and in extreme distress, two days
after.   Had he succeeded, he would have been hailed as
the deliverer of his country; but being unfortunate, he
speedily afterwards perished on the scaffold as a rebel †.

The execution of the Duke of Monmouth was followed
by scenes of atrocious cruelty, which, for the honour of
human nature, we are disposed to believe to be without
a parallel.   In the latter end of August the barbarians
Kirk and Jefferies were dispatched into the West on a
commission, not to execute justice, but to gratify the

The expe-
dition of
Kirk and
Jefferies
into the
West.

---

* At Taunton he was also proclaimed King.   To this measure, however, he consented with great reluctance.   From the first he declared on
all occasions, that he came for the sole purpose of procuring redress for
the grievances of the nation, and it appears evidently to have been in
compliance with the wishes of others, and in opposition to his own inclination, that he assumed regal authority.   See particularly Welwood's
Memoirs.

† Dr. Burnet's History of His Own Times, vol. i. p. 640.   Dr. Welwood's Memoirs, ed. 1710, p. 146–148.   The Life of James II. collected
out of Memoirs written by himself, and published from the original Stuart
MSS. in Carlton House, by the Rev. J. S. Clarke, LL.B. F.R.S., vol. ii.
p. 24–29. Dalrymple's Memoirs, part i. p. 61–75, Appendix, p. 128–135.

BOOK
II.

brutal malignity of revenge and arbitrary power, in defiance of all law and equity; nor were these ministers of
tyranny remiss in the execution of their vindictive purpose.
And that their proceedings were a source of high gratification to James is evident; for there is no reason to
doubt the truth of Dr. Burnet's statement, that the King
had a particular account of the proceedings of Jefferies
sent to him every day, took pleasure in relating them in
the drawing-room to foreign ministers, and at his table
called this "Jefferies' campaign *." After satiating his
appetite for blood at Winchester, Salisbury, and Dorches-
ter, he proceeded to Exeter, where two hundred and
forty-three were in custody for their adherence to Monmouth. Of these about eighty, it is said, suffered in this
city, and their mangled quarters were exposed on trees
by the sides of the roads, to the great terror of passengers.
From scenes so revolting we turn with horror, and are not
surprised at the fatal results to the perpetrators †.

The Revo-
lution of
1688.

James, it seems, was elated not a little by these instances of success, and was thus encouraged to proceed
from one measure of oppression and insane tyranny to
another, till at length his career of injustice terminated
in his own ruin, by producing the Revolution of 1688;
a transaction justly considered the pride and boast of
Englishmen, as having done so much without bloodshed
towards the recognition and establishment of the rights
of the people. By participating in the commencement

* Burnet's History of His Own Times, vol. i. p. 648. Dalrymple's
Memoirs, part i. p. 77. Jefferies after his return was also created a peer,
and invested with the dignity of chancellor.

† Hume, whose partiality to the Stuarts is well known, concludes his
account of these atrocities with the following statement :—" Even those
multitudes who received pardon were obliged to atone for their guilt by
fines, which reduced them to beggary; or where their former poverty
made them incapable of paying, they were condemned to cruel whippings
or severe imprisonments. Nor could the innocent escape the hands, no
less rapacious than cruel, of the chief justice. Prideaux, a gentleman of
Devonshire, being thrown into prison, and dreading the severe and arbitrary spirit, which at that time met with no control, was obliged to buy
his liberty of Jefferies at the price of fifteen thousand pounds; though he
could never so much as learn the crime of which he was accused."

of this happy event Devonshire was distinguished at the time. The Prince of Orange, supported by invitations from many of the principal nobility, the most respectable part of the clergy, and the unanimous good wishes of the Protestants generally in England, set sail from Helvoetsluys on the 21st of October, with a fleet of fifty-one ships of war, eighteen fire-ships, and about three hundred and thirty hired transports, and with an army little short of thirty thousand. For more than two days and nights the most violent tempests ensued, and they were compelled to return into port with some loss and considerable damage. In order to abate the vigilance of the King, and induce a state of fancied security for the present, exaggerated reports of the magnitude of this disaster were circulated in their gazettes by the States of Holland, and reason was given to believe that the Prince would not be able to carry his purpose into effect till the ensuing spring. James, it seems, was caught by the bait; for no sooner were his fears allayed for the present, than he began to retract some of the numerous measures of reform, which his terror of the approaching expedition had suddenly extorted *. It was now, however, too late for any measures either of conciliation or of rigour to avail him: he was no longer the object of the confidence or the fear of the great majority, of his subjects. But such was the activity and perseverance of the Dutch, that in about eight days the fleet was completely refitted, and again set sail with a favourable wind. The voyage was prosperous, and met with no oppposition. The English fleet consisting of about thirty-four sail, under the command of the Earl of Dartmouth, was at the Nore, but did not venture out till after the Prince had passed. The wind, it is true, was against them; but the sailors were well known to be disaffected, and their admiral did not venture to confide in their exertions against so formidable an opponent, whom they might be disposed to favour. As the

* Dr. Burnet's History of his Own Times, ed. 1724, vol. i. p. 784.

Prince passed Dover and Calais, his fleet extended in a line across the Channel within a league of each of these places.   The West of England appearing to be the most favourable quarter for his landing, he proceeded to Torbay, and arrived there on the 4th of November, the day of the month on which the Prince was born and had been married, and which therefore he wished to render more remarkable by landing on the English shores for the deliverance of the country.   The preparations however could not be completed in time ; but the next day the landing commenced, and the 5th of November again became memorable by one of the most celebrated and fortunate events in English history.   The landing occupied three days ; and instead of opposition, the Prince, upon coming on shore at Brixham, was hailed with the loudest acclamations of joy by a large assemblage of people, who brought supplies of provisions for the troops, for which they were paid their demands in full.   The Prince's ship on his arrival had English colours with the following motto: THE PROTESTANT RELIGION, AND LIBERTIES OF ENGLAND; and underneath, I WILL MAINTAIN IT. He also hoisted a red flag previously to his landing.

The Prince of Orange lands at Torbay.

Arrival at Exeter.

On the 7th, the Prince sent an officer with some troops to search Tor Abbey, and other houses inhabited by Roman Catholics, for arms and horses*.   He himself went to Ford House, the residence of Sir William Courtenay, near Newton Abbot, and on the 8th proceeded with the

---

* In the interesting account of the whole proceedings, by one who was present, in the Harleian Miscellany, an amusing anecdote occurs in the following words :—" Nor shall it be forgotten that there was a priest and some others upon a watchtower" (at Tor Abbey), "when we arrived at Torbay, to discover what our fleet was ; and discovering white flags on some of our men of war, the ignorant priest concluded we were French, which they had so long expected with great impatience : and having laid up great provisions for their entertainment, the priest ordered all to the chapel to sing *Te Deum* for the arrival of their forces.   But being soon undeceived on our landing, we found the benefit of their provisions ; and instead of *Votre serviteur, Monsieur,* they were entertained with *Yees Mynheer, can ye Dutch spraken?* Upon which they all ran away from the house, but the Lady Cary and a few old servants." Harleian Miscellany, vol. i. p. 449.

greater part of his army to Exeter. The description of his
public entry into the city on that day, as given by one who was present, published in the year 1688, and preserved in the Harleian Miscellany, may be thought interesting, and shows the confidence which the Prince felt in the success of his expedition. In the van the Earl of Macclesfield, with two hundred horse, the greater part of which were English gentlemen, richly accoutred and mounted on Flanders steeds, with head pieces and body armour. Attendant upon these were two hundred blacks, from the plantations of the Netherlands in America, with embroidered caps lined with fur, and plumes of feathers. Next followed two hundred Finlanders in bear skins, the common clothing of that climate, with black armour and broad swords. After these, fifty gentlemen, and as many pages to attend and support the Prince's banner, bearing the inscription GOD AND THE PROTESTANT RELIGION. These were followed by fifty led horses, trained to war, and accompanied by two grooms to each. Next came the Prince himself on a white charger, in complete armour highly wrought, with a plume of white feathers in his helmet, and forty-two running footmen by his side. The Prince was followed also by two hundred gentlemen and pages mounted. The next in succession were three thousand Swiss with fusees, and then five hundred volunteers, with two led horses to each. After them the chief officer with six hundred guards completely armed; and the rest of the army brought up the rear. The Prince on his entrance into the city as well as on his march was every where received with the most cordial welcome and triumphant acclamations by the people.

He was lodged at the deanery, having ordered the advanced guard to Clist Heath, and arranged the quarters of the army in a manner completely satisfactory to the inhabitants. The majority were stationed at Ottery and Honiton, and other parties dispersed to various places in the vicinity. The whole of the Prince's forces amounted to about thirty thousand, all picked men, and many of them personally present at the siege of Buda. But so correct was their discipline, so singular the civility and good conduct of the soldiers, and so exact the payment for whatever supplies of provisions they received, that though the city was crowded to excess, the greatest order and regularity prevailed throughout during the whole of their stay*. On the 9th the Prince went to the cathedral to return thanks for his safe arrival, and ordered *Te Deum* to be sung. After the service, Dr. Burnet, his chaplain and afterwards bishop of Salisbury, read the Prince's Declaration to the congregation; and the next Sunday the Doctor preached in the cathedral from the last verse of the 107th Psalm, " Whoso is wise and will observe these things, even they shall understand the lovingkindness of the Lord."

The common people flocked to the Prince's standard, new levies were made with rapidity, and many more might have been raised, had they been considered to be necessary.

Discouraging reception.

From the magistrates and the gentry however the Prince met with a very different reception at first from that which he had been led to expect. The bishop of Exeter, Lamplugh, on the news of the Prince's approach had fled with great expedition to the King, by whom he was created for his loyalty Archbishop of York: the dean and most of the resident clergy followed his example. When, two days before the Prince arrived, Captain Hicks was sent to Exeter with a party of horse, though many of the common people joined him, the mayor put him under arrest, and confined him in the Guildhall, as the people would not allow him to go to prison; and the next day, when Lord Mordaunt and Dr. Burnet came to the city with four troops of horse, they found the west gate shut against them; and when having gained an entrance by menaces Lord Mor-

* " That none of the disorders usually attending the presence of armies took place I am sure," says the writer of the account," for I was an eye witness of the whole order; and when we marched away from the city, the joy of the inhabitants was turned into dulness and cloudiness." Harleian Miscel.

-daunt requested the mayor to meet the Prince and preside over the city under him, he refused, assigning for a reason, the obligation he was under to the King by his oath. Alderman Tuthill and one other member of the Corporation only declared in the Prince's favour *. The Prince had been given to understand that all the gentry of the West would join him at his landing; but for nine days after scarcely any individual of note came in. These circumstances appeared so unfavourable to the Prince, that he began to doubt of the success of his expedition, and at a council of war held on the occasion it was in fact proposed that he should reimbark for Holland. The scene however soon began to assume a more favourable aspect. The hesitation of the gentry of the county arose, not from want of inclination in favour of the Prince, but evidently from timidity, from doubts of his success, and from terror excited by the rigour of the existing Government, exemplified in the recent outrages of Kirk and Jefferies. At length Mr. Burrington of Sampford, a major of the militia, took courage to wait upon the Prince, and the ice being broken, the gentlemen of Somerset and Devonshire came forward in great numbers, and soon afterwards several others of greater distinction followed their example. Lord Colchester, eldest son of Earl Rivers, accompanied by Lord Wharton, Colonel Godfrey, and James How, Esq. came over to the Prince with part of the Life Guards and some other troops. Lord Cornbury, colonel of the Royal regiment of dragoons, with some of his forces, and afterwards the Earl of Abingdon, Mr. Russell, brother of Lord Russell, and Captain Clargis, with various others, declared in his favour. In short, it soon became evident that the whole of the Protestant part of

The Prince joined by many of the Devonshire gentry.

---

* Even the Presbyterians stood aloof on this occasion, and would not allow their minister Mr. Ferguson to celebrate the arrival of the Prince in their chapel. They shut up the place, and carried away the keys; but the minister, having more courage than his flock, broke open the doors by force, and preached from the text in Ps. xciv. 16. "Who will rise up for me against the evil doers?" He was not however much regarded by the Prince's attendants.

BOOK
II.

the community in England were decidedly ready to contribute as they could to the success of his undertaking. His court was kept, whilst at Exeter, with magnificence, consisting not only of foreigners, but of upwards of sixty of the nobility and gentry, who had come to attend him, and who vied with each other in the splendour of their equipage.   An instrument of association, drawn up by Dr. Burnet *, was numerously signed in the cathedral on the 17th of November †.

The garrison of Plymouth now declared for the Prince, under the command of the Earl of Bath, whom the opposite party, it is said, had designed to poison.   And Pendennis Castle in Cornwall was held for him by several gentlemen in that county, who took the command of that

The Prince
leaves
Exeter.

garrison alternately; so that the whole country westward being in a state of safety, the Prince left Exeter on the 21st, having stationed a small garrison in the city under the command of Sir Edward Seymour, whom he appointed the governor.   He was accompanied by many gentlemen of Devonshire and Somerset; and having dined that day at Ottery, he advanced to Axminster, where he remained four days.   Thence he proceeded on his expedition, which happily terminated in his elevation to the throne of Great

* This instrument was expressed as follows :—" We do engage to Almighty God, and to His Highness the Prince of Orange, and with one another, to stick firm to this cause and with one another, in the defence of it, and never to depart from it, until our religion, laws and liberties are so far secure to us in a free Parliament, that we shall be no more in danger of falling under Popery and slavery.   And whereas we are engaged in the common cause, under the protection of the Prince of Orange, by which means his person is exposed to danger and to the desperate and cursed designs of Papists, and other bloody men ; we do therefore solemnly engage to God, and to one another, that if any such attempts be made upon him, we will pursue not only those that make them, but all their adherents, and all we find in arms against us, with the utmost severity of just revenge in their ruin and destruction, and that the executing any such attempt (which God of his infinite mercy forbid!) shall not deprive us from pursuing this cause which we do now undertake, but it shall encourage us to carry it on with all the vigour that so barbarous an attempt shall deserve *."

† Dr. Burnet's History, vol. i. p. 793.

* Life of William III., p. 137.

Britain, together with his consort, by the free choice of a grateful people*.

After this great transaction few events of importance occur in the general history of the county. In July 1690, the French fleet was drawn up in Torbay, and the whole of the forces of Devonshire were collected to oppose their landing. Several of their ships separated from the fleet, and made towards Teignmouth. After cannonading the town, they landed seven hundred men, plundered East and West Teignmouth, and a village called Shaldon. They also burnt or destroyed one hundred and sixteen houses, together with eleven ships and barks in the harbour. They violated the churches, destroyed the cattle, spoiled the merchandise as well as other property, and by these means occasioned a loss of about £11,000†.

It must not be omitted here that the celebrated Duke of Marlborough, who made so conspicuous a figure in the reign of Queen Ann, was a native of Devonshire, having been born at Ash in the parish of Musbury, the seat of his maternal grandfather Sir John Drake.

In the year 1719, in consequence of the preparations made by the French for the invasion of England, many regiments of horse and foot were sent into the West of England, three of which came to Exeter, and encamped during the summer on Clist Heath‡.

In 1779 the appearance off Plymouth of the combined fleet of France and Spain occasioned great alarm, espe-

* For the whole of these proceedings of the Prince of Orange in Devonshire, see two letters in the Harleian Miscellany, both the writers being present on this occasion, and published the same year, vol. i. p. 449. Dr. Burnet's History of His Own Times, vol. i. p. 780–790. Dalrymple's Memoirs, vol. i. p. 159; and the History of the Life and Reign of William III. p. 137.

† Lysons's *Mag. Brit.*, vol. vi. part ii. pp. 489, 490.

‡ Jenkins's Exeter, p. 202.

BOOK
II.

cially on account of the Dock-yard and the great number
of prisoners of war then collected at that port.   The prisoners were removed to Exeter under a guard of volunteers
collected by William Bastard, Esq., who commanded them
on their march. For his spirited exertions on this occasion,
the King, without any previous communication of his design, ordered a baronet's patent to be made out for him.—
The citizens of Exeter raised a corps of volunteers to guard
the prisoners who were confined in the county bridewell *.

Camp on
Woodbury
Down.

During the expectation of an invasion by the French in
1798, several regiments of volunteers were raised in
Devonshire, and the next year cannon were brought from
Plymouth to Exeter for its defence, and a camp was formed
on Woodbury Down, the park of artillery being stationed
within the ancient entrenchments.   Similar preparations
took place in 1803, and a camp was again formed on
Woodbury Down, Lieutenant-general Simcoe having the
chief command of the district †.

Napoleon
in Ply-
mouth
Sound.

Finally, the year 1815 was rendered remarkable by the
fall of Napoleon Buonaparte, who arrived on the coast of
Devon, a prisoner in the Bellerophon, which came into
Plymouth Sound; and on the 6th of August, without being
permitted to land, he went on board the Northumberland,
and on the following day proceeded to his final destina-
tion at St. Helena.

* *Ibid.* p. 218. Lysons.   † Jenkins, p. 226.   Lysons.

[The part contributed to this work by Mr. Brayley, Jun. will commence with the next Book.]

BOOK III.

OUTLINES OF THE GEOLOGY, PHYSICAL GEOGRAPHY, AND NATURAL HISTORY, OF DEVONSHIRE.

[By E. W. Bᴇᴀᴛʟᴇʏ, Jun., A.L.S., Lecturer and Tutor in the Physical Sciences in the Schools of Hazelwood and Bruce Castle.]

CHAPTER I.

INTRODUCTION.

IN commencing a section of this work which is designed, expressly, to be appropriated to the delineation of the physical structure and the natural productions of the County to which it relates; regarded both with respect to their interest in a scientific point of view, and their importance in connection with the arts and with commerce; some explanation of the views with which these subjects are brought forward, in so prominent a manner, in a topographical work, appears to be expedient.

BOOK III.

In the numerous publications on county and local Topography which have distinguished the descriptive literature of the present century, the Geological Structure and the Natural History of the counties or districts which have formed, respectively, the subjects of those works, have usually been treated in a manner altogether incidental and subordinate. With very few exceptions, some particulars of the mining history of the place or county described; a dry list, or perhaps a description, in language

Local Natural History, &c. hitherto neglected in Topographical Works.

CHAP.
I.
_____

which in science has become obsolete, of its more striking mineral productions; and an equally meagre catalogue of the rare plants indigenous to the vicinity; together with, in some instances, a few notices of insects and shells; have comprised all that has been imparted on these subjects in such works. It is true, indeed, that the class of publications alluded to has furnished not only several useful compendiums of local natural history, but also some valuable contributions to the stores of original knowledge,

Exceptions.

especially in geology; of which the earlier volumes of the " Beauties of England and Wales," a work which has formed in other respects the prototype of so many additions to topographical literature; the "Magna Britannia" of Messrs. Lysons; and Shaw's "History of Staffordshire," as containing Mr. Keir's able memoir on the geology of the southern portion of the Dudley coal-field, may be cited as examples. When these, however, have been excepted, (and but very few additions can be made to the foregoing list,) an examination of our numerous esteemed works on county and parochial history, will be found to verify

Causes of this neglect.

the statement which has just been made. It is not difficult to discover some at least of the reasons why such has hitherto been the case. The collection of particulars relating to the ancient history and former condition of counties and cities, rather than the acquisition and communication of knowledge respecting their existing state and resources, has been the object of topographical researches. The importance of the former species of information, it cannot be designed, in this place, to question or to undervalue; but the remark may be submitted, that, while it forms in reality only one department of Topography, it has too generally, perhaps, been regarded as the whole, to the neglect of subjects more immediately involved in the actual state of the places under consideration. And to this circumstance, it would appear, in addition to an erroneous impression, that the history of nature is a less important and less interesting branch of general knowledge, than the political and civil history of

man, and that of the arts which he has cultivated,—an impression, however, which the progress of knowledge is
now gradually dispelling,—the comparative disregard of
local natural history, in topographical publications, may
in a great degree be ascribed.

But another cause for this neglect of, or at least inadequate attention to, the physical history of the localities described by the topographer, and one which has contributed to it in an equal degree with that which has been
explained, may be found in the history of science itself.

Those branches of natural knowledge with which the
topographer possessing justly extended views of his subject is principally concerned, have not taken a form in
which they could be adequately available for his purposes,
until within that very period during which topographical
literature has become so copious and so popular. Of these
departments of knowledge, Geology is one of the most important; but although many of the facts respecting the
distribution of the mineral masses composing the crust of
the earth—that portion of our planet's substance which
is open to the cognizance of man—which constitute the
basis of this science, had been discovered towards the commencement of the present century, yet, so far as it formed
a subject of general inquiry, Geology consisted, at that
time, of little besides crude and unfounded speculations
on the original formation of the earth, and detached
points of knowledge respecting local peculiarities in its
structure. At the same period, the kindred branches of
Natural History—Botany, and Zoology, were nearly confined, as objects of general interest, to the recognition and
description of individual and insulated species; and their
reference to a certain station in an artificial arrangement,
which, however useful it might be in leading the student
to distinguish those species from each other, gave him no
information whatever as to their probable station in nature, and the functions they fulfilled in the vegetable and
animal worlds. While such was the condition of these
sciences, it is obvious that the detail of local circum-

Further
causes.

CHAP.
I.

stances, often in the unintelligible language of the miner or the quarryman, with lists of observed substances and species, without regard to their philosophical interest, or to their relations with the structure or productions of other districts of the country, or other regions of the globe, was all that could be expected from general writers on Topography. A gradual change, however, has taken place. As the last thirty years have witnessed the publication of so many splendid and elaborate works, detailing the History, and describing the Antiquities and Architectural Beauties, of so many of our counties and cities; so have they seen all the sciences concerned in the investigation of nature, assume an interest, and evince a utility, which they never possessed at any former period in the history of human knowledge. Thus the advance of Topography has not been preceded by that of Natural Science; but their progress has taken place during the same period and nearly by equal steps; so that the cultivator of the former could not, until the present time, have found the existing information on Geology and Natural History, such as could enable him to confer upon his local details a generally interesting and scientific form.

Present state of scientific knowledge as applicable to topography.

At the present epoch in the pursuit of knowledge the case is widely different. We now see the laws according to which are arranged the various mineral masses and strata composing the crust of the earth, in one country, extended with success (though not without exception) to large portions of the globe, and some of them even to nearly its entire surface. We find the phænomena of one district made subservient to the explanation of those occurring in others; and thus, in many different points of view, the interest of truly philosophical inquiry is imparted to those researches in Geology, which are necessarily confined within very narrow limits. Nor have the improvements in Botanical and in Zoological Science been less extensive, or such as are less applicable to the purposes of the Topographer and his readers. The more general laws of the distribution of plants over the surface of the earth

Drawn by T. H. Shepherd.   Engraved by W. Brooke.

EXETER.

Drawn by W. Westley

TAVISTOCK, FROM FITZ FORD.

Engraved by W. Floyd

Drawn by A Glennie

CHAPEL & HOSPITAL OF ST JOHN, EXETER.

London Jennings & Chaplin 62 Cheapside 1830

Engraved by W Deeble

Drawn by A Glennie

Engraved by W Deeble

CHAPEL & HOSPITAL OF ST JOHN, EXETER.

London, Jennings & Chaplin 62 Cheapside 1830

Drawn by T. M. Baynes

Engraved by A. M. Cuttle

NEW BRIDGE NEAR HOLNE.

ON THE DART.

being now understood, the physical grounds of the existence of particular species or genera in particular situations, may be explained, and the interest of extended
views of nature given to a local catalogue. The labours
of Zoologists of almost every age and every country have
also been concentrated, and united with the results of a
deep insight into the natural arrangement of animals which
has been recently attained ; and the knowledge acquired
by these means of the larger groups into which animals are
assembled by their natural and more general characters,
and of the relations of these groups to the vegetable clothing and physical structure of those portions of the globe
which they respectively inhabit, places the local and provincial history of animated beings in a position having
similar advantages.

   Such were the reflections which led to the introduction
into the present History and Topography of Devonshire,
of the ' Outlines of the Geology, Physical Geography, and
Natural History' of that County, which will now occupy
several successive numbers of this publication. It has
been deemed expedient to commence this portion of the
work with an explanation of the views with which it has
been introduced, as well as with a sketch of the subjects
to which it will be chiefly devoted, both on account of
the novelty of the design, and of the periodical mode of
publication of the work.

   These OUTLINES will be divided into four sections, de- Proposed
scribing, respectively, the Geology and Mineralogy, Phy- arrange-
ment of
sical Geography, Botany, and Zoology of the County of these Out-
Devon. It will be the endeavour of the writer, in considering lines.
each branch of his subject, so to unite familiarity and per-
spicuity of explanation with scientific detail, as to render
this portion of the work available for the use of general
readers and residents in the County, at the same time that
it may serve as a compendium of the Physical History of
Devonshire for the man of science. It is hoped, therefore,
that this intention, which is inseparable from the nature and

BOOK
III.

design of the work of which these Outlines form a part, will be a sufficient apology to the scientific reader for the explanations and accommodated details on various subjects, which, though well known to him, it will be necessary to describe, in order to adapt the following pages to the perusal of the general reader.

Geology of
Devon.

The GEOLOGICAL division will commence with a view of the formations, or assemblages of rocks and strata, believed to have been produced respectively during one general condition of the earth's surface at a former. period, which are presented within the limits of the County; as the granite and metalliferous slate of Dartmoor, the grauwacke of the central and northern portions of the County, the new red sandstone in the vicinity of Exeter, the greensand of the Blackdown Hills, &c. Each of these formations will be concisely described so far as correct information upon it has been published or can be obtained, nearly in the order adopted in the description of formations by the Rev. W. D. Conybeare, in the " Outlines of the Geology of England and Wales," by himself and the late Mr. William Phillips. Thus the history of each will commence with an account of its nature and local extent; which will be followed by particulars of its subdivisions, and brief notices of its extent into the contiguous and the neighbouring counties, or of formations equivalent or analogous to it in other districts of the British Islands, or in other countries of the globe. Its chemical and external characters and mineral contents will next be considered, particular attention being given to such mineral substances as are of importance in the arts, and which may be connected with the trade and commerce of the County; such as the granite of Dartmoor, the whetstones of Blackdown, the limestone of Plymouth, &c. To this, in the history of several formations, will succeed an enumeration of the organized fossils they contain, or of those remains of animal and vegetable life which record the existence of successive races of organic beings in the seas and on the surface of the earth, in former conditions of the globe; such as the Fossil Corals, and Crinoidea or stone-lilies, of the Plymouth limestone, the Fossil Shells occurring in the greensand of Blackdown and Haldon, and the bones of an extinct species of Hyæna, and of other quadrupeds in the caves of Oreston and Torquay. Under this head will be given references to Sowerby's Mineral Conchology, and to other works in which figures of the Devonian organic remains have been published. What may be termed the *constitution* of the formation having thus been described, its elevation and thickness, and the altitudes of the hills consisting of it, the inclination to the horizon of the plane of the beds which compose it, if it be stratified; the agricultural character of the soil which it produces, and the phænomena of water and springs which it presents, will be successively noticed; and the description will be concluded, in some instances, by local details.

This part of the work will consist of an arranged and condensed view of the memoirs and other sources of information on the Geology of Devonshire, which have resulted from the labours of Dr. Berger, Dr. Macculloch, the late Rev. J. J. Conybeare, Mr. Greenough, Professor Sedgwick, Mr. De la Beche, Mr. Hennah, and other geologists, combined with information which is at present scattered through various works not expressly devoted to scientific subjects.   With these will be interwoven the results of an actual examination of some of the more interesting tracts, made by the present writer in 1825, especially of the neighbourhood of Exeter; with reference, particularly, to the relations of the new red sandstone to the masses of amygdaloidal trap which it contains.

The review of the geological formations existing in Minerals. Devonshire, will be followed by a descriptive catalogue of such of its more useful and remarkable MINERAL PRODUCTIONS, as have not been noticed in the preceding division.   Among these will of course be enumerated the celebrated Lignite of Bovey; the recently-discovered Magnetic Ironstone of Hay Tor; the Haytorite, or remarkable

z 2

pseudomorphous calcedony of the same locality, exhibiting, in great perfection, the crystalline forms belonging to a very different mineral; the Tourmalines of Bovey, and the ores of Copper and Tin which the County affords. Some particulars of the comparative strength and durability of the materials for building furnished by Devonshire, will also be introduced in this place, if not anticipated by the mineralogical history of the formations in the first division. The subjects of the second division naturally lead to that of the Mining History of Devon, to which the third division will be devoted. This will comprise some account of the extent and economy of the principal mines, as well as of the disposition of the mineral veins in which they are worked. The history of the progress of mining in Devonshire, together with that of the Stannaries, and some particulars of the quantities of copper and tin yielded by the mines, will also form a part of this portion of the Outlines.

As those magnificent configurations and diversities of surface which mark the tropical regions of the globe, and also characterize every country that is traversed by chains of lofty mountains, are not found in any part of England, and as Devonshire presents even a less near approach to them than the neighbouring County of Cornwall, and much less so than several of our north-westerly counties, the Physical Geography of Devon, so far as relates to the configuration of the surface of the country, will be best considered in connection with its Geology. But its most important characteristics will be reassembled in a short section introductory to a view of the HYDROGRAPHY and METEOROLOGY of Devonshire, or of the disposition and physical history of its streams and springs, including the mineral springs, or those which are impregnated with saline materials*; and that of the principal atmospheric variations and phænomena to which Devonshire is subject.

Physical
Geogra-
phy.

* Copious details respecting the topographical distribution and local history of the rivers of Devonshire having already been given in the General Description of the County, Book I. Chap. II., the notice of them here will be confined to their physical relations.

The division relating to Physical Geography will be concluded by a general review of the united results of the influence of configuration of surface, distribution of waters, and atmospherical phænomena, on the physical history of the County.   This part of the subject will naturally lead to the distribution of organic beings over the surface, of which the GEOGRAPHY OF THE PLANTS OF DEVON-SHIRE will form the leading portion, and will be followed by notices of some of the rarer and more remarkable indigenous plants.   On this branch of the subject an entire work has recently appeared from the pens of the Rev. Mr. Jones and Mr. Kingston, entitled *Flora Devoniensis:* it comprises a descriptive catalogue of plants growing wild in Devonshire; or rather two such catalogues, one in which the species are arranged according to the Linnæan system, and another in which they are distributed in the approximate natural method of Jussieu and Decandolle.   From this valuable work the materials for the Botanical division of the Outlines will chiefly be selected, but information derived from other sources will be interwoven with them; and since an arrangement representing, or approximating to, the true natural system of plants, is the only one which can be employed in an exposition of the Botanical Geography of any district, that alone will be adopted here, with perhaps some slight modifications with respect to the Cryptogamous plants, as proposed by Professors Agardh and Fries.

The Outlines of the ZOOLOGY of Devonshire, constituting the fourth section, will commence with some general observations on that subject, which will be followed by notices of the principal classes and orders of animals that are found in the County; together with catalogues of some of the more interesting minor groups of Invertebrate Animals peculiar to the district, or abundantly existing within its confines; and descriptive notices of rare individual species, especially if of late discovery.   In the arrangement of this section it will be endeavoured to preserve the Linnæan classification of the Vertebrated Ani-

CHAP. I.

Geography of the plants of Devonshire.

Zoology of Devon.

mals and of some others, so far as the larger groups are
concerned, at the same time that the principles of the
natural distribution of animated beings recently discovered,
and now pursuing with so much zeal by many of the most
instructed zoologists in England, will in no instance be
neglected.   In this respect the provisional combination
with the Linnæan System of an approximate natural method will be imitated, which has been adopted in the
catalogues of the Museum and Vivarium of the Zoological
Society, and in the publications on Zoology which have
appeared under the auspices of its Council and Officers.

By this means the views and sentiments of two classes
of scientific readers will be met, without inconvenience to
either, and without departure from that mode of treating
the subject which the general reader will require.   On
the one hand, the naturalist, or the amateur of natural
history, who has been accustomed strictly to adhere to
the method of Linnæus, will not be repelled by the groups
and the terminology of a method entirely novel ;—whilst,
on the other hand, the student, whose knowledge has
been obtained in the modern British school of Zoology
will be gratified by finding constant reference to those
new discoveries in the science, which supply the deficiencies of the Linnæan arrangement, and contribute still
further to establish the fame of its illustrious author, by
evincing how extensive and how correct was his knowledge of the affinities, by which the links in the great and
interminable chain of animal existence are united with
each other.

The Vertebrated Animals of Devonshire, comprising the
classes of Mammalia, Birds, Reptiles, Amphibious animals,
and Fishes, will first be considered ; with appropriate references to Pennant, Bewick, and other authors on British
Zoology.   The multitudinous tribes of the Annulosa, including Insects and Crustaceous animals, with the Arach-
nida, or class of Spiders, and some others, will next be
passed in rapid review. Mr. Curtis's beautiful delineations
of British Insects, and Mr. Stephens's Illustrations of

British Entomology, with some of the works of Dr. Leach, will here be referred to for figures and descriptions of remarkable species.   The Radiated animals of Devon, the *Radiaires* of Lamarck, which will comprise the Echinida or Sea-Urchins, the Stellerida or Star-fishes, and other groups, including the *Actiniadæ* or animal-flowers; and the Acritous or least-organized animals, comprising some of the *Vermes* and most of the *Zoophyta* of Linnæus, will successively follow.   To these the Testaceous and other Mollusca will succeed in order; and the most interesting and rare shells found on the coast of Devon will receive their share of brief attention; the Works and Memoirs by Col. Montagu, Dr. Maton and Mr. Rackett, and Mr. G. B. Sowerby, being consulted, and cited for figures and further illustrations.   And with the succinct history of these classes, so far as relates to the Zoology of Devon, will be interwoven that of some minor yet highly important groups of animals, including, among others, the Annelida or worms having red blood, and the Cirripeda (*Lepas* Linn.) which appear to connect the primary groups into a series, without being strictly referable to any of them, so far, at least, as their organization and affinities are at present understood.

Some concluding inferences and reflections, and probably a few notes, supplying the deficiencies which may have been detected in the progress of the work, will then conclude the proposed " Outlines of the Geology, Physical Geography, and Natural History of the County of Devon."

Since the systematic arrangement of such a view as is here proposed to be taken of the physical history of any district of country, must be the same, whether the subjects be described at length or with brevity, the foregoing plan might, possibly, without some further explanation, be taken for the proposed contents of a voluminous work. On the contrary, however, all that can be attempted in the present case, will be a brief view of the history of each department of nature, as presented in that portion of our island, to describe which is the object of the present

Extent of these Outlines.

publication; accompanied with such references to sources of more detailed information, as will enable the local resident desirous of attending to the natural history of his own vicinity, or the scientific inquirer into the physical peculiarities of the County, to verify his observations or complete his knowledge, of the distribution within it of rocks and minerals, as well as of organized beings.

That the execution of the Outlines will fully meet the expectations which the foregoing syllabus of their proposed contents will in all probability excite, the author cannot pretend to infer. The novelty of the attempt to combine with Topographical History, a systematic view of the physical structure and natural productions of the County it describes, the periodical mode of publication of the work, and the professional engagements of the author, which allow a comparatively small portion of time only to be devoted to the necessary researches, will all conspire to render the execution inadequate to the design;—and the same circumstances, it is probable, will also have their influence in preventing an absolutely strict adherence to the plan of treating the subject, which has been proposed in the foregoing pages.

From the progress which has already been made, however, in assembling together the requisite authorities and materials, and from the assistance which several scientific friends have kindly engaged to contribute, he is induced to hope that, as a first attempt, at least, to introduce a new department into Topographical Literature, it will in some degree be worthy of the encouragement and attention of the general reader as well as of the cultivator of science.

VIXEN TOR.

CHAPTER II.

PRELIMINARY GENERAL REMARKS ON THE GEOLOGY
OF DEVONSHIRE.—INFERIOR ROCKS, AND THE DIS-
TRICTS IN WHICH THEY PREVAIL.—GRANITE AND
METALLIFEROUS SLATE.

For the purpose of taking a preliminary general view of
the Geological history of this County, we will suppose
ourselves, with Professor Sedgwick, surveying it from the
summit of the Haldon Hills.

We here find an alluvial cap containing many fragments
of common chalk flint; under which are the remains of
the greensand formation, and of the beds with which it
is usually associated.

From this elevation we command, on the eastern side,
the rich woodlands of the valley of the Ex. On the south-
west we have a country equally diversified and of the same
general aspect, though less exuberant in vegetation. To
the west and north-west, however, the face of nature is

CHAP.
II.

General
view of the
Geology
of Devon-
shire.

BOOK
III.
───
Granite
ridges.

completely changed. A succession of ridges, rising to an elevation considerably greater than any of the neighbouring hills, exhibits a singularly broken and rugged outline; and the whole appearance of the contiguous country forcibly impresses us with the idea of its barrenness and desolation. Almost any one, while surveying the outline presented by these elevations, though still seen on the distant horizon, would be led to conclude that this extremity of Dartmoor was of a composition entirely different from any of the hills he had left behind him.

At the eastern end of Dartmoor commences the great granitic ridge, which prevails, though not without considerable interruptions, through the mid region of Cornwall, and at length terminates in the broken cliffs of the Land's End. By whatever side we approach the moor, we find it flanked by hills of less elevation and of entirely different structure. The whole upper surface may be considered as making a rude approach to a broken table land of elliptical form, the longest diameter of which is more than twenty miles, and may be represented by a line drawn from Harford to Oakhampton.

Slaty
rocks.

From many of the higher parts of its western extremity we have a commanding view of the rich extent of country, which descends to the banks of the Tamar and the Tavy. This beautiful and picturesque region gains a double interest from being contrasted with the barren uniformity of the moor. The schistose rocks to the west of Dartmoor in some instances reach the elevation of eight or nine hundred feet. They are intersected by numerous mineral veins, which continue to be worked to great advantage, more especially in the neighbourhood of St. Mary Tavy and Beeralston. " In advancing to the west by the high moorlands which prevail throughout the middle of the peninsula, we find that the most elevated portions of the tract are composed of granite."

With the exception of these, almost all the country extending from Dartmoor to the Land's End, and bounded to the north and south by the Bristol and English Channels,

may be referred to one formation.   The prevailing rocks
of this formation are known in the West of England by
the provincial name Killas.   Granite is the fundamental
rock of the whole region.

" All the widely extended moors, more especially those
in which the granite rocks predominate, are of a wild and
dreary aspect.   They are thinly covered with vegetation,
and that often of the very worst quality; and in some
instances nearly half the surface is occupied by granite
bowlders, the remains of larger masses of the same kind
which have gradually disappeared through the corrosive
action of the elements. After descending from the granite
ridge to the killas, we often find a country almost destitute of foliage, and in few respects more inviting than the
one we have left behind.

" One who is attracted by the grand and more rugged
features of nature, will find many of the high tors and
masses of decomposing granite, which lie scattered about
the moors, well deserving of his examination."

Inferior Rocks: Granite, and the Rocks associated with it.

A crystalline aggregate of quartz, felspar, and mica,
forms by far the greatest part of the fundamental rock in
the region about to be described.   Varieties, arising from
the loss of one of these ingredients, or from the addition
of some other mineral, are by no means uncommon.   As
these, however, form the exception, any further consideration of them will be postponed till we have given some
account of the more prevailing rock.   Keeping therefore
in mind its most general character, the granite of the West
of England may be described as coarse-grained, and of a
grayish or yellowish colour, derived from the felspar, which
is the predominating ingredient.   When examined on the
great scale, it is often found porphyritic; the three constituents forming a granular base, in which are imbedded
large crystals of felspar. We may observe also that these
large crystals often exhibit a bright clear fracture, while
the felspar of the base is dull, earthy, and decomposing.

BOOK
III.

Crystals of
felspar in
them.

The large prismatic crystals are not unusually of that structure which Haüy calls hemitrope; and their recent fracture sometimes exposes small specks of mica, arranged within the prisms, in a figure which represents the section of a rhombohedron, and to which they have no doubt, been determined by the crystalline forces exercised at the consolidation of the mineral in which they are imbedded. The felspar is often crystallized in forms which are perfectly exhibited. Twin crystals arising from the intersection of two rhombohedrons, and hexagonal tables, are among these varieties. The granite bowlders on the moors afford most favourable opportunities for examining such appearances; but their smooth rounded surfaces make it exceedingly difficult to detach from them illustrative specimens for the cabinet. Of the other two constituents, quartz and mica, the former is always amorphous, and the latter generally presents the appearance of abraded fragments, rather than of regular crystals. These phænomena may be considered as the imperfect forms of a disturbed crystallization, and caused by the simultaneous consolidation of the heterogeneous ingredients.

Fissures in
the gra-
nite.

Wherever any natural section of the country exposes an extended surface of the granite, we find portions of it divided by fissures, which often, for a considerable extent, preserve an exact parallelism among themselves. These masses are not unfrequently subdivided by a second system of fissures, nearly perpendicular to the former; in consequence of which structure the whole aggregate becomes separated into blocks of a rhombohedral form.

The cliffs near Tol-Pedn-Penwith, in Cornwall, which in many places make a rude approach to a columnar structure, are divided into prismatic blocks, of such regularity, both in their form and arrangement, that they convey a striking resemblance to some piece of gigantic architecture. This peculiarity of form and structure acts powerfully on our associations; and leads us to do homage to the works of nature by contrasting them with the petty operations of human skill. This separation of the mass

by nearly parallel fissures is considered as indicating the
first stage of decomposition.

By the action of the atmosphere the fissures become enlarged; the solid angles at the points of separation gradually disappear; the rhombohedral blocks approach the
spheroidal form, and, no longer affording a firm support
to each other, the whole mass becomes ruinous, and forms
an irregular heap of rounded fragments.   Some part of
the cliffs between the Land's End and Cape Cornwall afford
striking examples of this second stage of decomposition.
From the upper part of the cliff being more exposed to
atmospheric action than the portions immediately below
them, we not unusually find these rounded masses resting
on blocks which still preserve the tabular form.   These
spheroidal blocks will obviously rest in that position in
which their lesser axes are perpendicular to the horizon:
it is also clear that if any mechanical force be applied to
them, they will, on its removal, restore themselves to the
position of permanent equilibrium.   Many thousand rocks
which are thus circumstanced, might, by an adequate force,
be made to vibrate on their point of support.   The celebrated Logan-Stone of Castle-Trereen, in Cornwall, is
above sixty tons in weight, and is poised on so firm a pivot,
that it may be made to oscillate through a sensible arc by
the mere force of the hand.   Many examples of the forms
assumed by granite during its first progress towards disintegration, are to be met with among the tors and higher
parts of the interior.   But by far the greater portion of
these moors exhibit the rock only in its second stage of
decomposition, where the soil is continually interrupted
by the naked surfaces of great bowlders, which are but
the nuclei of still larger blocks which once formed a continuous mass above the present surface.

Nearly all the granite of the West of England which
has of late years been so extensively used in our metropolis, is procured from these bowlders.   The indestructible
nature of one of the component parts of granite, and the
structure of the whole by which it is preserved from decomposition in one direction rather than another, are cir-

BOOK
III.

cumstances favourable to the duration of buildings formed of such materials. Still, Prof. Sedgwick thinks that stone procured from rocks which present such evident traces of decomposition, ought not to be used without most suspicious examination.   In addition we may remark, that many of the houses in Cornwall which have been built of granite, are continually damp from the penetration of moisture through the earthy part of the stone ;   and this is unfortunately the case even where the greatest possible care has been taken in the selection of the materials and in the construction of the walls.

Under the thin vegetable soil of the moors we may frequently find earthy siliceous beds, obviously derived from the granite, which may be considered as an exhibition of that rock in its last stage of decomposition.

Rocks associated with the granite.

We shall now proceed to describe some of the rocks which are usually associated with the granite. Among the most common varieties may be mentioned,

1st, Those which arise from the addition of a fourth mineral (as, for example, schorl or oxide of tin), so disseminated as to become a true constituent of the mass.

Quartz and felspar alone.

2nd, From the disappearance of one of the component parts.   A beautiful example of this may be seen at the foot of Dartmoor, between Ivy Bridge, and Harford. The rock immediately in contact with the schist is composed of bright red felspar and quartz, presenting some traces of that aggregation which forms the variety called Graphic granite.

Schorl rock.

Schorl rock (that is, a granular compound of quartz and schorl) is by far the most striking of all the mineral masses associated with the granite. We shall here enumerate some of its most common varieties.

1. Granular quartz rock, with deeply striated prismatic crystals of schorl, of a coal black colour, and without regular terminations, uniformly disseminated through the mass *. It is most commonly of finer texture than the gra-

* In one instance Professor Sedgwick saw the striated crystals with regular terminations. They were obtained on the east side of Dartmoor, but he did not find them *in situ*.

nite; but varieties may be found, especially on the north side of Dartmoor, in which a very coarse granular base contains crystals of schorl several inches in length.

2. Where the schorl rock is porphyritic, containing flesh-coloured crystals of felspar. These crystals are often decomposing. In some instances they have disappeared altogether, and the base then resembles a scoria.

Specimens have been obtained from the south side of Dartmoor, &c.

Blocks presenting some of the above-mentioned varieties, lie scattered about the surface in many parts of Devonshire and Cornwall, especially near the junction of the killas and granite. They form the whole of that magnificent mass of rocks near Roach, and in that neighbourhood are so widely extended, as almost to assume the characters of a distinct formation. In general, however, we do not find them *in situ;* but they seem to be undecomposed fragments of veins, or irregular masses which were once imbedded in the granite. This opinion is confirmed by the appearance of the western cliffs, which are irregularly traversed by veins of schorl rock varying from the fraction of an inch to many feet in thickness.

Such a description of the great formations of the County will necessarily embrace those varieties which are strictly of contemporaneous origin, whether they present themselves in the form of veins, irregular concretions, or imbedded masses. Accordingly, those mineral aggregates only are described which have appeared in some of the above-mentioned forms, and are supposed to be coeval with the granite. They might perhaps, without impropriety, be considered but as modifications of the granite; produced at the consolidation of the mass by the prevalence of certain ingredients in one part rather than another; or by the anomalous action of crystalline forces, arising from disturbing causes with which we are unacquainted. These opinions seem to gain great confirmation, when it is recollected that perhaps all the ingredients of these anomalous rocks are occasionally found disseminated

BOOK
III.
___

Dr. Mac-
culloch on
the granite
of Devon
and Corn-
wall.

Shaugh
Rick.
throughout the mass, and then appear to form a true constituent part of the granite.

The granite of Devonshire and Cornwall is in general
split by fissures in different directions, but most commonly
tending to the perpendicular and horizontal. By these it
is divided into masses of a cuboidal and prismatic shape.
Of the exceptions to this rule there is one among many
other instances, in Shaugh Rick near Plymouth. If we
examine a rock of this kind near the surface of the soil,
we shall find that the fissure is a mere mathematical plane,
separating the two parts, and that the angles are sharp and
perfect. If we now turn our attention to granites which
from their greater elevation above the present soil appear
to have been longer exposed to air and weather, we shall
find, as the first step to change, besides the wasting of
the surface, a gentle rounding of the angles, such as is
exhibited in the Vixen Tor on Dartmoor, and also by
many others in the same tract. By degrees the surfaces
which were in contact, and which in the Vixen Tor remain
at present in contact, become separated to a certain distance, which goes on to augment indefinitely, and the
prisms or cuboids become separated into detached masses.
We witness in the granites of this aspect which remain
unchanged in their places, an aggregated mass of cuboids.
As the wearing continues to proceed more rapidly near the
parts which are most external, and therefore most exposed,
the masses which were originally prismatic acquire an
irregular curvilinear boundary, and the stone assumes an
appearance resembling the blocks which constitute the
Cheesewring in Cornwall, a grotesque pile occupying the
highest ridge of a hill to the north of Liskeard, forming
part of the same granite chain; supposed by Borlase to
be a Druid-sculptured image of Saturn. If the centre of
gravity of the mass chances to be high, and far removed
from the perpendicular of its fulcrum, the stone falls from
its elevation, and becomes constantly rounder by the continuance of decomposition, till it assumes one of the various spheroidal figures which the granite bowlders so

often exhibit. A different disposition of that centre will
cause it to preserve its position for a greater length of
time, or in favourable circumstances may produce a Logan
stone, and to this cause the celebrated Logan at Castle
Trereen in Cornwall is undoubtedly to be attributed.

CHAP.
II.

The changes which the bowlders thus formed undergo
in their places of rest, by their more rapid disintegration
at the angles than at the sides, are sufficient to prove that
their spheroidal shape may be produced by the chemical
action of air and water, without the necessity of any mechanical violence.

Granite
bowlders.

That the wearing of these granites on the surface arises
from the action of water, will be evident on examining
the stones themselves, and the result of their disintegration. Whenever a stone is disintegrated by the most usual
process, the increased degree of oxidation of the iron which
it contains, a change may always be observed to have taken
place, from the surface downwards, to a more or less considerable depth in the stone. Sometimes even the whole
mass of rock will appear to have undergone this gangre-
nous process at once, and to have become a bed of clay
and gravel. But in the case of the granite now under view,
it is evident that the change is merely superficial, and
that no process of increased oxidation has taken place.
Indeed many of the varieties, of which the mica and felspar
are nearly white, contain so little iron that they are hardly
subject to decomposition from this cause, however much
they may, in such particular cases as that of the granite of
St. Stephens in Cornwall, resolve entirely into gravel and
porcelain clay. The most satisfactory proof, however, that
the mere agency of water is sufficient to disintegrate this
granite, is presented by the rock basins.

Origin of
these
changes.

We need not hesitate in admitting the solution of granite in water to an extent capable of producing this effect
of disintegration; since we know that silica (or the pure
earth of flints, of which the quartz in granite entirely consists, and which forms the greater part of the felspar and
mica) is soluble in that fluid by natural means, as the si-

Action of
water.

liceous deposits of the Geysers of Iceland evince, however imperfectly we have been able to imitate the process in our laboratories. It is also not improbable that the quantity of potash (nearly 16 per cent.) which enters into the compo sition of felspar, may confer on it a similar property, and that even in a greater degree, although direct experiments are wanting to prove this fact. Whichever of these bodies (the quartz or the felspar) is acted on in the case of this disintegration, the quantity of matter actually dissolved is probably very little; we can even conceive it possible that the mere alternation of the states of moisture and dryness, combined with frequent changes of temperature at the surface, may be sufficient to produce this effect without any actual solution of the substance of the rock.

Change of figure.

It is a matter of more difficulty to assign the cause of the changes of figure which the masses undergo; by what process Nature *mutat quadrata rotundis*.

Whether the fissures, as originally existing in the granite, are to be considered as the effects of contraction produced in the mass by the evaporation of water, or by the abstraction of heat, must depend on the conclusions which shall ultimately be adopted, relative to the aqueous or igneous origin of this rock. But in whatever way we suppose the fissures to have been formed, we have still a difficulty unsolved; and that is, the tendency they exhibit to wear more rapidly on the angles and edges than on the sides, and thus to assume the spheroidal forms which facilitate the ultimate ruin and migration of the summits.

That this would be the consequence of a gradual action merely mechanical is undoubted, as the mass must ultimately acquire that figure which, being the last result of the action of decomposition, is the one which will offer the greatest resistance to further change. In a chemical view, the same must also to a certain extent hold true; since any given particle, supposed cubical, and placed at the angle or edge of the mass, will be exposed to the action of the solvent on two or more surfaces, while that on the side of the mass is exposed but to one: hence the angular body must

ultimately change its figure, and approximate to a spheroidal form. It is easy however to see that the influence
of this cause will be retarded in a quickly increasing ratio,
and that it is insufficient to account for the extreme change
of form suffered by granitic masses. If it were sufficient
in the case of granite, it should equally produce a determination to the spheroidal form in sandstones having a
prismatic fracture. But in these we see that the process
of superior waste at the angles and edges, soon ceases to
produce an effect in modifying the figure of the mass,
and that sandstone never assumes the decidedly spheroidal
forms which are exhibited by granite.

If we now suppose the hardness of a mass of granite, or
its resistance to the disintegrating power of air and water,
to vary in any given ratio at certain distances from the centre, it is evident that the effect of chemical action on the
surface, will be to change the figure of that mass, and that
the ultimate effect will be to disclose the sphere inscribed
within that cube.

Let us consider how far the facts bear us out in this
supposition :

De Luc has observed in his Geology, that granite sometimes decomposes into spheroidal forms, and he describes
piles of this rock in Silesia, resembling, as he says, Dutch
cheeses. I need not quote more authorities for a fact witnessed by innumerable observers. In our own island of
Arran, nodules of spherical granite are found in the valleys
which descend from Goatfield, decomposing on the surface
in crusts, and marking decidedly the very construction
which my supposition requires, in a much greater degree
than is requisite for the purpose. Similar granite balls
have been seen in other places, so that their existence is
well ascertained. It is certain that these balls, now rendered spherical by decomposition, have been quadrangular
masses; and hence we may step, without any great hazard
of unsound footing, to this general conclusion,—that these
masses of granite, which show marks of wearing on their
surface, with rapidities proportioned to their distance from

Spheroidal
forms in
granite.

BOOK
III.

Spheroidal
concre-
tions in
granite.

a central point, have had their hardness, and probably
their crystallization or formation, determined from that
centre, or have a concentric structure.

It will be an additional support to the inference from
this mode of decomposing, that such is the structure of
this granite, to cite some instances which Dr. Macculloch
brings forward in support of his explanation, as given in
the note below *. These are, the spherically-disposed gra-

* The analogy of this circumstance to the similar balls formed in basaltic rocks is illustrative of both the cases, and probably both will equally
tend to confirm the opinions which have been held relating to the igneous
origin of these substances. Thus, if for the sake of argument I may be
allowed to assume that granite is of igneous origin, it will be easy to explain the peculiar appearances exhibited by that formation of granite,
which, like those of Cornwall and Arran, and many others, is separated
into cuboidal masses. " Here we must conceive, that in a homogeneous
mass of fluid matter, crystallization had commenced from numerous centres at the same time. While there was yet space for the formation of
successive solid deposits round any set of these imaginary centres, a
spherical or spheroidal figure would be the result. As the surfaces of
these spheroids approached each other, the successive crusts would interfere, and the remaining intervals would be filled by portions of spheroidal crusts, until the cuboidal figures of all the contiguous masses were
completed, thus forming that aggregated mass of cuboids which we witness in the granites of this aspect which remain uninjured in their places.
We need not be surprised that this regularity is not more constant, nor
the forms more perfect, as we are unacquainted with the numerous circumstances which may determine the several centres of crystallization,
or which may interfere with the ultimate regularity of the resulting
masses. It is certain from chemical experiments, that the fact which is
the basis of the foregoing supposition, occurs in various instances of the
cooling of slags and of rocks artificially fused, as Mr. Watt's experiments
(on the fusing of basalt, &c. *Phil. Trans.* 1804.) have so well shown.
But in these experiments, certain as they are, we are unacquainted with
the causes which determine the places of the several centres of crystallization; and though equally unacquainted with those which may have
influenced the centres on which the granite masses were formed, we may
yet from analogy understand how the irregularity of these masses may
have been caused by a corresponding irregularity in the position of their
centres".

We can also easily conceive that in certain cases, the peculiar circumstances of which lie equally hid from us, the approximation of the spheres
of crystallization may have caused the crystalline polarity of the several
masses to interfere with each other, so as to have produced in many cases
an irregularity still greater than this, and in some instances even entirely
to have obliterated the appearance of central tendencies. " To the chemical facts above adduced in support of this explanation, I might subjoin,
what every one's mind will immediately suggest, the illustration which the
commenced spheroidal forms of the Cheshire rock salt, and the igneous
explanation of the forms of basaltic columns, add to this supposition."

nite of Corsica, or Napoleonite, which exhibits the constituents of granite formed round numerous centres, and producing those beautiful specimens still so rare in the cabinets of collectors. Similar radiating tendencies in the smaller parts have been noticed by Saussure, and Professor Jameson has described them as existing in Arran. Dr. Macculloch has also witnessed a similar disposition in the mica which is included in the granite veins near Portsoy; and the same structure is well known to exist in that variety of granite which is called Tyger granite, in which the hornblende or schorl forms radiating spheres.

Dr. Macculloch concludes by suggesting in aid of his explanation, the spherical structure of certain varieties of granite, already mentioned in the text in describing the structure of the granite of Dartmoor.

The following is Dr. Macculloch's account of rock basins, which also occur in Devonshire as well as in Cornwall. "On the flat surfaces of these stones are frequently to be observed excavations, assuming some curved figure with rounded bottoms. Occasionally they are circular in their boundary, and as regularly spheroidal internally as if they had been shaped by a turning lathe. They are of various depths, and they may be sometimes observed to communicate with each other. Their artificial appearance was sufficient to convince of the truth of his system regarding them, this strenuous supporter of a worship [Dr. Borlase], which must on his hypothesis have required a priesthood sufficient to exclude all other population, if every rounded cavity which the granite exhibits was a pool of lustration.

"Their true origin is easily traced by inspecting the rocks themselves. On examining the excavations, they will always be found to contain distinct grains of quartz and fragments of the other constituent parts of the granite. A small force is sufficient to detach from the sides of these cavities additional fragments, showing that a process of decomposition is still going on under favourable circum-

Rock basins.

stances.   These circumstances are the presence of water,
or the alternate action of air and water.   If a drop of water
can make an effectual lodgment on a surface of this granite, a small cavity is sooner or later produced.   This insensibly enlarges as it becomes capable of holding more
water, and the sides as they continue to waste necessarily
retain an even and rounded concavity, on account of the
uniform texture of the granite.   In time, the accumulated
gravel is blown away by the winds, although in the deeper
hollows it may often be found forming considerable accumulations."

First ap-
pearance
of granite
in the
South of
Devon-
shire.

Kitt Hill is the nearest place to the sea from the mouth
of the Hamoaze, where granite, in Devonshire, is found *in
situ*.   This little hill, though insulated, must be considered
as a dependency of the mountains of Dartmoor: it is
situated on the southern skirt of the granitic mountain-
plain of the low range of Cornwall.

The sides of Kitt Hill are gently inclined; that on the
east is the most abrupt.   The north and south sides are
the most extended, and may be considered as the water-
sheds.   The upper part of the hill is a true granite, composed of crystals of white felspar, quartz, and mica.   From
Callington to Plymouth, by Beer Alston, Beer Ferris, and
Tamarton Folliet, as far as the point where the high road
to Tavistock joins, the granwacke slate continues.   Its
stratification is very distinctly seen at the passage of the
Tamar near Calstock, and of the Tavy near Beer Ferris.

At Calstock the strata are cut more abruptly on the
left bank, and at Beer Ferris on the right bank, from which
we may infer that the depth of the Tamar and the Tavy is
not the same at both banks, the depth of a river being in
general increased as its banks become more precipitous.

The grauwacke slate also continues in the road from
Plymouth to Ivy Bridge.   On approaching the latter place
we find pebbles, and even adventitious blocks of granite,
which being brought down into the plains, by the rivers
which flow from the highland of Dartmoor, show that that
district is formed of primary rocks.

Of the Mountain Plain of Dartmoor Forest.

When we trace up the courses of the rivers which flow through Devonshire, we find they all rise in an elevated and extensive plain situated nearly in the middle of the county, and upon which the adjacent rocks, gradually rising as they approach it, are found to rest. The south and north sides are the water-sheds of the mountain plain. The Tavy, the Plym, the Yealme, the Erme, the Avon, and the Dart, flow down the southern side; the two Oakments and the Taw run to the north: there is only the Bovey on the south-east, and the Lyd on the west, and these are both very small streams.

Dr. Berger entered Dartmoor Forest by the valley of the Erme, which opens at Ivy Bridge. This little valley is at first contracted and deep, with a rapid ascent. The general direction is nearly from north to south, which is the same with the course of the river flowing through it. Thus it appears that these valleys, which are all similar to each other, are perpendicular to the mountain plain. Dartmoor.

Leaving the bed of the river Erme to the left, about five minutes walk from Ivy Bridge, we pass some farm-houses at the bottom of a small detached hill, situated N.N.E. of Ivy Bridge, and thence to the top of the hill is about two miles and a half by the nearest road. This small hill, the only abrupt face of which is towards the south, is situated on the exterior line of the mountains of Dartmoor, on the first plain from the sea coast. The upper half is composed of a rock which Dr. Berger calls a porphyritic granite, and the lower part, as well as the base, is of grauwacke. He found the summit to be 1130 feet above the level of the sea, and the greatest height to which the grauwacke rises on its sides is 631 feet.

There is on the right bank of the Erme another small hill, equally rounded in its outline. Kitt Hill is situated further in the interior of the country than the small hill above Ivy Bridge. The distance of the latter from the

BOOK
III.

Valley
of the
Erme.

coast is, in a direct line, scarcely nine miles, whereas Kitt Hill is at least thirteen.

In proportion as the valley of the Erme rises, it continues to open, insomuch, that at three miles and some furlongs from Ivy Bridge northward, the river is no longer confined in a narrow channel, but flows over a plain gently inclined towards the south.

This mountain plain, at Harford Church, which is 658 feet above the sea, is entirely granite. We leave the grauwacke behind, about half a mile nearer the sea, and in ascending the valley of the Erme the point of termination is very distinctly seen, particularly on the left bank. At the junction there are veins or shoots of granite of different lengths and breadths, and they appear to penetrate into the grauwacke. The two rocks are certainly contiguous, and in immediate contact the one with the other. The grauwacke near its termination loses its slaty character, as may be seen on the sides of the hill above Ivy Bridge, where it attains nearly the same height as in the last-mentioned place.

The primary rock of this district is a true granite, composed of felspar, quartz, and mica, and its crystals of felspar are sometimes two or three inches long. From Harford Church the country assumes quite a bare and alpine appearance, presenting a vast plain extending beyond the visible horizon. The face of the country is formed by swellings and undulations gradually overtopping each other without ever forming very distinct mountains. There is neither vegetation nor any human dwelling; we tread upon a boggy soil of very little depth, and scarcely furnishing sufficient food to support some dwarf colts, wild as the country they inhabit.

Source of
the Erme.

The Erme rises about nine miles north of Ivy Bridge, and 1131 feet above the level of the sea, the land gradually rising as we approach its source. This, however, is not the most elevated point of this part of Dartmoor Forest; Dr. Berger judged that point to be near a place three miles south-east of Two Bridges, where some tin

BABICOMBE.

NEAR TORQUAY DEVON.

Drawn by T H Williams

Engraved by T Higham

VIEW FROM THE PARAPET OF THE PUBLIC ROOMS, TEIGNMOUTH, DEVON.

mines were worked, and where the oxide of that metal, constituting the mineral called *tinstone*, is found disseminated in the granite, as one of its integrant parts, forming an example of the first variety of rocks associated with the granite, as described in p. 264.

Two Bridges is fourteen miles to the north of Ivy Bridge. Until the erection of the Prison, during the late war, there was but one house here, and that is an inn, which stands nearly in the middle of this vast mountain-plain, which contains, Dr. Berger states, nearly three hundred and fifty square miles of surface *. Two Bridges is 1148 feet above the level of the sea. To the north of this place the granitic country appears to extend as far as to the neighbourhood of Oakhampton; but Dr. Berger does not assert this positively, as he did not trace it himself over the whole of that extent; he can only say, he observes, "that, according to the course of the rivers, the only mountain of any consequence which appears to me to rise above this mountain-plain, and which is, without

CHAP.
II.

Two
Bridges.

Extent of
Dartmoor.

* Dr. Berger appears to have comprised, in this estimate, the commons which slope down from the elevated plain of Dartmoor itself, to the extent of two miles on every side. Walkhampton Common alone contains 10,000 acres, or nearly 15¼ square miles.

Five other estimates of the extent of Dartmoor have been made, all differing materially from the foregoing, as well as from each other. The discrepancies have no doubt arisen, in great measure, from the surveyors and others by whom they have been made, assuming different limits as those of the Moor itself, exclusive of its dependencies; and also, it is probable, from some difference in the methods adopted by each for estimating the superficial extent of the many highly-inclined surfaces presented by the elevations of the Moor. Thus in Mr. T. Gray's survey, made in 1796, and quoted by Lysons, Dartmoor is stated to contain 53,644 acres, or nearly 84 square miles; Fraser, as quoted by Dr. Maton, computes its extent at 80,000 acres, or 125 square miles; in 1798 another survey gave 96,000 acres, or 150 square miles; and it has also been estimated at 100,000 acres, or 156 square miles.

As the improvements which have successively been made in the art of surveying land, have always shown that former surveys of undulating and highly-inclined tracts have given estimates of their extent less than the truth, we may infer from the above statements that the estimate of 130,000 acres, or 203 square miles, for the superficial extent of Dartmoor itself, exclusive of the surrounding commons, as given in a report made some years since to the House of Commons, may be relied upon as the most correct; and as agreeing, when the commons are taken into the account, with Dr. Berger's statement.

BOOK
III.

doubt, the highest point of all that part of the country, is
Craumere rock, where the two rivers Oakment and Dart
have their source."

Dr. Berger bent his course from Two Bridges to
Launceston in Cornwall, by St. Mary Tavy, Brentor,
and Lifton, making a circuit of the exterior boundary of
that part of Dartmoor forest. As long as the mountain-
plain continues, the country preserves the same appearance; and all along the road between Two Bridges and
Tavistock, for the first six or seven miles, we find on the
surface of the ground great numbers of granite blocks;

Blocks of
granite on
the Moor.

these probably come either from the tors, or are produced
by the rock on the surface splitting in that manner, in
consequence of the continued action of external agents.
Several of these blocks are so firmly fixed in the ground
from which they project, and are besides so uniformly
spread over the surface in every direction, that they cannot be supposed to have been transported by a current
to the place which they now occupy *.

First ap-
pearance of
the metal-
liferous
slate.

At the distance of three miles and a quarter from Tavistock the *Metalliferous Slate* begins to appear in a very
distinct manner, and at the height of 1129 feet above the
level of the sea †. From this place the country lowers

* See Prof. Sedgwick's and Dr. Macculloch's account of these blocks,
and of the cause of their present figure, p. 252–254, and p. 256–261.

† As Dr. Berger's observations were made above twenty years since,
at a period when the nature and distribution of the British rocks were
but little understood, it has been necessary to make a few corrections in
his statements as given in the memoir from which the above account of
Dartmoor is derived. He appears to have confounded together, under
the names of grauwacké and grauwacké-slate, two distinct rocks; to one
of which, belonging apparently to the *Submedial* or *Transition series* of
geologists, those denominations rightly apply; while the other, which is
termed, in the text, metalliferous slate, is one of the *Inferior series* usually
called the *Primary rocks*, and has generally received the name of clay-
slate. The subject is still involved in considerable obscurity, so far as
relates to the respective boundaries and relations to the subjacent granite, of the grauwacké and the metalliferous slate; and it is difficult, in
some instances, to ascertain, without an actual examination of the localities mentioned by Dr. Berger, of which of these rocks he is speaking.
Where it could with certainty be inferred that he is alluding to the
metalliferous slate, provincially termed *Killas*, the name of that rock has
been substituted above, for grauwacké; but still in several cases in which

with a pretty quick descent towards Tavistock; and the
change of rock here is accompanied by so complete a
change in the vegetation, that it is impossible not to
be struck by it. Nothing can be more remarkable than to
see on the skirt of this mountain-plain, towards St. Mary
Tavy and Brentor, highly cultivated valleys, succeeded
by rich pastures, which rise as high as the line of superposition of the grauwacké upon the inferior rocks, above
which there is nothing but bare and naked rock.

About a mile from St. Mary Tavy, near the place
where the roads join which lead from Plymouth to Oakhampton, and from Tavistock to Two Bridges, there is a
bed of greenstone of some feet in thickness, in the metalliferous slate; it decomposes into a green earth. With
regard to the slate itself, the direction and inclination
of its strata continue the same; it only contains more
quartz as we approach St. Mary Tavy, and becomes at
the same time less slaty.

St. Mary Tavy is 648 feet above the level of the sea.
A copper mine was worked here at a great depth, and
amongst the rubbish Dr. Berger found grauwacké and
schistose limestone, similar to that at the mouth of the
Plym, heaped one above the other; which shows that the
epochs of formation of these two rocks are nearly coeval,
since we find beds of the one included in those of the
other *. From St. Mary Tavy to Launceston, by Bren-

Bed of
green-
stone.

Grau-
wacké and
limestone.

the latter name has been retained, from defect of evidence to authorize
its change, it is probable that the rock alluded-to by Dr. Berger is in
reality the metalliferous slate. This may be the case with the junction of
the granite and the "grauwacké" observed in ascending the valley of the
Erme, as mentioned in p. 264; for although no clay-slate is indicated in
Mr. Greenough's geological map of England and Wales, as reposing on
the south-eastern flanks of Dartmoor, yet the appearances described by
Dr. Berger, are characteristic rather of clay-slate than of grauwacké.
The same may perhaps be said respecting the small detached hill,
N.N.E. of Ivy Bridge, mentioned in p. 263. The passage of the Tamar,
near Calstock, alluded-to in p. 262, is very near the line of junction of
the grauwacké with the metalliferous slate: the stratification there exposed is probably that of the latter rock.

* The spot here mentioned by Dr. Berger appears to be on or near
the line of junction of the grauwacké with the metalliferous slate; and
as the former rock frequently contains calcareous beds, hence the asso-

BOOK III.

Grau-wacké slate.

tor and *Lifton*, we cross successively the river Lyd and the Tamar, continuing in the grauwacké-slate formation, to within a mile of Launceston. The strata of the grauwacké-slate are very distinctly seen at the ferries of those two rivers *. It is succeeded by a schistose limestone, having a very fine paste of a dark blue colour and dull lustre, dividing into large flags, which are put to the same use as slate, and which Dr. Berger says he should have taken for such, if he had not found that the stone effervesced with acid †.

Mr. Prideaux's memoir on the granite of Dart-moor.

In 1828, Mr. John Prideaux, member of the Plymouth Institution,—the same gentleman, we presume, whose ingenious and well-directed efforts to fix, accurately and definitively, some important equivalent numbers in Chemistry, have lately appeared in the New Series of the Philosophical Magazine and Annals of Philosophy,—published a " Geological Sketch of the Country between the rivers Plym and Tamar, from the Granite of Dartmoor, southward to the Sea." From this publication we shall extract, with a few slight alterations and omissions, those portions which relate to the Granite-formation; thus concluding our series of abstracts of memoirs respecting this part of the Geology of Devonshire.

Aspect of the Dart-moor gra-nite dis-trict.

The granite of Dartmoor, from Mist-Tor to Hey-Tor, and south of that line, has the following characters, which probably belong to the whole. It is entirely mountainous, the highest elevations being on the borders, on which some of them attain an elevation of nearly 2000 feet. The

---

ciation of it with a limestone resembling that of Plymouth, as described above. It is, therefore, the grauwacké, not the metalliferous slate, which is shown, by the phænomena alluded-to, to be coeval with the limestone.

* St. Mary Tavy is situated near the northern termination of the metalliferous slate; and Dr. Berger, therefore, in travelling to Launceston, must have crossed the line of junction of that rock with the grauwacké. At the ferries over the Lyd and the Tamar, taking Mr. Greenough's map as the authority, the strata are those of the latter formation.

† " Observations on the Physical Structure of Devonshire and Cornwall," by J. F. Berger, M.D. of Geneva.—Transactions of the Geological Society, vol. i. p. 116–122.

valleys run in various directions, but have a tendency, upon the whole, to the north and south line.   The hills rise often steep, sometimes precipitous; their sides are scantily clothed with long grass, except where rushes of moss indicate subjacent bog; and are often strewed with loose blocks of granite, from the magnitude of fifty tons, or even greater than that, down to the size of a flag-stone. A crag, called a Tor, usually projects at the summit of the hill, "having a very striking appearance of stratification; the fissures being sometimes horizontal, more commonly a little inclined.   This stratified character is not less general in the quarries; where, although there are none of those marked divisions, indicative of intermissions in the original deposition of the rock, the stone always comes out in beds.   The dip is different in different hills, but seems to have a prevailing tendency towards east and south *."

CHAP.
II.

Supposed
stratifica-
tion of the
granite.

* The appearance which Mr. Prideaux here ascribes to stratification, as many geologists have shown, arises only from the parallel disposition of the fissures in the granite, which have been produced by the action of the elements upon a peculiar structure in the rock, and the nature and formation of which, as explained by Professor Sedgwick and Dr. Macculloch, have already been noticed in a former part of the present chapter. The error of regarding granite as a *stratified* rock has now for a considerable period been relinquished in geology; and it is a little unfortunate, perhaps, that in a memoir designed for the information of local inquirers and students, it should thus have been retained.   The expression that in the quarries " there are none of those marked divisions, indicative of intermissions in the *original deposition of the rock*," is also exceptionable as tending indirectly to convey an impression that the materials of granite, in the process by which that rock was formed, were *deposited* from a liquid in which they had been previously suspended, or in other words that granite is a *sedimentary* rock; whereas it is known to be an exclusively *crystalline* one; and whether we regard it as being of aqueous or of igneous origin, its elements must have been in a state of *chemical solution*, effected, in the one case by the agency of water, or in the other by that of heat.

As these Outlines may probably fall into the hands of some students of geology in Devonshire, who are engaged in the task, now so important in British Geology, of ascertaining the peculiarities in the nature and distribution of the rocks in their own respective districts, it may be useful to cite a few observations on the supposed stratification of granite, from the works of two eminent Geologists, both well acquainted with the rocks in the West of England.

Dr. Berger, in the memoir which has already been quoted, when noticing the celebrated rocks at Castle Trereen, in Cornwall, says,

Not only are the hills higher on the borders of the
Moor, but frequently the granite seems harder in those
places, and also of closer texture. Hey-Tor, Sheeps-Tor,
Collard-Tor, and Pen-Beacon will illustrate this remark;
as well as Calstock, in Cornwall, the granite of which belongs to a more westerly projection.. We must except, however, as will presently appear, the hill-sides in immediate
contact with certain rocks adjoining the Moor. The hardness and tenacity vary, from such as almost to defy the
tool, to those which permit the stone to fall to pieces by
the blow of a hammer, or even to be cut down with a spade,
like gravel. The colour is not much more uniform, being

"I am satisfied that the Logan-stones formed at one time only one
complete mass of granite, which, by the action of the atmosphere and
other external agents, has split into irregular blocks : the greater part of
these, though separated on all sides from each other, have remained in
their original position, but now appear as if they had been placed one
above another. It appears to me that it is in this way granite disinte-
grates in low primitive countries, and this appearance has I believe been
often mistaken for strata, and has given rise to the idea that true granite
is stratified, an opinion which I cannot adopt, even after having visited
those places where Saussure thought he had discovered the strongest
proofs in favour of the [alleged] fact."—Trans. of Geol. Soc. vol. i. p. 149.

Dr. Macculloch, whose elaborate and accurate works have laid so extensive and so firm a foundation for the investigation of our crystalline
rocks, and of those immediately associated with them, in his memoir
on the granite Tors of Cornwall (Trans. Geol. Soc. vol. ii.), from which
we have already quoted an account of the structure of the granite of this
chain (p. 256 et seq.), has the following detached remarks upon the subject : "The appearance of the perpendicular fissures on approaching
the Logging rock from the isthmus is so remarkable, that we might for
a moment fancy it the result of stratification, as geologists have in other
instances been tempted to suppose :" p. 67. "Whatever disputes and
doubts may have existed relating to the stratification of granite in general, I believe there is no one now who conceives the granite of Cornwall,
more than that of Arran or Mont Blanc, to be stratified :" p. 74.

The same writer, in his "Geological Classification" of Rocks, a work
which should be in the hands of every one who undertakes to describe
their structure or their mineral nature, says, in p. 225, "In conformity to
the general practice of geologists, confirmed by my own limited experience, I have considered granite as unstratified"; and in the next page,
after having noticed the apparent want of definite form in granite masses,
when they are continuous for a great space, he adds, "At other times,
they are disposed in large definite bodies, not unaptly compared to feather
beds, separated by fissures or joints. When these masses possess a large
dimension in two directions only, they often resemble the beds of stratified rocks, and have sometimes been mistaken for true strata."

however generally pale-gray or whitish in the mass, with
a shade of red or yellow; but it is found, from being almost black with schorl, also of a pure shining white; and
some occurs of a rich red, superior in beauty, Mr. Prideaux observes, to any Egyptian granite he has seen;
particularly where it contains tourmaline. That this
granite is metalliferous everybody knows; tin being the
most common product. Copper sometimes occurs; and
in a few instances manganese has been mentioned, the
geological relation of which to the rock Mr. Prideaux
states he does not know, the miners having reasons for
concealing it.

The granite of this portion of Dartmoor is rich in
schorl, and poor in mica, " consequently less impregnated
with magnesia, and perhaps more subject to the operation of the weather than is common to that rock—circumstances which may help to explain its comparative
fertility in grass *." In summer it feeds great numbers
of cattle, and in extremely hot and dry weather, when the
verdure elsewhere is burnt up, it assumes the appearance
of great verdure; its humid soil and cold, atmosphere,
which at other times give it a pale and hungry aspect,
then contributing to its fertility.

The close crystalline texture of the rock, obliging the
condensed vapours and rain to run over its surface, is

* In order to substantiate the inferences here drawn from the paucity
of mica in this granite, it must be first shown that the mica of the Dartmoor granite, and especially of those varieties which are less subject to
decomposition, belongs to the subspecies or variety of that mineral which
contains magnesia. For aught we know at present, the mica in the granite of Dartmoor may be the *aluminous* variety; in which case, of course,
its copious occurrence will not impart to the rock any properties depending upon the presence of *magnesia*. It is stated by Brongniart (art.
MINERALOGIE, *Dict. des Scien. Nat.*) that the aluminous mica has a vitreous lustre, and is not attacked by sulphuric acid; but that the magnesian mica has a fatty lustre, and is acted upon by boiling sulphuric acid.
The mica of the Dartmoor granite may be examined by these tests; but
a complete analysis of it, which Mr. Prideaux must be fully adequate to
furnish, would be far more satisfactory; especially since it has not hitherto
been shown, so far at least as the present writer is aware, that there is
any connexion between the quantity of combined magnesia in a rock,
and its liability to undergo decomposition.

probably the cause that the valleys are boggy; the bogs
extending, in numerous cases, up the sides of the hills
and over their summits. These bogs, though dangerous
to cattle, are not without their value; being the great
repositories of native fuel, an important article in these
bleak regions, where the fire-side is often agreeable in an
evening in July.

Boundaries of the granite.

The outline of the granite, from Tavistock to Hey-Tor
southward, may almost be traced by the coppice, which,
clothing the declivities of the slates and other rocks that
abut against it, disappears suddenly where the gritty soil
of the granite commences.

Entering the Moor from Tavistock, we must pass a
mountain of hornblende-rock [greenstone?] called Cocks-
Tor, before we reach the granite at Staple-Tor. Thence
the latter rock runs a little westward of south to Pu-Tor,
two miles; to Crip-Tor, east one mile; to Sheepstor,
south five miles; whence it leaves a deep curve, occupied
by a hill of schorl-rock, with some slates (Ringmoor-
Down), and comes out again at Wigford-Down. At

Dewerstone.

Dewerstone, the southern angle of this down, and the
south-west point of the Dartmoor granite, it is finely exhibited in a nearly vertical cliff, probably more than a
hundred and fifty feet in depth, down to the bed of one of
the branches of the Plym *. From hence, east-south-east,
about two miles to Collard-Tor; north by east, three miles
to Pen-Beacon; east, one mile and a half, and as
much south, to Blatchford-Hill; and about south-east by
south, to the Western Beacon, full four miles. This is
the southernmost point: thence about two miles north-
east by north, to Ugborough Beacon; about four miles,
in a concave line, north by east, to Shipley-Tor; thence a
little westward of north, about seven miles, to the Dart;
north-east by north, about four miles to Withycombe;

* In the annexed engraving of "the Dewerstone rocks" (published
with No. 8.) this cliff is represented as seen from a picturesque point of
view in the valley of the Plym: many of the characteristic appearances
of granite, as described in the present chapter, may be observed in this
view.

south by north, about the same distance to Rippon-Tor; and doubling back north-east by north, three miles to Hey-Tor. The Trigonometrical Survey may be referred-to for these points.

Gneiss, or the rock formed by a lamellar arrangement of the component minerals of granite, Mr. Prideaux remarks, has no where occurred to him within this range; but the slate, where in contact with the granite, is often micaceous; as at Meavy, Shaugh, Black-Alder Tor, Hey-Tor, and other places. These micaceous slates extend but a little way from the granite; clay-slate succeeding, though usually separated by an intervening valley. At Black-Alder Tor, the mica-slate merely covers the granite like a peel.

Mica-slate, &c.

In several places the Moor is extended by high hills of considerable dimensions, consisting of various aggregates of schorl, quartz, and clay-stone or slate. Ringmoor-Down, parts of Wigford and Roborough Downs, Crownhill-Down, and several others, are of this kind. In some cases these rocks are compounds of decided crystals of quartz and schorl; in others, of the same minerals in a granular form; sometimes of particles so minute, as to be with difficulty distinguished by the aid of a microscope, forming a hard, nearly black, stone; and most commonly consisting of this black variety, striped with veins or spotted with crystals of white quartz, and sometimes with veins or small portions of clay-stone or slate. This rock yields a poor soil, but a much better one than granite; the natural herbage on it affects a deep brown colour, from short shrubs and furze. All the varieties are known to the miners by the name of *caple*, and yield both tin and copper. Lead also, which Mr. Prideaux has not heard-of as occurring at all in the granite, is found, though in very trifling quantity, in this schorl-rock.

Schorl-rock.

Mr. Prideaux was unable to find a point of contact between these rocks and the granite; but as the black variety often runs in distinct veins into the latter rock, they probably do not pass into each other by gradual transition.

Junction of the schorl-rock and granite.

Loose blocks of each lie tumbled together about the hills at Blatchford and elsewhere. The road from Cadover Bridge to Cornwood runs over a long hill, between Saddlesborough and Trowlsworthy-Tor, where not only blocks, but gravel of each rock, mingled together, seem to form the hill, without either rock occurring in an entire state; and it is difficult to say which predominates.

Systematic account of the Granite-formation in Devonshire.

Having now concluded a series of abstracts of some of the most important memoirs on the Geology of Devonshire, given nearly in the words of their respective authors, so far as relates to the present branch of that subject, we shall proceed to a systematic description of the Granite-formation of this County; referring to those abstracts for information already communicated, and detailing some portions of its history which have not yet been considered.

We find in Devonshire only two decided rock-formations belonging to the group usually termed the *Primary rocks,* as having been formed prior to all those which repose upon them, but which group, in conformity with the nomenclature introduced into this part of geology by Mr. Conybeare, we have, in the heading of the present chapter, termed the "INFERIOR ROCKS." These two are the GRANITE; and the killas or clay-slate, for which, from its forming the great repository of the metallic ores, both in this County and in Cornwall, and also for the purpose of distinguishing it from the superincumbent grauwacké-slate, belonging to a distinct group of rocks, we have adopted the appellation of the METALLIFEROUS SLATE.

Associated with the formation last mentioned, and apparently subordinate to it, we find many masses and beds of greenstone, hornblende-rock, porphyry, &c., nearly if not quite identical, as to their mineralogical characters, with some of the rocks belonging to the Overlying or Trap family, and having relations to the contiguous rocks, which, in conjunction with that identity, render it difficult to assign them their true place in the geological series.

The Granite, as being the lowest of these formations, will first claim our attention; and its *General Nature* having already been stated, as described by Prof. Sedgwick and Dr. Berger, we shall proceed at once to an account of its

Local Extent, and Lines of Junction with the Incumbent Rocks.—With the slight exceptions of Lundy Island on the north-eastern coast, and the islet of St. Nicholas in Plymouth Sound, the granite, in Devonshire, is confined to the elevated tract called Dartmoor Forest, and its borders. It occupies, however, a very considerable portion of the southern and eastern part of the county, in a form nearly approaching to that of an isosceles triangle, the apex of the figure being directed about south-south-east, and the base ranging east and west, but verging considerably to the northward. The apex of the triangle would be situated somewhere between the Tory brook and the Yealme river, a short distance north of the parallel of Ugborough; and its base would extend from a prolongation of the granite in the direction of Trusham, and distant about two miles to the north-west of that place, to a point situated a few miles southward of Oakhampton.

The absolute northern extremity of this granitic tract, near Oakhampton, is not far distant from the centre of the County; while its southern extremity approaches the sea within about seven miles, and appears to be situated between two and three miles north-east of Plympton Earle[*]. Its greatest length, measured from the southern extremity to the rounded eminence about three miles east of Moreton Hampstead, the line of which is nearly parallel to the eastern side of the supposed triangle, is about twenty-four miles; and the distance from the southern to the north-western extremity, along a line

Marginal notes:

CHAP. II.

Local extent.

Form of the granitic tract.

Its dimensions.

---

[*] This statement is made on the authority of Mr. Greenough's map : Mr. Prideaux, in the tract already quoted, and apparently without being aware that a more southerly extension had been depicted by Mr. Greenough, states that the southernmost point of the granite is the hill called the Western Beacon, several miles to the eastward of the spot mentioned above.

intermediate between the western side of the triangle and
the perpendicular, about twenty-three miles.   The greatest breadth of the formation, from the eastern termination already defined, to the western, situated a little to
the east of Sourton, along a line south-west of the base
of the triangle, measures nearly twenty miles.   The area
of this single tract is probably equal to that of all the
granite tracts in Cornwall taken collectively ; it is therefore the most extensive district occupied by that rock in
South Britain.   The dimensions just stated would give
about two hundred and forty or fifty square miles for
the area ; which, on comparing it with the superficial extent of Dartmoor itself, as given in the note to a former
page, would appear rather to be within than to exceed the
truth.

Configura-
tion of its
outline.
Unlike the geographical outline of Dartmoor itself,
the boundary of this tract is not deeply sinuous, but,
when viewed on the large scale, gently undulating ; for
the line of junction of the granite with the superincumbent slates appears to intersect, indifferently, and in an
abrupt manner, the hills and valleys on the borders of the
Moor, the alternation of which gives to the geographical
outline its extreme sinuosity.   This abrupt intersection
has evidently arisen either from the deposition of the
slates upon the granite, posterior to its formation, and,
to a great extent, posterior, also, as it would seem, to the
existing distribution of its surface into hills and valleys ;
or from the upheaving and protrusion of the mass of granite from below, after the deposition of the slates.   The
boundary, however, is much more sinuous in the comparatively short space occupied by the line of junction with
the metalliferous slate, on the western side of the Moor,
than it is throughout the northern and eastern sides, on
which reposes the grauwacké.   This circumstance indi-
cates a closer connection between the granite and the
former species of slate, than between the same rock and
the grauwacké; a fact which accords with the other relations of those rocks.

The boundary of the granite may be stated as follows : —Commencing from the southern extremity as above defined, near the apex of the triangle, it forms an irregular curve ascending the valley of the Yealme to a short distance, crossing that river ; it then crosses the ridge separating the valleys of the Yealme and the Erme, crossing the latter river also, and approaches the high road from Plymouth to Exeter, which, from a short distance beyond Cadleigh to the base of the long hill west of Ashburton, ranges closely along the boundary, crossing, successively, several branches of the Aume and of the Dart. From the southern foot of this hill its general range is nearly north-east, to the eastern extremity of the base of the triangle, by Buckland, Ilsington, and Lustleigh, the first and last of which places are upon the granite. From this point it extends, towards the north and east, by Bridford and Moreton Hampstead, both situated also upon the granite; the course of the westerly and greater branch of the river Teign indicating its outline, by flowing at the base of the granite hills. The edge of the granite then ranges, nearly in a straight line, parallel to the base of the triangle, from a point distant about a mile and a half south-west of Drewsteignton, to very near Belstone, where a ridge of greenstone, about two miles and a half long, as it were penetrates the granite. Its direction thence, about south-west, is nearly marked by the road from Oakhampton to Sourton, at the average distance of a mile. After this the boundary becomes more sinuous, but preserving a general southern direction, west of Peter Tavy, Sampford Spiney, and Walkhampton; at distances of between one and two miles from those places, all which are upon the metalliferous slate. It then ranges, still southerly, but towards the east, by Meavy and Shaugh Prior, until we again arrive at the southern extremity near Plympton Earle; thus completing the circuit of the formation.

From a point in the valley through which flows the eastern branch of the Plym, the incumbent rock, on the south-

Boundary of the granite.

Incumbent rocks.

ern, south-eastern, and northern sides of the granite district, appears to be grauwacké; but on the northern boundary, within about three miles and a half south-east of Belstone, we enter upon the line of junction with greenstone, which continues for a few miles, until we have arrived at the western side of the prolongation above mentioned, when the grauwacké recommences, and continues for a short distance, until it is again interrupted by the greenstone of an eminence south of Oakhampton, on which a logan-stone is marked in Mr. Greenough's map. After passing this, the grauwacké extends to a short distance south-west of Elmdon, where the the greenstone begins again, and continues to a point between three and four miles east of Lydford, at which the grauwacké again appears, and continues until we approach within about the same distance north and a little east of St. Mary Tavy. From this point to that in the valley of the Plym, at which we commenced, the superincumbent rock is metalliferous slate. It is evident from the relative disposition of the granite and metalliferous slate in Devonshire, as well as in Cornwall, that the latter rock, wherever it exists, reposes upon the granite; but after quitting Dartmoor, the granite does not reappear at the surface until we arrive at Hingston-Down, west of the Tamar, and consequently in Cornwall; at the western extremity of which is Kitt-Hill, described in p. 262, but there erroneously stated to be in Devonshire. Ocular evidence, however, that the granite is subjacent to the slate in the intervening tract, also, has been obtained at Morwell-Down, on the eastern bank of the Tamar, where the slate has been pierced through, and the granite beneath it discovered. .

Mineral characters of the granite.

Mineralogical Characters, Structure, and Mineral Contents of the Devonshire Granite.—Many particulars respecting the mineralogical history and the structure of this granite have already been given, as stated by Professor Sedgwick, Dr. Macculloch, Dr. Berger, and Mr. Prideaux. To these we may add the following :

Throughout the tract the extent and boundaries of CHAP. which have been described in the preceding section, Gra- II. nite, or one of those rocks, which, in a geological point of view, must be regarded merely as varieties of that, is found in compact masses or beds beneath the soil; in many places also protruding above it in the form of Tors, and scattered over the surface in detached blocks and fragments of every size. Generally speaking there are two varieties of the granite itself, the white and the red, according to the colour of the felspar, which is the predominating constituent *. Both varieties generally contain black mica; and when the mica is wanting in either, it is commonly replaced by schorl. When worked for the purposes of building, it is provincially termed Moorstone. The blocks are readily cleft by wedges, and the smaller ones thus obtained are shaped to the intended forms by the use of a heavy pointed-hammer or pick. It is worked in this manner, when newly detached from the rock, with considerable facility; but upon exposure to the atmosphere it becomes extremely hard; probably in consequence of the escape of water previously existing in its interstices. The granite of Dartmoor has been used to a considerable extent in the construction of New London Bridge.

At Troulsworthy, in the parish of Shaugh, through an Granite of extent of about fifty acres, a very fine red variety occurs, Troulswor- much resembling some kinds of Egyptian granite. This thy. admits of an exquisite polish, as may be seen in the tables formed of it at Saltram and Mount Edgecumbe, and in the chimney-pieces of the Duke of Bedford's cottage at Endsleigh.

The granite of Ivy-Bridge is of a dead white; it is Granite of composed of a very large proportion of felspar, chiefly in Ivy-Bridge.

* It seems probable, from the researches of the late Mr. W. Phillips, that much of what appears to be red felspar in this granite, will be found, upon accurate examination, to be in reality Cleavelandite, or that felspathic mineral the alkaline constituent of which is *soda*; instead of *potash*, as in common felspar.

long prismatic crystals, nearly pellucid quartz, some schorl, and a few scarcely discernible specks of mica.

The base of the porphyritic granite, forming the upper part of the hill near Ivy-Bridge, described by Dr. Berger, (see p. 263,) is a beautiful kind of felspar of a brick-red colour, (probably Cleavelandite,) confusedly crystallized ; in which are imbedded crystals of vitreous quartz, hornblende, and tender steatite of a greenish yellow.

We may conclude this part of the subject by stating, for the information of students, that the varieties of granite found in this tract appear chiefly to belong to the following heads of Dr. Macculloch's " Synopsis of granite*." Future investigations will probably supply many other varieties ; and also determine whether those of each kind which contain Cleavelandite, must not be considered as distinct from the rest.

First Division.

Synopsis of
the Devon
granite.
Of two ingredients.

B. Quartz, and felspar.

b. The quartz, or felspar, or both, imperfectly crystallized and influencing each other's forms. Graphic granite.

Second Divison.

Of three ingredients :

A. Quartz, felspar, and mica.

a. An uniform mixture of the different ingredients.

b. Distinct additional crystals of felspar imbedded in the general mixture : porphyritic granite.

d. The quartz, or the felspar, or the mica, or all of them crystallized.

Appendix.

D. Schorl and quartz, sometimes with felspar. Schorl rock.

---

* " Geological Classification of Rocks," by J. Macculloch, M.D. F.R.S. p. 234–242.

The facts and arguments by which Dr. Macculloch has inferred the *concentric-spheroidal structure* of the granite of the West of England, from the phænomena of its disintegration, and the consequent change of form of its masses, have already been cited, p. 256–262 ; as well as Prof. Sedgwick's and Dr. Berger's account of the fissures in that rock, which denote the earlier stages of its decomposition, p. 252–253, and p. 269.   Some further remarks may here be added, arising from a general review of this interesting subject, so far as relates to the actual configuration of the granite masses, and the suppositions which have been entertained that their forms are the result of human ingenuity and labour, exerted, at a remote period, in the support of idolatry and superstition.

Some curious changes in the opinions which have been held by mankind on subjects of this description, have been induced by the progress of knowledge; and these changes, it is pleasing to observe, evince the progressive *amelioration* of error,—if we may be allowed the expression,—the gradual substitution of less grievous and mischievous aberrations from truth, for those which were more so,—preparatory to its entire removal.   In the times of Classical Antiquity, every natural phænomenon and production that was not understood, especially if it was of great extent or magnitude, and presented marks of regular structure, was attributed to the immediate agency of the gods; or among those nations with whom mythology had not assumed so systematic and in some respects so refined a form, it was ascribed to the strength of giants or the magic of enchanters ; and not unfrequently also, under popular impressions of another kind, such objects have been attributed to that simulation of miraculous power, which superstition, in almost every country, has delighted in awarding to the " foul fiend."   But in modern times natural phænomena of the same description, which the existing state of science has not afforded the means of explaining, have almost uniformly been regarded as the works of ancient nations ; and in this country, principally as those of the

Marginal notes: CHAP. II. Concentric structure of the granite. Changes of opinion on the origin of granite tors.

Accurate
description
of a gra-
nite coun-
try, by the
Author of
Waverley.

" Muckle-
stane
Moor."

Druids, or of the people at least whose operations were
instigated and directed by them.

In one of those productions of the "Author of Waverley," which have given to Fictitious Narrative, as a branch
of literature, a rank equal to that which the Plays of
Shakespeare have obtained for the Drama, is a most admirable and *picturesque* sketch—if that term be applicable
to the scenery of nature when verbally delineated—of
some of the appearances presented by a granite district,
which also portrays, at once, the antiquarian mistake of
modern times, and the legend of superstition by which it
was preceded.

Those persons who have visited any granite country, and
still more those who have resided in one, will not fail to
recognize in the scenery of " Mucklestane Moor," and its
vicinity, as described in that exquisite *petite Romance* called
"The Black Dwarf," a most accurate representation of the
appearances and objects which such a country exhibits.
The " remote and inaccessible recesses" which sheltered
the deer pursued by Hobbie Elliot, the " cleugh or wild
ravine" into which that undaunted borderer followed
the game, the " extensive waste" or moor "interspersed
with marshes and pools of water" over which he returned,
" the deep purple of the broad outline of heathy mountains
which surrounded this desolate spot,"—are all characters
or accompaniments of a district occupied by this rock, and
bounded by those geological formations which are usually
incumbent upon it.   It was on a visit to the granite tract
westward of Penryn in Cornwall, which belongs to the
same chain as that of Dartmoor, and has in all respects a
similar character, that the present writer was first struck
with " the truth of nature," even in these comparatively
unimportant features of his narrative,—fraught as it is with
so much deep moral interest,—which is displayed by the
" Mighty Wizard of the North."   The descriptions of scenery in The Black Dwarf, must have been drawn, we presume, from the granite moors of Scotland ; but we find,
in their applicability to those in the West of England,

an evidence of the marked and obvious distinctions of primary districts wherever they occur, and of the influence of the geological structure of a country on the character of its scenery.

We might not however recognize in "Mucklestane Moor" so perfect a picture of a granitic waste, were it not rendered complete by the "huge column of unhewn granite, which raised its massy head on a knoll near the centre of the heath"—and by the ground about the pillar being "strewed or rather encumbered, with many large fragments of stone of the same consistence with the column, which, from their appearance as they lay scattered on the waste, were popularly called the Gray Geese of Mucklestane Moor." We behold in the objects thus described—in terms not less appropriate than romantic—a Granite Tor, and the Boulders resulting from its degradation, by the natural process detailed in the commencement of our present chapter. But the author, when he afterwards recites the "supplementary legend" of witchcraft and *diablerie* with which tradition, "in the days of other years," had supplied the place of "the real cause of its existence," is true to his character as a modern Antiquary, in stating that the pillar was raised "perhaps to tell of the mighty dead who slept beneath, or to preserve the memory of some bloody skirmish;" thus exemplifying, at the same time, the errors which have prevailed on such subjects both in ancient and in modern times, together with the comparative harmlessness of the latter, however distant they may all be from the truth.

We have been induced to make this digression, from the desire of enlivening our graver details of the physical history of Dartmoor, with an allusion,—in strict keeping, we hope, with the subject before us,—to the genius and the knowledge of a writer, whose works are the delight equally of the unlettered and the learned—of the superficial and the profound. We must now return, however, to matters of science :

"Entering on studious thoughts abstruse."

CHAP.
II.

Granite
Tor on
Mucklestane
Moor.

BOOK
III.

Distinct
spherical
concre-
tions in
granite of
this for-
mation.

To the examples of obvious spherical structure in granite which are adduced by Dr. Macculloch, in support of his inferences regarding that of Devon and Cornwall, we may now add an instance, described by Professor Sedgwick, in the Memoir before quoted, as occurring in the granite of the same formation in Cornwall.

" Among the varieties of aggregration" presented by the granite of the West of England, this eminent geologist observes, " may be mentioned the strange appearance of nodular concretions, which abound in some part of the cliffs west of Castle Trereen.   Were it not for their situ- ation, they might be mistaken for rounded masses derived from the ruins of some other rock.   A more minute ex- amination proves them to have been contemporaneous with the rock in which they are imbedded, and composed of the same elements.   They are sometimes so nearly homogeneous, that it requires an examination with a lens to make out their granular texture.   But even in these instances, a fracture will often show the crystals of felspar, passing from the surrounding granite into the imbedded nodule, without any apparent interruption in their form*."

This kind of spherical structure, we may remark, is ex- actly that which is produced by the cooling of slags and of rocks artificially fused, as referred to by Dr. Maccul- loch, in p. 260 ; and its existence, therefore, gives addi- tional confirmation to the theory, that, in granite also, this structure has been produced by the cooling and crystalli- zation of the materials of that rock, from a state of ig- neous fluidity.

Vixen Tor.   The Vignette at the head of this chapter, represents the Vixen Tor, on Dartmoor, which has been selected by Dr. Macculloch, as exhibiting the first step to change ef- fected by the action of the weather in the form of gra- nitic masses, in the " gentle rounding of the angles" of its constituent blocks.   This Tor crowns an eminence on

* Transactions of the Cambridge Philosophical Society, vol. i. p. 101.

the western bank of the Wallcombe river, about a mile CHAP.
south of Merrivile Bridge.   II.

A singular pile, not far from the north-eastern extre- Bow-
mity of the Moor, and about two miles due south from man's
North Bovey, the lower portions of which are in a similar Nose.
state to the blocks of the Vixen Tor, while its upper stones
have begun to exhibit the curvilinear boundary marking
the further progress of partial disintegration, is called,
from the grotesque projections on one side, "BOWMAN's
or BOWERMAN's NOSE." It is represented in the subjoined engraving.

BOWMAN'S NOSE.

The Cheesewring, in Cornwall, is cited by Dr. Maccul- Little Mis
loch, as affording the most complete example of a Granite Tor.
Tor, in which decomposition has fully advanced to the

BOOK
III.
___

stage exemplified by the upper blocks of Bowman's Nose. A near approach to the configuration of the Cheesewring is presented by

LITTLE MIS TOR.

This Tor, like the former, is on the western side of Dartmoor, but on a hill distant about two miles from the Prison, in a north-westerly direction, and east of the river Wallcombe.

Rocking
Stones:

We must now mention some of the Logan or Rocking Stones which either still exist, or have formerly existed, in this tract. The mode of their formation, and the origin and nature of their mobility, have already been explained, p. 253 and p. 256.

One of these "self-poised" rocks, perhaps the most celebrated in this County, is thus commemorated by the Bard of the Moor:

> . . . . . . " And near the edge
> Of the loud-brawling stream a Logan stands,
> Haply self-poised, for Nature loves to work
> Such miracles as these amid the depths
> Of forest solitudes.   Her magic hand
> With silent chisel fashion'd the rough rock,
> And placed the central weight so tenderly,
> That almost to the passing breeze it yields
> Submissive motion."   CARRINGTON'S DARTMOOR.

This Logan is seated in the channel of the river Teign, *in the Teign.* being poised on another block belonging to a mass of granite below.   Its figure is very irregular, though approximating, of course, to the spheroidal.   In some places it measures six feet in height, or thickness, in others seven feet, and at the western extremity ten feet; by about eighteen in length. Mr. Polwhele states that in his time it was easily rocked with one hand, but that the extent of its motion did not exceed one inch, if even it equalled that quantity.   It has now almost ceased to oscillate.

At Holy Street, near Chagford, on the same river, was *at Holy Street.* another rocking stone, of smaller dimensions, but which, according to the same writer, was more easily set in motion, and described a greater arc.   This has become immoveable.

Mr. Polwhele has also described a third logan, as existing in the parish of Withycombe, between the Church *at Withycombe.* and Rippon-Tor.   He states its diameter to be eleven feet; and that "it is called the *Nutcrackers,* having been the resort of the common people, during the nut season, for the purpose of cracking their nuts."

There is another large rocking stone at Lustleigh *at Lustleigh Cleve.* Cleve, three or four miles north of High-Tor.

A fifth logan once oscillated on the slope beneath High *at High Tor.* Tor; on the summit of the tallest peak of that mass of granite is a rock-basin.——The process by which Rock- *Rock Basins.* basins have been formed has been described in p. 261, as ascertained by Dr. Macculloch.

"The number of rock-basins" in this tract, observes Mr. Burt, in his Preface to Carrington's Dartmoor, "is comparatively few; as, though there are numberless rocks and tors, yet all of them do not possess this distinction. Willistone and Blackstone rocks in Moreton ; Sharpitor, Pentor, Miltor, Beltor, Nestor, Heytor, several rocks at Holne, and Mistor Pan, exhibit them in greater or less perfection."

A number of rock-basins also exist on the level summits of the smaller tors and blocks which diversify the slope from Gidleigh Park to the river Teign, towards the north-eastern extremity of the moor.

Mr. Moore's opinion of the artificial origin of rock-basins examined.

The writer of these Outlines might be considered liable to a charge of inattention to his friend the Rev. T. Moore, Author of the topographical and principal part of this work, were he to omit noticing the remarks on the origin of rock-basins, which are contained in the first Chapter of Book II., relating to the original population of Devonshire, at p. 75.

The regularity of form of these cavities, which is adduced, by Mr. Moore, as a proof of their being artificial, is a consequence of the tendency of the action which produced them, to extend itself equally in every direction; which the "uniform texture of the granite" (to which, merely, it is ascribed by Dr. Macculloch,) would necessarily permit it to do. Mr. Moore also brings forward, as militating against the truth of Dr. Macculloch's explanation, that the rock-basins "are found only on the tops of the tors, and sometimes on the logan-stones ;" and he inquires, resuming this argument, " If the basins were excavations produced by natural causes, why are they not found on numerous other rocks and in different situations?" In reply to this it may be stated, that, in the granite of the Scilly Islands, and in the millstone-grit of Ashover in Derbyshire, (which is associated with the coal-measures, and belongs, consequently, to a very different group of rocks,) these basins do actually occur on the perpendicular sides of the rocks. That they should be sometimes found on the logan-stones, is also a consequence of their origin from natural causes ; since the same action of the elements, which, operating on the

TEIGNMOUTH, DEVON.

Drawn by T H Williams

London Published by N Jennings & W Chaplin Cheapside &c

Engraved by W Deeble

Drawn by W.H. Bartlett

Engraved by R. Wallis

WASHING ROCK, WEST POINT.

angles and edges of the blocks of granite, has pro- CHAP.
duced the logans—which Mr. Moore correctly remarks II.
" are clearly inartificial,"—operating on their exposed
surfaces, has formed rock-basins.　Hence, it would be
remarkable indeed, if rock-basins were not sometimes
found upon logan-stones.　An instance has already been
cited of the occurrence of rock-basins on other species of
rock besides granite ; and it may be mentioned, in addition, that there are deep cavities of this description on the
horizontal and slightly-inclined surfaces of the magnificent
mass of schorl-rock at Roach in Cornwall; in many of
which the present writer has found grains of quartz and fragments of crystallized schorl, resulting from the action that
produced them ; which is a circumstance parallel to that
related of the rock-basins in granite, by Dr. Macculloch.
It may also be useful to remark, in further explanation of
the process by which these cavities, in whatever rocks they
occur, appear to have been formed, that, on the declivities
of Roach rocks, where the water could not lodge, it has
worn deep channels, instead of producing basins.

How far the Druids, or other sacerdotal orders among
our more remote ancestors, may have appropriated these
results of atmospheric origin to their own purposes,—
how far it may be true of the officiating Druid, that,

" . . . . to wondering crowds
And ignorant, with guileful hand he rocked
The yielding Logan"— •

is a distinct question ; and one into which it is unnecessary here to enter.

But as the writer has found that other antiquarian The same
friends are unwilling to resign, altogether, that notion of opinion
the origin of these excavations, which, in the hands of by others.
Dr. Borlase and his compeers, has given rise to so imposing
a pageant of the ceremonies of Druidism—and are still desirous of attributing to the " Druid" the skill by which

" . . . . the rocks
That crest the grove-crowned hill he scooped, to hold
The lustral waters," †

it may not be out of place to state briefly the results of

* Carrington's " Dartmoor."　　　† Ibid.

an examination, made in the autumn of the year 1825,
of all the rock-basins upon the Tors or Carns which crown
the summit of Carnbrea Hill, near Redruth, in the sister
county; and the granite of which is part of the same formation as that of Dartmoor.

Results of
an exami-
nation of
the rock-
basins at
Carnbrea
in Corn-
wall.

With the exception of not finding the sides of the
basins crumbly, this examination verified every part of
Dr. Macculloch's statement, as given in p. 261; while
several minor facts were ascertained, which, though not
adverted to in Dr. Macculloch's paper, are nevertheless
entirely confirmatory of his opinion. Thus it was found
that wherever the form of the cavity, and the direction
and inclination of the surfaces of the rock, were such as
to have admitted the water to remain for the longest space
of time, in those situations the basins are always deeper
than in others; and that where the water has escaped from
one basin to another situated below it, a passage has been
worn, which in some cases has nearly converted the two
basins into one. In one instance, the thickness of an
immense slab of granite, much resembling that which
Borlase calls the "Sacrificing Stone," having on its upper
surface six or seven rock-basins, has been cut through in
several places; and the continuation of the process which
formed the basins will eventually divide the slab into
several blocks. In this manner many of the basins have
been destroyed, by the process which originally produced
them. The *side* of one basin has been completely perforated, while its *edge* has been left entire, forming an arch
which extends over the aperture. Basins of every size and
stage of formation and destruction, may be found on almost
every Carn. The water, collected from the rains, in the
basins on the so-called "Sacrificing Stone," as it flows
from the upper into the lower cavities, is manifestly wearing for itself a course which, in process of time, will completely unite all the basins into one great irregular cavity.

Conclusive
evidence
of their
natural
origin.

These circumstances are clearly indicative of the natural process, still going on, by which these curious excavations have been produced, and by which also they
will eventually be destroyed. But perhaps the most

palpably-undeniable evidence that they cannot have been artificially formed, may be found in the circumstance, which Dr. Macculloch has not mentioned, viz. that many of the rock-basins on Carnbrea are crossed by the veins of porphyry and porphyritic granite which traverse the Carns; and which, offering a much greater resistance to the action of decomposing agents than the granite itself, have been left in the basins in the form of ridges, their edges only having been rounded by the action of the elements. This fact is obviously conclusive; since the Druidical sculptors, who must have possessed the skill required to render some of the basins accurately spheroidal, if they were indeed the artists of them, would not have left these unsightly ridges in other basins.

The "indications of design," stated to be afforded by "the peculiar form" of these cavities, are all, when strictly examined, evidences that they were produced by the natural process which has been described by Dr. Macculloch, and illustrated in the preceding remarks. This is also the case with every particular among those which have been so elaborately described by Borlase, as evincing the Druidical origin and application of these basins; and the fallacy of some of which has been acutely pointed out by the author of "Philosophy in Sport made Science in Earnest," in the additional notes to that ingenious work, vol. iii. p. 170 et seq.

Nothing remains to be said, in this place, on the alleged Druidical origin of rock-basins; but the writer is unwilling to quit so interesting a subject, regarding it in a scientific point of view, without adverting to some inferences which have recently occurred to him, drawn partly from the researches of Dr. Macculloch and other geologists, and partly from his own very limited observations, respecting the structure and origin of the granite of this formation. Dr. Macculloch has attributed the "even and rounded concavity" of the rock-basins, to the "uniform texture of the granite;" and agreeably to this opinion, it has been attributed, in the foregoing remarks on Mr. Moore,

Probable
connexion
of the
figure of
the basins
with the
structure
of the rock.

to the equality of action permitted by this uniformity; as
being, perhaps, the more strictly accurate mode of stating
the fact. But may not this figure, which, in some instances, as Dr. Macculloch has remarked, is as " regularly
spheroidal internally as if they [the basins] had been
shaped by a turning lathe," be in reality, principally
owing to that spherical or rather spheroidal structure, the
existence of which, in the same granite, has been rendered so highly probable by that eminent geologist? For
it appears to be obvious that the same variation, in some
given ratio from the centre, of the resistance to disintegration of a mass of granite, which has led to the separation of granite of this formation into cuboidal blocks,
as explained in p. 256—261, will, when one surface only
of the rock is acted upon, give rise to cavities having a
figure which is precisely that of the rock-basins. And
indeed it would appear that some further cause than the
uniformity of texture of the granite, must in reality operate in the formation of these basins; for if that only
were the reason, the granite should be as much acted
upon in a direction perpendicular to its surface, as in those
directions which are parallel to it; and the depth of the
basins ought always to be equal to their diameters, or
nearly so; which, so far as the writer's knowledge extends,
is seldom, if ever, the case. And the occurrence of the
rock-basins on the vertical faces of the granite at Scilly,
would seem to be a further corroboration of this idea; for
it is difficult to conceive how the action of water could
produce such cavities in this situation, unless it were aided
by the tendency of the rock to disintegrate more easily in
certain directions, with respect to the planes of its surfaces, than in others.

That
opinion
confirmed
from the
appear-
ances at
Roach, in
Cornwall.

The form and appearance of the rock-basins on the
horizontal summits and ledges of Roach rocks, and the
deep channels on their highly-inclined surfaces, may
perhaps be mentioned as affording some degree of support to the foregoing conjecture. Here the basins are
very deep, and their outline is comparatively irregular;

while the channels which the water has worn on the declivities, do not, so far as has yet been described, occur upon granite, under the same circumstances. Now, supposing the form of the basins, as they exist in granite itself, to be connected with the concentric structure of the rock, the facts just mentioned are what we might have expected to find in a mass of schorl-rock like that of Roach. For although a process of disintegration has undoubtedly taken place with it, and is still proceeding, it tends to produce rather angular and pyramidal, than cubic and spheroidal blocks. From observation, therefore, we appear to have no evidence of the concentric structure of this particular mass of schorl-rock; and this negative result may be confirmed from theory; since the felspar, on the predominance of which, in granite, all the phænomena attendant upon and succeeding its presumed original state of igneous fluidity, must have been greatly dependent, is almost entirely wanting in this rock, which is unusually uniform in constitution, consisting merely of quartz and crystals of schorl, intersected by a few veins of the former mineral ; and being referable, with little exception, to the first variety of schorl-rock described by Professor Sedgwick in p. 254. The summit of the eastern rock only, at Roach, consists of the second or porphyritic variety, from which however the imbedded crystals of felspar have disappeared, leaving the rock in a state resembling a scoria ; specimens of which are described by Prof. Sedgwick as obtained from the south of Dartmoor.

Another circumstance in the history of rock-basins appears deserving of further inquiry. Although it is very true that rock-basins do occur on the inclined and even vertical surfaces of granite, in some places, yet by far the majority of them, in Cornwall and Devonshire, at least, are found on horizontal or gently-inclined surfaces. Has this fact any connexion, it may be asked, with the structure of the rock? and does it indicate any determinate relation between the direction of the axes of the spheroidal structure and any of the surfaces of the beds composing

Probable relation of the axes of the spheroidal structure to the surfaces of the beds of granite.

BOOK
III.

the masses of granite? Dr. Macculloch observes, (Classification of Rocks, p. 227,) that "the great laminæ, or beds of granite are often vertical, as well as horizontal or inclined; and it thus presents continuous smooth precipices laterally, while, above, it terminates in sharp peaks." Now the beds of granite in Cornwall and Devon are horizontal, or inclined;—and we find the rock-basins on their upper surfaces, which are parallel to the direction of the beds:—are the granite beds of Scilly, presenting basins on their perpendicular faces, placed in a vertical position?

Modification of these views by considering schorl-rock as a local variety of granite.

If we view these rocks on the grand scale, and consider the schorl-rock merely as a local modification of granite, which, in a strictly geological sense, is undoubtedly the truth, we may infer that the appearances at Roach,—which have been regarded, above, as indicating the absence of the spheroidal structure in that mass of rock,—are merely the consequences of the vertical position of its constituent beds; and the general aspect of these rocks gives indeed some weight to this supposition, agreeing as it does with the character, described, in the foregoing quotation, as resulting from that disposition of the beds. But in this case, the conjecture that the form of the rock-basins in true granite is connected with the spheroidal structure of that rock, will perhaps derive still farther support, from the difference of form in the rock-basins at Roach, which must, under this view, be regarded as excavated in the summits of the vertical laminæ; while the channels have been worn in their edges and sides. Still further would it seem, from this view, that the position and nature of the rock-basins is in some manner connected with the direction of the axes of the spheroidal structure existing in the rock.

Time required to change the figure of granite-rocks by disintegration.

To conclude, for the present, these remarks on the geological history of rock-basins:—Mr. De La Beche, in the explanation of his "Sections and Views illustrative of Geological Phenomena," just published (July 1830), after quoting Dr. Macculloch's paper as explaining the

Views taken from it of the Vixen Tor, the Cheesewring, and the Logan at Castle Trereen, observes, " Looking at these drawings, and taking into consideration the comparatively little waste which the objects they represent now suffer, it would seem to require a long lapse of time to produce the effects we here witness." In this opinion every one must agree; but the present writer would suggest, from a few observations of his own, that more rapid, though far less extensive changes, are effected by that particular species of action, which has produced, and is now producing, as well as destroying, rock-basins; and the effect of which in dividing masses of granite and changing their figure, is well exhibited in the Tors of Carnbrea.

The whole of the foregoing remarks are submitted, with much deference, to the consideration of geologists; as hints, merely, for future investigation, by those who have it in their power to institute extensive researches in this science.

The valuable minerals which Devonshire affords, we shall briefly notice under the heads of the rocks that contain them, reserving the detail of the quantities afforded, and the works undertaken to procure them, until we mention the mines of the County. The granite hills of Dartmoor have produced tin, probably for many ages, and traces of stream-works and mines are to be seen on every part of this immense waste. On every hill, as high as water could be diverted, the ground has been turned over by the help of these artificial torrents, the veins or lodes taken away to a certain depth, and the stream-works in valleys and bottoms, formed by deposits from the backs of the lodes, were made productive by washing away the alluvial matter in which the small fragments of tin-ore lay imbedded.

The tin veins or lodes in the granite in this county run in an east and west direction, and dip or underlie, in various angles, to the north. They are generally small, and, where they have of late been followed, not very

Mineral contents of the granite.

Stream-works on Dartmoor.

Tin veins.

CHAP.
II.

BOOK
III.

productive. The metal is of the finest quality,' admixture with other inferior metals being rare.   Besides the
east and west veins, others are found which run either
north or south, or on points of the compass between these;
they are called by the miner cross-lodes, cross-courses,
or caunters ; they are generally filled with white quartz,
called whiteacre, and traverse or heave the east and west
veins, and are therefore to be deemed veins of a later
formation.   If we except the stone itself, which is justly
esteemed as one of the best in nature for the purpose of
building, where durability is to be regarded, few valuable minerals beside tin are to be found in the gra-

Copper
vein in
Morwell-
Down.

nite mountains of Devon. In Morwell-Down, before mentioned, a copper lode has been found to pass from the
slate to the granite.

*Aspect of the Country occupied by this Formation; Form
and Height of Hills and Tors, &c.*

Aspect
of the
granite-
country:
heights of
hills, &c.

Many particulars belonging to this head have already
been recorded in the foregoing pages of this Book, and
need only to be referred-to at present.   In the extracts
from Professor Sedgwick's memoir on the formations immediately associated with the primitive ridge of Devonshire and Cornwall, given in pages 250–255, are noticed
the rugged outline of the granitic ridges, the barren uniformity of appearance of the contiguous country—the
wild and dreary aspect of the downs, half-covered with
granite bowlders, and the singular forms of the Tors.   In
the abstract of Dr. Berger's paper, the general aspect of
the country seen on approaching Dartmoor on the south-
western border, is described, together with the entrance
to the Moor by the Valley of the Erme, its bare and alpine character, the altitude of various hills and sources
of rivers upon it, the character of the surface, the contrast
presented by the highly-cultivated tracts of grauwacké,
reposing upon the flanks of the granite, &c.   From
Mr. Prideaux's " Geological Sketch," has been extracted in pages 268–274, some account of the general

aspect of the Dartmoor granite country itself; mentioning the appearances of the surface consequent on its comparative fertility in grass, in some places, the bogs in the valleys, the disappearance of the coppice on the surounding slates, wherever they meet the granite, the aspect of the south-western boundary of the Moor, and the character of the eminences of schorl-rock which are prolonged from it at certain points. Lastly, the nature of the outline of the granite, formed by its junction with the grauwacké and the metalliferous slate, and the forms and appearance of several of the most remarkable Tors, have been mentioned in the preceding section, pages 276 and 284—288.

Mr. Moore has also had occasion to notice many features which might otherwise have been described in the present section, in the First Book of this work, containing the " General Description" of the County; a circumstance which has arisen from the fact that so considerable and so important a part of the County is constituted of the granite formation we are now describing. Thus in Book I., Chap. I., relating to the picturesque scenery of Devonshire, &c. he has described the scenery which the granite-moors present, stated the altitudes of many of the Dartmoor hills, and noticed the views of the surrounding country which their summits afford. In the succeeding Chapter on the rivers and springs, he has described the scenery on the courses of the rivers Teign, Becky, Dart, and Lyd; also noticing many of the Tors.

A few additional particulars will here be mentioned, in order to complete the subjects of this section.

The mean elevation of Dartmoor, according to the Ordnance Trigonometrical Survey, is 1782 feet above the level of the sea; while that of the most commanding eminences of slate around it, is only 737 feet. The altitude of Cosson Hill, which is the highest point of this tract, is stated at 2090 feet. This elevation, though much inferior to that of the felspathic rocks of Snowdon, or the granite and porphyry of Ben Nevis, has an effect upon the climate of

Mean elevation of Dartmoor.

BOOK III. the whole district, as well as upon that of the contiguous country, which is eminently characteristic of a mountainous region. In the winter season the snow remains upon Cosson Hill after it has disappeared from every other part of the Moor.

Inclination. The predominating undulations of the surface are in the direction, nearly, of north-west and south-east: both sides of the Moor have nearly the same degree of inclination; the rivers on the northern side falling into the Bristol Channel, and those on the southern into the British Channel. On the west the slope is gradual, but on the east rather abrupt. Precipitous acclivities occur only at the immediate line of junction with the slates.

High Tor. The two elevations of exposed granite known by the name of the High Tor Rocks, which are peculiarly bold and massive in character, rise to nearly 1600 feet above the level of the sea, and their summits afford one of the finest panoramic views in the County *.

High Tor granite-quarries. "The Haytor [or High Tor] quarries, situated round the base of the rocks whence they derive their name, have obtained a high repute amongst architects, for the size, durability, and fineness of texture of the blocks produced from them: 200 or 300 men are usually employed there, a great part of the stone being worked to the shape and fineness [of surface] required, on the spot: it is conveyed to the Stoner canal by means of a railway of seven or eight miles in length, formed of the same materials: this winds down amongst the neighbouring hills, and crosses Bovey Heath, joining the canal-head at Ventiford, whence it is conveyed to the new wharf at Teignmouth, and there shipped to the extent of several thousand tons annually, chiefly for the metropolis†." In these quarries the rhom-

* The High Tor "has been erroneously spelt Haytor: the mistake probably originated in considering them as in the hundred of Heytor, and as giving name to it, which is not the case; they are in the hundred of Teignbridge."—Kingston's Mineralogy of Teignmouth and its Vicinity, published in the Guide to that place.

† Kingston's Mineralogy of Teignmouth. See also the section on the rail-roads of Devonshire, in Book I. Chap. III. of the present volume, pp. 75, 76.

bohedral structure of the rock may be observed with great advantage.

Hounter Tor, and also several others in the immediate vicinity of High Tor, present very broken and picturesque outlines ; and their appearance, when viewed from a certain distance, closely resembles that of extensive castellated ruins.

Agricultural Character.—The general character of the soil in this district is either sandy or peaty, more frequently a mixture of both : it includes what may be considered, on the whole, as the least fertile portion of the County, having the additional disadvantage of a cold and humid climate : nevertheless, it can boast of many sheltered coombes and widely extended vales, which have a kindly and productive soil, and possess considerable beauty and fertility. To the Botanist, perhaps, this is the most interesting portion of the County, "the wildest and most exposed parts of it yielding him a rich harvest of *Cryptogamous Plants*, that he might in vain search for elsewhere *.

"In wood," according to Mr. Prideaux, "this rock appears to be unproductive. A few young plantations of fir do not yet appear to suffer more than might be expected from the climate ; some fine trees are found about the borders of the streams ; and trunks of considerable dimensions have been dug up from the bogs : but it is said by gentlemen possessing estates on the granite (and my observation agrees with it), that trees, after reaching a certain height, rise no further ; spreading and twisting their branches, without proportionate increase of trunk. Wistman's-wood, a plot of oaks supposed to be of a thousand years' standing, the largest less than a man's waist, and within twenty feet high, is an extreme instance†."

* *Flora Devoniensis*, p. 201.
† Geological Sketch, &c. p. 22. In the Preface to Carrington's " Dartmoor," a subject is discussed at some length, which it may be useful to mention in this place, as connected with the Agricultural Character of the Dartmoor granite. The Rev. J. P. Jones is stated to have expressed, and supported by various arguments which are cited in the Preface, the

CHAP.
II.

Hounter
Tor.

Agricultural character.

The only place met with by Mr. Prideaux at which the soil on the mica-slate covering the granite, (as before described,) was sufficiently extensive for cultivation, was at Hey-Tor, where it appeared to yield good crops of corn.

Water and springs.

Phænomena of Water and Springs.—Many of these have been noticed by Mr. Moore in Book I. Chap. II. on the Rivers and Springs : we shall add a few general re marks under the present head.

In Dartmoor, or on its immediate borders, according to Mr. Burt, there are no fewer than five principal rivers, twenty-four secondary streams, fifteen brooks (besides others, perhaps, which are without names), two small lakes, and seven considerable heads of water; in all, fifty-three collections of that fluid which is so universally necessary to the healthy existence of organized beings.

---

following opinion respecting Dartmoor, as a *habitat* of forest-trees:— "With respect to Dartmoor being once covered with trees, I am decidedly of opinion that there were never any trees of consequence growing there." Mr. Burt, however, the author of the Preface, controverts this opinion, and brings forward various citations from ancient records, relating principally to the partial *disforestation* (as the relinquishment of the old forest-rights by the King was termed) of Dartmoor, together with inferences drawn from them, in support of his own view of the subject. A careful examination of these citations and inferences has led the present writer to conclude, on the contrary, that, though parts of this tract may have been wooded, yet, generally speaking, Mr. Jones's opinion must be correct. The documents cited by his opponent afford no proof of the existence of any trees of consequence; and there is no mention of timber, except that of the green oak which the Venville men were forbidden to take off the forest, and which implies neither the existence of large trees, nor that of extensive woodlands. To these may be added the more important and conclusive fact, that neither acorns nor mast of any kind are even once alluded to as food for hogs; an omission which could scarcely have occurred, had Dartmoor really been a *forest;* receiving that term, as we now commonly do, in the sense of an extensive wood: for at the æras of the documents in question this was the most important product of forest-lands. The allusions to wild-beasts, and to the chase, contained in those documents, merely prove the district to have abounded with herbage and the lesser arborescent plants, forming, in their rank native luxuriance, thick *cover* for the animals. The ancient history of this subject, in short, seems fully to confirm the inferences which a modern naturalist would be disposed to draw from the geological character of the soil; and these would accord entirely with the opinion expressed by Mr. Jones, as quoted above.

The streams flow onward, down the sloping flanks of the Moor, principally towards the north and the south, to fertilize and embellish the valleys which have been excavated in the transition and secondary formations of the County, which surround, and, as it were, insulate this primary tract.

CHAP. II.

Most of the streams are at intervals broken and diverted from their course by the masses of rock with which their beds are bestrewed. They are further subject, like mountain-streams in general, to instantaneous and violent risings, which are attributable to two causes,—the bursting of water-spouts in the uplands of the Moor, and the rushing down the declivities, into the nearest streams, of the torrents produced by the heavy rains to which this region is subject. After the rains, the same streams often appear, in shallow places, of an amber colour; and, where deeper, of a dark brown, resembling that of coffee-grounds. The colouring-matter, as Humboldt has suggested, when describing certain rivers in South America which present a similar appearance, is probably some combination of carbon and hydrogen, derived from the grasses and other plants through which the waters filter in their descent; or, in this case, from the peat of the bogs, the state of chemical change in which frequently imparts to water a brown hue, arising from the solution of some extractive matter. The same appearance is presented by most highland and forest waters throughout the world. In the Poems of Ossian it is thus alluded-to :

" Red through the stony vale comes down the stream of the hill."

" An allusion to the same fact," Mr. Burt remarks, "may be inferred from the names Cherry-brook, Blacka-brook, Redford-brook, and Red-lake *."

Many of the springs on Dartmoor, perhaps indeed the greater number, issue from the extensive peat-bogs which have been formed in the ravines and deep hollows in the

* Notes to Carrington's "Dartmoor," p. 112–113.

BOOK
III.

surface of the granite, and thus appear to be collected upon, and not within, the rock. There are instances, however, of a different kind; one of which may be observed at the eastern foot of Ugborough Beacon, where a fine spring gushes directly from the granite, at the rate, probably, of two hogsheads in a minute. " Such as these," Mr. Prideaux remarks, " may perhaps owe their origin to another condition of the granite, where the crystals of quartz and felspar are incoherent, and the schorl has very much disappeared, forming a sort of gravel, many yards in depth. Such a bed, of great extent, lies on one side of Hessary-Tor, near the Prison*." In beds of this description, much water would necessarily be collected.

Gneiss at
the Eddy-
stone.

The Eddystone rocks consist of granite, which Mr. Prideaux describes as having a very decided and rapid dip towards the south-west. Here the proportion of felspar gradually increases, the obvious structure of the granite becoming laminar at the same time; and we find the rock upon which the Lighthouse is erected to be composed of *Gneiss*, being the only spot in this primary tract in which that rock occurs †.

Metalliferous Slate; and the Grauwacké immediately associated with it.

Before we commence the systematic description of the Metalliferous Slate, and of the rocks with which it is immediately associated, either of contemporaneous origin, or reposing upon it in the ascending order of geological position, we shall continue the abstract of Mr. Prideaux's memoir; now selecting those portions of it which relate to

* "Geological Sketch," &c. p. 21.

† As Mr. Prideaux has stated his belief that the Eddystone is the only locality of gneiss in England, it may be well to remark that that rock exists much more extensively in Cumberland, as one of the members of the series of crystalline schistose masses which form the centre of the Skiddaw region. See "Proceedings of the Geological Society of London," No. 10, p. 122.

the metalliferous slate and the grauwacké in immediate connection with it.

At Collard and at Walkhampton, the slate in contact with the granite is not spangled [with mica]; but has a general glimmering surface approaching to that of talc, without the unctuous feel of magnesian minerals. This slate is not unfavourable to agriculture. On Yanadon-Down, from the Western-Beacon to Ugborough-Beacon, and in a larger tract from Deane to Holne, a hard stony slate bounds the granite. This rises into steep and high hills, unfertile, except in wood. It dips regularly away from the granite, at different degrees of declivity, but generally steep.

For a great part of the way from Ugborough-Beacon to Deanywood, and again on the northern side of the Dart, the granite is bounded by a rock which runs into all its creeks and bays, and rises into hills of inconsiderable altitude. This is a killas, with the texture of fine clay-slate, but having little of its laminar structure. Its appearance here differs from that of ordinary grauwacké; but it is known to the country people by the same appellation—" Blue Dun," and it sometimes passes into more decided granwacké, at a distance from the granite. Its dip is very regular, as it reposes upon the sides of the granite; but Mr. Prideaux was unable to discover the absolute line of junction with that rock. "In many places," he observes, "the separate rocks jutted out within thirty yards of each other; yet a detached fragment only could be found, wherein they are in contact. In this fragment the division is an abrupt line; the killas deep iron-gray; the granite pale buff, with the aspect of imperfect crystallization, distinguishing the granite of veins in Cornwall. In several parts where this killas is the boundary, the same condition of the granite occurred; and also where it comes in contact with the stratified iron ore at Hey-Tor [High Tor?]."

This killas is highly fertile, differing singularly from the adjoining granite. In no place is this more remarkable than at Buckland, on the Dart, where the killas runs in a trough between two eminences of granite. The vivid green of the turf in this trough, and the rich wood running up the acclivities, contrast strikingly with the pale herbage and the bald crowns of its overtopping neighbours. The same rock appears amidst the slate in Holne parish, and its superior fertility is marked by the greater value of the land. On the estate of Yolland, at the foot of Shipley-Tor, some fine trees appeared in the midst of the granite; but on approaching them, they were found to be growing on a patch of this killas, not a tree spreading out to the granite on either side.

Morwell-rocks.

"I have heard of no metallic veins in this rock; and, although it does not exhibit any striking marks of stratification, presents no vestiges of organic remains, and lies immediately on the granite, it appears to me to be a transition rock, belonging to the grauwacké family."

To the south of the slate which reposes on the southern side of the granite of Calstock (in Cornwall), are Morwell-rocks (which are in Devonshire). These consist of very hard primary slate; having in some parts a striated or fibrous, in others a sort of glimmering and speckled, appearance. Thence down the Tamar, almost as far as Saltash, in Cornwall, we find a succession of pale gray slates, dipping south, and gradually becoming tinged with green, and softer, as we proceed southward. At Cotehele, also in Cornwall, we have the deep iron-gray slate only, spangled in some places with mica. Its laminæ are pretty freely separable, and it breaks into rhomboids; it is connected with, if not traversed by, beds of hard gray stone, consisting of fine-granular quartz and schorl, having also a rhomboidal fracture in the large, but a granular one in the small. This slate seems to dip away from the western granite, from which it is three or four miles distant. The beds of granular stone strongly resembling grauwacké, are probably a crystalline deposit; for Mr. Prideaux found no indication that the slate did not belong to the primary class. After passing Pentilly (south), the slate

is lower in texture; has a brownish colour, and every
appearance of the transition slate which alternates with
the limestone of Plymouth.   Near Saltash we have, on
both sides of the river, beds of granular grauwacké, included in the slate, with a few thin beds or veins of
limestone; and this alternation continues on the eastern
bank down to Plymouth dock-yard, where the limestone
formation commences.   In fact, the eastern bank of the
Tamar, from the weir-head downward, is generally slate
dipping south; and it is remarkable that the dip increases
as we recede from the granite; the strata of Morwell-
rocks deviating scarcely ten degrees from the horizontal
line, and those near Saltash approaching almost as near
to the vertical.

A line drawn from the granite of Calstock to that of
Sheep's-Tor, will lie east by south, and pass, Mr. Prideaux believes, entirely over slate, varying both in dip
and in line of bearing, each hill often differing in these
respects from the next.   Sometimes it is disturbed, in
the same hills, by clefts and veins.   These irregularities
might have been expected from the position of the slate
between two granite eminences, as already mentioned.
This slate varies in colour; it is whitish, greenish, gray,
and red: that which is characterized by the former two
colours rises high, is pervaded with quartz, and is little
productive; the gray slate is soft and fertile; and the
red, where not too cold from its elevation, is perhaps still
more favourable to agriculture.   Upon the former lies
much of the fertile soil towards Tavistock; upon the latter, much of that round Walkhampton.

Just north of this line, on Morwell-Down, are blocks
of coarse porphyry, containing rhomboidal crystals of
reddish-buff felspar; the rock occurring to the miners,
probably, *in situ,* underneath the slate; for though these
blocks lie about upon the slate for some miles, Mr. Prideaux did not meet with the rock itself.   The same porphyry, however, is found at Grenofen, three miles further
east, and about a mile north of the line above-stated;

Coarse
porphyry
on Mor-
well-
Down.

BOOK
III.

where it is quarried for mending the roads. It occurs
again, and in larger quantity, about Walkhampton. It
breaks into flat pieces, and seems to yield to the weather.
The superincumbent soil, at Grenofen and Walkhampton,
is fertile; but whether from greater elevation, or from the
porphyry being covered with hard slate, this character
does not appear on Morwell-Down. North of Grenofen,
the slate prevails both eastward and westward; the country about Tavistock, however, still needs geological investigation, for which it presents an interesting field.

Peninsula
between
the Tamar
and Tavy
consists of
slate.

Southward of the line from the granite of Calstock to
that of Sheep's-Tor, the entire peninsula between the
Tamar and the Tavy, consists of slate, dipping almost
uniformly to the south, and becoming softer and less
elevated as it proceeds southward from the granite. In
the northern part of this peninsula, a portion of the slate
is gritty and whitish; other portions are softer and gray;
but more generally it is hard and greenish, with veins of
white quartz, "and strewed with snow-white bowlders of
the latter substance, retaining sufficient marks of their
origin; which having withstood the atmospheric depredations on their kindred-slate, were probably rolled about
and rounded by the Deluge*." Some very large and heavy
masses still retain their native position, protruding their
white shoulders through the slate. These bowlders disappear before we reach Beeralston; and the hill-tops,
wild and unproductive from the hardness of the stone and
the want of shelter, present a striking contrast to the lively
green of the prospect towards the south, down the valleys
bordering the Tavy, and the wooded sides of their low
hills, all composed of soft slate.

Bowlders
of quartz.

The slate of this peninsula is metalliferous; the country

* The present figure of these quartz bowlders has more probably been
the effect of disintegration, than of the cause here assigned by Mr. Prideaux; if indeed it be not their original form, when existing as concretions, or as detached portions of veins, in the slate. Had they been
rounded by diluvian agency, they would not have remained upon the
rock of which they once formed a part, but would have been rolled far
distant from it, by the action of the waters; as in all other cases in which
fragments of rock have been rounded by diluvian attrition.

being pierced with mines of tin, copper, lead, and silver, from Tavistock nearly to the confluence of the two rivers.

To the East of the Tavy, and between that and the Mew, the elevated and wild tract bearing several names, may be generally included under the term of Roborough-Down. Distinguished from the neighbouring granite, by the greenness of its bordering valleys, and by the copse which clothes its declivities, it is again a slate-formation. The predominant dip is at least 40° westward of south, but the position is a good deal disturbed; and the slate is intersected by other rocks in several places.

At the point where the road turns off to Dartmoor Prison, just above the western elbow of the river Mew, is a remarkable projecting rock, rising out of the slate. It consists of quartz, laminæ of slate, iron-ochre, and schorl; forming one of the aggregates termed *caple* by the miners. It appears to be a vein pervading the slate, and to have derived its prominence from its superior power of resisting the weather. It runs nearly westward across the Down, exhibiting the general dip of the neighbourhood, though it is probably less than twenty feet wide; similar appearances, on a smaller scale, occur in other parts of the Down.

To the south of this rock, and extending from a point nearly opposite Hoo Meavy to Bickham, is a bed of a singular porphyry, without defined dip; bowlders of which are strewed about the Down so extensively, as to have acquired for it the name of " Roborough-Down stone." Its fresh fracture is almost white, but turning brown by the action of the weather, and is full of small cavities, seldom exceeding one-tenth of an inch in diameter. Minute crystals of pure quartz are thinly disseminated in it; and the cavities, which, when regularly formed, appear to be cubical, contain, in some instances, remains of the matter with which they were originally filled. The cement, forming nine-tenths of the stone, has an earthy fracture; yields, when scraped, a powder sparkling apparently with mica, and is very imperfectly fusible before

CHAP. II.

Roborough-Down.

Projecting mass of slaty schorl-rock.

" Roborough-Down stone."

the blowpipe. It is perhaps mica, in a very fine-granular form. The same rock appears again, at Harewood, west of the Tamar, where it is quarried, but the quarry presents only loose blocks as it were buried.

Schorl-
rock.

At the south-eastern angle of the Down, towards Shaugh and Bickleigh, we have the hard black or marbled aggregate of quartz and schorl; and lower down, approaching the river, a gritty slate, spangled with mica. Mr. Prideaux was unable to find either of these rocks exposed in such a manner, as to enable him to distinguish its relative position; though the black schorl-rock often protrudes angularly through the turf, and detached fragments of both cover the ground.

Slate coun-
try be-
tween the
Plym and
Tamar.

After leaving Roborough-Down, the whole country between the Plym and the Tamar, for two miles south, is slate; generally hard, with a regular southerly dip; traversed by a single bed of compact felspar, which is cut through by the rail-road near Fancy, where it is not above thirty feet wide, and by broad veins of quartz.

About two miles south of Bickleigh, the river Plym cuts through a bed of excellent roofing-slate, worked to a considerable extent on both its banks. Cann-Quarry, the eastern working, presents a beautiful picture, when viewed from the rail-road. This slate has the conformable steep southerly dip; its natural surface is clothed with wood.

Green-
stone.

A short distance to the south of this bed of slate, the rail-road, cut out of the hill-sides parallel to the river, lays open an extensive mass of greenstone. As the slate approaches this rock, its laminæ are slightly contorted, and it becomes pale green, a colour which continues where the rock loses its slaty form and becomes fine-granular. As the grain becomes coarser, the colour deepens, until the rock acquires a deep green hue, and a rough granular texture; small blades of white felspar appearing in some parts, and black spots of hornblende becoming evident when a piece of the stone is breathed upon. In one place is an appearance of dip to the south-westward, about 80°; but the lines of cleavage are in general too irregular to llow of our having much confidence in their indications. This greenstone rises into hills, not so high as those of the slate, the soil upon it being fertile. The twin hills on which the houses of Rock and Estover stand, are composed of it; and it appears to terminate with them. It is bounded, everywhere, by slate, passing into it by the gradual transition above-described, wherever the junction appears. The greenstone seems to have been an intruder; not however exhibiting the decided marks of igneous action which are stated frequently to accompany that rock.

At nearly the same parallel a formation of grauwacké Grauwacké. commences; its northernmost point being near Knackers-knowle, where it is mixed with a soft slate; each often passing insensibly into the other, and forming the high ground which branches out a mile and a half west by north to Honiknowle; again the same distance west to Pennycross; and again three miles south-west to Swilley, where it is extensively quarried. The southern boundary runs in a curved line to the summit of Townsend Hill, where a ridge appears to mark the limit, and thence, across the limit, to a hill just south of the village of Crab-tree, in the quarry at which a similar ridge is seen to indicate the line of separation from the slate. The greatest breadth of this grauwacké, from north to south, may be two miles; from east to west it runs four miles at least; and as we find it again just behind Saltram, it is probably connected with the similar rock, which appears, as already stated, to follow, in some places, the outline of Dartmoor. Here, as elsewhere, the soil on the grauwacké is of distinguished fertility; and particularly where it is in contact with the slate.

This grauwacké, which is here called "Dunstone," is "Dunstone." generally compact, and hard enough to make a good road-stone. In mass it suffers from the weather; particularly where it happens to present an eastern face, south of the granite; mouldering and becoming honey-combed, the hollows containing ochreous matter. Amygdaloidal granules of limpid crystallized carbonate of lime are often

BOOK
III.

disseminated in it, and sometimes others of black schorl. Veins of quartz, accompanied by pulverulent black oxide of manganese, often occur, especially in the slaty portions; and the latter substance occasionally fills the pores of the exposed rock, instead of the ochreous matter above mentioned. This rock is very fusible before the blowpipe, which circumstance, in conjunction with its susceptibility of being acted upon by the weather, seems to indicate the presence of an alkali.

Junction of the dunstone and southerly transition slate.

A distinction appears to exist between the slate belonging to the dunstone, and the transition slate to the south of it, particularly the blue variety. At Crabtree, this blue slate comes in contact with the dunstone, (which at this point is granular,) with an abrupt line of division; and yet this same slate occurs in amygdaloidal concretions in the body of the dunstone itself. They are concretions, and not included pebbles, because their surfaces are ill-defined, and the laminæ of widely-distant nodules are parallel with those of each other, and also with those of the rock itself. This seems to mark a particular disposition to separation; whilst the dunstone-slate often passes so gradually into the compact rock, that two observers can scarcely agree where the line of separation should be drawn.

A detached bed of grauwacké is quarried behind Mount Tamar House, half a mile to the south of St. Budeaux. It runs through the slate, in thin beds or veins, to Saltash, as before observed. This grauwacké is granular, and has so great a resemblance to the greenstone last named, that, judging from this district only, Mr. Prideaux would have felt disposed to assign to these rocks an allied origin.

No metallic veins in the greenstone or grauwacké.

No metallic veins have been observed, in either the greenstone or the grauwacké. A hard black rock, with veins of white quartz, called by the country people "Blackacre," and very different from grauwacké, sometimes caps the hills of slate. This is most conspicuous at Warleigh-Tor, where it is conformable to the slate, and where, in some parts, it is laminated. Mr. Prideaux ob-

serves that it is "perhaps nothing but slate, with a large CHAP.
proportion of silica;" but it may with greater probability II.
be regarded as a variety of schorl-rock, consisting chiefly Schorl-rock?
of that mineral in a compact state.

The bed of clay-slate at Cann-Quarry seems to draw a Slate of Cann-Quarry.
line of distinction between the harder schist, traversed by
broad veins of quartz, which lies north of that bed, and
the softer and more fertile, which extends to the southward. To the latter character there is perhaps an exception at St. Budeaux; where, although not deficient in
fertility, the slate assumes a hard and somewhat nodular
texture, much resembling that of Morwell-Rocks. At
this spot it rises high and steep, and looks like a hill of
primary slate protruding through the transition rocks. It
is accompanied by two other insulated rocks; each appearing in one small point only, within the tract described
by Mr. Prideaux. The first of these is a felspar-porphyry, Felspar-porphyry.
with numerous cracks, having a decayed appearance, and
full of spicular crystals of schorl, sometimes an inch in
length. It rises at the corner of a field, just where the road
to King's Tamarton branches off from that leading from
St. Budeaux to the Saltash turnpike; and it dips to the
south-east, or even to a more easterly point; the strata
around it dipping westward of south. The other rock Rock of compact mica?
appears at the angle where the St. Budeaux road joins
the turnpike road; occupying, like the former, the corner
of a field, as a sort of quarry. It exhibits rounded masses,
looking not unlike granite bowlders, some projecting from
the soil, where that is cut down to a vertical face, others
standing up from the rock beneath. In the latter is some
appearance of cleavage, corresponding with the dip of the
country. The projecting blocks look as hard as any others,
but some of them may be entirely disintegrated by a kick;
and when cut down with a spade, they exhibit concentric
lines, and thus appear to decay in irregular balls, from
which their bowlder-like aspect doubtless originates. The
soil formed of the disintegrated rock, looks something like
a soft micaceous sand; but on being compressed, and

shaken loose again, the glistening lustre disappears, and
it becomes a soft, free soil.   Around the rock it appears
to be very fertile; but there is no clear indication how far
the former extends beneath. The rock itself is composed
of a very fusible brown mica, with a semi-metallic ____,
and granules of white felspar; whence its gra____
pearance is also partly derived.

Junction of the slate and the transition-limestone.

To the southward of the grauwacké, the count___
cupied, until we reach the limestone, with si____
south, and covered with a fertile soil. At the L____
we see at once the different form of the hills of
limestone; the difference of the altitude they r____
attain; the alternation between the two rocks ____
of junction; and also, after continued dry weath____
however, is a rare condition at this spot, situate____
between the Atlantic Ocean and the granite distric____
difference of character of their soil, as evinced b____
colour of the turf. As the slate approaches the lime___,
tabular masses of limestone are included in it; a___ as
the latter rock becomes predominant, it is pervaded by
slaty laminæ for a considerable distance. The two rocks
appear to be conformable in position, where in contact;
but at other points the limestone is less regular in dip than
the slate. The limestone hills are much less elevated than
those of the slate, and whilst the latter rise gently from
the south, and fall steep to the northward, those of the
limestone assume a contrary inclination. The soil on the
limestone is thin, and dries quickly; that on the slate is
deeper, and is retentive of moisture; the former being the
most fertile, except in dry weather.

Disturbed stratification on the south.

Hitherto we have found a tolerably regular disposition
of the strata, from the granite upwards: further south,
on the sides of Plymouth harbour, we find the greatest
disturbance.

At Mount Batten, the limestone is nearly vertical; in
some places even overhanging to the south. The hill
south of the Mount consists of soft slate, dipping generally southward, though in some places the dip is

DEVONSHIRE

irregular; and at the back of the hill the slate appears to dip north-east, under the limestone at Turnchapel.

A similar formation, with dunstone, occurs at Mount Edgcumbe, where, however, the stratification is less disturbed, dipping westward of south. The southern part of Mount Edgcumbe corresponds with Staddon-heights; both rising to considerable and nearly the same heights, and both being composed of slate, dunstone and red-sandstone, in well-defined strata.

General Characters and Nature of the Metalliferous Slate.—This rock, distinguished from the adjacent and probably incumbent grauwacké slate, by the veins of metallic ores which it includes, and also by the veins and beds of the porphyritic substance provincially termed Elvan, with which it is also intersected, (or possibly, in certain situations, interstratified,) belongs to that formation which has usually received the names of Argillaceous Schist and Clay-slate. The simple varieties of it are formed of a peculiar indurated clay, while the coarser or compound kinds contain, in addition, quartz and mica, and sometimes, perhaps more frequently than is generally supposed, the mineral called Chlorite. Its schistose or slaty texture allows of its division into thin laminæ, which, in general, have a shining surface, and sometimes a more or less silky aspect. The cross-fracture or surface exposed by breaking the rock in the direction across that of the laminæ, is dull and fine-grained, or in some degree earthy; and as the late Mr. Phillips has observed, "it often possesses the aspect of plates of chlorite, of which the larger planes are disposed with sufficient regularity to impart fissility *." Sometimes this slate has a soapy or greasy feel, arising, probably, from an admixture of talc with the indurated clay forming the basis of the rock. Its colours are grey, blueish, greenish-grey, and reddish-brown. It naturally divides into portions having a rhom-

General characters of the metalliferous slate.

---

* "Outlines of Mineralogy and Geology," edit. 1826, p. 153.

BOOK
III.

boidal or a prismatic form, devoid, however, of the regularity of crystallization. Like the other rocks of the Inferior or Primary class, it contains no organic remains.

"The slates (*killas*) of Cornwall [and Devonshire], which are generally understood to be clay-slate, are celebrated for their abundance of mineral veins, and for *dykes of porphyry* (*elvan* of Cornwall); and it is somewhat remarkable that no mineral veins or dykes of porphyry have yet been observed in that County [or in the County of Devon] in any decided grauwacké, which however is not wanting: clay-slate is also rich in metals in other countries *."

In Devonshire, this rock passes, by insensible gradations of texture, from the compact form, interspersed with mica, in which it occurs in the vicinity of the granite, through roofing and other slates varying in hardness, down to the

Associated rocks.

state of an incoherent clay. Other rocks, as already mentioned, in characterizing the Primary district of this County, p. 274, also appear to belong to the same formation; and are sometimes interposed between the granite and the slate, sometimes incumbent upon them. These have chiefly a syenitic or a porphyritic character, but in some instances, it would appear, are referable to what has been called flinty slate or siliceous schist; their variations are so numerous and so undefined, that to assign with precision their respective characters and limits would be a most difficult if not an impracticable task. Occasionally, in this formation, viewing it as a whole, rocks of very distinct character succeed each other in an abrupt manner; while in many instances the passage from one form to another, takes place, as mentioned above, by a very gradual change of texture and mineral constitution †.

Local extent.

Local Extent, Boundaries, &c.—The metalliferous slate occupies a tract between the granite described in the preceding section and the river Tamar; and it is situated,

* Phillips's " Outlines," as before quoted, p. 154.
† Kingston's " Mineralogy of Teignmouth."

consequently, almost wholly, to the west of that formation. The figure of this tract is nearly that of a trapezium, having one right angle, which is directed about south-east, and from which a small portion of the slate extends beyond its general southern boundary, nearly in the form of a parallelogram. It constitutes a comparatively small part of the area of the County, and is contained, entirely, in its south-western division. The longest side of the trapezium extends from a point about a mile west of Meavy, in a general direction of nearly due north, to a point situated about the same distance south of Lydford. The shortest side, forming a right angle with the longest, extends from the same point near Meavy, in a direction a little northward of the parallel of that place, to the Tamar; while that river forms the undulating third side, which has a general direction of south-east and north-west, and terminates on the eastern bank of the stream, at the distance of about a mile to the south-west of Milton Abbot; whence the fourth side of the trapezium ascends towards the north-east, until it reaches the northern termination already mentioned. The metalliferous slate, therefore, does not extend, on the north, so far towards the centre of the County as the granite does; nor does it reach, on the south, to so near the sea.

The extreme length of this formation, from south to north, being also that of the longest side of the trapezium, is about thirteen miles and a half; which is also very nearly the length of the diagonal from the south-eastern to the north-western termination. The breadth, measured from the western extremity of the peninsula formed by the acute flexure of the Tamar north of Hengston Down, to a point situated about a mile north-east of Sampford Spiney, is between nine and ten miles; to which the distance from the north-western extremity to a point situated between one and two miles east of Peter Tavy is nearly equal. The least breadth, (or length of the shortest side of the trapezium,) measured from the south-

BOOK
III.

_____

western termination, to the granite east of Meavy, is about
seven miles; and the length of the north-western side of
the trapezium and boundary of the formation, about nine
miles.   The area may be estimated at about a hundred
square miles.

Extension
of the me-
talliferous
slate into
Cornwall.

Such are the dimensions of this formation, as developed
in the County of Devon; but the river Tamar is here
regarded as the boundary of the metalliferous slate, only
because it separates this County from that of Cornwall.   It merely intersects this formation, which extends from its western bank, and continuously, though
with insulated tracts of granite occurring within it, as far
west as to Cape Cornwall, which is a few miles north of
the Land's End, and to the southern extremity of the
coast of Mount's Bay; the formation being divided, at
St. Ives' Bay on the north, and the Mount's Bay on the
south, and embracing, in two narrow arms, the granitic
extremity of Cornwall. Above half the area of that County
is constituted by this rock, chiefly on its north-western
side, but it reaches to near Mevagissey on the south.

Bounda-
ries.

Commencing our survey from the Tamar, at the north-
western angle of the trapezium, situated near Milton Abbot, we find the line of junction of the metalliferous slate
with the grauwacké, to proceed, in an undulating form,
in the general direction of about north-north-east, to
about a mile south of Lydford, the northern extremity of
the formation.   This line either forms the water-shed of
the adjacent country, or runs parallel to it at a very small
distance; the streams descending on one side, towards
the south-east, to increase the Tavy and the Tamar,
and on the other, towards the north-west, in contribution
to the Lyd.   From the point just mentioned it begins
to bend, with a regular curvature, and passing a hill
of greenstone, towards the south; until it reaches the
source of one of the southernmost streamlets of those
which unite to form the Lyd.   Here the granite forms the
adjoining rock, and the boundary is consequently the

same with that of the granite, from Peter Tavy to Meavy, described in page 277; until it reaches a point about a mile south-west of Meavy, whence it ranges, for between two and three miles only, towards the south-east, until it arrives at a point in the valley of the eastern branch of the Plym, which forms the south-eastern extremity of the formation. Thence the metalliferous slate is bounded by the Plym, which flows in a south-westerly direction, and continues to separate it from the grauwacké, as far as the point from which the two branches of that river take their origin, which is the extreme southerly termination of the slate. From hence the direction of the boundary is towards the north-west, marked by the western branch of the Plym, which thus forms the common boundary of the metalliferous slate and the grauwacké, until we arrive at a point within a mile to the south-west of Meavy, whence it proceeds, nearly north-west, for about the same distance; and it then extends for about five or six miles in a straight line, and very nearly due west, until it reaches the Tamar, at the south-western angle of the trapezium. On the south-west, as already stated, the Tamar forms the boundary, so far as the County of Devon is concerned. The extreme western point of the tract, in Devonshire, is the extremity of the peninsula formed by the acute flexure of the Tamar, which has already been noticed; but the north-western angle of the trapezium is nearly if not quite as far west. The south-eastern extremity forms the extreme eastern point, but many parts of the line of junction with the granite extend as far in that direction. The metalliferous slate is bounded, on the north-west and on the south, entirely by the incumbent grauwacké, as it is on the east by the subjacent granite; while the formation, on the remaining south-western side, as already mentioned, is prolonged nearly to the Land's End.

A range of limestone and calcareous slate extends from a few miles west of Launceston in Cornwall, passes the Tamar into the County of Devon, and proceeds in a cur-

CHAP.
II.

Calcareous slate.

BOOK
III.

vilinear form towards the north-east, until it nearly reaches Oakhampton. In Mr. Greenough's map, a portion of this range, on its north-western flank, from near Stewford to the north-eastern extremity, appears to be represented as belonging to the metalliferous slate: it does not, at any point, exceed five or six miles in width.

Hills of green-stone, &c.

A hill of greenstone near the northern extremity of this formation has already been noticed. At the north-western angle of the trapezium, near Milton Abbot, another hill of this rock occurs: there are others again near the eastern boundary, but these are surrounded by the granite, of which, probably, they are merely modifications, and do not interrupt the continuity of the metalliferous slate. In the neighbourhood of Sampford Spiney and Whitchurch, however, rocks of this description occur, which are entirely surrounded by the metalliferous slate. Mr. Greenough represents a mass of syenite or greenstone in the midst of the slate, as extending, near or upon the line of the Tavy, from near Tavistock to the vicinity of Mary and Peter Tavy. Its outline will admit of being inscribed within a parallelogram with very little addition of area; its length appears to be between two and three miles, and its greatest width not to exceed one mile.

Cock's-Tor.

The hill upon which is Cock's-Tor, situated about a mile and a half south-east of Peter Tavy, exhibits the junction of the greenstone with the slate, in a ridge near the summit. "This ridge," Mr. Prideaux states, speaking of the slate, "still preserves its laminar structure, but instead of its argillaceous aspect, has assumed that of flint, and gives fire under the hammer. In many places it is become ribband jasper."

Mr. J. Taylor on Morwell-Down.

Mr. John Taylor, F.R.S., communicated to the Geological Society, in 1816, an account of the geological phænomena observed in driving the tunnel of the Tavistock Canal through Morwell-Down. From this, as published in the fourth volume of the Transactions of that Society, we extract, as follows, whatever relates to the metalliferous slate and its mineral contents; with a few deviations in arrangement.

Morwell-Down is a hill lying between the river Tamar and the river Tavy: the latter, rising in the forest of Dartmoor, and passing the town of Tavistock, flows on the eastern side of Morwell-Down, and falls into the Tamar a few miles nearer Plymouth. The neck of high land separating these rivers, extends southward from Morwell-Down, and includes the parish of Beer, in which are situated the Beer-alstone lead and silver mines, not far from the point of the peninsula; the lode or vein worked in those mines crossing a part of that peninsula from north to south. In pursuing the Tavy towards its source, the country rises irregularly, and the rocks are found to consist of the killas or metalliferous slate, until we reach the borders of Dartmoor: the same appearances are observed on taking a survey of the hills situate between the eastern bank of the river and the granite range of Dartmoor.

In the valley through which flows the little river Wallcombe, and near the point at which it falls into the Tavy, a remarkable change of the rock occurs; the side of a very abrupt hill, on the top of which is West Down, in the parish of Whitchurch, being composed of a considerable cluster of detached masses of granitic rocks, which are piled upon each other in the most picturesque manner, and form a lofty and steep bank to the river. The metalliferous slate occurs in the same hill, on each side, and is the only rock observable in the hill which rises from the opposite edge of the valley.

Granitic rocks of Whitchurch.

Morwell-Down is one of the highest hills in the central part of this slate district; its elevation being about 700 feet above the tideway in the river Tamar, which washes its base.

This district of metalliferous slate is everywhere intersected by veins, or as they are technically called *lodes*. Those which are worked for copper or tin have universally a direction of from north-east to south-west, or nearly so;

Veins in the metalliferous slate.

BOOK
III.

those which run in other courses have all the appearances of belonging to a newer formation, and are generally unproductive of metallic ores, if we except two instances, one of which is the lode on which the Beer-alstone mines are working to a considerable extent, and the other is the lode in Wheal Betsey Mine, in the parish of Mary Tavy, both producing lead and silver.

Mining in
this district.

During great part of the last thirty or thirty-five years this district has been the scene of very active exertion in the pursuit of mining, and the most spirited efforts have been made for tracing the veins, and instituting trials upon them for the discovery of their contents. These efforts, as in most similar cases, have been attended with very variable success, though on the whole the result has been a favourable one. On many lodes considerable sums of money have been expended, without discovering sufficient quantities of ore to repay the disbursements, and on many others the loss has been heavy; but in other instances, though the smaller in number, mines have been established which have produced large quantities of ore, principally of copper, and have paid the adventurers very handsome profits. The most important of these mines are the following: Wheal Friendship, in the parish of Mary Tavy; Gunnis Lake and Drake Walls mines, which however are at Calstock, on the Cornish side of the Tamar; Wheal Crowndale, on the banks of the Tavy, below Tavistock; Beer-alstone mines, in the parish of Beer; Wheal Betsey, in Mary Tavy; Wheal Crebor, at the foot of Morwell-Down, discovered in consequence of driving the tunnel through that hill; and some others of inferior note.

Produce of
the mines.

Exclusive of the produce of Gunnis Lake copper mine, and that of the Beer-alstone mines, the former of which has been very considerable, the mines just named returned, between the years 1805 and 1815, from 3000 to 4000 tons of copper ore annually, and the quantity raising at the latter period was at the rate of at least 5000 tons in

the year.   A considerable quantity of lead has also been
raised at Wheal Betsey, and of tin at Drake Walls.

All the lodes that have been worked are in the killas
or metalliferous slate, except that of Gunnis Lake, where
the copper ore is found in granite. The ores of this mine
differ very much from those of the other mines : in the
latter the copper occurs almost entirely in the form of
copper-pyrites or yellow-copper-ore, yielding, in the form
in which it is raised, from 5 to 15 per cent. of metal ;
while in Gunnis Lake are found, besides copper-pyrites,
carbonates and arseniates of copper, grey-copper-ore, &c.
This fact is the more striking, since the vein worked in this
mine is certainly the same as that which is worked at
Wheal Crowndale and Wheal Crebor, in which it traverses
the killas, while at Gunnis Lake it passes into the granite.

About the year 1802, when the mines of this district
were assuming an importance they had never before attained, and when their prospects were such as to encourage
fresh adventurers, the proprietors of the principal of them
were led to think of the scheme of driving a tunnel through
the hill, which is the subject of Mr. Taylor's paper. The
chief inducements to this undertaking were, that Morwell-
Down was known to be traversed by numerous lodes, which
might be discovered and worked by piercing through it,
and that while a tunnel might be carried in such a direction as to cross them all, it might make practicable " a
navigation" or means of conveyance by canal, from the
vicinity of Tavistock and the adjacent mines, to the
river Tamar, where the produce of the neighbourhood is
shipped.

In 1803 an Act of Parliament was obtained for cutting
a canal from the town of Tavistock to Morwelham, a quay
on the river Tamar, and the driving of the tunnel was
immediately begun. A canal from the north end of it to
the town of Tavistock was soon after cut, by which means
a copious stream of water was obtained from the Tavy,
which was carried across a valley upon an embankment
fifty feet high, and afforded the means of working an

[margin note] Tunnel of
the Ta-
vistock
Canal.

overshot water-wheel of immense power, which was required for sinking the requisite shafts on the hill through
which the tunnel was to pass. This tunnel, which passes
through hard rock for the length of nearly a mile and three
quarters, and for the greater part at a depth of about 390
feet from the surface of the hill, was an undertaking of no
small enterprise; but after many obstacles had been surmounted, it was completed in the year 1817 *.

It does not often happen that the operations of the miner
lead to so much geological discovery as might be expected;
the works he undertakes follow the course of the veins he
is exploring, or are confined within a small space bordering upon it. As the veins are sought after in but very few
varieties of rock, the number of those varieties which are
laid open to view is generally inconsiderable, when compared with those actually existing in the mining districts.
A tunnel, however, of such an extent as that mentioned,
in such a district, crossing the direction of the metalliferous
veins, and passing at such a depth beneath the surface,
could hardly fail to prove an interesting object to the
geologist as well as to the miner.

Facts as-
certained
during the
progress
of the
tunnel.

"Two facts have been ascertained by its progress :

"1st. Relative to the rocks, that the killas of which the
hill is mainly formed, is traversed by beds of other rocks,
the direction of which is inclined to that of the metalliferous veins, and which have a pretty uniform dip or underlay to the north.

"2nd. Relative to the metallic veins or lodes, that they
traverse all the strata, and that they have a remarkable
difference in their dip or underlay on the two sides of the
hill; those on the north side dipping to the north, and
those on the south side to the south."

Beds in-
tersected
by the
tunnel.

The following are the strata which have been passed
through, commencing at the north end of the tunnel; the
provincial names of the different rocks being given as
they are generally used by the Cornish miners:

* Further particulars of this tunnel will be found in Book I. Chap. III.,
on the Navigation of the Rivers and Canals of Devonshire, at p. 67.

fathoms.

Killas ...	Metalliferous Slate ...	311
Elvan ...	Chlorite and Quartz ...	11
Killas ...		23
Grouan ..	Clay-Porphyry	6
Killas ...		12
Grouan ..	Clay-Porphyry	26
Killas .... ⎫		
Do. with veins of Quartz ⎭	.....	436
Elvan ...		15
Killas ...		3
Grouan ..	Porphyry	7
Elvan	{ Quartz, granular and crystalline ..... }	12
Killas ...		408

1270 Entire length
of the tunnel.

The directions of all these beds seem to be parallel to each other, and to range nearly east and west *.

It was not to be expected that any great proportion of the number of mineral veins intersected by the tunnel would turn out productive of ore, or at least that they should be so at the exact point where the tunnel crossed them. One or two, if rich in ore, might render the speculation a profitable one ; and it is somewhat extraordinary that the

* The situation of the granitic rocks in the parish of Whitchurch, noticed in p. 319, would seem to point out a connection between them and some of the beds of porphyry, &c. above described. The line of direction of the latter would lead us to this point, and there are strong grounds for inferring that these rocks form part of one of them. " It is however rather extraordinary," Mr. Taylor observes, " that it should have escaped notice in the deep valley of the Tavy, where it must pass, and where I have little doubt it will be found, from a recollection of the general features, though unfortunately it did not occur to me to look for it at the time when I could have done so.   It may likewise probably be traced through Morwell-Down to Gunnis Lake Mine.

" I do not venture to decide on what this rock should be called ; in describing the strata of the tunnel I have assumed that it is porphyry. That which occurs in the Wallcombe Valley has much more the character of granite, and so I should incline to call it."

The porphyritic rocks in the neighbourhood of Walkhampton, have been noticed also by Mr. Prideaux : see pp. 305, 306.

Wheal
Crebor
mine.

first which was discovered, at the commencement of the
work, at the north end, in 1803, should have been one of
that description. It is called Wheal Crebor lode, and in
1816 had already been worked about 60 fathoms deep
under the level of the tunnel, and had produced, down to
that time, between 8000 and 9000 tons of copper-ore; its
direction, as usual, is from north-east to south-west, and it
has been traced to be the same vein that is worked at
Wheal Crowndale mine to the east, in killas ; and at
Gunnis Lake mine to the west, in granite ; at both of
which very large quantities of ore have been raised. The
lode at Wheal Crebor is in some places fourteen feet wide,
while in others it does not equal so many inches. It is
traversed by cross veins, which *heave* the lode, as the
miners call it, or abruptly throw it out of its original direction, for a few feet. In 1816 this mine was producing
nearly 4000 tons of ore in the year. It is now upwards
of 80 fathoms deep *.

The next lode found in following the course of the
tunnel southward contained tin, but not in any great
quantity. Still further south is a lode called Wheal Geor-
giana, which has produced some rich copper ore in the
porphyry, in which it was discovered by carrying on the
tunnel. It has been pursued into the killas, but in this
rock it appears to be less productive of metal.

Cross-
lodes.

The lodes near the centre of the hill are intersected by
two cross-lodes or cross-courses. The killas, on each side
of one of these, occurs in a remarkably altered state, as a
soft clayey substance, so incoherent as to have rendered
the preservation of a passage through it, until it was securely arched, very difficult.

Number of
veins, &c.

The engraving annexed to Mr. Taylor's paper exhibits
a section of Morwell-Down on the line of the tunnel;
showing the relative position of the beds of killas and
porphyry, and of the veins and cross-courses which intersect them. Nineteen veins and two cross-courses are
represented.

* Wheal Crebor mine has already been noticed, in p. 68.

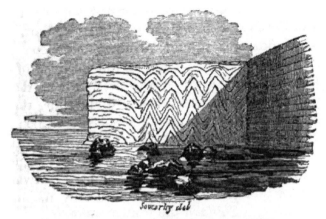

GRAUWACKE OF HARTLAND POINT.

CHAPTER III.

SUBMEDIAL OR TRANSITION ROCKS OF DEVONSHIRE: —GRAUWACKÉ AND TRANSITION LIMESTONE.

Grauwacké, in Contorted Strata, of the northern coast of Devon.—The late Rev. J. J. Conybeare, brother of the still more eminent geologist of that name, to whose exertions we are indebted for so great a portion of our knowledge of the Secondary rocks of England, has described the remarkable and characteristic contortions of the grauwacké, as it occurs on the northern coast of this County, in a paper which is inserted in the second volume of the Transactions of the Geological Society. From this paper, entitled " Memoranda relative to Clovelly, North Devon," are derived the following particulars on the subject.

The small fishing-town of Clovelly is situated in a narrow and precipitous ravine on the north coast of Devon, about 22 miles to the westward of Ilfracombe, and has attracted much notice from the singularly picturesque scenery of its site and more immediate environs, the general character of which much resembles that of Lynton, upon the same coast, so frequently described by

CHAP.
III.
_____
Contorted
grau-
wacké of
Clovelly.

modern tourists.   The best access to the town, from the
Hartland road, is by a private carriage-way cut through
the grounds of Sir James Hamlyn Williams, Bart.   This
not only commands several advantageous views of the
lofty and well-wooded ravine along the declivity of which
it winds, but offers in many places, where the rock
has been cut away for the purpose of levelling the road,
striking instances of that remarkable configuration of the
strata, which is said to be characteristic of the grauwacké
formation.   To that class all the rocks of this neighbourhood may probably be referred.   The principal varieties
are those known throughout Devonshire by the appella-
tions of *Dunstone* and *Shillat;* the former answers pretty
accurately to the description usually given by mineralogists of that species of grauwacké in which the fragments, supposed to be cemented together by the inter-
vention of a paste resembling the matter of clay-slate, are
too small to be discerned even by the aid of a considerable magnifier.   The latter alternates with the former,
and is evidently the finer grauwacké-slate of the same
nomenclature.   Of these rocks, the coast between Clovelly and Hartland Point presents the most magnificent
and interesting sections which were met with in the
course of their tour in this district by Mr. J. J. Conybeare
and his companion Mr. (now the Rev. Professor) Buckland;
both varieties sometimes alternating in distinct and well-
defined strata, sometimes appearing to graduate into each
other, and the compact species assuming the external
configuration of greenstone or serpentine.   The strata
inclined in every direction and describing the most capricious and picturesque forms, both curved and angular,
open an abundant field of instruction to the geologist,
while they present difficulties of which neither the theory
of original deposition on an unequal surface, nor that of
subsequent dislocation, appears to promise any plausible
solution *.

*Dunstone
and shil-
lat.*

* " Professor Jameson (Syst. of Min. vol. iii.)," observes Mr. J. J.
Conybeare, " has ascribed these appearances to crystallization. As we

The average height of the cliffs, as far as Messrs. Conybeare and Buckland could judge by the eye, is 130 or
140 feet; they are traversed in many places by steep
ravines running from north to south, and numerous outlying masses of rock show themselves above the sea at a
small distance from low-water mark, a character uniformly presented by the stratified rocks along the whole
of the northern coast.

In some parts the compact grauwacké was wanting for
a considerable distance; in such cases the forms which
the slate had assumed were rather angular than curvilinear. In the sections of those which have been called
saddle-shaped strata, it was usually observed that the dip
was more precipitous on the western side. In neither
variety of the rock could any traces of organic remains be
discovered, nor could any imbedded fragments be perceived that should indicate their having been formed
from the *debris* of an earlier rock. The strata are covered
by numerous veins of opaque white quartz, but no appearances of any other mineral substances occurred.

After stating these facts Mr. J. J. Conybeare refers to the
drawings accompanying his paper, as representing faithfully the flexures and contortions of the rock. From one of
these, representing some remarkable flexures and curva-
tures in the grauwacké of Hartland Point, we have copied
the vignette which is prefixed to the present chapter. An-

Nature of
the flex-
ures and
contor-
tions.

---

are always accustomed to regard terms of science as retaining (where the
contrary is not expressly stated) the precise sense in which they have
hitherto been uniformly received, the use of this expression is perhaps
not strictly correct. The external appearance of these rocks is certainly
not that of a mass of crystallized matter; and that the phænomenon itself
is not invariably connected with the process of crystallization, is evident
from the consideration that those rocks which are the most highly crystalline in their texture are the most free from these singular configurations.
That these appearances, however, may have been effected by a process of
nature, somewhat analogous to crystallization, and depending possibly
upon the same remoter causes, is perhaps the most satisfactory hypothesis
that has hitherto been offered on the subject, and such I apprehend to be
the opinion of the school of Werner, though somewhat obscured by the
adoption of a term implying identity of operation, in a case where the utmost
which can be fairly assumed to exist, appears to be a striking analogy."

other represents some highly-inclined strata, converging in
acute angles, consisting alternately of grauwacké and grauwacké slate, and including among them a comparatively
thick stratum which presents a nearly equable elliptical
curvature. In another compartment are shown numerous
strata of various thickness converging nearly at right
angles to each other, but forming obtuse angles with the
horizontal line of the base of the cliff. A fourth variety
of appearance is formed by highly-inclined strata, all
nearly parallel to each other; three of them exhibiting
angular arrangement, themselves inclined to the planes
of stratification, which, when the three strata are viewed
collectively, present a zigzag configuration. Between
these three are beds, the laminæ of which, apparently,
are nearly parallel to the main system of highly-inclined
strata.

" Although these singular contortions," Mr. J. J. Conybeare observes, " are not entirely confined to the dunstone and shillat of Devonshire, they yet occur much
more constantly in that rock than in the metalliferous
schist of Cornwall. In travelling westward we appeared
to lose them gradually. At Boss-castle, where the rock
evidently approaches nearer to the character of killas (as
it is termed by the miner), they still appear pretty frequently: at St. Agnes they are much rarer and less
capricious."

Grauwacké and associated Limestone of Exmoor.—In
the Third Volume of the Transactions of the Geological
Society, is a " Sketch of the Geology of the South-
Western part of Somersetshire," by Leonard Horner, Esq.
F.R.S. F.G.S., who now fills the office of Warden of the
University of London. This memoir relates to the structure of a tract, part of which is included within the county
of Devon; and the general views it contains, therefore,
so far as they relate to the formation and appearances now
under consideration, may be appropriately introduced in
this place.

In the western portion of Somersetshire, and partly within

Mr. L.
Horner on
the grau-
wacké of
the Ex-
moor Fo-
rest dis-
trict.

the adjoining county of Devon, there is a large district of high land, the greater part wild and uncultivated, extending about 30 miles from east to west, and about 16 miles between north and south; the highest and wildest part being known by the name of Exmoor Forest. In appearance and structure it is very similar to a great part of Devonshire and Cornwall, and may be considered as the termination of the schistose rocks which prevail so much in those counties. It is divided into several ranges of hills, distinguished by particular names. The longitudinal direction of these hills, with the exception of the Quantock hills, which are in the county of Somerset, is nearly east and west: there are numerous lateral branches from each central ridge, forming small steep valleys, or gulleys, which terminate in the great valleys that divide, and are parallel to, the principal ranges. These gulleys, called Combes in the country, when richly wooded, form some of the most striking features of the beautiful scenery for which this coast is so celebrated.

Aspect of the country.

The whole of this mountainous country has a smooth undulating and rounded outline, nowhere rugged or presenting any cliffs or precipitous faces, except on the sea shore, where sections have been formed probably by the action of the tides. The whole country is so covered by vegetation, either in the form of heath and turf on the high land, or of the more luxuriant productions of the valleys, that very few opportunities occur, in the interior, of ascertaining the nature of the rock on which the soil rests; but the cliffs on the sea shore afford such an ample field for studying the mineralogical structure of the country, that the scattered observations in quarries, may be more strongly relied upon and more easily connected.

From the Parrot, which enters the Bristol Channel at Huntspill Level in Somersetshire, to Barnstaple Bay in Devonshire, there is no river of any magnitude: the great water-shed is to the south, and the Ex, one of the most considerable of those rivers which fall into the English Channel, rises in Exmoor Forest.

The whole of the mountainous part of this district is formed of a series of rocks differing very considerably in mineralogical characters, but which the repeated alternation of the several varieties, and the insensible gradations that may frequently be traced of one into another, connect into one common *formation*.   A great proportion of these have the structure of sandstones, the component parts varying in size from that of mustard seed to such a degree of fineness, that the particles can with difficulty be discerned.   Quartz and clay are the essential component parts of all the varieties, but in different proportions. The quartz in some instances prevails to the entire exclusion of any other ingredient, forming a granular quartz-rock : it is more abundant in the aggregates of a coarse grain, clay being the chief ingredient in those of a close and fissile texture.   They have all an internal stratified structure, which is less apparent in those of a coarse grain (and in a cabinet specimen scarcely discernible), but which becomes gradually more distinct as the texture becomes finer, and at last the rock graduates into a fine-grained slate, divisible into laminæ as thin as paper, and having the smooth silky feel and shining surface of the clay-slate of a primary country.   Alternations of the fine-grained slaty varieties with those of the coarsest structure, in many successive strata, and without any regularity of position, are of constant occurrence ; and frequently without any gradation from one structure into the other.   In some instances portions of slate are contained in the coarse-grained varieties.   Scales of mica are frequent, and they all contain oxide of iron in greater or less proportion ; and to the different states of this oxide their various colours are no doubt to be ascribed.   The prevailing colours are reddish brown and greenish gray, and there are many intermediate shades and mixtures of these colours. Some of the slaty varieties are of a purplish hue, and this is occasionally spotted with green.   Of the specimens collected by Mr. Horner, those of a coarse grain and of a dark reddish-brown colour, did not effervesce with acids; those of a pale reddish-brown colour, and of a greenish-grey colour, all effervesced, and some of them briskly. None of the varieties of actual slate showed any signs of effervescence. The magnet was not affected by any one of the series. Mr. Horner did not discover a trace of any organic body in either variety; but in many places great beds of limestone full of madrepores are contained in the slate, the limestone and slate towards the external part of the beds being interstratified. Veins of quartz, which are often of great magnitude, are of constant occurrence, being sometimes accompanied by calcareous spar and ferriferous carbonate of lime; veins of sulphate of barytes, also, are not uncommon. Thin layers, composed of quartz, chlorite, and ferriferous carbonate of lime, are often interposed between the strata of slate, and pyrites is sometimes disseminated through the mass of the rock. Copper, in the states of sulphuret and of malachite or green carbonate, and iron in the form of veins of hæmatite, are frequently found, and nests of copper-ore of considerable magnitude have been found in the subordinate beds of limestone.

"Those who are acquainted with the geology of Devonshire and Cornwall," Mr. Horner observes, "will recognize in these characters a great similarity between the rocks which I have been describing, and those which have of late been designated by several mineralogists by the term *grauwacké*. I am fully aware of the unwarrantable extension of this name, and of the great want of precision which has been the consequence of applying it without pointing out the mineralogical structure of the compound; but I feel in common with many others the difficulty of finding a less objectionable term by which the series of rocks in question may be distinguished, when it is necessary to speak of them collectively. As the word [*grauwacké*] by itself conveys no theory, and as these rocks have a closer connection with that class to which the term was originally applied, than with any other, I shall call the series of rocks which I have described, a

Application of the term *grauwacké*.

grauwacké formation, hoping that the description I have given will in some degree remove that want of precision which is the chief objection to the word. To those however who may give to it the theoretical meaning which this word implies in the Wernerian system, I must again point out the alternations of quartz-rock, and of a clay-slate, with beds of limestone full of organic remains. The clay-slate cannot be distinguished from that of a primitive country."

Contortions of the grauwacké.
In every part of the district in which the slaty varieties of grauwacké prevail, the ends of the inclined strata, as they rise to the surface, either become vertical or are very much twisted. In this instance, contrary to what must probably have been the case with the flexures in the same rock at Clovelly, as described at the beginning of this chapter, the contortions appear to have taken place after the induration of the stone, for they are not in the form of curves, but are in general a succession of sharp angular twistings, with a fracture at every angle. The strata in general, as they approach the surface, are also very much traversed by those imperceptible cracks, which make the rock, as soon as it is moved from its bed, break down into polygonal fragments of various dimensions. Hence are probably derived those loose fragments which are to be found under the surface-soil all over the district where this formation occurs, and even at the summits of the highest hills. In the ravines formed by the streams in the lower parts of Dunkery Beacon, in Somersetshire, there are sections of some yards in depth where nothing is seen but these fragments, imbedded in a loose red sandy soil, which is doubtless produced from the decomposition of the fragments themselves. The angular shape of the fragments is an additional proof that they have been produced on the spot, and that they are not materials transported from a distance.

Dip of the strata.
In a country covered by vegetation, and where the rock is so liable to partial irregularities, it is exceedingly difficult to form any general conclusions as to the bearing and

dip of the strata. Every geologist must have observed, that the external shape of a hill is not always a certain guide in determining the bearing of the strata that compose it, and that in many places other causes must have operated in producing the external forms which the earth now exhibits. "I believe, however," Mr. Horner states, "that the general bearing of the strata in question, may be stated to be between east and west, and that the dip is more generally to the south than to the north."

In several parts of this district there are found, as already stated, very considerable beds of limestone which are contained in the slate. Their occurrence in detached spots, and their appearance in those quarries in which they are most extensively wrought, seem to point out that they are not regular strata conformable with those of the slate above and below them. Flattened spheroidal masses of the same kind of limestone are frequently found, completely enveloped by the slate, and very similar to the balls of clay-iron-stone in slate-clay, but thinning away at the edges much more than those do. The great masses of limestone appear to occur in the same way: they have an irregular bedded structure; and very often layers of slate, frequently of considerable thickness, are interposed between the beds. They appear to be confined to the places where the slaty varieties of the grauwacké formation prevail.

Mr. Horner's observations were principally confined within the limits mentioned in a former paragraph, p. 323; but he had also an opportunity of making a cursory examination of the country, partly situated in Somersetshire, and partly in Devonshire, which extends from Porlock in the former county, to Ilfracombe in the latter; the rocks of which are connected with those previously described. His route was from Porlock, by Culbone, and Withycombe farm, which are in Somersetshire, by Countesbury to Lynton, which are in Devon, and thence, in the latter County, through the Valley of Rocks, by Slattenslade, Trentishoe, Combe Martin, and Berry Narber, to Ilfracombe.   A very great part of this tract of country is entirely concealed by vegetation; but wherever the rock is exposed, Mr. Horner found some variety of the grauwacké formation identical with those he had left behind. In that part of the road which is eastward of Lynton, the coarser-grained varieties are most frequent; but westward of that place the slaty varieties predominate, very often resembling some kinds of iron-grey clay-slate found in primary countries.   Towards Ilfracombe this appearance becomes still more decided, and in a cabinet specimen it would be impossible to tell the difference.   But beds of limestone with very decided indications of organic remains, contained in this slate, show that it is of secondary formation, and at the same time afford a useful lesson of the inadequacy of mineralogical characters alone, to determine the geological nature of a rock.   These limestone beds are found between Berry Narber and Hele; their resemblance to those described by Mr. Horner in the former part of his paper, both in internal composition and in the accompanying slate, leave no doubt of their belonging to the same class.   When struck with a hammer, the limestone emits a slight bituminous smell, a circumstance which Mr. Horner did not observe in the limestone of the other places he mentions, and it is traversed by very large veins of a transparent and very beautiful calcareous spar.

Transition
lime-
stone of
the North
of Devon.

Transition Limestone of the North of Devon.—Some of the strata of this limestone in the northern part of the County, have been described by Mr. Hawkins, in his Sketch of the Geology of Devonshire published in Lysons' Magna Britannia, in nearly in the following terms.

In the map which accompanies Vancouver's *Agricultural Survey of Devonshire*, are traced four or five parallel courses or stratified beds of limestone, which extend through a great part of the Exmoor district, in a direction nearly east and west; two of them from the vicinity of Ilfracombe, and two from Barnstaple Bay, towards South Molton.   The existence of one of the former is merely inferred from what Mr. Vancouver had observed on the cliffs at one end of the course, and at a place southward of Lanacre bridge, in Somersetshire. He traces the other from the cliffs a little to the westward of the parish of Ilfracombe, eastwardly to Berry-Narber lime-works, thence north of East Downe, and south of Kentisbury to the Challacombe lime-works, the specimens from all which places, he says, correspond in colour, which is a greyish brown: the texture of the rock is very close, and it is more glossy in its fracture than other limestone, and is interspersed with minute veins of calcareous spar. It is not easy to distinguish it, at first sight, from the hard slaty rock.

The next stratum of limestone, according to the same authority, composes a part of the promontory that projects northwardly in the parish of Fremington, and occasions that sudden bend in the river Taw, opposite to Heanton House. Mr. Vancouver supposes that this continues through the parishes of Braunton, Heanton-Punchardon, and Barnstaple, but that no part of it extends to the south of the Taw. The fourth stratum, or bed, crops out, he observes, near St. Anne's Chapel, in the parish of Heanton-Punchardon; passing thence eastwardly through the parish of Fremington, where it does not exceed five feet in thickness, and is inclosed in a stratum of hard blueish building-stone (grauwacké?), occasionally veined with quartz; thence through Bickington, Bishop's Tawton, Swimbridge, the northern part of Filleigh, and the southern part of Molland Bottreaux, West Anstey, and through the parishes of Dulverton and Shilgate, in Somersetshire. It consists of a stratum of transition limestone, of from ten to twenty feet in thickness, highly but irregularly inclined, and imbedded in a stratum of hard blueish building-stone (grauwacké?) like the preceding, which it greatly resembles.

Southward of this line, and near Instow, is another stratified body of limestone, from one to three feet in thickness, extending eastwardly through the northern

BOOK
III.

parts of the parish of Harwood, thence in the same direction through the parishes of Chittlehampton, South Molton, the northern parts of Bishop's Nympton, by Ward's mill, through the parishes of East Anstey and Brushford. This, which resembles the preceding, Mr. Vancouver says, is inclosed in a compact bed of thick slate or flagstone (grauwacké slate ?). These beds of limestone contain occasionally organic remains, but not in great abundance: near South Molton, Mr. Buckland found fragments of encrinites and of coralline bodies, and also a perfect nautilus in the limestone quarries of Filleigh.

All these limestone beds have a general agreement in their dark blue colour, and other characters, and are all of contemporary formation with the grauwacké-slate with which they alternate. The appellation of transition limestone may therefore, with strict propriety, be applied to them. Marshall speaks of the black limestone of the quarry at Filleigh, which probably belongs to Vancouver's fourth course, and again of the same black limestone near Dulverton. Several courses of limestone, of a similar nature, are pointed out by both these writers, to the eastward of Exmoor, on the borders of the County. The very strong resemblance which all these stratified masses of limestone bear to those which are described by Vancouver on the north and south of Dartmoor, leads to a conclusion in favour of their common origin.

Anthracite
in the
grau-
wacké of
Chittle-
hampton.

Mr. Vancouver next notices a bed of culm, anthracite, or stone-coal, in the parish of Chittlehampton, varying from four to twelve inches in thickness, which follows the general direction of the strata of grauwacké in which it is imbedded; and veins of copper ore in the parishes of Swimbridge and North Molton. According to a report made by Mr. Gullet, who, in the year 1790, re-opened the old mines at Combe Martin, there is a considerable number of lead veins in that part of Exmoor, which lies on the southern side of the entrance to the Bristol Channel.

Engraved by J. Henshall

Drawn by T. Allom

CASTLE HILL, DEVONSHIRE.

THE SEAT OF THE RIGHT HONOURABLE HUGH EARL FORTESCUE, F.S.A. D.C.L. LORD LIEUTENANT OF THE COUNTY OF DEVON.

TO WHOM THIS WORK WITH HIS LORDSHIP'S PERMISSION IS MOST RESPECTFULLY DEDICATED

BY THE PROPRIETORS.

HATFIELD HALL, HERTFORDSHIRE.

Grauwacké and associated transition limestone of the country extending around the base of Dartmoor from Exeter to Plymouth.

From the memoir of Dr. Berger before quoted, "On the Physical Structure of Devonshire and Cornwall," we derive the following account of the transition rocks of the district examined by that geologist, in the former County. A few alterations have been made in its arrangement, for the purpose of adapting it to the purpose we have at present in view.

Dr. Berger on the grauwacké from Exeter to Plymouth.

In going to Thorverton by Cowley Bridge, on the summit of a hill which overlooks Exeter, and is almost close to the town, the grauwacké is met with *in situ*. It is of a grayish colour, with very distinct and separate grains, breaking spontaneously into rhomboidal fragments; it is harder in some places than in others; when tender, it splits in the manner of slate, and assumes quite the character of that species of rock. It occurs in strata, dipping north-west, at an angle of about 70°. The same grauwacké formation is met with to the N.N.E. of Exeter, on the road to Bickleigh, Silverton, Rew, and Cross Hill; at Cross Hill the direction and inclination of the strata are very distinctly seen. From Cowley Bridge the grauwacké extends as far as the neighbourhood of Upton Pyne, but in this district it can only be distinctly seen on the summits of the hills; it is lost in the bottoms of the valleys, and is there succeeded by the red argillaceous sandstone, or "new red sandstone." This is particularly the case at Upton Pyne, a village five miles north of Exeter on the right bank of the Exe.

Characters of the grauwacké.

The country between Exeter and Plymouth, by Chudleigh, Ashburton and Ivy Bridge, is quite hilly, the whole being a continual ascent and descent as far as the neighbourhood of Ivy Bridge. The red argillaceous sandstone continues from Exeter for some miles on that road: it is succeeded near Chudleigh by a vast number of flint pebbles, which appear to be scattered over the surface of the

Geological route from Exeter to Plymouth.

BOOK
III.

Transition
Limestone
of Ply-
mouth.

ground : between Chudleigh and Ashburton, there occurs a blue compact limestone, traversed by numerous veins of calcareous spar. At every step the extremities of the strata of this rock may be seen cropping out, and fragments of it are mixed with the soil. In the neighbourhood of Ivy Bridge a formation commences, which occupies a prodigious extent in this part of England—slaty and compact grauwacké. At Plymouth, however, the cliffs on the shore are of limestone.

The range of tolerably high cliffs which extends from Stonehouse Pool, between Plymouth and Devonport, and thence along Catwater, ascending the right bank of the Plym as far as the Lary Bridge, together with Mount Batten, and probably also the island of St. Nicholas[*], are formed of a compact limestone. It occurs in strata rising N.N.W., at an angle of about 65°; it breaks with a semi-conchoidal fracture into large flakes, is of a yellowish white colour, and, when quarried, is blasted with gunpowder. It contains cavities lined with calcareous spar, or with stalactites, and filled with an ochreous earth. It is frequently also traversed by veins of calcareous spar of a wedge-shape, wider at the bottom than at the top, and which generally occupy the whole height of the cliffs. On the side of Catwater, this limestone is of a blueish colour and a crystalline grain; it is here also frequently intersected by veins of calcareous spar. The cliffs near Stonehouse, being much exposed to the action of the sea, afford very distinct proofs of its effect on the most tender parts of the rock. It has made in several places erosions or crevices of various extent, which have been afterwards filled by a gravelly sand thrown up by the sea, and which has, by drying, become so coherent, that one might be led into error, by conceiving that the sand alternates in beds with the limestone.

It is however near the eastern end of the Lary Bridge, on the left bank of the Plym, that the transition limestone

* See note to p. 342.

is found in its true character. There is a quarry belonging to Lord Borringdon which is an excellent spot for studying it. This limestone is blackish brown; rhomboidal plates of calcareous spar may be seen disseminated through the mass, and it suddenly assumes in the same stratum all the characters of a shining slate : the rock in this last state effervesces less briskly with acids.

Though the cliffs at Stonehouse are of limestone, nevertheless Mount Edgcumbe, which is only separated from them by the Hamoaze, belongs to the grauwacké formation. We here find that rock, passing, from the state of a coarse argillaceous sandstone, of a reddish colour, not effervescing, and stained by oxide of iron, to that of a fine-grained grauwacké-slate, with red veins, giving it the appearance of ribbon-jasper. It occurs in strata, dipping S.S.E., at an angle of about 65° or 70°, which is nearly the same as that of the limestone cliffs of Plymouth Harbour. The stratification is best seen on the south side of Mount Edgcumbe, about half way up; and especially from the *Great Terrace* to the *Arch*, and beyond that on the way to the zig-zag walk. At the top of the hill the grauwacké becomes less distinctly stratified, and begins to separate into rhomboidal pieces. Maker Heights, the altitude of which is four hundred and two feet above the level of the sea, Rame Head, Higher Blinck in Whitesand Bay, precisely in the meridian of the Edystone Lighthouse, and consequently in Cornwall, all belong to the grauwacké formation.

Grauwacké and associated Transition Limestone, and other rocks, of Plymouth.—The following is an abstract of the concluding part of Mr. Prideaux's paper, relating, chiefly, to the neighbourhood of Plymouth. " No organic remains," Mr. Prideaux states, " are found in the rocks northward [of the slate in the immediate vicinity of the Plymouth Limestone]; nor in the slate, until just about its junction with the limestone. Even there they are so rare, that I have met with none *in situ;* but encrinal columns have been found in the slate by the Rev.

CHAP. III.

Grau-wacké of Mount Edg-cumbe.

Mr. Prideaux on the Transition Rocks of Plymouth.

2 H 2

BOOK
III.

Richard Hennah, F.G.S. In the limestone they are abundant; and, in the copious collection of that gentleman, offer novelty as well as variety to the investigator. In the hope that this paper will be soon followed by one from him, on the organic remains of our limestone, I leave that part of the subject entirely in his hands; conscious that from inclination as well as opportunity he is better qualified for it than myself*."

Limestone
of Cat-
down, &c.

Catdown and Teat's Hill are entirely limestone, which, very soon after passing from the slate, assumes a reddish hue, from the presence of a siliceous substance of that colour. This substance shortly appears in mass, in the character of the old red sandstone [?]; alternating with the limestone, southward, though much less strikingly than the slate does to the north. The Hoe also is limestone, as well as some of the south part of the town; but it is the mere ridge next the sea, in this place, for the new houses in Lockyer-street are founded on slate. Westward, it passes further inland. The New Crescent is founded on the alternation of slate and limestone; and at the back of Mill Bay we have the latter rock extensively quarried, and rising into respectable hills. As we proceed to Devonport, we have the limestone on the south side of the road, and the slate on the north.

Geological
site of De-
vonport.

A very small part only of the town of Devonport stands on limestone; the grauwacké running so far towards the south, in that locality, as to form the hill on which the new Town Hall is built. The westerly termination of the limestone is Bunker's Hill, in the Dock-yard.

Two dis-
tinct for-
mations of
limestone
in Devon-
shire.

According to Mr. Prideaux, " there is a marked diversity in our [Devonian] limestone; in texture, position, and contained animal reliques. The eastern is probably the oldest, and the western the newest deposit: but the consideration of this subject may more properly belong to Mr. Hennah's paper. I will only observe here," Mr. P. continues, " that if it prove so, our limestone is a different

* A brief view of the results of Mr. Hennah's investigations will be found in the succeeding abstract.

formation from that further east, which Mr. De La Beche
refers to the carboniferous series.   This is also probable
from its direction here, which is rather southward of east,
as well as from the more crystalline appearance of the
stone."

Devil's Point, parallel with an outlying rock at Mount
Edgcumbe and with the peninsula of Mount Batten, is the
southernmost projection of this limestone.   It not only
includes in its aggregation a considerable quantity of red
sand, but it is traversed by conformable beds of the red
sandstone itself, in an unmixed state, one of which, twenty
feet in thickness, was laid open in digging away the
ground for the new Victualling Office, and beds of inferior dimensions are visible in several places.

As just stated, there is a small deposit of limestone at
the northern angle of Mount Edgcumbe, and on the opposite side of the harbour is Mount Batten, a hill of the
same rock : these two outliers form a line from east to
west with the projection of limestone at the Devil's Point
and at the quarries of Oreston.

The soil upon the limestone is abundantly productive,
in our moist climate.   The rock is not metalliferous in
any part of this range*.   It contains numerous cavities,
lined, in many cases, with stalactites of delicate and
beautiful forms.   In some instances they are partly filled
with clay, in which, occasionally, are interspersed bones
of various animals, having the characters of diluvian
reliques†.   More frequently these caverns contain water;
the largest, under the quarries by the Marine Barracks,
forming an immense reservoir of fresh water, into which
a stream is heard to pour.   Its extent is so great, that a
boat was required in order to survey the interior; but it
is at present inaccessible.

A ridge of dunstone or grauwacké runs through the
limestone hill south of Mount Batten, towards St. Nicho-

Chap. III.
Devil's Point.
Mount Edgcumbe and Mount Batten.
General characters of the limestone.
St. Nicholas's Island.

* Some remarks on this subject will be found in page 348.
† An account of the bones found in these caves will be given in the
section on the Diluvium and Alluvium of Devonshire.

las's Island, which, according to Mr. Prideaux, consists of dunstone, much disturbed in position, the predominant dip being northward, unless the strata overhang [*]. The adjoining reef of rocks, called the Bridge, appears to correspond; and, as might be expected, a similar formation occurs at Mount Edgcumbe, where, however, the stratification is less disturbed, dipping westward of south. The southern part of Mount Edgcumbe corresponds with Staddon-Heights; both running high, to nearly the same elevation; and being alike composed of well-defined strata of slate, dunstone, and red-sandstone, mingled together, and

Phæno-
mena of
the sand-
stone.

dipping at different angles and in different directions. On the eastern side, flakes of sandstone, several yards in length, and eight inches in thickness, and copiously veined with white quartz, have slid off, and lie rolled together, for a hundred, or two hundred yards along the coast. These rolls look, from innumerable cracks on the convex side, as if they had fallen in a tough state, from igneous semi-fusion. Such appearances, on a smaller scale, occur also at the island; but not on the Mount Edgcumbe

Boveysand
Bay.

side. Turning the point into Boveysand Bay, there is a projecting ridge of very hard limestone, over which the sandstone and slate hang saddlewise. "It looks as if it had heaved the others, till the strata fell over, as above described; a case not very probable, as the corresponding formation at Mount Edgcumbe reaches the same level, without any similar appearance." In the country behind

Country
behind
Staddon-
Heights.

Staddon-Heights, Mr. Prideaux found a rock which bore the appearance of a passage from the grauwacké into the red-sandstone; but it was so covered with turf, that he could not trace the one into the other.

Shag-rock.

To the south of Boveysand Bay we find red-sandstone, dipping irregularly to the south-eastward. A ledge, called the Shag-rock, projecting from it into the sea, and consisting of white quartz, with streaks and patches of red

---

[*] We shall have occasion to return to the subject of the constitution of St. Nicholas's Island.

sand, appears to have been a vein, the superior hardness of which has resisted effectually the action of the sea, by which that part of the rock which contained it has been destroyed. On the western side of the harbour we find the same sandstone, occupying Cawsand Bay and the hill behind, "but standing nearly vertical, the strata running south-east and north-west, but diverging a good deal on both sides." The Cawsand Bay sandstone is deeper red, and has little cavities, some of which are filled with white nodules; and the same white substance also variegates and interlines it; looking, in some places, not unlike mortar. The northernmost beds of sandstone break into obtuse rhomboids, fit for street paving, for which purpose that on the eastern side is quarried.

From the south of Cawsand Bay to the Rame-Head, the coast is formed by grauwacké and grauwacké slate, in very distinct vertical strata. In one place where the ends of the strata appear, two or three feet in thickness, they look not unlike basaltic columns, when viewed at some distance. The rock called the Mewstone, on the eastern side, does not correspond with this; being composed of red sandstone and a rather gritty slate, full, in some places, of pale greenish nodules, which are perhaps organic remains, for such have been found on that side of the harbour, both in slate and in sandstone. This rock is equally dissimilar in the dip of its constituent strata, which is about 45° in the direction of about south by west. The strata have been laid open in such an extraordinary way, by the action of the sea and of the weather, that they look as if displayed by art, in tables for exhibition. Unlike the exposed heights of Staddon and Rame, the face of the Mewstone, corresponding to its dip, is by the direct impact of the sun's rays, and its lower level, covered with luxuriant vegetation, and perfumed, in summer, by numerous wild flowers.

Here these formations end; the coast, for some miles east and west, being composed of slate and sandstone.

CHAP. III.

Sandstone of Cawsand Bay.

Grauwacké of the coast from Cawsand Bay to the Rame-Head. Mewstone.

BOOK
III.

The rocks
above the
old red
sandstone
wanting in
this tract.
Inclina-
tion of the
hills.

In the tract of country now described, the whole series of rocks, from the old red-sandstone upwards, is wanting.

It has before been observed that the hills of mixed slate and sandstone, forming Staddon-Heights and Mount Edgcumbe, though irregular in formation and a mile distant from each other, rise to the same altitude. The same fact may be stated of the limestone, which, though intersected in several places, forms a ridge, from Mount Wise to the quarries of Oreston, which is almost as level as the top of a wall. The limestone hills have a gentle ascent on the northern side, but dip rapidly towards the south: the character of the slate and grauwacké hills is the reverse of this; the grauwacké often showing its place by a ridge along the hill. The whole country, with the exception of the small part constituted by the lime-stone, rises gradually towards the granite.

Direction
of the val-
leys.

Mr. Prideaux concludes by observing, that "the prin-cipal water-courses, the Tamar, Tavy, and Plym, cannot be taken as indications of the general direction of the valleys. Amongst the greatest irregularity, east and west, corresponding with the general run of the strata, have the predominance. And if the north and south val-leys of the Plym and Tavy, be principally, and that of the Tamar partially, the effects of heavy currents, at, or prior to, the general deluge; some of the smaller valleys in that direction are original; the strata lying in different positions, on the opposite sides. That of the Compton Brook may serve as a familiar example."

Transition
Limestone
of Ply-
mouth.

Mr. Hennah on the Transition Limestone of Plymouth.
—From a publication by the Rev. R. Hennah, F.G.S., Chaplain to the Garrison of Plymouth, a gentleman who has long been meritoriously engaged in the investigation of the geology of this particular spot, we derive the fol-lowing particulars of the formation of limestone at Ply-mouth, usually referred to the Transition or Sub-medial series.

The formation of limestone at Plymouth may be regu-

larly traced, on the south side, in an uninterrupted line,
forming, as it were, a barrier against the encroachments
of the sea, from the Passage-house at Cat-Down to the
Devil's Point leading into Hamoaze *. On the north side,
the following points will be sufficiently exact for the present purpose. Commencing from a spot near the Lary
Bridge, it may be traced westward over Cat-Down to the
Breakwater Inn, in Cat-Down Lane, and Fareham-place,
from thence to near the Pottery at Coxside, and into
Sutton Pool: still proceeding west, it is found again on
the opposite side of the water, near Foxhole Quay, running
near Cat-street, and the north side of the Parade; it then
turns a little south, and appears about the entrance into
Mill-Bay Lane, when it keeps its course westward, nearly
in the direction of that lane, until it arrives at Mill Prison;
afterwards it may be traced, in an irregular line, towards Extent.
the north-west, from the Mill-Prison to the Turnpike-gate
at the eastern end of Union-street, Stonehouse; it then
takes a westward direction, and runs nearly parallel with
that street, on the south side, to Stonehouse Bridge. On
ascending from the bottom of the hill, at the west end of
Stonehouse Bridge, towards Devonport, it is visible on
both sides of the road, over a great part of it, at least;
but, at the top of the hill, it is lost on the north side, and
is only visible towards the south.   From hence it makes
a short turn towards the south-west, passing near the
southern angles of George's Square; and may be seen,
accordingly as the ground permits, taking a direction still
westward, by Pembroke-street, which is situated between
the eminence on which the new Town-Hall is built, and
Mount Wise; it then enters the Dock-yard, and sinks
into the sea somewhere near, if not in, the Mast-pond, at
its southern extremity.   It rests on clay-slate [metalli- Subjacent
ferous slate, killas?] alternating with it, at the place of rock.
junction, in a remarkably distinct manner; tabular masses

* Mr. Hennah omits mentioning Mount Batten, Hooe Lake, and
Oreston, to which the limestone extends, as being on the other side of
the water, and without the prescribed limits of his survey.

of limestone, of a few inches in thickness, and many feet in length, appearing in considerable numbers, as may be seen near the western side of the Lary Bridge, as well as in other situations.

Elevation,
Dip, and
Bearing.

It has an average elevation of one hundred feet above high-water mark; and it extends in a direction nearly east and west; or to speak, perhaps, with greater accuracy, it varies a little to the north-west and south-east, with an inclination or dip towards the south or south-west. In *breadth* it does not appear anywhere to exceed, if indeed it approaches to, half a mile; but in length it extends many miles. Sinking into the sea, at the extremity of the Dock-yard, and at the Devil's Point, it appears again, although for a short space only, below Mount Edgcumbe, and at the back of the Passage-house at Cremill Ferry; after which it does not appear to be visible in this neighbourhood, further west, except in small patches or in detached rocks. "From the quarries at Oreston, however," Mr. Hennah observes, "it may be traced in a direct line, and with little interruption, eastward, as far as Petty Tor, in Babbacombe Bay, where it finally disappears, and is lost in the sea."

Colour.

The colour of the Plymouth limestone varies considerably, although the prevailing one is a light blue or gray, changing, at times, into a much darker shade, or becoming nearly black. These tints again are frequently intermixed, and marbled with an indefinite variety of red and other colours. This variegation, joined to its susceptibility of receiving a very high polish, from its hard and close-grained nature, renders it of some consequence to the stone-cutter and to the public, for slabs and chimney-pieces, "many of which require only to be seen, to be much and deservedly admired." In illustration of this remark, Mr. Hennah refers his readers to almost all the foot-pavements in the three towns of Plymouth, Devonport, and Stonehouse, which are composed of blocks taken from the quarries in the limestone; and which, after a shower of rain, present "most striking specimens of marble,

curiously marked with veins of different colours, and
beautifully shaded:—not unfrequently, too, full of animal
remains of various kinds."

The Limestone of Plymouth, generally speaking, contains magnesia, but in an extremely variable quantity.
"Although not professing myself a chemist, nor pretend-
ing to great accuracy," Mr. Hennah remarks, "yet I have
been enabled to submit certain portions of the rock to
the test; so as to ascertain the fact, and to produce the
following results.   From one hundred grains of the pure
and very transparent crystal [of the calcareous spar occurring in the limestone?] I obtained a very small proportion of magnesia;—and, from the common gray limestone, the produce of one hundred grains was rather more,
amounting to about six or seven grains.   But, from a
hundred grains of a brown, iron-coloured, limestone, selected from the Dock-yard, the hollows of which were
filled with small rhomboidal crystallizations, the proportion
of magnesia was considerable, being nearly twenty-one or
twenty-two parts in a hundred:—and lastly, from the red,
calcareous stone, from the eastern end of Mount Wise,
the quantity of this substance, although not so great as
in the last-mentioned specimen, was, nevertheless, about
eight parts in a hundred."

Mr. Hennah has occasionally found quartz, of a milky
colour, and usually amorphous, though sometimes assuming a regular crystalline form, and possessing tolerable
transparency, mixed with, and lying on the surface of the
limestone, at different points: particularly among the
rocks at the Devil's Point, at Bunker's Hill in the Dock-
yard, and in the red calcareous stone at the western end
of Mount Wise; which latter, he observes, "is full of
small cavities, variously shaped, occasioned," he considers, " by the decomposition of the animal-matter with
which they were once filled;—of shells, for instance, and
of what much resembles the pulley or screw-stone of
Parkinson [Organic Remains], Vol. II. Pl. 15. Fig. 6."
These curious hollows are not unfrequently lined with

Marginal notes:

Contains
Magnesia.

Included
Quartz.

calcareous formations, accompanied by perfect quartz crystals, each quite distinct, the one from the other. But instances of meeting quartz in conjunction, or blended, with the lime, are not common, nor does the quartz occur in large quantities.

Does not contain metallic veins.

This limestone formation, Mr. Hennah states, "appears to be entirely free from all *metallic veins;* and I have not seen, nor have I heard of anything, tending to what miners would call a *lode,* of any of the metals, having ever been discovered in any one of the quarries that have hitherto been opened. It is true, that indications of the presence of *iron* and also of *manganese* may occasionally be seen, as a colouring matter, in particular spots; but always thinly spread, and never in any quantity. In a single instance, I have observed spots of pyrites, in fragments of limestone and slate, taken out of a well, that was sinking at the back of the houses on the south side of Union-street, Stonehouse. And I have been told, that in digging another well, near the public-house on the road leading from Plymouth to Cat-Down, the sign of which gives a view of the Breakwater, particles of pyrites were observed by the workmen employed, and also a *glimpse of copper;* but, not having seen it myself, I cannot vouch for the accuracy of the statement; and I am inclined to think that the circumstance is extremely problematical, and that the men, in reference to the last-mentioned substance, more particularly, were deceived."

Animal Organic Remains in it.

A great variety of Organic Remains, such as Madreporites, Corallites, Trochites, Entrochites, Encrinites, Orthoceratites, Serpulæ, and Shells, both Univalves and Bivalves, are blended with, and form a very considerable part of, the contents of the calcareous rocks of Plymouth. These organic remains are more distinctly visible, and abound most, at those points where the limestone and the clay-slate alternate with each other, previously to their entire separation, and to their taking their respective regular courses.

Mr. Hennah's late researches.

A paper by Mr. Hennah was read before the Geological

Society, in the Session 1829–30, entitled "On the Animal Remains found in the Transition Limestone of Plymouth." This was the last of a series of communications by the author on the same subject; and in this he endeavoured to classify all the organic remains found by him in the Plymouth Limestone. In this arrangement there are enumerated several genera of Polyparia, or Corals, as above mentioned, including Spongia?, Stylina, Caryophyllia, Turbinolia, &c.; several species of Crinoidea, or Stone-Lilies; and genera of Conchifera and Mollusca, including the univalves and bivalves alluded to in the preceding notice. After a detailed description of many species in each of the above classes, Mr. Hennah concludes, that as the number of Zoophytes, which form the lowest class of the animal-kingdom, bears a very large proportion to that of the Shells, the Plymouth limestone must be considered to be one of the earliest deposits containing organic remains. But he states that great obscurity still involves the relative distribution of these animals in their order of superposition *.

In the Transactions of the Geological Society, Second Series, Vol. III., is a memoir by Mr. De La Beche, "On the Geology of Tor and Babbacombe Bays." From this we now select, with some slight alterations for the sake of compressing the information, those portions which relate to the transition rocks, and also to the Mountain or Carboniferous Limestone.

The following is a general sketch of the coast belonging to the tract of country described in the memoir. There is no beach to the cliffs from near the Ness-point, at the mouth of the Teign, to Hope's Nose, the northern point of Tor Bay, with the exception of the bottom of a few coves, and the Babbacombe-sands, and their continuation the Oddicombe-sands, for they are shingle-beaches. The cliffs plunge directly into the sea, and are well seen only from a boat. The coast is equally bold from Hope's Nose

* Proceedings of the Geological Society, No. XIV. p. 169.

to Torquay, with the exception of Meadfoot-sands, which are, however, backed by a high broken hill. After passing the hill between Torquay and Tor Abbey, the coast assumes a milder character; the cliffs, where they occur, are of no great elevation; and there are extensive sands both at Paignton and Goodrington, separated by Roundham Head. Further south, low cliffs intervene between Goodrington-sands and the Broad-sands. Beyond the low rocky land of Galmpton Point, the cliffs are bolder, and continue so to the Berry Head, being, in a few places, broken into coves, the most considerable of which is occupied by the harbour of Brixham. This range of coast is backed by hills, varying in height from 200 to 500 feet. Furland Hill, between Brixham and Dartmouth, is 589 feet above the sea, according to the Ordnance Survey.

Mountain Limestone.

The rocks of this district to which Mr. De La Beche gives the name of Mountain Limestone, have usually been referred to the transition limestone of English Geologists, that is, a limestone which occurs beneath the old red sandstone; they, however, rest upon that rock, contain fossils that have been discovered in the carboniferous limestone of other places, and, though a matter of minor importance, mineralogically resemble it:—they are, moreover, separated from the old red sandstone by a shale, which may be considered the equivalent of the lower limestone shale. These limestones occur in beds from a few inches to several feet in thickness; the usual colour is gray, varying in intensity; they are frequently traversed by calcareous veins, and, in texture, vary from compact to semi-crystalline, the latter predominating in the vicinity of trap, and when the strata are much disturbed. The semi-crystalline limestones afford a great variety of beautifully tinted marbles, not so well known, nor so much employed for ornamental purposes, as they deserve to be.

These limestones are, here and there, interstratified with shale: they also rest upon a considerable thickness of argillaceous shale, into which they seem to pass. The

shale is usually reddish in the upper part, brownish gray CHAP.
in the lower and larger portion; and it strongly reminded III.
Mr. De La Beche of the shale similarly situated in Pembrokeshire.

The most abundant organic remains in this limestone Organic
are encrinites and corals.   Trilobites also occur; and in Remains.
the vicinity of St. Mary Church a very singular fossil,
which Mr. De La Beche was unable to refer to any known
class of organic bodies, but which Mr. Broderip thinks
may have probably belonged to the *Tunicata*, a group
including the marine animals best known under the name
of *Ascidiæ*.   Shells also occur in it, including species belonging to the genera Cardium, Megalodon, Terebratula,
Spirifer, Natica, Euomphalus, Bellerophon, Turritella,
Murex?, Buccinum, Pleurotoma, Nautilus, and Orthoceras.

The Limestones of St. Mary Church, Babbacombe, Limestone
and the northern side of Tor Bay encircle the old red on the
North side
sandstone, which extends from Meadfoot-sands towards of Torbay.
Upham.   The section on the south side of Meadfoot-sands shows the limestones resting on old red sandstone.
The quarry at the south-west points, opposite a rock called
the Shag Rock, is worked in gray and reddish compact
limestone, dipping south-west: beneath, is an argillaceous
shale, reddish in the upper part and gray in the lower;—
the latter is slightly micaceous. This forms the cliff from
the point to a short distance east of the place where the
road descends to the beach; and to this succeeds a red
siliceous grit traversed by veins of quartz, and containing
iron.   The cliff composed of red grit is much concealed.
The limestones in the vicinity of Torquay are much disturbed, as are also, more or less, all the stratified rocks
of the district.   These beds are observed to be contorted
along the whole coast, from the town to the point opposite
the Shag-rock; they seem, however, to have a general
dip away from the old red sandstone, between which and
the body of limestone the argillaceous shale is always interposed.

BOOK
III.

Dip, &c.
of the
lime-
stones.

So much confusion exists in this vicinity, that no regular dip of the limestones can there be determined.
They dip south-south-west at an angle of 35° near the
Turnpike, and at the quarry near the Baths to the south-
west. They are perpendicular, with a north and south
direction, at the little hill near Tor Moham, at the Chapel
Hill, and under Torwood House. At Stantaway Hill,
between Tor Moham and Upham, the calcareous slate
and limestones are much confused. At Butterhill quarry,
the limestones are much disturbed. On the new road from
Torquay to St. Mary Church, at the entrance of the rocky
defile, irregular, detached and arched strata, have a very
picturesque effect, the arch appearing to be almost a work
of art. The coast also from Babbacombe to the Black
Head, exhibits confused strata of limestone and argillaceous shale; at the latter place we may observe a thick,
bent stratum of limestone included in the solid trap: this
limestone is very crystalline. Hope's Nose, with the
Leadstone, Oarstone, and Thatcher Rocks lying immediately near it, is composed of limestone which is much contorted at the cove north of the Thatcher. This mass of
limestones is detached from the limestones on the west,
that is, above the level of the sea; and, beneath, they are
probably connected with the Torquay beds, for the Thatcher
Rock is composed of them. Kent's Cavern, lately celebrated on account of the remains of Elephants, Rhino-
ceroses, Hyænas, Bears, Deer, Wolves, &c. found in it,
is situated in these limestones.

From Barton the limestone extends along the hill to
King's Kerswell, where Exeter Red Conglomerate covers
it for a short distance: but at the lower part of the village
on the old Dartmouth road, the limestones again come in,
and are continued to the top of the hill, where a quarry
exhibits their contortions.

The limestones on the south of Torbay, like those on
the north, are greatly disturbed, as may be seen along
the coast from the Berry Head to Saltern Cove, near
Goodrington. At Marstink quarry, near Paignton, thin

strata of semi-crystalline limestone dip north about 20°. At Saltern Cove, limestones are mixed with, and disturbed by, Trap, which has greatly altered the character of the limestone at the points of contact. In one of the projecting points the altered limestone does not effervesce freely with acids; it contains corals. Reddish shale, resembling that on the north side of Tor-Bay, and similarly situated beneath the limestone, occurs much contorted at the western point of Saltern Cove. In some places it is traversed by quartz veins.

The general character of the *Old Red Sandstone*, as it occurs in this district, is best exhibited near Cockington. Between this place and Livermead Sands, are two quarries of chocolate-coloured, micaceous, siliceous, and very compact sandstone. In both a slaty variety, splitting easily in the line of the laminæ, which are filled with mica, is mixed with compact and micaceous beds, which vary in thickness from a few inches to two feet. The strata are much confused, some are curved, and some dip in all directions. In its great hardness, in its colour, in being micaceous, and in general appearance, it differs entirely from the red sandstone associated with the "Exeter Conglomerate" of the Corbons and Livermead. After passing Livermead on the road to Paignton, a new cut exposes a slaty variety of this rock, apparently passing into grauwacké. Among the strata are a few of the more compact and solid sandstones.

Thick beds of old red sandstone are observable on the rise of the hill west of Cockington, on the old road to Totnes, but they are quickly covered up by "Exeter Conglomerate," which latter continues to conceal it as far as a small rivulet about half-a-mile east from Ockham, where it again emerges. From the vicinity of Ockham to Westerland, this rock passes gradually into grauwacké slate, losing its red colour, but preserving its mica. At Collaton Kirkham, the same slaty and compact varieties are seen as in the Cockington quarries; their dip is east-north-east, at an angle of about 20°, the beds being some-

CHAP. III.

Old Red Sandstone.

times curved. They are much more highly inclined in the same vicinity. Exeter red conglomerate covers these rocks on the same hill, and contains rolled pieces both of its slaty and compact varieties. The old red sandstone passes into grauwacké on the high hill north-north-west of Paignton.

The red compact sandstone beneath the argillaceous shale at Meadfoot-sands, very much resembles the Cockington compact old red sandstone. At Hope Farm, the resemblance between the two will be found most striking; and there can be no doubt that the limestone shale rests upon it in the vicinity: in fact, the wedge-shaped mass of old red sandstone extending from Meadfoot-sands and Hope Farm towards Upham, is bounded by a mantle of argillaceous shale.

Meadfoot-sands.
The sandstone and slate of Meadfoot-sands may almost be considered as the passage of old red sandstone into grauwacké, or they may be the old red sandstone strata altered by the vicinity of trap. Beneath the red grit of the Meadfoot-sands is a gray, compact, fissile, and very micaceous sandstone, resembling in everything but colour the semi-schistose varieties of the Cockington red sandstones. Their angle of dip varies considerably; it is at first towards the south-west at about 65° or 70°. These strata rest upon, and pass into a slaty rock resembling the old red sandstone schist of the vicinity of Ockham, in everything but colour. They are here dark-coloured. These rocks traverse the point of land, named at its extremity Hope's Nose; and upon them the limestone of that place appears to rest. Small trap veins are observable both in this rock and in the red grit of Meadfoot-sands.

Grauwacké.
Between Ockham and Westerland, the old red sandstones pass into grauwacké; at the latter place is a quarry of grauwacké rather micaceous. It contains the vertebral columns of encrinites, corals, and bivalve shells. The schist is used to line the interior of the neighbouring lime-kilns. The dip is east-south-east, about 45°.

CHAPTER IV.

SUPERMEDIAL OR SECONDARY ROCKS OF DEVONSHIRE:
—NEW RED. SANDSTONE, AND INCLUDED AMYGDA-
LOIDAL TRAP:—GREEN SAND.

THE *New Red Sandstone* formation is by some also termed the *Red Rock*, or *Red Ground*. It is a very extensive deposit in England, stretching, with little interruption, from the northern bank of the Tees in Durham to the southern coast of Devonshire. Its texture is very various. It appears sometimes as a reddish marle or clay, sometimes as a sandstone; sometimes the clay and sandstone are interstratified, or pass the one into the other; and it will further appear that it is associated with, or contains beds of, a conglomerate consisting of masses of different rocks cemented by marle or by sand. When this deposit appears as a sandstone, its characters differ greatly in different places; it is occasionally calcareous, and sometimes of a slaty texture. Above all, this extensive deposit is remarkable for containing masses or beds of gypsum; and the great rock-salt formation of England occurs within it, or is subordinate to it, in Cheshire and Worcestershire. In some counties the strata of coal dip beneath it.

" Although it would perhaps be generalizing too hastily," Mr. Conybeare remarks, " to assert that these beds invariably follow in a constant order, yet it may be safely stated as a general truth, that the red marle containing gypsum usually occupies the higher, the sandstone the central, and the conglomerate the lower portions of this deposit; but the most remarkable of the subordinate beds connected with this formation are those of amygdaloidal trap, which occur in it in Devonshire." The general composition of the beds of this formation is argillaceous, argillo-siliceous, with a variable proportion of

CHAP.
IV.

New Red
Sandstone.

General
Characters.

Order of
the beds.

calcareous matter, sometimes effervescing weakly with acids, sometimes not at all.

The marle and sandstone are often red, but vary in their hue from chocolate to salmon-colour; they are not unfrequently variegated, exhibiting streaks of light blue or verdigrise, buff, or cream-colour. Mr. Polwhele has stated that the soil of Marlborough, in this County, which is situated on the New Red Sandstone, is so red, that the butchers at Dodbrooke market know the sheep that come from that quarter by the colour of the fleece.

Mineral constitution.

According to Mr. Greenough, the sandstone itself of this formation consists of rather fine grains of quartz, with a few specks of mica, cemented by clay and oxide of iron; it contains galls of clay, is friable, and affords large tracts of sand. The beds generally differ in colour, and though it rarely happens that any great variety of colour is seen in the same bed, yet between Exeter and Exminster in Devonshire, the white and red layers of sand are strangely mixed. The slaty character of the sandstone is mostly derived from particles of mica which are generally gray, and lie in detached spots, not in regular layers. It occasionally passes into slaty marle. Generally, it is unfit for the purposes of architecture, but in some places it has sufficient tenacity and hardness to be used for building.

New Red Sandstone Conglomerate of Honiton:

Towards Honiton, the new red sandstone is in the state of a coarse-grained gravel, almost entirely disintegrated. It contains rounded pebbles, some of which are two or three inches in diameter: it then approaches to a conglomerate pudding-stone; but near Exeter, it assumes the appearance of an arenaceous sandstone, and becomes more compact and uniform in its texture and composition. The city of Exeter is situated in a kind of hollow encircled by hills not very elevated, nearly all of the same height, and which become gradually lower as they approach the coast. One of these hills, situated eight or nine miles N.N.W. of Exeter, near the village of Thorverton, is seven hundred feet above the level of the sea. This hollow or basin

opens to the S.S.E., and, as is frequently the case in
England, a river, which at the distance of a few miles
from its mouth would rather deserve the name of a brook,
suddenly enlarges near the sea to a considerable width.
The Exe, at the place where it flows into the open sea,
suddenly again contracts, and forms a narrow strait.

Several quarries which have been opened in the neighbourhood of Exeter deserve the attention of the geologist.

The quarry of Heavitree is situated about a mile and a
half from Exeter, on the road to Honiton.　It is worked
to the extent of a quarter of a mile in length, and at present, to the depth of about ninety or a hundred feet, in a
plane intersecting that of the strata.　The rock worked in
this quarry is a conglomerate evidently stratified; the
strata are from six to eight feet in thickness, and dip
south-east at an angle of about 15°.　As long as this rock
preserves the character of conglomerate (Exeter Red
Conglomerate of De La Beche), it is compact and tenacious, and according to the statement of the quarry
men, it hardens more and more by exposure to the air.
But as soon as it passes to the state of an arenaceous
sandstone, it becomes tender and friable.　It is very common to see blocks of it in this last state, and sometimes
of great size, included in the middle of the conglomerate.
The cement of this rock is argillo-ferruginous, and by
itself does not effervesce with acids, as it is easy to prove
by making use of pieces of the pure sandstone for that
purpose; but it produces so brisk an effervescence from
the intimate mixture of calcareous particles, that it might
be very easily mistaken for limestone.　The substances
which enter into the composition of this conglomerate are
numerous; and it may first be remarked, that these pieces
are of very different sizes and forms, sometimes swelled
and rounded, sometimes pointed with sharp angles, from
very minute grains to the size of several inches in diameter.
There are found in it rhomboidal crystals of calcareous
spar, and crystals of felspar, most frequently of an opake
white, and decomposed; pieces of flint [chert]; grau-

wacké; yellowish limestone; rolled masses of a species of porphyry somewhat resembling the antique, the base of which is of a reddish brown colour, not effervescing with acids, and containing numerous, small and well-defined crystals of felspar imbedded in it; pieces of a rock which is itself compounded, having the appearance of a porphyry, the base earthy, and including small grains of quartz, crystals of felspar, and pieces of blueish carbonate of lime; and a whitish tender steatite, in small angular fragments.

of Poncham.

Poncham quarry is situated about two miles N.N.E. of Exeter. It is of much less extent than that in the parish of Heavitree. Dr. Berger was not able to determine either the direction or the inclination of the strata. The rock itself is an amygdaloid, the nodules of which are chiefly calcareous, small and uniform; the base does not effervesce with acids, and when breathed upon, it has the smell peculiar to clay. It is much stained by oxide of iron, which tarnishes the lustre of the calcareous nodules and veins contained in it.

Manganese of Upton Pyne.

At Upton Pyne, a village five miles north of Exeter on the right bank of the Exe, a mine of black oxide of manganese is worked in open day. The red argillaceous sandstone, at the place where the mine is excavated, forms a stratum several feet in thickness from the surface; below this is a conglomerate pudding-stone, the same that is found in the parish of Heavitree, but quite disintegrated: then, a reddish compact felspar in mass, containing a few laminæ of calcareous spar, and some crystals of quartz. This last rock forms the roof of the mine. The direction of the vein of oxide is from east to west, dipping towards the north, with an inclination of three feet in six. Of the black oxide of manganese several varieties are met with, together with ferriferous carbonate of lime. The red argillaceous sandstone occupies the surface of the country from Upton Pyne to Thorverton.

Amygdaloid of Thorverton.

There are three or four quarries at Thorverton, and these not far distant from each other. They are all in the same rock, viz. a calcareous amygdaloid, the nature of which, however, varies considerably in different places. In some places the nodules are small, and very closely united in clusters at the base, forming a nearly homogeneous mass, with here and there nodules of a much larger size imbedded in it. In other places the nodules are about the bigness of a pea, all of the same size, and consist of rhomboidal sparry laminæ. There are other places where the base of the amygdaloid has the appearance of a sandstone, in which a small number of calcareous nodules are imbedded, externally coloured green by steatite, and exactly resembling those which enter into the composition of some of the amygdaloids of Derbyshire, and of the Pentland Hills near Edinburgh.

From the vale of Taunton in the south of Somersetshire, the principal mass of the red marl, sandstone, and conglomerate, proceeds south into Devonshire, its line of junction with the transition chains ranging a little west of the river Tone, and afterwards nearly following the Exe, and ranging between it and the Culm as far as Silverton, about five miles north of Exeter. There is, however, an insulated and outlying group of transition hills within this tract, surrounding Collumpton both on the north and south. From Silverton, a long tongue of this formation runs in westwards among the transition hills along the valley of Crediton, whence the junction trends round by Upton Pyne and Pinhoe to Exeter, proceeding thence with a nearly uniform southern course by Chudleigh and the river Teign, to the Channel, at the south-west angle of Tor-Bay, where it ends ; that portion of it which ranges between the river Teign and Tor-Bay being indeed only a tongue of this formation lying among the transition formations, since at Babbacombe and the northern cape of Tor-Bay, insulated groups of transition limestone skirt it on the east, as does the great transition district on the west. Mr. Conybeare observes, on this point, " Mr. Greenough's Map has however given rather too great an extension to these eastern groups, and made them cut off the red marle of the middle of Tor-Bay from the main tract of the formation, with which we have however been assured that it is continuous." The formations of red marle, sandstone, and conglomerate occasionally associated with amygdaloidal trap, occupy a great part of East Devon between the line of junction just described and the overlying platform of green-sand which crowns the ridges proceeding from Black Down Hill. The red marle has also a corresponding cap of overlying green-sand along Haldon Hill on the west of Exeter.

In the cliffs about half-way between Seaton and Sidmouth, according to Dr. Kidd, the red marle contains gypsum, very much resembling the mineral called Mountain Leather; nor was it difficult to trace on the spot, he states, the gradual transition of the transparent crystalline gypsum into this amianthiform state. The red cliffs of Budleigh Salterton near Sidmouth, which are of considerable height, and also those of Sidmouth itself, consist of alternations of argillaceous beds of sandstone and of breccia (conglomerate); and the red strata on the western side of the Exe near Dawlish, are alternately soft and stony, but always intermixed more or less with strata of breccia; and they are inclined in various directions.

Amygdaloidal Trap of the vicinity of Exeter. "Along a line of from five miles north to five miles south of Exeter, many points occur," Mr. Conybeare states, "in which masses of this rock are found interposed between the beds of this [the new red] sandstone. As these points nearly follow the junction of the red-sandstone and transition districts, the trap must occur towards the lower part of the sandstone series; that it is, however, associated with the sandstone, and not, as might have been supposed from this circumstance, with the transition series, is said to be distinctly proved by clear instances of its alternation with the former. The points along which it occurs, are, proceeding from north to south, 1. Near the mouth of the tongue of red marle which, as has been observed, penetrates among the grauwacké chains towards

Drawn by G. B. Campion

Engraved by James Ryall.

WATERMOUTH, NORTH DEVON

OAKHAMPTON CASTLE, DEVON.

Drawn by G. B. Campion.

Engraved by H Wallis.

Crediton, and close to its north edge, in a group of quarries lying near Killerton, Silverton, and Thorverton.
2. On the south edge of the same tongue of red marl at
Upton Pyne, Poltimore, and Poucham.   3. A little north-
east of Exeter, and again south-west of it in going to
Ide.   4. Near Dunchidiock.

Dr. Berger's account of this rock, as it occurs at Thorverton, has already been given.

The late Rev. J. J. Conybeare has given the following
more precise mineralogical description in the Annals of
Philosophy, New Series, for September 1821.

The general aspect of this rock is that of a granular
mass, rather loosely compacted, of a purplish-brown colour, more or less intense, given most probably by the
oxide of manganese in which it abounds.   In this paste
are imbedded, or rather intermixed, in such quantities as
to form a very considerable part of the whole mass, minute portions of calcareous spar, mica, or chlorite, in a
state of semi-disintegration, and indurated clay (litho-
marge ?), sometimes tinged by copper, and sometimes by
manganese.   This latter substance, as well as the calc
spar, frequently traverses the rock in small veins.   The
cells of the amygdaloidal portions are filled or lined with
brown oxide of manganese, with calc spar, and a coarse
jasper.   The nodules of the latter are not remarkable
either for their size or beauty.   The character of the rock
is so obscured by this abundant admixture of substances
apparently adventitious, as to render it very difficult to
pronounce with any certainty as to its essential constituents.   "These we should, I apprehend," Mr. J. J.
Conybeare remarks, "in the present state of our knowledge, assume to be granular or earthy felspar, and one
or more of the following : hornblende, augite, bronzite, or
hypersthene, probably the second of these.   My specimens
do not afford distinct indications of any of them.   The more
compact portions fuse before the blowpipe, sometimes into
black glass more or less slaggy, sometimes into a dirty
white enamel more or less mixed with black patches."

CHAP.
IV.

Amygda-
loid of
Thorver-
ton.

The same obscurity which is attached to the mineralogical characters of this rock seems to extend in some
measure to its relations with the conglomerate in which
it occurs. In some places it covers, and in others is
covered by, sandstone. On the road from Killerton to
Silverton, near a house occupied (in the year 1812) by
Mrs. Brown, Mr. J. J. Conybeare saw it resting on the
large-grained conglomerate; and at one of the Radden
quarries, near Thorverton, covered by a sandstone bed of
from three to ten feet in thickness. Its line of separation
from the sandstone is sometimes tolerably distinct. In
one quarry at Thorverton a line of sandy clay, not quite
a foot thick, prevents their actual contact. " At other
places, especially at the Radden quarries, the two substances appear to pass so insensibly into each other, as to
induce for the moment a conjecture that both were the
result of a common deposition, modified in its characters
by the partial intrusion of some extraneous matter."

At the Radden quarries was also noticed the occasional
tendency of this rock to split into basaltiform balls; and
in one spot it was observed to be traversed by nearly horizontal veins of its own substance, differing slightly from
the mass by their greater compactness, and the largeness
of the nodules which they contained. The veins of extraneous matter were mostly vertical, or at very high
angles.

Green-
sand for-
mation.

The *Green-sand formation*, taking a general view of its
characters as it exists throughout England, consists of
loose sand, and of sandstone. The sand is siliceous, but
the cement, when the rock occurs in the form of sandstone, is generally calcareous. Both sand and sandstone
mostly contain minute portions of a substance which has
been termed *green earth*, (which has not been chemically
examined, but very probably derives its colour from the
protoxide of iron;) and very commonly spangles of mica;
subordinate beds and masses of chert, and veins of cal-

Its general
characters.

cedony, usually occur; and also frequently alternating
beds and nodules of limestone, which in the Isle of Wight

is termed *Rag*, and which is identical with the Kentish
Rag.   Beds of clay also form occasional separations in
this formation.   In the series of these beds, chert, flint,
and calcedony continually pass into each other by insensible gradation; owing to their hardness they are often
discoverable on the summits of hills, as at Leusden, Pilsdon, &c.   Its flinty and calcedonic varieties are much
more frequent in the West of England, than in the eastern part of Kent, in which this formation also occurs to
a considerable extent; but they are very commonly met
with in Surrey; the most beautiful are found near Charmouth in Dorsetshire.

The differences of appearance which characterize different beds of this formation, and often indeed affect all
its beds in particular localities, arise, first, from a difference of texture, which passes from a very coarse-grained
sandstone, and even a distinctly conglomerated rock containing large rounded fragments of quartz, to the finely
granular form: of which latter variety, the quarries of
Blackdown, in Devonshire, which principally supply England with whetstones, afford the best examples; and
secondly, from the greater or less quantity of the green
particles; these often prevail to such a degree, as to impart to the rock its predominating aspect; often they are
so few, as to permit it to assume a grey or even a buff
colour.   In some beds, also, the sand is deeply coloured
by brown oxide of iron; a circumstance which gives
weight to the opinion that the green particles owe their
colour to an oxide of the same metal.   In the latter case,
it is difficult if not impossible to distinguish the individual beds from those of the (in many places, though we
believe not in Devonshire) subjacent formation of iron-
sand.

It does not appear that any certain order of superposition can be traced to any distance in the varieties above
described, but that they continually pass into one another,
and are irregularly blended; a constant uniformity of
character can hardly, from the circumstances of the case,

*Different
beds it
presents.*

BOOK
III.
be expected in extensive depositions, so obviously mechanical in their origin.

Organic
Remains.
The *Organic Remains* of this formation are extremely
numerous; and often when, as at Blackdown, in this
County, imbedded in the more siliceous varieties of its
rocks, occur in a state of preservation equally singular
and beautiful; the original calcareous matter of the fossil
being entirely replaced by an infiltration of calcedony. In
this state, it is often easy to detach them completely from
the loose sandy matrix; and they then appear, although
having undergone a thorough conversion of substance, with
all the sharpness and character of recent specimens*.

Of the higher animals no remains have yet been found
in the greensand; except a few teeth of fishes, both of
the conical and lanceolate figure. Of the Testacea, or
Shell-fish, the remains are so numerous, that the quarries
of Blackdown alone afford 150 species.

Local ex-
tent.
On the confines of Dorset and Devon, the greensand
presents many high and insulated masses, constituting
what are called outliers, or insulated hills, which have
been rendered insular by the intervening masses of the
same formation with which they were once continuous
having been swept away by some violent convulsion.

Black
Down.
Thus, it forms the summit of Leusden and Pilsdon Hills,
and the extensive Table-land of Blackdown, which stretches
far to the west, covering great part of the eastern division
of Devonshire, being subdivided by many valleys into
several long ridges. In the course of its progress to the
south-west, the greensand overlies, in succession, the terminations of the oolites, and the lias, and becomes, in the
western part of Blackdown, immediately incumbent on
the newer red sandstone, described in the preceding
portion of the present chapter.

Haldon.
Still further westwards, and beyond Exeter, we have

* "Shells converted into calcedony, and containing agates in their
cavities, occur near Exeter, in the whetstone-pits of the green-sand formation, at Black Down Hill; and shells, entirely converted to red jasper,
in sand of the same formation, at Little Haldon Hill."—Professor Buckland, Proceedings of Geol. Soc. No. 12. p. 150.

another outlying mass of this formation capping the long
range of Haldon Hill, which is divided only by an intermediate valley from the granite of Dartmoor; "a singular instance (in this island)," Mr. Conybeare observes,
"of the near juxta-position of primitive and very modern
rocks."

The greatest elevation of Blackdown is 817 feet above
the level of the sea, and that of Haldon is very nearly the
same. At the former locality the strata of greensand are
200 feet thick. The surface of this formation, in Devonshire, remains, for the most part, in the state of unreclaimed heath *.

CHAPTER V.

ORGANIC REMAINS BELONGING TO THE DILUVIAL
ÆRA:—CAVERNS IN THE PLYMOUTH LIMESTONE,
CONTAINING THE BONES OF LAND MAMMIFEROUS
ANIMALS.

THREE deposits of bones have been discovered at Oreston,
near Plymouth, by Mr. Whidbey, in removing the entire
mass of a hill of transition limestone, for the construction
of the Breakwater. The first of these is described by
Sir Everard Home and Mr. Whidbey, in the Philosophical
Transactions for 1817. They were found in a cavern
fifteen feet wide, twelve high, and about four feet above
high-water mark; it was filled with solid clay (probably
diluvial mud) in which the teeth and bones were imbedded,
and was intersected in blasting away the body of the rock
to make the Breakwater. The state of the teeth and bones
was the same with that of those found in the caves of
Kirkdale and Kirby Moorside, &c.; they were much
broken, but not in the slightest degree rounded by attrition, and Sir Everard Home has ascertained them to
belong exclusively to a species of Rhinoceros. A similar

* "Outlines of the Geology of England and Wales," p. 127–133.

discovery of teeth and bones was made in 1820, in a smaller cavern, distant one hundred and twenty yards from the former, being one foot high, eighteen feet wide, and twenty long, and eight feet above the high-water mark; a description of its contents is given in the Philosophical Transactions for 1821, by the same gentlemen; it contained no stalactite (or deposition of calcareous sparry matter), which abounds in many of the adjacent caverns. Sir Everard Home describes these teeth and bones as belonging to the Rhinoceros, Deer, and a species of Bear.

Bones discovered in 1822.

A third, and still more extensive discovery, was made in the same quarries in the summer of 1822, by the intersection of other apertures in the middle of the solid limestone, containing an immense deposit of bones and teeth imbedded in a similar earthy matrix to that in which they were found in the two former cases. On this discovery being communicated to Professor Buckland, that gentleman went immediately to Plymouth, accompanied by Mr. Warburton; and he found the circumstances to be nearly as follows: In a vast quarry, produced by the removal of an entire hill of limestone, for the construction of the Breakwater, there is an artificial cliff ninety feet in height, the face of which is perforated and intersected by large irregular cracks and cavities, which are more or less filled-up with loam, sand, or stalactite. These apertures are sections of fissures and caverns that have been laid open in working away the body of the rock, and are disposed in it after the manner of chimney-flues in a wall; but they attracted no attention till the discovery of bones in them in 1822. Some of them have lateral communications with adjacent cavities, others are insulated and single; some rise almost vertically towards the surface, others are tortuous, passing obliquely upwards, downwards, inwards, and in all directions, in the most irregular manner, through the body of the rock. Apertures of the same kind occur in continual succession in the limestone of the natural cliff that forms the shore from Oreston to

Stonehouse; and at the latter place, immediately on the north side of the Marine Barracks, is another large quarry, in the face of which Prof. Buckland found four apertures of the same kind leading also into caverns, the floor of all which was covered with a deep bed of mud, over the surface of which was spread a crust of stalagmite; but as these caverns have not been examined, no bones have as yet been found in them. The occurrence, however, of fissures and caves, more or less filled with mud, sand, fragments of stone and stalactite, is universal in the limestone rocks of this district, whilst the dispersion of bones through them is partial. The caves of Kent's Hole and others near Babicombe and Torbay are notorious examples of this kind.

These fissures and caverns are so connected, so often confluent and inosculating with each other, and so identical as to their contents, that there appears to be no difference as to the time or manner in which they were filled; indeed, something intermediate between a cavern and a fissure, which we may call a cavernous fissure, is the more common form under which they occur. In many of those which are nearly vertical, the communication with the surface is obvious; whilst in others that traverse the rock obliquely, it can be seen only where their upper extremity intersects the surface of the rock; and if this happens not in a cliff, but along the level face of the country, it is usually so completely filled and covered up with earth, as not to be discoverable unless by approaching it through the caverns from below. We have in this circumstance, a satisfactory reason why so many cavities, having at first view no apparent communication with the upper surface, are intersected in working the central and deepest portions of these limestone rocks.

In almost all the cavities there occurs a deposit of diluvial detritus, consisting of mud and sand, and angular fragments of limestone; these substances sometimes entirely fill up the lower chambers, and are usually lodged in various quantities and proportions on the shelves and

CHAP. VI.

Connection of the caverns with each other.

Diluvial detritus.

ledges, and lateral hollows of the middle and upper regions. The composition of the mud, or earthy portion of this diluvium at Plymouth, differs in some degree from that of the cave at Kirkdale, in Yorkshire, having been derived from the detritus of strata of a different character; it is of a redder colour, and looser texture, and less calculated to protect the bones in it from the access of atmospheric air and water. In one large vault at Oreston, where the quantity of diluvium is very great, it is stratified, or rather sorted and divided into laminæ of sand, earth, and clay, varying in fineness, but all referable to the diluvial washings of the adjacent country. It is also partially interspersed with small fragments of clay slate and quartz. The sand and loam are in many places invested with, and cemented together by, stalagmite, but not so firmly as in the Gibraltar breccia, and in much of that which occurs in the bone caves of Germany: portions of bone and single fragments of rock are also found occasionally incased with a thin crust or coating of the same substance; but, generally speaking, it is not sufficiently abundant to hold the mud and bones together in a solid mass, after they are moved from the cave.

Quantity
of bones.
It was in one of these oblique apertures in the then existing face of the rock at Oreston, and at about forty feet above the bottom of the quarry, that the congeries of bones, skulls, horns, and teeth now to be described, was discovered in the summer of 1822. Mr. Whidbey had collected fifteen large maund baskets full of them before Prof. Buckland's arrival; these have been sent to the College of Surgeons, and distributed to various public collections. In the upper parts of the cavity from which they were taken, were seen appearances of as many more still undisturbed, and forming a mass which entirely blocked it up, to an extent which could not then be ascertained; those already extracted had been discovered in a hollow, which apparently formed the lowest part of a cavernous aperture descending obliquely downwards. Ascending this aperture from its lowest point, it was pursued upwards

many feet through the solid rock, till it became narrow, and was entirely obstructed by a mass of bones, fragments of limestone, and mud.

The bones appeared to Professor Buckland and Mr. Warburton to have been washed down from above at the same time with the mud and fragments of limestone, through which they are dispersed, and to have been lodged wherever there was a ledge or cavity sufficiently capacious to receive them, or a strait sufficiently narrow to be completely obstructed by them; they were entirely without order, and not in entire skeletons; occasionally fractured, but not rolled; apparently drifted, but to a short distance only from the spot in which the animals died; they seem to agree in all their circumstances with the osseous breccia of Gibraltar, excepting the accident of their being less firmly cemented by stalagmitic infiltrations through their earthy matrix, and consequently being more decayed; they do not appear, like those at Kirkdale, to bear marks of having been gnawed or fractured by the teeth of hyænas, nor is there any reason to believe them to have been introduced by the agency of these animals. The only marks Prof. Buckland saw upon them were those pointed out to him by Mr. Clift, of nibbling by the incisor and canine teeth of an animal of the size of a weasel, showing distinctly the different effect of each individual tooth on the ulna of a wolf, and the tibia of a horse; and a few pits or circular cavities produced by partial decomposition on one surface only of the tibia of an ox, exactly resembling those which occur on many of the bones from the cave at Kirkdale.

These pits must have been formed before the bone was imbedded in mud in the lowest recesses of the cave, and probably whilst it lay exposed in some upper cavity of the rock. The weasel's teeth also must have made their impressions on the bones of the wolf and horse before they were buried in diluvial mud, and probably whilst these dead animals lay in the same situation with the tibia of the ox.

CHAP.
V.

Attendant circumstances.

The bones, when half dry, on being thrown out of a
basket on the floor, had the smell of a charnel-house, or
newly opened grave. On examining the spot where they
lay yet undisturbed in the mud of the cave, we found
some of them decomposed, and crumbling under the touch
into a blackish powder, and all extremely tender and
frangible, and of a dark brown colour whilst wet; but on
drying they acquired a greater degree of firmness and a
whiter colour. They retain less of their animal gelatine
than the bones at Kirkdale, and when dry they ring if a
blow be given to them, and are absorbent to the tongue.
On some of them there are marks of extensive disease*.

Marks of
disease in
the bones.
Mr. Clift has discovered in two of these bones from
Oreston (the metatarsus and metacarpus of an ox) extensive enlargement by ossific inflammation, arising probably
from a kick or blow; and also cavities and swellings produced by abscesses in both sides of the under jaw of a
wolf. This jaw is represented in the subjoined figure,
copied from an engraving in the Philosophical Transactions, after a drawing by Mr. Clift.

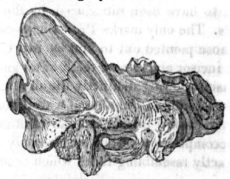

These bones, Mr. Clift informs us, in his paper on the
subject in the Philosophical Transactions for 1823, belonged to several distinct genera; namely, the bos, or ox,
the deer, the horse, the hyæna, the wolf, and the fox.
The cavities which contained them communicated with
each other, and the bones of the different graminivorous
animals were found mingled together in the same cavity;

* Buckland's Reliquiæ Diluvianæ.

but those of the carnivora at a considerable distance from
each other; the bones of the hyæna having been discovered in the lowest cavern shown in the annexed longitudinal section, and those of the wolf and fox in the gallery furthest to the right.

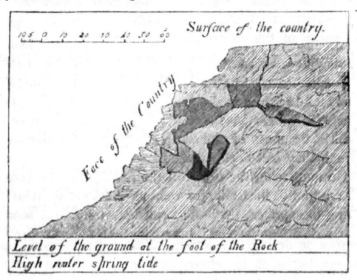

Some of the bones and fragments of bones which lay
on and near the surface of the clay, have acquired a thin
crust of stalagmite, but in none of them does it appear to
have penetrated beyond the surface : the greater number
were imbedded in the stiff clay, which adhered so firmly
to them, that many were broken by the workmen in separating them from the matrix; and others have fallen
to pieces since their exposure to the air; but a great proportion of the cylindrical and other bones, of the graminivorous animals in particular, are still as perfect in form
as at the time of the death of the animals to which they
belonged, and do not exhibit the least appearance of
having been gnawed or otherwise mutilated. The clay
still adhered so firmly to the surface of many of these
bones, that, unless removed with considerable caution, the
outer layers separated along with it, and showed that but
little animal matter remained ; and on submitting some
of these fragile portions to the action of dilute muriatic

BOOK
III.

acid, they almost entirely dissolved, leaving scarcely any trace of animal matter.

"Is it not therefore probable," Mr. Clift inquires, " that the clay immediately surrounding the bones, which is of a darker colour as well as more tenacious than that in which no bones were found, may have abstracted a large proportion of the animal matter, and be the principal cause of the extremely fragile state of the bones? for they are now so absorbent, that if the largest of them be applied to the surface of the tongue, they adhere so firmly as to support their whole weight. In this, they resemble those bones which were discovered in 1816, and 1820; most of them being as white and fragile as though they had been calcined."

On immersing the bones of the carnivorous animals in water, more effectually to remove the clay without injuring the surface, they effervesced strongly, and became nearly of a black colour, but recovered their former appearance on drying. A similar effect was produced, but in a less degree as to colour, on the bones of the bovine animals, and on those of the horse.

All the bones from these caverns at Plymouth, which have come under his observation, Mr. Clift informs us, are clearly referable to animals of known and still existing genera, as will appear by the following enumeration: but it is a curious circumstance, that, with the exception of the very few belonging to the deer, they all appertained to animals entirely differing from those found in the immediate vicinity in the former instances.

Animals.

Of the bovine genus, there are specimens of the bony core of the horns belonging to three individuals of different size; all of them remarkably short, conical, and slightly curved, and standing in a nearly horizontal direction from the head. They evidently do not belong to very young animals, and from the appearance of these alone, a very small species would be inferred; but numerous specimens of the teeth, of the os humeri, ulna and radius, os femoris, tibia, os calcis, metacarpus and meta-

tarsus, and phalanges, clearly prove that they belonged
to individuals considerably larger than the average size of
animals of that genus at the present day.

The number of bones collected affords sufficient grounds
for supposing them to have belonged to more than a dozen
individuals, varying considerably in their age.

Of smaller ruminants there are a few portions of the
cylindrical bones belonging to one or two individuals,
which are too imperfect to admit of being very satisfactorily identified, but apparently are those of a deer; and
some others belonging to very young animals in which
the epiphyses had not been united, and consequently the
bones had not acquired sufficient distinctness of character
to allow of our speaking decidedly concerning them; but
they have been most probably those of a calf or fawn.

Of the horse, the bones are satisfactorily identified by
various specimens of the teeth, the large cylindrical bones,
the os calcis, metacarpus and metatarsus, first and second
coronary bones, the sesamoid or nut-bone, and particularly by the terminal phalange or coffin-bone of the foot.
From the number of these there must have been twelve
or fourteen individuals of not less than fourteen hands
high ; one of the metatarsal bones measuring eleven inches
and a half in length.   Some of these animals, from the
worn state of the teeth, appear to have been very aged.

Of the hyæna, there are bones and teeth which belonged to at least five or six individuals of various ages.
Among these, is a part of the right side of the lower jaw,
in which remain one of the shedding molar teeth, and two
permanent ones which had not sufficiently advanced in
their growth to have protruded through the gum, but are
still inclosed within their alveolar cavities.   This is represented in the subjoined figure.

Among them also is part of the right side of the lower jaw of an adult animal, with the teeth in a good state of preservation. This specimen was discovered in the lowest cavern marked in the section in p. 371.

There are likewise detached specimens of the canine teeth and molares of individuals of very large size: and the posterior part of a skull of uncommon magnitude, which corresponds most exactly in form with that of a hyæna, and must undoubtedly have belonged to that animal, but measures twice as much from every determinate point to another, as a recent full-grown hyæna's skull.

Gigantic
hyæna's
jaw.

The following is an outside view of the left side of the lower jaw of an hyæna of very large size, (probably belonging to the skull just-mentioned,) in which the teeth are considerably abraded by masticating hard substances.

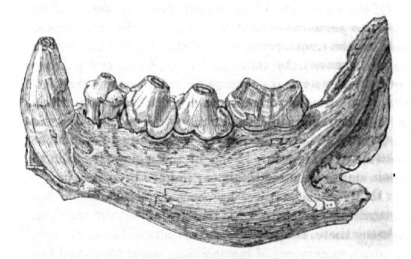

Of the wolf there are some bones of several individuals, which were found in the gallery before mentioned. There are two large portions of the lower jaw, containing nearly all the teeth in good preservation, and perfectly agreeing in size, in form, and arrangement, with those of a full-grown recent animal. The os humeri, also, is perfectly similar, and has the rounded aperture through its lower extremity, to receive the curved process of the olecranon. A few very small fragments of shell were found,

apparently allied to the genus Ostrea; but they are too
minute to admit of even that being positively ascertained.
A single valve would produce more than all the fragments
in question: when applied to the tongue they do not
adhere, and their pearly surfaces have all the compactness
and lustre of a recent shell.

Of the fox there were subsequently found a few verte-
bræ and two canine teeth from the lower jaw, which correspond perfectly in size and form with those of a recent
animal ; but are equally fragile and absorbent with those
of the other animals *.

Mr. Cottle, of Bristol, made a large collection of bones
from the same cave during a visit to Plymouth in the
summer of 1822.   He added the tiger to the list of animals before discovered in it.   The following is a list of
the remains in his possession.

18 jaws of horse,	2 jaws of deer,
2 jaws of ox,	5 jaws of wolf,
9 jaws of hyæna.	

Single teeth, 188 of horse,	5 of wolf,
26 of ox,	35 of deer,
2 of hyæna,	50 of ox or deer, not ascertained.

2 tusks of tiger; one $3\frac{2}{4}$ inches long, the other $3\frac{1}{4}$: one
from the upper, the other from the lower jaw.

Bones: 300 large and small, chiefly of the horse; none
of them are gnawed, many are quite perfect, and the majority of them slightly broken.

Osseous breccia: 33 specimens, containing teeth and
bones cemented by stalagmite.

From this list it appears that the bones of the horse
greatly predominate in the collection made by Mr. Cottle:
in that sent to the College of Surgeons, and described in
the preceding pages by Mr. Clift, those of the ox were
much more numerous, being nearly equal to those of the
horse; but whatever be the disproportion of their numbers,
the bones and teeth of all the animals are found con-

* Phil. Trans. 1828.

fusedly mixed together in irregular heaps, and not in entire skeletons, nor arranged in different parts of the cavern according to the difference of their species.

Origin of
these re-
mains.

. Professor Buckland, after describing, in his Reliquiæ Diluvianæ, these caverns and their contents, proceeds to consider, in the following terms, the time and circumstances under which the bones were introduced.

-. " I have already stated," he observes, "that there is no evidence like that at Kirkdale to show the animal remains at Oreston to have been collected by the hyænas; no disproportion in the number of the teeth to that of the bones; no destruction of the condyles and softer parts, and abundance in excess of fragments of the harder portions; no splinters of the marrow-bones; no friction or polish on the convex surfaces only of the curved bones; no marks of large teeth; no album græcum; and no dispersion of bones along the horizontal surface of a habitable den: but, on the contrary, a deep hole nearly perpendicular, and bones quite perfect, lodged in irregular heaps in the lowest pits, and in cavities along the lateral enlargements of this hole, and mixed with mud, pebbles, and fragments of limestone, in precisely the same manner as I shall hereafter show them to be lodged and mixed, in the caves and fissures of Germany and Gibraltar; and as they would have been, supposing they were drifted to their present place by the diluvian waters, from some lodgment which they had before obtained in the upper regions of these extensive and connected cavities. That they are of antediluvian origin is evident from the presence of the extinct hyæna, tiger, and rhinoceros; but there still remains a difficulty in ascertaining what was the place from which they were so drifted; 1, Are they the bones of animals that were drowned, and their bodies drifted in entire by the waters which introduced the mud and pebbles? Or, 2, had they laid some time dead on the antediluvian surface of the earth, till they were washed in at the Deluge? Or, 3, were they derived from the animals that had fallen into the open antediluvian fissures, and there perishing, remained as entire skeletons in the spots

Drawn by T H Williams

Engraved by H Wilkes

HOLCOMBE HOUSE, DEVONSHIRE.

THE SEAT OF THE RIGHT HON. LADY LAEL TIPTOE.

TO WHOM THE PLATE IS RESPECTFULLY INSCRIBED BY THE PUBLISHER

Drawn by T. H. Williams.

Engraved by H. Wallis.

WATCOMBE, DEVONSHIRE.

London, Published for the Proprietors by Wrightson & Webb, 1832.

on which they died, till they were drifted on further by
the diluvian waters into the lowest recesses and under-
vaultings with which these fissures had communication,
and there mixed up, in irregular heaps, with mud, pebbles, and angular fragments of limestone, all falling down
together with them to the places of their present inter-
ment, and producing in this short transit that quantity of
fracture to which they have been submitted?

"1. On the first of these hypotheses, had they been
drowned, and the carcases drifted in by the diluvian waters,
we should have found the skeletons more entire, and the
bones less broken, and less confusedly mixed together,
than they are; and we should neither have had the marks
of nibbling by the weasel's teeth on the bones of the wolf
and horse, nor the hollow pits arising from partial decay
on one surface only of the tibia of the ox; for neither of
these effects could have been produced on bones surrounded with a bed of mud.

"2. To the second hypothesis, that they had laid
as dead bones on the antediluvian surface, till they were
drifted from thence into the fissures, I would reply, that
in a land inhabited as this was by wolves and hyænas, it
is not likely that any carcases would have laid long on
the surface, without at least the softer portions of the
bones being eaten off by the hyænas, and thus we should
have found them lacerated, rather than perfect, in the
place to which they have since been drifted; they might
also in this case have been expected to be more or less
rolled, and to have lost their angles by friction, which does
not appear to be the fact. Another objection also arises,
from this circumstance, that the bones of dead animals
exposed on the surface of the earth, without any protection of soil or gravel, are soon destroyed by minute insects, and continual atmospheric changes; and were it
not so, the world would by this time have been spread
over most abundantly with the bones of the myriads of
animals that have died on its surface, and received no

Marginal notes:

CHAP.
V.

Examina-
tion of the
first hypo-
thesis:

of the se-
cond:

burial, since the period of the last retreat of the diluvial
waters.

" 3. The third hypothesis is that which I propose as
most probable, viz. that the animals had fallen during the
antediluvian period into the open fissures, and there perishing, had remained undisturbed in the spot on which
they died, till drifted forward, by the diluvian waters, to
their present place in the lowest vaultings with which
these fissures had communication. This explanation is
supported by the strong fact, that animals at this day do
fall continually into the few fissures that are still open,
and that carnivorous as well as graminivorous animals,
lie in nearly entire skeletons in the open fissure at Duncombe Park, each in the spot on which it actually perished, upon the different ledges and landing-places that
occur in the course of its descent, and from which, if a
second deluge were admitted to this fissure, it could only
drift them downwards, and with them the loose angular
fragments amidst which they now lie, to the lowest chambers in which the bottom of this fissure terminates. The
teeth marks of the weasel, and the pitted surface of the
tibia, will on this hypothesis have been effects produced
on the bones as they lay dead within the fissures (for a
weasel might find access by minute crevices to the interior
of such fissures,) and the wolves and hyænas may have
either fallen, like the horses, oxen, and deer, by accident,
into these natural pitfalls, or have been tempted to the
fatal experiment of leaping into them by the carcases of
the other animals, whilst they lay yet undecayed within
the fissures. The proportion of individuals collected at
Oreston, (the graminivorous being very much in excess
beyond the carnivorous,) is, as far as it goes, consistent
with this hypothesis; and if this solution appears fanciful,
it is one that need not be urged, for by the same accident that dogs at this day fall into the open fissure at
Duncombe Park, no less than sheep and deer, might the
wolves and the hyænas also of the antediluvian world

have fallen, as well as the horses and oxen, into the chasms which then in countless numbers crossed their paths, whenever they ventured on the perilous regions of the hollow and fissile limestone; and possibly some of them, whilst in the very act of pursuing their prey, may have dashed (like our less ferocious dogs in pursuit of game) into the chasms, which became the common grave of themselves and of the victim they were too eager to devour. And however new and unheard-of the existence of such fissures may be to those who have never visited or lived in a country composed of compact limestone, it is matter of painful notoriety to the farmers in Derbyshire, that their cattle are often lost by falling into the still open fissures that traverse the districts of the Peak; and it is no less matter of fact, that similar accidents are avoided in the mountain limestone countries of Monmouth and Glamorganshire only by walls carefully erected round all the open chasms, with which there also the same rocks are intersected.

"In speaking of the bones at Oreston in my former paper on Kirkdale, I had expressed a decided opinion that the caverns in which they occur must have had some communication with the surface through which the bones may have been introduced; and Mr. Whidbey has since found reason to adopt the same opinion in a further account of this third discovery to the Royal Society."[*]

* Reliquiæ Diluvianæ, p. 76–80.

CHAPTER VI.

DEPOSIT OF LIGNITE OR WOOD-COAL, OF BOVEY HEATHFIELD.

BOOK
III.

Dean
Milles's
account of
the Bovey
Coal:

Stratifica-
tion of the
Bovey
Coal:

THE beds of Lignite which are interstratified with beds of clay, of sand, and of gravel, at Bovey Heathfield, constitute one of the most interesting minor formations which the geology of this County presents. But although the chemical and mineralogical investigation of the wood-coal itself, has contributed in a great degree to the elucidation of the natural processes, by which vegetable substances become converted into coal, yet the geological history of this formation is at present very imperfectly understood; and the best accounts perhaps which have been given of it, are, that by Dean Milles, written about seventy years since, and a notice by Mr. Kingston published during the present year, 1830. Of these as well as of the various memoirs which have appeared on the chemical and mineralogical history of the " Bovey Coal," as it has most generally been termed, we shall now give a connected view.

We commence with some extracts from Dean Milles's " Remarks on the Bovey Coal," given in the Philosophical Transactions for 1760; and dated Feb. 28 in that year.

The Bovey Coal "is found on a common surrounded with hills, called Bovey Heathfield, in the parish of South-Bovey, 13 miles south-west of Exeter, and 3 miles west of Chudleigh.

" The uppermost of these strata rises within a foot of the surface, under a sharp white sand, intermixed with an ash-coloured clay, and underlies to the south about 20 inches in a fathom. The perpendicular thickness of these strata, including the beds of clay, with which they are intermixed, is about 70 feet. There are about six of

each, and they are found to continue eastward, in an uninterrupted course, to the village of Little-Bovey, a mile
distant, and probably extend much further.   The strata
of coal near the surface are from 18 inches to four feet
thick, and are separated by beds of a brownish clay,
nearly of the same dimensions, but diminishing in thickness downwards, in proportion as the strata of coal grow
larger; and both are observed to be of a more compact
and solid substance in the lower beds.   The lowermost
stratum of coal is 16 feet thick; it lies on a bed of clay,
under which is a sharp green sand, not unlike sea sand,
17 feet thick, and under that, a bed of hard close clay,
into which they bored, but found no coal. From the sand
arises a spring of clear blue water, which the miners call
mundic water, and a moisture of the same kind trickling
through the crevices of the coal tinges the outside of it
with a blue cast.

CHAP.
VI.

" Some small and narrow veins of coal are found intermixed with, and shooting through, the beds of clay, forming impressions like reeds and grass, and very similar to
those, which are generally found on the tops of coal
mines.   The clay also (at least that part of it which lies
nearest to the coal) seems to partake of its nature, having
somewhat of a laminous texture, and being in a small degree inflammable; and amongst this clay, but adhering
to the veins of coal, are found lumps of a bright yellow
loam, extremely light, and so saturated with petroleum
[Liquid Bitumen or Mineral Oil] that they burn like seal-
ing-wax, emitting a very agreeable and aromatic scent.

Impres-
sions of
Plants in
it?

" Bright
yellow
Loam in
it:"

" Though the substance and quality of this coal, in its
several strata, are much alike, and it is all indiscriminately used for the same purposes; yet there is some
difference in the colour, form, and texture, of the several
veins.   The exterior parts, which lie nearest to the clay,
have a greater mixture of earth, and are generally of a
dark brown, or chocolate colour; some of them appear
like a mass of coal and earth mixed; others have a laminous texture, but the laminæ run in such oblique, wa-

Varieties
of the Coal:

ving, and undulating forms, that they bear a strong resemblance to the roots of trees, of which kind I have seen some specimens from Lough Neagh in Ireland, which seem to be the same sort of fossil.

"There are other veins of this coal, which lie more in the centre of the strata, and abound most in the lowest and thickest bed, the substance of which is more compact and solid : these are as black, and almost as heavy, as pit coal; they do not so easily divide into laminæ, and seem to be more strongly impregnated with bitumen : these are distinguished by the name of stone coals, and the fire of them is more strong and lasting than that of other veins.

Wood-coal or Board-coal.

"But the most remarkable and curious vein in these strata is that, which they call the wood coal, or board coal, from the resemblance which the pieces have to the grain of deal boards. It is sometimes of a chocolate colour, and sometimes of a shining black. The former sort seems to be less impregnated with bitumen, is not so solid and heavy as the latter, and has more the appearance of wood. It lies in straight and even veins, and is frequently dug in pieces of three or four feet long, and, with proper care, might be taken out of a much greater length. Other pieces of the same kind are found lying upon them, in all directions, but without the least intermixture of earth, or any other interstices, except some small crevices, by which the pieces are divided from each other, in all directions. When it is first dug, and moist, the thin pieces of it will bend like horn, but when dry, it loses its elasticity, and becomes short and crisp. At all times, it is easily to be separated into very thin laminæ, or splinters, especially if it lie any time exposed to the heat of the sun, which, like the fire, makes it crackle, separate, and fall to pieces. The texture of this fossil consists of a number of laminæ, or very thin plates, lying upon each other horizontally, in which small protube-

Spar in the Wood Coal.

rances sometimes appear, like the knots of trees; but, upon examination, they are only mineral nuclei, which occasion this interruption in the course of the laminæ;

and pieces of spar have been sometimes found in the
middle of this wood coal.

"Though the texture of this coal is laminated, yet it
does not appear to have any of those fibrous intersections,
which are observed in the grain of all wood. This coal
easily breaks transversely, and the separated parts, instead
of being rugged and uneven, are generally smooth and
shining, in which even the course of the laminæ is hardly
discernible.

"They dig this coal in an open pit, together with the
clay that is mixed with it; and though it lies very close
and compact in its original bed, yet it is so easily separated, that they can afford to sell it for half a crown a ton
at the pit. The smaller coal is separated from the clay
by a screen, or grated shovel; the larger, which rises
sometimes in pieces of above an hundred weight, is piled
up by hand. There is hardly any other use made of it at
present, but to bake the earthenware of a manufacture
erected at South Bovey, and for burning of limestone,
which rising in great quantities at the neighbouring town
of Chudleigh, the coal is carried thither, and they return
with limestone to the pit, which they burn there, for the
use of the Northern parishes, to whom it lies more convenient than the kilns of Chudleigh.

"The fire made by this coal is more strong and lasting
according to its different veins: those which lie nearest
to the clay, having a greater mixture of earth, burn
heavily, leaving a large quantity of brownish ashes; that,
which they call the wood-coal, is said to make as strong
a fire as oaken billets, especially if it be set on edge, so
that the fire, as it ascends, may insinuate itself between,
and separate the laminæ. But that of the stone coal is
accounted most strong and durable, being apparently
more solid and heavy, and probably also more strongly
impregnated with bitumen. One of the proprietors of
this coal made an experiment of burning it in the fire-
engines [Steam-Engines] of Cornwall, to which it might

BOOK
III.

have been transported without much trouble or expense, being only four miles distant from the navigable river Teign; but the heat of the coal was not sufficiently intense, and the consumption of it too great, to answer the purpose. When this coal is put into the fire, it crackles, and separates into laminæ, as the cannel coal does into irregular pieces, burns for some time with a heavy flame, becomes red-hot, and gradually consumes to light white ashes. Though the transverse crevices made in it by the fire give it the external appearance of a wooden brand, yet, if quenched when red-hot, the unconsumed part does not look like charcoal, but seems to be almost as smooth and solid, as when first put into the fire.

Its smoke.

" The thick heavy smoke, which arises from this coal when burnt, is very fetid and disagreeable ; entirely different from that aromatic scent of the bituminous loam, which is found adhering to it, but much resembling that of the asphaltum, or bitumen of the Dead Sea. The whole neighbourhood is infected with the stench, which is wafted by the wind to the distance of three or four miles. When burnt in a chimney (as it is sometimes in the neighbourhood), the offensiveness is lessened by the draught: however, it is found, by those, who live continually in the smoke of it, not to be unwholesome; nor is it in the least prejudicial to the eyes, like the smoke of wood. The most shining and solid pieces of this coal have not the least degree of electrical attraction."

Mr. Hatchett's account of the Bovey Coal:

The next account of the Bovey Coal which attracted the attention of naturalists was given by Mr. Hatchett, at an early period of his important researches on the Bituminous substances. It is nearly as follows :

The Bovey Coal is a dark brown, light, brittle substance, which, in texture and other external properties, much resembles wood which has been half-charred. It is not found as scattered logs or trunks, but forms regular strata.

The pits are on a heath which is flat and sandy; the

stratum of sand is however but thin, after which a pale
brownish gray clay is found, mixed with quartz pebbles.
This prevails to about six feet, at which depth the first
stratum of the coal commences.   The quality of this is
however much inferior to that of the subsequent strata,
which in all amount to seventeen, producing a depth of
nearly seventy-four feet from the surface.   Between each
stratum of coal is a stratum of clay. The direction of the
strata is from east to west, and the inclination or dip is
from north to south.   The inferior strata are thought to
afford the best coal, .and the coal is more solid and of a
better quality towards the south.   The thickest stratum
of coal is from six to eight feet.

The Bovey Coal burns readily with a flame like half-
charred wood : it does not crackle, and, if but moderately
burned, forms charcoal ; or if completely burned, it leaves
a small quantity of light ashes exactly similar to those of
wood.   The smell of it when burning also resembles that
of wood, with a faint disagreeable odour.   It is certainly
very remarkable that this substance should form regular
strata, although it possesses the texture and most of the
properties of wood ; and that these strata do not exhibit
any of those irregularities on their surfaces, which might
be expected on the supposition that they were formed by
the roots, trunks, and branches of trees, long buried in
the earth.   It is also difficult to imagine wood to have been
transported and deposited in this place at seventeen different periods, and yet it must be allowed that these strata
have been formed by successive operations.   " I must
confess," Mr. Hatchett observes, when describing these
circumstances, " that after having twice visited and examined the spot expressly for the purpose, I still find
myself utterly unable to offer any opinion upon the subject."

The characters of bitumen are but little apparent in the
Bovey Coal, and the superior strata even appear to have
lost a portion of their combustible principle, while the inferior strata possess it.   The lower parts also of these

CHAP.
VI.

Considera-
tion of its
origin.

strata are more compact and more combustible than those parts which are immediately upon them *.

There is a remarkable kind of fossil wood, which much resembles the Bovey Coal, and in like manner is arranged among the bituminous woods, which is found in Iceland, and called by the inhabitants *Surturbrand*. This is rather harder than the Bovey Coal, but in every other respect is the same. It also forms strata many feet in thickness; but it is very extraordinary that these strata appear to be formed of trunks of trees, which, in their transverse section, exhibit the concentric circles of their annual growth, with this difference, that the trunks have been so compressed as to be nearly flat, so that the circles appear like parallel lines connected at their extremities by a short curve. Mr. Hatchett did not observe such an appearance at Bovey; but this would depend upon the position of the trunks of the trees, in respect to the section of the strata. " Chaptal, Troil, Bergman, and many others, have been of opinion that the surturbrand is wood which has been charred by the heat of the lava. But I cannot discern," says Mr. Hatchett, " why it should be supposed that it has been acted upon by fire, any more than that the Bovey Coal has been subjected to the effects of the same agent. The qualities of the two substances are the same; and as (from Archbishop Troil's and Professor Bergman's account) the surturbrand is stratified, I think we may venture to pronounce that the circumstances under which they are found, are also similar. The whole, therefore, of the opinion in favour of fire, appears to rest on the volcanic nature of Iceland; but it surely would be going too far were we to ascribe to fire all the phænomena which are observed in volcanic countries."

Bovey Coal, like the surturbrand, resembles half-

* Not far distant from the pits, to the westward, is a bog of considerable extent, where peat is cut, and decayed roots and trunks of trees are found, which do not, however, in the least approach to the nature of the Bovey Coal. Whether this bog has been in any manner connected with the formation of the latter substance does not at present appear.

charred wood; and it appears to be in a state nearly
similar, but it does not follow from this that fire has been
the cause.

Carbon is known to be one of the grand principles of
vegetables, and also as that which is the most fixed, excepting the small portion of the earths contained in them.
As a fixed principle, carbon appears to form, in great
measure, the vegetable fibre; and after a certain degree
of combustion, (by which the other principles have been
dissipated,) it remains, and the particles of it keep the
same arrangement which they possessed when the vegetable was complete.

If, however, the combustion has been carried on with
the free access of air, the carbon enters into combination
with oxygen, and becomes carbonic acid.

We have many examples in which carbon is formed, or
rather, liberated, from those substances with which it was
combined in vegetables; and these are now explained as
effects similar to those of combustion, although fire has
not been the cause.   In both cases the carbon has been
freed from the more volatile principles; and under circumstances not favourable to the union of carbon with
oxygen, the former must necessarily remain more or less
undiminished.

During the combustion of vegetable matter, the more
volatile principles contained in the vegetable fibre (which
with carbon also form the resinous and other similar substances) appear to be first separated; and in proportion
to this separation, the other more fixed substance, which
we call carbon, is developed.

Thus, by the progress of combustion, wood becomes
brown, and afterwards black; so that the state of the
wood shows the degree of combustion to which it has
been subjected, or, in other words, how far the separation
of the other principles from carbon has been effected.

Combustion is therefore a species of analysis by which
the principles of vegetables are separated, according to
their affinities, and according to their degree of volatility.

CHAP.
VI.

Develop-
ment of
carbon
from vege-
tables.

By this operation hydrogen and azote (if it be present in the vegetable) are first disengaged and form new combinations, while the carbon is the last which is acted upon; so that unless a sufficient quantity of oxygen be present, it remains fixed and unchanged.

But the same separation of the vegetable principles happens, whenever vegetables, in the full possession of their juices, are exposed to circumstances which favour the putrid fermentation.—As in combustion, so by the progress of putrefaction does the vegetable lose its colour, become brown, and afterwards black; at the same time a gas is discharged, which is composed of hydrogen, azote, and carbonic acid.

When combustion is long continued with the free access of air, the whole of the carbon is dissipated in the state of carbonic acid; but in the process of putrefaction a considerable portion of carbon commonly remains even long after the putrid fermentation has ceased. Although, therefore, it is as readily developed by putrefaction as by combustion, it is not, however, when liberated from the other principles, so speedily dissipated by the former as by the latter process.

According to the degree of combustion, within certain limits, the carbon is more or less apparent, and the like prevails according to the degree of putrefaction; so that whenever the causes which have promoted this species of fermentation have ceased, the vegetable substance will remain with more or less of its first principles, and with more or less visible carbonaceous matter, according to the degree of putrefaction which has prevailed, and the vegetable substance will consequently have the appearance and properties of wood which has been charred more or less.

Conclusion drawn from this subject.

"To this cause, therefore," Mr. Hatchett observes, after reviewing the facts we have described, "I am inclined to attribute the formation and appearance of the Bovey Coal and Surturbrand; and I believe that the portion of oily and bituminous matter, which I have obtained from them by distillation, is nothing more than the remainder of the vegetable oils and juices which have been partly modified by mineral agents *.

The first volume of Parkinson's Organic Remains of a Former World, published in 1804, contained some further particulars of the geological history of Bovey Coal, which were communicated to Mr. Parkinson by Robert Scammell, Esq. of Bovey. Among these is the following list of the beds of coal, giving their respective thickness.

Strata of Coal.	Ft.	In.	Strata of Coal.	Ft.	In.
No. 1.	1	0	No. 11.	0	6
2.	1	6	12.	2	0
3.	2	0	13.	1	2
4.	1	6	14.	1	3
5.	2	0	15. The great bed in four floors {	2	0
6.	0	9		1	2
7.	0	4		1	4
8.	1	0		1	0
9.	1	0	16. The little bed ...	1	0
10.	1	9	17. The last bed......	2	7

The lower coal-strata, it is also stated, furnish the best and strongest substance for burning. The shaft, from the surface of the ground to the bottom of the last coal-stratum, at this time was seventy-five feet deep. It had been bored thirty-three feet still deeper, but nothing had been discovered but a kind of muddy clay, intermixed with sand. The disposition of the strata, it is observed, is displayed by the method of working them : the workmen begin at the top, and clear away to the distance of eight or ten fathoms, and work down, in a perpendicular direction, through the various strata, to the bottom of the shaft; then recommence their operations. The direction of the strata is from north to south ; the inclination or dip tending to the latter. This inclination is computed to be about one foot in six ; the leading part is from east to west. The northern part reaches to the surface, within one hundred yards of the shaft, where it is cut off by a bed of sand ; to what depth the southern extremity reaches had not

* Transactions of the Linnean Society, Vol. iv. p. 138—143.

been ascertained; however, it had been found to extend
a quarter of a mile. The eastern portion had been clearly
found to extend upwards of seven miles, by the experiment of repeated boring; whilst the western had not, as
yet, been traced further than two miles.

"The Bovey Coal is now [1804] used for supplying
the steam-engine, for burning lime, and, occasionally, for
giving the earthern-ware its first burning; it is not now
used for domestic purposes, the sulphurous[?] gas it emits
being, not only extremely disagreeable, but injurious to
the health of the inhabitants. It has been said, that exposure to the influence of the sun and atmosphere, for

Action of
the atmos-
phere on
the Bovey
Coal.

some months, has deprived it of this pernicious quality;
but this is not warranted by experience; even seven years
has only lessened, but by no means destroyed it entirely.
It certainly undergoes considerable decomposition; the
different laminæ cracking and peeling off, from the evaporation of the contained moisture; it then weighing
considerably lighter."

The coal has some peculiarities, with respect to its
appearance. From this circumstance, the workmen have
divided it into three species or varieties, which they call
stone coal, board coal, and *knotty coal.*

"From every observation and inquiry I have made," Mr.
Scammell remarks, "it does not appear, that any substance
of a vegetable form has ever been discovered, either in the
coal strata or incumbent strata: no leaves, pine-nuts, or
anything of a similar nature.

"Solid bitumen [Retinasphaltum?] has often been met
with in the coal and argillaceous strata; and it has been
remarked, that the coal, taken up after this substance has
been found, is always of good quality. A species of spar
has been sometimes, though rarely, found in the middle
of a portion of the coal. The iron *pyrites* is met with
very frequently. There are springs impregnated with
ferruginous matter, depositing an ochre, which is sometimes used in the pottery.

"It appears, upon inquiry, that the space of time *from*

the Bovey coal being first worked, to the present [year 1804] is a period of upwards of ninety years.

"The spot now [1804] worked for the Bovey Coal, is situated in low boggy ground, which extends several miles : it is said to be the lowest in the county, but this is an assertion not true. To the south of the shaft, about a quarter of a mile, is a bog, from which have been taken (several feet below the surface) many trees of the fir kind ; several eighteen inches in diameter, together with pine-nuts, but no traces of coal."

About the same period Mr. Hatchett was led to re-examine the Lignite of Bovey, in continuation of his researches on the change of some of the proximate principles of vegetables into bitumen. Having made experiments upon a species of schistus from Iceland, which consisted, in part, of the leaves of the alder, he found that these leaves, though apparently reduced almost to the state of charcoal, as they existed in the schistus, nevertheless retained some part of their original proximate principles, namely extract and resin. This, of itself, was undoubtedly a remarkable fact; but if it were unsupported by any other, Mr. Hatchett perceived, the only inference would be, that the schistus was most probably of very recent formation, and had been produced under peculiar circumstances. He was desirous, therefore, of discovering some similar cases, which might serve as additional corroborative proofs, of the gradual alterations by which vegetable bodies become changed, so as at length to be regarded as forming part of the mineral kingdom.   The Bovey Coal, he had ascertained, exhibited a series of gradations, from the most perfect ligneous texture, to a substance nearly approaching the characters of pit coal, and on that account, distinguished by the name of Stone Coal. For this reason, as well as from a certain similarity in the external characters of the substance composing the leaves in the schistus, to those of the Bovey Coal, he was induced to make the latter also a subject of chemical inquiry.

Continuation of Mr. Hatchett's researches.

For chemical examination Mr. Hatchett selected some of the Lignite which had a wavy texture, and rather a glossy fracture; the quality of this sort being apparently intermediate between the others, as it retains completely the marks of its vegetable origin, while, at the same time, it possesses every perfect character of this species of coal.

Analytical
Distilla-
tion of the
Bovey
Coal.

200 grains of the Bovey Coal yielded, by distillation,

Grains.

1. Water, which soon came over acid, and afterwards turbid, by the mixture of some bitumen 60
2. Thick brown oily bitumen 21
3. Charcoal 90
4. Mixed gas, consisting of hydrogen, car- } estimated at... 29
   buretted hydrogen, and carbonic acid }

————

200

The charcoal, in appearance, perfectly resembled that which is made from recent vegetables. By incineration, about 4 grains of yellowish ashes were left, which consisted of alumina, iron, and silica, derived most probably from some small portion of the clay strata which accompany the Bovey Coal. But it is very remarkable, that neither the ashes obtained from the charcoal of the Bovey Coal, nor those obtained from the leaves of the Iceland schistus, afforded the smallest trace of alkali, which recent vegetable matter always contains[*].

A great similarity appeared in the products obtained from the Iceland schistus and the Bovey Coal, in some further experiments; with the single exception, that the leaves contain some vegetable extract, which Mr. Hatchett could not discover in the Bovey Coal. "They agree however," he observes, "in every other respect; as they both consist of woody fibre in a state of semicarbo-

[*] This fact, as far as related to the Bovey Coal, had been also noticed by Dr. Milles. But wood, however long submerged, is not deprived of alkali, unless it has more or less been converted into coal; for Mr. Hatchett afterwards made some experiments on the wood of the submerged forest at Sutton, on the coast of Lincolnshire, and found it to contain potash.

nization, impregnated with bitumen, and a small portion of resin, perfectly similar to that which is contained in many recent vegetable bodies ; and thus it seems, that as the woody fibre, in these cases, still retains some part of its vegetable characters, and is but partially and imperfectly converted into coal, so, in like manner, some of the other vegetable principles have only suffered a partial change. Undoubtedly there is every reason to believe that, next to the woody fibre, resin is the substance which, in vegetables passing to the fossil state, most powerfully resists any alteration ; and that, when this is at length effected, it is more immediately the substance from which bitumen is produced. The instances which have been mentioned corroborate this opinion ; for the vegetable extract in one of them, and more especially the resin which was discovered in both, must be regarded as part of those principles of the original vegetables which have remained, after some other portions of the same have been modified into bitumen."

As an additional confirmation of this opinion, Mr. Hatchett gives an account of a very singular substance, which is found with the Bovey Coal. In the remarks of Dean Milles, quoted in a preceding page, a substance is noticed, termed by that writer "a bright yellow loam, ... saturated with petroleum." This substance Mr. Hatchett had also observed, when he visited the Bovey Coal-pits in 1794 and 1796. At that time it was scarce, but he determined that it was a peculiar bituminous substance, and not loam impregnated with petroleum as Dr. Milles had supposed. Having afterwards received a considerable quantity of it, he was enabled more fully to ascertain its real nature and properties.

The following is an abstract of his observations.—This substance accompanies the Bovey Coal in the manner described by Dr. Milles, and is found in masses of a moderate size. The colour is pale brownish ochraceous yellow. The fracture is imperfectly conchoidal. It appears earthy externally, but, when broken, exhibits a

CHAP.
VI.
_____

The Bovey Coal imperfectly carbonized wood.

Retinasphaltum.

slight degree of vitreous lustre. The fragments are irregularly angular, and completely opaque at the edges. It is extremely brittle. It does not apparently become softened, when held for some time in the hand, but emits a faint resinous odour. The specific gravity, at temperature 65° of Fahrenheit, is 1·135. Some specimens have dark spots, slightly approaching in colour and lustre to asphaltum; and small portions of the Bovey Coal are commonly interspersed in the larger masses of this substance. When placed on a heated iron, it immediately melts, smokes much, burns with a bright flame, and yields a very fragrant odour, like some of the sweet-scented resins, but which at last becomes slightly tainted with that of asphaltum. The melted mass, when cold, is black, very brittle, and breaks with a glossy fracture.

By distillation, 100 grains of it afforded,

Grains.

1. Water slightly acid 3
2. Thick brown oily bitumen, very similar to that which was obtained from the Bovey Coal, but possessing slightly the odour of vegetable tar 45
3. Light spongy coal 23
4. Mixed gas, composed of hydrogen, carburetted hydrogen, and carbonic acid (by computation) 29

The coal yielded about three grains and a half of ashes, which consisted of alumina, iron, and silica, with a trace of lime.

Analysis of the Retin-asphaltum.

Upon analysis it appeared that this substance accompanying the Bovey Coal, was one of a peculiar and before unknown nature; being partly in the state of vegetable resin, and partly in that of the bitumen called Asphaltum, the resin being in the largest proportion, as 100 grains of the substance afforded

Resin 55
Asphaltum 41
Earthy residuum 3
                           ——
                           99

" Thus we have an instance," Mr. Hatchett remarks, " of a substance being found under circumstances which constitute a fossil, although the characters of it appertain

partly to the vegetable, and partly to the mineral kingdom." To this substance Mr. Hatchett gave the name of
Retinasphaltum, indicating its nature as a compound of
resin and bitumen ; and under this name it has accordingly been described in systematic works on mineralogy *.

In the second volume of the Transactions of the
Geological Society (1st Series) is an elaborate and valuable paper by Dr. Macculloch, on the chemical history
of the bituminous substances. In this paper, after describing the nature of the truly bituminous substances,
which appear to form a series, from naphtha, through
asphaltum, to common coal, and in which all traces of
organization or resemblance to vegetable and animal inflammable matter, have so thoroughly ceased, that we are
fairly entitled to give their several species a rank among
minerals, Dr. Macculloch proceeds to make the following
observations on the class of substances to which Bovey
Coal belongs.

" But there is yet another division of inflammable
and subterraneous substances connected with these, of
which the claims [to be ranked among true minerals]
may appear doubtful. Retaining as they do, the traces
of organization, and that sometimes in great perfection,
it may be often questioned whether they do not more
properly rank with the fossil remains, than with the minerals properly so called. They are well distinguished by
the name of Lignites. At one end of this series is placed
jet, in which the traces of vegetable origin are nearly
obliterated. Surturbrand and the several varieties of
brown coal [to which species Bovey Coal must be re-

CHAP.
VI.

Dr. Mac-
culloch on
the Lig-
nites.

---

* Phil. Trans. 1804, p. 390—405. At the conclusion of his paper Mr.
Hatchett mentions an inflammable substance then recently discovered
near Helbra, in the county of Mansfield, in Germany, which, as described
by M. Voight, appeared to be very similar to the retinasphaltum of Bovey.
Retinasphaltum has since been found in layers, about 1-16th of an inch
thick, in the coal of the Great Coal-formation, in several places in the
southern part of Staffordshire. The coal, where the retinasphaltum
occurs, is chiefly composed of mineral charcoal, and the layers of retinasphaltum are parallel to those of the coal.—Phillips's Mineralogy, p. 375.

BOOK
III.
___

ferred], including Cologne earth, connect it gradually with submerged wood and peat. The experiments I have already related, prove that the substance resembling bitumen, which is produced by the action of fire in the ordinary way on vegetables, differs from it essentially, and it has been seen that solubility in naphtha is the readiest criterion by which these substances can be distinguished. To assure myself of the accuracy of this test, I mixed the petroleum of coal with the black oil of wood in several proportions, and by the application of naphtha separated the one from the other. By this simple method therefore I expected to detect not only the progress of bituminization from simple turf to jet, but to assure myself whether, in the examinations hitherto made by others of these different substances, any mistake had arisen from confounding the vegetable bitumen with true bitumen, when distillation was used to investigate their nature.

" Vegetable turf in all its varieties, as well as brown coal, gave a considerable colour to lixivium of potash, but the same menstruum produced no effect on jet or surturbrand. Nor had naphtha or alcohol any action except on the resinous lignite of Bovey, from which they extracted the resinous matter which that variety contains.

" I therefore subjected these different substances to distillation, trusting that by the produce, I should ascertain, not only the fact, but the progress of bituminization.

" Submerged wood, from peat mosses in Cumberland, gave a brown oil, smelling of the wood tar, and refusing to dissolve in naphtha. In this case, therefore, no appearance of a change towards bitumen was exhibited. A compact pitchy looking peat gave an oil, which had a fetid smell, neither resembling that of wood-tar, nor bitumen, and which was very slightly soluble in naphtha.

" The Bovey brown (board) coal, produced an oil of a peculiar smell, but most resembling that of wood-tar, and much more soluble in naphtha than the preceding. Having a larger quantity of this, I separated the soluble part by naphtha, and in the remainder or insoluble oil, the smell of

wood-tar was powerful, notwithstanding the strong odour
of the naphtha. Here then the progress of bituminization
had advanced another step.   The resin of this wood, on
which a particular name [*retinasphaltum*] has lately been
bestowed, I consider as an adventitious and accidental
substance, [?] and the natural produce of the tree, now probably unknown, which occupies these alluvial [?] strata,
as other lost productions of nature are detected in other
alluvial soils *."

The best account which has yet appeared of the geological situation and circumstances of the Bovey Coal, is
given by Mr. Kingston, in his Mineralogy of Teignmouth
and its vicinity.   It is substantially as follows :

The Bovey Clay and Coal formations commence at the
base of the granite hills, in a large natural basin of irregular form, about seven or eight miles in circumference ;
situated in the parishes of Hennock, Bovey Tracey, Ilsington, and Teigngrace, and nearly surrounded by hills of
considerable elevation. The surface of this basin is known
by the name of Bovey Heathfield, and is at the average
altitude of 50 feet above the low-water sea-level.   The
formations are continued from this, through a natural
opening, in a south-east direction, to Teignbridge and
Kingsteignton, and thence across the Teign by Newton,
and by Ford at the base of Milburn Down, and might
probably be partially traced, in that direction, to the sea-
coast near Goodrington.

The Clay formation is composed, principally, of deposits
of clay of different degrees of purity, from that of a coarse
and gritty quality, to the finer marketable sorts, alternating horizontally with other deposits consisting of sand and
gravel ; the whole being formed, apparently, from the debris of the primary hills which bound the formation on
the west.   Debris from the Green Sand formation, apparently water-worn, also occurs, sparingly, on the surface,
at the eastern side of the formation.

CHAP.
VI.

Retinas-
phaltum.

Geological
History of
the Bovey
Coal de-
posit.

* Trans. of Geol. Soc. 1st Series, Vol. ii. p. 17—18.

" These deposits consist chiefly of five clay beds of various widths, running parallel with as many alternating ones of gravel, whose width varies from 50 to 100 feet; the loose head of earth and gravel on these varies considerably, from 5 or 6 feet, to 25 or 30 ; beneath this incumbent stratum, the clay beds lie, not in a straight level manner, but undulating, like the waves of the sea; beneath the four westernmost beds (which are worked to depths varying from 30 to 80 feet)* the Bovey Coal runs ; under the most eastern or pipe-clay (which is also frequently worked to the depth of 80 feet) white quartz and sand are found."

The Bovey Coal which passes under this, occurs in stratified beds, which have the collective thickness of seventy feet ; and near the Pottery in the parish of Bovey, where the largest body of the coal appears to be situated, and where it approaches to within five or six feet of the surface, they dip, at an angle of 24 or 25 degrees. At this spot are six beds, of various thickness, " interposed between brownish clay"; in this clay small veins of coal resembling reeds and grass are found, as mentioned by Dean Milles, and also pieces of the *retinasphaltum*: the whole is covered by a loose gravelly head. " The main beds of this formation appear very obviously to consist of the wood of Dicotyledonous trees imperfectly mineralized."

We have seen that down to the period of Mr. Scammell's observations (cited in p. 390), no vegetable organic remains had been discovered in connexion with the Bovey

Coal, but Mr. Kingston states, that "some distinct scales, apparently of cones belonging to the Pine family, are occasionally met with in this deposit ;" and that he has also been favoured by J. G. Croker, Esq. "with specimens, in a very perfect state, [from this formation] of a small one-celled capsule, or drupe, resembling that of the genus *Myrica*," or Candleberry Myrtle.

* " Near the S.E. corner of the Heathfield, this formation was bored to the depth of 200 feet through continuous layers of clay, varying in colour and texture, in an unsuccessful search for black [or common] coal.

· This will be the proper place to introduce Mr. Conybeare's view of the natural operations by which he conceives the Bovey Coal deposit to have been formed.

Mr. Conybeare considers the Lignite of Bovey, as well
as that of the banks of the Rhine, between Cologne and
Bonn, to be of "Diluvial" origin. These lignites, he
states, are "associated with accumulations of gravel apparently resulting from the last great catastrophe that
has affected the earth's surface, but unconnected with
the order of causes still acting."* In noticing the theoretical deductions concerning the origin of the Great Formation of true coal, such as that of Newcastle, &c., he
observes, that, " the partial filling up of lakes and æstu-
aries offers us the only analogies in the actual order of
things with which we can compare the deposits of coal
[forming part of the Great Coal-formation] ; for in such
situations we often find a series of strata of peat, and sometimes submerged wood, alternating with others of sand,
clay, and gravel, and presenting therefore the model of a
coal-field on a small scale, and in an immature state.

" The Lignites of Bovey Tracey, which seem evidently to have been accumulated (but at an earlier period)
in the filling up of an æstuary, are disposed in regular
strata, alternating with clay and gravel evidently derived
from the detritus of the neighbouring granitic chains. The
thickness of the beds in this instance, and the structure
of the whole deposit, give it a still nearer resemblance to
a regular coal-field. We must here suppose the wintry
torrents to have swept away a part of the vegetation of
the neighbouring hills, and buried them [it] in the æstuary,
together with the alluvial detritus collected in its course;
the latter would, from its gravity, have sunk first and
formed the floor ; the wood would have floated till, having
lost its more volatile parts by decomposition and become
saturated with moisture, it likewise subsided upon these,
being perhaps also loaded by fresh alluvia drifted down

* " Outlines of the Geology of England and Wales," p. 328.

BOOK
III.

Œconomi-
cal appli-
cations of
the Bovey
Coal.

upon its surface; the reiterated devastations of successive seasons must have produced the repetition and alternation of the beds *."

We shall now terminate our account of this remarkable and interesting substance, the Lignite of Bovey, by some particulars of its present œconómical applications, given in the terms of Mr. Kingston :

" The chief use to which the Bovey Coal is applied, is the manufacture of an inferior description of earthen-ware, at the potteries on Bovey heath; it is also used as fuel, in the cottages of the neighbouring poor, but its difficult and imperfect combustion, and the fœtid gas emitted during the process, prevents its being used to any great extent for domestic purposes; many experiments have been made to render this article more extensively useful, but hitherto without any approach to success, the large proportion of earthy and incombustible matter it contains, having hitherto proved an insurmountable obstacle; the charcoal produced from it is of excellent quality, but not in pieces of sufficient size and compactness to stand a blast.   It would be a most important advantage to the neighbourhood, if any means could be devised to make it available in the smelting of iron; the chief difficulty to overcome appears to be, the getting rid of the ashes, which by their rapid accumulation, prevent a sustained white heat from being kept up in the furnace.   We have ourselves," Mr. Kingston concludes with remarking, " made some unsuccessful experiments for this purpose, nor do we yet quite despair of seeing some plan devised to overcome the difficulty—and here we cannot but call to mind with esteem and regret the late Mr. Hatherleigh, to whose spirited exertions the neighbourhood, on this and many other accounts, is so much indebted."

* " Outlines," p. 346.

CHAPTER VII.

BOTANY OF DEVONSHIRE.

It does not appear that any peculiar vegetable features distinguish from each other the various geological formations which we have seen this County to include. The *Cistea, Conyza squamosa,* and one or two other plants, Messrs. Jones and Kingston have observed, "seem to affect the limestone; the *Clematis* also appears to grow more luxuriantly amongst the crevices of that rock than elsewhere; whilst the *Iris fœtidissima* and the *Elm* prevail most in the new red-sandstone: still neither these, nor any other species, so far as we are aware, are exclusively confined to any particular formation."

The most striking local difference which actually does occur in the character of the Devonian Flora, and which seems to confirm the foregoing statement, is that which results from a comparison of the plants growing along the extensive ranges of the sea-coast and cliffs, with those of the more interior parts of the County. Each of these tracts is distinguished by its own peculiar botanical features; but these exist independently of the nature of the strata, and the same plants may frequently be traced along the whole of the coast-line, whether the cliffs consist of sandstone, limestone, or slate, all of which are found alternating with each other on the southern shores of the County. If the investigation be pursued further, along the shores of Cornwall, the same plants may still be found in the serpentine formation of the Lizard district, and in that part of the granite range which forms the rocks around the Land's End. Thus the most characteristic *Botanical* division of the County, would be, into the central inland portion, and those on either side of it, bordering on the sea. That there is a great difference,

BOOK
III.

not only between the mean annual temperatures of these tracts, but also a much greater variation in the mean temperatures of the different months of a year, in the former, than in the latter, experience sufficiently proves. These differences arise from the elevation and exposure of the one, as well as from the large extent of boggy and unreclaimed surface which it includes; and from the sheltered and cultivated state of the other, together with its proximity to the ocean. The extent of these differences, however, cannot at present be determined, from the want of data sufficiently accurate and extensive.

Numerical views of the Plants of Devonshire.

According to the researches of Messrs. Jones and Kingston, which are the most extensive that have yet been made in this County, the entire number of Phænogamous plants spread over its diversified surface, amounts to 774 species, belonging to 84 natural orders, and arranged in 343 genera. Of these, 187 species, belonging to 15 orders, and arranged in 59 genera, belong to the Monocotyledonous class: 587 species, belonging to 66 orders, and arranged in 284 genera, to the Dicotyledonous class. The number of species contained in the former class, therefore, as compared with the latter, is nearly as one to 3·2; the Monocotyledons thus forming rather less than one-fourth, and the Dicotyledons rather more than three-fourths of the whole.

The proportions of the different natural orders, as respects, first, their own class, and, secondly, the total number of Phænogamous plants, according to the statement of the same Botanists, are as follows:

I. MONOCOTYLEDONOUS CLASS.

	No. of Species in each Order.	Relative proportion of its own Class.	Ditto of total Phænogamous Plants.
Graminéæ	74	$\frac{1}{3}$ between $\frac{1}{14}$ and $-\frac{1}{14}$	
Cyperaceæ	48	$+\frac{1}{4}$	$-\frac{1}{14}$
Junceæ	16	$+\frac{1}{14}$	$-\frac{1}{14}$
Orchideæ	13	$+\frac{1}{14}$	$-\frac{1}{14}$

	No. of Species in each Order.	Relative proportion of its own Class.	Ditto of total Phænogamous Plants.	
Fluviales	10	$-\frac{1}{10}$	$-\frac{1}{10}$	CHAP. VII.
Aroideæ........	8	$+\frac{1}{10}$	$+\frac{1}{10}$	
Asphodeliæ	5	$-\frac{1}{10}$	$\frac{1}{10}$	
The remaining 8 orders of the Monocotyledonous Class together .	13	$-\frac{1}{10}$	$-\frac{1}{10}$	

II. DICOTYLEDONOUS CLASS.

Compositæ.....	72	$-\frac{1}{6}$ between $\frac{1}{10}$ and $\frac{1}{10}$	
Cruciferæ......	44	$-\frac{1}{10}$ between $\frac{1}{7}$ and $\frac{1}{10}$	
Leguminosæ ...	39	$\frac{1}{10}$	$+\frac{1}{10}$
Umbelliferæ....	37	$+\frac{1}{10}$	$+\frac{1}{10}$
Rosaceæ and Pomaceæ	36	$-\frac{1}{10}$	$-\frac{1}{10}$
Labiatæ	35	$+\frac{1}{10}$	$-\frac{1}{10}$
Scrophularinæ & Orobancheæ .	31	$\frac{1}{10}$	$\frac{1}{10}$
Caryophylleæ & Lineæ	31	$\frac{1}{10}$	$\frac{1}{10}$
Corylaceæ and Salicineæ	28	$\frac{1}{10}$	$+\frac{1}{10}$
Ranunculaceæ ..	20	$-\frac{1}{10}$	$+\frac{1}{10}$
Polygoneæ	18	$+\frac{1}{10}$	$\frac{1}{10}$
Chenopodeæ ...	15	$\frac{1}{10}$	$+\frac{1}{10}$
Boragineæ	13	$\frac{1}{10}$	$+\frac{1}{10}$
Primulaceæ and Lentibulariæ .	13	$\frac{1}{10}$	$+\frac{1}{10}$
Geraniaceæ and Oxalideæ....	13	$\frac{1}{10}$	$+\frac{1}{10}$
Rubiaceæ......	11	$-\frac{1}{10}$	$-\frac{1}{10}$
Hypericinæ	9	$\frac{1}{10}$	$\frac{1}{10}$
Semperviveæ....	9	$\frac{1}{10}$	$\frac{1}{10}$
Solaneæ	8	$-\frac{1}{10}$	$-\frac{1}{10}$
Euphorbiaceæ ..	8	$-\frac{1}{10}$	$-\frac{1}{10}$
Papaveraceæ ..	7	$\frac{1}{10}$	$-\frac{1}{10}$
The remaining 39 orders containing altogether	110	between $\frac{1}{4}$ & $\frac{1}{3}$	$\frac{1}{4}$

The Glumaceæ, it appears from this comparative enumeration, form very nearly two-thirds of their own Class;
together with the Compositæ they constitute one-fourth
of the whole of the Phænogamous plants of Devonshire;
and the Cruciform, Leguminous, Umbellate, Rosaceous,
and Labiated plants, constitute one-fourth more among
them.

The Cryptogamous Plants enumerated in the *Flora
Devoniensis* amount altogether to 666 species, of which
the natural orders Lycopodineæ, Marsileaceæ, Equise-
taceæ, and Characeæ, contain each a single species only.
The Filices include 22 species, Musci 174, Hepaticæ 30,
Algæ 147, and the Lichens 141; the Hypoxyla, Fungi,
&c., comprehending the remaining 148 species; making
the total number of Devonian Plants described 1440
species.

The Flora of the whole of the British Isles contains
about 1350 species of Phænogamous Plants, of which
about 370 are Monocotyledons, and 980 Dicotyledons.
They are distributed among the great natural orders nearly
as follows: Gramineæ 120 species; Cyperaceæ 70;
Compositæ 120; Umbelliferæ, Cruciferæ, Leguminosæ,
and Caryophylleæ, 60 each; Labiatæ and Scrophularinæ,
50 each; Ranunculaceæ 36; the remainder belonging to
the less extensive orders.

"The principal genera belonging to the British Flora,
of which we can boast no exemplars," the authors of the
Flora Devoniensis observe, "after excluding

Stipa	Carum	Epimedium
Lagurus	Borago	Asarum
Cyperus	Alyssum	Staphylæa
Crocus	Isatis	Xanthium
Leucojum	Doronicum	Cyclamen
Echinophora	Calendula	Œnothera
Tordylium	Amaranthus	Chrysocoma,
Imperatoria	Datura	

which have but a doubtful claim to rank as indigenous

plants, and therefore, though we have habitats for some of them as undoubted as any, we have omitted noticing them, are

Sesleria	Juniperus 1	Sibbaldia
Hierocloe	Empetrum	Cherleria
Tofieldia	Selinum	Dryas
Anthericum	Ligusticum	Trollius
Eriocaulon	Pyrola 5	Oxyria
Malaxis	Polemonium	Swertia
Corallorhiza	Azalea	Trientalis
Cypripedium	Menziesia 2	Impatiens
Goodyera	Andromeda	Linnæa
Convallaria 4	Arbutus 3	Rhodiola
Pinus 1	Subularia	Erigeron 2
Taxus 1	Hesperis	

Genera not found in Devonshire.

" These are for the most part confined to more northern or more alpine regions than ours, as is likewise the case with the greater part of the genus Saxifraga, of about 12 British Species of which we only possess one.

" The greater part of the others are rare or local plants: we annex the situations where the chief of them are most generally found growing, to show the chances there may be of finding them in a wild state in this country, and the likeliest places to search for them.

"Names of Genera.	Most usual Localities.
Fritillaria	Pastures, midland counties, local.
Paris	Woods, eastern and northern counties.
Hippuris	Muddy ponds, rare.
Tillæa	Dry heaths, Norfolk and Suffolk.
Hippophae	Eastern coast.
Buffonia	Heaths, rare.
Buxus	Chalky hills.
Asperugo	Old rubbishy places.
Hottonia	Ponds.
Phyteuma	Chalky pastures.
Atropa	Eastern and northern counties.
Thesium	Chalky cliffs and downs.
Herniaria	Southernmost coast of Cornwall.

Names of Genera	Most usual Localities.
Athamanta	Cambridge, local and rare.
Danaa	Cornwall, ditto.
Cicuta	By streams, eastern counties.
Tamarix	Cornish coast.
Parnassia	Wet pastures, Wales, and N. & E. counties.
Althæa	Marshes near the sea.
Frankenia	Salt marshes on the eastern coast.
Aristolochia	Woods, &c. in several counties.
Monotropa	Woods, parasitic on roots of trees, &c.
Comarum	Bogs, northern and eastern counties.
Actæa	Woods, Yorkshire.
Delphinium	Cornfields, &c.
Adonis	Ditto, counties round London.
Stratiotes	Slow streams, &c. eastern counties.
Sagittaria	Ditto, Thames, &c.
Limosella	Muddy places, occasionally flooded.
Lathræa	Woods.
Astragalus	Calcareous and hilly pastures.
Pisum	Dorsetshire coast.
Lactuca 3	Borders of fields, &c.
Prenanthes	Rocks and old walls.
Cineraria 2	1 species in marshes, 1 on hilly pastures.
Bryonia	Hedges, &c. midland counties.

BOOK III.

"Except where the number of species is placed after the generic name, they each include but a single British one."

Species deficient in the Devonian Flora. Among the genera belonging to the Devonian Flora, the greatest deficiency will be found in the following; *Carex, Juncus, Veronica, Vaccinium, Rubus,* (of all these the species wanting are chiefly alpine plants,) *Campanula, Dianthus, Silene, Salix.*

The authors of the *Flora Devoniensis,* from whose pages the contents of the present chapter have entirely been selected, terminate their view of the Geographical Distribution, &c. of the plants indigenous to this County with the following remarks : "We shall conclude this part of our volume, by briefly noticing another view in which the vegetable features of a district may be contemplated;

namely, the preponderance of particular families or species, which often almost exclusively occupy large tracts, and have as natural a tendency to encroach and extend themselves, as others have to remain scattered and unobtrusive.   Thus, the grasses constitute an order the most widely and profusely spread of any ; and the *furze* and *heath* may be instanced as species that often cover a large surface : the *oak* also may be observed spreading itself, to the exclusion of everything else, along the sides of many of our coombes, both in the granite and slate formations.   But this part of the subject having been carefully attended to in the former portion of the volume, any further detail would be superfluous.   Illustrations, on a grand scale, of what we have been here observing on, are still to be met with in many parts of the world, where the preponderance of certain families of plants, or even occasionally of single species (of the *social* kinds), not only give a peculiar and decided character to the landscape, but have also a powerful influence on the conditions and character of men ; and though in countries long reclaimed and cultivated this has become less obvious, it remains to most of them a subject of considerable importance."

Preponderant Families or Species.

Having now given a comprehensive synoptic view of the Geology of Devonshire, (including some details relating to certain branches of its Mining and Mineralogy,) and a brief sketch of the Botany of the County, we must here terminate the distinct consideration of its Physical Structure and Natural History. The unexpected length to which it has been found requisite to extend the Outlines of the Geology of this County, as the most generally interesting and important part of its Physical History ; and the necessity of not encroaching too much on the space allotted to the Topographical and Historical facts which this work is designed principally to communicate, render this par-

Conclusion of the Physical History of Devon.

tially abrupt termination unavoidable. In order, however,
to supply, in some measure, the defects which may ensue
from this deviation from the original (somewhat too extensive) plan, illustrations have been prepared of some kind
subjects of interest in Mineralogy and Zoology, which
will be introduced in the descriptions of the places
which they occur.

———————————

[The part contributed to this work by Mr. Brayley, Jun. terminates
here.]

Drawn by G.B.Campion.

Engraved by James Ringley

TAWSTOCK HOUSE, DEVONSHIRE.

THE SEAT OF SIR BOURCHIEL WREY BAR. TO WHOM THIS PLATE IS RESPECTFULLY INSCRIBED
BY THE PUBLISHERS

LOVELY COURT, DEVONSHIRE

BOOK IV.

AGRICULTURE, PRODUCTS, MANUFACTURES, TRADE AND COMMERCE.

CHAPTER I.

AGRICULTURE AND PRODUCTS.

N the importance of agriculture it is perfectly unnecessary to expatiate; and in reference to this subject, Devonshire is admitted to be one of the finest and most valuable counties in the kingdom. In extent 1,600,000 acres, "it is equal," as Mr. Frazer has observed*, "to the whole extent of the Genoese territories, not inferior to the Balearic Islands, which were once a monarchy, and twice the size of Algarve, which is so still." A large proportion of it indeed is in a state of barrenness, and unproductive; but the cultivated districts abound with the richest soils and the most luxuriant vegetation; nor can it be doubted that nothing is wanted but judicious and persevering attention to suitable means of improvement, to render productive a very considerable portion of what now lies waste, with sufficient remuneration for the labour and expense of cultivation. The climate, moreover, is in the highest degree salubrious, and from its warmth and moisture more propitious to vegetation than that of any other county. The mildness of its winter is scarcely surpassed in any other part of Europe; so that green-house plants,

CHAP.
I.

---

* Agricultural Survey, p. 1.

as the Fusia, the Myrtle, and Magnolia, flourish in the
open air with a luxuriance and vigour to be observed in
no other part of the island.

Scarcely any department of useful occupation and œconomy requires or admits of greater improvement than
agriculture ; and, although there are many intelligent and
enterprising individuals who have done much for the benefit of husbandry in this country by the introduction of
important improvements, what has been done in this way
does not appear to have generally affected the system
prevalent in this district : this is said to be of great antiquity, and appears to remain in a great measure stationary.
On all these accounts the agriculture of the county is an
interesting subject, and will receive more attention here
than is usual in works devoted to topography *.

Western
district.

In treating on this subject, the county will be divided
into districts, as has been done in other instances, beginning with the Western, or that portion of it which is
bounded on the west by the Tamar, on the south by Plymouth Sound and its estuaries, and on the north and east
by Brent Tor with its surrounding heaths, and part of
Dartmoor ; comprising an extent of country about twenty
miles in length from north to south, and ten in width from
east to west.

In this district some barren tracts are found, though
comparatively not extensive. The tide flows to its centre ; and though its elevation is nowhere great, yet on account of the narrowness and depth of the larger valleys,
whose sides, covered with wood, rise abruptly from the
streams by which they are watered, as well as the hills and
wider spaces between the valleys being rent and broken
in a manner peculiar to the western counties, the surface
varies in the extreme. Here indeed is no extent of vale

* In drawing up this account of the agriculture of Devon, much use
has been made of Marshall's " Rural Economy," and Frazer's, but especially Vancouver's, " Surveys," as well as the works of other writers:
much valuable information has also been obtained from respectable private correspondence. More particular reference in general is not thought
to be necessary.

land, the parts in cultivation consisting of a perpetual
succession of hills, with here and there a narrow bottom
or combe *, intersected by streams of greater or less extent. This is much spoken of as the region of picturesque
beauty. There are, however, two or three drawbacks,
namely, the want of lawn or vale land, and also of the
lake, or any extent of water, which might give softness
to the scenery, and by contrast and variety add greatly
to its beauty or its grandeur.

The hills here are covered with the fruits of cultivation,
and the lofty fields waving to their very summits with the
rich gifts of harvest afford no slight gratification to the eye.
Farms of this kind indeed are numerous throughout a large
portion of the county, and the climate is admirably suited to the surface. The soil being generally thin upon
rocks of granite, limestone, schistus, red sandstone, &c.,
would be liable to be soon parched but for the frequent
falls of rain, which usually afford a supply of moisture
sufficient even in these elevated situations for every purpose of vegetation. For these reasons the pastures, especially those on the hills and rising grounds, produce a
fine, sweet, and nutritive grass ; whilst at the same time
they are free from the abundance of rank weeds which
flourish on the strong flat lands of other counties. On the
higher lands the turf is as smooth and fine as a garden
grass-plat ; and if a succession of hot days or weeks
should occur, which even here does occasionally happen,
and change the surface into a russet brown, a very few days
of rain restore the beautiful verdure, which yields a short

* The word *combe* or *soombe*, so often occurring in the accounts of
Devonshire, signifies a valley surrounded by hills on all sides but one.
These combes are generally narrow at the top, and widen as they descend
to the lower grounds. They have not been formed by the streams,
which have taken their course as the surface gave them direction. It is
however a striking remark, that at the tops of the combes the principal
rivers take their rise in bogs formed by the water issuing from among
the rocks, and creating a profuse vegetation. The clumps of moss growing here are large, various and beautiful beyond the conception of persons who have not seen them : they are found rising three or four feet
in height.

BOOK
IV.
_____

but delicious nutriment to the cattle. Notwithstanding the benefit of cultivation, and the decay of vegetable matter, the soil here must remain perpetually shallow through the constant wearing down of the surface to the lower grounds, which of course are rich in proportion, and exhilarate the eye with fertile valleys, large orchards, and picturesque scenery.

Soil.

The species of surface soil in this district is remarkable on the whole for its uniformity. It does not properly class with any of the ordinary descriptions, as clay, loam, sand, or gravel; but is silty or muddy, consisting chiefly of perished slate-stone rubble, or slate reduced by the action of the atmosphere to its original state. A portion however of loamy mould is found mixed with it in various degrees, and hence the quality varies, though the species is the same. Small plots of land occur upon the upper branches of the Tavy equal to the best in the kingdom. The prevailing depth of soil is from five to ten inches. Rocks, however, and fragments of rocks, are everywhere in abundance. This singular species of soil is absorbent, not tenacious, and highly favourable to purposes of husbandry.

Subsoil.

The subsoil is universally stony, nor are beds of clay, loam, or gravel, as in other districts, to be met with here. It consists of soft slaty rock or schistus, frequently mixed with a species of crystal, or quartz, provincially called *whiteacre*, generally white, but sometimes tinged with red, in blocks or fragments of various sizes. Hence, though this is the region of rains *, from the absorbent

* Tavistock is admitted to be one of the most rainy places in the kingdom. Plymouth has also obtained a similar character; and travellers who have visited it, will probably be unanimous in maintaining the justice of this imputation. The inhabitants of this port itself, however, insist upon its falsehood, and account for the general prevalence of the notion, by admitting that the rains are more frequent there than in many other places; but they affirm at the same time, that they are neither so violent nor of such long duration as elsewhere. In their defence of their climate, some allowance may be made for local partiality. However, by the account received by the writer of the quantity of rain that fell in this district in 1828, from an inhabitant of Tavistock, who keeps a rain guage, it appears that though the quantity of rain which fell at the

nature of the soil and substratum, aided by the perpetual
recurrence of declivities, the surface is soon dry; nor is
the cultivation of the land ever impeded by the moisture,
except in seasons unusually wet.   To this it may be
added, that the water which filters through the slaty and
limestone rocks is remarkable for its fertilizing quality.

CHAP.
I.

As a subject connected with agriculture, it may be remarked, that the manors of this vicinity are generally
small, more than one being frequently included in the
same township.   The manor courts are regularly held,
and well attended ; the rents appropriated to the manors
being usually paid in these courts.   In this district the
inquests of the manors also have cognizance of the weight
of bread, which is considered as an excellent custom.

Manor
courts.

The population of the country in this district is much
below the general average; the employment is chiefly
agricultural, and the quantity of the produce greatly exceeds the consumption.   The villages are few and small,
farm-houses and numerous cottages being scattered over
the area of the townships.   There are, however, several
considerable towns in the district besides Plymouth and
Devonport, at which latter places, by means of the extensive population, the Government dock-yard and stores,
together with the shipping and the sea, a ready and ample
vent is found for the extra produce.   Of this produce,
wood forms no inconsiderable portion.   Of the inclosed
lands, a large proportion is in grass, perhaps two thirds;
the rest being occupied by arable lands and orchards.
The animals are of the ordinary domestic kind, but some

Population
and pro-
duce.

---

latter town was greater, that which fell at Plymouth was less, than the
average of the whole kingdom. The winds here are generally active,
and often violent; so that, if the clouds are brought up by them from the
sea in great numbers, they are speedily carried over, and moisture is
never suffered to stagnate. Nothing like a London fog is ever seen here,
and the town on the whole is reckoned healthy. The reason why Tavistock abounds so much with rain, may be found in the following circumstance : two opposite ranges of hills, beginning near the sea at some
distance from each other, gradually approach till they almost meet near
the town, thus forming a sort of funnel, by which the winds and consequently the clouds are conducted towards that place, where, being ar-
rested by the hills, they discharge their contents in unusual quantities,

BOOK
IV.

The roads.

of them, which will be hereafter described, of a very superior breed.

The roads, so important to agriculture, in West Devonshire as well as in the rest of the county are in excellent condition; nor is anything necessary to render them everywhere equal to the best in the kingdom, but labour and judgement, as abundance of valuable materials is at hand. Risdon's account of them in his time* is well known. "They were," he observes, "rough and unpleasant to strangers travelling those ways, which are cumbersome and uneven, among rocks and stones, painful for man and horse; as they can best witness who have made trial thereof. For be they never so well mounted upon horses out of other counties, when they have travelled one journey in these parts, they can, in respect of ease of travel, forbear a second." To this it may be added, that all material improvements are of very modern date. The first turnpike roads were made about the year 1753; but it was a considerable time after this that the spirit of improvement affected the roads of Devonshire. Within the last twenty years, by levelling the hills, filling up the hollows, and making shorter cuts instead of narrow windings as before, and by a judicious use of the materials best adapted to the purpose, great amelioration has been effected, and Devonshire has received its full share, in this instance, of the benefits derived from knowledge and experience. Further and great improvements, however, are still wanted, and in various instances throughout the county are at present taking place. In numerous quarters the roads, especially leading to the villages and farms, are much too narrow; and at the same time having high banks on each side, with coppice-wood on the tops of them, are kept almost constantly wet: less than a century ago they were mere gulleys worn by the streams. The ancient inhabitants, to whom we are indebted for the first formation of roads before inclosures took place, paid little or no attention to the choice of a level, but went

* Two hundred years ago. Risdon died in 1640.

from place to place as nearly as possible in a direct line
over the hills where they intervened. The British roads,
as well as the Roman, were usually straight. These lines,
in many places, are continued to the present time, and
hence arises the steepness for which, in Devonshire, they
are remarkable. The roads in this county can never be
brought to a dead flat, nor is it desirable they should be.
Some descent, especially where the rains are so frequent,
is necessary to keep them dry; and it is remarkable,
that horses on the roads in hilly countries, through the
relief that is afforded by the frequent interruption of their
speed, and the opportunity given in their ascent and descent for the exercise of different muscles, do not tire so
soon as on continued levels. Still, however, great inconvenience and increased expense arise from the perpetual
recurrence of steep declivities in the roads of Devonshire;
and much advantage would be derived from more regard
to levels, and from generally winding round the lofty eminences instead of passing over them.

The cultivated lands in Devonshire are universally in- Inclosures.
closed. But some of those which are now open, have in
former periods been evidently ploughed, for the furrows
remain, with traces of the fences, and even of buildings;
so that these spots must have been formerly inclosed, but
again thrown open through the failure perhaps of the population in the vicinity. Mr. Marshall, however, supposes this circumstance to have arisen from an ancient
custom, prevalent here and peculiar to this county, for the
lords of the manors to possess the privilege of letting
portions of the common lands within their respective pre-
cincts, for one or more crops, and then suffering the land
to revert to a state of grass and commonage. This might
be an excellent custom at first, in order to secure the
cleansing and cultivation of the country: the lands in a
wild state having been gone over in this manner, out of
them might arise the present inclosures.

Having mentioned the fences, it may be proper to de- Danmoni-
scribe them, as forming one of the most remarkable fea- an fences.

tures of the rural œconomy of Devonshire. These fences universally consist of a mound of earth, sometimes flanked with stones eight, ten, or more feet in width at the base, and sometimes nearly as high, but narrowed at the top to six or even four feet. This is covered with coppice-wood, as oak, ash, sallow, birch, and hazel, which is cut at fifteen or twenty years growth, and at more perhaps than twenty feet in height, besides the mound, forming altogether a barrier about thirty feet high. The origin of these fences cannot be traced. When the forests were cleared away, it is probable they might be adopted to supply the want of fuel. At any rate the age of most of them is great beyond memory. Being on several accounts admirably adapted to the nature of the country and the climate, they still continue to be formed; nor indeed is any other method of raising 'live' fences in general use in Devonshire. The benefits of these fences are obvious: they form an insuperable barrier to cattle; and by their shade and shelter afford no unsuitable protection in a country so much abounding with hills, and so exposed to the wind and frequent rains, as Devonshire. The most important advantage, however, attending them is, that they furnish a necessary supply of fuel, often when no other can be had. The county produces no coal for common use; but many farms that have no woodlands nor any other fuel, are nevertheless amply supplied by these fences, besides perhaps pales, and cord-wood, faggots, and oak-bark. This therefore is a valuable crop in addition to an excellent fence. It may also be added, these fences are everlasting, with ordinary care, as they will increase rather than diminish with years. Their disadvantages, on the contrary, are so great that it is difficult to say on which side the scale preponderates. The first cost, about two shillings per yard, is considerable. The large space of ground which they occupy, and the injury which is done by their drip and shade to the roads and the crops, as well as the quantity of soil which is consumed in their formation, are serious considerations: not less than twenty-five feet can be reckoned for the width of the waste; nor is the mischief arising to the arable crops, by the obstruction which they present to the free circulation of the air, to be overlooked. They are said also to be liable to be torn down by the cattle of the next field. However, in hilly countries, with large fields, and without other fuel, they appear to be decidedly preferable. Much of the injury done to the crops might be obviated by preventing the coppice-wood on the mounds from spreading, by frequently cutting the sides of it, and suffering it to grow upwards only.

By the traveller these fences are justly complained of as an intolerable nuisance; for though he may be encompassed by the most extensive views and the richest scenery, all prospect of the surrounding country is completely shut out: nor will the sportsman think he has less reason for complaint. Against an invading army indeed they might afford an excellent protection; but, happily for this country, this is an advantage which needs not to be urged as a reason for their preservation. In some situations in the county the common low hedges of other quarters might be introduced with great propriety, and in several instances this plan has of late been adopted.

In the distribution of the land to its proper uses, as those of woodlands and farms, little has been done in general, probably since the laying out of townships; but in this there is considerable merit. It is desirable, that farms in the same district should be of various sizes to suit the convenience of different occupiers. Small farms have hitherto been generally prevalent in Devonshire, and are now perhaps too numerous; but it is not uncommon to observe two, three, or more of them thrown together and in the occupation of the same individual. The laying out of farms is commonly judicious. They lie well about the homestead, which is placed, not in the villages, but, as it ought to be, in the centre of the farm. The situation of the farm-house is in most cases well chosen, as on the side of the valley, or near the head of a combe or dell, where there is suitable shelter and a

Distribution of the land.

BOOK
IV.

rill of water.   Mr. Vancouver, however, contends, that
half-way up the hills would be infinitely more suitable, because more convenient for the conveyance of manure and
the produce of the lands.   When water is not on the spot,
leats, that is, rills or small canals, are cut for the purpose of
procuring the necessary supply.   This expedient, it seems,
has been employed from time immemorial; and if the leat
be conducted in a proper direction, it may be rendered of
admirable use by serving the purpose of irrigation to the
neighbouring lands.

Cobb-
walls.

The frequent recurrence of cobb- (that is, earth-)walls
throughout the county has an unsightly appearance, if
they are not plaistered, which however is often the case,
rough-cast being here well understood, both in theory and
practice.   The material of which farm-houses are built,
is usually stone; but the out-houses, and even the walls
of the farm-yard, are of earth, covered with thatch,
wherever stone is not to be had with convenience.   Numerous cottages and many of the dwelling-houses in the
villages are of the same materials.   Nor is it uncommon
to observe houses in the towns two stories high, built with
a frame of wood, filled up with cobb, and covered with
slate or thatch; and if plaistered and white-washed, they
have a tolerably decent and respectable appearance.   With
the abundance of stone in Devonshire, and lime for cement,
there can be no necessity surely for adopting a mode so
slovenly in the erection of inferior dwellings; nor can any
thing but the spirit of improvement be wanting to remedy
the evil.

Letting of
farms.

A few of the owners of lands are also the occupiers:
but in the disposal of farms an ancient practice, common
to the West of England, and formerly in very general use
here, still in some instances prevails, being indeed one of
the most distinguishing features of its rural œconomy.   The
farms, instead of being let to tenants, as in other counties,
at an annual rent equivalent to their value, are sold, generally for three lives, named by the purchaser, or for ninety-
nine years, provided any one of the parties so named sur-

vive that period; a small annual rent, however, being reserved by the owner of the land, together with an heriot, or other forfeiture on the death of the nominee, similar to those attached to the copyhold tenure, which indeed this very much resembles. It is also usual to put in fresh lives, as the preceding ones drop off, receiving a fine or adequate purchase for the addition of a fresh life. The first purchase is usually made at a species of auction, in which the seller fixes his price, and the highest bidder has the refusal. This kind of tenure is eagerly sought after by the farmer, as the land becomes, in some sort, his own property, and descends to his successors; and, if indeed he possess a suficient supply of ready money to stock his farm as it ought to be, and if at the same time he be endowed with industry, intelligence, and skill in his occupation, much benefit may be the result, both to himself and the public, from the permanency of this mode of tenure. The chances, however, are against all this, and on the whole, the disadvantages seem greatly to preponderate. The occupier has usually spent the whole of his property in the purchase, and has probably been obliged to borrow: the consequence is, that he has not the means of procuring sufficient stock and manure for his farm; and if he happen at the same time to be negligent, ignorant, and improvident, the farm is ill-managed, the land impoverished, and the produce deficient; and for these evils there is no remedy, as the landowner has no power to interfere. Accordingly, for these reasons, and others that are obvious, this system is on the decline; and many farms are now let upon the common plan of an annual rent, with or without leases for a term of years. The form or conditions of the leases, which it has been the practice to adopt, are said also, in many instances, to be absurd and mischievous, restricting the occupiers to antiquated modes of cultivation, and precluding the introduction of modern improvements and discoveries, which are frequently valuable. Knowledge surely travels slowly enough at the tail of the plough, and it must be quite superfluous to throw obstructions in the way of improve-

BOOK
IV.

Tithes.

The wood-
lands.

ments in agriculture, which, whilst nothing admits of more, usually, from the influence of prejudice and ignorance, receives less, or with greater difficulty.

The pressure of the tithe system is at present a subject of general complaint throughout the country, and is now said to be felt in a peculiar degree in Devonshire. It is stated to have been for a long time the practice in this district for the rector, whether lay or clerical, to send individuals through the parishes before the harvest, for the purpose of estimating the value of his tithes, and if the owner of the crop agrees to the valuation, he reaps the whole; if not, the tithes are taken in kind, which however seldom happens : but in either way the discouragement to agriculture is similar.

A considerable portion of the county is occupied by woodlands, which appear to be deserving of more attention than is commonly paid to them. A stranger indeed on a cursory and general view, from the constant succession of bare hills and the absence of trees in the hedge-rows, might be disposed to come to a different conclusion; but by directing his attention to the sides of the hills, the lower grounds and the margins of the rivers, he would find that this district is not deficient in this kind of produce. The species of timber-trees generally prevalent are the oak, the ash, the beech and the sycamore, with the elm on superior soils. The oak, however, is emphatically the timber here. The coppice wood consists of oak, birch, sallow, hazel and chestnut; the last being found in wild situations with every appearance of being a native. The wild cherry is also found in the coppices, but little or no hawthorn, which does not seem to be indigenous in the county. The history of these woodlands extends to time immemorial, and cannot be traced, as planting appears not to have been the fashion of this district. Their situations are in general eligible; small portions of them might indeed be advantageously converted into farms; but in most instances, the land which they occupy could not be applied to better purposes.

The writers on the subject * represent the management **C H A P.**
of the woods and coppices to be of the worst description. **I.**
The period of cutting the coppices is from twenty to
twenty-five years, and the usual mode of disposing of the
produce is by auction, which is hazardous and uncertain.
The ancient law, that a certain number of young trees in
each acre of coppice-wood should be left standing, is more
or less complied with here; but by evasion at the next
cutting these are taken down, and others left standing in
their stead; so that though there may be much coppice-
wood, little timber remains. A few pollards only are found
in the hedge-rows. After the common woods are cut
down, the oak is peeled standing, and this practice proceeds through the summer. This method, if convenient,
is still bad in husbandry; and wood, moreover, cut in
winter, before the fluids begin to circulate, would without
doubt be more durable than in the state in which it is cut
at present. The market for bark, after the county is
supplied, is Ireland; but the price is enormous, and bids
fair to extirpate the timber for ship-building altogether.
It is also to be lamented that so little attention is paid
in this district to the training of timber. Planting indeed
has latterly in some instances been attempted, but might
be carried with profit to a much greater extent. The chief
species proper for planting on the sides of the valleys,
sheltered from the frequent and cutting winds, is the oak.
The beech flourishes in exposed situations, as well as the
birch. In those that are most exposed the larch alone
is preferable, and if used in ship-building would be planted
with the prospect of great advantage. The Spanish chestnut is spoken of as indigenous in Devonshire; and this is
proved by the vast quantity of this wood found in old
buildings in the county. In several parks it flourishes
most luxuriantly. Why is it not more cultivated now?

Agriculture, however, or the cultivation of the land, is Hus-
the most important, as it is the most extensive branch of bandry.

---

* See particularly Marshall and Vancouver.

rural œconomy, and more immediately connected with the
means of human subsistence; but to do justice to this
topic, as it relates to Devonshire, would far exceed the
limits to which such an article, in a work of this kind,
must of necessity be confined.

Origin of different systems of husbandry.

The indications of a different origin for the rural œconomy
and the methods and implements of husbandry adopted
in the various provinces of the kingdom, are too obvious
and striking to be mistaken; and this circumstance would
constitute an interesting part of their history, if the extent
of this work would allow the subject to be pursued.
Whether the origin of these peculiarities may be found in
the ancient practice of the different settlers, or of their
conquerors, or in the different degrees of progressive improvement, it would now be sufficiently difficult to determine. The probability is, that each of these sources has
contributed to their production. Devonshire husbandry,
however, is by no means the least remarkable for its dis-
tinctive and singular customs, and for the slowness with
which it assimilates to the improved management of other
counties; circumstances which arise, no doubt, from the
remoteness of the situation, and the little intercourse which
operating farmers have here an opportunity of holding
with experimental and practical agriculturists in the best
cultivated districts. The chief obstacles to improvement
are unquestionably the want of information, and the almost
invincible attachment to ancient customs which the smaller
farmers especially in general discover;—evils greatly to
be deplored in an occupation so important as theirs, and
which by the introduction of improved management might
be rendered so much more beneficial to the community.

Singularities of Devonshire husbandry.

The principal singularities of Devonshire husbandry, as
enumerated by Mr. Frazer, are the following:—the life-
leasehold tenures; the general smallness of the farms;
the peculiar management of coppice-wood; the extraordinary nature of the fences, suggested probably by the
want of fuel, and the exposure of the country to the winds,
in consequence of the perpetual hills; the general pre-

valence of earthen walls in the farmeries, the gardens, and the cottages; no fixed time or place for the hiring of servants; the practice of putting out parish apprentices to husbandry; the carriage of agricultural produce and manure on horseback, and the absence of wheel-carriages; many, if not most, of the old implements of husbandry, particularly the plough; the practice of "beat-burning" for wheat and turnips; several singularities of the harvest, particularly the "arish-mow"; housing or stacking corn by hand, and winnowing in the open air; the sowing of wheat, and the culture of turnips without hoeing; watering the slopes of hills; orchard grounds; the singular method of raising cream; the shepherding and shearing of sheep without previous washing; and especially the breed of cattle, a beautiful and distinct variety, probably descending from the original native stock without mixture.

A brief notice of some of these subjects, which have not been already adverted to, is all that our limits will admit. And in the first place, a description of the common Devonshire plough (called in the county *zewl**) may perhaps be interesting to agriculturists, if not to antiquaries. The following is Mr. Vancouver's account of it. " The common Devonshire plough, made by a hedge-row carpenter, and seldom exceeding in cost fifteen shillings, irons included, is much used; and candour must allow, that its performance is very superior to what might be expected from the very rude appearance it makes, either at work, or lying out of use on the ground. It is a swing-plough, with a beam about seven feet long, lying nearly parallel to the head and heel of the plough: at the end of this beam is occasionally fastened a horizontal graduated iron, to which the team-band is affixed, and regulates from the line of draft the direction of the plough, either to the land or to the furrow. It is constructed to enter the land obliquely, and at an easy angle; and though there is little

The old Devonshire plough.

* Query *tool!* Marshall.

BOOK
IV.

apparent curve in its breast or mould-board, the strait
pieces of board (of which these are made) are placed and
continue so far backward, that in all cases, but particularly in whole ground, the furrow is lifted up and whelmed
completely over. The shares used in these ancient ploughs
differ in their forms according to the kind of work to be
performed with them. When the land is designed to be
ploughed clean, and to a good full pitch, a long pointed
share with a small fan or wing is used : when parting is
required, the wing of the share is considerably enlarged;
and when *velling* is performed, the wing of the share is
turned upward, forming a sharp comb upon its outside
angle." The annexed engraving of the old Devonshire
plough is copied from Mr. Vancouver's Survey.

Paring
plough.

Mr. Vancouver's description of the paring-plough now
in use may also be added. "This, which is meant to
supply the place of the breast-plough, or ancient paring-
shovel, has a wide-winged flat share, measuring about
fourteen inches from the land side to the angular point of
its right side or cutting wing. In the beam of this plough,
and preceding a sharp comb welded on the coulter margin
of the share, is a sliding foot, so fixed as to regulate the
precise thickness of slice intended to be pared. The share
and comb of this machine being kept very sharp by frequent grinding, enables it to perform its business well."
This writer also strongly recommends a thrashing machine
of improved construction, made by Baker of Exeter, and
other wheel- or mill-wrights in the county, costing, exclusively of the large frame timber, about forty guineas,
and now very prevalent in most parts of the county ; the
power being usually four horses, though water power, if
to be had, is of course preferred. The remainder of the
implements of husbandry peculiar to Devonshire, which
we have not room to notice here, are described by Messrs.
Marshall, Frazer, and Vancouver.

Labouring
oxen.

The ancient patriarchal custom of yoking oxen to the
plough still prevails both in Devonshire and Cornwall.

THE OLD DEVONSHIRE PLOUGH.

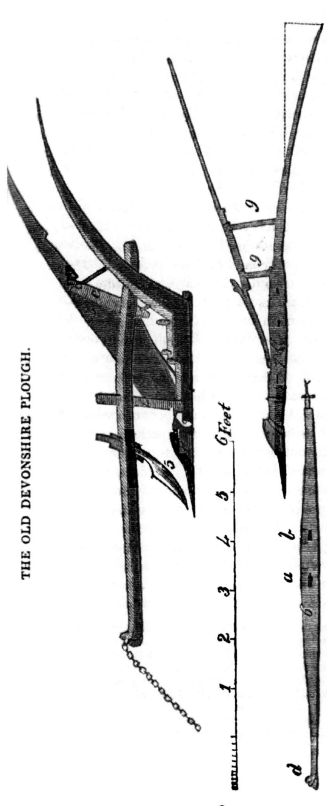

No. 1. The beam made of ash and bound with thin iron between the spill (4) and coulter (5) to prevent its splitting.——2. Land-hall or handle, made of oak, ash, or elm grown similar thereto, about four inches thick at the foot and beam mortice.——3. Furrow-hall or handle, made of 1¾ inch board, and nailed to the spill (4) and the cradle-piece (c).——4. The spill, made of ash, 1¾ inch thick by 3 inches in width.——5. Coulter about ¾ inch thick, and 2¼ inches in width at the neck, which is kept in place by wooden wedges, and when fixed it hangs over the share-point about ¾ inch towards the land.——6. Showing the top part of the beam, with the spill and coulter mortices a and b, and staple d to draw the plough by.——7. The sole-piece or chip, showing the splay of the two halls or handles, together with the share, and cradle-pins (9.9).

BOOK
IV.

Much of the field work is done by them, and they are occasionally seen upon the roads. The flesh is more esteemed
when the ox has been worked from two to four years.
Mr. Marshall speaks in the highest terms of the yoke for
these animals, as light and easy in its construction, and
possessing a contrivance by which the draft of the weaker
ox is relieved. In West Devon the native breed in use
is somewhat too small for the labour of the plough; but
the north, where this animal is larger, supplies the best
working cattle in the kingdom *.

Horse
carriage.

A remarkable feature in the rural management of this
county, is carriage of every kind on the backs of horses.
Hay, corn, fuel, stones, dung, lime, &c., and the produce
of the fields, are all conveyed on horseback : sledges, or
sledge-carts, are also used in harvest time, drawn chiefly
by oxen. Fifty years ago a pair of wheels was scarcely
to be seen on a farm in the county, and at present the
use of pack-horses still prevails, though on the decline.
This must have been the original mode of conveyance,
and the reason of its long continuance here evidently
arises, in part at least, from the hilliness of the country.
The same practice, however, does not occur in other hilly
districts, and its prevalence in modern periods in Devonshire must be attributed in a great measure to the original
want of judgement in laying out the roads, as well as to
the backwardness so common in the introduction of agricultural improvements. There may be many farms in
Devonshire in which the use of pack-horses ought never
to be laid aside; but there are others, consisting of some
hundreds of acres, where wheel carriages can be used with
as much ease and advantage as in any other county, and
the use of them is now being gradually introduced.

* The tone, or tune, with which the driving of the oxen is accompanied, is mentioned by agricultural writers as remarkable, and as resembling the chanting of the cathedral service; nor is it improbable that
it might originate in the Roman Catholic service, to which the people of
this county were formerly so much attached. The ploughboy is the
counter-tenor through the day, and the ploughman at intervals chants
the hoarser notes. This is supposed to animate the team; and it is certain that no where is so much cheerfulness observed in ploughing as in
Devonshire. The team is said to stop when the chanting ceases.

The manner in which horses are furnished for carriage is sufficiently remarkable to be described. Long crooks are generally fixed to pack-saddles for the purpose of removing corn, hay, straw, turf, or faggots. Having a form corresponding with the curve of the saddle, they descend rather below the line of the horse's girth, and there curving outwardly, form a bottom of from twenty inches to two feet in width, and then rising with a small inclination inward ascend to the height of about two feet eight inches or three feet above the line of the horse's back and withers. Within these crooks, which are two ascending on each side of the pack-saddle, there is no difficulty in placing any load equal to the strength of the horse. Stronger crooks are used for the heavier carriage, as poles, timber, &c., and for dung, stones and gravel, wicker baskets or pots, open at bottom, large enough to contain $1\frac{1}{2}$ cwt. of rotten dung each. Lime is carried in bags on the horse's back, and sometimes loose in horse-carts.

Mules are also much esteemed as beasts of burden; and being particularly suitable for this county, great numbers of them are employed for carriage, chiefly of coals and lime on the hilly roads. They are sometimes worked in teams. When bred from a Maltese parent, they are of a large size, and exceedingly fleet.

Mules.

The practice of " *beat-burning*," as it is called, that is sod-burning, has been mentioned before as one of the peculiarities of the husbandry both in Devonshire and Cornwall. It corresponds indeed with the paring and burning of other districts, but the method of conducting it is altogether different, and is confined to these counties, where it has been used in breaking up land from time immemorial. In the age of Risdon and Camden it was called " Denshiring," because peculiar to Devonshire, and the name is still known in the county*. This practice, in one respect at least, appears to be of real service, as it renders the land beautifully clean. Wherever the land is foul, it may

Beat-burning.

* The method is described, with its peculiarities, in Frazer's Survey and Marshall's Rural Economy.

BOOK
IV.

consequently be used with great advantage, and might be made a valuable instrument of improvement in bringing waste lands into cultivation; but in general a suitable rotation of crops, and common care in keeping the land clean, would render this practice unnecessary.

Irrigation.

The custom of irrigating grass-land is probably more ancient in Devonshire than in any other county. Mr. Marshall supposes it to have been brought from the Continent, where it has been in use from time immemorial. And when the great utility of the practice is considered, and when it is at the same time remembered how obvious this is rendered by experiment and observation, and how much water of a fertilizing quality abounds in this county, it is only extraordinary that irrigation is not become universal, wherever it is capable of being applied. The best example of improvement in this instance, as well as others, is James Templar, Esq. of Stover, who has converted considerable tracts of unproductive land, consisting of poor, thin, black mould, on a subsoil of cold clay, into fertile fields and meadows, chiefly by irrigation after previous draining. This was effected by means of a canal, extending from the sea to Bovey Tracey, with a branch to Newton Bushel. This canal is made to serve the double purpose of furnishing conveyance for limestone, potter's clay, Bovey coal, &c. and at the same time of giving fertility to the adjacent lands. Water of the most fertilizing quality appears to be that which is impregnated with calcareous matter; and as there is great difference in the qualities of waters, chemists, by analyzing them and making their properties known, might render an essential service to agriculture. As the Roman agriculturists made great use of irrigation*, particularly in their corn-fields as

---

* Quid dicam, jacto qui semine cominus arva
Insequitur, cumulosque ruit male pinguis arenæ?
Deinde satis fluvium inducit, rivosque sequentes;
Et cum exustus ager morientibus æstuat herbis,
Ecce, supercilio clivosi tramitis undam
Elicit: illa cadens raucum per levia murmur
Saxa ciet, scatebrisque arentia temperat arva.
                    VIRGIL. *Georg.* lib. i. l. 104.

well as grass-lands, when parched up by the heats of
summer, it is very possible the practice in Devonshire
might be derived from this people during their possession of the island.

From the uncertain state of the weather and the hu-
midity of the atmosphere, the time of harvest varies extremely here; but on an average of years, Devonshire is
ten days or a fortnight later than the midland counties.
The old method of cutting the wheat is by a kind of mowing with one hand by a hook, longer and broader than the
common sickle, and without teeth. The standing corn is
hewn down with the right-hand, and supported by the
left. This practice was in use in Kent and Surrey, but is
considered slovenly, and difficult to be done well: the
general method with the common sickle is therefore now
getting into use.

But one of the most remarkable singularities of harvest
in the West, is the "*arish-mow*" as it is called, that is,
collecting the corn into small stacks in the field, where it
stands some weeks to dry and harden before it is housed;
a clean and expeditious method of "saving the corn,"
admirably adapted to a climate where the weather is so
precarious, and no doubt originally suggested by this circumstance. The work-people bind not only the wheat
but the barley and oats in sheaves, which are collected
together in considerable numbers, and arranged upon
each other, with the heads inward in the form of a pyramid or cone, to shoot off the rain. Thus the grain is secured, and the wind finding an easy passage through the
stack, dries it thoroughly before it is conveyed to the barn.
This, we are told by some, is a Roman custom, and that
the name *arish* is derived from *aridus*, dry, whilst others
derive it from the Saxon.

Mr. Vancouver's account of the reaping and harvesting
of wheat is too singular and amusing to be omitted. "The
wheat being ready," he observes, "amounting from ten
to twenty acres, notice is given to the neighbourhood that
a reaping is to be performed on a particular day, when,

BOOK
IV.

as the farmer may be more or less liked, an indefinite number of men and women assemble in the field, and the reaping commences after breakfast, which is seldom till between eight and nine o'clock. The company is open for additional hands to drop in at any time before twelve, to partake of the frolics of the day. By eleven or twelve o'clock the ale or cider has so much warmed and elevated their spirits, that their noise, jokes and ribaldry are heard to a considerable distance, and often serve to draw together auxiliary forces within the accustomed time. The dinner, consisting of the best meat and vegetables, is carried into the field between twelve and one o'clock, and is followed by plenty of ale and cider. At two the pastime of cutting the wheat is resumed, and is continued without interruption, except the squabbles of the company, until five, when what are called the drinkings are taken into the field, and under the shade of a hedge-row or a large tree, the panniers are examined, and bunns, cakes, and all such articles are found, as the confectionary skill of the farmer's wife could produce, for gratifying the appetites of her customary guests at this season.

"After the drinkings, which continue for half or three quarters of an hour, the amusement of harvest is continued, with binding up the sheaves till the evening. This done, a small sheaf is bound up and set upon the top of one of the ridges, when the reapers retiring to a certain distance, each throws his reaping-hook at the sheaf, until one more fortunate or less inebriated than the rest strikes it down. This is accompanied by the utmost stretch and power of voice by the whole company, uttering words very indistinctly but somewhat to this purpose; *We ha in! we ha in!* * This noise and tumult continues about half an

---

* There is no puzzle here for the antiquary. *In*, or rather *en*, is generally used by the working people in the West for the pronouns *him* and *it*. *Ha* is no doubt an abbreviation of *have*, as in some other counties. The exclamation therefore is, *We have it! we have it!* meaning, We have gained the object in pursuit, or We have done what we intended. The frolics of rustics, especially after drinking, are often like those of children.

hour, when the company retire to the farm-house and sup, which being over large portions of ale and cider enable them to carouse and vociferate until one or two o'clock in the morning. The next day the company proceeds to a neighbouring farmer's, and a similar scene is repeated. No wages are paid the reapers on these occasions; but an invitation is given them to the farmer's house to partake of a harvest frolic, and at Christmas open house is kept for three or four days and nights. On the whole this custom is deserving of reprobation, as very expensive, and leading to great excesses." It is said to be still continued in some parts of the county, but, like many other ancient practices, is gradually yielding to modern improvements.

THE SOUTH-HAMS.

The natural boundaries of that portion of the county which is known by the name of the South-Hams, are Dartmoor and the heights of Chudleigh on the north; Plymouth Sound on the west; Torbay on the east, and the English Channel on the south; the whole being nearly in the form of a triangle, the base of which on the sea-coast being about thirty miles, and the perpendicular fifteen: but including the rich vale of the Dart towards Ashburton, it may form an area of about 250 square miles, or 160,000 square acres.

The estuaries with which it is deeply indented, and which are filled by the tides, afford great facilities for inland navigation. In an agricultural view it is to be considered as an upland district, the bolder swells, which may be termed heights, although but hillocks when compared with the mountains that overtop them on the north, being in the centre. When viewed from Dartmoor, whence almost every acre may be seen, this district seems to be flat; but in crossing the country it is found to be billowy in the extreme. The whole is well supplied with excellent water, rills being often found even near the summits of the hills. The climate here is more mild and salubrious than

BOOK
IV.

Soil.

Subsoil.

Town-
ships.

Roads.

in any other part of the island.   Violent winds, however,
and heavy rains, chiefly from the south-west, are not unfrequent.

With regard to the fertility of the soil, few districts in
the kingdom can be placed in competition with the South-
Hams. A rich loam abounds in the vicinity of Ivybridge,
and thence to Kingsbridge the soil is uniformly fertile: even on the tops of some of the hills the grass is
abundant; on their sides is excellent corn land, and the
bottoms are luxuriant meadows. In this quarter the red
soil occasionally appears. From Kingsbridge to Totnes
the land is of a similar description, except in the higher
swells, where it is of inferior quality. In this part the red
soil abounds, and the water is deeply tinged of a similar
colour. In the environs of Totnes the soil is rich in the
extreme, even to the summits of the hills. From Totnes
to Ivybridge the land, though of the same character, is
not perhaps of equal value. On the whole the general
quality of the soil, though in various parts of it too shallow,
is that of extreme fertility.

The subsoil in the west of the South-Hams consists
chiefly of slaty rock, or slate-stone rubble. A vein of
limestone or marble runs along the south; in different
parts of its area a deep red ochrey loam is observed; and
at the foot of the Dartmoor hills gravel abounds. These
are incidental variations. The land is in general clean,
sound, adapted either to corn or grass, and inclined to
absorbency in the extreme.

Some of the townships in the northern part of the
South-Hams are very large, arising perhaps from the
unreclaimed state of the lands when the divisions were
formed, the inclosures being probably of modern date.

The most frequented turnpike roads in this district are
greatly improved, and are now in excellent condition, with
the exception of being too narrow in some places, especially when the high fences are taken into consideration.
But the roads to the small towns, villages and farms, are
wretched; crooked, extremely narrow, and being often

PLYMOUTH, DEVON.

Drawn by G. B. Campion.

Engraved by James Ryan(?)

carried over the tops of the hills, are sometimes too steep
even for sledges.

The whole of the district is in a state of permanent inclosure, with Danmonian fences and small square fields,
except where the roads wind between them, showing apparently that the country was inclosed at once from a
state of common pasture. Woods abound on the banks
of the Dart, but elsewhere scarcely a coppice is to be seen,
and not a tree in the hedge-rows. From these circumstances, together with the general roundness of the hills,
a considerable part of the South-Hams is not remarkable
for picturesque beauty. The banks of the Dart, the scenery
below Kingsbridge, that both below and above Ivybridge,
and the view from Modbury churchyard, however, are
splendid exceptions. The northern margin is also finely
diversified.

The general size of the farms here is much too small to
admit of extensive agricultural improvement. Happily the
tenure of farms by life-leases in this district is now getting
out of use, as the capital being devoured by the original
fine, the want of exertion generally attending the payment
of a small rent, and the prospect of losing all interest in
the property when the last life is in the wane, are causes
operating powerfully against permanent improvement.

But though the system of leasing estates for lives
may be said on the whole to be rapidly declining, there
are still very extensive districts held by this tenure.
There are few landlords now indeed, unless in very neces-
sitous circumstances, who grant additional lives: most
proprietors are suffering the lives of former leases to run
out; and as the estates come into possession, it is the present custom to grant what are termed rack-leases for fixed
periods, at a full annual rent, without purchase-money for
the lease. The periods vary in different districts, as seven,
fourteen, or twenty-one years, and in other instances ten.
In all cases in which more than one period is mentioned
in the lease, it is optional with either party to determine
with respect to the continuance of the lease, at the ex-

piration of either of these terms, but not at any intermediate time.   Poverty and the law of entail have each contributed their aid towards giving perpetuity to the old
custom, generally prevalent in the generation preceding
the present, of letting farms for three lives at the nomi-
nation of the purchaser.   A person whose property consists almost exclusively of land which is entailed, has often
no other method of providing for his remaining family, or
of effecting a just distribution of his property.   It is however a fact, that in the ordinary circumstances of entailed
property, the practice of leasing for lives is declining.   But
there are cases (not indeed strictly of entailed estates) in
which the present possessor does not feel much, if any,
interest in the welfare of his successor; and in these instances we find the system of life-leases still obtains.   This
is strikingly exemplified in the case of ecclesiastical bodies and some other corporations.   They often sell leases,
it is true, for a certain period, as perhaps for twenty-one,
or thirty years, instead of lives; but the principle and its
operation are of a similar kind *.

Improved
state of
the hus-
bandry.

The general system of husbandry in this district is
similar to that in the western, which has been already described.   Greater improvements, however, in the methods
of agricultural management are said to be introduced here
than in any other part of the county.   In this quarter intelligent and well-informed agriculturists have done much
for the prevalence of a better system than that formerly
in use.   Agricultural Associations, moreover, and Horti-
cultural Societies, have been formed in several parts of
the county, and there seems to be a general disposition
to give encouragement to such institutions.   This is
a propitious circumstance.   If " he who causes two
blades of grass to grow where one grew before is a bene-
factor to his country," how much good may reasonably
be expected from the association of gentlemen who unite
science to practice and independent thinking, for the ex-

* From information communicated by an intelligent resident in the
county.

press purpose of rendering the earth as productive of the means of human subsistence and comfort as possible!

VALE OF THE EXE.

The district usually included in the Vale of the Exe being bounded by an extremely irregular outline, it is difficult to calculate its extent. By a random estimate it may be supposed to contain about 200 square miles. It may be considered as extending from the sea along the banks of the estuary and the river, as far to the north-east as Tiverton, and on the north beyond Crediton. On the west it is bounded by the extremities of Dartmoor, or rather by the unproductive lands in the vicinity of the forest. Near the sea it is contracted by Haldon on the west, and on the east by a range of unproductive lands between the Otter and the Exe. It is termed a vale district, because it partakes more of this character than any other part of the county; and round Ottery, the Clists, along the eastern banks of the estuary, and near Exeter, much of the country is of the true vale description. But between Tiverton and Exeter there are elevations of considerable magnitude; and between Exeter and Collumpton, as well as in other parts, there is much billowy surface.

There is considerable variety in the soil throughout this district, showing the origin of its formation in the several instances to be different. From Honiton to Exeter there is much deep, strong, good land, partly brown, and in part having a strong tinge of red. This is the first red soil observed on entering the West of England. Round Exeter the soil is a reddish deep loam, having the quality of singular fertility: north of the city it varies in productiveness according to the substrata. When the rock does not rise too near the surface, it is fertile to the summits of the higher swells. On the south, between Exeter and Topsham, there is much fine land, chiefly arable, of the first quality, and essentially different from the siliceous soils of the county. From Exeter to Nutwell by Heavi-

Vale of the Exe.

Soil.

tree and Bishop's Clist, the soil and substratum are inclined to red, intermixed with gravel, the whole hardening
in some places into a sort of pudding-stone, used for ordinary buildings.   In the environs of Nutwell are some
strong red land; much dark, pebbly loam of tolerable
quality; some light sandy soil, and some still poorer,
black and moor-like.   Above Woodbury a cold, weak,
woodland soil prevails.   From Exeter in the direction of
Tiverton the hills in general are covered with light turnip
and barley land; but in the intervening part of the Vale
the strong red loam abounds, very suitable for wheat and
beans.   About Bradninch is a rich vale of grass land.   In
the environs of Tiverton the general soil is red, and of
superior quality; and towards Maiden Down, through Halberton, is also a portion of red soil, with a fine rich vale.

Subsoil.   The lands in the Vale, as elsewhere, are of course characterized by the strata beneath.   The strong red soil
covers a subsoil of clay, or loam of the same colour.   The
strong brown soil is also incumbent upon earth of a kindred colour inclining to black; and the rich productive
lands round Exeter, and towards Tiverton, &c. have a
peculiar kind of earthy gravel for their basis.   On the west
the same soil on the higher lands is incumbent on a sort
of slaty rock or schistus, rising near the surface.   But
the prevailing subsoils of the high grounds in the area of
the Vale is a red sand, and in an instance between Tiverton and Maiden Down is found a variegated substratum,
composed of thin layers of red and white loam and sand,
resembling what is seen in Gloucestershire and the red
lands of Nottinghamshire.   These instances suffice to
show that the Vale of Exeter is formed from different
materials*.

The red marly loam prevalent in parts of this district
and the south of Devon, is not exceeded in fertility by

---

* Mr. Marshall, to whose work the writer is chiefly indebted for this
account of the soils, observes, that from Stoke Hill, about a mile north
of Exeter, these various soils may be distinguished by their productions
in an interesting point of view.

any in the island, and is usually of considerable depth. According to Mr. Frazer it consists of firm rocky marl, easily friable when exposed to the air or water; feels greasy or soapy in the hand, and effervesces in acids. It contains much calcareous earth; produces rich grass, as well as strong crops of corn, but is more suitable for feeding bullocks. Trefoil springs up everywhere spontaneously; and irrigating the surface renders the grass wonderfully luxuriant. Intervening downs, especially in the east, serve extremely well for sheep. Towards the eastern extremity a rich stratum is found upon white chalk, and there also blue marl prevails.

In the Vale of the Exe the climate is much more favourable than in West Devon, and the rain much less, the clouds from that quarter being intercepted by the hills. The seasons are forwarder, and so mild is the weather, that near Exeter the grass grows freely in general through the winter months. The inhabitants consider the Vale as the richest and finest country in the world; and indeed a stranger upon entering it cannot fail to be struck with the healthy, vigorous, and luxuriant appearance of every species of vegetable production, especially the trees and shrubs. The elm flourishes, and arrives at great magnitude here as well as along the valley of the Yealm. The growth of the myrtle has been mentioned before, as a singular proof of the mildness of the climate and fertility of the soil; and Mr. Vancouver has stated that Mr. Hutchinson of Dittisham had in his possession, about twenty years ago, the stump of the double-flowering, broad-leaved species of this shrub, whose cross diameter measured about eight or ten inches. The head was luxuriant in proportion, so that being near the house and causing dampness, it became necessary to cut it down. He also observes, that Lord Clifford had a red cedar cut down in his park at thirty years growth, which afforded boards twenty-two inches in breadth and twelve feet long. These instances are sufficient to show the extraordinary strength of vegetation in this vicinity.

The villages about Exeter are surrounded with trees, which give a rich and beautiful appearance to the country. The fields are remarkable for their smallness, indicating early inclosure; but the mounds of the hedge-rows are not so high as in the south and west, and are besides generally furnished with trees, which, however, the land being of great value, are unfortunately lopped, oak as well as elm, close to the stems, leaving only a small portion of foliage at the top;—a practice which greatly injures their growth, and entirely destroys the beauty of their appearance.

The towns are generally populous, cheerful, and finely situated, particularly Exeter and Tiverton; and many of the cottages are neat in their appearance. Farm-buildings, however, are without plan, and meanly constructed, earth and straw being the chief materials. The walls of the farm-yards and gardens are of "*cob*," or strong red loam mixed with gravel, which becomes hard like stone, and if kept dry will last for ever, as they have been used from time immemorial. The walls are from fourteen inches to two feet thick. Barns and dwelling-houses of almost every size are constructed of these materials, even in the environs of Exeter itself.

Inland navigation.

The only inland navigation in the Vale is by means of the estuary, and a canal thence to Exeter. But if the projected canal from the city, through Crediton to Oakhampton, should be completed, and another thence with collateral branches to Torrington, where it would join the Bude canal and also one already constructed by Lord Rolle to Bideford, Devonshire would be nearly unrivalled in the means of internal transfer. Scarcely a farm in the county would be more than one day's journey from water carriage, and the advantage to the land would be incalculable.

Although in the remote parts of the county there still exists that blind and absurd partiality to old practices, which is the greatest enemy to all improvement, yet in the vicinity of Exeter and other large towns, as well as in

many extensive districts, the husbandry is excellent, and
the farmers are ready to listen to useful suggestions, or to
adopt any improvement that may fairly promise to be be
neficial.

NORTHERN DISTRICT.

The Northern district is an extensive tract between the
Bristol Channel and the mountains of Dartmoor, together
with the Vale of Exeter, including Oakhampton, Hatherleigh, Hartland, Torrington, Bideford, Barnstaple, South
Molton, Dulverton, and Ilfracombe. In so large an extent
of country such is the variety of soils, that the limits of
this work will not allow a minute and particular description
of them all, nor of all the remarkable features of the husbandry in this quarter.

The principal soils in the county are briefly described by
Risdon, and, observes the Introduction to that work, "with
sufficient accuracy for such an account; but the proportion
of each in point of extent is not mentioned. They divide
naturally into four sorts, the first of which is found to occupy the smallest space. ' On the east side of the shire
the mould standeth upon white chalk, which is passing
good for sheep and corn.' The second is the red land,
which surrounds Exeter, and extends considerably east
and west of it : this soil, he observes, 'is most natural for
pasture of beasts, though it is plentifully furnished with
corn'. The third is the peat soil, of which Dartmoor
furnishes the principal example. The fourth, which per-
vades by far the greater part of the county, though varied
in its appearance by continual admixtures, is what of late
has obtained the name of *Dun-land*. It is furnished probably by the decomposition of the schistus rock on which
it lies, and is found in almost every state, from the most
fertile to the most sterile." This it is which appears to be
most prevalent in the north.

After admitting that the land in the south of the county
is of such value, and so fertile that it may be called the
Garden of Devonshire, Risdon also observes, that "in the

CHAP.
I.

The north-
ern di-
strict.

Soils.

north and west parts the land is more lean and barren,
except about towns, where the husbandman by improvement hath enforced fertility ; and near the sea, from whose
shore sand is carried to better their grounds both for grain
and grass, otherwise so churlish and unthankful to the
husbandman's labour, that it hardly affords rye and oats;
for moors and hills are intractable for tillage : only in a
few places of the inland, a vein of red land soil showeth
itself, which indeed is accounted chief, as most nourishing
the grass cast into it, that seldom it frustrates the husbandman's hopes." But with respect to the sterility of
the north, Risdon must either have been greatly mistaken,
or cultivation since his time has made wonderful improvements, for great quantities of valuable land are now to be
seen in this district as well as in the western.

The general aspect of the country is billowy like the
south, and the greater part of it has now at least assumed
an appearance of great fertility and luxuriance. Some
notices of the principal soils in particular spots are all that
our limits will allow to be given ; and for a more particular
description we must refer to Marshall's Rural Economy
of the Western Counties, and to Frazer's, but especially
Vancouver's, Survey.

Oakhamp-
ton.

Beginning with Oakhampton, we cannot omit noticing
the ruins of the ancient castle, occupying a peninsular
hillock, and facing the bold, woody steeps on the borders
of Dartmoor, which are divided from it by the western
branch of the Oke. The scenery partakes of the alpine
character. The castle is situated upon slate rock, like
that, says Mr. Marshall, of the west and south. In the
vicinity are fertile swells, covered with grass, stocked with
excellent cows of the northern breed, but producing little
corn. On the road to Torrington, seventeen miles, cultivation extends to a short distance from the town; the
soil apparently good, on a slaty subsoil, fit for any purpose of agriculture. Further onward is an inclosed upland country with some red soil, succeeded by highly
improvable commons, with patches of excellent wheat.

Thousands of acres of dwarf furze are to be seen, which ought to be supplanted by wheat, beans and clover. Some timber trees are observed. The subsoil of these commons is a red clayey gravel.

The environs of Hatherleigh, a mean market-town, with houses chiefly of red earth and thatch, some of which are whitewashed or rough-cast, consist of red-soiled inclosures, with a subsoil of rubble, red as ochre. Between Hatherleigh and Shipwash is a finely wooded country, which is succeeded by a wild flat of marsh land, in a state of great neglect. *Hatherleigh.*

The inclosures of this district resemble those of the south, except that the mounds of the fences are not quite so large. The woodlands are extensive, the oak being the prevailing timber, much of which is fine. Coppices are also frequent. Arable crops of wheat and oats are small in proportion to grass and furze, nor are they very abundant. The method of sowing and preparing the land is similar to that in the south.

The general character of the soil throughout the northern parts of the parish of Hartland, is that of a light, tender loam, resting on a substratum of clay. In the vicinity of Torrington is also a loose free loam of good quality on a deep rubble subsoil. This town, large, neat and lively, situated on the eastern bank of the Torridge, is surrounded by many family residences which adorn the neighbourhood. The view from the east of the castle is uncommonly fine, over a wooded amphitheatre, richly diversified, with a lengthened bend of the stream in the middle. *Hartland.*

Bideford, seven miles from Torrington, is situated in a rich and beautiful country. The old road crosses a well-wooded valley. The general surface being divided into hill and dale, the upland soil is strong and good, on a subsoil of brown rusty rock. The whole appearance of the country is Danmonian, bearing considerable resemblance to the south-western district. Carts as well as pack-horses are in use here for the conveyance of lime and sea-sand. The town itself is remarkably forbidding, with houses meanly *Bideford.*

built, situated at the side of a steep hill. The bridge is
an extraordinary erection, described by Marshall as a thick
wall, with here and there a Gothic archway to let the water
pass. The views here, however, are worthy of the pencil;
on the north grand, and on the south highly picturesque.
The country is wholly inclosed, and the fields large : the
produce chiefly grass, and but little corn. Large herds
of cattle and flocks of sheep are indications of larger farms
than in other parts of the county. On the north side of
the town is a rich loamy soil to the very summit of the
hills. From this quarter is an admirable view of Barnstaple Bay, with its finely diversified coast. The entire
environs are studded with houses.

Climate.
The climate of this district is much less favourable than
in the south. The north-east winds are extremely injurious : the fences of coppice-wood are cut down by them.

State of
husban-
dry.
The state of husbandry in this district is much superior to that of some other parts of the county. A laudable
industry is observable in collecting and preparing manures.
This quarter greatly resembles the south of Devon, both
with regard to natural character and agricultural management, except in a manifest superiority in the breed of cattle
and horses, as well as in a more general use of wheel-
carriages.

From Bideford to Barnstaple, eight miles, is a broad
billowy district, consisting of rounded swells, with deep
narrow valleys. The materials of these hills are chiefly
decayed schistus, on rusty rubble of the same character.

Banks of
the Taw.
On the banks of the Taw are branches of marsh land
of reddish clay, stocked with cattle, but admitting of great
improvement. In the wide valley of this river, the land
in general is cold and swampy, with rushy inclosures and
rough furze ground. There is also much oak-wood, but
the timber is greatly injured by the wind and cold substratum. Nearer Barnstaple are seen excellent cattle
grazing on rich marshes. The whole country is inclosed
in large fields, with Danmonian fences, and the farms appear to be larger. Barnstaple is a populous and better

built town than Bideford. Pilton is a pleasant village adjoining Barnstaple. A bold promontory rising abruptly in the centre of the broad valley above the town, severs the Taw from the brook of Pilton. The scenery is finely picturesque. Draining, burning, and fallowing the cold rough lands of this quarter, would obviously be an improvement. Above Barnstaple is a rich flat of meadow or marsh lands nearly a mile wide, evidently formed by the tide and floods, and well stocked with beautiful cattle.

In the district round Ilfracombe, Combe Martin, South Molton, and along the borders of Somersetshire, the soil appears to be of a light sandy colour on a stratum of dunstone. On the road from Barnstaple to South Molton, eleven miles, the lofty swells are productive, like those of the South-Hams, to their summits. At Filleigh, Earl Fortescue's noble demesne breaks at once upon the eye with its fine woods and water. The farmery is large; and herds of young cattle, with flocks of sheep, are seen feeding on the grounds about the house. Near is a quarry of limestone not less than fifty feet deep, similar to Chudleigh marble, but not quite so dark. The country is inclosed and the soil good, but the roads in this quarter are much complained of.

South Molton is situated on a rounded hill among similar elevations equally beautiful and productive. The soil is a rich loam on a slaty rubble, or soft-checkered rock. This is one of the finest farming districts in the kingdom. Not an acre of unproductive land is seen in the vicinity.

The inhabitants of North Devon are in general intelligent and civilized; and the state of husbandry on the whole superior. To the management of live stock—horses, cattle and swine—in this district, more than ordinary attention has been paid for a considerable length of time.

The number of individuals who possess extensive landed property in Devonshire is not large. Some of the principal proprietors are, the Duke of Bedford, Earl Fortescue, the Earl of Mount Edgecumbe, Lord Rolle, Lord Clifford, Lord Courtenay, Lord Graves, Lord Morley, Lord Clinton,

Sir Bourchier Wrey, Sir John Kennaway, Sir T. Dyke Acland, Sir H. Davy, Sir L. V. Palk, Sir A. Chichester, Sir John St. Aubyn, the Hon. Newton Fellowes, E. P. Bastard, Esq., R. W. Newman, Esq., and ——— Waldron, Esq. The rest of the land is very much divided. A large portion of it is in the hands of respectable yeomen: other estates belong to the Sees of Exeter, York, and Salisbury; to the Dean and Chapter of Windsor, the Universities, and the Duchy of Cornwall,—forming together no inconsiderable portion of the whole county. In no other part of England, it is said, are the care and management of estates deputed so much to attorneys and unqualified persons as in Devonshire; and from the want of knowledge, and the interested views of these persons, it is also affirmed, much detriment to agriculture results.

I cannot refrain from inserting here the following passage from Mr. Vancouver's Survey, to the correctness of which, I must beg leave to add, my intercourse with the natives, whether personal or by correspondence, as far as it extends, bears ample testimony. "It has been remarked by Mr. Frazer, and the author of this report most cordially agrees in the observation, that there is an openness of heart and mildness of character in the inhabitants of Devonshire, which probably is not to be excelled in any part of England. A general urbanity of manners, and desire to please, and meet the wishes of the stranger, prevail among all classes of the community, from the peer to the peasant; even in those who compose the lower order of society, and among whom we are to find both male and female servants."

MANURES.

Food of plants.

Soil, we are told by scientific men, as applicable to the growth of vegetables, consists, in general, of the following predominant parts: calcareous or lime earth; siliceous or flinty earth; argillaceous, or clay; magnesian and carbonaceous matter from the decomposition of vegetables, which is commonly called mould. The vegetable power, says Mr. Haywood, depends on the latter altogether. He observes, however, that the use of lime is most important in agriculture, as vegetation depends upon the calcareous principle: yet he adds, lime is not a manure, but an alterative, as it does not form any part of the food of plants, but assists the decay of vegetable matter, and prepares the soil for the purpose of vegetation*. But the intelligent and scientific editor of Risdon appears to have adopted, with Kirwan in his valuable work on Manures, a different principle; for he says, " Certain plants require calcareous mixture in the soil more than others, and of course withdraw more of the same principle in their growth. Those plants which it is the farmer's object to cultivate are of the sort which require it in the greatest degree: lime forms a principal constituent part of grain: clovers have a part of it in their formation, as well as some other valuable grasses; while the inferior kinds of herbage are found on analysis to contain little or none of this primitive earth.

" Hence we see why lime produces such effects on a soil where it does not naturally exist; why grain may be grown, as Risdon says, ' where formerly such never grew in any living man's memory;' and why, on the other hand, lands that have been fertilized by the valuable addition of lime, are again made barren by the practice of taking crop after crop of corn, which rapidly withdraws this nutritious principle, and leaves the ground unfit for the production of anything but the inferior grasses. This is the prominent evil of Devonshire husbandry in the arable lands, and no opportunity should be lost of exposing and reprobating it†."

Agricultural chemistry, however, appears to be yet in its infancy; and accordingly Mr. Haywood admits that on the subject of the food of plants it is evident little is known by chemists. And it is perfectly true, as observed in the Introduction to Risdon, that " practice is often be-

* Haywood on the Science of Agriculture, &c.; with Strictures on the works of Kirwan and Sir Humphry Davy.
† Introduction to Risdon, p. v.

fore science in its operations; and a casual experiment has
established the value of a measure before the reasoning
upon it could commence. This is precisely the case with
the use of lime in Devon as a manure. We find by Risdon, that in his time this practice was new. 'Of late,'
he says, 'a new invention has sprung up, and been practised, by burning lime, and incorporating it for a season
with earth, and then spread upon arable land, hath produced a plentiful increase of all sorts of grain among us,
*where formerly such never grew in any living man's me-
mory.*' That the greater proportion of Devonshire soils
is defective in calcareous mixtures, will better appear from
the nature of the rocks, the decomposition of which has
furnished these soils." Hence the value of lime in the
cultivation of land in Devonshire is obvious, whatever be
the mode in which it operates.

Sir Humphry Davy observes, "It is not known what
was the precise time when lime came into common use as
a manure in the cultivation of land. A substance which
had been applied with success in the improvement of
gardens, would be soon tried in farming; and in counties
in which marl was not found, calcined limestone would be
naturally used as a substitute. The old writers on agriculture had no correct notion of limestone or marl, nor of
their effects;—the necessary consequence of their little
skill in husbandry. Calcareous matter was considered by
the alchemists as a peculiar earth, which, in the fire, became combined with inflammable acid; and Evelyn and
Hartlit, and still later Lisle, in their works on husbandry,
have characterized it merely as a hot manure, of use in cold
lands. It is to Dr. Black of Edinburgh that our first distinct
rudiments of knowledge on the subject are owing. About
the year 1755, this celebrated Professor proved, by the
most decisive experiments, that limestone, and all its modifications, marble and marls, consist principally of a peculiar earth united to an aërial acid, and that the acid is
given out in burning, occasioning a loss of more than 40
per cent., and that the lime in consequence becomes caustic.

These important facts he immediately applied with equal
certainty to the explanation of the use of lime, both as a
cement and manure." But whatever be the nature of its
operation, it is important for the purposes of agriculture
that practice has established its utility. If lime is within
a convenient distance, little else is in general sought after
in Devonshire as manure : the farmers in the county consider it as best adapted to their land, and consequently as
the most beneficial. It is a striking remark of the distinguished writer just quoted, that " Nature has, in her wisdom, so placed the materials of which she formed the surface of the ground, that there may be always discovered,
near any soil, some subsoil, or matter most suitable for the
land adjoining." In many counties this remark is applicable to marl; in Devonshire, to lime, as few parts of the
county are placed at a very inconvenient distance from some
vein or other of this rock. It must be added, that lime
may be used injudiciously and to excess, and in that case
would do injury, and not good.

CHAP.
I.

We learn from Risdon, that in his time the method of
applying the lime was by mixing it with earth, and letting
it remain in this state for some time before spreading it
on the land : and this method is still continued. A compost is formed of lime, earth, and burnt ashes, in the proportion of forty-eight Winchester bushels heaped to an
acre, with ten or twelve parts of earth and ashes to one
of lime. The earth is taken from near the edge of the
fields, by turning up three or four deep furrows about
Christmas, to lie for compost. Another method is by
spreading the lime in powder upon the soil, reduced to a
fine tilth, and mixing them with a roller, or by harrowing,
till the whiteness of the lime disappears. The latter method
is the least expensive, and the most complete. The price
of lime is regulated by that of the culm with which it is
burnt, and which is brought from Wales.

When lime cannot be procured with facility, or is too
expensive for the farmer, sea-sand has been used from time
immemorial as manure. It is of two kinds;—one, found
at the mouth of the rivers, is a compound of common sand

Sea-sand.

and mud; the other seems to be clear fragments of broken shells without mixture, in appearance resembling bran. It has been usual to mix it in the proportion of 200 seams (400 bushels), with earth, mud or rotten dung, to the amount of 120 seams; in the mixture of which no care or labour are spared. This compost is reckoned by good farmers an excellent manure, and even more desirable than lime. The latter kind of sand is preferred: and Mr. Parkes is of opinion, that the beneficial operation of this sand undoubtedly depends upon the presence of calcareous matter; but at the same time he observes, " We are borne out by unequivocal facts in believing that the sea-salt with which it is impregnated contributes materially to its fertilizing power *." To this it may be added, that the shells of which sea-sand consists, may possibly contain animal matter of an unctuous or oily quality, which may contribute to the fertility of the soil †.

Soap-ashes act powerfully upon the land, and contri-

Soap-
ashes.

* See A Letter to Farmers and Graziers on the Advantages of using Salt, by S. Parkes, F.L.S. p. 59; and also Dr. Paris's Memorial in the Transactions of the Royal Geological Society of Cornwall, Vol. i.

" From evidence it appears," says Mr. Parkes, " that a great portion of the land in this kingdom might, by the proper use of salt, be made to produce double. It destroys weeds, grubs, worms, flies, and insects, and at the same time gives extreme luxuriance and verdure to grass lands when rightly applied. Great care and judgement, however, are necessary in the use of it; since, if applied in too great quantities, it would inevitably do much injury."

Mr. Haywood's remarks on this subject are, that " sea-salt never can contribute as an article of food to the increase of any vegetable. It acts only as a chemical agent, by destroying and facilitating the decomposition of animal and vegetable matter, and by its deliquescence it may in some instances increase the fertility of the soil." He also observes, that sea-salt may contribute to promote vegetation, just as mustard, cinnamon, &c. assist in promoting the digestion of the food of animals; that is, by stimulating the action of vegetables.

† Some years ago, much was said about the wonderfully fertilizing quality of oyster-shells, when reduced to powder, or nearly so. The writer is not acquainted with the result of experiments with this material: but if sand, consisting of small shells or their fragments, proves to be a useful manure, why should not the shells of oysters, or of other larger fish, if pulverized, be found to serve the same purpose? May they not possess calcareous or saline qualities, in addition to animal matter in their pores, which would have a tendency to assist vegetation? If so, this article may be had in abundance everywhere, without expense, except in collecting and preparing the shells for use. The experiment seems to be worth a trial.

bute greatly to its fertility, but, from their bulk and weight, can seldom be used at a distance from large towns, unless their conveyance be facilitated by water-carriage. A soap manufactory has been established in Plymouth a considerable number of years by Mr. Thomas Gill; it is now in full work, and making many thousand tons of ashes yearly. At first, the farmers being unacquainted with their value, they lay on hand; but at present they meet with a ready sale. Whether as a manure or an alterative, they are highly beneficial, and are much used in Devonshire.

It is much to be regretted that hitherto the agriculturists of Devon have remained unacquainted, at least practically, with the benefits of bone-manure, which is said to be the richest now known. Bones have been shipped off from Plymouth by the vessels which bring coals and timber from the North, and have generally ascended the Humber to fertilize the lands in the counties of York, Lincoln, and Nottingham, instead of enriching the soil on which they were raised. The small cellules of bones are filled with an oily or mucilaginous substance, which appears to be exceedingly conducive to the growth of vegetables. If they are not reduced too small, and the decomposition is allowed to take place gradually, their fertilizing quality retains its power three or four years; but if reduced to powder, a much smaller quantity is used at once, and must be repeated more frequently.

Bone manure.

Some twenty or thirty years ago, the farmers in the North employed boys to break the bones with a hammer; they were afterwards reduced by a horse-mill into small pieces: but at present, by the irresistible power of steam, the large thigh-bone of a horse or bullock, in less than half a minute, is made to pass through a succession of iron rollers, drawn gradually nearer to each other, until the fragments come out in a form not greatly exceeding dust in magnitude. The conveyance and distribution of this article on the land is performed with less difficulty and expense of labour even than lime,—an advantage which would be felt in a peculiar degree in Devonshire.

Individuals in the North have acquired considerable property by preparing the bones for the purpose of agriculture; and it is highly desirable that persons of enterprising spirit and some capital would set on foot similar undertakings in Devonshire, as there can be little doubt such projects would contribute not less to the benefit of the projectors themselves than that of the farmers in the county. If steam should be thought too expensive where coal is dear, water-power at least abounds in this district, and might be sufficient for the purpose.——The writer, however, has just been informed, that very recently a gentleman in Plymouth has begun to collect bones, and reduce them to powder for the use of the farmer.

It is now about fifty years since the attention of the farmer was turned to the use of bones as manure; and though at first the article was not appreciated, because the proper method of applying it was not known, by degrees its value and importance have been established beyond dispute. When the object is to derive from it the greatest benefit in the shortest time, it is used in the form of dust; and in that state it offers the advantage of being drilled in together with the seed by a machine constructed for the purpose. Thus a saving is effected in the quantity, and the manure is made to act immediately upon the plant which it is intended to benefit. It has been found to be most useful in light lands, such as are adapted to the growth of barley and turnips. Not like ordinary manure, which passes quickly through the soil, especially in rainy weather, bones, from their lightness, being suspended or kept near the surface, will continue to fertilize the land, as is generally supposed, during a complete course of crops, or about four or five years. The quantity of bone-dust commonly made use of, is from twelve to twenty bushels per acre, drilled in with turnip-seed, and sometimes with wheat and barley. Besides the light soils, there are large tracts of peat soil where great quantities of bone manure are profitably employed. In such soils, bones are used in the first year with rape-seed, and the crop is usually abundant: the sheep are turned on in the winter season, and are in a short time well fattened. This in all probability is succeeded the next year by a valuable crop of corn, and sometimes by another the following year. This kind of management, besides its productiveness, is attended with much less expense than any other system of tillage that can be adopted: the cost of the manure is not half that of stable- or yard-dung, whilst at the same time the labour in conveying it to the land and laying it on is less.

Bones are used in prodigious quantities on the higher lands and the wolds of Lincolnshire and Yorkshire, where, but for the introduction of this manure, the farmers must have been long since ruined. They are also much used even on those soils which lie upon or near a substratum of limestone; and with great success on clay, the land having been first well reduced; and thus excellent crops of turnips have been obtained where the growth of them was thought impracticable. Grass lands have been also found to receive great benefit from their application. In short, bone manure has become so indispensable in the districts where it has been introduced, and the demand has so much increased, as to render the trade of procuring and bruising the bones highly profitable. There are persons in the North of England who have realized two, three, and even five thousand pounds yearly by preparing them for use, though competition has at present much reduced the profits of this employment. Thousands of tons, however, are annually imported into the northern parts of our eastern coast from France, Holland, Germany, and other quarters, and the demand is increasing. Yet still it is to be regretted, that farmers in many parts of the kingdom, and especially in Devonshire, from want of experience, are altogether ignorant of the benefit to be derived from this cheap and valuable manure.—We have dilated on this subject more than was intended; but its importance, it is hoped, will serve as a sufficient reason *.

* For the substance of these remarks on bone-manure, the writer is indebted to a respectable correspondent at Plymouth.

BOOK
IV.
_____
Soot.

Soot, as in other places, is used in Devonshire as a manure, and approved of; because, from the smallness of its particles, it is precipitated immediately by the first shower of rain, when scattered on the grass or corn; and being taken up by the plants, furnishes them with a nutricious or stimulating supply of nitre and ammonia, and renders it unnecessary for them to send out their capillary roots in search of food, or enables them to do so with greater activity and vigour.

Farm-yard manure.

On the subject of green crops, it has been remarked by several writers on Devonshire husbandry, that too little attention is paid to them by farmers generally in the county. The great principle of Nature, that of producing much in order to produce more *, obvious as it is, they are said either not to understand, or to disregard. On account, perhaps, of the natural fertility of the soil, they appear to overlook the consideration, that were they to grow finer crops of vegetables, they would be enabled to maintain more cattle, raise more dung and more straw, which would furnish the means of accelerating the increase of their produce still further indefinitely. It may probably be attributed to this oversight, that the manure afforded by the farm-yard and the stable is said to be ill managed and much neglected. Lime is a most valuable improver of arable lands, but there are some soils for which it is not suitable, or which may be overcharged with it; and on grass-lands it is not the custom to use it at all †. The farm-yard and the refuse of Plymouth, Exeter, and other towns, afford large supplies of rich manure, which is represented not to be turned to the best account. In the farm-yard especially there is much waste, and there is room for great improvement, both in the management and arrangement of it, particularly in forming receptacles for the dung, and above all for the

* " See dying vegetables life sustain,
  See life dissolving vegetate again."—POPE.
† Mr. Marshall, however, mentions an instance in which he saw it used in the north of Devon on land laid down with grass.

drainings; for it is asserted by the ablest writers on agriculture, that the urine of cows and horses is even more
fertilizing than their dung *. The skill of the farmer,
moreover, is discovered in suiting his manures to his
crops; and when any of them has not answered his expectations, to have recourse to others: and in Devonshire especially his wisdom would appear in paying more
attention to green-crops—to turnips, clover, mangel-
wurzel, sainfoin, vetches, &c.

It has been observed before, that the knowledge of
chemists on agricultural subjects is still defective: it is
so especially with respect to the food of vegetables, or the
manner of preparing and applying it; and it ought not to
be overlooked, that the intelligent and well-informed practical agriculturist will probably do more, by judicious experiment and observation, towards improvement in the
management of land, than the most scientific man without
practice. Not, however, that chemical knowledge on
agricultural subjects is to be despised. Scientific writers
on these as well as other topics, give publicity to important discoveries, and supply a variety of valuable information; and if knowledge thus obtained be united to
practice and experiment, the result may justly be expected
to be in the highest degree beneficial.

The cultivation of land is divided into two important
operations. The first, the adapting, improving, or correct-
ing the surface and the subsoil, where this can be done,
so as to receive and regulate a due supply of water, and
afford a proper accommodation for the roots of vegetables.
The second, to furnish such plants as the soil may be
adapted to support, and the necessary and suitable food
to maintain them in health and vigour. The office of the
root of vegetables is to collect and appropriate the food

The object
of agricul-
tural ope-
rations.

* Alkaline salts, according to Mr. Haywood, contribute greatly to
fertility, not by serving as food for plants, but by acting chemically on
the soil, dissolving and increasing its divisibility, changing its composition, and otherwise exerting an influence upon it. The urine of cows
and horses, he observes, contains a portion of alkaline salts, and is therefore more fertilizing than their dung.

which is to be consumed in the formation of the sap and organized parts; and one purpose, at least, of the leaves is to throw off the excrementitious matter by perspiration *.

The food of plants is held in solution by water. The roots take up this liquid, and have the power of decomposing and appropriating it to the use of the plants, whatever food it may contain; and hence the value of judicious irrigation. It is evident that different vegetables require different food, or rather, perhaps, food differently composed and prepared, if all their food consist of similar ingredients. Vegetables may be divided into three classes; namely, land, fresh-water, and sea-water vegetables. None of them will grow out of their proper element; and different soils are essential to different plants, as well as different exposures, as in valleys, by the side of hills, to the north or south, &c. To the absence of proper attention to these circumstances must be attributed, in a great measure, the want of good plantations and abundant crops.

The following observations, containing the substance of some of Mr. Haywood's remarks, will not, it is presumed, be considered either unimportant or unnecessary. Mucilaginous, gelatinous, saccharine, oily, extractive fluids, and solutions of carbonic acid in water, in their unchanged state, contain almost all the principles necessary for the life of plants. But there are few cases in which they can be applied as manures in their purest form. Such substances must generally be reduced by fermentation or some other process, before they can be taken up by the roots. No substance is more necessary to plants than carbonaceous matter. The more solid part of vegetables, if reduced by dry distillation, or burnt in a close vessel, will become charcoal, retaining the same figure or organic

* Sir Humphry Davy affirms that the absorption of carbonic acid gas, and the production of oxygen, are performed by the leaf. Mr. Haywood, however, maintains, that it is irrational to suppose that plants receive their food by the leaves as well as the roots, and adduces proofs to show that the leaves are not furnished with organs adapted to this purpose. The leaves, he observes, serve to eject oxygen, &c., which affords no nutriment to the plant.

disposition. Carbon, therefore, constitutes the grand sta-
mina of plants, and enters into every part of them. How,
then, to collect, to prepare, and to apply this substance, is
the grand desideratum; and this is still a perplexing subject to philosophers. Whatever constitutes the food of
vegetables, must be reduced to a suitable form, or be
placed in a state of minute divisibility. Passing through
the earth, water dissolves or combines, and carries with it
carbonaceous or earthy matter necessary to the support
of vegetables. Carbon therefore must be applied in that
state which admits of its perfect solution in water. It is
evident, however, that some other agent is essential to
fertility than carbon; for black soils, which are wholly
vegetable, and therefore carbonaceous, are sterile; but
with the addition of lime they become fertile; and lime,
if it do not supply food to vegetables, may act chemically
upon the soil. Of the former of these substances, carbonic acid is the most complete solution: this, however,
is not found in sufficient quantities. It is formed, says
Sir Humphry Davy, in a variety of processes of fermentation and combustion, and in the respiration of animals:
and he adds, as yet no other process in nature is known
by which it can be consumed, except by means of vegetables. In this view of the subject, however, Mr. Haywood maintains that Sir Humphry Davy is mistaken; for
that there are other means of consuming it, appears from
this eminent writer himself; and in its application to the
food of vegetables, he prefers the theory of Kirwan, namely,
that carbonic acid gas is heavy, and therefore sinks down,
is absorbed by the dews and the soil, and finds its way
into the plants, as food, by the roots. Dr. Priestley has
proved, that plants surrounded with it will not thrive; but
if it be applied to their roots, they flourish.

The great object of the application of manures, is to
render them capable of affording as much suitable matter
as possible for the food of plants; and that in a slow and
gradual manner, so that the nutriment may be entirely
consumed in forming the sap and organized parts. Vege-

Applica-
tion of ma-
nures.

BOOK
IV.

tables, moreover, it must be observed, are as much affected by the quality and quantity of their food, as animals. A surfeit will disease and destroy them, not less than a total want of nutriment, or the application of such as is of an improper quality.

Sir Humphry Davy thinks that vegetable manure should be used at the beginning of the fermentation, to prevent loss. But Mr. Haywood, again, adopts a different opinion, and gives his reasons in support of it. Dung, he maintains, should be spread upon the surface immediately after sowing the seed, and lie a year. It would in this case decay, and thus set carbonic acid gas at liberty, which from its weight would descend, and contribute to the nourishment of vegetables; whilst the hydrogen, which is injurious to plants, would escape. Which of these methods, however, is preferable, practical agriculturists are the best qualified to judge; and the difference of opinion among the ablest chemists shows how much safer it is to place dependence on actual experiment in agriculture, than on this branch of science in its present state.

Having thus treated much more largely on the subject of manures, on account of its importance, than was originally intended, we shall proceed to give some account of the animals of the county.

DOMESTIC ANIMALS.

The breed
of cattle.

The breed of cattle in Devonshire is justly reckoned the most beautiful, and on the whole perhaps, as some persons think, the most valuable in the island. There are several varieties in different parts of the county, but all springing from the same original stock, which has probably undergone less alteration than any other breed in the country. That of North Devon is the most excellent, and is generally celebrated. The young heifers of this district, with their taper legs, the small features of their countenance, the exact symmetry of their general form, and their clear coats of dark red, are pictures of elegance. The full-grown cattle are not so large as many others, but

Engraved by James Sargent

full of flesh in proportion to their size. Their superiority for grazing and for draft is demonstrated by the great demand for them, and the high price which they obtain; but for the use of the dairy they are not in equal estimation, the secretions, from the nature of the animal, being appropriated more to the production of fat than of milk. For labour, this breed is nowhere excelled in docility, activity, or hardihood, of which the use generally made of them is sufficient proof, the ploughing of two acres of fallow land being the common day's work of four. The full-sized North Devon cow, when fattened to its frame, will not exceed eight score per quarter; and the ordinary average of the ox, at five years old, and equally well fed, not higher than three score per quarter above the weight of its fattened parent.

The following minute description, both of their excellences and defects, in Mr. Vancouver's technical style, may not be unacceptable. Their excellences are as follow: "The head small, clear, and free from flesh about the jaws; deer-like, light and airy in the countenance; the neck long and thin, and the throat free from jowl or dewlap; the nose and round the eyes of a dark orange colour; the ears thin and pointed, and tinged on their inside with the same colour that is always found to encircle the eyes; horns thin, and fine to the roots, of a cream colour, tipped with black, growing with a regular curve upwards, and rather springing from each other; light in the withers, resting on a shoulder a little retiring and spreading, and so rounded below as to sink all appearance of its pinion in the body of the animal; open bosom, with a deep chest or keel preceding and between the legs; small and tapering below the knee; fine at and above the joint, and where the arm begins to increase it becomes suddenly lost in the shoulder; the line of the back straight from the withers to the rump, lying completely on a level with the pin or huckles, which lie wide and open; the hind-quarters seated high with flesh, leaving a fine hair-ham, tapering from the hock to the fetlock; long from the

CHAP. I.

Their excellences.

rump to the huckle, and from the pinion of the shoulder to the end of the nose; thin loose skin, covered with hair of a soft and furry nature, inclined to curl whenever the animal is in good condition and in full coat, when it also becomes mottled with darker shades of its permanent colour, which is that of a bright blood-red, without white or other spots, particularly in the male. A white udder is sometimes passed over, but seldom without objection."

Their defects.

Such are stated to be the excellences of form in the North Devon cattle: but as no animal is perfect, the following are mentioned by Mr. Vancouver as their defects, of which, however, few animals of this species have less: "The sudden retiring of the vamp from behind the huckle to a narrow point backwards; the great space between the huckle and the first rib; the smallness of the angle inwards, at which the ribs appear to be projected from the spine or back-bone, often giving the appearance of a flat-sided animal, and in its being so much tucked up in the girth as to show an awkward cavity between the keel and navel, the line of which, it is presumed, should always be found to hold a position as nearly as possible parallel with that of the back from the withers to the loin. The animal, however, is generally well grown, and filled up behind the shoulder."

South Devon cattle.

The cattle of South Devon are more bulky, and want the elegance of their Northern kindred, owing no doubt, in part, to their mixture with other breeds. Those of the West are said to be a mixture of the North Devon with the old Marlborough red, the former being the original native stock. The most beautiful specimens of this justly esteemed animal are always to be met with in Earl Fortescue's grounds; Sir Bourchier Wrey's; Thomas Acland's, Esq. of High Bray; the Rev. Mr. Quaterly's, of Molland; Mr. Stoneman's, of Woodhouse, near Torrington; Mr. Nicholl's, of Heanton Court House; Mr. George Burton's, of Harewood; and with many other respectable gentlemen and farmers in North Devon. Great efforts have been made of late years for the improvement of the stock, by selecting the most perfect specimens for breeding ; whereas formerly a very absurd practice prevailed in the county, of fattening for sale the calves that were most inclined to feed, and retaining those of an inferior kind for the purpose of raising stock. Great numbers are driven into Somersetshire, half-fed, and, being fattened in the extensive pastures of that county, are sent forward to London and Bath, or are returned for the Exeter market. The demand for the navy and merchant-ships is also large, and is chiefly supplied by lands in the neighbourhood.

The general temperature of the climate, the peculiar herbage of the county, and above all the plenitude of its pure and rapid streams, may probably be stated as in a great measure the cause of that striking peculiarity of form and colour so faithfully indicative of the other excellences observable in the cattle of this district ; and if so, it becomes a question, whether they would thrive so well, and retain their qualities in so great a degree, if removed from their native fields. One of the tenants, however, of Mr. Coke of Norfolk, is said to have greatly improved these naturally beautiful animals. The King of Denmark had some of the improved breed sent over to him a few years ago, and they are now in great request in all parts of England.

Supposed causes of their superior excellence.

Many are fed in the county; and Mr. Vancouver states, that some experiments have been made by Earl Fortescue, and other spirited individuals who have devoted much attention to agricultural improvements in this district, in stall-feeding oxen on potatoes and hay. The result is not known to the writer. Artificial food, moreover, might possibly render the cattle of Devonshire much more profitable than at present. It merits consideration, whether oil-cake, for instance, which is not now used in the county, if added to the rich food of their hills and meadows, might not be found to be productive of great profit. The farmers of the Northern counties, who hold large farms, and are well-informed as well as practical men, know well the value of this article. A respectable correspondent of Ply-

Artificial food.

mouth informs the writer, that a friend of his, who farms a large and valuable estate near the city of Lincoln, and who united intelligence to experience, was accustomed to say, that by feeding his cattle on oil-cake, the whole expense was returned to him by the increased value of the manure which they furnished. It may be granted, indeed, that the flesh of animals is in some instances affected by the nature of the food which they consume : still, however, experience is adduced to show the futility of the prejudice too commonly prevalent against feeding cattle with a portion of oil-cake, and the notion often expressed, that it gives a yellow tinge to the fat ; for, as in other markets, so in those of Devonshire, carcases, usually of the Jersey breed, are occasionally seen of a deep yellow, when no oil-cake has been used ; and in other counties, where it is generally employed, no dissatisfaction with it exists.

Horses.　　The horses of this county, in their general character, bear a strong resemblance to the cattle.　Their colour is dun or red, more or less dark, seldom deep.　They scarcely ever exceed fifteen hands in height, and, by their lightness and agility, are well formed for the roads and lands over which they are destined to toil.　The heavy horses of the eastern parts, and especially the more bulky Flemish breed, could not work in Devonshire.　The Exmoor poneys are small, hardy animals, bred on the moors, and useful for running in light vehicles.　They are probably an original race.　Mules, it has been before observed, are also much used in the county.

Sheep.　　Of the sheep we have only to remark, that the original native breed has been crossed by all the best varieties in the kingdom, and is now esteemed one of the most excellent.　There is also a small variety that pastures on the downs, the hind quarters of which seldom exceed ten or twelve pounds.　Their flesh is highly esteemed, as remarkably sweet and tender.　In the Vale of Exeter, the common house-lamb breed prevails ; and this city is considered to have one of the best supplied markets in the kingdom both for beef and mutton.

DAIRY.

There is one peculiarity common to the dairies of Devonshire and Cornwall, which must not pass without notice; namely, the method of raising what is known by the name of Devonshire, scalded, or clouted[*] cream—an article which stands unrivalled as an addition to pastry and coffee, and for which there is consequently great demand. The method of preparing it is as follows:—the milk, after standing some hours in ordinary pans, either of brass or earthenware, is placed, undisturbed in the same vessels, generally over the wood embers of the common hearth, but sometimes over a fire of charcoal, and even of common coal, in stoves fitted up for the purpose, or on iron plates; and remains in that state, warming very gradually, till it approaches nearly to boiling heat,—the proper degree of heat being indicated by pimples, or blisters, rising on the surface of the cream: the smallest degree of ebullition mars the process, which is therefore properly termed *scalding*: the fire should consequently be regular and moderate. The cream, thus raised, remains on the milk for some time, till it is wanted for use, or for making butter, which is effected by stirring the cream with the hand, without the use of the churn. The origin of this practice is unknown; but it is singular that the art of preparing an article of luxury so universally esteemed, has not found its way into other counties, when, for aught that appears,

* A corruption, no doubt, of *clotted*; the cream being so denominated from the closeness of its texture. Mr. Marshall, however, thinks it was originally named *clouted*, from its tough, *cloth-like* texture,—a conjecture not very probable.

The following is Horne Tooke's derivation of the word; and, though not so absurd as the derivation of *napkin* from *diaper*, with which he elsewhere amuses his readers, has still, as I apprehend, no application to clouted cream. *Clouted*, it seems, signifies cut or divided into small pieces:—how can this apply to clouted cream?

" *Clough, Clout*, as well as *Cleeve, Cleft, Cliff, Clift*, and *Cloven*, are the past participle of Cliopian, findere, *to cleave*."

" *Clouve, Clough*, cleaved or divided—into small pieces. *Clouved, Clouv'd, Clout*."

" *Clouted* cream is so called for the same reason."

Tooke's *Diversions of Purley*, by R. Taylor, vol. ii. p. 178, 179.

it may be raised with equal facility in any part of the
country. There are instances of its having been made in
London, or its vicinity, where the milk is often poor[*].
The butter made from this cream is highly esteemed as
of superior quality; but the milk, by the process, is rendered lean and blue; and though Devonshire is distinguished for the excellence of its cream and butter, it is
also remarkable for the inferiority of its cheese.

CIDER[†].

History of
cider.

Cider and the growth of apples being of so much importance in Devonshire husbandry, these subjects have a
peculiar claim upon our attention, and may be treated of
more copiously than others of inferior consequence. There
seem to be no data for showing when this country became noted for this beverage: orchards are not mentioned
in Domesday Survey, nor in records two or three centuries
succeeding[‡]. It appears, however, from a passage in
Hoker's MS. Survey of Devon, written in the sixteenth
century[§], that a considerable variety of apples were then
grown, and orchards are not mentioned as a novelty.
Among thirteen sorts, one is mentioned as the cider fruit.
Herrison, contemporary with Hoker, in his description of
Great Britain prefixed to Hollinshed's Chronicle, inti-
mates, that cider and perry were then preferred to the
more delicate kinds of drink, and were made in Sussex,
Kent, and Worcestershire: Devonshire is not mentioned;

[*] The writer can assert from his own knowledge, that it was lately
made at Islington, in the neighbourhood of London, by a native of Devonshire; and, having used it both there and in the county of Devon, he
has not been able to perceive any difference in the quality. Wherever
common cream is produced, clouted cream may also be made. The
failure of attempts to produce it has arisen solely from want of sufficient
knowledge of the only method by which it can be made, or from unskilful
management.

[†] In French *cidre* or *sidre*, Italian *sidro*, Spanish *sidra*; all spelled
with the *i*.

[‡] See Lysons's Mag. Brit.

[§] Quoted by Mr. Polwhele from the Portlege Collection, since dispersed.
In the Chronicles of the Canongate, by Sir Walter Scott, we read, that
cider was known in Scotland much earlier—in the fourteenth or fifteenth
century. Vol. iii. p. 3.

but the reason of this omission might be, that this county was too remotely situated to fall within the range of the writer's observation. A great increase of orchards, however, soon afterwards took place in the county; for Westcote, early in the following century, says, "They have of late years much enlarged their orchards, and are very curious in planting and grafting all kinds of fruits for all seasons, of which they make good use and profit, both for furnishing their own table and the neighbouring markets; but more especially for making cider,—a drink both pleasant and healthy, much desired of seamen for long voyages, as fitter for beverage than beer, and much cheaper and easier to be had than wine." His friend and contemporary Risdon, in similar language, observes*, that "such plenty of cider is made in Devonshire, as many copyholders may pay their lord's rent with their cider only, which is found a drink very useful for those that navigate long voyages; whereof one tun serveth them instead of three tuns of beer, and is found more wholesome drink in hot climates." Upwards of two centuries ago, therefore, cider was plentiful in the county; and Mr. Marshall states†, that one of the orchards of Buckland Priory is said to be the oldest in the county; and this is spoken of as being about two hundred years old. It is still stocked, and in full bearing.

Large quantities of cider are made for exportation, and much of it is sent to London, Newcastle-upon-Tyne, Sunderland, Leith, Swansea, Liverpool, and thence by canals into Yorkshire. There is great difficulty in stating anything like an average produce throughout the county. The mean, however, of several statements given to Mr. Vancouver, upon a period of seven years, varying from two and a half to five hogsheads per acre, would equal that of three hogsheads and two-fifths per acre throughout the county; the average price, in the year 1808, being fifty shillings per hogshead of sixty-three gallons. This

Quantity made in the county.

* Risdon's Survey, p. 7.
† Marshall's Rural Economy of the Western Counties, vol. i. p. 212.

BOOK
IV.
average, however, will not serve at present: about forty
shillings, or even lower, might be quoted for what would
be called good cider. The best cider has sometimes risen
as high as three guineas, and at others the worst has
been sold even as low as five shillings a hogshead at
the press.   The year 1820 was remarkable for its abundant produce; 10,265 hogsheads having been sent in
that year from the ports of Exeter and Dartmouth, the
former including Teignmouth, and the latter Salcombe,
exclusive of what was shipped by the makers, and not
liable to duty.

Quality.
The cider of the South-Hams is preferred, and it is
there only and in the vicinity of Exeter that it is prepared
for exportation.   At Dunkeswell and Church Staunton,
however, cider is made equal to that of the South-Hams.
Mr. Frazer, in 1793, mentions an orchard of three acres
at Staverton, which produced 80 hogsheads; and in full
years 8000 hogsheads have been produced in this parish.
Dartington also, and some of the neighbouring parishes,
produce an abundance of cider of the richest quality. The
year 1829 was distinguished by the extraordinary plenty
of its fruit, the quantity of cider made in that year being
greater than was ever known before. At the press, much
was sold at ten shillings a hogshead, and in some instances
at five.   The cider tax operated formerly to reduce the
number of apple-trees, thousands of which were cut down
at the time when it was imposed, and great discontent was
the consequence; but the removal of this tax will now enable the farmer to pay more attention to the production
and the excellence of this favourite beverage, and we may
reasonably expect a reduction of the former prices.

Value of
this article
to the
farmer.
Besides the large quantities that are exported, the chief
beverage of the farmers and their families in Devonshire is
cider; and great use is also made of it in the villages and
towns. Malt-liquor is comparatively little known among
them, and the best especially, the old friend and companion of British hospitality, is extremely rare in the county.
There is not, perhaps, a district in England so ill served

with this nutricious, pleasant, and wholesome beverage as Devonshire; a deficiency much regretted by persons who come to reside here from other quarters. The vineyards and olive-groves of Palestine were not more valuable, however, to the natives of that country, than are the orchards of Devon to the farmer; for not only do they furnish supplies for his family throughout the year, but, as in Risdon's time, many of them are enabled to pay their rent, and even add to their income besides, by the produce of the cider-press.

The cider in general use in the county is that which has undergone the vinous fermentation, and has consequently become strong and hard, which, though it agrees with the natives, seems much too acid to strangers, and in them causes flatulency and the colic, frequently to a serious and alarming degree. The sweet cider is obtained, not from different fruit, but by checking the fermentation by repeatedly racking it off, preparing the casks by burning brimstone in them, and other arts. This is prepared for the metropolis, and for general exportation; but it does not suit the taste of the inhabitants of Devonshire, nor, as it is said, does it afford the nourishment and strength which it yields when properly fermented *. The nature of the soil appears generally to have little effect on the quality of the cider, for the prime sorts are produced on soils of directly opposite qualities; and though its value does depend, in a great measure, on the properties of the fruit, it is fermentation that has the greatest influence in determining its quality. Without a perfect vinous fermentation, there cannot be a vinous liquor: hence the impropriety of mixing together in the cider-press different sorts of apples, because many of them ferment at different

Fermentation.

* The effect of the cider upon working men is said to be relaxing; and another and a still worse effect, Mr. Marshall observes, is what is called the Devonshire colic, which is like that of Poitou. This is to be attributed, he adds, not to the lead which is used in the cider presses, but to the cider itself, or rather, perhaps, to a vile spirit called " necessity," which is drawn from the grounds or lees of the fermenting-room, and which is very pernicious.

BOOK
IV.

Care in the
choice of
fruit.

Planting
and ma-
naging
orchards.

periods *. Excessive fermentation also deprives the cider of its strength.

Valuable as a good orchard is to the farmers of Devonshire, but little care, it is said, has been used to raise such fruit as is best adapted for cider. Much more attention, however, is now paid than formerly to the grafting of stocks with the best sorts. For this purpose, rich sweet fruits seem to be preferred by the most capable judges. The red-streak is a favourite apple. However, it may be stated, that the finest table fruit, or the sorts used for cooking, are not those that are most suitable for the cider-press. Many of the poorer apples make excellent cider; and one of the most celebrated is so hard and bitter that even the swine are said to refuse it. But the names of the different sorts vary so much, that those in use in one parish are not understood in the next.

In planting an orchard, care should be taken to place all the trees of the same sort or quality in rows, by which means the fruit, ripening at the same time, can more readily be kept separate, and be milled, and the juice expressed and fermented without mixture;—objects of the first importance, as the mixing of the fruits is found to produce, according to a preceding remark, unequal and repeated stages of fermentation, thus exhausting the strength and deteriorating the liquor. Sheltered situations are usually chosen as fittest for orchards, nor is there a valley in the South-Hams without one. Mr. Vancouver's opinion, however, is deserving of attention;— namely, that an elevated situation for orchards, if sheltered from the cutting winds, is preferable; because, being above the fogs, they are the less liable to receive injury from the frosts. In planting the trees, the subsoil is of the greatest importance: if cold, tenacious, and abounding with stagnant water, it is of course altogether unfit for the purpose, and underdraining is essential. Or when

* See MacCulloch on Wines. Occasionally, but not often, the cider is boiled, and two hogsheads thus reduced to one. This is the finest of all; strong, and luscious in taste.

the subsoil is bad, a stone flooring, through which the
roots cannot penetrate, about a foot and a half under the
surface, is recommended. A substratum of granite gravel
is not found unfavourable to the growth of the tree; but
a moist loam or clayey bottom is said to produce a superior and richer cider *.   Planting potatoes in orchards is
extremely injurious to the trees; but dressing them with
manure, in the same manner as mowing grounds, or applying to each tree annually a compost of dung, lime, and
way-soil, about a horse-load to two trees, is found to contribute wonderfully to their vigour and the increase of the
crop.   In training the young trees, which is an affair of
great importance, one perpendicular shoot, with a sufficient number only of horizontal branches, should be suffered to grow.   It is also an error of the greatest magnitude, but a very common one, to allow the trees to stand
too near each other, and the branches to grow as thickly
as they please; thus, whilst the object is greater abundance of fruit, less is in fact obtained, and that defective
in size and flavour.   The grass, moreover, under trees
thus planted and thus neglected becomes rank and of no
value †.

The Pear is not particularly cultivated in Devonshire,
as the soil in general does not appear to be suitable for it.
Perry, consequently, is not one of the products for which
the county is remarkable.

* "The most approved method of planting," says Mr. Marshall, "is
to remove the soil down to the rock, which is seldom deep, and to cover
this with eight or ten inches of a compost of fresh earth and sea-sand.
Upon this compost the inverted turf is laid, and upon the latter the
young trees are planted, and the whole is finally covered with the ordinary earth."
The canker, which does great injury to the trees, and which appears
to arise from the too great richness of the soil, or too much dressing with
manure, producing a surfeit, this writer also observes, is probably best
cured by common river-sand, or that of Roborough Down.
† It is singular that the misletoe is not found in Devonshire, where
apple-trees abound so much, nor, it is believed, in Cornwall. If this
were the case in ancient times, it is unfavourable to the supposition of
the prevalence of the Druidical superstition in this district.

The great variety of soils in Devonshire, the mildness of the climate, and the strong tendency of vegetation to luxuriate, afford opportunities for the introduction of every species of grain and grass in use by agriculturists, as well as for the fattening and rearing of cattle, to great advantage. Our limits do not allow us to treat at large of all the products of the county, and of the whole of those which might be added with increasing benefit. The following brief notices, relative to past as well as present times, must suffice. Westcote says, that whereas considerable quantities of corn used to be exported from the county, such was the increase of manufactures in his time, and the county had consequently then become so populous, that much grain was imported, and in one year (1610) the imports of this article amounted in value to £60,000. Frazer in 1794 mentions Kingsbridge, Dartmouth, and Modbury, as remarkable for the production of barley, and states that this grain was then exported from Salcombe in incredible quantities. From this port were also then exported 2468 quarters of wheat, 558 of wheat flour, and 357 of oats; all of them being sent coastwise. Great quantities of corn were also grown in the neighbourhood of Hartland, Bideford, and Ilfracombe, from which ports considerable exportations of this article took place. The chief corn-markets are at Exeter, Tavistock, Barnstaple, Plymouth, and Kingsbridge.

In 1770 Moreton Hampstead was remarkable for the growth of large quantities of potatoes, which were sold for the use of Plymouth, &c. at a market then held at Two Bridges. They are now planted in abundance in all parts of the county, and for the most part are mealy and of excellent quality.

Formerly rye was cultivated in the county very extensively. This is proved by the rye-straw used in old thatched buildings, and is countenanced by the vestiges of ancient cultivation to be traced in all the extensive moors and commons, notwithstanding the soil and substratum are not altogether suitable for this grain. At present there are no crops of rye in the county.

Hemp also, in former periods, was grown in great quantities in the parish of Combe Martin; and in the reign of Elizabeth it is mentioned as of consequence. It has long ceased to be cultivated here. Flax at a later period was one of the principal commodities of Devon*; and still in the parish of Halberton, and in the adjacent parishes towards Somersetshire, it is cultivated to a considerable extent†. If this article were manufactured in the county, for which purpose there are great facilities, extraordinary advantage would, doubtless, be the result.

Hops, Mr. Vancouver observes, seem to spread spontaneously, and occupy a place in most of the sheltered hedge-rows of the county: they are even cultivated, moreover, in the vale through which the Yeo runs, in the parishes of Littleham and Monkleigh. The cultivation is exceedingly limited, and conducted in a very humble manner; but from the mildness of the climate, the many sheltered situations, the richness of the soil, and the plenty of hop-poles at hand, it is reasonable to infer that hops might be cultivated in this county with prodigious profit. Probably no district of the kingdom is more favourable to the growth of this plant.

The wool of Dartmoor in the reign of Edward I., when manufactures were so little known in England, was exported in considerable quantities. In modern times, in which the manufacture of cloth is carried on to so great an extent, wool is become an article of importation.

Butter is sent in great quantities to London from Honiton, Axminster, and other places. Mr. Lysons‡, in

* Campbell's Political Survey, vol. i. p. 340.

† Mr. Vancouver mentions the following remarkable circumstance:— A permanent pink tinge accompanies flax grown upon red land, which no bleaching, washing, or chemical preparation yet discovered, has been found sufficient to discharge: bleaching, indeed, instead of removing, rather increases the colour.

‡ For many of the particulars here stated relative to the produce of the county, the writer is indebted to Lysons's Magna Britannia.

1820, states, on the best authority, that no less than 1500 dozen pounds were sent weekly to London from Honiton alone, and about 300 dozen for the supply of the towns on the southern coast of Devon.

Even the vegetable productions of the rocks of the county, in a commercial view, might be rendered profitable. Lichens are used by dyers. We are told, that from the year 1762 to 1767 inclusive, 100 tons of the *Lichen tartareus* were collected in Devon for the purpose of making it into orchil. Many tons of this, and the *Lichen parellus,* applicable to the same purpose, have been formerly gathered in the vicinity of Oakhampton. After the rocks have been well stripped, many years are required to renew the crop. It is at present plentiful.

Gardens.

In no part of England are kitchen-gardens laid out on a more extended scale, or to better purpose. Notwithstanding the cob- or earth-walls, they abound with wall fruit of the finest quality; and all kinds of vegetables for the table are equally excellent and abundant. Among others the white broccoli has a claim to be noticed. It begins to be plentiful in April, and in May arrives at a size and excellence unknown in other counties. Solid heads that measure eight or ten inches in diameter are very common. In Dunsford's History of Tiverton the following singular statement occurs. In the year 1789 a broccoli plant, in the garden of Mr. Henry Dunsford of Fore-street, grew to the height of eight feet, measured thirteen feet and a half in diameter (from each extremity of the leaves of course), and forty feet and a half in circumference. Figs ripen to perfection, and are commonly sold in Exeter and Plymouth markets. The parish of Beer Ferrers has long been noted for fruit, as cherries, strawberries, pears and walnuts. Goodleigh is noted for cherries, by which the market at Barnstaple is supplied. Christow also abounds in the same fruit. Paignton, on the Torbay coast, is famous for a large but very sweet and early cabbage, which takes its name from the village, and which is also grown in great quantities in Cockington and the adjoining parishes for the markets of Plymouth and Exeter.

CHAP.
1.

ON THE AGRICULTURE OF THE MOORS AND COMMONS, BUT PARTICULARLY DARTMOOR.

THERE are large quantities of waste land in various parts of Devonshire, besides Dartmoor, which admit of cultivation, and which would furnish sufficient remuneration for the necessary labour and expense. Among these is the common of Great Torrington. Some years ago, as Mr. Vancouver states, with the consent of the inhabitants about thirty acres of this waste were granted to a company for the purpose of establishing a woollen manufactory; and the remainder of the inclosed waste amounts to about 260 acres. The south-east part, lying east of the Bideford old road, contains about thirty-five acres, and is composed of a reddish or cedar-coloured loam, on a deep under-stratum of clay, mixed with coarse rubble: the south part, bounded by the river Torridge, consists of a thin gray loam, lying close upon the shillot rock. Its lower parts are subject to springs, of which, however, they might easily be relieved by draining. A further part of this common, called Hatchmoor, is composed of a wet gray loam, on a woodland clay, lying ultimately on the shaly rock. The whole is capable of great improvement, and the loss sustained by suffering it to remain in its present state, as estimated by Mr. Vancouver, is very considerable.

The improvement of Hatherleigh Common, in extent about 463 acres, is also of importance. A large portion of its northern side consists of a rich cedar-coloured loam, applicable to the culture of the most productive green crops, the best grains and pulse. Its present value is seven shillings an acre; its improved value Mr. Vancouver estimates at thirty-five shillings, after clearing the expense of inclosure.

The Dowland, Dolland, and Hallacombe Moor would also pay well for the expense of improvement, the soil in

Moors and commons.

many parts being found to consist of a tender hazel loam, or a deep, dry, and open subsoil; and a gray moist loam of moderate depth on a yellow wood clay. Some wet and boggy places occur on the hanging sides, which might be easily cured by draining.

Whitten Down is attached to particular estates, and would pay well for inclosing. The same may be said of Ilton Moor, lying between the parishes of North and South Tawton.—All these are but specimens, similar to many other large tracts of moors and commons, chiefly in the north of Devon.

The high down overhanging the church and village of Cadbury is capped with an old fortification, called Cadbury Castle. ' From this spot the views are rich and very extensive. The works consist of a deep ditch and rampart, inclosing about two acres of ground. In the area, or terra plain, of this inclosure, when Mr. Vancouver saw it, a rank growth of spurry and fleabane seemed completely to overpower a very indifferent crop of turnips, showing, however, that the exterior, which is a furze brake, is capable of improvement with proper cultivation. Welland, Lenard and Goose Moors in the parishes of Welland and Halberton; the common of Holcombe Rogus, called Durly Moor; Beer Down in the parish of Uplowman; Chimbery Down in the parish of Hackworthy; Bampton Down, and a number of wastes and commons of more or less extent, would answer well for inclosing, provided they were afterwards properly cultivated. Of this, however, there is little room for expectation, whilst such large tracts of the old moorlands, either for want of means or inclination, lie in a state of neglect.

DARTMOOR.

The rights pertaining to Dartmoor.

Dartmoor is itself a subject for a volume of no small interest and curiosity; but at present we are concerned with it only in an agricultural view*.

* For the extent of Dartmoor see above, p. 263 note (4to edit. p. 186); also the Preface to Carrington's Dartmoor, p. x.

The forest of Dartmoor is parcel of the Duchy of Cornwall, which, it is well known, belongs to the Prince of Wales, except that when the King has no son the royalty reverts to the Crown. The following account of the rights pertaining to this royal domain is extracted from Carrington's Dartmoor, as the best that can be obtained. "After the general disafforestation," says Mr. Burt*, "for some time the purlieus of the forest of Dartmoor were devoted to the purposes of the chase, and had officers over them, called rangers; but gradually they became more or less cultivated, as we see them at the present day. Many of them belonged to parishes lying in what is called *venville*, which paid annually for the cattle, when trespassing within the forest bounds, certain compensations, entitled *fines villarum*, thence corrupted into *fin vil* and *venville*. The names of the venville parishes are Sheepstor, Walkhampton, Sampford Spiney, Sampford Courtenay, Whitchurch, Peter Tavy, Mary Tavy, Meavy in part, Chudlipps' Town in Tavistock, Taverton Tithing, Shaugh Prior, Dean Prior, Widdecombe, Manaton, North Bovey, Chagford, South Tawton, Gidleigh, Throwleigh, Sourton, Bridestow, Belstone, Holne, Buckfastleigh in part, Lamerton, Lydford, Oakhampton, South Brent, Ugborough, Cornwood, and Harford. In the 17th of Elizabeth an account was taken of the fines, which had then grown to be fixed rents, and they amounted to 4*l*. 11*s*. 4½*d*. They are payable at the court baron, held by the deputy steward of the forest, originally at Lydford Castle, but since its being ruinous, at Prince Town, Dartmoor, where homage jurors are sworn in, surrender taken, and grants made to the free and customary tenants.

"The venville men are considered as the King's special tenants, do suit and homage to his courts, and there present all defaults in and about the forest. They are liable to the feudal service of driving the Moor for trespasses on each quarter of the forest, once yearly in each quarter, with an additional one in the eastern quarter for colts,

* Preface, p. xxviii.

after receiving notice through the forest-reeve from the
deputy auditor, who fixes the exact time, which is somewhere between New and Old Midsummer day; being entitled for their trouble therein, and in further consideration
of their fines and rents, to depasture their bullocks on the
Moor, which they do chiefly in summer at 2d. per head
annually by day, and if by night 3d., their young cattle
at 1½d. per head, and as many sheep as they choose to
send at 3d. per score; and if they depasture more cattle
than they can winter by night, they are expected to pay
for the excess as strangers, and they themselves employ
persons to look after their cattle. It is understood that
the venville men have a right to take away anything off
the forest that may do them good, except vert*, and also
to fish in all waters, and to dig turf in any place. They
are further exempt from tollage in all fairs and markets
throughout England, except London, Totnes, and Barnstaple; and the Duchy steward gives them an exemption
under his hand for all the produce of the venville estates,
and they are free from an attachment by any officer, except
for the yearly rent of 4d. at Michaelmas and Christmas.
Yet with all these privileges it is singular, that none of
the parishes lying in venville can make a rate for repairing
and constructing roads, except Lydford. By the survey
of the 25th of Edward I., among the issues of the forest
are included 4l. 10s. for fines of the villagers (the venville fines) and pasturage of cattle; 11s. 3d. for twenty-
seven turbaries at 5d. each; 4l. 14s. for pasture of 487
horses at 2d. per head; and 2s. 3d. for pasturage of hogs,
with an allowance to the bailiff for hemp, which proves it
was cultivated on Dartmoor at that early period.

Privileges
and duties
of custo-
mary te-
nants.

"Besides the venville estates there are thirty-five ancient tenements on the Moor, held by copy of court roll,
the persons residing on them being called customary
tenants, and doing suit and service to the courts, and
bound, like the venville men, to assist at drifts. The names

* Mr. Burt, after Risdon, p. 223, translates vert by "green oak," which
he considers as one argument for Dartmoor having been formerly wooded.

of these holdings are, Brimps three tenements, Hexworthy three, Riddons one, Bellever one, another Bellever one, Dunnabridge five, Baberry three, Pizwill three, Runnage two, Lower Marepitts one, Hartaland one, Huccaby one and a half, another Huccaby three and a half, Broom Park one, Brown Berry one, Sherberton three, and Prince Hull one, which formerly enjoyed a privilege, supposed to be peculiar to the forest of Dartmoor, that of entitling the proprietors, upon death or alienation, to a new take, which it was customary for the reeve and homage jury to set out on application, subject to 4s. 4d., the fees of the reeve and steward, and a quit-rent for 1s. 8d. or 2s. to the Duchy. Chapple, in his MS. Collections on Devon, notices the same custom and its abuse. 'The customs of those who hold of the venfield court, on the borders of Dartmoor, is,—if the grandfather or father of the tenant has held the same tenement successively, he may have a new take (as they term it) or perpetual addition to his tenement of eight moor acres in the skirts of the forest, exclusive of rocks, bogs, and mines intermixed therewith, for which they generally take care to reckon a sufficient quantity of ground, and are to pay for this eight acres only 4d. per acre yearly, but not till this new take has been presented and duly entered in a court where the venfield men are jurors, and the bounds and limits of the ground so taken determined by their verdict; in consequence whereof, fifty, sixty, or even eighty, or more acres have been sometimes taken, in the name of rocky and miry ground, intermixed with the eight acres of pasture ground thus granted, which rock and mire being accounted waste, the tenant has the benefit of it for draining only, and the removal of such rocks as can be removed, after blowing them up with gunpowder, or otherwise.' From the practice of this deception the custom is discontinued, and no new takes have been allowed since 1796.

" The customary tenements descend by will, the father having the power of bequeathing them to any one of his sons, or even to a daughter. The owners enjoy a right of

2 s 2

BOOK
IV.

turbary, and have the privilege of depasturing as many cattle as they could winter; but most of them, in lieu thereof, have accepted allotments for ninety-nine years absolute, under an Act passed in the third year of George IV. for making inclosures and improvements on the forest, at the yearly rent of 3*d.* per acre for the first thirty years, 4*d.* per acre for the next thirty years, and 6*d.* per acre during the last thirty-nine years, subject to a proviso, that if no improvements shall be made in the way of cultivation within the first thirty years, the allotments become for-

Allotments to others.

feited to the Duke or the Crown. Others (not the free and customary tenants) had very large allotments made them when the Marquis of Hastings (then Earl of Moira) came into office, at the yearly rent of 1*s.* per acre, which continued for some time, but is now reduced to 6*d.* per acre yearly, during the remainder of their several terms of ninety-nine years. The leaseholders likewise hold for ninety-nine years absolute, upon the same terms as the free and customary tenants; but application for such leases increasing under the foregoing Act, the Duchy has latterly demanded 1*s.* per acre.

"It is remarkable, that in a spot not very productive of corn, and less so in former times than now, the act of seizin on surrender should be made by delivering a *mote of reed*. At the drifts before spoken of (which mean an

Drifts.

exact view, taken to know what beasts are within the forest marks or boundaries, and that none be there but such as are entitled, and that the forest be not trespassed on by strangers or foreigners,) estrays are impounded at Dunnabridge, whence borderers must redeem their cattle, and any belonging to the towns of Barnstaple and Totnes are immediately forfeited, whether whole-eared or not, whilst all whole-eared cattle, found at any time in the forest, are also forfeited. The sheep belonging to the renters of the forest are exempted from being impounded as estrays, on paying 3*s.* 4*d.* yearly to the Duchy."

Privilege of others besides

Besides the stock of those who have thus a right of pasturage on the Moor, considerable numbers of cattle and sheep are annually sent by others from various parts of the county, who pay a small acknowledgement to the Crown or the Prince, and to his lessee or tenant for taking care of them*. The whole number, however, is small, compared with the extent of the forest. None are bred on the Moor; and the pasturage of them is confined to the summer and autumn, the climate in the winter being too severe.

CHAP.
I.

those who have a right of pasturage on the Moor.

From the small sum that is paid for this privilege, it would appear, on a superficial view of the subject, to be of considerable advantage to those who avail themselves of it. Mr. Frazer, however, expresses great doubt whether any real benefit accrues from keeping stock on the Moor at all. In the article of sheep, he affirms, this practice may be proved to be extremely unprofitable; insomuch that the most intelligent farmers in the neighbourhood have given it up altogether. He gives an instance on the estate of a large farmer near Dartmouth, who formerly kept many sheep on the Moor, but found they did not pay common interest for his money, the profit amounting to not more than $2\frac{1}{2}$ per cent.; whereas by purchasing good rams, keeping the same ewes, and pasturing them on his own estate, the profit was greatly increased. Another instance is that of Mr. King of Dean Prior, who made a similar experiment, with a still more beneficial result.

Little advantage of keeping stock on the Moor.

It can scarcely be made a question whether a very large proportion of Dartmoor does not admit of profitable improvement by suitable and judicious cultivation. The experiments already made seem to afford sufficient encouragement to this expectation. The chief obstruction appears to be the climate; but even this is capable of amelioration, as will be hereafter shown. The soil of the un-

Improvement of Dartmoor.

---

* When Frederick son of George II. was Duke of Cornwall, " this prince," says Mr. Burt, " demised the forest of Dartmoor to Abram Elton, Esq. and Mrs. Mary Haywood, for a long term of years, determinable on the death of three persons; and Mr. Elton and Mrs. Haywood, by their steward, licensed persons as priors, or herdsmen, in the four quarters, for taking in all sorts of cattle to depasture, and collecting the usual fees."

reclaimed land is represented to be considerably above par*, when compared with the mountain soils of the rest of the island, and to be superior to that of the Highlands and of the North of England. And though the peat bogs occupy a large proportion of the Moor, and there are many parts where the land is half-covered with stones and bowlders, there are also extensive tracts of the upper grounds, which have a loamy soil nearly free from stones, and of sufficient depth for cultivation, wanting nothing but a more genial climate, and a proper supply of manure, to render them valuable arable lands; and in some of the marginal commons the soil is of a better quality.

The forest itself rises with a bold majestic grandeur over all the surrounding heights, which command an extremely rough and broken region in this part of the county. After attaining the summit of the waste, though the surface is still billowy, it will be found to spread into what may be considered, in comparison with the leading features of the country below, an extended plain; the mean height of which is given by Colonel Mudge at 1782 feet,—an elevation of no less than 1045 feet above the highest hills of the adjoining districts. But though the effect of this elevation on the climate must be obvious, it is not the only cause of its severity. Much of the evil must be attributed to the superabundant moisture with which the atmosphere here is constantly charged; and hence it becomes an interesting subject of inquiry, whether, and how far, this may be corrected. As Mr. Vancouver, in his valuable Survey of the county, has treated this subject with his accustomed knowledge and ability, the substance of his ideas may not be unacceptable to the reader †.

Climate and soil.

The coldness of the climate depends greatly on the quantity of moisture suspended in the atmosphere. The whole surface of Dartmoor, including the rocks, is gene-

* Marshall's Rural Economy of the Western Counties, vol. ii. p. 24.
† In order to show the effect of this mountainous elevation on the climate of the adjacent country, Mr. Vancouver has referred (page 280)

rally of two descriptions; the one, a wet peaty moor, or
vegetable mould, but affording good sheep and bullock
pasture during the summer season; the other, an inveterate swamp, absolutely inaccessible to the lightest and
most active quadruped that can traverse the sounder
parts of the moor. From personal observation, Mr. Vancouver found that when the sun and wind had been acting
for several hours with the greatest force, their combined
powers did not penetrate within several inches of the bottom, or through the luxuriant vegetation, which was still
charged with an extraordinary portion of moisture, clearly
observable on every fibre where the sun had not been
able to dart a ray, or the wind to penetrate, and exhibiting drops from the dew or shower. This multiplied surface of aqueous matter, as well on the depasturable parts
of the forest as on its more extensive swamps and red
bogs, amounts, he observes, to the extent of the forest
thrown into a lake; and riding at that height for the
production of aqueous vapour, it must have a wonderful
effect in increasing the cold of the climate; and hence
the obvious source of those cold and blighting winds
through the country below, becoming from the nature of
things more injurious every year. The most elevated
part of the forest, in which the principal rivers have their
sources, consists of one continued chain, answering in

CHAP.
I.

Bogs.

to two registers,—one kept at Ilfracombe, and the other at Oakhampton,
which are as follow:

	Jan.	Feb.	Mar.	Apr.	May.	June.	July.	Aug.	Sept.	Oct.	Nov.	Dec.
Ilfracombe	53	$48\frac{1}{4}$	52	$57\frac{1}{2}$	$62\frac{1}{4}$	$64\frac{1}{4}$	$65\frac{1}{4}$	66	$61\frac{1}{4}$	62	$58\frac{1}{4}$	$56\frac{1}{4}$
Oakhampton	$34\frac{1}{4}$	$36\frac{3}{4}$	$41\frac{1}{2}$	$43\frac{1}{4}$	$50\frac{3}{4}$	$55\frac{1}{4}$	62	$63\frac{1}{2}$	$57\frac{1}{4}$	$46\frac{1}{2}$	41	$39\frac{1}{2}$
Difference	$18\frac{3}{4}$	$11\frac{1}{2}$	$10\frac{1}{2}$	14	$11\frac{1}{2}$	$9\frac{1}{4}$	$3\frac{1}{4}$	$2\frac{1}{2}$	4	$5\frac{1}{2}$	$17\frac{1}{4}$	$16\frac{3}{4}$

The average of these monthly differences of depression is $10\frac{1}{2}°$, on
Fahrenheit's scale, between Ilfracombe and Oakhampton; and so much
is the latter under the influence of a colder climate. This difference of
temperature cannot be attributed to the difference of elevation between
the two places, as that at any rate does not exceed 180 or 200 feet.
Ilfracombe, it may be added, is also situated more than half a degree of
latitude north of Oakhampton. As these facts are the result of data,
they cannot be mistaken.

every respect the character of an Irish bog. This district every summer teems with a luxuriant growth of the purple melic-grass, rush, cotton-grass, flags, rushes, and a variety of other aquatic plants, the annual growth of which and subsequent decay, have at length raised this part of the forest from five to forty or perhaps fifty feet above the plain or foundation on which it originated. A quantity of vegetable matter, thus accumulating every year, performs the office of a large sponge, in retaining a still further increase of water, and thus the bog will be, imperceptibly indeed, but in fact annually, increasing in bulk and height, so long as its base may be able to sustain it. In some places, however, it appears to have been overcharged, as prodigious slips, several acres in breadth, have parted at different times from the great field or body of morass above, thus forming frightful chasms from the surface to the bottom, or former resting-place of the bog. These slips would of course occur more frequently on the sides of the hills, were they not in some measure prevented by the granite rocks, or moor-stones, which rise out of, and occupy a considerable part of the beds of those morasses; all of which are formed of the remains of light aquatic vegetables, intercepted by about eighteen inches of black peat-earth from the bed of the bog, consisting of white or yellow clay, intermixed with granite rocks, the decomposing parts of the latter forming partial spots of granite gravel, all highly retentive of water.

Soil of the depasturable parts.

The depasturable parts of the forest consist of a black moor-soil, from eighteen inches to two feet in thickness, generally forming peat below, always highly charged with moisture, and ultimately resting upon a reddish-coloured, argillaceous loam, called fox-mold, and which is also retentive of water in a very considerable degree.

Vegetation.

The spontaneous vegetation of this part of the forest, among many other herbs and grasses, consists of the purple melic-grass, mat-grass, downy oat-grass, bristle-leaved bent, eye-bright, bulbous-rooted rush, common tormentil, smooth heath-straw, common bone-binder, cross-

BARNSTAPLE, DEVON.

London, R. Jennings & W. Chaplin, Cheapside 1831

WARDOUR LODGE, DEVONSHIRE, WILTSHIRE.

leaved heath, common heath or ling (dwarf), milkwort, dwarf dock, and the *Agrostis vulgaris* in very large quantities. "The disturbing of this herbage," says Mr. Vancouver, "however inferior it may appear to the refined agriculturist, is on no account to be recommended or permitted."

Though it may not be necessary, in giving a general description of the covering of the forest, to make a greater distinction than that of black peaty moor, and red spongy bog, still a number of gradations occur, all of which, as they approach the character of red bog, will require a longer time to exsiccate and bring forward to a state of profitable cultivation.

The first step, however, towards the improvement of the Moor, is the formation of proper roads, or the repairing of those that already exist; and for this purpose the best material is everywhere found on the spot. The want of convenient roads to the peat-pits is attended with much loss of time to the farmer, as well as danger to the poor who subsist by digging and collecting peat fuel for the country below. None of the parishes in venville, it has been before observed, have the power of making a rate for the formation and repairing of such roads, with the exception of Lidford, in whose boundary the whole of the forest is included; and as the parochial disbursements in these parishes are said to fall lightly, it is worthy of consideration whether an application to Parliament, to enable the inhabitants to accomplish this valuable improvement, would not be desirable and well advised.

As the means of draining the bogs and of bringing them into a state of cultivation are of so much importance, an outline of the method proposed for this purpose by the same able and experienced improver may not be unacceptable to the reader. Many ages have elapsed in the accumulation of these morasses to their present bulk; and though not by equally slow, it is still by gradual means only that they can be reduced, so as to render them an important object in the great field of national territory. But though a long period

CHAP.
I.

Gradations of soil.

Improvement of the roads.

Draining the bogs.

may be required for this purpose, as our author observes,
the method is plain, easy, certain, and efficient.

In the first instance, out-fall drains should be formed;
and from the unevenness of the surface, in no case whatever could want of proper situations for this purpose occur.
These, judiciously planned, and executed so as to receive
the water from other drains on the surface of the morass,
would be beginning the attempt at the right end, and the
most substantial benefits might be expected to be the result. The surface drains should be made at first one foot
(or spit) deep and one wide, and intersect each other at
a rod apart over the whole surface of the bog. By these
drains the descending waters would immediately escape,
and, the annual supply once checked, the morass would
gradually become more firm and consistent on the top;
and when this was accomplished, as many of the foot-
drains as should be found necessary might be preserved,
deepened, and enlarged, and serve as the direction for
subsequent inclosures and subdivisions of the Moor *.

The water being discharged, the soil would gradually

* Mr. Vancouver gives an interesting account (Survey, p. 285) of the
result of a similar method adopted by him in improving a large tract of bog
in King's-County, Ireland, which, after sinking as much as four feet, in
two years after the out-fall drain, which was twelve feet wide, was finished,
cattle roamed over and browsed upon it with ease and perfect security,
where the footstep of man before was not admissible. In the course of
these operations, some circumstances occurred which are remarkable
enough to deserve insertion here. The bottom of the drain was formed of
a retentive clay, or gault, above which, in many places, there was a
depth of twelve or fifteen feet of red bog and turf moor, under which,
and on the bed or resting-place of the bog, there were distinctly to be
seen ridges and furrows, the indisputable remains of ancient cultivation.
In other places on the bed of the bog were found considerable quantities of yew, oak, and pine, all of which appeared to have been more or
less exposed to the action of fire. The more valuable pieces of this timber were easily discovered by probing with a spit, and then raised out of
the bog. One of the oaks measured fifty-five feet in length, and twenty-
two inches in diameter at the butt end. Some of the yew was cut into plank,
and made into beautiful furniture; and the remainder, together with the
oak and pine, was applied to building and agricultural uses. In addition
to these, upon the clay at the bottom of the out-fall drain were found
the dash and lid of a hand-churn, and a large crane-necked brass spur,
with a rowel at least an inch in diameter; the whole serving to show that
the formation of the bog was not of so ancient a date as its depth might
naturally suggest.

undergo a change from the red spongy state, by the alteration of the vegetable matter, to that of the black moor or
peaty character. When sufficiently strong to support a
yoke of oxen, the paring-plough should be applied two or
three times successively in the reduction of the red spongy
substance, taking care always to deepen the drains as the
surface lowered and became more compact and solid. The
intelligent conductor of these improvements must be the
best judge of the time when a trial of a crop should commence. Probably the attempt should be made after the
third or fourth paring and burning, merely by sowing
rape- or cole-seed in July upon the spread ashes, about
half a peck to the acre; on which occasion neither ploughing, harrowing, nor bush-harrowing, is in the smallest degree necessary.

The red bog being thus reduced and cultivated, repeated paring and burning afterwards can produce no possible
injury to such a substance. It will afford the means of
producing abundant crops of cole-seed, turnips, flax, potatoes, cabbages, pease, beans, and every sort of leguminous vegetable that can be used and appropriated in a
green state; and this process may be continued without
danger till the morass and the former adventitious covering is reduced within a foot or fifteen inches of the ordinary bed or stratum of natural earth. A few oats, provided they were put in proportionably early, might perhaps be brought to ripen at a late period of the season.
Hemp would probably be found, towards the completion
of the improvement, to answer very well: but neither this
nor oats should be attempted in the early stage of the process. Raygrass, or *hievre*, would also flourish very soon
after the second or third crop of cole-seed; and as the
mass of bog below obtained relief from saturation, clover
and other valuable grasses might be cultivated upon it
to advantage.

As the improvement advanced, it would be of the first
consequence to mix carefully and incorporate with the
surface small but frequent portions of the understratum

of white or yellow clay : the enlarging of the out-drains might furnish a supply of it. This should by no means be omitted, as it would operate to produce firmness and consistency, so requisite to the vegetable matter which constitutes the surface.

Improvement of the depasturable parts. While these works are carrying on upon the red boggy parts, the depasturable portions of the Moor should be relieved of their superfluous water by foot-drains, intersecting each other at two or perhaps three rods apart, and the water conducted by them into out-fall drains properly disposed and constructed to receive it.

The moor-soil thus drained, would readily assimilate frequent and light dressings of its understratum, fox-mould, which, thus applied in small quantities, would gradually incorporate with the surface-mould and improve its herbage.

No consideration, however, should induce the Council of the Prince, or the Crown, to permit this species of moor to be broken up to any further extent than may be necessary to its drainage ; for, the present covering once destroyed, ages would not supply it again with an herbage equally valuable.

Lime necessary. As the whole of the forest will stand in need of the calcareous principle,—and as an inexhaustible supply of strong peat fuel may always be procured upon the Moor, were roads properly laid out from Bridestow, Oakhampton, and Holne or Buckfastleigh lime-works, the stone might be carried into the interior of the Moor, and calcined in kilns, properly constructed, to almost any extent, and with incalculable advantage.

Canals on the Moor. But if it were possible to extend canals into the interior of the Moor, these of course would be preferable; and of the practicability of such plans, some writers who have paid attention to the subject are fully persuaded. In this view they have observed that the elevation of this district is not so formidable as it may appear to the common observer. The sources of the rivers are not above eight or nine hundred feet above the sea-level. In the descent from these heights there are valleys, through which canals CHAP. might be carried for miles together; and it has been sug- I. gested that a canal might be formed on the most exten- sive summit-level that could be found, for boats carrying only a few tons. Another canal might be formed on the next lower level, and the boats passed from the one to the other by means of an inclined plane and machinery, in case water for the·locks could not be spared, which however there is not much cause to fear. In this man- ner a series of canals communicating with the sea might be extended to all parts of the waste, by which lime, sea- sand, &c. would be conveyed to the interior, and granite, copper, &c. returned *.

Railways, however, are now superseding the use of Railways. canals, and in this district especially would, doubtless, be preferred, where granite, of which they might be form- ed, is on the spot, and where the experiment, though with iron, has already been tried, from Plymouth to Prince Town, with so much success.

To remove the rocks and stones with which an exten- Removal sive part of the surface is so profusely encumbered, would of the stones. be a task for a race of giants; and yet much improvement might be effected in various places, even with respect to this formidable obstacle to cultivation. In the words of Mr. Prideaux, a large proportion of these loose stones "may be easily split or blown up with gunpowder and removed; and when this is once done, it is done for ever†."

To colonize the Moor, as Mr. Burt observes ‡, erect cottages for labourers, with sheltered stables and courts for cattle; and to form the whole into a separate parish, divided into villages or hamlets, with chapels or churches for each, would, no doubt, be important preliminary steps towards the improvement of the whole. The success of Inter- ference of any attempts of this kind, however, must depend alto- Govern- gether on the interference of Government. In the fifty- ment ad- visable.

* See Frazer's Survey, p. 628.
† Communications to the Board of Agriculture, vol. v. p. 48.
‡ Notes to Carrington's Dartmoor, p. 118.

fifth year of His late Majesty George III., an Act was
passed, for vesting in the Crown certain parts of Exmoor,
and for inclosing that forest. Why might not suitable
measures be also adopted by Government for the improvement of Dartmoor; and, it may be added, with respect
likewise to the other extensive waste lands in various
parts of the county, which in many instances are said to
be capable of being converted into productive and profitable tracts of land? The emoluments of the Duchy of
Cornwall were originally designed, no doubt, as a handsome allowance to the King's eldest son; and they were
in former periods considerable : but at present the reduction of their value is so material, that the profits arising
from Dartmoor especially are unworthy of notice. And
when it is considered how much they are capable of aug-
mentation by the use of suitable means for the cultivation
and improvement of a large portion of this waste, it appears to be an object worthy of the attention of the legislature,—more so, at least, than the colonization of far distant countries. The wisdom of adopting the proper measures for this purpose will appear more manifest, when it
is recollected how much the supply of agricultural labour
exceeds the demand, and how greatly preferable it would
be to employ the superfluous hands in the improvement of
such wastes as Dartmoor, to suffering them to remain a
wretched and useless burden on public industry.

Causes of
the failure
of former
attempts at
improve-
ment.

Some years ago, indeed, the rage for improvement was
great, and Government patronized plans for this purpose.
These attempts, however, soon proved to be failures,—and
no wonder *. The speculators in these undertakings were
in general but little versed in agriculture; and having in-
spected the country in a very cursory manner, were altogether mistaken with respect to the soil of Dartmoor, the
produce for which it is adapted, and the methods to be
pursued for its improvement : scarcely any one in the

* See Observations on the Scenery and Antiquities of Moreton-Hamp-
stead and the Forest of Dartmoor, by the Rev. J. P. Jones, of North
Bovey, p. 59.

neighbourhood had anything to do with these plans. CHAP.
These failures afford no discouragement to future attempts I.
under the direction of judgement, knowledge, and adequate experience. Under efficient management, and with
more ample means, efforts may still be made that will be
crowned with success; and the time may come when it
will no longer be said of this solitary waste,

"Yet lone, as if some trampler of mankind
　Had still'd life's busy murmurs on the wind,
And, flush'd with power, in daring Pride's excess,
Stamp'd on thy soil the curse of barrenness;
For thee in vain descend the dews of heaven,
In vain the sunbeam and the shower are given;
Wild DARTMOOR! thou that, 'midst thy mountains rude,
Hast rob'd thyself with haughty solitude,
As a dark cloud on Summer's clear blue sky,
A mourner, circled with festivity." •

Something considerable, however, has been effected by Improve-
private individuals in the way of improvement; and what ments by
has been already done is sufficient to show the practica- duals.
bility of doing much more. A good road has been made
some time from Moreton to Tavistock, with branches to
Ashburton and Plymouth, for which an Act was obtained
in 1772, chiefly through the exertions of Mr. Turner, then
steward to the Duke of Bedford; though, strange as it may
appear, not without strong opposition by the towns of
Bodmin, Launceston, and Oakhampton. The late Mr.
Heywood of Maristow joined that road at Two Bridges,
from the rock on Roborough Down. The principal improvers have been, the Rev. Mr. Vollans, upon 3000 acres;
the late Sir Francis Buller, who held about 2000 acres,
and planted 40,000 trees; Sir Thomas Tyrwhitt, who
has 2000 acres; the Rev. Mr. Bray, the holder of 900
acres; the Rev. Mr. Mason, of 600 acres; Thomas
Sanders, Esq.; and the late Mr. Gullet, who was a
great improver, and built the farming part of the house at
Prince Hall (then one of the ancient tenements and a ruin
of the former building), the better apartments being added

• Mrs. Hemans's Prize Poem on Dartmoor. A few copies only were
printed for the Royal Society of Literature, by whom the prize of 50l.
was offered for the best poem on the subject, and awarded to this lady.

by Sir Francis Buller, who inclosed the best of the ground (which has been since improved) as well as some extensive takes, and built the inn at Two Bridges. July 26th, 1822, an Act was passed, enabling His late Majesty to make leases for absolute terms of ninety years, for building upon, and the improvement of, waste lands, parcels of the Duchy. Messrs. Thomas and John Hullett were also improvers, having purchased grants made by the Duchy to Mr. Paterson and others, which, on the death of Mr. Thomas Hullett, were sold to the Rev. Mr. Vollans. Messrs. Hullett built Post Bridge, and had a large estate in its vicinity *.

Sir T. Tyrwhitt's improvements.

But of all the improvers, there are none to whom the welfare of the Moor is so much indebted as to Sir Thomas Tyrwhitt. In everything relating to this subject he has taken an active part with indefatigable perseverance. In 1785 he commenced his operations on what Mr. Burt calls the very worst part of the forest; which at great expense, by means of draining, and sowing artificial grasses, he has amended considerably. The cultivation of flax having been begun by Mr. Saunders, Sir Thomas followed the example with success, and received a medal on this account from the Bath Agricultural Society. Tor Royal was entirely formed by him in 1798, with its adjoining fields, plantations, and garden, to which there was no road when he undertook the work: he soon made, however, the present one, as well as another to unite the Plymouth to the Tavistock road. In short, to this gentleman all the late improvements on Dartmoor must be referred. But his efforts in promoting the formation of the railway surpass all his other attempts, and well deserve, as no doubt they will secure, the gratitude of posterity.

The railway.

This grand undertaking was first projected by Sir Thomas with a view to accelerate the cultivation of the Moor, and the conveyance of granite for architectural and other purposes; and he employed Mr. William Shillibeer of Walkhampton, surveyor, to mark out the line. In the

* Carrington's Dartmoor, Notes 6 and 9.

early part of 1818, having matured his plans, he submitted them to a special meeting of the Chamber of Commerce at Plymouth; and after they had received the approbation of that useful body, he presented them to the public in a pamphlet, and speedily obtained sufficient encouragement to proceed. The first Act of Parliament for carrying the work into execution passed July 2nd, 1819; and subsequently, two others were obtained, for the improvement of the line, and the excavation of the tunnel; and under their authority subscriptions were raised to the amount of 39,983*l.*, principally by the influence of Sir Thomas Tyrwhitt, who himself subscribed upwards of 3000*l.* The total length of the line from Prince Town to Sutton Pool is twenty-five miles, two quarters, and six chains. The tunnel is in Higher Leigham estate, at the twentieth mile from Prince Town, and measures in length 620 yards, in height 9 feet 6 inches, and in breadth 8 feet 6 inches; its greatest depth under ground being 109 feet. The part completed (being more than twenty-three miles) was opened for public use, with a procession, September 26th, 1823; and the remaining short distance was soon afterwards finished. Any just idea of the grandeur and picturesque beauty of the scenery through which the railway passes, would be very imperfectly conveyed by an attempt at verbal description. The benefits, however, which the merchant and the trader, the manufacturer and the agriculturist, may expect from the undertaking, are of greater importance, and Dartmoor itself may possibly hereafter be no longer doomed to sterility. To Sir Thomas Tyrwhitt the measure is indebted for its origin; and the spirited proprietors, together with all who were concerned in the management and execution of the undertaking, in defiance of all obstacles, have achieved a task which reflects credit, not only on themselves, but on the port of Plymouth, and indeed on the country *.

* Sir Thomas Tyrwhitt was formerly Lord Warden of the Stannaries in Devon and Cornwall. Holding also the office of Black Rod, in the discharge of its duties he received the distinguished praise of a select.

The extensive war-prison on Dartmoor, which will be hereafter described, is at present unoccupied, the supply of inmates for whom it was erected having happily ceased. It furnishes accommodation for a large number of individuals, no less than 10,000 prisoners at one period of the late war having been inclosed together within its walls. Is it not, then, possible to apply it to some useful purpose in connection with the improvement of the waste? Some time ago it was indeed intended to occupy the prison with convicts, with a design of employing them in effecting this object; and subsequently a school of industry within its walls was projected; neither of which projects, however, it is to be lamented, has been carried into execution.

> "............. Silent now,—
> How silent! that proud pile, where England held
> Within her victor gripe the vanquished foe!
> O here full many a blooming cheek was blanched,
> O here full many a gallant heart was quelled
> By stern captivity; protracted till
> Hope almost ceased to bless the drooping brave!
> At eve the exile stretch'd him on his couch;
> And while the tear stood trembling in his eye,
> As night fell on him, thoughts of Home awoke
> The bitter, unregarded sigh. To him
> Sweet spring no pleasure brought;—the summer ray

committee of the House of Commons, for his generous and disinterested conduct in exercising the patronage of this office, by forbearing to sell, according to antecedent usage, the situations of several officers employed under him;—a forbearance which involved the voluntary relinquishment of more than 9000*l.* He has, on all accounts, a just claim to the high encomium of the excellent poet of "Dartmoor."

> "............. The civil wreath,
> Tyrwhitt, is thine; distinguished 'mid the band
> Of British patriots, glowing with the love
> Of country and of man. The noble thought
> Was thine, to rescue from the withering hand
> Of Desolation the vast waste, so long
> A proverb and a by-word in this isle
> Of beauty—this famed isle—her children's boast,
> And envy of the nations! Nor in vain
> Th' attempt, for Enterprize and Science, led
> By thee, their mighty energies combine
> Auspicious."

The preceding account of the railway, &c. is the substance of Mr. Burt's, which is of course the best, as he was clerk to the undertaking. See Note 7 to Carrington's Dartmoor. In the present work some account of the railway has been already given, p. 75 (4to edit. p. 52).

Gilded the waste in vain; and when the deep
And ruthless winter capp'd the cloud-wreath'd Tor
With snow, and loud the highland tempest howl'd,
He heard and shuddered." •

Instead of the repetition of scenes like these, what a gratification would it be to every mind from which the common feelings of humanity are not estranged, to know that this gloomy and now useless building were devoted to the arts of peace, and rendered subservient not only to the shelter but support of thousands, by means of useful and productive occupation! It was in the anticipation that the prison was about to be appropriated to some such valuable use, that Mrs. Hemans wrote the following lines; and there is so much that is admirable in the spirit and the poetry of the passage, that, notwithstanding its length, I cannot resist the temptation of extracting it, especially as but few copies of the poem were printed, nor does it appear to have been published.

" It is a glorious hour when spring goes forth,
O'er the bleak mountains of the shadowy North,
And, with one radiant glance, one magic breath,
Wakes all things lovely from the sleep of death;
While the glad voices of a thousand streams,
Bursting their bondage, triumph in her beams!
" But *Peace* hath nobler changes! O'er the mind,
The warm and living spirit of mankind
Her influence breathes, and bids the blighted heart,
To life and hope, from desolation start!
She with a look dissolves the captive's chain,
Peopling with beauty widowed homes again:
Around the mother, in her closing years,
Gathering her sons once more, and from the tears
Of the dim past, but winning purer light,
To make the present more serenely bright.
" Nor rests that influence here. From clime to clime,
In silence gliding with the stream of time,
Still doth it spread, borne onwards, as a breeze
With healing on its wings, o'er isles and seas:
And as heaven's breath call'd forth, with genial power,
From the dry wand, the almond's living flower,
So doth its deep-felt charm in secret move
The coldest heart to gentle deeds of love;
While round its pathway nature softly glows,
And the wide desert blossoms as the rose.

• Carrington's Dartmoor, p. 37.

" Yes! let the waste lift up the exulting voice!
Let the far-echoing solitudes rejoice!
And thou, lone Moor! where no blithe reaper's song
E'er lightly sped the summer-hours along,
Bid thy wild rivers, from each mountain source,
Rushing in joy, make music on their course!
Thou, whose sole records of existence mark
The scene of barbarous rites, in ages dark,
And of some nameless combat; Hope's bright eye
Beams o'er thee in the light of prophecy!
Yet shalt thou smile, by busy culture drest,
And the rich harvest wave upon thy breast!
Yet shall thy cottage-smoke, at dewy morn,
Rise, in blue wreaths, above the flowering thorn,
And, midst thy hamlet-shades, the embosom'd spire
Catch from deep-kindling heavens their earliest fire."

Whatever may be thought of the prophecy, the poetry at least will be admired.

Notwithstanding the severity of its climate, the Moor, it is well known, is singularly healthy, not only to the natives, but even to others; and though the site of the prison is at least 1400 feet above the sea-level, by returns to Parliament it was found that the mortality was proportionably less among the prisoners than in any English town with an equal population. And if it be observed that these unfortunate individuals were generally in middle life, and therefore less subject to mortality than infancy and age, there were other circumstances in their condition unfavourable to health, by which this would be counteracted; such as long confinement, want of occupation, mental suffering, &c. However, independent of the state of the prisoners, there are sufficient proofs of the healthiness of the climate of the Moor : sickliness and epidemic disorders are not so common here as in other places, and the inhabitants are consequently remarkable for robust health and longevity.

Cultivation of flax.

Flax has been mentioned as suitable for cultivation in this district; and experiment has given sufficient confirmation to this opinion. It has also been remarked, that hemp as well as flax are indigenous to the Moor; but the Rev. J. P. Jones (the distinguished botanist of Devon) observed, in answer to an inquiry of Mr. Burt's, that

" hemp is not a British plant, and therefore cannot be
found growing naturally on the Moor ; nor have I ever
found flax growing wild there." But we learn from
Campbell, that flax was formerly one of the principal commodities of Devon ; and " the trials of it upon the Moor,"
says the writer just mentioned, "by Sir Thomas Tyrwhitt
and Mr. Sanders of Exeter, fully warrant the expectation that it might be again successfully and more extensively cultivated. In 1817 and the following year, during
an unusually dry season, the former planted it on Tor
Royal, and had an ample produce. In the following year
he repeated the experiment; but the weather being not
so favourable, the return was less. The metropolitan
school * being then in contemplation, he kept the flax with
a view of having it manufactured by the children; but
the design unfortunately fell to the ground. In 1819
R. R. Sanders, Esq. the present owner of Brimps on the
East Dart, sowed, without impoverishing the soil, twenty-
four acres of flax, with a slight admixture of lime ; and
by the aid of a person conversant with the subject, prepared the produce for spinning. This gentleman's father,
the late Joseph Sanders, Esq., was decidedly of opinion
that thousands of acres in the forest of Dartmoor are well
adapted for the growth of flax and hemp. Sir George
Yonge was a decided friend to the same cultivation, and
introduced a Bill, since repealed, for granting a bounty
to the growers of flax. He afterwards applied, but inef-
fectually, to the Chancellor of the Exchequer, for the
purpose of reviving the Bill, which is equally expedient

* When this School of Industry was projected, a public meeting was
called in 1820 for the purpose of carrying it into execution, at which
Mr. Brougham [now Lord Brougham and Vaux] announced, by desire
of the late King, a princely donation of 1000*l.*, and an offer of a grant of
part of the waste. The children were to be orphans, rescued from the in-
famy and ruin of the streets of London. Either this, or the previous design
of occupying the prison with convicts for the improvement of the Moor,
would surely have been preferable to suffering the building to remain, as
at present, useless, and exposed to decay. May we not be allowed to hope,
that it is not reserved for a purpose similar to that for which it was
erected?—See Carrington's Dartmoor, note 15.

BOOK
IV.
now as ever, the woollen trade having declined, and the linen one offering itself as a promising substitute *.

"The best mode of rearing flax is on old ground, after paring and burning the sward, and letting it lie fallow for some time. The Dutch raise flax on the stiff clay of Zealand. In France any soil is indiscriminately chosen for cultivating it, and every cottage has a patch of hemp for domestic uses. In Switzerland the most mountainous districts are appropriated to flax. In Ireland a bounty was given on the importation of flax and hemp dressers. The profit to the grower may be estimated at 10*l.* per acre, besides affording employment and subsistence to the industrious. In time, by the adoption of the like means, every moorman might have a plot of flax or hemp, and this would consequently lead to a linen manufacture†."

Whether Dartmoor formerly abounded with wood?
It has been disputed whether Dartmoor has at any time been generally wooded. Mr. Polwhele, whose notions however, as well as his descriptions, have often more of poetry in them than truth, imagines that the Moor in former times was luxuriantly covered with wood;

"When the bleak waste a robe of forests wore,
And many a crested oak, which now lies low,
Wav'd its wild wreath of sacred miseltoe ‡;"

and he observes, that every year young trees spring up spontaneously, but perish before they can rise high enough to escape the bite of cattle. And Mr. Burt, who has so much knowledge of what relates to this district, has written

* Mr. Prideaux, in a communication to the Board of Agriculture in 1806 (vol. v. p. 47.), mentions, that some land which he had recently inclosed from the moors, bore excellent flax and hemp; but having few or no labourers to manufacture it, he was obliged to desist from cultivating it: and he proceeds to observe, "I am certain that many thousands of acres of these uncultivated moors would produce excellent flax. In a future period, should the machines be of general use for spinning wool, which is the employment of the greater part of the poor in Devon and the east of Cornwall, flax enough might be produced for supporting the labour of the poor, whenever the machines become general, and the thousands now paid to the Germans may be saved."
† Carrington's Dartmoor, note 16.
‡ Mrs. Hemans's Prize Poem.

much and with great energy in support of this opinion. But the Rev. J. P. Jones, whose judgement on the subject is certainly entitled to respect, adopts the opposite side of the question with equal decision. He has observed * : " The soil and climate of Dartmoor are so unfavourable to the growth of trees, that there is not the least probability to support the idea of its heights ever having presented a sylvan appearance. The inspection of Westman's Wood, combined with the extreme difficulty which has attended all recent attempts at planting, must convince every one that Dartmoor presented at all times the same barren appearance. The discovery of an occasional trunk of a tree proves nothing. It might have been brought there, and deposited by some accidental cause; a flood, for instance. Many are led away by the word forest. It strikes me, however, that the word *foresta*, as explained in Spelman's Glossary, means any large tract, inclosed or terminated by certain limits, and set apart for game. Trees do not appear to be a necessary accompaniment of a forest." In reply to this it is argued, that although the Moor may not, generally speaking, be favourable to the growth of timber, it is certainly not so adverse as to preclude this altogether. Joshua Hepworth, Esq., agent to the Rev. Mr. Vollans, a gentleman possessed of much agricultural experience, considers the land and climate of Dartmoor as not worse than those of the Yorkshire wolds, nearly the whole of which are inclosed and cultivated; and Mr. Shillibeer, a competent judge of the capabilities of Dartmoor in every point, affirms, that in each of its four quarters several places exist adapted for planting; and that the peat earth is well suited to the growth of certain shrubs at least, as the *Arbutus Rhododendron*, &c. is well known, as it is extensively used by nurserymen and gardeners for that purpose. The best

* In his " Observations " before quoted, p. 57; and preface to Carrington's Dartmoor, p. 18. Geologists give it as their opinion, that the soil of the granite regions is incompatible with the growth of timber; but Mr. Marshall has observed that a substratum of granite gravel is not found to be unfavourable at least to the growth of apple-trees.

proof, however, that the Moor is fit for the growth of trees in certain parts and to a considerable extent, is the success of several attempts in modern times at plantation on its surface. Many thousand trees, it is true, have perished, or are in a state of decay, particularly those planted by the late Sir Francis Buller. But failures of this kind, being attributable to an injudicious mode of planting, or to want of care and sufficient protection to the young trees, weigh little in opposition to the more successful attempts of others. At Brimps may be seen fine ash, larch, &c., and also oak, whence some have been sold as timber; and at Tor Royal and Swincombe, Sir Thomas Tyrwhitt has flourishing plantations. On Bear Down estate, near the river Cowie, a large number of firs, &c. have been planted by the Rev. Edward Bray, which are doing well: and on Stover, the property of George Templar, Esq. are quantities of thriving Scotch firs and other trees, together with the Spanish chestnut; and though not on the forest, these may serve to show what may be done on soil quite as unpropitious for planting. In the parishes bordering on the Moor many trees are also seen to flourish, as in those of Manaton, Chagford, Gidley, and Throwleigh, where there is oak timber of considerable dimensions.

Wistman's
Wood.

With respect to Wistman's Wood, the diminutive appearance of the trees is by no means decisive on the point in question. This solitary relic, as it is supposed to be by many, of the woods formerly existing on the Moor, stands on a slope near the West Dart, on the north-west of Crockern Tor, a mile or more above Two Bridges, and consists of scrub, or dwarf trees, chiefly oak, whose stunted roots, finding scarcely a covering in the thin granite soil, or being entirely exposed on the bare surface of the rocks, obtain in such a situation little nutriment for their support. There are several patches of wood near each other, covering an extent of several acres. The trees seldom exceed ten feet in height; the branches are long and straggling, nor are their trunks large, although from the vast accumulation of moss, together with thorns, brambles, and other parasites, they have assumed a bulky appearance. Unpropitious, however, as the situation of the Wood unquestionably is, it has withstood the tempests of the Moor and the disasters of its climate many centuries: it is supposed to be a thousand years old. Many of the trees are now dead, and the remainder hastening to decay. This, however, cannot in justice be considered as a fair specimen of the timber which the forest may be capable of producing, since there are many and extensive portions of it far better adapted to planting; and at any rate it may serve to show that this desolate waste may have produced at least stunted trees.

But that parts of the forest were once wooded, one of the strongest proofs appears to me to be the discovery of the trunks of trees in the bogs; notwithstanding Mr. Jones says this proves nothing. "That many trees," as remarked in the notes to Risdon*, "did anciently grow upon this extensive tract, is evident from the fragments of trees occasionally found in the bogs." And, says Mr. Burt†, "At sundry times the trunks, branches, and roots, even the leaves of trees, chiefly oak and birch, have been discovered, some two, some six or eight feet, beneath marshy soil in the Moor, particularly at Taw Marsh in the north quarter. On exposure to the sun and air, they grow almost as hard as Brazil wood." Mr. Jones supposes they may have been brought to the spots where they were found, by some accidental circumstance, as a flood, for instance. But if they have been discovered at any considerable height on Dartmoor, it is difficult to conceive what flood since the days of Noah could have raised them to such an elevation; and if they have been washed down by inundations, they must have grown on still higher ground in the forest: by what other accident they could have been deposited in the bogs, it is equally difficult to imagine. The only rational supposition appears

* p. 406.
† Notes to Carrington's Dartmoor, p. 155.

to be, that they must have grown on the spot where they have been found.

With respect to the meaning of the word forest (*foresta, forestis* and *forestum*) applied to Dartmoor in ancient documents, Mr. Jones's reference to Spelman does not appear to answer the purpose for which he intended it; as that writer includes woods or groves in his definition of a forest, and afterwards quotes the "Constitutiones Canuti Regis de Foresta," in which that monarch forbids the cutting down of trees in the forest without royal permission. One of the ancient officers, moreover, invariably attached to the forest was Custos sylvarum *. Manwood's opinion on the subject is expressed in his treatise on the Forest Laws with the utmost clearness and precision: nor will Manwood's authority be considered as of little weight, for the work itself discovers a complete knowledge of the subject in all its branches. "A forest," according to his definition, "is a certain territory of woody grounds and fruitful pastures, privileged for wild beasts and fowls of forest †, chace and warren, to rest and abide in, in the safe protection of the King, for his princely delight and pleasure; which territory is bounded by certain limits, known either by record or prescription, and also replenished with wild beasts of venery, or chace, and with great coverts of *vert*, for the security of wild beasts to have their abode in, for the preservation and continuance of which place,

* Spelman's definition of *foresta*, &c. is as follows: "Exteris sæpe occurrit pro saltu et sylva, simpliciter. Anglis vero ampla est ruris portio, deserta plerumque, et *nemorosa*, alendis feris regiis exposita: nullo sepimento, ut certis terminis, certisque legibus, magistratibus, judicibus, officialibus et ministris valde insignis et communita." The adverb *plerumque* seems properly to belong to *deserta*; but if it be extended to *nemorosa* also, still the circumstance of the forest being a shelter for wild beasts, the law against the cutting down the trees, and the appointment of an officer called the Keeper of the Woods, demonstrate that trees were originally a necessary appendage to the forest.

† "The wild beasts of forest," Manwood observes, "are five, and no more; namely, the hart, the hind, the hare, the boar, and the wolf; wild beasts of chace are also five, the buck, the doe, the fox, the marten, and the roos: the fowls of warren are the pheasant and the partridge;" nearly all requiring the shelter of trees.

together with the vert and venison, there are certain particular laws, privileges and officers belonging to the same, mete for that purpose, that are only proper for a forest, and not to any other place;" and one of these officers he states to be a keeper of the woods. He afterwards proceeds to show that woods and *vert* were indispensable to a forest, as without them beasts of chace would have no shelter, and consequently desert the territory. By *vert*, he also expressly states, are meant trees, woods, bushes, and such like underwood. Spelman's definition of this word also includes green trees as well as herbage. If therefore these authorities be allowed to be sufficient, there is no room for doubt that the districts to which the word forest was originally applied abounded with woods; and it may be moreover observed, many extensive tracts of land in the island, besides Dartmoor, that were once covered with trees, have still retained the name, though long denuded of these ancient appendages.

To all this may be added the following remarks by Mr. Burt, which he considers to be decisive on the subject. " By an account taken of the Dartmoor issues, in the 25th of Edward I., Ralf de Comber was fined 12*d.* for a dog taken in the forest at the time prohibited; Joel Kyr and two of his companions 6*s.* for a trespass *in the wood;* and Elias de Christinestone 6*s.* 8*d.* for being found in the forest at the time prohibited. The use of the word *wood* in this account, is plainly affirmative of the point in question: but there is, if possible, a more powerful, nay, an unanswerable corroboration of it in the expression *assartare* in John's charter* of liberties to Devon, which means to root, or grub up plants and trees by the root, &c., in which sense this interesting document undeniably uses it; thereby intending to render the disaforestation of parts severed from Dartmoor forest more complete†." The inference from the whole therefore appears to be unavoid-

* " A.D. 1203. An. 5. Johan. Carta de comitatu Devon' deaforestand' exceptis Dertemora et Exemora." Cart. Antiq. in Turr. Londin. K. 12. a copy of which is intended to be given in the course of this work.
† Preface to Carrington's Dartmoor, p. 20.

able, that in former periods Dartmoor was at least partially covered with trees. However, my intention was merely to state the arguments advanced on both sides, and to leave the reader, who may have better information on the subject, to form his own conclusions.

The method of planting, and the trees suited for the purpose.

As it is the opinion of those who are best acquainted with the Moor, that large portions of it are suitable for planting,—whenever this may be attempted, it can only be accomplished gradually, and by methods better adapted to the purpose than those which were made use of for plantations that have failed. Draining will of course be necessary in the first instance, as well as wider and deeper pits than heretofore for the reception of the young trees, the clayey substratum being cleared away, and a better soil being substituted, in which the plants might find nothing repulsive. Thick planting is also recommended, that the trees may form a shelter for each other; and especially each plantation, which should not be too large, should be surrounded by stone walls or turf embankments, sufficiently high not only to keep out intruders, but to afford some protection from the winds. A plantation being once formed, this also would afford shelter to another in its vicinity, and thus by degrees an extensive tract might be covered. The larch, Scotch fir, and birch, would no doubt be most suitable for the purpose; but many others may be added, of which the planter will be the best judge, as the silver, black, red and common spruce firs, Weymouth pines, mountain and common ash, holly, beech, sycamore, Spanish chestnut, oak, &c.

Other waste lands.

All round the forest are vast tracts of waste land, besides those in the north already adverted to. Walkham Common, among others, may be mentioned, comprising nearly ten thousand acres, formerly included in the forest. On Roborough Down are extensive commons, as also many thousand acres near Bridestow, in the neighbourhood of which is a lime rock, and which might be rendered good arable and pasture land. High-Tor Down and Haldon, if divided and inclosed, would prove to be as good sheep-walks as any in the kingdom. "Full one-fifth of Devon," says Mr. Frazer, "is waste land, amounting to 320,000 acres; all of which, except some parts of Dartmoor, are capable of improvement. 150,000*l.* additional rent might be made of these, and the additional produce would amount to half a million. This estimate, however, is probably below the reality." Mr. Prideaux also observes, in his communication to the Board of Agriculture, "That the county of Devon, if properly cultivated, and manure could be had in greater plenty, would produce double the quantity of corn it now does. The greatest obstruction, however, to improvement is the tithes." And speaking of his own efforts in this way, he says, "These improvements answer my most sanguine expectations; and I hope they will serve as a stimulus to others, as so many thousands of acres, well worth cultivating, lie in a state of nature, and without cultivation, except upon a bad plan. They pare and burn a few acres, plough very shallow, apply no manure, take one crop of wheat and two of oats, and then sow grass seeds. This method reduces the land to greater sterility than before." Having purchased land, covered with heath and furze, which at that time was let at sixpence an acre, he inclosed four or five hundred acres in fields, some twenty, some fifteen, and others about twelve acres each; made good hedges, and planted; built on one piece a dwelling-house, two barns, two ox-stalls for thirty oxen, a stable, &c. in the course of six years. He states that his crops had been wonderful, and the price of corn and cattle was then (in 1806) greatly in his favour. He also inclosed and improved another piece of land of superior quality, worth about 3*s.* an acre, which produced excellent flax and hemp, &c. After the course of cultivation which he intended to pursue, he had hopes that his land would be worth to a tenant 20*s.* per acre. On this land, he proceeds to state, that he was able to feed a large number of cows and sheep yearly, where no sheep had ever been fed, as the land had not been drained, nor had wheat or clover been sown on it before.

"I am sorry," observes this gentleman, "that the county of Devon is so much behind with respect to inclosing and improvement in agriculture, that not a single Act had then been passed for that purpose. Notwithstanding the importance of its local advantages from the vicinity of Plymouth and Devonport, which afforded so ready and profitable a market for its produce, more than one half of the county is uncultivated *."

Local Customs.

The following singular customs, as connected with the rural œconomy of the county, and mentioned by several writers as still more or less prevalent among the working farmers and their labourers, may be introduced here with propriety.

Harvest customs.

It was formerly a custom almost universally prevalent, for nearly the whole population of the villages to flock to the reaping, and the singular proceedings on these occasions have been already described†. In scarcely any parts of the county is this mode of gathering in the harvest now prevalent; but on account of the expense,— for though no wages are given, the entertainments on these occasions amount to considerable sums,—hiring reapers for the purpose has of late years become general, if not universal. Mr. Lysons, in his account of Cornwall, having described a singular custom prevalent in that county at the close of the harvest, mentions another that resembles it in the western extremity of Devonshire. Mr. Brand relates,—as he observes ‡, on the authority of the clergyman of Warrington, a parish in Devonshire on the Cornwall side of the Tamar,—that the ears of corn are tied up into a curious figure, which they call "a knack." This is brought home with great acclamations, the labourers shouting "A knack! a knack! well cut, well bound, well shocked," &c. It is then hung over the table in the farmer's house, and

* Communications to the Board of Agriculture, vol. v. p. 47; and vol. vi. part i. p. 192.   † p. 429.
‡ Mag. Brit. vol. vi. part i. p. 354.

kept till the next year, the owner preserving it with the
greatest care, and refusing on any account to part with it.

He also observes that the *Yule* or Christmas log is still
burnt in some parts of the county; and in others they
have the custom of burning, on Christmas eve, a large
faggot of green ash.   Mummers also go about at the
Christmas season, in some places, acting a kind of rude
drama on the subject of the exploits of St. George.

The following is also Mr. Lysons's account of a custom,
which, he says, is still prevalent in most parts of the cider
district, of what in former times was called "wassailing the
apple-trees," and which in some parts of the county is still
called "watsail."   The custom was accompanied by the
superstitious belief in the words of an old poet;

> "That more or less fruit they will bring,
>   As you do give them wassailing."

This ceremony at some places is performed on Christmas eve; at others on Twelfth-day eve.   It consists in
drinking a health to one of the apple-trees, with wishes
for its good bearing, which generally prove to be successful, as the best bearing tree in the orchard is selected for
the purpose.   It is attended with the singing of some
verses applicable to the occasion, beginning

> "Health to the good apple-tree!"

The potation consists of cider, in which are put roasted
apples or toast.   When all have drunk, the remainder of
the contents of the bowl is sprinkled over the apple-tree.
The Saxon term "wassail," which, it is well known, implies drinking health, is thus defined in the glossary of
the Exmoor dialect: "A drinking-song sung on Twelfth-
day eve, throwing toast to the apple-trees in order to a
fruitful year; which seems to be a relic of the heathen
sacrifice to Pomona."

The peasantry of the county do not appear to be remarkable for a quarrelsome and pugnacious disposition;
but the athletic exercise to which they are most addicted
is that of wrestling.   By this custom they, as well as the

Cornish men, have been distinguished from time immemorial, and it is still pursued with great avidity and emulation by the young farmers and labourers in the country. Whenever the progress of knowledge and civilization shall find its way among them, we rejoice in the conviction that all pastimes of this class, which at best are mere exhibitions of bodily strength and agility, and are too generally attended with much brutality and great excesses, will gradually give way to amusements more worthy of men, who ought at least to be ambitious of distinction by means of their understanding, their humanity and benevolence, as well as by their courage in defence of what is right. However, as this is one of the remarkable customs of the county, some account of it may be expected here : the following is the substance of that given by Mr. Vancouver*. A purse of six, eight, or ten pounds, having been made by persons of more property than the rest, a day is appointed for the meeting, generally near some village or market town. A ring being formed with stakes and ropes from fifteen to twenty yards in diameter, in this the winner must toss or throw down five of his antagonists. They are allowed to take hold any where above the waistband. The contest sometimes continues ten or fifteen minutes; much activity, strength, adroitness, and it may be added brutality also, are displayed, for the shins are seen to be streaming with blood from the sharp and violent blows which they receive from each other; and though the kicks are on no account permitted to be given above the knee, it sometimes happens that a leg is broken by them.

It is customary to shake hands before and after the contest, which is rarely followed by boxing or by any grudge or ill-will. It generally begins about two or three o'clock in the afternoon, and so well matched are the combatants, that the victory is frequently not declared till after midnight, in which case the ring is properly lighted, and precautions taken to secure fair play.

The moor-men are most celebrated for their capacity of

* Survey, p. 40.

Drawn by C. B. Compton.

Engraved by Jn.º Rolph.

VIEW ON THE BANKS OF THE GANGES ABOVE BENARES. 1826.

Drawn by G.B. Campion.

Engraved by Langley.

BICTON, DEVONSHIRE.

THE SEAT OF THE RIGHT HONOURABLE LORD ROLLE TO WHOM THIS PLATE IS RESPECTFULLY INSCRIBED

enduring excessive kicking upon the shins. The ill effects which might be expected to result from such violence, are soon carried off by their excellent habit of body and the peculiar temperament of their constitution.

In the outset of the play every man who becomes a standard for the purse must first throw two men on their back, belly, or side. Eight of these standards must be made from the primary competitors for the single play; and when the standards are thus made, they each receive a crown. Of these eight, four must fall; the other four then engage, two of whom must fall; when the remaining two enter to decide the purse, and the second best man, or he who is thrown last, usually receives about one in five upon its amount. Three triers or conductors of the lists are appointed, who decide all disputes immediately and without appeal *.

How far preferable to this are the amusements of the peasantry on the Continent, consisting chiefly of music and dancing in the open air!

* A remarkable work on this subject was published more than a century ago, with the title " Προγυμνασματα, The Inn-Play: or Cornish-Hugg Wrestler. Digested in a method, which teacheth to break all holds, and throw most falls mathematically, by Sir Thomas Parkyns of Bunny, Bart. Nottingham, 1714." with a 2nd edit. in 1784. There is nothing in it worth extracting. It consists chiefly of minute directions for the play. It serves to show, however, the constant progress of civilization and improvement. It was written by a Baronet, who was a great admirer of this practice, and who laments greatly that it was then much on the decline among gentlemen, in comparison with former periods. No gentleman would now be seen to practise it; and we trust, in the further progress of improvement, the time is not far distant when none will be found to give it encouragement.

A LIST

OF

SOME OF THE PROVINCIALISMS

Formerly at least prevalent chiefly among the common people of the county, though now probably, from the influence of modern improvement, gradually getting out of use.

————◆————

Agest, terrified.

All abroad, open. " The door is *all abroad.*"

An, than. " More *an* that;" more than that.

Aneest, near. " I won't go *aneest* en."

Aprill'd, soured, turned sour.

Apurt, sullen.

Arrishes, stubbles.

Arrish Mows, field stacklets.

Ausney, to anticipate bad news.

Avroar, frozen, frosty.

Barker, a rubber, or whetstone.

Barton, a large farm, or demesne.

Been, a withey, a band, or twisted twig.

Being, because. " *Being* it is so."

Belwit, to upbraid.

Billid, distracted.

Biver, to shake or quiver.

Blast, miss fire with a gun.

Blid, blood.

Bowerly, blooming, comely. " A *bowerly* woman."

Butt, a close-bodied cart.

Cheese, the pile of pomage in cider-making.

Cladgy, waxy. " The potatoes are *cladgy.*"

Clitty, close, clotted. " *Clitty* bread;" close bread.

Clouted Cream, cream raised by heat.

Clome, earthenware.

Cob, mud or loam with straw.

Colbrand, smut in wheat.

Combe, a hollow between two hills, open at one end only.

Cousin Betty, a female who goes about the country to excite charity.

Cowslip, foxglove.

Crowd, a violin.

Cruel, very; as "*cruel* good," "*cruel* kind."

Culvers, pigeons.

Daps, an exact likeness. "The very *daps* of him."

Dashels, thistles.

Dinder, thunder.

Dirsh, a thrush.

Dishwater, a water-wagtail.

Drashel, a flail.

Dring, a crowd.

Drudge, a large team-rake.

'e, for *ye,* is commonly used after the imperative of *do;* as,"' do *'e.*"

Eart, sometimes. "*Eart* one, *eart* another."

Eet a voreoll (probably, *yet afore all*), notwithstanding.

Elsh, new. "An *elsh* maid," an uncouth girl.

En, un, or *'n,* him or it. "I told *en;* I bought *en.*"

eth, the termination of the third person singular of verbs, is in use, as are also *hath* and *doth.*

Eute, to pour out.

Fags, truly! indeed!

Fadge, to fare. "How d' ye *fadge?*"

Faries or *varies,* squirrels.

Fineney*, to mince. "Zit down to table, good now; doan't ye *fineney* zo."

Fitty, clever.

Fore-right, plain, honest.

Foreweened, difficult to please.

Forth, out of temper.

Frith, brush wood.

Fudgee, to contrive to do.

Frump, the upshot, the principal matter.

* The *f* is generally pronounced like *v.*

2 x 2

Fustiluggs, a big-boned person.

Galdiment, a great fright.

Galey or *goiley,* ground where springs rise.

Gally, to frighten.

Geowering, quarrelling. " *Geowering* and maundering all the day," scolding and grumbling.

Giglot, a female laughing or playing wantonly.

Gill, a quart.

Ginged, bewitched.

Girts, for groats, oatmeal.

Gurry butt, a dung sledge.

Haydigees, in high spirits, frolicsome.

Heal or *hell,* to cover with slates.

Hellier, a slater.

Hend, to throw.

Hoke, to wound with the horns.

Hoop, a bullfinch.

Junket, coagulated milk or curds, eaten with sugar, spices, and clouted cream.

Kex, dry stalks. Some plants, as hemlock, are called *kexies.*

Kit, a tribe, collection, gang.

Keezer, a sort of sieve.

Lamiger, lame, crippled.

Latch, fancy, wish.

Leat, an artificial rill or rivulet.

Lew, sheltered, defended from storms.

Lidden, a tale, theme, subject.

Limmers or *limbers,* shafts.

Linhay, an open shed.

Manche, to chew, to eat.

Mang, to mix.

Meech, to play truant.

Mixen, a dunghill.

Moot, to root out.

Maur, a root.

Northering, wild, incoherent.

Nummet or *nunch,* luncheon.

Ort, anything.

Pike, peek, or *pick,* a hay-fork.

Pilm, dust.

Pixies, or *pisgies,* fairies.

Plum, light and puffy : as, " *plum* soil."

Ray, to dress.

Readship, confidence, trust.

Reed, unbound straw of wheat.

Roily, to rail.

Roo, rough.

Rowl, a fair or revel.

Sar, to earn or get.

Sewl, or *zule,* a plough *.

Sham, I am.   " *Sham* agest to go in ;" I am afraid to
    go in.

Shave, I have.

Shell, shall.

Shippen, an ox-house.

Slapdash, rough coating of buildings.

Slataxe, a mattock with a short axe-end.

Skeer, to mow lightly over.

Skram, to benumb with cold.

Skrent, to burn or singe.

Skir, a swift, a black martin.

Small, low, shallow : as, " a *small* river."

Smeech, fine dust in the air.

Souant, fair, even, regular.

Spine, turf, sward.

Spire, reed.

Staff, nine feet, half a rod.

Steckle, steep.

Stroll, a narrow slip of land.

Stroyl, couch-grass, or other weed, raked out of the soil.

Survey, a sort of auction for farms.

Tack, a shelf.

Taffety, delicate, nice, dainty.

Tallet, the garret, a room next the roof.

* *s* before a vowel is commonly pronounced like *z*.

Tang, to tie.

Tilty, testy, soon offended.

Tine, to shut, to close.

Tongtree, the pole of an ox-cart.

Tor, a rude rack on the top of a hill.

Tucker, a fuller.

Tucking-mill, a fulling-mill.

Turf, peat.

Tut, a hassock.

Tutty, a flower, or nosegay.

Tut-work, piece-work.

Twily, troublesome.

Unket, dreary, dull, lonesome.

Untang, to untie.

Vad, the beam of the cider-press.

Vell, to separate the turf entirely from the soil.

Vitty, apposite, suitable.

Vinny, mouldy.

Vlother, incoherent talk, nonsense.

Want, a mole.

Ward, to wade.

Wardship, a wagtail.

Whitaker, a species of quartz.

Wish, inapt, bad, unfit; as, " *wish* weather."

Woodquist, a wood-pigeon.

Zart, soft.

Zoundy, to swoon.

CHAPTER II.

HISTORY OF MINING, AND NOTICES OF MINERALS.

THE history of mining commences with the earliest ac- CHAP.
counts of the island; nor is there any doubt that the II.
mines were among the first sources of commercial intercourse with foreign countries, and, consequently, of
civilization and general improvement to the ancient
Britons. The tin of Britain was in request in distant
parts of the world at a very remote period; and, as far as
we can ascertain, it appears to have been this metal that
supplied the first inducement to merchants from the Mediterranean, in their frequent visits to the West of England
especially. Of the early commerce of the Phœnicians
with the Danmonians, and afterwards of the Greeks and
Romans, in succession, some account has already been
given in the former part of this work, Book II. chap. i.
The exaggerated notions which the Romans especially
had formed of the quantity of the precious metals supposed to abound in this country, are mentioned by historians among the principal incentives of that people to
their first attempts upon the island *.

That the Romans, after their conquest of the island,
employed themselves in mining operations in the western
counties, there seems to be no evidence.   The Saxons,
moreover, appear to have neglected those hidden trea-
sures; and this may account for the circumstance of no
mention being made of the Devonshire mines in Domesday Survey,—the agents of the Conqueror, when they
surveyed the county, having found no such works in ope-

* It is stated on good authority that the miners have repeatedly found,
in the course of their operations, shovels, spades, and mattocks, all made
of oak or holly; proofs sufficiently clear, that the mines were worked
before iron came into use in this country; and, consequently, not by
the Saxons, as the Cornish tradition is, but by the aboriginal Britons.

BOOK
IV.

ration. Subsequently, however, the Normans are said to have practised mining in the country, after its complete subjugation, with advantage. We find, indeed, that so early as the reign of Richard I., the mining of Devonshire was one of the principal resources of the earldom of Cornwall. In the 10th year of that King's reign, the earldom being then in the Crown, William de Wortham accounted to the Exchequer for the "ferm" and issues of the tin-mines of Devon and Cornwall; and in the 14th of King John, the same individual accounted for the sum of 100 marks for the ferm of the stannaries in Cornwall, and 200*l.* for that of Devon; from which it appears, that the mines of the latter county were at that time more productive than those of the former.

It should seem, however, that the mines were then not so productive as they soon afterwards became; for in the next reign, that of Henry III., the immense wealth which enabled Earl Richard, in 1257, to purchase the title of King of the Romans, was attributed by the old foreign historians to the revenue which he derived from the mines of his earldom. And in the same reign a charter was granted, in 1250, to the miners of Devon, commanding all knights and others, of whom the miners held, that they should not exact from them other customs and services than they ought and had been accustomed to do; nor to vex them contrary to the liberties they had before enjoyed under the charter of the King's predecessors, but maintain them in their said liberties *. During this reign also, Walter de Bathe, sheriff of Devon, accounted to the Exchequer for 25*s.* 1*d.* as the profits for black mineral, and 29*s.* 9*d: pro minera dealbanda,* or refining the ore and tin sold †.

In the beginning of the reign of Edward I. the mines seem to have been neglected; but Edmund, the elder son of the King, and Earl of Cornwall, willing to restore what

* Pat. Rot. in Tur. Londin. 35 Henry III.; and Lysons's Mag. Brit.
† Black tin is the ore before it is smelted; white tin, the pure metal after smelting.

had produced so large a portion of the revenues of his domains, made some important grants to the miners, which were confirmed by the King, by a charter, in the 33rd year of his reign *. By this charter, for the advancement of the stannaries, he frees the tinners of all pleas of the natives touching the court, and from answering before any justices, &c., save only the keepers of the stannaries (pleas of land, life, and member excepted); neither are they to be kept from work, but by the said keeper. It indemnifies them from tolls, &c., gives them liberty to dig tin and turf anywhere in the said county, and to turn water-courses at their pleasure, with many other privileges. By this charter also, the Devonshire stannaries became separated from those of Cornwall, though still retaining in common one Lord Warden; and the courts, or stannary parliaments, were thenceforth appointed to be held at Crockern Tor instead of Hengist Hill.

The lead mines of Devonshire and Cornwall are more enriched with silver than those of any other part of the kingdom. The produce of the mines of Combe Martin and Beer Alston, is said to have been unusually great in the reigns of Edward I. and II., and to have much enriched the Treasury of those monarchs. In the year 1293, William de Wymondham accounted to the Treasury for 270 lbs. of silver raised in Devonshire, which was given towards the portion of Eleanor, the King's daughter, then married to the Duke of Barr. In the year 1296, in which three hundred and sixty miners were impressed out of Derbyshire and Wales, there was great profit from the Devonshire mines †.

In the year 1326, near the close of Edward II.'s reign, it appears that the mine of Byrlande, which Mr. Lysons supposes to have been Beer, was in the King's hands; certain

* See Laws and Customs of the Stannaries, part ii., by Thomas Pearce, Gent. London, 1725; and Introduction to Risdon.
† Lysons's Mag. Brit., and Fuller's Worthies, which latter writer quotes from records in the Tower.

persons being empowered to elect miners in the counties of Cornwall and Devon, and to bring back such as had deserted from the works *.

In the early part of Edward III.'s reign there was a grant to the inhabitants of Devon, of liberty to dig for gold or silver in their own lands for two years, giving an account to the King's clerk †.

In 1337 the profits of the coinage of tin to the Earl of Cornwall, in the county of Devon, were 273*l.* 19*s.* 5¾*d.* In the year 1373, and the two following years, the coinage of tin produced, on an average, only 127*l.* per annum ‡.

In the 32nd of Edward III., the King granted exclusive license to John Ballantine and Walter Balbolter, to search for gold, silver, and copper, in all his mines in Devonshire, for two years §. This might be an experiment, for at the end of two years the King took the mines into his own hands; and in 1360 a writ was issued, authorizing certain persons to take up so many miners and working men as should be necessary to work in the King's mines in Devonshire, allowing them reasonable wages, according to the custom of the country; to arrest and imprison such as should resist, till they should give security to serve the King in the said mines; and to buy and provide timber at the common price‖. In 1361, John Wolf was made controller of the King's mines in Devonshire ¶: in 1730, a writ was directed to the masters of the King's mines in the county of Devon, empowering them to take eight men (miners, &c.) out of the county of York, and six miners from the counties of Nottingham and Derby **.

* Pat. Rot. 19 Edward II. m. 18. Mag. Brit.
† Pat. Rot. 12 Edward III. Mag. Brit.
‡ Mag. Brit.
§ Pettus's Fodinæ Regales; or, the History of the Laws and Places of the chief Mines and Mineral Works in England, p. 13.
‖ Pat. Rot. 34 Edward III. part i. m. 9. Mag. Brit.
¶ Pat. Rot. 35 Edward III.
** Pat. Rot. 44 Edward III. part ii. m. 2. dors. Mag. Brit.

Richard II., in 1377, appointed Henry de Burton, by himself and his deputies, to search all mines of gold and silver in the counties of Devon, Cornwall, &c., as well in the banks of rivers and in rivulets, as in other places in the said counties, where it might seem to be most for the King's advantage; and also to elect and take, wheresoever they might be found, such labourers and workers as should be necessary for digging and works; and to imprison such as should resist *. In the 8th of the same reign, license was granted to Richard Wake, clerk, to dig for gold and silver in the King's mines, in the county of Devon, for ten years, paying tithes to the church, and one-ninth to the Exchequer †. In 1405, Henry IV. granted a lease of his lead-mines, containing silver, in the county of Devon, for ten years, on condition of paying yearly nine pounds of pure silver,—William Charleton, the prior of Pilton, being appointed controller ‡. In 1427, John Duke of Bedford had a lease of all mines in England for ten years, paying tithes to the church, a fifteenth to the King, and a twentieth to the lord of the soil : and in 1438, the 17th of Henry VI., on the expiration of the Duke of Bedford's term, John Solers obtained a lease of all mines of gold and silver in Devon and Cornwall, and of all mines of lead containing silver or gold, for twenty years, paying to the Crown a fifteenth of pure gold and silver §. In 1440, Richard Curson, Esq. had a twenty years lease of all mines of gold and silver in Cornwall and Devon, with wood and underwood requisite for the purpose of proving and refining metal ‖. In 1451, John Bottwright, the King's chaplain, was made controller of the mines in these two counties ¶; and the following year a lease of them was granted to the same individual, to be held during good behaviour, paying to the Crown the tenth part of pure gold

* Pat. Rot. 1 Richard II. part i. m. 2. Mag. Brit.
† Pettus, p. 14. Pat. Rot. 8 Richard II.
‡ Pettus, p. 15. Pat. Rot. 7 Henry IV.
§ Pettus, p. 15. Pat. Rot. 17 Henry VI.
‖ Mag. Brit. Pat. Rot. 19 Henry VI.
¶ Pettus, p. 16. Pat. Rot. 30 Henry VI.

BOOK
IV.

and silver, copper, tin, and lead, with power to let them for twelve years *. In 1454, Alured Cornburgh was appointed controller; and in the following year a lease was granted by the King of all his mines of gold and silver, and of all other metals containing gold and silver, within the counties of Devon and Cornwall, to the Duke of York, for twenty-one years †. And John Bottwright, before mentioned, in 1457, being governor of the mines of Beer Ferrers, soon afterwards, as appears by a record in the Exchequer (an. 36 Henry VI.), made complaint, that Robert Glover, by command of Roger Champernoun, lord of the manor, took away 144 *bouls of glance* ore, valued at 15*l.* 6*s.* 8*d.*, and made profit of the same, without anything allowed to the King, to the King's damage of 100*l.* ‡ The same year, soon after the accession of Edward IV., all the King's mines in Devon and Cornwall were leased to Sir John Neville, of Montague, at the usual rent of 110*l.* §

In 1471, the quantity of tin raised in Devon was 242,624 lbs., the profit to the Duke being 190*l.* 17*s.* 11$\frac{1}{4}$*d.* at the rate of 1*s.* 6$\frac{3}{4}$*d.* per hundred weight; and in 1749 the profits were 166*l.* 9*s.* 5$\frac{1}{4}$*d.* ‖

Henry VII. appears to have paid great attention to the mines of his kingdom, and by their means to have added greatly to his revenues. In the first year of his reign, he appointed Jasper Duke of Bedford, and other persons of rank, commissioners and governors of all his mines of gold, silver, tin, lead, and copper, in England and Wales; and Sir William Taylor controller for twenty years, paying to the King a fifteenth of pure gold and silver, and to the lord of the soil an eleventh: and the prosperous condition in which he left the Treasury at the time of his death, is attributed, in part at least, to the produce of the mines ¶.

---

* Pettus, p. 16.   Pat. Rot. 31 Henry VI.
† Pettus, p. 17.   Pat. Rot. 34 Henry VI.
‡ Pettus, p. 17.   Rees's Cyclop. art. *Mining.*
§ Pat. Rot. Edward IV.
‖ Lysons's Mag. Brit.
¶ Pettus, p. 19, and Pat. Rot. an. 1 Henry VII.

In the year 1510, the 2nd of Henry VIII., a charter of statutes respecting the Devonshire tin-mines was continued, and afterwards printed at Tavistock, August 20th, 1534, being the 26th of the same reign. This singular book, consisting of sixteen leaves quarto, was communicated by the Rev. Joseph Sandford, of Baliol College Oxford, to Mr. Ames, who takes notice of it in his History of Printing. In 1531 and 1535, the 23rd and 27th of the same reign, acts were passed for making "*hatches and tyes*," to prevent the choking of rivers by stream works, at the ports of Plymouth, Dartmouth, and Teignmouth in Devonshire, and Falmouth and Fowey in Cornwall *. From this latter circumstance, it is reasonable to infer that the stream-works on the rivers of both these counties were carried on very extensively.

In the reign of Edward VI. the mines appear to have been neglected, and were not likely to receive more attention under the bigoted and tyrannical government of his successor. We read, however, that in 1557, the 5th of Mary, an order or letter was addressed by the Lord Chancellor Hows to John Trelawnye, Thomas Trefre, John Tredenick, and William Carnesewe the elder, to take the charge of the mines discovered in the counties of Devon and Cornwall by Burchart Cranice, *Almaine*†.

Elizabeth oppressed and paralysed the industry of her subjects by the most impolitic and unjust monopolies; but the mines of the kingdom in general, which she considered well calculated to enlarge her resources, partook of the benefit which the fostering care of this economical and sagacious Queen extended to whatever might contribute to the prosperity of her government. With this view, Germans, who appear to have been more skilful in mining than the natives of this country, were invited over to open mines in different parts of the kingdom; and on the 10th October, in the 6th year of this reign, grants

* Preface to Carrington's Dartmoor.
† *Ibid.* p. 54.

BOOK
IV.

were made of the mines of eight counties, including Devonshire and Cornwall, besides those in Wales, to Houghsetter and Thurland; and the next year, further grants were made to William Humphreys and Christopher Schutz, a German, of all her mines in England and Ireland not included in the former patent. A corporation, moreover, which still exists*, was also organized in 1568, the 10th of the same reign, under the denomination of The Society for the Mines Royal, which had certain grants and privileges in several counties, and of which William Earl of Pembroke was the first governor; and so important was the object of the society considered, that, besides this nobleman, Sir Nicholas Bacon, then Lord Keeper, the Duke of Norfolk, Robert Earl of Leicester, William Lord Cobham, Sir William Cecill, Sir Walter Mildmay, Sir Henry Sidney, Sir Francis Jepson, Sir William Gerard, and twenty-nine other persons of distinction, both natives and foreigners, were appointed members. By means of a joint stock, this society is said to have effected great benefit both to the Exchequer and themselves†. It does not appear, however, that they had any power to interfere in the tin-mines of Devonshire, which continued under the jurisdiction of the stannaries; but it is observed, in the Preface to Risdon ‡, that it is probable Houghsetter and Thurland worked mines in this county for copper, as well as for lead and silver. Evident traces, it is added, of ancient works have lately been discovered on a copper lode at Crowndale, near Tavistock; and it is remarkable, that the name of the place, so very unlike most others

* The usual history, says Mr. Lysons, of Royal mines, has been, that they were first worked at the King's expense: when they became less productive, they were farmed out: afterwards, when abandoned by the lessee, permission was granted to individuals or companies, who were more enterprising, to work them: hence arose the Company for Working the Mines Royal. The power which this society once possessed having been much abused, was justly considered as highly injurious to the liberty of the subject, and has been abridged so as to render it nugatory.

† Pettus, p. 20.   ‡ p. 18.

in the neighbourhood, is similar to the names to be found connected with many of the mines in Germany *. It is generally believed, that the lead and silver-mines at Beer Ferrers and Combe Martin were extensively worked in this reign; though, as to the former, it is certain, from the extract above quoted from the records of the Exchequer, that it had existence long before. These mines, however, are not noticed by any contemporary writer on the subject †. In the 16th of this reign, a new act was passed, for the preservation of the havens in the counties of Devon and Cornwall, which had been greatly injured by the rubble descending from the tin-works. This was intended to confirm and enlarge the two acts on the same subject in the 23rd and 27th of Henry VIII.; and the penalties were increased, because, as the preamble states, the former acts not having been put in execution, redress of the grievances complained of had not been obtained ‡. Towards the close of this reign, however, in 1602, the profits of the coinage of tin in Devonshire amounted only to 102l. 17s. 2$\frac{3}{4}d$.§ It was in this reign also, that Sir Walter Raleigh was appointed Lord Warden of the stannaries of Devonshire and Cornwall.

From Risdon, who wrote about the year 1630, we derive no information respecting the state of the mines in his time; for he merely observes : " Out of the bowels of the earth there are found and digged sundry rich mines and minerals; some of tin and lead, some of iron, and other metals : and in following those veins of tin, some have lighted on silver, against Cicero's affirmation, that denieth any such to be found in Britain." But as he describes the daily " labourers in tin-works," whom he calls " Spadiards," as forming one class of the labourers of the county, it seems probable that the tin-works on

* Mr. Lysons says the Combe Martin mines were re-opened in the reign of Queen Elizabeth, under the direction of Sir Bevis Bulmer, a skilful engineer, much esteemed by the Queen and her ministers.
† Introduction to Risdon, p. 18.　　　‡ Pearce, p. 242.
§ Lysons's Mag. Brit., and Doddridge.

BOOK
IV.

Dartmoor employed a considerable number of hands. Webster, who wrote a treatise on metals about the year 1670, mentions the tin-mines of Devonshire as being productive, and gives particulars of some situated on the hills above Plympton, which he had from a person of the name of Creber, of that place, who was one, as he says, that had wrought in the tin-mines, and all his ancestors before him *.

In the reigns of James I. and his successor Charles, the whole amount of tin raised annually in Devonshire and Cornwall, was from 1400 to 1600 tons. Mr. Bushell, a celebrated mineralogist of that time, and a pupil of Sir Francis Bacon, strongly recommended the working of Combe Martin mines to the Long Parliament in 1659†. But it is probable that the civil wars, which harassed the western counties especially for a considerable time, greatly injured the working of the mines; for in a note of Mr. Scawen of Molinick, who was vice-warden of the stannaries, quoted by Dr. Pryce, it appears that the tin revenues were very small. We find also, that the records of the stannary laws previously made, were destroyed during those commotions, at the time when the Prince's Exchequer at Lostwithiel was plundered and burnt‡. Fuller, moreover, who wrote soon after the Restoration, observes, that the mines of Combe Martin had not recovered their former credit. They do not appear to have been opened before the close of that century, and then without success.

In the reigns of Anne and George I., the produce of tin had again become considerable, and amounted, one year with another, to something more than 1600 tons; so that in the space of 110 years, its mean proportion was equal to 1500 tons per annum. Afterwards, a gradual increase took place in the ensuing thirty years; for, in 1742, a proposal was made by the Mines Royal Company in London, established in Elizabeth's reign, to raise 140,000l. for the purpose of encouraging the tin

* Introduction to Risdon, p. 19.   † Lysons's Mag. Brit.
‡ Pearce.

trade, by farming that commodity for seven years at a certain price. A company of Cornish gentlemen were appointed to consider the proposal; and they reported, that the " quantity of tin raised yearly in Cornwall, on an average for many years last past, had been about 2100 tons."

The chief part of the tin raised from the year 1700 to 1800, was produced from the mines in Cornwall alone; as, although Devonshire had yielded in ancient times a large proportion of the tin, yet before this period the mines, or rather stream-works of the latter county, had become exhausted in a great measure, and were incapable of producing any notable proportion of ore *.

When Chapple wrote his review of Risdon, in 1770, it would appear, that mining had scarcely existence in Devonshire; for in alluding to Risdon's account of the tinners before mentioned, he tells us that no such labourers were then in the county. It is highly probable, however, that Chapple did not make sufficient inquiries into the subject, for mining was certainly carried on in it in his time. Early in the eighteenth century, the lead mines in Mary Tavy were worked by Mr. Moore, who was also employed in searching for copper in this and some of the adjacent parishes. Not long after this period, mining again started into notice; but the first efforts that were made for its revival, were not such as to put it upon the respectable footing upon which it has since stood. Some small quantities of tin, which were produced from a mine in Dartmoor by certain poor men, about fifty years since, attracted the notice of speculators, who engaged in numerous undertakings of this kind; and not finding in the neighbourhood a sufficient number of persons of the same views with themselves, endeavoured to obtain support in London, and with some success. Many mines were thus set to work; but for want of skill or discretion, they generally proved unprofitable †.

* Rees's Cyclopædia.   † Introduction to Risdon, p. 19.

Mr. Lysons informs us, that the average quantity of tin raised in Devonshire for six years, ending at Michaelmas 1820, was 1171 blocks, weighing 586 cwt. 9 lbs, and yielding a duty of 45*l.* 17*s.* 9*d.* Of the tin-mines then at work, Vitefer in North Bovey, Ailsborough in Shipstor, and Whiteworks in Lidford, he adds, were upon a large scale. The former had been productive, but was then on the point of being abandoned : Gobbett, in Widdecombe-on-the-Moor, was about that time at work: Wheal Union and Bottlehill in Plympton St. Mary were then worked also for tin and copper. There were besides some stream-works and small mines near Dartmoor, that were then carried on by labouring miners on their own account. The old stream-works of Plympton were renewed some years before, but had been neglected since 1805 *.

* The following table of abandoned tin-mines was communicated to Mr. Lysons by J. Taylor, Esq.

Parishes.	Names of Mines.	When last worked
Ashburton	Whiddon Down	1810
North Bovey	Peckpits	
Lidford	Bachelors' Hall	1810
Widdecombe	Huntington	1810
	Brimpts	1807
Walkhampton	Nuns	1810
	Keaglesborow	1810
	Gad's Hall	1780
	Whitemoor Mead	1790
Mary Tavy	Wheal Jewel	1791
	Wheal Unity	1795
	Wheal Saturday	1809
Tavistock	Devil's Kitchen	1795
Whitechurch	Wheal Surprise	1795
	Concord	1795
	Concord East	1795
Walkhampton	Wheal Mary	1795
Shaugh	Wheal Sidney	1795
Buckland	Furzehill	1798
Sampford	Grimstone	1805

These had been abandoned before 1815 : since that time, East Poldice in Buckland, Wheal Greenofen in Whitechurch, and Wheal Lucky in Sampford Spiney, have been abandoned. These were worked but a short time.

The tin-mines at present in work, says Mr. Burt (1826), are Vitifer in North Bovey, and Ailsborough in Sheepstor, which has a smelting-house, where 100 blocks were coined for Michaelmas quarter 1824.

The Combe Martin mines, after being closed some time, were again opened in 1813, and continued to be worked for four years, during which 208 tons of ore were shipped for Bristol; but the quantity of silver obtained not being found sufficient to pay the expense of working, they were given up in the month of August 1817 *.

The mines of Beer Alston and Beer Ferrers are remarkable for the length of time for which at different periods they have been worked, and for the quantity of silver which they contain; the silver in each ton of lead being from eighty ounces to one hundred and twenty †. This may be supposed, as mentioned before, to be the mine which in a record of Henry VI. is called Bir-lond. Either this, or the mine at Beer Ferrers, was worked, in the reign of Charles II., by Sir John Maynard; but, as it is said, without success. In 1783 or 1784 this mine was again opened by Christopher Gullet, Esq., and the silver produce of the year 1784 and 1785 amounted to 6500 ounces ‡. Extensive preparations were also made for reopening Beer Alston mines about 1809; and the undertaking was divided into 3000 shares of 100l. each. It has been said that some time after the last opening, 6000 ounces of silver were produced in six weeks. The mines are described as 110 fathoms deep, and running under the Tamar §. The Beer Alston and Beer Ferrers mines are contiguous upon two lodes or veins. They have not answered to the adventurers; and the whole has

* Lysons's Mag. Brit.

† Information given to Mr. Lysons by Mr. Taylor. An article in Rees's Cyclopædia states, that in one the portion of silver is 70 ounces in the ton, and in another 170. Mr. John Hitchins speaks of 140 ounces as the greatest quantity occasionally occurring in the ore in South Hooe mine at Beer Alston.—Mag. Brit.

‡ From information of John Hawkins, Esq., communicated to Mr. Lysons.

§ Rees's Cyclopædia.

been again abandoned, except the mine called South Hooe[*].

Wheal Betsy lead-mine, in Mary Tavy, which had been worked eighty years before, was re-opened about 1806, and has been a productive concern. The quantity of pig-lead obtained from it was in 1822 between 300 and 400 tons in a year, and the silver from 4000 to 5000 ounces, although a ton of the lead yielded only twelve ounces[†]. This mine is drained by large water-wheels, and is about sixty fathoms deep, with good promises of continuing productive[‡].

About the year 1787, Mr. Gullet, above mentioned, re-opened a lead and silver mine at Newton St. Cyres; but it was abandoned after a trial of five or six years. The proportion of silver in this ore is said to have been thirty ounces in a ton[§].

There are said to have been old iron-mines at Rattery, and near South Molton. Vancouver mentions, that a considerable quantity of rich iron-stone was sent annually

---

[*] Mag. Brit.

[†] From the information of Mr. Taylor to Mr. Lysons. The pig-lead is smelted at the mine: some of the produce is sent away in ore.—Mag. Brit.

[‡] Other mines worked about 1820, were Wheal Prosperous, in Hennock; Wheal Mary, in Mary Tavy; Birch Cleve, Buttspile, and Wheal Ezenedge, in Beer Ferrers parish.—Ibid.

[§] From the information of J. Hawkins, Esq. to Mr. Lysons. The lead veins or lodes in Devon range from north to south, crossing the usual direction of the copper and tin mines. It is said, that there have been mines formerly at Ilsington: lead ore has been found at Rattery: lead is found accompanying the copper in Wheal Friendship. At one time this was the only lead ore raised in the county.

The following list of lead mines abandoned before 1815, was communicated to Mr. Lysons by Mr. John Taylor.

Parishes.	Names of Mines.	When last worked.
Yarnscombe	(Unknown)	1794
Berry Narbor	Berry Mine	1809
Lidford	Wheal Mercy	1810
Beer Ferrers	Wheal Resolution	1795
————	North Hooe	1795
————	Furze Hill	1785
————	Whitsum	1785
————	Lockeridge	1785
————	Wheal Unity	1805

from the neighbourhood of Combe Martin to South Wales.
Upon inquiry, Mr. Lysons found that this was from the
year 1796 to 1802, and it was sent to the iron-works at
Llanelly. The quantity sent in seven years was 9293
tons : none has been shipped since 1802 *.

We have seen, that in early records, copper-mines in
Devonshire are mentioned; but it appears, that the raising of this mineral in the county, with any advantage, is
of recent date. Little attention seems to have been
paid to it before the year 1726; but, about that time,
some attempts were made to work several mines in which
this metal was found. It was not, however, till the commencement of the present century that they began to be
productive. Mr. Polwhele, indeed, in his History of
Devonshire, published in 1798, speaks of copper-mines
at Ashburton, Wood Huish in the parish of Brixham,
Sampford Spiney, and a mine at Oakhampton, worked
some years, but long since deserted. Of these mines he
promised to give. a more particular account, but omits
doing this in the subsequent part of his work; and upon
inquiry at Oakhampton, Mr. Lysons could not find that
any copper-mine had ever been worked there with success.
About the period, however, when Mr. Polwhele's work
was published, part of the county of Devon began to
attract notice as a mining district, namely, that which
borders upon the Tamar; and which must therefore be
considered as a branch of the great mineral country on the
other side of the river, the features of both being nearly
alike, their productions very similar, and the system of

* The following is a list of the quantities shipped in each year :—

Date.	Tons.
In 1796	116
1797	1584
1798	1336
1799	1012
1800	2114
1801	2024
1802	106

From the information of Walter Locke, Esq. of Ilfracombe, to Mr.
Lysons.

operation in Devonshire being borrowed from Cornwall. But previously to 1800, it is supposed that the copper-mines in Devonshire, chiefly situated within a few miles of Tavistock, had not yielded altogether, in any one year, more than 100 tons of fine copper; and even this was, at that time, a recent occurrence. The rise in the price of the metal, gave a great stimulus to the exertions of the miners; and from this time the quantity of ore raised rapidly increased *. Several copper-mines were worked near Tavistock; many hands were employed, as well as some of the most extensive and powerful water-engines in the world; and, as exhibiting the best proof of the value and importance of the mineral produce of this district, Mr. J. Taylor, in the Introduction to Risdon, gives the following statement of the exact return of these mines, as far as the year 1810; the same gentleman enabled Mr. Lysons to carry on the account from that period to the year 1820, and has also favoured the present writer with the continuation of it to this time. The whole is as follows:

	Copper Ores.			Fine Copper.				Value.		
	tons.	cwt.	qrs.	tons.	cwt.	qrs.	lbs.	£.	s.	d.
1801	1078	18	0	136	6	3	23	12878	6	1
1802	2204	6	0	252	12	1	21	22950	0	0
1803	2486	0	1	288	4	1	2	36581	16	9¼
1804	2578	17	0	283	16	1	3	29119	9	11¼
1805	3832	16	2	332	0	2	16	43130	16	7
1806	4542	13	0	412	0	3	6	50714	10	8
1807	3916	5	0	394	15	1	6	36526	6	5¼
1808	3308	3	0	346	6	3	21	26894	2	3¼
1809	3206	7	2	361	19	3	4	35245	11	6¼
1810	3747	2	3	358	1	3	5	39568	3	1 †
1811	3540	0	0	325	13	0	0	31517	15	0
1812	5321	1	1	506	15	2	7	40340	18	11
1813	5020	3	2	475	10	2	22	39076	16	11
1814	5743	3	3	473	5	3	8	45772	12	3
1815	4691	5	0	371	10	2	17	30581	13	9
1816	3650	14	3	319	5	1	26	21270	4	6
1817	3390	8	2	287	2	3	0	21093	12	7
1818	4053	15	3	407	16	0	0	40496	2	9
1819	3776	10	1	374	16	1	9	36418	9	7
1820	4037	3	1	463	11	3	24	39593	15	11 ‡

* Pryce's Mineralogia Cornubiensis, and Lysons's Mag. Brit.
† Introduction to Risdon, p. 21.   ‡ Mag. Brit.

	Copper Ores.			Fine Copper.				Value.		
	tons.	cwt.	qrs.	tons.	cwt.	qrs.	lbs.	£.	s.	d.
1821	3894	15	1	455	19	1	26	33670	16	2
1822	4941	20	3	524	5	1	4	40220	6	10
1823	4568	14	3	495	2	1	14	39969	18	6
1824	5106	20	3	526	19	0	19	41311	9	7
1825	4673	0	0	502	10	3	0	48461	2	9
1826	4229	0	0	447	17	3	0	36187	13	3
1827	3821	0	0	455	18	3	0	35321	19	2
1828	3244	0	0	351	2	0	0	27711	18	8
1829	3597	0	0	345	13	0	0	26135	17	0
1830	3914	0	0	332	10	0	0	23426	15	10

When his History of Devonshire was published (1822), Mr Lysons informs us, that the principal copper-mines then at work, were Wheal Friendship, in Mary Tavy; Wheal Crowndale, in Tavistock; Wheal Crebor, near the tunnel on the Tavistock canal *; East and West Liscombe, on the west; and a mine at Buckfastleigh.

Wheal † Friendship mine, he further observes, which also produced some lead, was at that time very productive of rich copper ore. It had been worked for twenty-five or twenty-six years, and was then 170 fathoms deep. Wheal Crowndale, which was discovered in 1799, was rich in ore for about ten years; but of late it had been so very unproductive, that it was then nearly abandoned: it was 110 fathoms deep. Wheal Crebor was very rich about 1811 to 1819, when it became unproductive; but further discoveries had been lately made, which promised to render it more productive: it was about eighty fathoms deep. East Liscombe, discovered about 1818, had lately become productive; and a large water-wheel was erected to drain the mine, for the purpose of prosecuting further discoveries: it was about fifty fathoms deep. Wheal Tamar, near the river of that name, had been worked about thirty years, and was rich in copper ore for a short time, but had not of late years been productive. This was the only copper-mine in the county which had a steam-engine, the

* For an account of the construction of the tunnel of the Tavistock canal, see p. 321 of this work.

† Wheal (or rather huel) is said to be derived from the Cornish language, and to signify a work or mine.

BOOK
IV.

others having been worked by very powerful over-shot water-wheels, some of which are from forty to fifty feet diameter. The four last-mentioned mines, Wheal Crowndale, Wheal Crebor, East Liscombe, and Wheal Tamar, are on the same lode, which ranges as usual from east to west, and are included in a space of about four miles in length. There were other copper-mines which had been tried, or were at that time (1822) being explored, but were not considered as entitled to particular notice.

The copper-mine at North Molton is said to have been worked many years with good success : it had been abandoned before 1778. Vancouver speaks of it as having been re-opened, and worked about the year 1815 ; but it was not found to answer to the adventurers, and has since been wholly abandoned *.

* We extract also the following list of mines at work about 1815, but which had not been productive, communicated by Mr. Taylor to Mr. Lysons, for his History of Devonshire in the Magna Britannia.

Parishes.	Mines.	
North Molton	The old mine	Since again given up.
Mary Tavy	Wheal Hope	}Soon given up.
———	North Wheal Crebor	
———	Wheal Georgina	{Produced some copper, but not of importance.
Bickleigh	Wheal Henry	}Unsuccessful.
Tavistock	Wheal Burn	
———	William and Mary	{Produce small, given up, but re-opened the last year.
———	George and Charlotte	
———	Wheal Impham	}Given up.
———	South Wheal Tamar	

The ore of North Molton mine was plentiful in 1729, and sold then at 6l. 10s. per ton, a good price at that time. Woodward.—This mine is said to have produced specimens of gold.

The following is another list of abandoned copper-mines, drawn up about 1815, and furnished by Mr. Taylor to the same work.

Parishes.	Names of Mines.	When last worked.
Ashburton	Ausewell Wood	1810
Molland	Molland Mine	1770
Oakhampton	Wheal Oak	1808
Bridestow	———	1809
Tavistock	Wheal Bedford	1812
———	Wheal Adam	1806
———	Wheal Peter	1811

SHREWSBURY, FROM KINGSLAND.

Drawn by G. B. Campion.   Engraved by James Tingle.

This brings the history of copper mining in Devon down to 1820.

At the present time (1831) the state of mining in the county is at a low ebb. Various copper lodes have been tried since the period to which the preceding accounts relate; and though ore has been found in many, the quantity has not often been sufficient to pay for the working of them.

The character of the lodes in Devonshire seems to be that of having a few rich masses, such as have occurred at Wheal Friendship, Wheal Crowndale, and Wheal Crebor, but not of being generally enriched, as in many parts of Cornwall. The annexed tables of produce, &c. will show some decline since 1820 * : the number of mines however

CHAP. II.

State of mining in 1831.

Parishes.	Names of Mines.	When last worked.
Tavistock	Great Duke	1813
————	Wheal Tool	1812
————	Holming Beam	1810
————	Marquis	1812
————	Wheal Tavistock	1810
————	Wheal Smith	1810
Whitchurch	Wheal Surprise	1812
Buckland Monachorum	Virtuous Lady	1807
———— ————	Crackern Beam	1807
———— ————	Wheal Charlotte	1807
Whitchurch	Wheal Carpenter	1803
Lamerton	Wheal Capeltor	1803
Owlacombe mines, near Ashburton, were abandoned about		1815

* *Produce of Wheal Betsy Mine from 1821 to 1830 inclusive.*

Date.	Silver.		Pig Lead.				Lead Ores.			Litharge.				Value.		
	oz.	dwt.	tons.	cwt.	qr.	lb.	tons.	cwt.	qr.	tons.	cwt.	qr.	lb.	£.	s.	d.
1821	4202	0	317	1	2	3	105	15	0	40	0	0	0	8927	16	11
1822	3178	0	250	13	1	3	418	10	0	0	10	0	0	10635	6	1
1823	5704	10	261	3	3	11	220	10	2					8553	11	0
1824	5870	0	482	16	3	9	450	12	2					16922	18	11
1825	4448	10	473	5	2	12	1195	8	0	3	7	2	27	12786	0	½
1826	6368	0	400	18	1	26				22	0	0	0	10101	5	7
1827	5742	0	494	16	1	14				5	12	3	4	10623	7	4
1828	7109	15	523	16	0	11				2	3	3	19	10644	4	6
1829	5869	10	416	16	2	21				1	13	1	20	7213	10	0
1830	4810	0	378	12	0	12				1	14	0	0	6253	10	2
							Cop. Ores.									
	52302	5	4000	0	3	10	0	13	1	77	1	3	14	102661	10	11

BOOK
IV.

is more reduced than the produce itself.　The only ones now in effective working being, Wheal Friendship, Wheal Franco, and the Virtuous Lady, for copper; and Wheal Betsy, for lead *.

THE STANNARY COURTS.

History of
the Stan-
nary
Courts.

The administration of justice, as it relates to the tin mines in Devonshire and Cornwall, is in the hands of the Stannary Courts, which are courts of record in these counties.　They are held before the Lord Warden or his substitutes, by virtue of a privilege granted to workers in the tin mines, to sue and be sued only in their own courts, in order that they may not be drawn from their employment by lawsuits in other courts.　The peculiar privileges of the tinners, and the laws by which they are governed, are more ancient than the time of Edward I., as appears by two charters of King John, and Richard King of the Romans, now in the Tower†.　They were confirmed, however, by a charter of Edward; were fully expounded

Produce of Wheal Friendship Mine from 1821 *to* 1830 *inclusive.*

Date.	Copper Ores. tons. cwt. qrs.	Lead Ores. tons. cwt. qrs.	White Tin. cwt. qrs. lb.	Amount. £. s. d.
1821...	2665 17 0	53 7 0	0 0 0	28361 7 9
1822...	2831 18 1	25 10 0	4 2 10	29871 17 10
1823...	2471 7 1	24 16 0	21 1 2	25571 6 7
1824...	2884 14 1	0 0 0	1 2 6	27966 10 8
1825...	3285 8 2	0 0 0	252 0 4	38696 0 7
1826...	3114 15 0	0 0 0	116 2 18	33619 0 2
1827...	2627 6 3	0 0 0	296 3 12	28621 15 10
1828...	2670 4 1	0 0 0	64 2 5	25603 12 8
1829...	2167 12 2	0 0 0	38 1 26	19250 9 7
1830...	1931 2 2	21 2 2		15678 10 10
	26650 1 1	124 15 2	795 3 25	273240 12 6

The above account is made up to Michaelmas in each year. The last year is estimated, the accounts not having been closed at the Mine till December.

* For this account of the present state of mining in the county, and the annexed tables, I am indebted to John Taylor, Esq., F.R.S., &c.
† Laws and Customs of the Stannaries; in Two Parts—Part 2nd by Thomas Pearce, Gent.; also Inst. 231, 232 ; and Rees's Cyclopedia.

by a private statute 50 Edward III.; and since explained by a public Act, 16 Charles I. c. 25. According to these Acts, while the miners are employed in and about the Stannaries, they can be impleaded only in the Stannary Courts in any matters, except pleas of land, life and member. No writ of error lies hence to any of the courts of Westminster, as was agreed by the Judges in 4 James I. An appeal, however, lies from the Steward of the court to the Under-warden, and from him to the Lord Warden, and thence to the Prince of Wales, as Duke of Cornwall, when he hath had livery and vestiture of the same. Thence the appeal lies to the King himself in the last resort. The Lord Warden has two deputies, or vice-wardens, one for each county, who officiate as Judges in the respective courts.

Prince Arthur, eldest son of Henry VII., made certain constitutions relative to the Stannaries, which the tinners refusing to observe, and taking greater liberties than their charter allowed, the King, after Prince Arthur's death, made that a pretence to secure the Stannaries in his own hands; but finding them not so productive as he expected, he was content to accept of 1000*l.* in lieu of all the pretended forfeitures; confirmed the privileges of the tinners; and at the same time granted by charter, that no new laws affecting the miners should be enacted by the Duke and his Council, without the Stannary Courts, consisting of twenty-four jurats or jurors for each county, chosen by the mayors, or chief magistrates, in the proportion of six for each of the stannary towns, those for Devon being Chagford, Ashburton, Plympton, and Tavistock *. The meeting of these Stannators, as they are called, who are some of the principal gentlemen of property in the mining districts, is called a Stannary Parliament, and on their assembling they choose a Speaker. Every Act of these courts must be signed by the jurors, the Lord Warden or his deputies, and the Duke himself in his privy council, or by the King: it then has all the authority, with regard to stannary affairs, of the supreme legislature.

Stannary Parliament.

* Pearce, Pref. p. 10.

These parliaments, or general assemblies of the tinners, have been summoned by the King's warrant, directed
to the Lord Warden, occasionally, as the circumstances
of the times have called for new laws, or a revision of
the old. Anciently they were held at Crockern Tor, on
Dartmoor; and when the Earl of Bath was Lord Warden, he was attended at this assembly by three hundred gentlemen well mounted. Mr. Polwhele, writing
about the year 1795, observes, that the president's chair,
the jurors' seats, &c., remained entire, cut out in the rude
stone; but that it had been for a long time customary to
open the commission and swear the jury on the site of the
ancient court, and then to adjourn to the court-house at
one of the stannary towns. Indeed the custom of even
opening the court at Crockern Tor has been for many
years disused, and the seats have been destroyed by the
removal of the stone for building materials. The Stannary
prison was appointed by the charter of Edward I. to be
Lidford Castle, which continued to be such till it became
too ruinous for the purpose. A complete table of the
Stannary laws made at Crockern Tor, in the reigns of
Henry VIII., Edward VI., and Elizabeth, may be seen
in the work of Pearce before referred to. The horrid
state of the prison, and the unjust severity with which
the laws were formerly administered, were subjects, it
seems, of well-founded complaint, and gave rise to the
expression " *Lidford law*—punish a man first, and try
him afterwards." The last of the Stannary parliaments
was held for both the counties, at Truro in Cornwall,
in 1752, and continued by adjournment to the 11th
of September 1753. On this occasion the ancient privileges of the miners* were confirmed; and among other
things it was enacted, that the working tinners should
pay no tithes out of their wages, but 16*l*. 3*s*. 4*d*. in
lieu thereof to the Bishop of Exeter, for the tin and tin-

* The laws, franchises, and liberties, relating to the Stannaries of Devon and Cornwall, depend partly upon royal charters, partly upon
common right, and in part upon customs and usages. An account of
them is contained in the before-mentioned work of Mr. Pearce, edit.
1750.

ners of both counties,—a compensation first allowed by King John to the church of St. Peter and the Bishop of Exeter, and confirmed by Edward I., as well as other succeeding Kings; that they should be free of tollages in fairs and markets; that they should be exempt from serving as jurors, except in the Stannary courts, saving for life, land, and limb, as heretofore; that they should sue foreigners at common law; and that all executions out of the courts should be good for a year and a day without renewal.

On the 11th of December 1786, a survey of the limits of the Stannary jurisdiction in Devon was taken at Moreton Hampstead, when Christopher Gullet, Esq. the foreman, produced an ancient manuscript book containing copies of former presentments of the bounds of the several courts, and many other records, appearing to have been made in June 1613. The jurisdiction of these courts, however, in both counties, has been much shaken by a decision in the Secondaries' Office in London, on Saturday, May 14th, 1825, in the case of Hall v. Vivian, the Vice-Warden, and others, before the under-sheriff and a special jury, to assess the damages sustained by the plaintiff, in consequence of his mining property being seized and sold, under Stannary process, in Cornwall. The damages were laid at 20,000l., but reduced by the verdict to 900l. the actual loss. Mr. Brougham (now Lord Chancellor) for the plaintiff, speaking of the jurisdiction of the Stannary courts, observed, that "it far exceeded in its sweep the sphere of the Court of Parliament, the High Court of Chancery, and all the other Courts in and about Westminster Hall, without a shadow of foundation for it, at least in the manner in which it had been acted upon." To this Mr. Denman, for the defendant, replied, that "the common custom only of Cornwall had been acted on; and he regretted that the plea of justification had been withdrawn from the record, as it would have been well supported by the custom and the facts." In his speech Mr. Brougham argued from the derivation

Limits o: the Stan- nary juri diction.

of the word stannary from *stannum*, 'tin,' or rather *stanna-
rius*, 'pertaining to tin,' that the privileges in question related solely to tin mines *.

ADDITIONAL NOTICES OF MINERALS, &c.

Minerals
in refe-
rence to
commerce.
Geological notices of the minerals in Devonshire have
been already presented to the reader in Mr. Brayley's account of the physical structure of the county, Book III.
chap. iv.   The following are some further particulars respecting them as they relate to commerce and the manufactures; and for which we are chiefly, though not entirely, indebted to the Magna Britannia of Mr. Lysons.

Manga-
nese.
Manganese has been found in great quantities in Devonshire; and within the last fifty years a considerable
trade has been carried on in that article.   It was first
found about the year 1770 at Upton Pyne, and this mine,
together with two others in the same lode at Newton St.
Cyres, for many years supplied the whole United Kingdom
with this article; it appears to have been the finest ever
raised.   For some years the consumption was inconsiderable, the use of it being confined almost entirely to
the manufacturing of what was called Egyptian ware in
Staffordshire, and in purifying glass.   The use of it, however, in bleaching, afterwards became considerable, and
from 1804 to 1810 the quantity shipped from Exeter
amounted to between two and three thousand tons per
annum.   The mines or pits at Newton St. Cyres failed
about 1810; and since that period the mine at Upton
Pyne has been exhausted.   New discoveries of this mineral, however, were made in the parishes of Doddescombsleigh, Ashton, Christow, &c. seven miles west of
Exeter, which are said to have produced from ten to
1500 tons per annum.   In 1821 they were still worked,
but the produce of the preceding year did not exceed 450
tons.   It was shipped at Exeter.   About the year 1815,
manganese mines were opened in the neighbourhood of

* Preface to Carrington's Dartmoor, p. lvi.

Tavistock, in the parishes of Coryton, Brent Tor, Lifton, Maristow, and Milton Abbot, from which considerable quantities were procured, and shipped at Plymouth. In the note below will be seen the produce of the Devonshire manganese mines in 1821 *. This mineral has also been found in the north of the county, in the parishes of Braunton and Morwood, but not in sufficient quantity to encourage speculation.

Antimony, from Pillaton in Cornwall, is exported from Plymouth, but is of rare occurrence in Devonshire : it has been found in an old copper mine in Buckland-on-the-Moor. Zinc and arsenic are equally rare. Cobalt occurs near Meavy and Walkhampton, but not in suficient quantities to become an article of commerce, except that about 1700lbs. of an inferior quality were procured from a mine at Sampford Spiney, and sold about the year 1820.

Amphibole has been found in an old copper mine at Buckland-on-the-Moor; and apatite in crystals, with tourmaline and quartz, at North Bovey. Tourmaline occurs at Woolleigh near Bovey Tracey, and in large crystals and loose decomposed granite near Moreton, and also shooting through quartz near Bridestow, between Oakhampton and Tavistock. Axinite is found, with garnets and epidote, in the bed of the Ockment, near Oakhampton. Chiastolite is also found in the bed of the Ockment and near Tavistock, and what is supposed to be loadstone, with garnets, near Ashburton. Touchstone occurs in a quarry

* Upton Pyne .... 30 Tons.
Ashton 130
Doddescombsleigh................................. 280
Christow... 16
Ilsington 15
Milton Abbot 250
Lamerton.. 150
Brent Tor 40
Coryton.. 280
Maristow 390
Lifton 250
Lew Trenchard 80

From information communicated to Mr. Lysons by —— Williams, Esq.

BOOK
IV.

Ochre.

producing slabs nine feet long by one foot thick, mentioned by Westcot as lying on the West Dart, but the place is not specified, and in small pieces on Teignmouth strand[*].

Ochre occurs in Mr. Templer's canal and the coal-pits of Bovey Heathfield, at Ashburton, near the banks of the Dart, in old mines at Ilsington, and also in large quantities in the parish of East Downe. In the year 1785 Mr. Pine Coffin set up a manufactory there for grinding it: umber, raised in Berry Narbor, was sent thither to be ground with it; and for three years forty-five tons, on an average, were shipped and consigned to London; but from difficulties which occurred in managing the concern, Mr. Coffin was induced to discontinue it. While the concern was carried on, these articles were much in use by the paper-stainers; the umber was esteemed to be of an excellent quality.

In the parishes of Hennock and Lustleigh, there is found in the granite a species of micaceous or peculiar iron-ore, known by the name of Devonshire sand. A few tons of this article were sent some years ago from Exeter to London, where it was used for writing sand, and various other purposes: it was sold at from three to eight guineas a ton.

Pipe-clay
and pot-
ter's clay.

Pipe-clay and potter's clay are found in inexhaustible quantities in the parishes of Hennock, Ilsington, Bovey Tracey, Teigngrace, King's Teignton, &c. Some years ago pipe-clay was also dug at Knighton, in the parish of Hennock, and manufactured into pipes on the spot. The manufacture has long since been given up, and the works abandoned. Both pipe-clay and potter's clay are now dug in great quantities on Bovey Heathfield, in the parish of King's Teignton, and are conveyed by the Stover canal to Teignmouth, whence they are shipped to most parts of the kingdom.

Potter's clay is used at the manufactory at Indio and Bovey Heathfield, and also sent to most of the manufac-

* Preface to Carrington's Dartmoor.

tories of earthenware. Potter's clay of superior quality has also been recently discovered in the parish of King's Teignton, which burns remarkably white, and is considered as a valuable discovery for the manufacture of china. About 20,000 tons of clay of the various sorts are annually exported from Teignmouth.

The clay-pits for the most part are the property of George Templer, Esq. They were first worked about the year 1730. The demand has greatly increased within the last fifty years, particularly since the Stover canal has been opened. The pits are open works, seldom exceeding 100 feet in depth, and are kept clear of water by common wooden pumps *.

China clay is also found a quarter of a mile due north of Ailsborough mine, which is three miles south-east of the Prison,—not equal to Cornish clay, but superior to that of Bovey Heathfield, of which blue-and-white ware is manufactured. It also occurs in some deep cuttings of the railway between Swell Tor and King's Tor. *China clay.*

Brown clay is raised in the parish of Fremington, and manufactured into useful coarse earthenware at the potteries of Barnstaple and Bideford.

Several attempts have been made to procure Coal in Devonshire, but always without success. Mr. Northmore sunk a shaft for this purpose near Exeter in 1818, but did not succeed, as was the case with his father, who had before made a similar experiment. It is the opinion of the most skilful geologists of the present day that coal does not occur in the strata of this county. It has been said to have been found in small quantities at Abbotsham, and elsewhere; but culm might have been mistaken for it. *Coal.*

Culm has been dug in the parishes of Tavistock, High Heanton, and Chittleham. At the two last-mentioned places the works were soon abandoned; but at Tavistock it was procured in great quantities, and of good quality, about the middle of the last century. The works had *Culm.*

* In boring for coal some time ago in the parish of Ilsington, the bed of clay was found to be 230 feet in depth.—Mag. Brit.

been given up, and re-opened about 1790; they were abandoned about 1800, on account of the water; at that time about ninety bushels a week were procured, the depth of the pit being about twenty-five fathoms. The culm is found at the depth of five or six fathoms; the veins, of which there are two, are about nine feet thick, and were supposed to be of great depth.

Bovey Coal was first dug for use early in the last century.—For a full account of this substance, see page 380 of this work.

Marbles.

Beautiful marbles abound in Devonshire, and occur in the lime rocks at Chudleigh, Bickington near Ashburton, Buckfastleigh, Denbury, Staverton, Berry Pomeroy, Waddon, Churston, &c., near Torbay, Babbicombe, St. Mary Church, King's Teignton, Drews Teignton, South Tawton, Yealmpton, Brixton, Oreston, &c.; and some years ago a good deal of the Babbicombe marble was polished and sent to London. That obtained from the Chudleigh and Harcombe rocks is manufactured into beautiful chimney-pieces, and sent from the port of Teignmouth.

Lime-
kilns.

So extensive is the use of lime as a manure in Devonshire, that not only are prodigious quantities raised from the limestone and marble rocks in various parts of the county, but there are at least twenty kilns between Wear Gifford and the mouth of Bideford harbour, for the purpose of burning lime imported from Wales, and three or four more scattered round the bay. There is indeed scarcely an inlet or creek, either on the northern or southern coast of the county, that is not supplied with a lime-kiln; and when the stone is not found in the vicinity, vessels are employed to convey it from the lime-rock districts. The immense quarries at Oreston near Plymouth and the adjacent parts, supply the kilns on the whole range of the Tamar, Tavy, and St. Germains rivers, as well as some other districts. The beautiful cliffs at Berry-head in Torbay, and at Babbicombe, furnish those on the Teign, the Exe, and the adjoining coast. The artist and

the man of taste may possibly turn from works of this kind
with something like disgust, lamenting that the ruthless
hand of commerce is permitted, with provoking unconcern,
to demolish by piecemeal the grand and magnificent ornaments of the coast, and that the owners of these splendid scenes, with the sordid love of gain absorbing all other
considerations, are literally retailing the picturesque and
beautiful by weight and measure ; whilst the friends of
industry and productive labour will observe only in such
operations a rich increase of agricultural produce, and
consequently of general benefit. Nearly the whole of the
south-western portion of Devon abounds with lime-works.
Those of Chudleigh especially, and its vicinity, are numerous ; and the rocks here have long been celebrated, not
only for their beauty, but the excellence of the lime which
they supply, which is remarkable for its extreme whiteness. In the centre, and towards the northern district of
the county, little lime-rock is found ; and the quarries in
that direction produce a darker kind of lime, which is not
so well adapted to every kind of soil. The principal of these
quarries are at Drewsteignton and South Tawton ; and the
large excavations near the present lime-works of the latter
place show that works of this kind have been carried on
there for a great length of time. Besides those already
specified, the following may be mentioned : namely, those
at St. Mary Church, Buckfastleigh, Bickington near Ashburton, Branscombe, on the southern coast; South Tawton,
Bampton, Canonsleigh, Hackworthy, Castle Hill, Swimbridge, Combe Martin, &c. Earl Fortescue, who owns the
works at Castle Hill, had formerly lime-works at Challacombe, but they have been discontinued. The great lime-
works at Swimbridge are on an estate called Marsh ; and
there are other smaller works in that parish and Landkey.
There are also several small lime-works in Combe Martin,
and those of J. D. Basset, Esq., which are on an extensive scale, as are those at Canonsleigh in Burlescombe.

There are quarries of good building-stone at Flitton, in
North Molton, in Ashwater, Lew Trenchard ; and at Great

Building-
stone.

BOOK
IV.

Cocktree, in South Tawton, and at Beer on the southern coast. That of the latter quarry exactly resembles the fine stone at Toternnoe in Bedfordshire. A considerable quantity of it is dug, and sent coastwise. It was used for the inside work of Exeter Cathedral. The clay porphyry, which occurs in detached rocks on Roborough Down, is said by Marshall to have been used formerly for the Gothic ornaments of most of the churches of Devon and the neighbouring parts of Cornwall.

Alabaster.

The alabaster which is found in the cliffs from Beer to Salcombe, Branscombe, and Sidmouth, makes good plaster of Paris; but it is in too small quantities to become an object of attention.

Slate quarries.

The principal slate quarries are, near Ivybridge; Cann quarry, about five miles from Plymouth; Lamerton, Lew Trenchard, Werrington (an insulated district of Devonshire west of the Tamar), Millhill, and other places near Tavistock, West Alvington, and Buckland Toussaints. Before the Dutch war, in 1781, great quantities of slate were exported from the Buckland quarries to Holland: this trade has not been renewed. A branch of the Tavistock canal has been carried to the Millhill quarries, the slate from which neighbourhood is exported to Guernsey and Jersey, and has also been sent to France, but not of late years.

Granite.

It is scarcely necessary to add, that granite of the best quality, lately used for bridges and public works, may be had in any quantity from the Dartmoor rocks; but on account of the difficulty of carriage, it was not till lately thought of as an article of commerce. The rail-road constructed from Plymouth to Prince Town on Dartmoor, and another made by Mr. Templer, from High Tor to the Stover canal, tend now greatly to facilitate this object. The granite is equal to that of Aberdeen.

Almost every variety of granite may be found on the moor. The red- or rose-coloured, admitting of an exquisite polish, may be seen at Troulsworthy, in Shaugh, and other places. The chimney-pieces of Ensleigh (the cottage of the Duke of Bedford), made by Mr. Kendall of Exeter, show to what perfection granite may be polished. It is not only possible, but probable, that the granite of Stonehenge was brought from Dartmoor, as there is no rock of the same kind to the east, and none nearer elsewhere on the west.

A considerable quantity of the whetstones which are sold by the name of Devonshire batts, are sent to Bridgewater, and thence by water to Bristol, Gloucester, Worcester, &c.; and some are exported from Topsham to London. They are formed from a soft sandstone on the side of Blackdown, within the parishes of Pea Hembury, Broad Hembury, and Kentisbeare, and which is worked on the spot into proper shape whilst wet: they are made also on the east side of Haldon, in the parish of Kenne.

Westcote mentions the magnets of South Brent as famous in his time, and Chapple speaks of them among the commodities of Devon; but they have long ceased to be considered as such.

Such are the products of the land;—those of the rivers, and the sea on both the coasts, are of too much importance to be omitted. The most valuable fishery of the rivers is that of salmon, which has produced considerable revenues to the proprietors, but has of late years declined in this county, as well as others, in consequence of the fish having been destroyed in the spawning season. Salmon is the produce of all the principal rivers; that of the Exe and the Dart is said to be most esteemed, but the largest quantities appear to be taken in the Tamar and the Tavy. The salmon fishery of the Tavy is attached to the lands of Buckland-Place, and the weir is a work of considerable magnitude and expense. The trap for taking the salmon is constructed on the same principle as that used for vermin, with an entrance large externally, but gradually contracted inwardly, so as to oppose the return of the fish after it has entered, though the internal orifice is not reduced so small as to render the return even of the largest impossible; for it is believed there is no instance of any

CHAP.
II.

Whetstones.

Produce of the rivers. Salmon.

that have once entered having quitted their confinement;
a circumstance which can only be accounted for by the
natural propensity of these fish, which directs them against
the stream, and prevents their giving up any advantage
which they have gained. The trap itself is twelve or fifteen feet square within, and is covered with planks, nearly
level with the top of the water. Opposite the entrance
in the upper side is an opening or sluice in the stone-work
or the rock, as a passage for the water. This opening is
furnished with two flood-gates, the one close, to shut out
the whole of the water; the other, a grating to suffer the
water to pass, and at the same to prevent the escape of
the larger fish. When the trap is set, the close gate is
drawn up, to afford a passage for the water through the
interior; but in order to take the fish when they have entered, this gate is again let down, and the trap is left
nearly dry. It may be observed, moreover, that the tunnel or narrowed entrance of the trap is placed somewhat
above the floor, so that before the salmon are seriously
alarmed by the fall of the water, it has sunk below this
entrance, and their retreat, if they were disposed to make
the attempt, is effectually cut off. The tunnel, like the
open floodgate, is made of strong wooden bars, far enough
asunder to admit the passage of the water, but not the
fish. The principal part of the salmon, however, is taken
by nets. The river Tavy, for nearly a mile below the weir,
is broken into rapids and pools, some of them very deep;
several of these are adapted to the sein, or drag-net, drawn
once or twice a day by four men, with horses to carry the
net, and dogs to convey the end of the rope across the
water, where it is too deep to be forded. In the Tavy the
fishing season commences in the middle or latter end of
February; but on the Tamar, not till several weeks afterwards; and closes in October or November, when the
weir is thrown open, and the fish are suffered to go up to
spawn.

Salmon
peal.

Salmon peal, or pail, is found in the Tavy, the Tamar,
the Axe, the Coly, the Otter, the Dart, the Arme, and the

Mole. Trout abounds in almost all the principal rivers. The Lamprey is found in the Exe and the Mole, but has not the same repute as the lamprey of the Severn.

The herring fishery on the northern coast of Devon, though never of much importance compared with the fisheries of Scotland, was formerly much more considerable than of late years, and constituted one chief source of employment for the poorer classes of Clovelly, Lymouth, &c. Both white and red herrings were then cured at Ilfracombe for exportation, and great numbers were sent to Bristol; but of late years the herrings have almost forsaken the coast. Considerable numbers have also been taken at Teignmouth in nets.

Herrings.

Pilchards also still frequent the southern coasts of Devon, as well as Dorset and Cornwall. For some years large quantities have been taken at Burrisland, in Bigbury Bay, and at two adjoining stations, called Clannaborough, and The Warren; they are cured on the spot, and sold to Cornish merchants. Some years ago a quantity was taken in the Bay large enough to produce about 7000*l.*, but since that time the fishing seasons have been less successful. There is also a pilchard fishery at Dartmouth, though on a smaller scale; and formerly there was another at Teignmouth. Pilchards taken on the Cornish coast are cured at Plymouth, and exported thence.

Pilchards.

Sidmouth is mentioned by Leland as one of the fishing towns of the county, but scarcely anything is done there in this trade at present. Westcote speaks of the fisheries at Plymouth as carried on in his time to a great extent, and says, that very often one hundred sail of fishing vessels, and sometimes double that number, were to be seen in the harbour. At present a considerable number of trawlers belong to this port, which supply the town with fish, besides what is sent to market at Bath and elsewhere [*].

Fisheries of Sidmouth and Plymouth;

[*] It is probable, says Mr. Lysons, that fish have been cured on the coast of Devonshire from a very early period. Numerous salt works near the coast are mentioned in the record of Domesday. About the middle of the last century, a brine for curing fish was made at Bideford, from rock-salt dissolved in sea-water, called salt-upon-salt.—Mag. Brit., vol. vi. part ii. p. 295.

BOOK
IV.

Teign-
mouth and
Torbay.

Teignmouth has a considerable fishery for whitings, mackerel, plaice, soles, turbot, &c. The great fishery, however, of the western part of England is now at Torbay. The number of decked fishing-boats at Brixham, according to Mr. Lysons, in the year 1822 was eighty-nine; that of open boats, sixty; and the number of men and boys employed in the fishery, about five hundred and forty. The number of tons brought to market weekly, was on an average one hundred and twenty; the annual quantity 6240 tons. The fish taken are chiefly turbot, soles, whiting, mackerel, &c. The Bath and Exeter markets are supplied from this fishery; and great quantities are sent by sea to Portsmouth, whence they are conveyed by land carriage to London.

Oyster-
beds.

The oyster-beds at Starcross, Topsham, and Lympstone, are productive of considerable profit. Oysters are brought from the Teign, from Weymouth, Poole, Saltash, &c. to these beds, and having been fed there for a time, are sent to the Exeter market. The young oysters from the Teign are also sent to be fed in the Thames, for London.

New-
foundland
fisheries.

The port of Bideford, as well as Topsham, had formerly a considerable share in the Newfoundland trade; but at present no port in Devonshire, except those of Teignmouth and Dartmouth, has much interest in this trade, and at the latter place it has of late years greatly declined. The small port of Torquay has had some concern in this trade, and a few ships are employed in it from Plymouth. From this latter port also a small number of vessels have been employed in the whale fishery.

CHAPTER III.

TRADE AND MANUFACTURES.

THE point of elevation and influence among the states of Europe, and consequently of the world, to which Great Britain has gradually risen, at present is certainly extraordinary and unparalleled. And to what is this superiority to be attributed? Though not entirely, yet chiefly, without doubt, to the excellence of her manufactures and the vast extent of her commerce, resulting from the industry, the ingenuity, and enterprising spirit of her natives; for these are the main sources of her wealth, and consequently of her power. The great seats, however, of her manufacturing and commercial importance are not to be found in the West of England. Formerly, indeed, during a long period, a large portion of the woollen fabrics of the country were produced in Devonshire and the neighbouring counties; but for many years this manufacture has been greatly on the decline, and at present is of little comparative consequence in the scale of national industry. Were an inquiry to be instituted into the causes of this decline, it would probably be observed, that the long duration or perpetual recurrence of war during the protracted reign of George III. operated more powerfully than anything else to the injury of the trade, diverting it into other channels, and thus reducing it to a state from which it has never been able to recover itself. But to this it may be replied, that the same wars would operate with equal force to the disadvantage of the trade and manufactures of other districts, where, however, they are still flourishing to an extent beyond all former example. Some other causes, therefore, must be sought for to account for this decline of trade in the West; and the principal of these are said to be, the absence of a spirit of enterprise in the na-

CHAP. III.

Chief sources of the wealth and prosperity of Great Britain.

Causes of the decline of the woollen trade in the West.

tives; the neglect of modern improvements, in machinery especially; and the facilities by means of which the manufacturers of other counties have excelled all others in the quality as well as the quantity of the articles they have produced, and consequently in the terms, so advantageous to the purchaser, at which they have been enabled to offer them for sale. But there is a natural disadvantage under which this county labours, and which appears to be an insurmountable obstacle to the extension of some of the principal manufactures at least; and that is, the want of coals, as a native production. No county in the kingdom, it is true, can boast an equal supply of water-power, which is less expensive than any other, and readily applicable, not only to machinery, but to other purposes of the manufactures: still it is observable that all the most successful manufacturing counties are also the coal districts; and so essential is this article in its various applications to the manufactures, but especially to that most valuable of all agents,—the steam-engine, that no district where it is wanting can be expected to enter into competition with those in which it abounds. How far the inexhaustible peat-bogs of Devonshire might be made to supply the place of coal-mines in manufacturing operations, is a question upon which the writer is not competent to give an opinion. Is Devonshire then to acquiesce in the failure of her trade as irremediable? Certainly not. There are various manufactures which might be carried on in this county with great success, and some for which it has advantages peculiar to itself; and which we may have occasion to specify. By the extent of her coast, moreover, and the number and excellence of her ports, facilities are afforded to commerce which few counties enjoy, and which it is rather singular have not been turned to better account.

The nature of the woollen trade, which has been so long carried on in Devonshire, has been gradually changed in the course of years, both as to the species of goods produced, and the manner in which the manufacturing process has been conducted. At present, it is principally confined to a species of fabrics called serges, or long ells, which are exported chiefly by the East India Company, and made according to their orders *.

The manufacture of woollen cloths in Devon, as well as in England generally, appears to have been derived from Flanders and the Low Countries. No mention is made of fulling-mills in this county in Domesday Survey; but from the mention of them in the records of Edward I., who granted charters to foreign merchants and manufacturers to settle in the kingdom, it is evident that cloth was then made at Exeter and Chudleigh. But it appears also from the Hundred Rolls, that the Dartmoor wool was at that time exported. Edward III. also, by the measures which he adopted for the encouragement of manufactures in this country, contributed not a little towards laying the foundation of our national superiority in this instance. He prohibited the exportation of wool, and gave great encouragement to weavers of woollen cloth, as well as dyers and fullers, from the Continent, who in his reign came to London, and afterwards settled in other parts of the kingdom. This took place about the year 1350. Some of these manufacturers were established at Bristol and Taunton, where one of them, John Kempe, a clothier of Flanders, is said to have established the cloth trade in this reign; and though there is no evidence that any of them settled in Devonshire, it is not improbable that the woollen trade extended from these places into this county : it is known that a wool staple existed in Exeter in 1354. From this period the

CHAP.
III.

Origin of the woollen manufactures.

* "Some of these," it is observed in the Introduction to Risdon, "after having been dyed in London of the finest colours, are sent to the China market. It is understood, that one of the uses which the Chinese make of these goods, is to extract the colour from them, which they apply to the dyeing of articles of their own manufacture; and that, for this purpose, the Devonshire serges are shredded, or cut in small pieces, and rendered useless as cloth. Such advantages does the possession of the sciences give to a nation, that while chemistry has enabled us to discover and imitate the process by which the inhabitants of the East have fixed the various tints upon their cottons, we oblige them to take our colours in the expensive, and to us profitable, form of an article manufactured of our staple commodity ! "—p. xxiii.

trade gradually increased in importance in the county, and several eminent clothiers not long afterwards were to be found in the principal towns *.

It appears that cloths called *raies* were made in the West in the reign of Henry IV., but the counties are not specified in the statute of 1409 ; and in the reign of Edward IV. (1450) kerseys are said to have been first made at Exeter, Honiton, and other towns in this district. During this reign, indeed, it would appear that the woollen manufacture was carried on to a considerable extent; for in 1463 the inhabitants of the hundreds of Lifton, Roborough, and Tavistock, petitioned Parliament to be exempted from the operation of an Act which prohibited the use of flocks in the manufacture of woollen cloths; stating, that they had been accustomed to use such mixtures from time immemorial, and that the cloth made by them could not be otherwise manufactured, on account of " the stubbornness of the wool," as it was made solely of the wool grown in these three hundreds; and they add, that if the Act should be enforced, the trade would be utterly destroyed. An exemption was in consequence allowed them, which is recognized in all subsequent Acts. In the statute of 1511 these cloths are exempted, by the name of *Tostocks*; and in a statute of 1534 they are called Tavistocks, or Werstern dozens. And it appears there was another species of coarse cloth, nearly similar, called *white plain streits*, or *streights*, and *white pinned streights*, to which the same exemption was allowed. They are spoken of in the statutes of 1513, 1553, and 1585 ; and in the statute of 1553 they are described to be of the nature of Tavistock cloths. It appears that they were made of the refuse of coarse wool, flocks, lamb's wool, and hair wool; that they were exported by the Devonshire merchants to Britanny, and bartered for dowlas, lockeram, and canvass. The statutes above mentioned prescribe their measure and weight †.

* Lysons, vol. vi. part i. p. 294. Introduction to Risdon, p. xxiii.
† Lysons, vol. vi. part i. p. 290.

The remark is obvious, that the bigoted, cruel, and persecuting reign of Máry was fatal for a time, not to some only, but to all the best interests of the country, and among others to trade and the manufactures. Never did these interests flourish less than during the short period of her melancholy and disastrous reign. Nor can we refrain from reminding the reader, of the illustration afforded by the Reformation, of the favourable influence which liberal principles in religion, by that event begun at least to be recognized, have uniformly exerted, not only on the progress of the sciences in general, but on every kind of improvement depending on the ingenuity, the skill, and industry of the people, in whatever way these sources of national wealth and prosperity may be exercised. Bigotry and superstition not only cramp the powers of the mind, and fetter its exertion in religion, but in every other department where the active and voluntary exercise of its faculties is required. Persecution, whether among Catholics or Protestants, throws the whole frame of society into disorder, and puts a check, at once equally fatal and extensive, upon whatever is beneficial to its welfare. Whenever the mind is left free to assert its native independence, and exert its powers without restraint in religion, it acquires an elasticity, a spring, which will not fail greatly to invigorate its efforts and aid its researches in all the branches of knowledge, skill, and ingenuity. It becomes a matter of habit to the mind, thus escaped from thraldom, to think freely, and to act with energy and independence on all subjects, whether religious, scientific, political, mechanical, or of any other description; and, if unobstructed by the ferocious and blind zeal of bigotry and fanaticism, the results will not fail to be most salutary and beneficial. Hence it is, if history may be credited, that the principles of Protestantism, and the progress of science, of industry, and the useful arts, are never failing companions. Hence it may be seen, that the countries where trade and commerce, as well as useful knowledge, have flourished most, are not such as Spain, Italy, and other portions of the

CHAP.
III.

The beneficial influence of liberal principles upon trade.

globe where the people are priest-ridden and held in religious subjection,—but Protestant England, as well as
other countries where religious freedom prevails ; and in
England, those classes of society which have been most
distinguished by the grand principles of the Reformation—
religious liberty and independence, and who have refused
most steadily to " prostrate the understanding " to priestly
domination,—these are the classes of society who have
also been most remarkable for their excellence in all
scientific improvements, in commerce and trade, in the
manufactures, and in all useful arts *.

Benefits
derived to
the trade
in En-
gland from
the perse-
cutions of
the Ne-
therlands.

Nor let these reflections be deemed either trifling or
irrelevant : they are of the first importance to the welfare of the country, and closely connected with our subject. The reign of Elizabeth was a grand æra of activity
in the manufactures and of commercial enterprise : the
cloth trade, moreover, in Devonshire particularly, had
arisen to considerable consequence; and this was the result, in a very great degree, of the causes to which the
preceding animadversions relate. It was to the persecutions inflicted by the Duke of Alva that England was
indebted for a vast accession of skill and industry, for
the improvement and extension of her manufactures. In
1567, having been appointed to the government of the
Netherlands, urged by the Pope, and with the sanction
of his master the King of Spain, he commenced his career
with the savage determination to eradicate the reformed
religion from the seventeen United Provinces at any sacrifice ; and with no remissness was he chargeable in
prosecuting the work of blood for which he was commis-
sioned. This monster had to boast, that during the five
years and a half that his power lasted, he had consigned
18,000 heretics, as they were called, to the public exe-
cutioner, besides the multitudes whom he had put to the
sword. Many thousands escaped ; and those of the Pro-

* It is a remarkable fact, that the woollen manufactures in the south-
western counties, as well as in other districts, were for centuries chiefly
in the hands of Protestant Dissenters.

testants who were unable to fly, if in any way aiding
others who were engaged in the contest, suffered every
species of torture. Flanders, in cultivated produce of
every description, is said to be the most fertile part of
Europe: its manufactures were also once the most flourishing and extensive; and had they been suffered to
proceed without interruption, and been cherished by its
Government, having cities and towns most advantageously
situated for commerce, with excellent ports and numerous
canals, it must also have become the most wealthy. The
seven United Provinces, with a soil less favourable and
an inferior natural produce, being able to secure their separation from the other ten, and maintaining their independence, avowing the reformed religion, and granting
universal toleration, did become rich and prosperous: but
Flanders was ruined. These savage persecutions destroyed
its trade, and expelled or annihilated its artizans. Thousands of families fled, most of them into England, where
many of their relatives and friends had settled before them. Happily for this country, Elizabeth had
the good sense and the virtue to accept the boon which
Philip, in his mad zeal in support of an absurd superstition, had rejected. To the Flemish exiles she afforded
the most effectual relief and protection; and as a large
proportion of these meritorious but unfortunate people
were the most skilful and industrious of the artizans of
that country, the Queen was furnished with the most favourable opportunity of introducing into England some
manufactures unknown in this country before, as well as
of carrying those that were already established to a state
of much greater excellence. Many English towns had
previously gone to decay, because rivalled and excelled
by Flanders in the manufacture of cloth, and because the
works established in England had been interrupted and
destroyed by similar persecutions during the short reign
of the unhappy bigot Mary. These towns were now re-
peopled, and their prosperity restored by the Flemings,
who brought with them,—not riches, but what was more
important, their skill, their industry, and their trade.

BOOK
IV.

Devonshire, among the rest, partook of the benefit[*]. Previously to this period, the fabrics manufactured in the county were for the most part the coarser and inferior sorts; and so little were they acquainted with the arts connected with the manufacture, that most of their cloths were sent to Flanders in the rough, whence, after being dyed and prepared for use, they were resold to their original possessors. Even the wool of this country had formerly been sold in its raw state to the Flemings, who returned it to England manufactured into cloth. At present, it is said, upwards of 1,000,000l. sterling is sent to foreign markets, for the purchase of fine wool for the use of the manufacturers.

Early importance of Tiverton as a manufacturing town.

We learn from the history of the woollen cloth trade, that Tiverton, at an early period, held the most distinguished rank as a manufacturing town. Its population was greatly increased by the Flemings; and by their skill and industry it flourished in a very high degree, till the town was destroyed by a dreadful fire in the year 1612. This calamitous event occasioned the dispersion of the industrious inhabitants, who carried their trade into other towns in the West, and particularly Exeter; though the trade of Tiverton afterwards revived, and became of considerable importance. In the year in which it was burnt down, the returns of this town were estimated at 300,000l.

---

[*] Dr. Toulmin, in his History of Taunton, p. 95, has stated after Fuller, respecting the numerous artizans that came over from the Netherlands, that "it was judged best, in order to diffuse the benefit of their art over the kingdom, to disperse them into different and remote counties; that they might establish in each different manufactures. The making of fustians was set up at Norwich; of baize, at Sudbury, in Suffolk; of sayes and serges, at Colchester, in Essex; of broad cloths, in Kent; of kerseys, in Devonshire; of cloth, in Worcestershire and Dorsetshire; of Welsh freezes, in Wales; of cloth, at Kendal, in Westmoreland; of Manchester cottons, in Lancashire; of Halifax cloths, in Yorkshire; of cloth, in Hampshire, Berkshire, and Sussex; and of serges at Taunton[a]." From Taunton the manufacture of the latter article would readily find its way into Devonshire; and Honiton is consequently said to be the town where it was first made in this county.

---

[a] Acta Regia, vol. i. 8vo, p. 195; and Fuller's Church History, Book III. p. 111, 112.

Drawn by W.H.Bartlett from a Sketch by H.Worsley

Engraved by W. Deeble

THATCHED COTTAGE, NEAR MILTON ABBOT, DEVON

THE SEAT OF HIS HON.[ble] THE EARL OF BEDFORD TO WHOM THIS PLATE IS MOST RESPECTFULLY INSCRIBED

BY HIS LORDSHIPS ...

London, Published by ...

HAREWOOD HOUSE

Drawn by W.J. Lea

Engraved by J. Rogers

annually; and in a brief granted by King James after the great fire, it is stated, that "their trade kept alway in work 8000 persons, men, women, and children;" and that "the said town had lately been accounted the chiefest market town in all the west part of this our realm of England, whereunto great recourse of people out of divers places, far and near, continually has made it, being the very nurse of all the parts of the country within many miles compass, both for their daily provision of corn, cattle, and manifold other necessaries, as also for many profitable and good trades used therein; and specially for their trade of clothing, whereon was bestowed weekly throughout the year, upon their market day, 2000 pounds at least in ready money, cloth-wool, and yarn, which wool and yarn was continually, by the inhabitants, converted into cloth; whereof there did grow and raise unto us for custom, subsidy, and aulnage, a great sum of money yearly." If the value of money at the time this brief was granted and at the present be compared, it will appear how much the returns of this town alone then exceeded those of the whole county now *.

The following extract † from Westcote, who wrote in the early part of the 17th century, shows the state of the woollen manufacture in the time in which he lived. After observing, that before the reign of Edward IV. only friezes and plain coarse cloths were made in Devonshire; and that one Anthony Bonvise, an Italian, in that reign, is said to have taught the art of making " *carsies* " (kerseys), and the women to spin with the distaff, he states: " For the *karsies* at first they only used Devon wool, which is more than any stranger travelling the country would suppose, since, except in Dartmoor, Exmoor, and such open grounds, the sheep are hidden by the high-grown hedges of the inclosures. Now they work Cornish and Dorset wools, and from other parts of the kingdom, and from London sent weekly (though by the new measure 150

* Introduction to Risdon, p. xxiv.
† Quoted also by Mr. Lysons.

BOOK
IV.
miles distant), Gloucestershire, Worcestershire, War-
wickshire, Wales, and Ireland ; all which is here wrought
into cloths and stuffs, wherein most towns have appropriated to themselves a several or peculiar kind.

" The late made stock of serges, or *perpetuanoes*, is
now in great use and request with us, wherewith the
market of Exeter is abundantly furnished of all sorts and
prices,—fine, coarse, broad, narrow ; so that the number
will scarcely be credited *. Tiverton hath also much
store of karsies, as (the neighbourhood of other markets
considered) will not be believed. Crediton yields many
of the finest sort of karsies, for which, and for fine spinning, it hath the pre-eminence †.

" Totnes, and some other places near it, hath besides
this a sort of coarse cloth, which they call Pynn Whites,
not elsewhere made. Barnstaple and Torrington furnishes
us *bayes*, single and double, and *fryzadoes*, and such like ;
and Pilton, adjoining, vents cottons and lyninge, so coarse
a stuff as there was a *vœ* (a woe) pronounced against
them in these words : ' And woe unto you, ye Piltonians,
that make cloth without wool.'

" At Tavistock there is also a good market for cloth, and
for other commodities of a like nature, without any great
difference. Ottery St. Mary, and diverse other places,
hath mixed coloured karsies ; Culmton, karsie stockings.
This might be enlarged with other pretty commodities
belonging to other towns, besides the generality of knitting
stockings, and spinning thread for women's working in
every town."

Trade to
the Le-
vant.
It appears, according to the statement of Mr. Lysons,
that the Devonshire kersies had acquired celebrity, and

* The market for wool and cloths, which had long been at Crediton,
was removed to Exeter in 1538.—Lysons.

† In another place, he says that it has become a proverb, " As fine as
Kerton (Crediton) spinning." " It is very true," he adds, " that 140
threads of woollen yarn spun in that town, were drawn through the eye
of a tailor's needle, which needle and threads were many years together
to be seen in Watling Street, in the shop of Mr. Dunscombe, at the sign
of the Golden Bottle."—Lysons.

were an important article of commerce to the Levant in the early part of the 16th century. Fine kerseys of various colours, coarse kerseys, and white Western dozens, were sent in English ships to Chio, and other ports in the Levant, from the year 1511 to 1534, by Sir John Gresham, Sir William Bower, and other London merchants, as we learn on the authority of Hackluyt. Each ship that sailed from those parts took from 6000 to 8000 kerseys. They were bartered to considerable advantage for commodities of the country, which bore a good price in England. Gaspar Campion, an English merchant residing in Ohio, writing in 1569, when the trade had been some time in the hands of the Venetians, strongly recommends the revival of a direct trade with this country *.

A statute of the year 1552 regulates the weight and measure of the Devonshire kerseys. By an Order of Council in the year 1587, the 29th of Elizabeth, it appears their value was rated at from 18s. to 3l. † The statute of 1593, the 35th of the same reign, speaks of them as having been formerly in great request, and of great price and estimation, both at home and in foreign countries; but then grown into discredit, in consequence of the frauds of the manufacturers, which it was the object of that statute to correct by the enactment of heavy penalties, a Royal proclamation, in consequence of complaints from the States of Holland, having been already issued for the same purpose ‡.

Westcote, speaking of the progress of the woollen manufactures, observes: "The gentleman-farmer, or husbandman, sends his wool to market, which is bought either by the comber or spinner; and they the next week bring it again in yarn, which the weavers buy; and the market following bring it thither again in cloth, when it

* Hackluyt's Voyage, vol. ii. p. 96, or p. 206 of the new edition: and p. 116 or 230, and 127 or 229. Mag. Brit. vol. vi. part i. p. 300.
† Hutchins's Dorset, vol. iv. p. 186.
‡ Mag. Brit., vol. vi. part i. p. 300.

BOOK
IV.

is sold either to the clothier (who sends it to London), or to the merchant, who (after it hath passed the fuller's mill, and sometimes the dyer's vat,) transports it. The large quantity whereof cannot be well judged at, but is best known to the custom-book, whereunto it yieldeth no small commodity ; and this is continued all the year through." The great increase of the woollen manufacture spoken of by this writer, was occasioned by the revival or the extension of the sale of English cloth in Italy, Turkey, and the Levant. Morrison, who was in Turkey in 1596, speaks of kerseys and tin as our chief articles of commerce with Turkey *.

Decline of
the trade
during the
civil com-
motions of
Charles I.,
and its
subsequent
revival.

The trade declined in some degree during the tempestuous times which followed the reign of James I.; but reviving in the reigns of Charles II. and William III. rose to its greatest height. A new æra about this time took place in the manufactures of the county, by the introduction of mixed worsted serges, which being found more profitable than the kerseys, shortly displaced them, and have continued the chief articles of the trade from that time to the present †. About the commencement of the 18th century the woollen trade in Devonshire began to decline, on account of the preference given in the markets of Holland, and other parts of the Continent, to the finer stuffs made at Norwich. An attempt to introduce the manufacture of the latter into this county was made about eighty years ago, and at first appeared likely to succeed ; but soon proved abortive. Some other articles were afterwards attempted, and for a time found a market in Spain and Italy. Almost perpetual war, however, has operated to the ruin of the manufacture, except that

---

* Itinerary, part iii. p. 127. Mag. Brit.

† In the fabric of the serges two distinct kinds of yarn are used : the one called worsted, probably from the place in the county of Norfolk, where it was first made, and which forms the chain or woof ; the other, of a softer twist, for the warp or shoot, is generally denominated yarn. Both the chain and the warp of the kerseys are the same, only more twisted.

portion of it which is required for the supply of our East India possessions, in addition to the very limited demands for home consumption *.

Brice, who published his "Topographical Dictionary" in 1759, speaks of the clothing trade as then somewhat on the decline : he observes, however, that the ordinary weekly sale at Exeter on a Friday was 10,000*l.* worth; and that Exeter was esteemed the greatest wool-market in England : and Mr. Lysons was assured, that about the year 1768 the exports of woollen cloths were above a million pounds in value annually. The trade suffered materially during the American war, but on the restoration of peace recovered itself in some degree; and the extension of exportation to the East Indies, which took place soon after, raised it again to considerable importance. In the year 1783 the East India trade took off not more than about 35,000 pieces,—each piece containing twenty-six yards. In 1789, the demand being then increasing, 121,000 pieces were bought by the Company; and from 1795 to 1805 the average of their purchases was from 250,000 to 300,000 pieces annually. After this their purchases began to decline, and on the renewal of their Charter in 1813 the demand became still less, and the prices they now offer leave little or no profit to the manufacturer. During the last war the woollen trade sustained the most serious injury in its foreign consumption; and notwithstanding the reduced scale of their purchases, more than two-thirds of the woollen cloths now made in the county are for the East India Company †.

At Tiverton, even so late as 1790, it is said, there were 1000 looms, 700 of which were in daily use, and 200 wool-combers. The trade has now deserted the place. At Newton Bushel, Chudleigh, Bampton, Oak-

---

* Introduction to Risdon, p. xxv.

† Mag. Brit. vol. vi. part i. p. 301. Introduction to Risdon, p. xxvi. The serges are of various descriptions, and of different degrees of fineness. The sort now chiefly manufactured for the East India Company is that called Long Ells.

hampton, Hatherleigh, Moreton Hampstead, Culmstock, Uffculme, and Ottery, also, the manufacture of cloth is nearly, if not altogether, annihilated. Before the late war, Exeter, and the towns of Crediton, Collumpton, and South Molton, with the populous villages of North Tawton and Bishop's Morchard, were principally employed in manufacturing coarse woollens for Spain, Portugal, Italy, and Germany. The long continuance of war, from time to time, lessened the demand for these foreign markets, or entirely destroyed it, and these places shared only with others the orders of the East India Company for long ells, &c. After the return of peace they again supplied the diminished demands for the same countries. The reduced manufactures of Exeter have been chiefly of plushes and estameans * for Spain.

Crediton especially, being a place of large population and extensive trade, continued highly prosperous till the great fire in the year 1743, which burnt down more than half the town. Nearly the whole of the yarn was spun in Cornwall and the Moor towns and villages, and brought to Crediton, where it was bought and wove. The cloth was afterwards sold to the merchants of Exeter and Tiverton; at which towns it was dyed, pressed, and finished. From Exeter and Topsham it was shipped for Flanders and Holland, and more recently for Spain and Italy; the serges being the material chiefly worn by the nuns, monks, and priests, in Catholic countries, as well as by others. From 1500 to 2000 pieces of serge were manufactured weekly. There is now only one manufacturer in the town.

To so low a state is the trade of this once flourishing town reduced, that the late contracts for the supply of the East India Company were made at cost prices, with no other view than to keep the poor employed, and thus prevent an alarming increase of the rates. Considerable

* Mag. Brit. vol. vi. part i. p. 302. The article of this name is a sort of fabric between a kerseymere and a shalloon: the pieces are thirty-two yards in length, and three-quarters of a yard wide.

quantities of serges from other places are sent to London to meet the demands of the American merchants, who carry them to China, and sell them sixteen per cent. below the Company's prices. Similar to this has been the fate of the trade in the other towns of the county, which were once places of great activity in this manufacture.

Collumpton, before the late war, manufactured considerable quantities of serges, plain and twilled druggets, sagatties, duroys, and estameans, which were shipped at Topsham, by the merchants of Exeter, for Holland, Germany, Spain, Portugal, and Italy. Since the peace, some cloths, kerseymeres, and estameans, with flannel and baize of various descriptions, have been made for the markets of Spain and Portugal, as well as for home consumption. The chief trade of Ashburton and South Molton has of late consisted in the manufacture of woollen goods for the East India Company. The woollen trade of Tavistock, Totnes, Kingsbridge, Modbury, Brent, Chagford, and Buckfastleigh, also consists chiefly of long ells for the same market. The largest factory of this article is that of Messrs. Berry of Chagford. The trade of Modbury and Kingsbridge has much declined. Barnstaple, formerly celebrated for its manufacture of baize, has now little or no trade in that article, or in the coarse serges which it formerly made for the American market. The general state of the woollen trade, as compared with that of its greatest prosperity, may be estimated by the entries at the custom-house at Exeter, as from this city the great bulk of woollen goods manufactured in the county are exported. In 1768, 330,414 pieces of cloth were exported from Exeter: in 1787, 295,311 pieces: in the year 1820, the number was 127,459 [*]. What is the quantity exported at present I have not been able to ascertain.

Some of the principal woollen manufacturers now are the following: Messrs. Richard Berry and Son, at Chag-

---

[*] Mag. Brit. vol. vi. part i. p. 303.

BOOK
IV.

The prin-
cipal ma-
nufactu-
rers at
present.

ford* and Ivybridge ; Messrs. Fox and Sons, Culm-
stock and Uffculm ; Mr. William Upcot, Collumpton ;
Messrs. Brown, Davy, and Sons, Collumpton ; Mr. John
Fulford, who manufactures about 500 pieces of serges
weekly at Crediton and North Tawton ; Mr. Richard
Caunter, Ashburton ; Messrs. Tozer and Co., Ashburton
and Buckfastleigh ; Messrs. Pearse and Sons, Stickle-
path ; Messrs. Maunder, Exeter and Exwick ; Messrs.
J. and W. Maunder, South Molton ; Mr. William
Hitchcock, South Molton ; Messrs. Bentall, Sons, and
Co., Totnes ; and Messrs. Gill and Co., Tavistock and
Horrowbridge.

The high price of English wool, and the fluctuating
state of the market, have also operated to prevent a more
extensive revival of the foreign trade ; but some of the
most intelligent manufacturers have expressed a hope that
it may be yet revived, either for the old articles, or for
others suited to the altered taste and habits of the country.
Besides the trade of the East India Company, long ells
are purchased for the private trade of India and have
been introduced into China by American and other foreign
vessels.   In the Western Times newspaper of Jan. 15th,
1831, is the following statement : " The orders for the
woollen goods from the East India Company this quarter
are more extensive than has been usual for some time
past ; at prices, however, it is said, that will leave but
little profit to the manufacturer.—We anticipate the destruction of this monopoly, and then our manufacturers
may again hope to flourish." It has since, however, been
observed more than once, that the woollen trade still continues dull.

·In the enumeration of the other fabrications of Devon-

* At these works, which have been established thirty years, the articles manufactured are long ells, or serges of various widths and qualities,
blankets, miners' cloths, &c. The number of hands employed at present
is 115 men, 127 women, 98 children, besides the weavers at Chagford,
and various surrounding parishes to the distance of sixteen miles and
upwards, which exceed 800 ; amounting in all to 1140 operatives.

shire, we shall mention first the celebrated manufactory of
carpets at Axminster, now in full employ. Unlike every
other fabric of the kind in England, and distinguished by
their superior beauty and durability, these carpets surely
need only to be better known to secure a much more extensive sale. They were first produced in 1755 by the
ingenuity of Mr. Thomas Whitty, the grandfather of Mr.
Ransom Whitty, the present proprietor of the works. The
following copy of a document which has fallen into our
hands, will serve to show how favourably they were received on their first appearance :

" This writing testifies, that Thomas Whitty of Axminster, in the county of Devon, did, on the thirtieth day of
March one thousand seven hundred and fifty-seven, produce before the Society for the Encouragement of Arts,
Manufactures, and Commerce, a carpet made on the principle of Turkey carpets, which was adjudged, by gentlemen whose opinion was on this occasion requested by the
Society, to excel Turkey carpets in pattern, colour, and
workmanship: and in consequence thereof he was rewarded
with a premium of twenty-five pounds.

" And it is hoped, that he will be careful to support
the character he has by this means acquired, by carrying
on, and endeavouring to establish a manufacture which
may be of so much use and advantage to the public.

(Signed) " FOLKSTONE, President."

That the preceding recommendation of this highly
respectable Society has been well supported by corresponding exertions, a splendid proof was afforded a few
years ago, by the manufacture of a magnificent carpet for
the palace of the Grand Seignor. The pattern was peculiar,
elegant, and rich, as well as totally unlike those that are
worked in the East: the size was immense, the carpet
measuring seventy-four feet in length by fifty-two in
width. The cost of it to the "Lord of the Crescent"
was more than a thousand pounds.

The peculiarities of the Axminster carpets are, that
they are manufactured in one piece, of any size or pattern,
and of any shape, however irregular: they will admit of

the execution of the most beautiful designs in flowers, fruit, armorial bearings, grotesque figures, or any other, so as to harmonize with the furniture of the room : the texture is also extremely durable, the evidence of which is exhibited in many which have been in use for fifty or sixty years. These carpets were never in higher repute than at present. His Majesty's palaces at Brighton and Windsor are graced by the labours of the women of Axminster, as are many also of the mansions and country-seats of the nobility and gentry.

The method by which these superb fabrics are produced is unique. They are worked in large perpendicular looms, by females, five or more on the same piece, who are guided as they proceed by a printed pattern placed before them ; having the coloured threads ready on needles, which they use singly, as the pattern requires. The nature of the stitch permits it to be cut, which gives to the carpet the softness of velvet, and by no means injures the texture. The thickness of these fabrics being greater than any others of the kind, and the quantity of raw material used in the manufacture of them being consequently large,—the labour, as the work is done by the fingers, being minute and tedious,—and considerable sums, occasionally thirty or forty pounds being spent on the pattern, the price of them is necessarily high. The returns, moreover, from an article so expensive, and so long in fabrication, must evidently be slow. About a hundred individuals, chiefly females, are now employed in the manufactory. It will give us great pleasure, if the information we are enabled to communicate of this not sufficiently known, but truly ingenious and valuable article of Devonshire fabrication, should not only be acceptable to the reader, but, by extending the knowledge of it, contribute in any degree to the benefit of the ingenious manufacturer*.

* In Westcote's time fine flax thread was spun at Axminster; and he observes, that Combe Martin supplied the whole country with shoemaker's thread, made from hemp grown there. Both these have been discontinued ; but there was lately a considerable manufactory of linen thread at Tukenhayes in Ashprington.—Lysons.

Honiton was formerly celebrated for the lace as well as the woollen manufacture; both of which are supposed to have been introduced, in the time of Elizabeth, by the emigrants from Flanders during the religious persecutions of that country. The highly flourishing state in which these trades continued for many years, received its first check in the beginning of the American war, about 1778. By this and subsequent wars the woollen trade especially received an injury here, as in all other towns in the county, fatal to its prosperity, and reduced it to a state from which it has never been able to recover. Nothing is now done at Honiton in this branch, but the manufacture of some worsted by one individual, which is preferred for knitting stockings: this furnishes employment for the children of a school, designed to train them up to be good servants, and is superintended by ladies.

The Honiton lace manufacture (formerly known by the name of bone-lace) is said to have been flourishing in the reign of Charles I. Westcote, speaking of Honiton, says: " Here is made abundance of bone-lace, a pretty toy, now greatly in request ; " and he speaks also of some being made at Bradninch. And says Mr. Lysons in 1822: " Some years ago, at which time it was much patronized by the Royal Family, the manufacturers of Honiton employed 2400 hands in the town and neighbouring villages: they do not now employ above 300*." Although the lace long

* It has been humanely remarked, as a melancholy consideration, that so much health and comfort are sacrificed in the production of this beautiful but not necessary article of decoration. The sallow complexions, the rickety frames, and the general appearance of languor and debility of the operatives, are sad and decisive proofs of the pernicious nature of the employment. The small unwholesome rooms in which numbers of these females, especially during their apprenticeship, are crowded together, are great aggravations of the evil. It is no wonder that the offspring of mothers in such circumstances, in a majority of instances are a puny, feeble, and frequently a short-lived race. The confinement of the children ten hours a day is too rigid ; and even then, if their task were not completed, it has been the custom not to release them, but to deprive them of the little time in which they should have been regaining the use of their cramped limbs. Another hardship, in the case of the Devonshire lace-makers, is said to have been, some time ago, the manner

BOOK
IV.

Bobbin-
net estab-
lishment at
Tiverton.

maintained its superiority, yet latterly, on account of its high price, and the introduction of bobbin-net by machinery, the trade has been greatly reduced. Recently, however, there has been a sudden and great revival. Our present estimable Queen, with a view to give encouragement to the industry of the country, a short time since was pleased to order a handsome suit of Honiton lace for a Court dress, which was got up, in a very superior style, by Miss Amy Lathy, who is now enabled to employ 200 individuals; and so much is the demand increased, that if it continue, employment will probably be found for a much greater number.

The demand for this lace, however, has been superseded in general use by an article made by machinery, called bobbin-net, or Nottingham lace, which resembles that made at Honiton, and is ornamented in a similar manner with sprigs. It is, however, more regular in its structure, and, if fabricated with the same material *, would be more beautiful; but being made of cotton or silk, and with far greater speed by machines, it can be sold at a much lower price. A large manufactory of this lace was established in 1816 at Tiverton, by Messrs. Heathcoat and Co. †, which affords occupation for numerous operatives, whose means of subsistence had failed on the removal of the cloth trade. We learn from Mr. Lysons, that in 1822 these works were employing about 1500 hands, including men, women, and children. They are still carried on with success, and, as we are informed on good authority, employ at present several thousand

---

in which they have been often paid for their labour, by the prevalence of the truck system; but we are happy to say that a law is now in progress for the abolition of this unjust and pernicious custom.—See Cooke's Topography of Devon, p. 105.

* The Honiton lace is made of fine thread imported from Antwerp, the market price of which was some years ago 70*l.* per pound. An inferior sort is made, in the villages along the coast, of British thread, called *Trolly* lace.—Lysons.

† These machines were not the invention of any individual, but were the result of many successive inventions and improvements. Mr. Heathcoat was one of the first who availed themselves of the inventions of others, and by his ingenuity contributed greatly to the state of excellence to which the machines are now brought.

workpeople in the town and vicinity. About the time
mentioned above, the largest factory in Tiverton, formerly
belonging to Messrs. Heathfield and Co., was purchased
for this manufactory by Mr. Heathcoat, who afterwards
added very considerably to the premises. The twisting
and preparation of the cotton and silk, together with the
machines by which the lace is manufactured, occupy the
principal part of the buildings. Bleaching- and gas-works
have also been constructed, as appendages to the factory, and brass and iron works established, which, besides supplying the factory, are a great accommodation to
the town and neighbourhood. The machinery is put in
motion by a water-wheel of one hundred horse power; it
is of the best construction, and large dimensions, being
21 feet wide, and 25 feet in diameter, and is made entirely of iron, except the float-boards. The machines by
which this lace is made are among the most ingenious of
any that are employed in the manufactures of the country,
and are well worthy the inspection of the curious.
They are, however, too complex, and admit of great improvements, which indeed are frequently taking place.
At any rate, they serve to show that the wonderful excellence to which British ingenuity and perseverance are capable of attaining in the construction of machinery for the
manufactories, is not exceeded, if equalled, by any other
country. Pieces of lace are made by these machines
from one to two, and in some instances three yards in
width, and of a convenient length. One machine will
produce in one minute a quantity of net, which, by the
method in general use twenty years ago, would occupy a
woman a fortnight in making. From the rapidity with
which the lace is made, the profits, eight or ten years ago,
were enormous, and large property was consequently accumulated by many manufacturers in a very short period.
This was the case with Mr. Heathcoat himself, who has
risen by his ingenuity and perseverance from the state of
a working mechanic to his present affluence and prospe-

rity.   This circumstance induced such numbers to flock into the trade, as to raise the quantity of the produce above the demand for it, and the prices in consequence are at present so much reduced, as to afford little encouragement to new speculations in this branch of manufacture.

Mr. Heathcoat's manufactory was first established at Loughborough, in Leicestershire, where it was conducted for seven or eight years, until his machines were destroyed by the Luddites, whose infamous operations had been previously carried on, in Nottingham especially, to an alarming extent.   This destruction was occasioned by an attempt of the proprietor to reduce the wages of his workpeople, which were then indeed extremely high, though not more in proportion than the vast profits of the masters themselves.   This, however, is one instance, among many, which serves to show the extreme folly, as well as wickedness, exhibited by the destruction of productive machinery; for Mr. Heathcoat, in order to be out of the reach of these lawless desperadoes, removed his manufactory to Devonshire, and consequently carried with him a large quantity of profitable employment from the neighbourhood where the shameful scene of destruction had taken place.   The insanity moreover of destroying machinery is alike obvious in all cases; for it is certain, that machinery, by the facility with which it increases the produce of the manufactories, and thus reduces the prices, adds so much to the extent of the consumption, that eventually more hands are employed than could by any other means find occupation. This is strikingly exemplified throughout England.   What would have been the state of trade in this country at present without machinery?

About the year 1821, as we learn from Mr. Lysons, a lace manufactory was about to be established at Raleigh *,

* There was formerly a large manufactory of woollen articles at this place, and another of cottons, calicoes, &c.   One of these was accidentally burnt down, a few years after the building of it, and the whole was discontinued.

in the parish of Pilton, near Barnstaple, and numerous CHAP.
cottages were then being built for the workpeople. This III.
establishment, we are informed, has been since conducted
on an extensive scale, but is now relinquished. Another
lace manufactory, we are also informed, is carried on by
Mr. Newberry, at Ottery St. Mary.

In the neighbourhood of Bradiford Bridge is a factory,
for a variety of wood-work and large toys, wrought by
circular saws and other curious machinery. The invention
originated with Mr. Furze, who parted with it to the present conductor of the works eight years ago.

There are several manufactories of gloves in this county, Manufac-
one on an extensive scale at Torrington, and another near ture of
Exeter, conducted by Mr. Tanner, who employs from 100 gloves.
to 130 individuals. And at Fordton, adjoining Crediton,
the extensive buildings formerly occupied by the woollen
manufacture, are now employed by Messrs. Davy in the
manufacture of canvass, duck, shoe-thread, ticklingburgh*, Hessians, &c. He employs from one to two
hundred hands. Weaving is also sent to Crediton from
Tiverton, Collumpton, and Launceston; lace from Tiverton to be mended, and gloves from Exeter to be made.

Several paper-mills occur in different parts of the Paper-
county. At Bradninch there are three; conducted by mills.
Messrs. Dewdney and Fremet, and by Messrs. John
Dewdney and Co. Those of the latter gentlemen, which
were at Heale Paine, in this parish, were burnt down in
1821, but have been since rebuilt, on an extensive scale,
for the manufacture of all kinds of writing-paper. There
are other paper-mills, at Weir and Exeter, belonging to
Mr. R. Cooper; at Huxham, by Messrs. Matthews and
Co.; and at Stoke Canon, by Messrs. Harris and Crags.

At South Bovey are two manufactories of white pottery, Potteries.
usually called in the county *clome*, formed of the fine
white clay which abounds in the marsh or common, as
well as pipe-clay. Blue-and-white ware is made at

---

* Ticklingburgh is a coarse linen cloth, chiefly for the use of the poor.

Indio in Bovey Tracy. A manufactory of an inferior sort of white ware was established here in 1772. The present proprietor is Mr. Steer, who employs about forty operatives, having been himself proprietor of the works thirty years. At Honiton, plant-stands and other coarse ware are manufactured : there are also potteries of brown ware at Bideford and Barnstaple; and the former of these towns has long been noted for a kind of earthen ovens, often used in the farm-houses and cottages of the county. Pipes, bricks, and tiles, are also made here, and a steam-engine is at work for grinding corn : about fifty individuals are employed in these works, and seventy in shipbuilding.

Iron-foun-
dry at Ta-
vistock.

At Tavistock are iron-works, and a foundry attached to them, where are manufactured anchors, ships' knees, axles, shovels, sythes, and a variety of edge-tools. Eight or nine overshot water-wheels give motion to the various apparatus required for this purpose. Chain cables are manufactured at Topsham, by Messrs. R. and D. Davy.

Plymouth has never been a town of manufacturing notoriety, and though some attempts to introduce manufactures into this town were made formerly, they soon failed. Sea-faring pursuits alone appear to be best suited to its situation. A manufacture of porcelain was once carried on at Plymouth by Mr. Cookworthy, who settled here in 1733, and first discovered the materials requisite for its composition. It continued to flourish for some years, but was afterwards removed to Bristol, and thence to Worcester, where, in consequence of subsequent discoveries and improvements, it is still flourishing. When the persecuted Protestants of France fled their country, Plymouth was one of the stations appointed for their residence: it does not appear, however, that they were ever distinguished here as manufacturers, though their number must have been considerable, as Stonehouse was almost peopled by them fifty years ago. The descendants of these Confessors are still numerous about the town, but are merged into English families. The most distinguished private manufacture at Plymouth now, is carried on under the firm of Welsford and Oldham, in which upwards of one hundred men and an equal number of women and children are employed in hackling, spinning, and weaving flax for canvass, ducks, sheeting, and other kinds of coarse linen, but especially sail-cloth, of which Government frequently takes by contract several thousand pieces in the year, for the use of the navy. This manufactory occupies extensive premises, and employs mills worked by the town leet. The principal of these buildings is situated without the old town, on a piece of land formerly called Stone Park. Several other persons are engaged in similar works, as well as in the worsted manufacture, but on a smaller scale.

Very recently, machinery for various purposes has been constructed by Mr. Ashby upon the lower part of the leet. It consists of circular saws for fine work, large perpendicular saws for rafters and beams, a mill for preparing ivory-black, and another for reducing bones to powder for the use of the farmers in the county, who, though still unacquainted with the real importance of this manure, are beginning to understand its uses; and the consumption, we trust, will eventually remunerate Mr. Ashby for the expense and risk of the speculation. The machinery is driven by an overshot wheel, which has power for more work than is at present assigned to it.

The reward of ingenuity and perseverance is seen very conspicuously in the success of the soap factory established at Plymouth a few years ago by Mr. Thomas Gill. Previously to this establishment, soap for the county was obtained from Bristol and from London; at present, by far the larger portion of what is used in the West is manufactured by this gentleman. An attempt was made originally to do the whole work by steam: but this not answering the purpose intended, the steam-engine is used for a part of the work only. The ashes, which are well known to be a valuable manure, instead of lying waste, as they did at first, are now eagerly sought after by the farmer.

CHAP. III.

Messrs. Welsford and Oldham's manufactory.

Mr. Ashby's machinery.

Mr. Gill's soap factory.

By far the most important works, however, in Plymouth, are those of Government. The Dock-yard is an
immense manufactory, forming the most important establishment known to a civilized country, especially an
island. The number of hands now employed is little
more than half of what it was in the time of war; but it
still amounts to about two thousand three hundred and fifty,
besides four hundred convicts *. The regular and good
wages which the artizans receive is a steady and valuable
stream of profitable income to the towns of Devonport
and Plymouth. The expenditure for the works of the
Dock-yard must evidently extend to a considerable amount,
besides that for the officers and men belonging to private
ships arriving in and going out of port.

The formation of this grand arsenal commenced in the
year 1691, during the reign of William III., previously
to which the artificers were accommodated on board vessels prepared for their use. Its improvements have been
progressive; and it is now acknowledged to be one of the
finest in Europe. Every department of this extensive
establishment will afford the most ample gratification to
the curiosity of the visitor. The various methods employed
in building and repairing ships, in forming masts of the
largest size, in twisting enormous cables, and forming
anchors of immense weight and dimensions, are displayed
on a scale of magnitude and efficiency, which, if equalled,
are certainly not excelled in any other establishment. In
devising the means by which the mechanical powers have
been employed to effect these arduous operations, human
ingenuity has been carried to an extent truly wonderful.
Many of the most difficult have been simplified and rendered more expeditious by recent inventions; among
which those of Sir Robert Seppings and Richard Pering,

---

* These unfortunate men, employed as labourers, are distinguished by
their dress of coarse brown cloth, and by a ring of polished iron on the
right leg. The latter is no hindrance to their employment, nor does it
appear that their labour is by any means severe. They take their meals
and sleep on board a large vessel, which lies alongside the quay, and
when their conduct is good, their term of labour is shortened.

Esq., are eminently conspicuous *. A more detailed description of this national establishment is intended to be given in its proper place, in a future part of this work.

COMMERCE.

In foreign commerce, notwithstanding its numerous and excellent sea-ports, and the great extent of its coast, Devonshire has never held a distinguished rank. The portion which it formerly enjoyed was limited chiefly to the export of the inland produce and manufactures, which were sent to different parts of Europe, the Levant, and Newfoundland ; and to the importation of articles of general consumption, such as timber, wines, grocery, &c., to which may be added the produce of the Newfoundland fisheries.· To obtain the exact returns of the exports and imports of the county seems to be impracticable; for if the officers of the Customs were disposed to give the information in their power, even their account would be incom plete, as many of the articles pay no duty. It may be said, in general, that the exports are still the natural produce of the county; as metals, principally copper, tin, and lead ; granite, limestone, or marble, manganese; pipe and potter's clay ; sythe-stones, timber, wheat, barley, oats, cider, butter; and manufactured articles, especially woollens of various kinds, chiefly the coarser sorts, for the East India Company ; paper, lace, and gloves.

Commerce.

The ports on the southern coast are, first, Axminster, which was opened about ten years ago for coasting vessels, bringing in a considerable quantity of culm for the neighbouring limeworks : Salcombe, which exports corn, cider, &c., and imports coals, &c.: Exeter, the principal exports of which are woollen manufactures, manganese, &c., and the imports wine, hemp, tallow, coals, grocery, &c.: Teignmouth, with the port of Exeter, exports granite, pipe and potter's clay, manganese, tim-

Exports and imports of the southern coast.

* " The Tourist's Companion, &c." by John Sandford, 1824, p. 105.

ber, cider, fish, &c. This is now the chief port for the Newfoundland trade; the other imports are coals, culm, deals, iron, groceries, &c. Torquay has some portion of the Newfoundland trade, and imports coals, culm, &c., in coasting vessels. Brixham exports great quantities of fish, and imports coals, culm, &c. Dartmouth exports woollen goods, cider, barley, &c., and imports dried fish from Newfoundland, coals, and merchandize in coasting vessels. Kingsbridge exports cider, corn, and malt, and imports coals from Sunderland. The principal exports of Plymouth are copper ore, silver, tin, and lead; antimony (from Cornwall), manganese, marble, slates, granite, lime-stone, pilchards, &c. The chief imports are corn, coals, and foreign produce. This most important port, possess-ing advantages for commerce so numerous and valuable, during the late war paid little attention to her foreign and colonial trade,—what was then done in this department being chiefly on account of the London, Liverpool, and Bristol houses. Nearly all the merchants of that time were agents for others, and purchased and transported the vast quantities of prize articles brought here for sale, under the direction, and for the exclusive benefit, of strangers. Since the conclusion of the war, the state of commerce here has altered materially. Those houses which stood the shock caused by the change from warlike to peaceable occupations, have been gradually extending their connections with foreign nations, and with our dis-tant colonial possessions. A considerable trade is now carried on with North America, the Mediterranean, and the Continent of Europe; and a direct intercourse has been opened with the West Indies, for the regular supply of colonial produce, on terms which must ensure a rapid sale, as the goods come directly from the planter, and are not burdened with the expense of immediate agencies, and the heavy port and warehouse charges of London and Bristol. Several vessels have already arrived with car-goes of rum, sugar, &c.; others will follow; and the re-sult, it is hoped, will be the conversion of the port into

Commer-
cial impor-
tance of
Plymouth.

a grand entrepot of West India produce, for the consumption of the West of England.

Coasting vessels, for the conveyance of goods to and from London, Bristol, Exeter, and elsewhere, are constantly employed in the trade, and take in and discharge their cargoes at the different quays in Sutton-pool. To this it may be added, that the *Eria* steam-packet keeps up a constant communication between this port, London, and Belfast; the *Brunswick* runs from hence to Portsmouth, but is generally laid up during the winter; and the *Sir Francis Drake*, during the summer, plies from Stonehouse to Guernsey, Jersey, and some parts of Cornwall *.

Finally, an institution must be mentioned, which in its design and tendency is well calculated to promote the objects adverted to, and which, from the ability and great respectability of the patronage by which it is supported, must have contributed not a little to this purpose. A Chamber of Commerce was established Dec. 28, 1813, by the merchants, ship-owners, &c., for the express purpose of giving increased vigour and extension to the foreign and domestic trade of the port, for which it possesses such decided and superior advantages, and which had been previously so much overlooked and neglected. The directors appointed were, His Grace the Duke of Bedford; the Right Honourable the Earl of Mount Edgecumbe; the Right Honourable Lord Elliot; the Right Honourable Lord Boringdon; the Right Honourable R. P. Carew, M.P.; Sir William Elford, Bart.; Sir Charles Pole, Bart. M.P.; Sir Massey Lopez, Bart. M.P.; Sir John Pering, Bart. M.P.; J. P. Bastard, Esq. M.P.; Benjamin Bloomfield, Esq.; Francis Glanville, Esq.; and John Harris, Esq.

The Managing Committee is chosen by the members, annually, by ballot; and there can be no doubt, that from their knowledge of the best interests of the port, and indefatigable exertions for its welfare, they must have proved

CHAP.
III.

Board of
Commerce.

* " The Tourist's Companion, &c." by John Sandford, 1820, p. 105.

an important and useful body to the commercial prosperity of the place.

On the northern coast of the county, Hartland exports corn, &c., and imports limestone and coals. At Bideford the foreign and coasting trade in the year 1829 was as follows :—eight vessels were employed in conveying wine, spirits, cordage, linen, cotton and woollen goods, hardware, &c., to the colonies : and 148 vessels, coastwise, with earthenware to Wales; corn to London, Bristol, and Wales; oak-bark to Ireland, and apples to Scotland. Eleven vessels arrived with foreign imports ;—timber from America and the Baltic, and wine from Spain and Portugal; and coastwise, 403 vessels imported spirits, sugar, coffee, &c., under bond from London, Bristol, and Plymouth; cattle from Ireland; coals and culm from Wales; and slate from Wales and Cornwall. Barnstaple exports timber, bark, &c., and imports coals and culm from Wales, and merchandise from Bristol. Ilfracombe exports oats, &c., and imports coals, groceries, &c. in coasting. And Combe Martin exports corn and bark*, and imports limestone and coals.

* Much less bark, however, is now exported from the county than formerly; the tanners, indeed, are beginning to import that article from Holland, and other parts of the Continent.

END OF THE FIRST VOLUME.

PRINTED BY RICHARD TAYLOR,
RED LION COURT, FLEET STREET, LONDON.

Drawn by G B Campion.

Engraved by J Henshall.

PLYMOUTH REGATTA.

Drawn by T.M.Baynes.   Engraved by W.Deeble.

THE BUTCHER ROW, EXETER.

London. R. Jennings & W. Chaplin, 6.ᵗᵉ Cheapside 1831.